BUSINESS, GOVERNMENT, AND SOCIETY

A Managerial Perspective

Text and Cases

McGraw-Hill Series in Management

Fred Luthans and Keith Davis, *Consulting Editors*

SIXTH EDITION

BUSINESS, GOVERNMENT, AND SOCIETY

A Managerial Perspective

Text and Cases

GEORGE A. STEINER

Harry and Elsa Kunin Professor of Business and Society
and Professor of Management, Emeritus, UCLA

JOHN F. STEINER

Professor of Management and Chair, Department of Management,
California State University, Los Angeles

McGraw-Hill, Inc.

New York   St. Louis   San Francisco   Auckland   Bogotá
Caracas   Lisbon   London   Madrid   Mexico   Milan
Montreal   New Delhi   Paris   San Juan   Singapore
Sydney   Tokyo   Toronto

To Our Students—
Past, Present, and Future

PERMISSIONS ACKNOWLEDGMENTS

The following company logos are reproduced with permission: Exxon (p. 3), Courtesy of Exxon Corporation; Kodak (p. 23), Courtesy of Eastman Kodak Company; The American Tobacco Company (p. 51), Courtesy of American Brands, Inc.; Dow (p. 117), Courtesy of Dow Chemical U.S.A.; Johnson & Johnson (p. 126), Courtesy of Johnson & Johnson; Hewlett-Packard (p. 154), Courtesy of Hewlett-Packard Company; J. C. Penney (p. 242), Courtesy of J. C. Penney Company, Inc.; NRA (p. 281), Library of Congress; Advanced Genetic Sciences (p. 320), Courtesy of Advanced Genetic Sciences, Inc.; Toshiba (p. 357), Courtesy of Toshiba Corp.; Heinz (p. 389), Courtesy of H. J. Heinz Company; Ford (p. 429), Courtesy of Ford Motor Company; Ohio Edison (p. 469), Courtesy of Ohio Edison Co.; Asarco (p. 511), Courtesy of Asarco, Inc.; IBM (p. 553), Courtesy of IBM Corporation; AT&T (p. 601), Courtesy of AT&T; Merck & Co., Inc. (p. 642), Courtesy of Merck & Co., Inc.; Trans Union (p. 697), Courtesy of Trans Union Corp.

Table 1-1 (p. 16), Copyright © 1984 by the Regents of the University of California. Reprinted from the *California Management Review*, Vol. 26, No. 3. By permission of The Regents.

This book was set in Palatino by the College Composition Unit
in cooperation with Waldman Graphics, Inc.
The editors were Alan Sachs, Dan Alpert, and Ira C. Roberts;
the production supervisor was Janelle S. Travers.
The cover was designed by Rafael Hernandez.
R. R. Donnelley & Sons Company was printer and binder.

BUSINESS, GOVERNMENT, AND SOCIETY
A Managerial Perspective
Text and Cases

3 4 5 6 7 8 9 0 DOC DOC   9 8 7 6 5 4 3 2 1

ISBN 0-07-061173-4

Library of Congress Cataloging-in-Publication Data

Steiner, George Albert, (date).
    Business, government, and society: a managerial perspective:
    text and cases / George A. Steiner, John F. Steiner. — 6th ed.
        p.   cm.—(McGraw-Hill series in management)
    Originally published as Business and society.
    Includes bibliographical references and index.
    ISBN 0-07-061173-4
        1. Industry—Social aspects—United States.   2. Industry
and
state—United States.   I. Steiner, John F.   II. Steiner, George
Albert, (date).   Business and society.   III. Title.   IV. Series.
HD60.5.U5S8   1991
658.4'08—dc20   90-44439

About the Authors

GEORGE A. STEINER is one of the leading pioneers in the development of university curriculums, research, and scholarly writings in the field of business, government, and society. In 1983 he was the recipient of the first Summer Marcus Award for distinguished achievement in the field by the Social Issues in Management Division of the Academy of Management. In 1990 he received the Distinguished Educator Award, given for the second time by the Academy of Management. After receiving his B.S. in business administration at Temple University, he was awarded an M.A. in economics from the Wharton School of the University of Pennsylvania and a Ph.D. in economics from the University of Illinois. He is the author of many books and articles. His latest books are *Strategic Planning: What Every Manager Must Know; Management Policy and Strategy: Text, Readings, and Cases* (with John B. Miner and Edmund R. Gray); and *The New CEO.* Two of his books received "book-of-the-year" awards. In recognition of his writings, Temple University awarded him a Litt.D. honorary degree. Professor Steiner has held top-level positions in the federal government and in industry, including corporate board directorships. Past president of the National Academy of Management and co-founder of *The California Management Review,* he is Harry and Elsa Kunin Professor of Business and Society and Professor of Management, Emeritus, at the University of California at Los Angeles.

JOHN F. STEINER is Professor of Management and Chair of the Department of Management at California State University, Los Angeles. He received his B.S. from Southern Oregon State College and received an M.A. and Ph.D. in political science from the University of Arizona. He has coauthored two other books with George A. Steiner, *Issues in Business and Society* and *Casebook for Business, Government, and Society.* His latest book is *Industry, Society, and Change: A Casebook.* Professor Steiner is a former chair of the Social Issues Division of the Academy of Management and currently serves as a member of the Advisory Board of the Edmund G. "Pat" Brown Institute of Public Affairs.

Contents

PART THREE   BUSINESS ETHICS

PART EIGHT   HUMAN RESOURCES

PART NINE   CORPORATE GOVERNANCE

Preface

This book, as its title explains, is about the interrelationships among business, government, and society. Today, these relationships are rapidly changing. Change comes both from forces in the business environment and from the actions of business. The impact of these changes has in many ways altered the attitudes, duties, and decisions of managers, particularly in larger corporations.

Although our central focus in this volume is on business managers, we write for a broader audience, including also university students, managers in government agencies, and socially concerned citizens. We believe that our topic is of arresting importance because the subjects examined here will, in one way or another, significantly affect the lives of all Americans.

This is not a book of broad abstractions; rather, it deals with specific issues. In this way we hope to help managers in business and government to better understand and deal with specific problems. We are equally concerned with helping students to bridge the gap between theory learned in the classroom and practice in the real world. We also try to provide them with a perspective which links courses such as business policy, management theory, and strategic planning to specific managerial issues.

COMMENTS ON THE NEW EDITION

Centuries ago Marcus Aurelius observed in his *Meditations:* "Time is like a river made up of the events which happen, and a violent stream; for as soon as a thing has been seen, it is carried away, and another comes in its place, and this will be carried away too." In preparing for this new edition we found that time had worked its way in almost every chapter. We have retained the basic framework, subject matter, and thrust of the preceding editions of this text. Furthermore, we believe that this edition, more than previous editions, contains much basic conceptual material that is not subject to early obsolescence by events. However, substantial revisions have been necessary to up-date and refocus the text in many areas.

Within the chapters, we have added extensive new material on current events, historical subjects, and academic research. During the revision process two chapters were eliminated, but their essence is retained in other chapters. A new chapter, "Corporate Global Competitiveness," has been added. As in the last edition, each chapter begins with a short incident involving a corporation (or, in two cases, a non-corporate organization) that illustrates key concepts. Those that are retained are updated, and six new company incidents are added.

As in the last edition, the reader will find one or more cases at the end of each chapter. Most deal with real companies or current situations. In all, there are 22 cases, most of moderate length. The cases are important learning tools which may be used as exercises for group discussion, springboards to research, or readings that illustrate chapter material. Six new cases have been added, and cases retained from the last edition are updated.

ACKNOWLEDGMENTS

This book would not have been possible without the research and published work of many people. We try to recognize inspirational and informative authors by citing, where appropriate, their works. We are deeply indebted to them.

Many people have made comments and suggestions concerning the preparation of this sixth edition, too many to name here. We do want to express our appreciation, however, to supporters in academic life, business, government, and elsewhere as follows.

Dick Anthony, the Business Roundtable; Rev. Willie Barrows, Operation PUSH; John E. Blodgett, Congressional Research Service; Robert Charleton, Dow Chemical Co.; Kent Dreyvestyn, General Dynamics Corporation; Fred Eiland, Federal Election Commission; James R. Glenn, Jr., San Francisco State University; Sister Mary Ann McGivern, Loretto Literary and Benevolent Association; John McGuire, General Dynamics Corporation; J. Duncan Muire, J. C. Penney Company, Inc.; Bruce Mulock, Congressional Research Service; Gilbert C. Nolde, Caterpillar Inc.; David A. Osterland, Ohio Edison Company; Eleanor Paradowsky, Merck & Co., Inc.; David Sampson, Manville Corporation; Harold B. Shore, Glendale Federal Bank; Kenneth O. Sniffen, Union Carbide Corporation; Vicky M. Suazo, Dow Chemical U.S.A.; George Trainer, Ford Motor Company; J. Fred Weston, University of California, Los Angeles; and Robert Wright, Pepperdine University.

The following reviewers provided many helpful comments and suggestions for this edition, and to them we are grateful: David M. Flynn, Hofstra University; James G. Frierson, East Tennessee State University; Charles Hamburger, California State University, Long Beach; John F. Hulpke, California State University, Bakersfield; Daniel R. Kane, George Washington University; D. Jeffrey Lenn, George Washington University; Charles H. Matthews, University of Cincinnati; Janice J. Miller, University of Houston; Osita Nwachukwu, Western Illinois University; and Ronald J. Sivitz, Pace University.

At the John F. Kennedy Library at California State University, Los Angeles, Murray J. Ross and Alan Stein gave valuable advice on the research process.

We are also grateful for guidance received from the staff of the College Division of McGraw-Hill, Inc., particularly June Smith, Alan Sachs, Dan Alpert, Ira C. Roberts, Suzanne BeDell, Kathleen Loy, George Hoffman, and Cathryn Sauer.

Finally, we give special thanks to Deborah Luedy and Jean W. Steiner for their support and encouragement.

George A. Steiner
John F. Steiner

A Framework for Studying Business, Government, and Society

Introduction to the Field

Every large corporation in the United States and many smaller ones are concerned with a wide range of forces in the business-government-society (BGS) interrelationship. Exxon provides a good example of its complexity.

Exxon was the third largest industrial company in the United States in 1989, measured by assets, and was surpassed only by General Motors and Ford Motor. In 1989 it reported assets of $83.2 billion, sales of $86.6 billion, and net earnings of $3.5 billion. It is the world's largest integrated oil company. It engages in virtually every major type of basic energy production, from exploration of oil and gas to mining coal, nuclear fuels, and other minerals. It refines petrochemicals and until 1987 also manufactured electric motors. It owns and operates fleets of ships, airplanes, and helicopters.

Exxon operates in more than 80 countries of the world and derives 50 percent of its earnings from abroad. It has business in every one of the fifty states, employs 135,000 people, and has 709,000 stockholders.

The above numbers give some indication of the complex role that a corporation the size of Exxon plays in society. There is no way, however, to picture briefly the extraordinary array of important BGS forces that flow to and emanate from a corporation such as this. The following thumbnail sketch may, however, help to focus on some of their dominant impacts.

The business environment is naturally of exceptional concern to Exxon. For one thing, it is in a highly competitive and volatile industry. In 1982, for example, when the oil price bubble burst, Exxon found its profits declining by $1.4 billion during the year. It had to close nine refineries, slash tanker capacity 25 percent, close 10,000 service stations, and drop 24,000 people from its payrolls of 180,000. Aside from carefully watching world oil price movements, Exxon is concerned with such changing current and future business conditions as foreign exchange rates, interest rates, the demand for gasoline and fuel oil, general economic levels throughout the world, and what its domestic competitors are doing.

The company is deeply intertwined with governments here and abroad. The federal government of the United States has roughly 300 primary agencies, and Exxon's operations are affected by all of them with but a very few exceptions. Aside from the more obvious agencies with which it is engaged (such as the Department of Energy and the Department of Interior), we note the Federal Communications Commission's (FCC) regulations of Exxon's offshore telecommunications, the Bureau of Indian Affairs in relation to drilling activities, the Maritime Administration and the use of Exxon's ships, the Interstate Commerce Commission (ICC) and pipelines, the Federal Aviation Administration (FAA) and jet engine fuel regulations, and the Securities and Exchange Commission (SEC) and security financing.

A major recent event created extraordinary new problems for Exxon. This was the 11 million gallon oil spill of its tanker *Exxon Valdez* in Alaska's Prince William Sound. This disaster and the issues it raised are presented in a case at the end of Chapter 15.

Like many other large companies in the public eye, Exxon has institutionalized the social point of view in its decision making, from top management policies down through the divisions. The company has had a reputation of being attentive to its social responsibilities, but that was tarnished by the bitter criticism it received as a result of the *Valdez* oil spill in Alaska. The company was accused not only of laxity in its ship operations but also of sluggishness in cleaning up the huge oil spill.

A prominent feature of its social posture for years has been its philanthropy. For example, the Exxon Education Foundation is the largest corporate donor to higher education in the United States, with total expenditures in 1988 of $49 million. In addition, each division of the company has an annual contributions budget for cultural and social giving.

A central theme of this book is that business managers cannot operate successfully in conflict with their environments. Exxon is an example of a large company that must deal successfully with a vast range of environmental forces if it is to prosper.

There are many ways to look at the interrelationships among business, government, and society. In this chapter we present the major conceptual models which people use in thinking about this interrelationship. A model is then presented to show how we determine the relative importance of an issue in the BGS field as a subject for our book. We conclude with comments about how we approach the study of the BGS field.

THE NATURE AND SPECTRUM OF BGS RELATIONSHIPS

In the BGS relationship, society is the all-encompassing concept. Both business and government are institutions operating within society. Individual components in society are constantly in motion and interacting to produce

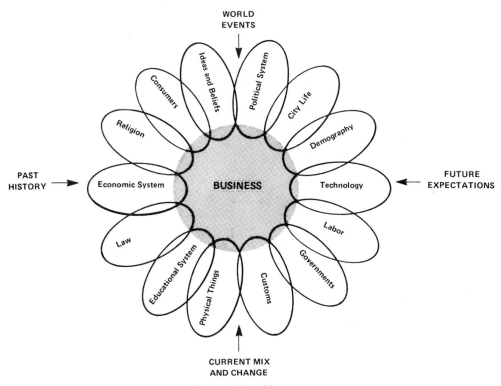

FIGURE 1-1   Business and its major societal areas of interrelationship.

changes. Business and government, of course, are in constant interaction. Both, however, influence and are continuously influenced by other aspects of society, such as changing social values, pressure groups, technology, intellectuals, workers, educational institutions, lawyers, consumers, prices, and so on. The mix of these interrelationships varies greatly from time to time.

Figure 1-1 conceptualizes one set of interrelationships between business and society. The ellipses include those areas of primary interest in this book. Additional areas of importance to business would include weather, natural resources, military events, language, medicine, geography, and agriculture. The illustration shows that history has an impact on the current mix of relationships in society. The mix and its direction of change are also influenced by current world events and by what is going on in this society at the present time. The changes are influenced as well by future expectations.

In examining the many interrelationships between business and society, one must distinguish among businesses. The business system is not a unified structure. There are giant firms that are larger, at least in terms of cash flows, than most governments of the world. There are also millions of small enter-

BUSINESS

The term "business" encompasses a broad range of action, from individual pursuits to the work of giant corporations. In this book, the term covers manufacturing, commercial, trade, and other economic activities of both individuals and institutions.

GOVERNMENT

Government encompasses a wide range of activities and institutions throughout our country, including school districts; local, county, state, and interstate governments; and the federal government. "Government" may be defined as the structures and processes through which public policies, programs, and rules are authoritatively made for society. In this book, we are most interested in the economic and regulatory powers of government, especially those of the federal government, and their impact on business.

SOCIETY

As used in this book, the term "society" means essentially what generally is meant when one speaks of this nation, or the American civilization. Inherent in this concept are three fundamental, interrelated parts that make up the abstraction of society. They are (1) ideas or beliefs, (2) institutions, and (3) material things.

Ideas include such things as attitudes, ideologies, and beliefs. They establish the broad goals of life expressed in terms of what is considered to be good, true, right, beautiful, and acceptable. These ideas and beliefs underlie and dominate the systems of institutional arrangements in society, of which business is one.

Institutions are those more or less formalized ways by which society tries to do something. Examples of institutional systems are the business system, the political system, labor unions, the educational system, the language system, and the legal system.

The third element in society encompasses tangible, material things such as stocks of resources, land, and all manufactured goods. These things help to shape, and are partly products of, our institutions, ideas, and beliefs. Our economic institutions, together with our stock of resources, determine in large part the type and quantity of our material things. As our types and quantities of material things change, so do our ideas and beliefs.

prises. (Most of the economic activity of the nation is conducted through several thousand of the largest companies, and for this reason a large part of this book is concerned with these companies.) Some companies do business only in the United States, while others operate in many foreign countries. Some companies are in service trades, and others only mine or manufacture. Some managers have committed their enterprises to improving the quality of life of their employees and people generally, whereas others feel their objective is only to optimize stockholder wealth. A business institution is not wholly an economic organization, for it has social as well as political characteristics. The discussion, therefore, considers all three of these aspects of business activity.

Different elements in society have different impacts on business, and vice versa. The title of this book, *Business, Government, and Society*, highlights the fact that of all institutions in society, the government is the most important influence on business today. Other elements of society, however, also exert strong influences on business either directly, as does new technology, or indirectly through government, as when people want to reduce the pollution of the environment by business.

MODELS OF THE BGS INTERRELATIONSHIPS

Everyone recognizes that BGS interrelationships are extremely complex. Individuals and groups view these relationships from different perspectives. Depending upon their perspective on business' relationship to its environment, people and/or groups may reach entirely different conclusions about any business-society issue. They may differ radically, for example, about the nature of business' power over society, the motivations of business leaders, the morality of executives, the role of business in society, the social responsibilities of the business community, and any other public issues involving business. Therefore, it is important to know the fundamental model, or conceptual framework, that people use in viewing the BGS relationship.

The following models frequently are used as basic frames of reference for viewing the BGS relationship. We believe that the first two models, despite their popularity, are seriously flawed and lead to irrational interpretations of factual information. Only the later models are sophisticated enough to provide constructive and accurate interpretation of a dynamic business system in a changing society.

THE DOMINANCE MODEL

The dominance model, Figure 1-2, is pyramidal and shows society to be hierarchical in nature. To those who subscribe to this model, business and gov-

FIGURE 1-2   The dominance model.

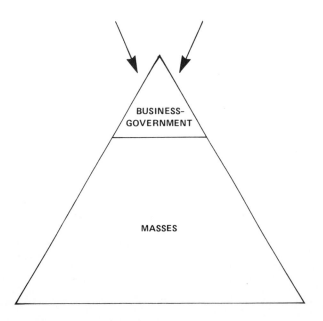

ENVIRONMENTAL FORCES

BUSINESS-
GOVERNMENT

MASSES

ernment act in combination to dominate the great mass of ordinary people. Environmental forces are transmitted to the bulk of the population by an elite establishment. Given this mental image of business, government, and society, certain conclusions and interpretations are likely to follow.

1 Society is hierarchical, and a small number of influential people and/or institutions dominate it. The business institution is one of these, and business leaders manipulate society from a fulcrum of great power in association with government.

2 Power mainly moves down from the top levels of society. Unlike democratic theory, which postulates that leaders serve the will of the people, the social hierarchy implicit in this model implies dominance by a small group of business managers, politicians, and the wealthy.

3 The policy-making process is dominated by the interests of business and the wealthy and is used as a tool to aggrandize the needs of these groups. Decisions are not widely consultative.

4 The role of business in solving and ministering to societal problems, such as housing, unemployment, pollution, income inequality, urban decay, traffic congestion, and women's rights, is paternalistic at best and exploitative at worst.

5 The political machinery is meshed with economic institutions, rendering any adversary relationship between business and government a fiction. A primary goal of government is to help business.

6 Human nature being what it is, those who dominate this societal hierarchy work to preserve the status quo because existing arrangements are to their benefit. They have little concern for reforming institutional arrangements to make them more participatory or for changing policies that benefit the rich, such as the tax system.

A number of leading intellectuals have subscribed to theories of the business-government-society relationship based on the assumptions of the dominance model. The "power elite" theory of the confluence of economic and business power popularized by the late sociologist C. Wright Mils, for example, parallels the dominance model.[1] Another version of the dominance model is the idea that business and government have formed a sort of monolithic power that tells people what they must do. This thesis is found in John Kenneth Galbraith's works,[2] and is adopted by others.[3,4]

Marxism provides another version of this theory in its central tenet that an elite ruling class that dominates the economy and other institutional forms has been present in every society. Contemporary Marxist thinkers in the United States see such domination by a small capitalist class that controls

---

[1]C. Wright Mills, *The Power Elite*, New York: Oxford University Press, 1956.
[2]John Kenneth Galbraith, *The Affluent Society*, Boston: Hougton Mifflin, 1958; *The New Industrial State*, Boston: Houghton Mifflin, 1967; and *Economics and the Public Purpose*, Boston: Houghton Mifflin, 1973.
[3]Charles A. Reich, *The Greening of America*, New York: Random House, 1970.
[4]Theodore Roszak, *The Making of a Counter Culture*, New York: Doubleday, 1969.

both government and the economy.[5,6] To those who subscribe to this symbol of the pyramid, the power of business is too great and the motivations of its leaders are selfish (and perhaps conspiratorial).

We believe that this model is far too simple. It is a gross distortion of reality, and the conclusions derived from it are largely erroneous, as will be demonstrated in the remainder of this book.

THE MARKET CAPITALISM MODEL

A second model, Figure 1-3, which has been popular with business managers and economists for more than two centuries, is the market capitalism model. This conceptual model visualizes the business system as substantially isolated from social forces in its environment and draws attention to the primacy of market economic forces. It depicts business and industry as existing in a market environment that is influenced and shaped both by business decisions inside the market environment and by impinging social, political, legal, and cultural forces. The market environment in the model acts as a buffer between business units and nonmarket environmental forces.

This conceptual representation of the business-society relationship implies conclusions and interpretations much different from those of the dominance model.

FIGURE 1-3   The market capitalism model.

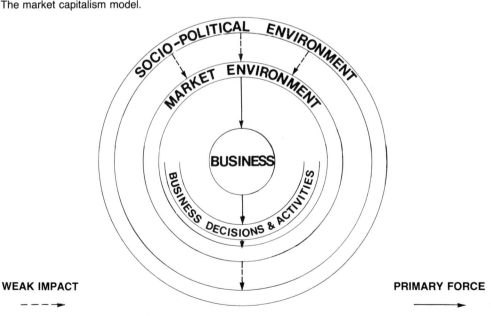

WEAK IMPACT   PRIMARY FORCE

- - - ➤   ———➤

[5]Douglas F. Dowd, *The Twisted Dream*, 2nd ed., Cambridge, Mass.: Winthrop, 1977.
[6]Holly Sklar, ed., *Trilateralism: The Trilateral Commission and Elite Planning for World Management*, Boston: South End Press, 1980.

1 Market performance is virtually the only accepted measure of social performance. Because business does not interact directly with the sociopolitical environment, managers concentrate on market goals, not social goals.

2 Market performance justifies or legitimizes the existence of the business unit. Its contribution to society is directly related to the performance of its primary economic function. Noneconomic goals or performance measures are not legitimate guideposts for judging contributions of business.

3 Managers should define the interests of their companies narrowly, as profitability and greater efficiency in using scarce resources.

4 Efficiency in economic transactions is the highest good, superseding abstract notions of social justice such as altruism.

5 Government, not business, has primary responsibility for ministering to social problems. Government institutions are assigned the task of monitoring and adjusting the nonmarket environment of business.

6 Business should respond to market forces of supply and demand and not be subjected to political pressures or government-imposed regulations that cut economic efficiency. Business makes its primary contribution by providing a surplus for society as a result of profitable operations. It can do this best when unhindered by government.

7 Business executives should accept social values as given and do not have a responsibility to work for the resolution of social problems unless these problems register on business firms through market forces or government regulations.

We believe that this model, like the dominance model, has serious drawbacks and does not illuminate fully the role of business in society today. There is validity in parts of the model, but the emphasis is distorted in light of realities. Today, for example, the social responsiveness of business is not as limited as this model would indicate, and many of the assumptions that derive from the model are under attack, as will be discussed in later chapters.

THE BUSINESS ECOLOGY MODEL

Ecology is concerned with mutual relations between organisms and their environments. Business ecology, as shown in Figure 1-4, refers to the relationships of business with various elements in society. We prefer this model because it promotes understanding of the realistic relationship of business units to other elements in society.

The business ecology model depicts the business-society relationship as a system of interactions. In this conception, units of business activity are energized by inputs of various kinds. These inputs, which have consequences for both the system and its environment, include economic and sociopolitical demands made by governments, pressure groups, and individuals; and also supports, or attitudes and actions that legitimize the business system. The business system is oriented toward preserving itself, maintaining the integrity of its boundaries, and increasing its control over the environment. On the basis of these inputs, then, the business system creates products and

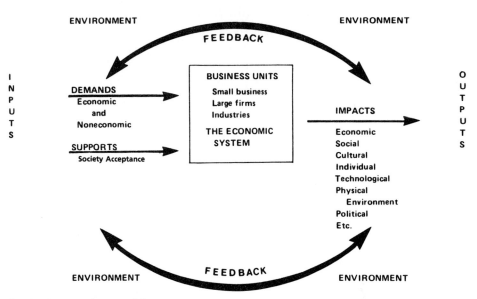

FIGURE 1-4   The business ecology model.

takes actions that affect major areas of society. The impacts influence various groups, individuals, and institutions in society and lead them to make new demands and increase or decrease their support of business.[7]

What conclusions can be reached with the business ecology model?

1 Unlike models that show business dominating the environment or existing in partial isolation from it, this model clearly implies that business is integrated into the environment and must respond to many forces impinging upon the business system.

2 Society is not basically hierarchial or dominated by a small group but is an interacting network of influences. Any group in the environment may have potential influence on business, and many different forces, social as well as economic, affect executives' decisions.

3 Broad and underlying public support of the business enterprise depends on its adjustment to many different environmental forces. To survive, business must react to a mixture of social and economic forces.

4 The basic function of economic efficiency can still be recognized as essential to the continued survival of the business system, but this basic economic primacy is seen to coexist with continued response to the social environment.

5 The business ecology model shows that the business-government-society relationship will evolve continuously and that business must adjust continuously.

[7]David Easton, "An Approach to the Analysis of Political Systems," *World Politics,* April 1957, set forth a similar model.

6 The model implies that support for business will be greatest when the impacts of the business system on its environment are more positive than negative, that is, when benefits provided are greater than costs imposed.

This model provides a sound basis for focusing on the two central themes of this book: (1) the way in which the environment is changing the managerial task, and (2) the way in which the role of business in society is changing.

THE DOMINANT FORCE MODEL

Figure 1-5 is another way of looking at the business ecology model in Figure 1-4. It is designed to show the dominant flows of influence in the business-government-society relationship as far as business is concerned. This model shows that the main influence on business comes from changes·in societal values, expectations, needs, and demands. These forces influence business through the political processes that affect the private sector. They also influence business directly to the extent that business responds voluntarily to them.

Changes in values, expectations, needs, and demands arise from many forces. One is the changing environment of people, which includes of course, economic well-being, the physical environment, working conditions, and so on. Business both influences this environment and is influenced by it. Government leadership also influences the environment and social response to the changing environment. Business operations may influence public values, expectations, demands, and needs.

This obviously is a dynamic model of influence. The forces operate differently and with varying impact, depending upon a wide range of factors such as the subject or issue under review, the power of competing groups, intensity of public feelings, and effectiveness of government and business leadership.

Over a long period of time, there have been major changes in the dynamics of influence. For example, fifty years ago business paid attention almost solely to stockholder interests and market economic and technical forces. Today such forces are still important but are matched by the influence of government and pressure groups.

What overarching conclusions can be drawn from this model?

1 The BGS relationship is extremely dynamic in its flow of influences.
2 Business responds to its environment.
3 Environmental changes are the most important influences on business.
4 Business is a major initiator of change in its environment, especially through its introduction of new technologies and products.

THE STAKEHOLDER MODEL

This model is presented to underscore the point that businesses, especially the larger ones in the public eye, are confronted with many constituents who

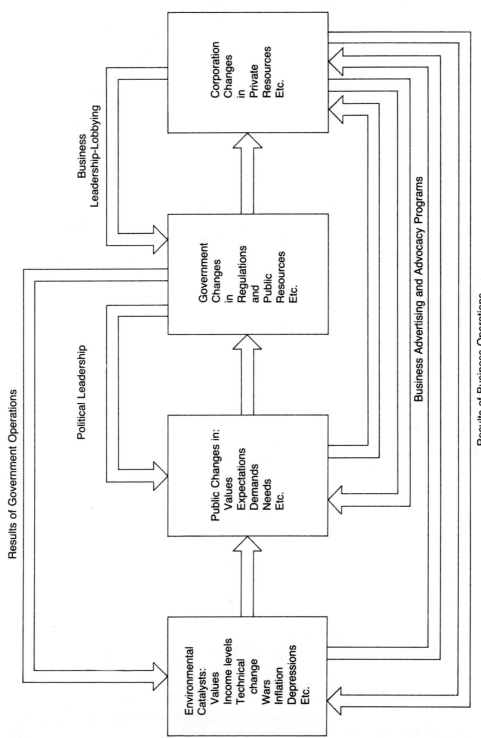

FIGURE 1-5 Dominant forces in the business-government-society relationship. (*Source:* Reprinted with permission of The Free Press, a division of Macmillan, Inc., from *Corporate Power and Social Responsibility* by Neil H. Jacoby. Copyright © 1973 by The Trustees of Columbia University in the City of New York.)

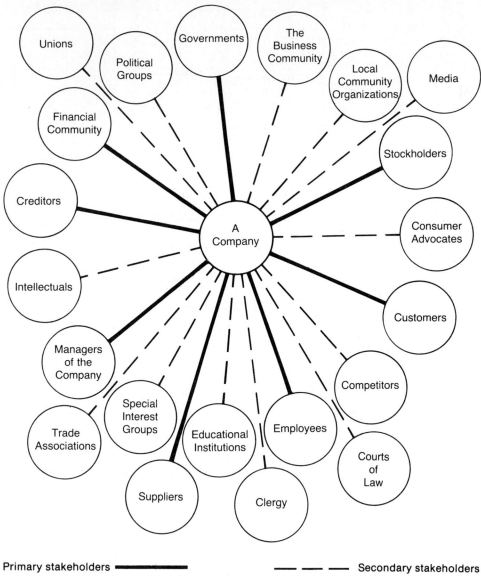

Primary stakeholders ━━━━━━━━   ━━ ━━ ━━ Secondary stakeholders

FIGURE 1-6   Stakeholder groups of a large corporation. (*Source:* Reprinted with permission of Macmillan Publishing Co., from *Management Policy and Strategy*, 3rd ed., by George A. Steiner, John B. Miner, and Edmund R. Gray. Copyright © 1986 by Macmillan Publishing Co.)

believe they have a stake in the operation of a business; hence the name stakeholder.

Every one of the constituent interests identified in Figure 1-6 has multiple parts, and each may present its own set of demands on a company. For example, the circle "governments" covers numerous governments, foreign and domestic.

Influence is not one-way. Stakeholders can be influenced both directly and indirectly by what a company does. A company may affect union workers directly by closing a plant, and it may influence people in a community indirectly by increasing employment. Influence can be both positive and negative. Stakeholder pressures on a company may be direct, as for example when a bank demands specific actions to protect its loans, or indirect, as when a stakeholder successfully gets government to force a company to act in the interests of the stakeholder (for example, environmentalists get laws passed to reduce pollution by public utilities).

A very small company typically has few constituents of important concern to it (usually stockholders, customers, employees, and the bank). A very large company has many stakeholders, and there will be great variations in the degree to which managers will yield to each of their interests. A pharmaceutical company, for example, will be very receptive to the demands of physicians who use its products. A coal-burning utility will be highly concerned about the expectations of environmentalists.

What conclusions can be drawn from this model?

1 Every large corporation has a variety of constituents who have an interest in the way the corporation operates.

2 A large corporation seeks to react appropriately to stakeholders, who are seen as having important actual or potential impact on the operations of the corporation.

3 The corporation will seek to influence its stakeholders in accepting its decisions.

Managerial Attitudes about Stakeholders   The American Management Association recently sponsored a study of 6,000 managers. Part of the study concerned the importance with which three different levels of managers viewed a list of business stakeholders, including themselves. Table 1-1 shows that customers came first for top managers but not for supervisory and middle managers. The three levels of managers seemed less than humble, but quite candid, about their own importance. The table is striking with respect to the high status given employees, coworkers, and superiors in the company. The researchers concluded, "The stereotype of managers as running the nation's corporations for the primary benefit of their stockholders does not seem to be borne out by the data."[8] This does not mean, of course, that managers are less concerned with company profit than themselves or their colleagues in the business. Profitable growth is still a dominant objective of managers. What Table 1-1 shows, however, is that it is not the sole objective. It also can be hypothesized that managers understand very well that appropriate concern for major stakeholders will enhance profit potential.

---

[8]Barry Z. Posner and Warren H. Schmidt, "Values and the American Manager: An Update," *California Management Review*, Spring 1984, p. 207.

TABLE 1-1   THE IMPORTANCE OF VARIOUS ORGANIZATIONAL STAKEHOLDERS TO MANAGERS

	Supervisory managers	Middle managers	Executive managers
Customers	5.57	6.10	6.40
Myself	6.28	6.29	6.28
Subordinates	6.06	6.30	6.14
Employees	5.93	6.11	6.01
Boss(es)	5.72	5.92	5.82
Coworkers	5.87	5.82	5.81
Colleagues	5.66	5.78	5.75
Managers	5.26	5.56	5.75
Owners	4.07	4.51	5.30
General public	4.38	4.49	4.52
Stockholders	3.35	3.79	4.51
Elected public officials	3.81	3.54	3.79
Government bureaucrats	3.09	2.05	2.90

Scale of 1 to 7 (1 = lowest; 7 = highest).
Source: Barry Z. Posner and Warren H. Schmidt, "Values and the American Manager: An Update," *California Management Review*, Spring 1984, p. 205.

BUSINESS AND THE SOCIAL CONTRACT

Institutions, or systems, in society are not created and accepted as the result of some mystical conception. They exist in order to perform important societal functions. At any time there exists a working relationship between society and its institutions called the social contract. This contract is partly written in legislation but is also found in custom, precedent, and articulated societal approval or disapproval. Whether explicit or implicit, the social contract is the basis for institutional actions.

This fundamental interrelationship between business and society leads to a number of important conclusions. One is that the business institution operates, basically, to serve society's interests as society sees them. Another is that generalizations about the relationship between business and society in

If we view legitimacy...as the belief or perception by society that a particular social institution is appropriate or proper or consistent with the moral foundations of that society, we arrive at some rather interesting propositions. Satisfactory performance, for example, is not the only point. An institution regarded as legitimate by society can survive failure after failure of performance of social tasks without endangering its survival, but even satisfactory performance cannot guarantee survival if legitimacy is lost. Our American Revolution bears witness to that fact with regard to the institution of British Rule.[9]

[9]Edwin M. Epstein and Dow Votaw, *Legitimacy, Responsibility, Rationality: The Search for New Directions in Business and Society*, Santa Monica, CA.: Goodyear Publishing Company, 1978, p. 3.

the past may not be valid today or tomorrow. The social contract changes continuously. In periods of great change, such as we are witnessing today, there is more pervasive and fundamental rewriting of the contract than in tranquil times. Indeed, today there are many people who feel that the social contract is being rewritten in a fundamental way.

BOUNDARIES OF THE BGS FIELD[10]

This book sets forth the BGS field of study as we see it today. Our view, of course, is based on our fundamental focus—the managerial perspective. Others focus on public policy issues, or economics, or political science—areas that are subgroups in our approach.

As noted earlier, the BGS field covers an enormous territory. Figure 1-7 shows the frame of reference that we believe is useful in defining the BGS field for a text such as this. On the left is a scale of threats to the legitimacy of business. On the bottom line is a scale concerning the impact of a particular subject on the managerial function of business and/or the business role in society.

A high threat to the legitimacy of business would mean, for example, a force that could sap the vitality of business, weaken the broad acceptance of the business institution, or reduce the efficient functioning of business. A low threat on this scale would mean just the opposite. A high marking on the bottom scale would mean, of course, that management could be powerfully affected by the forces arising in a particular area.

We believe that the field of BGS should fundamentally focus on subjects in the upper right quartile of the matrix. The subject-matter of each of the chapters in this book is in this area, that is, government, social responsibilities of business, ethics, pollution, consumerism, and so on. Other topics that impact on management of business are excluded because they do not now appear in this area of the matrix. These include, for example, agriculture, national security, demography, and the money and banking systems.

The topics located in the upper right quartile remain in that position over comparatively long periods of time. They do change, however. Government, of course, is a more or less permanent resident in that area. Twenty-five years ago, pollution and consumerism would not have been found in this area. Forty years ago, the Korean War economy was prominent in the BGS relationship.

Although many of the topics remain dominant in the BGS domain, there is constant shifting of emphasis. For example, social audits were of high concern to business in the social responsibility area twenty years ago but are not a significant consideration today. Ten years ago, the basic question in the social responsibility area was whether business had social responsibilities. Now, the argument has been decided in the affirmative, and the focus of at-

---

[10]For a detailed discussion of the boundaries of the BGS field, with which we are in agreement, see Lee E. Preston, "Business and Public Policy," *The Journal of Management*, vol. 12, no. 2, 1986.

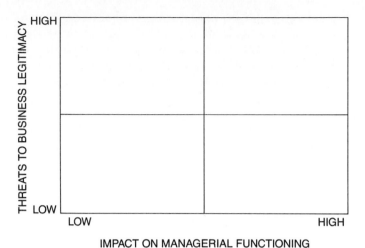

FIGURE 1-7   Matrix to define the BGS field.

tention has shifted to what business is doing to institutionalize the social point of view in decision making. In each of the chapters in this book will be found those topics which we consider at this time to be the more important ones to include in the BGS relationship for a book of this type and in the intellectual tool kit of students of this subject.

CHARACTERISTICS OF THE ANALYSIS IN THIS BOOK

As you have seen, the interrelationships among business, government, and society are many and can be approached in different ways. The principal characteristics of our analysis in this book are as follows.

FOCUS ON STRATEGIC MANAGEMENT

The central focus of this book is on the many powerful nonmarket forces in the business environment (external and internal) that significantly affect the management of individual firms and on the changing role of the business institution in society. It is widely recognized, especially in the larger corporations, that business firms cannot operate successfully over the long run in conflict with their environments. Managers of successful companies avoid this conflict through effective strategic management of their companies.

"Strategic management" is a term now in vogue. It describes the formulation and implementation of strategies that adapt a company to its changing environment. By strategic, management, we refer to the formulation of company missions, purposes, and objectives; the policies and programs to achieve them; and the methods needed to assure that they are implemented. In the past, strategic management meant essentially adapting to the economic and technical environments. Now it means adapting also to the sociopolitical environment. Indeed, these sociopolitical environmental forces are influences on corporate strategy as dominant as the traditional market forces.

The concept of strategic management does not imply that managements formulate strategies only in response to current events. Quite the contrary, it means that managers try to anticipate future environmental forces so that they can take proactive measures to deal with them.

More specifically, we are concerned with the way sociopolitical forces enter into the formulation and implementation of such strategies as the following:

- Those that spell out the social responsibilities of the company.
- Those that react properly to changing social values with respect to such matters as the nature of the company's products or the changing aspirations of the people in the organization.
- Those that respond appropriately to government regulations concerning such matters as pollution, product safety, and equal opportunity.
- Those that determine when and how the company will try to influence political processes in matters of concern to the company.
- Those that change the structure and processes by which the firm responds to environmental forces.
- Those that affect the ethical standards according to which decisions are made in a company.

This emphasis is based on our conviction that among all the disciplines that must be employed in studying BGS interrelationships, the managerial (especially its strategic management aspect) is the most appropriate one for BGS courses in schools of business/management/administration. Disciplines other than the managerial may be more appropriate in other academic departments and schools.

INTERDISCIPLINARY APPROACH WITH A MANAGERIAL FOCUS

A large number of disciplines must be considered in dealing with theory, practice, and policy issues in the business-government-society interface. The more prominent ones are economics, political science, law, philosophy, sociology, science, history, and management. Our approach is an eclectic one in which we attempt to use the most relevant disciplines associated with a particular theory, practice, or policy issue. It is possible to analyze the business-society relationship in an interdisciplinary way but with a dominant disciplinary orientation, such as economics, political science, or law. Our orientation, as we have said, is managerial.

COMPREHENSIVE SCOPE

We have sought to make this book comprehensive in scope. We have tried to cover the large canvas, sketching out all of the most important interrelationships among business, government, and other societal forces. This approach is in contrast to that of selecting and concentrating intensively and exclusively on a few areas such as business social responsibility, pollution, consumerism, equal opportunity, and antitrust. We believe that it is far better for students in a basic course to be exposed to the many dominant interrelationships, even if the exposure is often "light," than for them to dig deeply into only a few areas.

FOCUS ON THEORY

We have tried to emphasize theoretical concepts appearing to have some permanence and providing valuable normative guides for understanding environmental forces, the managerial responses to them, and the way in which the business role is changing. We recognize, however, that there is no underlying theory integrating the entire field, nor is there likely to be one in the foreseeable future. The field is extremely diverse, complex, and fluid, and there is no consensus about its precise boundaries.

One can say tentatively, however, that the beginnings of an underlying theory of business and its relationship to society are emerging, but the profile is not clear. There is growing agreement, for example, about the theoretical obligations of corporations to respond to social pressures. In a number of major areas, there are useful theories rooted in relevant disciplines. For example, there are tested political theories concerned with business power, technical theories concerned with pollution issues, legal theories concerned with manufacturer liability, and economic theories concerned with government regulations, to mention a few. We have sought to emphasize such theories where they are relevant to the subject matter of this book.

ISSUES, FACTS, AND CONCLUSIONS ABOUT POLICY AND PRACTICE

A central focus of this book is to examine and evaluate the more significant issues in the business-society nexus so as to come to conclusions about what appropriate policy and practice should be for business and/or government. One of our goals is to help students to identify the "correct" issues. This means asking the "right" questions and framing the "right" problems. What is "right" often depends upon who is asking the question. Nevertheless, students of this subject must try to get at the basic strategic questions. For instance, there is no question but that technological advance has had serious and unwanted side effects. Is the question how to slow down technological advance to reduce these side effects, as some people advocate, or is it, as others suggest, how to inject into decision-making processes incentives to avoid the unwanted side impacts? Or is it something else? Students of this subject should understand that framing the "right" question is often very difficult and that proposed solutions follow the question once it is asked.

Many times in this book questions will be asked and no answers given. This is because there are no answers. Even if there are no answers, we still are progressing if the right questions are posed.

Once the issues have been identified, what are the facts? Getting the facts may be extremely difficult. For example, what are the facts about the safety of nuclear power plants? What are the facts about the human and economic damage caused by various types of pollution? What are the facts about society's expectations of the social responsibilities of business? We do not have enough facts about these and many other crucial questions.

Once the facts are gathered, it is essential to use them in a proper context. For example, some critics charge that business has not really solved major social problems, and its failure to do so indicates more concern with profits than with social welfare. The first part of the statement is correct but not the second. The facts are correct—business has not solved major social problems—but the perspective of the critics is wrong. It is not business's responsibility to solve major social problems, with a few exceptions to be noted later.

Even with the right issue at hand and all the facts that are available, reasonable people may come to radically different conclusions about preferred policy on issues. The reason, of course, is that people come to the issues and facts with differing ideologies, values, and interests. The Attorney General of the United States looks at the antitrust law somewhat differently from the chief executive of General Motors. At the very least, however, reason is more likely to prevail in society when people can communicate about commonly identified issues and the real facts.

In some instances, but not all, we explain our position on the issue being examined. We do so not to intrude our views on the reader, but rather to help in the analysis, for this book is not designed to "sell" or "explain" one particular point of view. Its purpose is to identify outstanding theories, processes of decision making, and policy issues, and to stimulate full, informed, and thoughtful debate about them.

Because judgment is often the final determinant of one's position on a particular issue, it is not an excuse to ignore the facts of a case. A charming story about Michelangelo will illustrate this situation. When Michelangelo had completed his carving of David, the governor of Florence came to look at the finished piece. He was pleased with what he saw, but as he looked at it he mused, "The nose...the nose is too large, is it not?" Michelangelo looked carefully at David's nose and quietly answered, "Yes, I think it is a little too large." He picked up his chisel and mallet, and also a handful of marble dust, and mounted the scaffolding. Carefully he hammered, permitting small amounts of dust to fall to the ground with each blow. He finally stopped and asked: "Now look at the nose. Is it not correct?" "Ah," responded the governor, "I like it...I like it even better. You have given it life." Michelangelo descended, according to an old chronicle, "with great compassion for those who desire to appear to be good judges of matters whereof they know nothing."[11]

To deplore "shooting from the hip," so to speak, does not suggest as an objective to "know all there is about business and society." We agree with J.

---

[11]Louis Lerman, *Michelangelo: A Renaissance Profile*, New York: Knopf, 1942, pp. 168–169.

Robert Oppenheimer when he observed: "No man should escape our universities without... some sense of the fact that not through his fault, but in the nature of things, he is going to be an ignorant man, and so is everyone else." It is appropriate to approach the subject of this book with humility.

THE HISTORICAL PERSPECTIVE

To the extent practicable we set forth an historical perspective for discussion of major topics. We believe that one cannot fully understand the present—or the future—without some comprehension and appreciation of the past. With history as a base, it is easier for one to avoid being deceived by cliches, "red herrings," and irrelevant observations. As Justice Holmes once suggested, history is the first step toward an enlightened skepticism. Furthermore, it is important to know that there are historical causes for current events and that the pattern of future events is being shaped today.

History is not useful in the sense that a knowledge of chemistry is. But it can be at least as valuable in providing insights into how we got where we are today, the creditability of solutions proposed for burning current issues, and where we may be heading. "A moment's insight," wrote Justice Holmes, "is worth a lifetime of experience."

2

The Business Environment

Giant Eastman Kodak Company was jolted in the early 1980s because it improperly assessed its principal environments. For a century this company was the bluest of blue chip American firms. Gradually its great success led to complacency, contentment, an erosion of its entrepreneural edge, and a clouded focus on its changing environments.

The company failed to exploit the rapidly growing camera market outside the United States. In trying to play catch-up with Polaroid in instant photography, it used a process so close to Polaroid's that in 1986 it lost a suit brought by Polaroid for patent infringement. It had to cease production of its camera and recall those it had sold. It invented the technology for the videotape recorder, but thought it too expensive to mass market. The Japanese then took over, developed VCRs and camcorders, and became proficient in videotape. Similarly, Kodak had made 35mm cameras for years but failed to exploit that knowledge in new product development and saw the Japanese steal that market. Now Kodak sells 35mm cameras made in Japan and Hong Kong.

Kodak remained remote from the global marketplace, believing it could simply make products in the United States and sell them abroad without adaptations to local cultures. This resulted in missing the Japanese market, the second largest in the world for photo film. Up to 1985 its film packages sold in Japan were in English only. It failed in other ways to assimilate Japanese ways into its Japanese business and has been struggling to increase its sales there. For years Kodak set prices almost at will for most of its products, from film to flash bulbs. Now it is faced with strong foreign competitors, many of whom are more efficient producers than Kodak. Fuji Photo Film Co. of Japan, for example, has sales of $380,000 per employee, compared with

$140,000 for Kodak.[1] In the early 1980s the strong dollar hurt the company by foreign currency translation losses. Finally, problems have arisen with toxic waste disposal in the company's Kodak Park plant, which has been making film and other photographic products. It seems that highly toxic solvents have been leaching into Rochester's ground water for many years. The company knew contaminants were entering the wells of nearby homes but improvidently delayed informing residents until after news media found out and presented the story in a critical way.

The first shock to profits hit the company in the early 1980s. Profits reached a peak in 1981 of $1.2 billion and fell in 1986 to $374 million on sales of $11.5 billion. Colby H. Chandler was named Chairman and CEO of Kodak in 1983, and immediately set out to revive the company through a series of reconstruction programs. He cut costs—although not enough, in the minds of many analysts. He reorganized the company from a functional to a divisional and subsidiary structure. The company diversified from photographic film and equipment to other product areas. Today there are four business sectors: photographic and consumer products, information systems, industrial materials, and health. The diversification program included the acquisition of Sterling Drug Inc., for $5.1 billion; IBM's copier service business, and a number of independent film processors, such as Fox Photo and American Photo Group.

The restructuring increased sales and profits. It stimulated the introduction of a number of new products; some have been successful and others have failed. It has also significantly raised debt, and layoffs have cost Kodak the traditional strong loyalty it enjoyed for many years with its working people.

Sales and profits have risen, due partly to the acquisitions. In 1988, sales were $17 billion, which made Kodak the 25th largest company in the United States, and profits were at an all-time peak of $2.9 billion. However, profits fell sharply in 1989 to $529 million, a worrisome decline.

Colby realized he had to change the Kodak culture to keep pace with the rapidly moving environment. The critical question is whether he has changed things enough soon enough. The company clearly is struggling to regain its old sharp competitive edge. However, a better understanding of and quicker response to environmental changes should pay off.

As the story of Eastman Kodak suggests, for the student of BGS as well as for business managers, there is a continuous need to evaluate forces in the evolving environment of business. For the student, understanding the forces in the business environment provides a solid basis for comprehension of the nature of today's interrelationships among business, government, and society, and it provides insight into possibilities in the future. For business, the environment is the source of opportunities to be exploited as well as threats to be avoided. Those companies that do assess environmental forces on a

---

[1] Clare Ansberry and Carol Hymowitz, ''Kodak Chief Is Trying for the Fourth Time, to Trim Firm's Costs,'' *Wall Street Journal*, September 19, 1989.

continuous and more or less formal basis can take proactive measures to adapt to the changing environment. Those that do not are doomed to react to environmental impacts on their operations and will sooner or later falter.

Implicit or explicit in all that is in this book is the business environment. It is therefore useful to begin with a brief summary and a few illustrations of environmental forces influencing the BGS relationship and the operations of business.

The business environment, in broad terms, is the climate or the surroundings within which a firm operates. The broad concept loses consensus, however, when we move to a description of the environment, the forces operating in it, the perspectives from which it can best be viewed, and a structure that can be used effectively in organizing and facilitating managerial assessment of it.[2]

We find it convenient to divide the discussion in this chapter into two parts. The first pertains to the handful of fundamental underlying forces that have evolved over a long period of time and underlie shorter- and medium-range trends in the business environment. Second is the current environment of business. This we divide into two parts, the external and the internal environment.

UNDERLYING HISTORICAL FORCES CHANGING THE BUSINESS ENVIRONMENT

We believe that, in a broad sense, order can be found in the swirling patterns of current events; that there is a deep logic in the passing of history; and that the directions of change in the business environment are the product of elemental currents flowing in roughly predictable channels. In brief, change in the business environment is the product of seven deep historical forces.

THE INDUSTRIAL REVOLUTION

The first historical force is the industrial revolution. The breakup of small, local economies and the invention of new machinery and manufacturing techniques in the seventeenth century led to expanded markets and mass-production technology that combined capital, labor, and natural resources in dynamic new ways. The growth of mass consumer societies and a world economy in the twentieth century are but two recent echoes of this industrial "big bang." The ramifications of the industrial revolution ripple out through time to define the strategic business environment in many ways. For example, new and larger factories, massive capital accumulation, management techniques for organizing huge corporations, and the interdependence of world financial markets all articulate its centuries-old premise.

[2]R. T. Lenz and J. I. Engledow, "Environmental Analysis Units and Strategic Decision-Making: Field Study of Selected 'Leading Edge' Corporations," *Strategic Management Journal*, January–February, 1986.

DOMINANT IDEOLOGIES

The second historical force is the impact of dominant ideologies. A small number of powerful, well-developed doctrines define a world view for millions of people. In the United States, we largely adhere to ideologies of capitalism, constitutional democracy, and the great religions such as Catholicism and its offshoot, Protestantism. In the main, these ideologies coexist peacefully. But tensions frequently arise, for example, when the accumulation of great wealth and its translation into societal power may be justified by capitalism but conflict with tenets of constitutional democracy that give mass populations the right to check ruling classes in the exercise of power. These tensions among ideologies have ignited political movements and led to redistribution of power in society. Dominant ideologies also determine the broad cast of public opinion and social values.

INEQUALITY OF HUMAN CIRCUMSTANCES

The inequality of human circumstance is the third historical force. From time immemorial, societies have been marked by status distinctions, class structures, and gaps between rich and poor. Inequality is ubiquitous, as are its consequences—jealousy, demands for equality, and doctrines that justify why some people have more than others. The current emphasis on corporate social responsibility in the business environment is, in a general sense, based upon the need to mitigate the appearance of remote and greatly concentrated wealth.

SCIENTIFIC DEVELOPMENT

The fourth historical force is scientific development. The great scientific developments of civilization since Leonardo da Vinci in fifteenth-century Italy have been fuel for the powerful engine of commerce. From the water wheel to recombinant DNA, business has utilized new discoveries to more efficiently convert basic resources into equity. The development of the computer has brought changes in virtually every facet of the business environment and has had enormous consequences for management theory. Like the automobile in its time, it has changed our society.

NATION-STATES

The fifth historical force is the nation-state system. The modern nation-state system arose in an unplanned way from the wreckage of the Roman Empire. Today the world is a geographic mosaic of independent countries, each with a separate government to impose social order and economic stability over its territory. Each country asserts its own sovereignty, or right of self-determination. And in each there develop feelings of nationalism, or loyalty to a national identity. The dynamics of this system are a powerful force in the international business environment. Sometimes countries expand territories to encompass new markets or essential raw materials, as did Japan in the late 1930s. The nationalistic feelings of Palestinians deposed from Israeli territory have affected American companies in many ways, from oil companies that have been caught in Middle East conflicts to airlines that lose passengers afraid of terrorism. The international nation-state system is one of the major sources of turbulence in the business environment.

GREAT LEADERSHIP

The sixth historical force is great leadership. The innovations of great leaders change societies. In the third century B.C., Alexander the Great imposed his rule on the Mediterranean world and created new areas of trade for Greek merchants. In our time, Lee Iacocca earned laurels with the less sweeping act of restoring Chrysler Corporation to financial health by his management of the company. It has always been the case that a small number of individuals in any organization or society are a major force in bringing innovation and change.

CHANCE

The seventh historical force is chance or accident. Many scholars are reluctant to use the concept of random occurrence as a category of analysis. Yet some changes in the business environment can best be explained as beyond the control of business strategists because they are the product of the unknown and unpredictable. The first Tylenol murders occurred in September 1982, when seven people died from capsules filled with cyanide. This event, perhaps the work of one deranged person, was followed over the years by recurrent cyanide poisonings caused by product tampering. The result has been an important change in the production and marketing environments of food and over-the-counter drugs. No less perceptive a student of history than Niccolo Machiavelli observed that fortune determined about half of the course of human events and men the other half. We cannot prove or disprove this estimate, but we note it and are not foolish enough to try to improve upon it. The student of the world surrounding business must recognize the role of caprice.

THE CURRENT BUSINESS ENVIRONMENT

The total business environment is composed of many forces, as shown in Figure 2-1. The chart suggests that environmental forces influence one another and, potentially, every important functional area in a company. John Muir, the great conservationist, once said, "When we try to pick out anything by itself, we find it hitched to everything else in the universe." So it is in business. Any force that affects it turns out to have roots extending over a

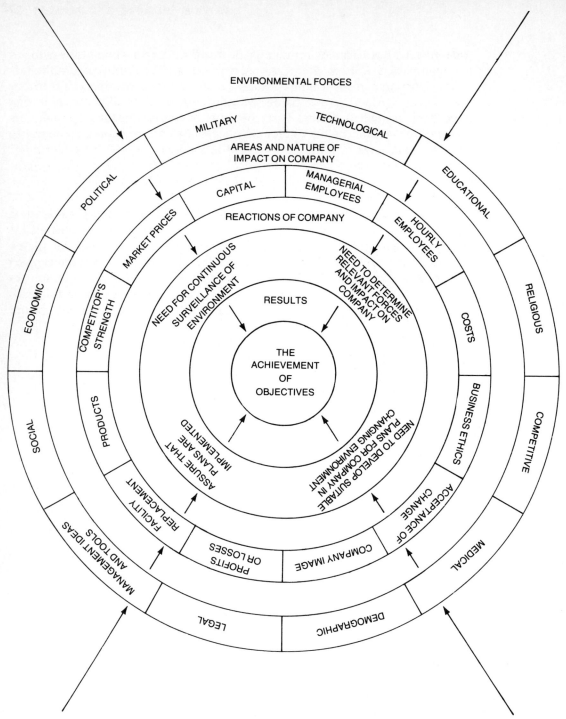

FIGURE 2-1 Environmental impacts on company planning. (Source: Reprinted with permission of The Free Press, a Division of Macmillan, Inc., from *Top Management Planning* by George A. Steiner. Copyright © 1969 by The Trustees of Columbia University in the City of New York.)

wide area. Economic forces, for example, can influence every one of the areas in the outer circle and every one of the areas in the middle circle of Figure 2-1.

This chart shows only selected external environmental forces. There are also internal environmental forces. Some of these are, for example, attitudes of people, the ways in which things are done in an organization, the systems and methods employed in a company, the skills of people, and the values which managers and employees hold. All of these are called the company culture. Such environmental factors are crucial to a company in its operations, including how it formulates strategy and whether the strategy can be implemented properly.

It is worth repeating a point made in Chapter 1, that business is not helpless in the face of environmental forces. Business can influence them, often powerfully. Also, business is an extremely flexible institution and can generally adapt to current and future environmental forces in such a fashion as to maintain its strength and vigor in the face of adverse changes.

Up to this point, we have spoken of environments in general. Our discussion will be simplified if we now narrow the focus to the four major external environments of business and to its internal environment (see Figure 2-2). Other environments may, from time to time, affect a business and, for a particular business at some point in time, may be of critical importance. Some of them are shown in Figure 2-1, and some will be discussed later. Each of these environments has international as well as domestic dimensions.

FIGURE 2-2   The major environments of business.

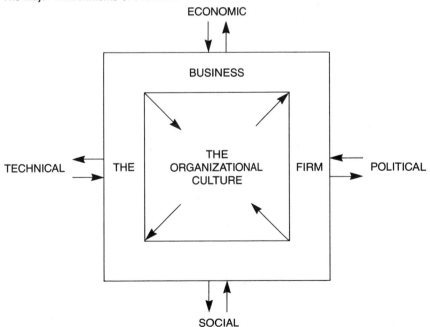

Even a very large company cannot make a penetrating assessment of all the current and evolving domestic and international environments that conceivably might affect it. There are simply too many forces involved. But it is not necessary for a company to make such a comprehensive evaluation. What is necessary is for a company to choose those significant forces in the environment that will likely have an important impact on its operations and devote as much energy as possible to understanding and projecting them.

Today's business environment is challenging managers in far more sophisticated and uncertain ways than ever before in recent history. We seem to be at a critical stage in the world's history, and in the next few years we expect to see important turning points in the post-Cold-War political, economic, social, and technical environments. It is no wonder that business executives are spending more of their time, indeed most of their time, dealing with environmental forces affecting their businesses. The requirement today is that managers throughout an organization, not just the chief executive officer and staff, be continuously committed to understanding and adapting to environmental developments that can affect the organization.

We turn now to a thumbnail sketch of the nature of each of the dominant environments of business and selected forces operating in them. We will dig in greater depth into these environments throughout this book.

THE ECONOMIC ENVIRONMENT

The economic environment covers a vast territory and is, of course, of arresting significance to business. The economic forces of concern to a company range from overall economic activity, as measured by the gross national product (GNP), to what a competitor is doing in a local market. We illustrate as follows a few dimensions of the scope, turbulence, complexity, and power of the economic environment of business.

Overall economic activity as measured by GNP has fluctuated widely from the end of World War II to the present. When GNP is rising robustly, it stimulates business growth and profitability. When it is growing slowly, or declining, business activity is depressed and profits drop or disappear.

The many different components within GNP tend to fluctuate much more than the GNP total. Thus, changes will vary more in such economic forces as consumer and wholesale prices, employment, wage rates, worker productivity, steel production, automobile sales, house construction, and inventories.

Every important economic force has an impact on a wide range of other economic forces, which in turn affect others. The patterns of change vary with time and in intensity. To illustrate, commodity prices have fluctuated significantly in recent years and will do so again in the future, a matter of concern to business as well as consumers. But when and by how much will prices change? What will be the economic implications? No one really knows. Major changes in the general level of commodity prices will affect interest rates, consumer purchasing, stock and bond prices, basic raw material prices, wage-rate demands, to mention but a few activities. Each of these forces affects other phenomena. For example, rising commodity prices tend to generate forces that lift interest rates. This, in turn, increases the cost of capital to business and dampens business borrowing for expansion. Rising interest rates also will bring a decline in bond prices. But rising, or lowering, interest rates result not only from commodity price increases. Higher interest rates can result from a too rapid expansion of general economic activity and rising demand for capital, a decline in savings, or rising interest rates in a major foreign country that attracts our limited capital.

These broad changes in the economic environment narrow down to specific impacts on an individual business and necessitate some difficult and often fateful decisions in dealing with them. For example, such questions as these must be answered. How will my costs of operations change? Wage rates? Raw materials? Health and benefit costs for my employees? Interest rates on my borrowing? What new competition will I face in the global market? How will the economic unification of Europe in 1992 affect my business? Will my competitors here at home steal my market? How can I expand the demand for my products? How much research and development expenditures for new products shall I authorize?

As important as the economic environment is to business, it is matched in significance by the technological, the political, and the social environments, to which we now turn.

THE TECHNOLOGICAL ENVIRONMENT

New technology can and often does change the entire way of life, thinking, values, habits, and even the political processes of a nation. The automobile is a classic example of a new technology that enormously affected every aspect of life in this and many other countries of the world. The United States has gone through one technological revolution after another and continues to do so. For example, in computer science, biotechnology, medicine, robotic factories, telecommunications, and microelectronics, to mention just a few, technology is new. The list of new technologies today is awesome. In the next two decades technology changes will reshape virtually every product, every service, every job in the United States. The forces generated will shake the foundations of the most secure businesses. The choices will powerfully affect options available to consumers, the rate and growth of different business sectors, the role of business in the world, and the standard of living in the United States.[3]

Since the 1970s, about every two and one-half to three years we have had a new generation of computers. The trend has been to make them smaller and smaller and cheaper and cheaper. This movement continues. The new use of lasers, for example, will produce computers with enormously greater power than those of today. Super-computers are still the size of a large piece

[3]See Office of Technology Assessment, *Technology and the American Economic Transition: Choices for the Future*, Washington, D.C.: Congress of the United States, Office of Technology Assessment, May 1988.

of living room furniture, but new laser technology and microelectronics will permit the same capacity to be put in a box the size of the current telephone answering machine.[4] Computers are moving from simple number crunchers to machines of insight and discovery. Soon they will be able to recognize handwriting. Engineers are now designing microsensors that are so small they can be inconspicuously inserted into the human body to snip tumors, repair artery walls, unclog blood vessels, and provide television transmission of interior conditions for diagnostic purposes.[5] Biotechnology is making it possible to produce drought resistant plants, disease resistant plants, bug resistant plants, new and improved fruits and vegetables, and larger farm animals.

These and many other new developments will open up astonishing opportunities for the alert business manager. They will also pose new threats. These threats may arise not alone from domestic competitors in the same industry, but from companies in unrelated industries, and from foreign competitors.

THE POLITICAL ENVIRONMENT

This environment covers a range of subjects, from federal government regulations to local party politics. The greatest concern to business in the area is, of course, the actions of governments. But the legal system and our pluralistic society also are of high interest to business. These three aspects of the political environment will now be examined very briefly.

THE GOVERNMENTAL ENVIRONMENT

There is today practically no aspect of business that governments cannot and will not regulate if the occasion arises and popular or legislative support exists. In recent years, governments have responded affirmatively to a wide range of public concerns about such matters as product safety, product labeling, advertising, minority employment, honesty, pollution, and worker safety, to mention a few. Accordingly, laws have been passed to deal with these concerns. These, when added to the accumulated volume of laws in the past, have resulted in more government control of business than at any peacetime period in our history. Furthermore, the direction of many of these laws has been to involve government in detailed managerial decision making. Government controls in the automobile industry over emission and safety standards are cases in point.

To the typical businessperson, government regulation is burdensome. Antipollution controls, for example, require vast expenditures of funds by many companies. Equal opportunity regulations influence the ways in which

---

[4]Lawrence M. Fisher, "The Vast Promise of a Laser Chip," *The New York Times*, May 13, 1989.
[5]Richard Lipkin, "Big Promise Held in Tiny Packages," *Insight*, April 18, 1988.

companies employ and treat people. Other laws force managers to act in certain ways with respect to product design, work environment, prices charged, costs of capital, and so on. An often overlooked cost of regulation is the time and energy managers and staff must devote to preparing reports for government.

Business is not only subject to the regulations of the federal government but also must deal with fifty state and hundreds of local governments. In addition, our companies that do business abroad are subject to foreign government regulations.

But governments support business as well. For example, the federal government helps business by making direct cash subsidies to individual companies; it gives business the results of government-funded research; it protects businesses from unfair domestic and foreign competition; and it opens up foreign markets for business by negotiating with foreign governments.

The significance of government in the business environment is profound. One CEO put it this way: "All of our skills at managing—financial manufacturing, marketing, research and development and the like—all these put together will not influence our destiny as much as what happens in political and economic arenas."[6]

THE LEGAL ENVIRONMENT

An executive of a large company remarked that not many years ago his principal legal worries centered on antitrust matters, and everything else was lumped together as a poor second. Today, however, he finds that there are many areas of great urgency, the priorities of which change from month to month, and that the number of problems as well as attorney and other legal costs have exploded. Indeed, he said facetiously, he has set a goal of having annual earnings five times the legal fees of the company!

Today, in addition to antitrust, other major areas of legal concern to business are securities and stockholder matters; consumer complaints; fair employment practices; product safety; worker safety and health; government contracts; and air, water, and noise pollution. Not only have legal actions against business in all areas increased rapidly, but potential liability for business has also risen explosively. Corporations are exposed considerably more than in the past to legal liabilities for injuries from their products. Also, directors, officers, and other managers of businesses are subject to vastly expanded legal liabilities for their actions and, often, for those of their subordinates. Not only do businesses find their liability insurance rates far higher than in the past, but many who are in exposed positions are unable to get any liability insurance.

The newly complex legal environment of business is due in part to increased government regulations, which foster suits against corporations for

---

[6]Robert Cushman, "Remarks to the New England Public Relations Society," Worcester, Mass.: Worcester Polytechnic Institute, February 27, 1980.

perceived violations of regulations. Also, courts of law have made it much easier for plaintiffs to get generous awards for injuries for which corporations in the past were not held liable.

PLURALISM

Ours is a pluralistic society, which means that it is composed of many semiautonomous and autonomous groups through which power is diffused. These groups exert pressure on governments to act in their interest, and much of the legislation that they influence governments to enact impacts on business. They also exert pressure directly on business to act on their behalf.

In the distant past, business managers could be successful if, working within the rules of the game laid down by government, they tried to satisfy only customers and stockholders. Today the managers of a large corporation must pay attention to a growing number of constituent groups. Dealing with the diverse, often conflicting, and often disruptive pressures of such groups consumes a growing share of managerial time, especially in larger companies. Pluralism will be discussed at some length in the next chapter.

THE SOCIAL ENVIRONMENT

The social environment includes such diverse forces as changing values, education, religion, labor union activities, and the customs and habits of people. Here we will examine only values.

CHANGING VALUES

Values are enduring beliefs that people hold about morals, equality, freedom, democracy, patriotism, and so on.[7] Values do not change easily, but over time they do change. When values change, the impact is felt in the ways in which business, government, and society operate and in how they interrelate. For example, in the 1970s there was an upsurge in public demand for environmental and consumer protections. These demands grew out of a rise in the values people held for a higher quality of life. There was a significant elevation, for example, in the values of a cleaner environment, higher-quality products, more equality in the workplace, safer products, and safer workplaces. The result was an unprecedented burst of federal legislation.

Over past centuries, some of the fundamental values associated with the BGS relationship have changed significantly, whereas others have changed

---

[7]There is no simple, generally accepted definition of the term "value." Professor Milton Rokeach of Washington State University (*The Nature of Human Values*, New York: The Free Press, 1973) defines value as a fundamental, relatively stable, prescriptive or proscriptive belief that a specific behavior or aim of existence is preferred to a different mode of behavior or aim. This belief is stronger and more stubbornly held than attitudes, fads, or opinions. Values, thus, are general guides that people hold to make decisions and to appraise the results of actions taken by institutions (such as governments or businesses) and people. They are powerful motivators of people and institutions in society.

surprisingly little. For example, public opinion polls clearly confirm that many values supporting the free enterprise system and the role of the business institution in society are still strongly held by most people. In contrast, it is also clear that more people are less willing than in the past to accept the unfettered operation of the free market mechanism and are demanding more and more government protection from its operation.

Following is a review of the current status of some of the underlying values held by people that relate most closely to the business system.

Individualism   Older beliefs associated with individualism centered on the freedom of the individual to pursue interests relatively unimpeded by government. Each individual, in this view, had an opportunity to achieve ends through his or her own efforts. Today, the older view of unrestrained individualism has been modified by concepts of equality, government protection of the individual against market forces, and more participation of individuals in organizations.

Laissez Faire   Throughout our history, a fundamental dogma of people in business, which has been accepted by an overwhelming majority of people, has been minimum government interference in the economic system. The term *laissez faire,* first used by the French, meant literally that government should "leave us alone." This old idea of limited government has been badly bruised in the current massive intrusions of government in the market mechanism. The classical freedom of people in business to operate in conformance with a comparatively unfettered open market mechanism is no longer a reality. The value is still strongly held, however, by many people and is a restraint on expanding government regulatory power.

Property Rights   As a direct result of increased government regulations, but also because of changing legal decisions reflecting new societal values, the rights of property owners have undergone considerable changes. Although entrepreneurs of very small businesses still enjoy considerable autonomy in their use of company assets, managers of the larger companies know full well that they are administrators of private property invested with a heavy public interest. The public is increasingly concerned about how larger companies operate. This concern is reflected not only in government mandate about how property will be used, but also in voluntary allocations of resources by managers, which reflect public as distinct from private interest. For example, managers today are well aware of the necessity to use company property in such a way as to reduce pollution of the atmosphere.

Profit   The old view of profit as the sole end of business is no longer accepted. Profit is still considered necessary by a majority, but attitudes about profit are changing. Society is coming more and more to expect that societal interest be considered as well as business self-interest in pursuing profit objectives. Business managers, especially in larger corporations, take the view today that concern for the interests of the dominant sociopolitical stakeholders in their companies is the best route to expanding profits for shareholders.

The Protestant Ethic   A central feature of the older concept of individualism was the so-called Protestant Ethic, which placed a high value on hard work, delayed gratification, thrift, loyalty, and obedience to authority. This ethic is being considerably modified by the attitudes of managers and other workers in enterprises. To oversimplify, today's workers place less value on hard work for its own sake. They want, generally, more meaningful jobs, greater satisfaction on the job, and opportunities for advancement. In contrast to the notion of delayed gratification, emphasis today is placed on achieving satisfaction, and this generally means, among other things, going into debt. The questioning of authority has replaced the former blind acceptance of authority. Loyalty to company has eroded in light of a widening acceptance of the view that any employee caught in a conflict between the company and the public interest should resolve it in favor of the latter.

Materialism   The striving of individuals to increase their possession and use of material goods and services has been a powerful motivator of business. Materialism has been a prime influence in our passion for productivity, efficiency, the spirit of competition, innovation, and growth—all of which, in turn, contributed to the extraordinary rise of gross national product that has been recorded since our nation's birth.

The motivation to acquire more material goods and services is still strong but is tempered by the desire for leisure, for a satisfying job even though it may pay a bit less than a stressful job, and for adventures that yield a more satisfying life. This desire does not mean subtraction from material accumulation goals, but addition to them.

Equality   Alexis de Tocqueville, the insightful nineteenth-century French observer of our society, saw equality as the dominant value in American society. Closely related to individualism, equality traditionally meant the elimination of inequalities among people with respect to opportunities for social, political, and economic growth. It meant that conditions should permit individuals, whatever their origins (although in the nineteenth century color was considered to be a question of another order and women were not in reality in the same position as men), to make a life on the basis of ability and character. It was the idea that everyone should have "an equal place at the starting line."

In recent years, the concept of equality has broadened to include rights to receive a wide range of political, economic, and social demands. The concept has further broadened to mean equality of results, or an equal outcome for all.

CHANGING ATTITUDES AND VALUES AFFECTING BUSINESS

We believe that there is general agreement about the following subtle, but pronounced, shifts in the thinking of people about the functioning of business. Consider how such shifts in attitudes and values change not only the internal functioning of a company but also how the firm relates to government and society generally, for example:

- From considerations of quantity ("more") toward considerations of quality ("better")
- From profligate use of resources to conservation
- From the concept of independence toward the concept of interdependence (of nations, institutions, individuals, all species)
- From free trade to managed trade
- From more government regulation to less government regulation and back to more government regulation
- From mastery over nature toward living in harmony with it
- From the primacy of technical efficiency toward considerations of social justice and equity
- From the dictates of organizational convenience toward the aspirations of self-development in an organization's members
- From authoritarianism and dogmatism toward participation
- From uniformity and centralization toward diversity and pluralism
- From the concept of work as hard, unavoidable, and a duty toward the recognition of leisure as valid in its own right

CRITICISMS OF BUSINESS

Criticism of business is discussed in depth in Chapter 4, so we will merely mention it here. There has always been criticism of business behavior and performance. There is nothing wrong with criticism per se. When expressed with good reason it can be effective in improving business performance. Excessive and ill-founded criticism of business, however, can have an adverse impact on the operation of individual businesses because it can lead to excessive government regulation. In this way, it can erode the foundations of the business institution.

Public attitudes toward business are not completely negative. For example, communities throughout the nation are courting business favor through such mechanisms as tax concessions, guaranteeing loans, providing cheap or free land, building access roads to plants, and providing retraining programs for workers. The reason, of course, is to get jobs for unemployed workers in the community.

OTHER EXTERNAL ENVIRONMENTS

Other business environments shown in Figure 2-1 should be noted in passing. For instance, universities are sources of challenge to business values as well as sources of valuable ideas, basic research, and skills needed by business. The state of the educational system as a whole affects business through the capabilities of students it has taught. Changing rates of fertility have an impact on business because of changes in the labor supply. The concentration of unskilled, poor, and uneducated people in some urban centers is complicating city governance and, in turn, raising demands for business aid to deal with the problems. It also erodes the environment in which business is done. Wars and threat of wars produce a wide range of impacts on business.

THE INTERNAL ENVIRONMENT OF A BUSINESS

The internal environment is not as extensive as the external environment, but it plays a cardinal role in the operation of a business. It can be described in several ways. One is to view it as being coterminous with the company culture, the general nature of which was noted previously. Another approach is to identify the main classes of people in an organization. This approach is shown in Figure 2-3. Each of the groups in the chart has different goals, beliefs, needs, and so on, which managers must coordinate to achieve overall company goals. The fundamental characteristics of the groups shown in the chart are readily known and need no further elaboration here. Later in the book, we will intensively examine the changing internal life of organizations.

BUSINESS'S IMPACT ON ITS ENVIRONMENTS

We have emphasized that business has both direct and indirect influence over virtually every important facet of this society. Its introduction of technology into society brings in its wake changes in values, which in turn affect what society believes and does. Because of its dominant role in society, there

FIGURE 2-3   Major stakeholders in the internal
business environment.

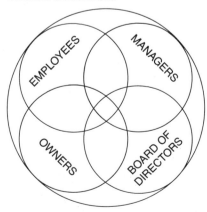

is a tendency for business values to be accepted. Being on time, for instance, is a business value that is also applied in nonwork situations. Rising affluence brings the occasion for changing social priorities. When a company decides to move from one community to another, its influence in these areas can be extraordinary.

The influence of business over its environments can be derivative and indirect or purposeful, as when business seeks to influence directly its environment. The activities of corporate political action committees (PACs), for example, have the avowed purpose in many instances of helping to elect politicians with a conservative, business point of view. The Business Roundtable, a group of chief executive officers of the largest corporations in the United States, has a purpose, among others, to promote legislation in the Congress that helps business. The Allegheny Conference on Community Development is a group of business people that initiated programs to clean up and develop the downtown area of Pittsburgh. These activities represent successful exercises of business power over its environment. But on other occasions, business power has been negligible. For example, when tax reform legislation was passed in 1986, it was passed over the "dead bodies" of legions of business lobbyists. They sought special favors for oil, real estate, mining, textiles, and so on and lost heavily, even though some concessions were gained.

IMPLICATIONS FOR BUSINESS AND THE BUSINESS INSTITUTION

All of these observations have vast and profound implications for the management of business enterprises and the future of the business institution. Currently, the management of business enterprises is significantly different from what it was ten to twenty years ago. Top managers of corporations spend a large part of their time today dealing with environmental problems. These include addressing social concerns of society, complying with new social legislation, communicating with legislators and government executives about proposed laws and regulations, meeting with various interest groups concerning their demands and/or grievances, and administering their organizations in such a way as to respond to the new attitudes of people working there. This agenda is in sharp contrast to that of a top executive of a major corporation twenty years ago, whose decision making was based almost wholly on economic and technical considerations.[8]

---

[8]For a study of this subject, see George A. Steiner, *The New CIO,* New York: Macmillan, 1983.

Asbestos Litigation "Bankrupts" Manville

It is said that when railways were first opened in Spain, peasants standing on the tracks were not unfrequently run over; and that the blame fell on the engine-drivers for not stopping: rural experiences having yielded no conception of the momentum of a large mass moving at a high velocity.

Herbert Spencer, (1884)[9]

On August 26, 1982, the Manville Corporation of Denver filed a voluntary petition to reorganize under Chapter 11 of the Bankruptcy Reform Act of 1978. Manville, like the rural peasants on train tracks, was caught dumbfounded by an unprecedented force in its environment—a surge of asbestos-related illness litigation. Underlying this litigation were more fundamental environmental changes, including new public attitudes toward product safety and new legal theories of product liability. Manville's bankruptcy declaration is a response that some admired as creative and others criticized as irresponsible. Everyone was surprised. Here is what happened.

THE ASBESTOS LITIGATION

When Manville filed for reorganization, it was financially sound. In 1981 it earned $60.3 million on sales of $2.2 billion and ranked 181st on the *Fortune* 500 list of industrials. In the first half of 1982, the company reported a loss of $25.1 million, due largely to a recession in the construction industry. Despite this loss, financial analysts were favorably impressed with Manville's low debt-to-equity ratio, and, under ordinary circumstances, the company would have had a sound future. Manville is the only company included in the Dow Jones industrial average ever to declare bankruptcy, and it is perhaps the healthiest ever to do so.

[9]*The Man Versus the State*, London: Watts & Co., 1940 (reprinted), p. 28.

Manville's burden is an avalanche of lawsuits by victims of diseases caused by exposure to airborne asbestos particles. Most of the victims are workers who used asbestos materials supplied by Manville and other asbestos manufacturers. The company argued that it could not pay future debts from anticipated claims in 16,500 existing asbestos injury lawsuits. These suits were being settled for an average $40,000 a claim; 500 new ones arose each month; and an independent study projected another 36,000 future claims for a total liability by the year 2000 of at least $2 billion and probably many times that amount. In addition, five large claims early in 1982 averaged punitive damage awards of $616,000 each—an unsettling augury. Punitive damages are awarded in excess of due compensation for injury to punish a corporation for flagrant misbehavior. Ordinarily, they are not covered by insurance. It became clear to a special committee of Manville directors, appointed to study the lawsuit problem, that Manville eventually could not pay all the claims against it.

Large awards arose, in part, because of two important changes in legal precedent. First, decisions in state courts in the early 1970s permitted injured asbestos workers to bring tort actions against asbestos suppliers. Earlier, workers could pursue wrongful injury claims only through state worker-compensation systems, where awards were far below the average for tort suits. Second, legal doctrines of product liability changed. Prior to the 1960s, the liability of manufacturers for their products was firmly grounded in the doctrine of negligent conduct. Under this doctrine a manufacturer had to be proven negligent or blameworthy in making or selling a product. The law, however, evolved toward the concept of strict liability, under which manufacturers could be found liable for harm to their consumers even if they were not intentionally or knowingly negligent or irresponsible. According to a newly evolved legal theory called strict liability, a manufacturer could be held liable for selling an "abnormally dangerous" product to a consumer even if no negligence in manufacturing the product was proven.[10] "Abnormally dangerous" means that a product is more dangerous than would be assumed by the average user unless warned otherwise.

As a result of the rise of strict liability, it became increasingly difficult for Manville to prevail in litigation. For example, in *Beshada v. Johns-Manville Products Corp.* in 1982, the New Jersey Supreme Court accepted the argument that Manville and other asbestos manufacturers could be held liable for asbestos injury even when it could not be proven that years ago the company was aware of asbestos dangers.[11] Symptoms of illnesses resulting from exposure to asbestos may not appear until 30 or 40 years after exposure. So in this and other cases, Manville had argued that scientific knowledge about asbes-

[10]See American Law Institute, *Restatement of the Law of Torts*, 2d., Washington, D.C.: American Law Institute Publishers, 1965, vol. 2, section 402A, pp. 347–48. Section 402A imposes liability for damages on anyone who sells a product in defective condition unreasonably dangerous to the consumer where the product reaches the consumer without substantial change and causes the consumer injury even though the seller has exercised all possible care in the manufacture and distribution of the product.
[11]90 N.J. 191, 447 A.2d 539.

tos hazards had not been sufficiently conclusive prior to the 1960s to require manufacturers to warn workers in industries where asbestos products were used. The court rejected this argument, stripping Manville of its primary defense.

These two changes in Manville's legal environment ensured rising settlement costs. In their wake, an entire industry developed to litigate asbestos cases, complete with its own publication, the biweekly *Asbestos Litigation Reporter*, and pressure groups such as the Asbestos Litigation Group (a coalition of 500 lawyers and thousands of plaintiffs suing Manville), the White Lung Association, and Asbestos Victims of America.

The growth curve in the number of lawsuits was astounding. The first against Manville came in 1968, and by 1973 there were only thirteen claims. By 1980, however, there were 5,000, and at the time of bankruptcy filing there were 16,500. In 1983, a total of 24,000 suits faced sixty manufacturers and suppliers; the long-term cost of this litigation was estimated to be $40 to $90 billion.

A Rand Corporation analysis of claims settled at the time of the bankruptcy filing showed that lawyers' fees were larger than awards to plaintiffs. For every dollar received by victims of asbestos illness, $1.71 went to lawyers' fees and legal expenses.[12] This arrangement was widely regarded by observers as a flaw in the legal system and unfair to asbestos victims. But the victims' attorneys were securing for them much larger awards than would have been received under worker-compensation systems—even after deduction of lawyers' contingency fees.

Adding to Manville's woes was the fact that its insurers refused to pay claims. Manville filed lawsuits against more than thirty insurers. Its current insurers resisted payment with the argument that, because of long latency periods common to asbestos diseases, the damage had been done in past years. Past insurers argued that coverage was invoked only by manifestation of symptoms, not by earlier exposure to injury. Manville countered with a "theory of continuous injury," under which insurers of all periods could be liable because both early exposure and later symptoms produce harm, entitling asbestos victims to compensation. In late 1986 Manville reached an out-of-court settlement with twenty-seven of its insurers for $730 million.

THE BANKRUPTCY PROCEEDINGS

When a company files a bankruptcy petition, it asks a bankruptcy court judge for protection from creditors until a future date, when it presents a reorganization plan to pay debts. The reorganization plan must be approved by 50 percent of creditors representing two-thirds of the dollar amount owed. The term "Chapter 11" refers to a section of the Bankruptcy Reform Act of 1978 that consolidates all reorganization sections of prior bankruptcy laws.

[12]*Rand Research Review,* "The Asbestos Tragedy: Costs and Compensation," Fall 1983.

In the past, a corporation could declare bankruptcy only if it was insolvent or unable to pay debts as they matured. In 1978, however, the insolvency provision was deleted from voluntary bankruptcy proceedings to relieve the courts of the burden of making financial calculations. Hence, while hard hit by changing legal doctrines of product liability, Manville was helped by a change in the bankruptcy laws allowing a company that *may* become bankrupt to petition for reorganization, rather than permitting only companies that *are currently* insolvent to petition.

In a newspaper advertisement the day after Manville's reorganization filing, Manville's chief executive, John A. McKinney, stated:

> To avoid Chapter 11, we would have had to strangle the Company slowly, by deferring maintenance and postponing capital expenditures. We would also have had to cannibalize our good business just to keep going. If recent trends had continued we would have had to mortgage our plants and properties and new credit would be most difficult and expensive to obtain. This is no way to go forward.

The petition for reorganization had the effect of stopping regular payments on interest and principal to large creditors such as Morgan Guaranty Trust, Bank of America, Chemical Bank, Citibank, Republic National Bank, Continental Illinois National Bank, Wells Fargo Bank, and Prudential Insurance Co. It also put the thousands of impending asbestos lawsuits in limbo, as Manville's financial liability was in doubt. "Bold," said *Time* magazine.[13] "Pretty creative," remarked a Harvard Law School bankruptcy professor.[14] A *Fortune* magazine writer called the move "a particularly daring example of the new uses of bankruptcy."[15] Others were less charitable. Manville was accused of "cold-hearted profit motives" and "murder" by a former asbestos worker, testifying at a House subcommittee hearing.[16] "Dubious and unusual at best," cried Senator Robert Dole (R-Kan.) in a next-day statement. "A shoddy effort to escape liability," said Representative George Miller (D-Calif.).[17] Both declared an interest in amending federal bankruptcy law to prevent similar abuse in the future.

Shortly after seeking Chapter 11 protection, Manville fought off legal challenges to the bankruptcy by asbestos victims. Then, between 1982 and 1986, a plan of reorganization was negotiated in the bankruptcy court. At first, Manville proposed a "limited pot" plan, which would have allowed the company to continue operation immunized from future legal claims while giving fixed compensation to victims from current assets. This plan was unacceptable to victims' attorneys and negotiations became deadlocked. Then, an at-

---

[13]James Kelley, "Manville's Bold Maneuver," *Time,* September 6, 1982, p. 18.

[14]Clemens P. Work, "Bankruptcy: An Escape Hatch for Ailing Firms," *U.S. News & World Report,* August 22, 1983, p. 66.

[15]Anna Cifelli, "Management by Bankruptcy," *Fortune,* October 31, 1983, p. 69.

[16]Gary Geipel, "Asbestos Lawsuits Paralyzed House Panel Told," *Los Angeles Times,* February 11, 1983.

[17]Ben Sherwood, "Probe of Bankruptcy Laws Pledged in Manville Case," *Los Angeles Times,* August 28, 1982.

torney representing future asbestos claimants proposed an "open-ended" plan in 1984. This plan, which was finally agreed to by Manville in 1986, created two trusts to settle and pay claims.[18] They were to be funded with a mixture of bonds, cash, stock, and future profits.

The first, the Personal Injury Settlement Trust, was funded with $2.5 billion for payment of health damage claims brought by present and future asbestos victims. Manville is scheduled to pay up to 20 percent of operating profits into this fund over a 22-year period beginning in 1992. The trust was funded in part with 80 percent of Manville's common stock, which made common shareholders the biggest financial losers. The second trust, the Property Damage Settlement Trust, was funded with $240 million in cash and insurance proceeds and will pay claims brought by owners of asbestos-containing buildings. Both trusts are run by trustees who operate independently of Manville management. In addition, Manville was to pay over $700 million to creditors and set up a $5 million charitable fund for deserving asbestos victims who did not technically qualify for compensation.

After lawsuits brought by Manville's common shareowners to block the reorganization plan went up to the Supreme Court, where they were denied a hearing, Manville finally emerged from Chapter 11 on November 28, 1988—six years and three months after filing.

During the long bankruptcy period, Manville restructured itself, divesting all asbestos operations and consolidating three operating groups—a fiber glass group, which makes insulation and auto parts; a forest products group, which grows trees, makes wine cooler cartons, grocery sacks, and folding cartons; and a specialty products group, which includes a variety of businesses from lighting fixtures for stadiums to palladium mines. The loss of asbestos plants has hurt Manville's earnings, because asbestos was the most profitable of its many businesses. Manville has been continuously profitable throughout bankruptcy (with the exception of 1982 and 1988, when losses were due to reorganization-related extraordinary charges against earnings). Questions have, of course, been raised about its ability to sustain funding for the Personal Injury Trust. In August 1991, Manville must begin payments of $75 million a year into this fund, and in 1992 it must begin to hand over 20 percent of profits in addition to the $75 million annual payments. In 1988, the company netted $89 million on $2 billion in sales, a 6.5 percent return on capital. It will be years before the full consequences of the plan are clear.

The payout to asbestos victims is now much lower than would have been the case under the pre-Chapter 11 torrent of litigation, and this is the key to Manville's survival. As a condition of emerging from the protection of Chapter 11, the company can no longer be sued by injured workers. And the end of lawsuits also brings with it the end of punitive damage awards.

---

[18]This complex plan, presented here in brief summary, is described in a 554-page document, United States Bankruptcy Court, Southern District of New York, *In re Johns-Manville Corporation, et al., Second Amended Disclosure Statement, Second Amended and Restated Plan of Reorganization, and Related Documents*, December 9, 1988. A concise summary of the bankruptcy negotiations is Stephen W. Quickel, "Triumph of Wile," *Business Month*, November 1988.

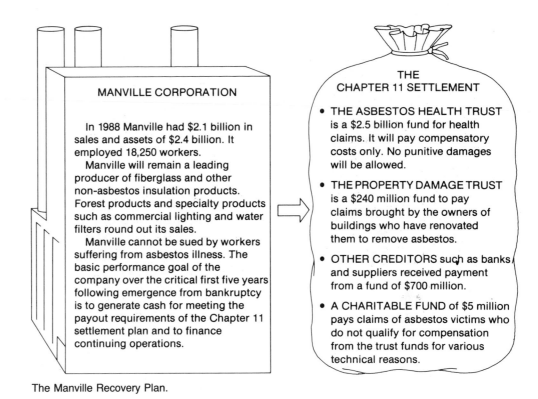

MANVILLE CORPORATION

In 1988 Manville had $2.1 billion in sales and assets of $2.4 billion. It employed 18,250 workers.

Manville will remain a leading producer of fiberglass and other non-asbestos insulation products. Forest products and specialty products such as commercial lighting and water filters round out its sales.

Manville cannot be sued by workers suffering from asbestos illness. The basic performance goal of the company over the critical first five years following emergence from bankruptcy is to generate cash for meeting the payout requirements of the Chapter 11 settlement plan and to finance continuing operations.

THE CHAPTER 11 SETTLEMENT

- **THE ASBESTOS HEALTH TRUST** is a $2.5 billion fund for health claims. It will pay compensatory costs only. No punitive damages will be allowed.

- **THE PROPERTY DAMAGE TRUST** is a $240 million fund to pay claims brought by the owners of buildings who have renovated them to remove asbestos.

- **OTHER CREDITORS** such as banks and suppliers received payment from a fund of $700 million.

- **A CHARITABLE FUND** of $5 million pays claims of asbestos victims who do not qualify for compensation from the trust funds for various technical reasons.

The Manville Recovery Plan.

During the reorganization period between 1982 and 1988 over 2,000 asbestos claimants died, their claims stalled by bickering in bankruptcy courts. A heartrending letter from a prominent asbestos-illness researcher, Dr. Irving Selikoff, to the *New York Times* in 1985 underscored the human tragedy behind the Chapter 11 gambit.

Death and disease are not held in abeyance by legal writs. The victims are barred from applying for the financial help needed to ease their difficulties. Men are dying of mesothelioma [cancer of the lining of the chest or abdominal cavity] or lung cancer, unable to seek medical care to ease their last days, and others are not able to afford the medical surveillance that could save their lives. Still others, short of breath, with asbestos lung scarring and no longer able to make a living, can't keep their families together.

It is hard to appreciate the terror of a woman whose husband has been sent home from a hospital with a tracheostomy tube in his throat, unable to afford a nurse, resuscitating him at each emergency, until the final episode. Or widows—of shipyard workers, steam-locomotive repairmen, construction workers, power and utility plant personnel, and other craftsmen—having used slowly accumulated retirement dollars for the illness brought on by asbestos.

Some have written me that they come close to begging in the streets. Others get along by visiting the children in rotation. Often, when I write a widow for scientific information, the reply comes from a trailer park: the house sold. After a lifetime of hard work, to die and to have his widow live in penury is a bitter final reward for a worker.[19]

Since Manville's exit from bankruptcy, the Personal Injury Trust has settled 14,000 claims at an average of $38,000 each, higher than the anticipated average of $25,000. There are 80,000 current unsettled claims left to deal with, and Trust officers predict that 200,000 new claims will be filed over the next 30 years by workers who are well now, but who will become sick from past asbestos exposure.[20]

ASBESTOS AND WORKER HEALTH

"Asbestos" is a generic term for a family of naturally occuring fibrous minerals. The first asbestos mine in North America was opened in Quebec in 1879 to tap huge Canadian deposits. In 1901, the Johns-Manville Corporation was born of the merger of two independent companies that made asbestos and insulation products. Over the years, the company became the world's largest producer of asbestos products.

World asbestos production increased from 20,000 tons annually in 1916 to 4.3 million tons at its high point in 1978.[21] In its heyday, asbestos had thousands of uses in industry and consumer products, and as an advanced industrial nation close to enormous Canadian deposits, the United States consumed about half of the world's processed asbestos. Asbestos has great value because its fibers are easily woven, do not burn, and conduct heat slowly. This makes it an ideal insulating and fireproofing material. Over the years, asbestos has brought many benefits to society. Many lives have been saved as a result of its fireproofing quality. The use of asbestos on brake linings has increased motor vehicle safety. And the use of asbestos in such products as paint and insulation has added comfort to modern living. No dollar value that can be balanced against the costs of health damage to workers has been placed on these overall benefits.

Harmful worker exposure occurs through inhalation of airborne asbestos particles. Once inhaled, the particles permanently attach themselves to lung tissue. Long-term exposure produces lung scarring, and an irreversible, chronic disease—asbestosis—progressively damages the lungs and makes breathing difficult. Asbestos exposure is also associated with lung cancer, gastrointestinal cancer, and mesothelioma.

Exposure to asbestos is extremely dangerous. Medical studies extending back at least fifty years demonstrate impairment of lung function, scarring of lung tissue, and increased risk of pulmonary neoplasia to be closely associated with heavy, prolonged exposure to asbestos. Indeed, it is a rare worker

---

[19]In Paul Brodeur, *Outrageous Misconduct: The Asbestos Industry on Trial*, New York: Pantheon Books, 1985, pp. 302–303.

[20]Cynthia F. Mitchell, "Manville Trust May Be Forced Into Stock Sale," *Wall Street Journal*, February 8, 1989.

[21]Samuel S. Epstein, *The Politics of Cancer*, revised edition, New York: Anchor Books, 1979, p. 80.

who survives to a ripe old age unimpaired after working for any length of time at a job where there is heavy exposure to airborne asbestos fiber. So dangerous is the fiber that asbestos illness has occurred repeatedly among family members of asbestos workers whose only exposure was the dust that came into the home on the worker's clothes at the end of the day.

After exposure, asbestos fibers remain in the lungs. They are sharp and tough and continue to produce scarring of the lung tissue that reduces the area available for exchange of gases and makes breathing difficult. Asbestos fibers also irritate bronchial cells, causing them to undergo morphological change and develop into cancerous, invasive cells. Because of the persistent presence of asbestos fibers in lung tissue, latency periods of up to forty years exist in asbestos-lung disease. Even after exposure to asbestos fibers ends, they continue to work their insidious task, until the disease becomes symptomatic years later.

It was not always known that asbestos endangered workers. The first evidence that business realized the dangers came in 1918, when some insurers in the United States and Canada refused to sell life insurance policies to asbestos workers. A number of early studies and accounts in the medical literature addressed a relationship between asbestos and asbestosis and lung cancer. A central issue in the asbestos-illness litigation against Manville and other asbestos manufacturers was whether managers at these companies knew about the dangers of asbestos and failed to warn and protect workers. It has been Manville's position that adequate knowledge of asbestos dangers was not present until 1964, with the publication of a major study of illness among asbestos workers. This assertion, that Manville was ignorant of the dangers until conclusive evidence was available in the 1960s, became known as the "state-of-the-art defense" in asbestos litigation, and all the other companies followed Manville's lead as co-defendants in numerous suits with Manville. Manville's lawyers were well rehearsed in tactics and testimony buttressing this position, and when Manville declared bankruptcy, the other defendants missed its courtroom presence.

Attorneys for asbestos victims sought to invalidate this "state-of-the-art defense" that was based on alleged ignorance. In taking depositions, information was uncovered that eroded Manville's position. One breakthrough was the testimony of Dr. Kenneth W. Smith, a former company doctor at one of Manville's Canadian asbestos plants. Smith reported, for example, that in the late 1940s, he had information that workers were getting sick and in 1949 sent a report to top officers showing that out of 708 workers whom he had X-rayed, only four had normal, healthy lungs. He further reported that he had withheld information from workers about their condition to avoid upsetting them and shortening their productive days with the company. Dr. Smith was able to document the fact that top company officers—including a future president of Manville—had seen his report, but did not act on it.

In another trial, attorneys for injured workers discovered that Raybestos-Manhattan, the largest U.S. manufacturer of asbestos-containing brake linings, had requested Metropolitan Life Insurance Co. to undertake health surveys of its workers and make recommendations about protecting their health in the 1920s. Metropolitan released a report in 1931 that demonstrated a high incidence of asbestosis among Raybestos-Manhattan workers and issued a strong warning about the health dangers of asbestos exposure. The report was discussed in 1933 at meetings of top officials of Manville and Raybestos-Manhattan, and those officials agreed to keep the information secret to avoid lawsuits. In 1977, an attorney for asbestos victims obtained copies of minutes of this meeting and was able to document for the first time a conspiracy among major asbestos manufacturers to hide evidence of health dangers to workers. The minutes of the 1933 meeting and other documents had been kept in a Raybestos-Manhattan vault for the intervening years, while Manville had destroyed its copies.[22] The discovery of this kind of information made it increasingly difficult for Manville to convince juries that its top officers were ignorant of asbestos dangers until 1964, led to record punitive damages, and ultimately forced the Chapter 11 declaration.

In the 1990s the dangers of asbestos are better known, and its use is declining. In the United States the Environmental Protection Agency first banned asbestos for nonessential uses in 1984 and since then the ban has expanded to cover more consumer products and industrial uses. Although auto manufacturers make asbestos-free disc brakes and non-asbestos brake shoes, millions of cars still depend on asbestos-lined drums. European countries use less asbestos today; imports fell 58 percent in the 1980s.[23] Canadian asbestos producers, however, have undertaken a campaign to promote asbestos. They argue that for many uses, asbestos exposure hazards are low and health risks minimal. The biggest markets for Canadian asbestos are now third world countries such as Thailand, South Korea, Bangledesh, and Pakistan.

THE BROADER QUESTION: COMPENSATING VICTIMS OF EXPOSURE TO TOXIC SUBSTANCES

Whatever else may be said of it, the Manville bankruptcy and reorganization stands as a precedent for compensating victims of environmental exposure to toxic substances. No party to it saw it as an ideal solution. During bankruptcy, Manville's top management fought the long-term transfer of company funds into the two trust funds, preferring a more limited, finite obligation paid in full upon emerging from Chapter 11. Owners of Manville's common shares were, of course, bitterly opposed to the reorganization plan because the value of their shares was diluted by four-fifths.

Manville has advocated an administered compensation plan in which other parties accept some financial responsibility. These other parties include the federal government, which operated shipyards where workers got heavy exposure to asbestos, and tobacco companies, because asbestos workers who smoke have a much higher risk of pulmonary illness. Both, argued Manville,

[22]Paul Brodeur, "The Asbestos Industry on Trial: II-Discovery," *The New Yorker*, July 1, 1985.
[23]Jonathan Dahl, "Canada Encourages Mining of Asbestos, Sells to Third World," *Wall Street Journal*, September 12, 1989.

also knew of asbestos dangers but failed to properly warn workers. Manville has supported legislation in Congress to reform product liability law by limiting punitive damage awards and reversing the trend toward strict liability. Manville was a victim of what some call the "piranha syndrome," in which plaintiff lawyers search for products that juries might find dangerous and then, working on contingency fees which give them a large percentage of any court awards, organize victims to attack the treasury of the corporation that made the product.

Lawyers for sick workers, on the other hand, saw the huge awards against Manville as just. Their contingency fees, they argued, allowed poor victims to be represented by skilled lawyers without having to pay huge legal fees in advance of monetary awards. In addition, they believe that the punitive damage awards against Manville set a precedent that will make other companies handling other toxic substances ultracautious about health hazards.

Sick workers have had to wait many years for compensation and instead of receiving six or seven figure jury awards, they have averaged $38,000. Many of them feel that Manville caused widespread cancer in the population, then waltzed away from harsh penalties by using bankruptcy as a business strategy and paying modest claims to the doomed through an administered system. For future asbestos victims, those who will become ill through the year 2020, some compensation from the post-Chapter 11 Manville is certainly preferable to none from a defunct firm.

MANVILLE: A BETTER COMPANY NOW?

Today Manville emphasizes worker health and safety. It carefully investigates health risks of all products it sells, uses warning labels so freely that it even puts a sticker reading "this creates dust" on every wood board it sells (because wood dust is carcinogenic), and indemnifies its customers against future health claims arising from its products.[24] The diatomaceous earth Manville mines contains crystalline silica, which is a probable carcinogen. Recently, in Japan, the company was advised that the word "cancer" was never used on warning labels, even on cigarettes and asbestos, and would scare customers. The Ministries of Health and Labor advised that an innocuous phrase such as "this product may be harmful" fully met social and legal expectations. But Manville went ahead and used a warning label noting the risk of cancer. Said W. T. Stephens, president and CEO of Manville:

> We concluded that the ethic of product safety and health stewardship has no cultural or geographic boundaries. Every worker and consumer of a potentially hazardous substance has the right to know the facts.
>
> This is a fundamental human right. This was a tough business decision because we stand to lose $20 million in sales to competitors who chose not to label.[25]

[24]Jagannath Dubashi, "Insulated From Reality," *Financial World*, June 27, 1989, p. 65.
[25]In "Preventive Management," speech to the 1989 Corporate Legal Health Program, Denver, Colorado, July 13, 1989, p. 3.

Stephens, who took over after the top management team which led Manville into bankruptcy was forced out as part of the reorganization, believes that Manville has been responsible. "I get a little hot under the collar when people say that Manville entered Chapter 11 to evade its legal responsibilities," he says. "Giving up $2.5 billion, 20 percent of your profits and 80 percent of your stock is not exactly walking away from the right solution."[26] In an interview with the *New York Times*, he noted that the company has been punished appropriately and that most of the people who made mistakes in years past are dead now.[27] In addition, he once observed that Manville has learned the lesson of anticipating change in the social environment of business. "Frankly," he notes, "my advice to business is to not focus on today's law on the books, but on the evolving laws of society as it emerges in the form of public opinion."[28] "The lesson is you'd better listen to society very carefully and don't sit back and hide behind today's law. A businessman has to worry about tomorrow's law."[29]

QUESTIONS

1 Did Manville make responsible use of the bankruptcy laws?
2 Was the Manville reorganization and settlement plan fair to all parties (including employees, shareholders, asbestos victims, insurers, and lawyers)? In principle, which plan was better for compensating asbestos victims: large court awards and settlements or the trust funds set up during reorganization?
3 Were Manville executives adequately punished for their actions?
4 Does Manville have an ethical right to continued existence? Is there a practical need for the company to stay in business?
5 Based on the Manville experience, is product liability law in need of reform?

[26]In George Melloan, "A Company Held Captive by the Plaintiff Bar," *Wall Street Journal*, October 4, 1988.
[27]William Glaberson, "Of Manville, Morals, and Mortality," *The New York Times*, October 9, 1988.
[28]In "Preventive Medicine," *op. cit.*, p. 1.
[29]In Melloan, *op. cit.*

3

Corporate Power and Legitimacy

The American Tobacco Company

James B. Duke was born in 1856 on a North Carolina farm. At the end of the Civil War his father returned home and found a shed of tobacco miraculously intact after the Union Army occupation and began selling the contents. Soon the elder Duke built a small factory to manufacture a brand of chewing tobacco named Pro Bono Publico (a Latin phrase meaning "for the public good"). Young James Duke entered the business with his father. He was a precocious, energetic boy who became the driving force behind the company.

During the 1870s James Duke's visions of grandeur for the little factory were thwarted by the dominance of a huge rival firm, the Bull Durham Co. Its brand of chewing tobacco, Bull Durham, was so dominant and well-entrenched that head-on competition seemed hopeless. So he decided on a new strategy. He would manufacture an unproven tobacco product—cigarettes. This was a venturesome move, because at the time cigarettes were a tiny segment of the tobacco market and their use was associated with degenerate, slightly effeminate dudes and dandies in big cities.

Duke brought ten professional tobacco rollers from Europe to his factory in North Carolina and set them to work. Each could roll a little over 2,000 per day. At first he had trouble selling his Duke of Durham brand. Tobacco shops refused to buy them because customers didn't request them. So Duke innovated in marketing strategy. In Atlanta, he put up a billboard of a famous actress holding Duke cigarettes in her outstretched hand. This was the first time a woman had been used to advertise cigarettes, and the novelty created demand. In St. Louis, Duke's salesmen found extreme prejudice against cigarettes. Tobacco shop proprietors simply would not buy. So Duke hired a young, red-headed widow to call on the tobacconists, and she got nineteen orders on her first day. Duke also advertised in newspapers, gave awards to dealers who bought his cigarettes, and orchestrated timely price cuts.

When a young Virginia engineer, James Bonsack, invented a mechanical cigarette rolling machine capable of rolling 200 per minute Duke negotiated an exclusive agreement to operate them. With the new Bonsack machines Duke simultaneously cut manufacturing costs from $0.80 per thousand to $0.30 and multiplied factory output many times.

To find new markets for this swollen output, he first tried to open New York City as a foothold in the East. There he ran into competition from local firms and he also encountered resistance to machine-rolled cigarettes among smokers. But both these barriers yielded to an array of ingenious promotional practices. He advertised widely. He put pictures of actresses and athletes in cigarette packs and numbered them so that compulsive collectors would want complete sets. He hired people to go into tobacco shops and demand his new machine-rolled Cameo and Cross Cuts brands. Immigrants entering New York were handed free samples. Dealers received secret rebates. He bankrolled a team called the Cross Cuts of Durham that played polo on roller skates and arranged for competing teams to be created in other cities so it could play in promotional matches.

Overseas, Duke's minions were at work also. One great conquest was China. At the time a few Chinese, mostly older men, smoked a bitter native tobacco in pipes. Cigarettes were unknown. Duke sent experts to Shantung Province with bright leaf from North Carolina to cultivate a milder tobacco. His sales force hired "teachers" to walk village streets showing curious Chinese how to light and hold cigarettes. He installed Bonsack machines in four huge manufacturing plants in China that soon ran 24 hours a day. And he unleashed on the Chinese the full range of promotional activities proven successful in America. At one time his cigarette packs contained pictures of nude American actresses, which proved to be a big hit with Chinese men. Duke turned China into a nation of cigarette smokers and to this day its population has one of the highest per capita smoking rates of any nation.

Back home, his tactics wore down competitors and in 1889 he engineered a combination of his firm and other large firms into the giant American Tobacco Company. As president, Duke built the company into a monopoly which controlled 93 percent of the cigarette market by 1900 and dominated the snuff, cheroot, and smoking tobacco markets as well. Duke ruthlessly swallowed or bankrupted 250 competing firms during the next 22 years and continued to spread the gospel of smoking around the globe.

Duke's monopoly lasted until 1911, when the Supreme Court ordered it broken up. Duke himself divided the giant trust into four independent companies—Ligget & Myers Tobacco Company, P. Lorillard Company, R.J. Reynolds Company, and a new American Tobacco Company. These firms, with the addition of Philip Morris, constitute the present-day oligopoly in cigarette manufacturing. After the breakup Duke retired from the tobacco industry, but started a new electric utility, Duke Power & Light, and made huge donations to a small North Carolina college which became Duke University.

Duke's career illustrates the power of commerce to shape society. His promotional practices accelerated the growth of smoking around the world. To find an outlet for the copious production of Bonsack machines he turned China into a nation of cigarette smokers. His monopoly defined the structure of the tobacco industry and destroyed the lives of rivals; its financial power flattened the comparatively feeble efforts of antitobacco leagues to publicize health hazards. Duke's ads made smoking glamorous and legitimized the tobacco industry. His bribes to legislators killed antismoking laws. And, due in large measure to Duke's forcefulness, the tobacco industry resuscitated the crippled post-Civil War southern economy and created a powerful, enduring political coalition in Congress. Duke shaped society with his business strategies, but encountered the limits of business power when the Supreme Court ordered his company dismantled.

THE NATURE OF POWER

As the story of the American Tobacco Company illustrates, American corporations wield enormous power in many ways and on many occasions. This power cannot be precisely measured, but there are abundant anecdotes, theories, and judgments about its exercise. In this chapter we discuss a variety of perspectives on corporate power.

Power may be defined as the ability of an individual, group, or organization to manipulate the behavior of other individuals, groups, or organizations in intended directions. Power may be actual manipulation or a potential that can be used at will. The exercise of power takes place on a spectrum of force from harsh coercion at one extreme, through strong influence in the middle, to mild persuasion at the other extreme. There are many sources of power. They include wealth, knowledge, arms, religious sanctity, social status, influence over public opinion, and legitimacy. Power is unevenly distributed, and all societies have mechanisms to control it and channel it into widely beneficial pursuits. These mechanisms include laws, police, cultural values, public opinion, and competing outcroppings of power.

In our society there is a strongly held view that the growth and exercise of power should be limited. The American social contract philosophy, the broad theory that explains the proper relationship between society and the powerful institutions set up to govern it, holds that ultimate power resides in the ordinary citizenry and is delegated to political, economic, and military leaders to act in the common interest. Popular thought has also long embraced the belief that power is evil. This is expressed in Lord Acton's celebrated dictum that "power tends to corrupt and absolute power corrupts absolutely." Traditionally, Americans distrust those who hold great power. This distrust is reflected in a 1985 Harris poll in which 56 percent of a nationwide sample agreed that "most people with power try to take advantage of people like yourself."[1] As a result of such attitudes many Americans are reserved in professing to seek or exercise power. Corporate leaders, for instance, speak of themselves as being "employees" or "agents" of someone or a group having

[1]Kenneth E. John, "A Feeling of Powerlessness," *Washington Post National Weekly Edition*, September 9, 1985.

power over them. This self-effacing tendency is exemplified in the words of Henry Ford II:

> Power is never monopolized by a few people at the top. Important changes almost always occur in little steps as the result of the complex interaction of many people at many levels all pulling in somewhat different directions. Everyone who pulls has some influence on the outcome and some share of power.[2]

SPHERES OF CORPORATE POWER

Corporate power is defined as the ability of a person, company, or business group to manipulate the business environment. There are six major spheres in which power may be exercised.

- Economic power is the ability of the holder to influence events, activities, and people by virtue of control over economic resources, particularly property. It is an ability to influence or determine price, quality, production, and distribution of goods and resources.
- Social and cultural power is the ability to influence social activities, values, and systems. It is the ability to influence social institutions, such as the family, and cultural values, mores, customs, lifestyles, and habits.
- Power over the individual affects individuals having direct relationships with a corporation (such as employees, stockholders, suppliers, and community members), affects the general characteristics of individuals, and affects concepts of individualism in society.
- Technological power is the influence over the thrust, rate, characteristics, and consequences of technology.
- Environmental power is the impact of a company's actions on the physical environment, as in air and water pollution, use of resources, and general community development.
- Political power is the ability to influence public policies and laws.[3]

These areas of power obviously are related. For instance, technological developments of corporations influence their own economic power as well as social and cultural values. Use of political power can, of course, increase a corporation's economic power. A coherent view of corporate power must encompass all six areas.

TWO THEORIES OF BUSINESS POWER

There is considerable disagreement about how much power corporations can exercise in these six spheres. Perspectives on business power cross a wide spectrum, but considerable attention and debate is focused on two basic positions.

[2]In *The Human Environment and Business*, New York: Weybright and Talley, 1970, p. 24.
[3]These spheres of influence are set forth in Edwin M. Epstein, ''Dimensions of Corporate Power: Part I,'' *California Management Review*, Winter 1973.

The first is the *dominance theory*, which holds that business is the preeminent institution in society and its power is inadequately checked. Hence, corporations are able to alter their environments in self-interested ways that may be detrimental to society. This was the thesis of Karl Marx, who wrote that unrestrained business power exercised by a tiny capitalist class results in the exploitation of workers and lower social classes.

The second is the *pluralist theory*, which holds that business exercises power in societies where other institutions such as government, labor, education, and public opinion also have great power. Hence, business power is counterbalanced, restricted, controlled, and sometimes defeated. This was the conviction of Adam Smith, who wrote that business power, constrained by market forces, results in a maximization of the common good without further control by government.

In the remainder of this section we first discuss two aspects of the dominance theory: (1) asset concentration as a *prima facie* source of unmatched power, and (2) the theory that a small, wealthy power elite has excessive influence. Then, we discuss the pluralist theory that emphasizes restraints on business power.

CONCENTRATION OF ECONOMIC POWER LEADS TO ABUSE

The idea that concentration of economic power results in abuse traces its roots back to the growth of American industry in the second half of the nineteenth century. Between 1860 and 1890 industrial growth decisively changed the face of American society. During that 30-year period the number of manufacturing plants grew from 140,433 to 355,415; the value of domestic manufactures rose from $1.8 billion to $9.3 billion; capital invested in manufacture rose from $1 billion to $6.5 billion; tons of coal mined annually grew from 13 million to 141 million; and yearly production of pig iron rose from 821,223 pounds to 9.2 million pounds. This skyrocketing industrial growth changed society. The population doubled from 31 million to 62.6 million; the number of wage earners nearly quadrupled, from 1.3 million to 4.2 million; and deposits in savings banks rose from $149.3 million to $1.5 billion.[4]

American life changed also. Large cities grew up around industry, bringing slums, crime, disease, impersonality, and other affronts to the folksy, rustic values of a largely agrarian country. Many social tensions were created, and the dislocations of industrial development were often blamed on business, which was the most visible force of societal change. Large companies, in particular, bore the brunt of public criticism. They sprouted like mushrooms. Immediately after the Civil War no company had a billion dollars of assets, but there were 318 by 1904.[5] Huge trusts such as James Duke's Amer-

[4]Figures in this paragraph are from Arthur M. Schlesinger, *Political and Social Growth of the United States: 1852–1933,* New York: Macmillan, 1935, p. 132. They may also be found in various editions of *The Statistical Abstract of the United States.*

[5]Thomas C. Cochran and William Miller, *The Age of Enterprise,* rev. ed., New York: Harper & Row, 1961, p. 190.

ican Tobacco Company manipulated national markets and wiped out small town competitors, usually family businesses.

The idea that concentrated economic power results in abuses finds its roots in protest movements that grew up to oppose business power in the nineteenth century. Of course, other eras of rapid industrial growth occurred between 1900 to 1929 and after World War II. Continued industrial growth has fostered continued belief in the dominance theory. A basic tenet of the theory is that economic power is concentrated in the hands of a few wealthy individuals and the leaders of giant corporations. Adherents insinuate that the financial power of giant corporations not only defeats market competition but, in addition, is converted into influence over the social, cultural, and political life of the nation in a way that is injurious to the public interest.

CORPORATE ASSET CONCENTRATION

The most frequent measure of the degree and extent of corporate economic power is asset concentration. The first creditable compilation of asset concentration data was made by a lawyer and an economist, Adolph Berle and Gardner Means, in 1932. They concluded, after an exhaustive study, that the 200 largest nonfinancial corporations in the United States in 1929 (less than .07 percent of all nonfinancials) controlled nearly 50 percent of all corporate wealth.[6] That level of asset concentration soon declined. By 1947, the ratio had fallen to 46 percent, and after 1963 it leveled off at 40 percent.[7] But the top 200 industrial corporations controlled 66 percent of all industrial assets in 1986; the top 100 controlled 55 percent.[8] A similar phenomenon exists with respect to oligopolistic concentration in specific industries, where the ratio of sales of the largest companies to total sales in the industry is often high.

Undeniably, assets are highly concentrated in large corporations, and the challenging question of who controls them is raised. When Berle and Means wrote *The Modern Corporation and Private Property* in 1932, many of the largest manufacturing and financial institutions were still controlled by the entrepreneurs who had created them or by their descendants. However, a gradual revolution that largely ended widespread family control was already in progress. As big corporations grew, new stock offerings diluted the equity of the founders and their families. Thus, the professional managers who ran the firms—and increasingly were the only ones who understood their complexities—assumed control in company after company. Although stockholders could formally exercise control over these professional managers, in practice, ownership in giant companies was so fragmented among a multitude of shareholders, each holding a small minority of shares, that concerted action from this quarter to control management was as unlikely as a large oak tree shedding its leaves in a neat stack on the ground.

[6]*The Modern Corporation and Private Property*, New York: Macmillan, 1932.
[7]J. Fred Weston, "Mergers and Economic Efficiency," *Industrial Concentration, Mergers, and Growth*, vol. 2, Washington, D.C.: U.S. Government Printing Office, June 1981.
[8]*Statistical Abstract of the United States*, 108th ed., Washington, D.C.: U.S. Government Printing Office, December 1987. Numbers calculated from data in Tables 858 and 859, p. 513.

In recent years, large institutional investors such as pension funds and mutual funds have come to own huge blocks of stock in top companies but have only rarely attempted to influence management decisions. They prefer instead to follow "the Wall Street rule" and to sell if confidence in management diminishes. Boards of directors, which in theory represent stockholders and supervise management, have in practice been dominated by management. In recent years both pension fund managers and corporate directors have grown more inclined to exercise influence over corporate managers. Nevertheless, managers of large corporations usually control corporate assets. Their exercise of power is, therefore, closely scrutinized by scholars and social critics who ask: To whom or what are these managers responsible?

Comments on the Theory   Concentration of economic power certainly exists. But it is often difficult to show where and how power derived from asset concentration has been abused. Critics of asset concentration claim that one important manifestation of its *prima facie* evidence of power is that where it exists profits are excessive, prices are higher, and competition is stifled. Our antitrust policy has been based on this so-called *structural theory,* namely, that when the degree of concentration in an industry exceeds some specified number, the conduct, behavior, and performance of those holding, this power can be predicted to be undesirable. That is prohibited by our antitrust laws and where present must be eliminated.

This structural theory has been conventional wisdom for almost 100 years, but a new antitrust orthodoxy challenges the structural theory. J. Fred Weston, an advocate of this new theory, concludes: "The empirical evidence is overwhelming that there does not exist valid support of the structural theory of antitrust. It has not been demonstrated that high concentration in an industry is associated with the unfavorable economic performance in any dimension."[9] This is the so-called *performance theory* which, as Weston notes, has been validated by voluminous empirical data. These two theories are discussed in more detail in Chapter 10.

The conclusions of the performance theory school demonstrate that the fact of possession of power does not prove abuse of power, at least in the economic realm. Certainly there is potential for the abuse of power in the concentration of assets. But the question of the use or restraint of corporate economic power as related to the public interest is complex. Concentrated power is not synonymous with either good or evil intent.

POWER ELITE THEORY

A variant of the abuse-of-power argument is that there exists a small elite of wealthy individuals who, by virtue of their control over economic institutions, constitute a power elite. Those who believe this argue that the concentrated power of wealthy, entrepreneurial families such as the Rockefellers,

---

[9]J. Fred Weston and Michael E. Granfield, *Corporate Enterprise in a New Environment*, New York: KCG Publications, 1982, pp. 182–83.

Mellons, Fords, and du Ponts is combined with the influence of the managers of the largest professionally managed corporations, top politicians, and top leaders in other walks of life to control the nation. The public believes in the existence of an elite. In a nationwide Harris poll conducted in 1984, 74 percent believed that there was "a group of powerful people who really run things in this country."[10]

The modern impetus for this theory came from the late sociologist C. Wright Mills, who wrote in 1956 of a "power elite" in American society. "Insofar as national events are decided," wrote Mills, "the power elite are those who decide them."[11] Mills described the American social structure as a single power pyramid. At the top is a small group of the economic-military elite. A second level of power immediately below consists of the lieutenants of the power elite, including politicians and professional corporate managers. The remainder of the pyramid is the large base, which is composed of an undifferentiated mass of powerless citizens.

Shortly after Mills wrote *The Power Elite*, another sociologist, Floyd Hunter, estimated the size of the top elite to be "between one and two hundred men."[12] More recently, political scientist Thomas R. Dye studied the exercise of power by a "national institutional elite" of 5,416 individuals in positions that control half of all industrial and financial assets, nearly half of the assets of private foundations and universities, the television networks, news services, leading newspapers, cultural organizations, and the various branches of government.[13]

A perennial student of elites, Professor G. William Domhoff, has written for over twenty years of a dominant managerial class in American society that perpetuates itself in power through social mechanisms, including inheritance of wealth, attendance at private schools, intermarriage, family offices, and government service. Domhoff argues:

> There is a social upper class in the United States that is a ruling class by virtue of its dominant role in the economy and government. . . . This ruling class is socially cohesive, has its basis in the large corporations and banks, plays a major role in shaping the social and political climate, and dominates the federal government through a variety of organizations and methods.[14]

Incontrovertibly, America has always had a wealthy upper class. Examination of tax records shows that in 1771 the richest 1 percent of Bostonians accounted for 44 percent of personal wealth in the city.[15] The post-Civil War years in America were called the Gilded Age in reference to the ostentation of a small upper class of entrepreneurial families which sought to display in-

[10]Kenneth E. John, "Defining the Power Elite," *Washington Post National Weekly Edition*, April 23, 1984, p. 38.

[11]*The Power Elite*, New York: Oxford University Press, 1956, p. 18.

[12]*Top Leadership U.S.A.*, Chapel Hill: University of North Carolina Press, 1959, p. 176.

[13]Thomas R. Dye, *Who's Running America?* Englewood Cliffs, N.J.: Prentice-Hall, 1976.

[14]G. William Domhoff, *Who Rules America Now? A View for the 80s*, Englewood Cliffs, N.J.: Prentice-Hall, 1983, p. 1.

[15]Kent A. MacDougall, "Progress is Harbinger of Inequality," *Los Angeles Times*, November 15, 1984.

credible fortunes they had made during the years of industrialization. They built busy, gothic mansions which were architectural monuments to their wealth. Fifth Avenue between 42nd Street and 92nd Street was New York's Gold Coast, lined with palatial residences such as Cornelius Vanderbilt's block-long townhouse. When Pierre Lorillard IV, the tobacco magnate, built Tuxedo Park in the 1890s on 600,000 acres north of New York City, the residents of the twenty-two houses there, in the understated patois of the elite, called their twenty-five-room mansions on five-acre plots "cottages." Vanderbilt's yacht, the *North Star*, had a library, a dining room, a stateroom furnished with Louis XIV furniture, and a false fireplace. J. P. Morgan's impressive steam yacht *Corsair* had a crew of eighty-five. Aside from conspicuous consumption, the elite separated itself from the common ruck in other ways, by favoring sports such as polo and yacht racing, by taking vacations in Europe and at exclusive resorts, and by throwing elaborate parties such as one in which cigarettes were rolled in $100 bills and ladies found gold bracelets as party favors when they opened their dinner napkins. As a group, the plutocracy also had a set of unique norms and customs. On New Year's Day, for example, society families prepared delicacies such as codfish tongues in black butter and waited for other members of society to come "calling." The time of day the caller appeared was critical, for if an important member of rarified society called very early, it indicated that other, more important, calls were being saved for the prime midafternoon hours. A special etiquette applied to riding in the elegant horse-drawn coaches that the rich paraded in on Sundays and holidays. On first passing another coach all parties bowed, on the second meeting everyone smiled, and on the third encounter politeness required averting the eyes.

Today, there is still a small elite of wealth in America. A government study revealed that in 1983, 0.5 percent of households accounted for 37 percent of the net personal worth of all American households. The study noted that these "super-rich" had increased their concentration of wealth over the past twenty years. In 1963, the top 0.5 percent of households controlled only 25 percent of net personal wealth.[16] National income figures show that the richest 20 percent of Americans received 44 percent of national income while the poorest 20 percent received only 4.6 percent.[17]

As in the past, today's "super-rich" are often ostentatious in their pattern of living. In 1989, the late Malcolm Forbes, publisher of *Forbes* magazine, threw a huge 70th birthday party for himself. He rented a Concorde, Boeing 747, and DC-10 to fly 800 celebrities from New York to his palace in Morocco. Actress Elizabeth Taylor, a special friend, flew over in Forbe's private jet, named the *Capitalist Tool*. The cost of the birthday party was $2 million. Real estate billionaire Donald Trump's yacht, the *Trump Princess*, has gold-plated bathroom fixtures, a waterfall, cinema, disco, swimming pool, three elevators, and a bullet-proof sauna (surrounded by 12 inches of lead).

---

[16]David M. Gordon, "Concentrated Wealth Poses Threat," *Los Angeles Times*, August 5, 1986.
[17]"Poverty in America Still Resists Resolution,"*National Journal*, November 4, 1989, p. 2719.

Scholars like Domhoff locate members of today's elite class through the Social Registers published for major American cities. Bibliographical information there reveals that many have attended such prestigious schools as Harvard, Yale, and Princeton. Many are also members of exclusive private clubs, such as the Links and Knickerbocker in New York, the California in Los Angeles, the Pacific Union in San Francisco, and the Somerset in Boston.

Members of the elite also attend exclusive private preparatory schools, such as Choate in Wallingford, Connecticut. Domhoff has compiled a list of such schools and considers a person to be a member of the upper class if he or she has attended one. Those who attend these prep schools are nicknamed "preppies." Most prep schools are in the Northeast and are either secular or Episcopalian, the religious affiliation identified by sociologists as most common in the American upper class. In addition to providing a first-rate education, prep schools are said to inculcate upper-class mores, to begin lifelong upper-class social contacts, and to mix old aristocracy with new money.[18] Graduates of prep schools make their way to elite universities, particularly Ivy League schools and small exclusive private schools, such as Vassar College or Finch College.

One function of the marriage institution, to elite theorists, is to perpetuate upper-class cohesion. Although marriage may be a way for the upper class to infuse its ranks with new ability, members of the elite often intermarry. Prep schools and upper-class social functions such as debutante parties bring adolescents approaching marriage together. Debutante balls follow a centuries-old English tradition in which the upper class of England presented its daughters to the royal court. One study of marriages that were reported on the society pages of the *New York Times* found that 68 percent of brides or grooms were from families listed in the Social Register or had attended an exclusive prep school. Twenty-four percent of the marriages were between two such individuals.[19]

Another device for concentrating wealth in the cream of the upper class, the families with great entrepreneurial fortunes, is the family office. The family office is a private organization set up by members of an extended family to manage family assets and financial affairs. Examples are T. Mellon & Sons, Rockefeller Family and Associates, and F. Weyerhaeuser and Company—family offices that manage the fortunes of the descendants of great businessmen. Family members allow the office to work their assets so that, rather than dissipating fortunes through inheritance, the sum is kept intact and leverage is gained. Family offices perform a variety of functions. F. Weyerhaeuser and Company, for example, employs thirty-one people in two offices in St. Paul and Tacoma and provides services that include

[18]Dennis Gilbert and Joseph A. Kahl, *The American Class Structure: A New Synthesis*, Homewood, Illinois: Dorsey, 1982.

[19]Paul M. Blumberg and P. W. Paul, "Continuities in Upper-Class Marriages," *Journal of Marriage and Family*, Fall 1975.

"paying bills, determining the "best policy" for home, auto, and life insurance, filing tax returns, managing individual portfolios, helping in estate planning, making travel arrangements, and coordinating political and philanthropic giving."[20] The Weyerhaeuser family convenes annually in Tacoma at a family meeting to discuss asset management and make financial decisions.

Finally, the elite of America are said to perpetuate their influence through government service, and there is much evidence that government service attracts wealthy executives and members of the upper class. One study of cabinet officers between 1897 and 1973 showed that 78 percent had been corporate officers or partners in corporate law firms, and 60 percent were listed in the Social Register.[21] A second study of cabinet officers, from the Kennedy cabinet in 1961 through Reagan's inaugural cabinet in 1981, showed that 60 percent came from business or from corporate law firms.[22]

Interlocking Directorates A device for further concentrating both economic power and social contacts among an economic elite is the interlocking directorate, in which directors of one or more corporations sit on the boards of other corporations. Basically, there are two types of director interlock. *Direct* interlock occurs when a director of one company sits on the board of a second company. *Indirect* interlock occurs when two companies that do not share a common director on their boards each have a director on the board of a third company. In the past, studies have shown significant director interlock among the largest corporations.

- In 1969 a Federal Trade Commission study showed a total of 1,450 direct and indirect interlocks among the 200 largest industrial corporations (Blumberg, 1975). In the same year, another study, this one of the 250 largest industrials, showed that only seventeen were not significantly interlocked and that this level of interlock was greater than in the 1930s.[23]
- A 1978 study by the Senate Governmental Affairs Committee of the 130 largest corporations—which controlled $1 trillion in assets, about one-fourth of all corporate holdings—showed 530 direct interlocks and 12,193 indirect interlocks. The study reported that each of the thirteen largest corporations reached an average of 70 percent of the 130 largest "through a total of 240 direct and 5,547 indirect interlocks."[24]
- A 1980 study of 797 large corporations showed 1,572 interlocks among 8,623 directors. The analysis showed that larger firms had more interlocks

[20]Marvin G. Dunn, "The Family Office: Coordinating Mechanism of the Ruling Class," in G. William Domhoff, ed., *Power Structure Research*, Beverly Hills, California: Sage Publications, 1980.
[21]Beth Mintz, "The President's Cabinet, 1897–1972," *Insurgent Sociologist*, Fall 1975.
[22]Gilbert and Kahl, *op. cit.*
[23]Peter Dooley, "The Interlocking Directorate," *American Economic Review*, June 1969.
[24]James L. Rowe, Jr., "Big Firms' Sharing of Directors Studied," *Los Angeles Times*, April 23, 1978.

and that interlocking was positively related to several measures of profitability.[25]

Interlocking is legally permissible and natural. A director of a prestigious company such as General Motors who proves competent may be invited to join the board of another company, such as General Electric, which seeks the business acumen of this person. If he or she accepts, the two companies are interlocked. Companies also seek to establish relations with other firms through shared directors. This is frequently the case with industrial firms seeking access to capital by inviting directors of banks to join their boards. In some cases, banks seek to have their directors or managers appointed to the boards of debtor firms when those firms become financially troubled.

The fear of corporate critics is that directors who sit on more than one board necessarily have knowledge of the affairs of another company and that this creates a conflict of interest. Allegedly, a small group with multiple ties to giant corporations has inordinate control over commerce because of widespread interlocking. Section 8 of the Clayton Act of 1914 prohibits interlocking directorates where two companies, by virtue of their location, market, and size, compete, and where the elimination of competition by agreement between them would constitute a violation of antitrust laws. In addition, there is an informal custom that directors should excuse themselves from the room when minor conflicts of interest arise. Periodically, directors resign when major conflicts occur, but legal action is rare. The Federal Trade Commission once asked Edmund Littlefield, a director of both Chrysler and General Electric, to resign from one board or the other because both corporations made air conditioners. The Supreme Court, on the other hand, recently allowed directors of BankAmerica and Crocker National Bank to remain on the boards of several life insurance companies that were in competition with banks for mortgage and real estate loans.[26]

Is interlocking on company boards and other leadership positions a method by which a small elite perpetuates its domination of national affairs? Two studies shed light on this question. One, by Michael Useem, looked at over 5,000 corporate directors and senior executives.[27] Among them, Useem found an "inner circle," a tiny inner elite of business leaders who served on

[25]Johannes M. Pennings, *Interlocking Directorates: Origins and Consequences of Connections Among Organizations' Boards of Directors,* San Francisco: Jossey-Bass, 1980, pp. 60 and 189. For some recent research on director interlock see, for example, Donald Palmer, Roger Friedland, and Jitendra Singh, "The Ties That Bind: Organizational and Class Bases of Stability in a Corporate Interlock Network," *American Sociological Review,* December 1986; R. Jack Richardson, "Directorship Interlocks and Corporate Profitability," *Administrative Science Quarterly,* September 1987; Mark S. Mizruchi and Linda B. Stearns, "A Longitudinal Study of the Formation of Interlocking Directorates," *Administrative Science Quarterly,* June 1988; William Roy and Phillip Bonacich, "Interlocking Directorates and Communities of Interest Among American Railroad Companies, 1905," *American Sociological Review,* June 1988; and Donald Palmer, "The Dual Nature of Corporate Interlocks," in Michael Schwartz, ed., *The Structure of Power in America,* London: Holmes & Meier, 1987.

[26]*BankAmerica Corp. v. United States,* 103 S. Ct. 2266 (1983).

[27]*The Inner Circle,* New York: Oxford University Press, 1984.

the boards of three or more major corporations. The "inner circle" is about 10 percent of all corporate directors, and Useem believes it is exceptionally influential in decisions at high levels of business, government, and civic life. In a second study, however, Thomas R. Dye identifies an inner circle but concludes that power over national resources is very fragmented. Dye identifies 7,314 top institutional positions in twelve different sectors of society. The people in these positions control half the nation's industrial and bank assets; control nearly half the assets of private foundations; dominate the media and cultural organizations; direct the federal government; and control the military. The 7,314 positions are held by 5,778 individuals. Only 15 percent of the top leaders are "interlockers" who hold more than one position. A tiny inner elite of one half of one percent of the individuals occupies six or more institutional roles and most interlocking occurs in the corporate sector. But because "specialists" far outnumber "interlockers" in powerful positions, Dye concludes that "[i]f there is a 'coming together' of corporate, governmental, and military elites as C. Wright Mills contends, it does not appear to be by means of interlocking directorates."[28] These two studies show that interlocking exists and that it can be interpreted in different ways.

An Evaluation of the Power Elite Model   The thesis that a small ruling class holds power in capitalist societies by virtue of its concentrated ownership of wealth has major weaknesses. First, statistical presentations of the number of corporate directors in the Social Register, director interlocks, concentration of assets, and similar phenomena do not themselves demonstrate either the real exercise of power or the negative public consequences of the condition they portray. It is correct that a small percentage of corporations controls disproportionate assets, but this fact does not, by itself, lead to the conclusion that such a state of affairs is grave. And even if members of an upper social stratum do occupy many positions of institutional power, it cannot be numerically proved that their decisions are bad for the public.

Second, there are many formal and informal restraints on the "power elite" or "governing class." The Constitution, laws, government regulation, and the court system are formal restraints. In addition, informal checks and balances set limits to the exercise of money power; educational and religious institutions train Americans in traditional ideals; pressure groups and public opinion counter wealthy interests; and environmental, civil rights, and consumer interests have forced large corporations to adopt respect for community as a major goal. Unlike in some European, Asian, and African countries, there has never been a tradition of deference toward elites in this country. Much public suspicion of wealth exists.

Competition and technological change have had impacts on the marketplace largely beyond anyone's control. The fates have not respected large

---

[28]Thomas R. Dye, *Who's Running America: The Bush Era*, 5th ed., Englewood Cliffs, N.J.: Prentice-Hall, 1990, p. 184.

J. P. MORGAN AND THE PANIC OF 1907

In the first decade of the twentieth century, J. P. Morgan (1837–1913), head of J. P. Morgan & Co. in New York, was often called the most powerful man in the country. He specialized in buying competing companies in the same industry and merging them into a single, monopolistic firm. He joined separate railroads into large systems. He combined smaller electrical concerns into General Electric in 1892 and consolidated diverse manufacturers into the International Harvester Company, which started with 85 percent of the farm machinery market. In 1901 he created the first billion dollar company when he merged competing firms to form the United States Steel Company with capitalization of $1.4 billion (it would not be until 1911 that the annual appropriations of the federal government reached $1 billion).

Morgan and two of his close associates together held 341 corporate directorships. He dominated American banking and finance in an era of finance capitalism. His power was very independent of government controls. At the turn of the century the Sherman Antitrust Act was unenforced, there was no national bank to regulate the money supply, and existing securities and banking laws were rudimentary. One awestruck writer said he was "a kind of unelected economic president of this country."[29]

In October 1907, panic swept Wall Street and stocks plummeted as anxious investors sold shares. Soon a number of banks suffered runs of withdrawals and were on the verge of failure. Liquidity, or the free flow of money, was fast vanishing from financial markets, and the nation's banking system was on the verge of collapse. So influential was Morgan that he commanded the New York Stock Exchange to stay open all day on October 24 to maintain investor confidence. To support it, he raised $25 million of credit.

There was little the federal government could do to ease the crisis. President Theodore Roosevelt was off hunting bears in Louisiana, an ironic pursuit in light of the crashing stock market. Without a national bank, the government had no capacity to increase the money supply and restore liquidity. Powerless, Secretary of the Treasury George B. Cortelyou traveled to New York to get Morgan's advice.

On the evening of October 24, Morgan gathered members of the New York banking elite at his private library. He played solitaire while in another room the assembled bankers discussed methods for resolving the crisis. Periodically, someone came to him with a proposal, several of which he rejected. Finally, a plan was hatched in which $33 million would be raised to support the stock exchange and failing banks. Where would this money come from? The Secretary of the Treasury was to supply $10 million in government funds, John D. Rockefeller contributed $10 million, and Morgan the remaining $13 million.

This action stabilized the economy. Perhaps it demonstrates that elite power may be exercised in the common good. It should be noted, however, that the panic of 1907—and other panics of that era—came after Morgan and other titans of finance repeatedly choked the stock exchange with the colossal stock offerings needed to finance their new combinations.

Morgan was widely criticized for his role in ending the panic of 1907. Conspiracy theorists, suspicious of so much power resident in one man, attacked him. Upton Sinclair, for example, accused him of inciting the panic for self-gain, a wildly erroneous accusation. In 1912, Morgan was the focus of congressional hearings by the Pujo Commission, which concluded that he led a "money trust" which controlled the nation's finances and that this was unfortunate. Death claimed him in 1913 just before Congress passed the Federal Reserve Act to set up a central bank and insure that no private banker would ever again be sole caretaker of the money supply.

---

[29] Alex Groner, *American Business and Industry,* New York: American Heritage Publishing Co., 1972, p. 213.

size more than small and have bankrupted giants as well as pygmies. For example, out of the 100 largest corporations in 1909, only thirty-six survived on the list until 1948. Between 1948 and 1968, only sixty-five of the top 100 companies continued to hold their rankings.[30] Today the winnowing continues. Between 1983 and 1988, the names of 143 companies were dropped from the well-known *Fortune* 500 list of the nation's largest industrials.[31] This was a period of great merger, acquisition, and leveraged buyout activity, and most of the dropped companies became part of other companies on the list or went private. Many, however, shrank and became too small in comparison with growing firms, and a few were liquidated or declared bankruptcy.

In defense of the elitist model, it has been argued by historians Will and Ariel Durant that throughout recorded history, the concentration of wealth in the hands of a disproportionately small number has been inevitable.[32] In the days when humans were hunter-gatherers, stratification theorists believe that a state of equality existed. When game was hunted and prepared by small bands, the fruits of this labor were widely and equally shared. After the emergence of agricultural civilization, however, material inequality greatly increased, as small elites of wealthy landowners emerged to dominate society. At this stage in the development of human civilization, class inequalities were greatest; the awesome gap between the rich aristocracy and the impoverished bulk of citizenry in the Roman Empire is an example. Mature industrial societies such as the United States are marked by less inequality than agricultural civilizations because the elite that controls productive assets must share rewards with a large class of technically knowledgeable workers, because population growth declines, and because of the development of egalitarian ideologies.[33]

Human inequality, although inescapable, requires continuous justification. Those at the bottom must somehow be convinced that their lot is fair, natural, or proper. How does the business elite in America accomplish this? In our society one palliative is that elites are checked by law and opinion, that high positions are open to the hard-working based on the merit of their achievement, and that much power resides in the common person and is only delegated to ruling institutions. Another rationale advanced by conservative economists is that the function of the rich should be to accept risk and invest money in projects that create opportunities for the classes below them.[34] The reward for accepting this risk is greater wealth, from which all classes benefit. An elite of wealth and power is essential for the continued growth of industrial society. Ideas such as these have proved serviceable in justifying the existence of a privileged, potent upper class.

---

[30]Neil H. Jacoby, *Corporate Power and Social Responsibility*, New York: Macmillan, 1973.
[31]John Paul Newport Jr., "A New Era of Rapid Rise and Ruin," *Fortune*, April 24, 1989, p. 77.
[32] Will Durant and Ariel Durant, *The Lessons of History*, New York: Simon & Schuster, 1968.
[33]Harold R. Kerbo, *Social Stratification and Inequality*, New York: McGraw-Hill, 1983.
[34]See, for example, George Gilder, *Wealth and Poverty*, New York: Basic Books, 1981.

PLURALIST THEORY

A counterpoint theory to asset concentration and power elite theory is that pluralism restrains business power. A pluralistic society is one that has many semiautonomous and autonomous groups through which power is diffused. No one group has overwhelming power over all others, and each has direct or indirect impact on all the others. The existence of power in many decentralized groups makes less possible the tyranny of a majority over a minority.

American pluralism is based on several historical factors. The first is the freedom of individuals to join associations, express desires, and seek fulfillment of interests. This freedom has been regarded as essential by Americans, for we are, as Tocqueville observed, "a nation of joiners." This right encourages the growth of new associations to meet new needs of society and individuals.

Second, our Constitution, which diffuses political power through many jurisdictions and branches of government, has given rise to an open system in which groups make their influence felt in many places. Groups shut out from one level or branch of government make their interests known elsewhere. After World War II, for instance, civil rights interests were *personae non gratae* in the legislatures of southern states and in a Congress where elderly southern committee chairmen dominated policy-making. Civil rights leaders such as Thurgood Marshall turned, therefore, to the courts and won a series of decisions in state courts favorable to blacks. They also won a number of landmark Supreme Court decisions, including *Shelly v. Kramer* and *McGhee v. Sipes,* the two 1947 cases which struck down restrictive covenants in deeds, and the famous *Brown* school desegregation case in 1954.[35]

Third, the heterogeneity of American peoples and interests has nurtured pluralism. Major native and immigrant groups press for their aspirations. Economic interest groups, including labor, business, agriculture, and consumer groups, are a permanent fixture of politics. And a rainbow of voluntary associations (whose size, permanence, and influence vary) compete in governments at all levels.

Pluralism is not found in all political systems. It was an alien concept in Rome, throughout the medieval world, and under early mercantilism. It was in the medieval world that widespread attacks on authority gave rise to the concept, but it was not until the end of the eighteenth century that the idea was made workable in practice. Pluralism and political democracy are handmaidens. If democracy is to survive, diffusion of power among groups must exist and be guarded.

A pluralistic society imposes immediate, close boundaries on the discretionary exercise of business power. Wise managers anticipate that their power often will be restricted, blunted, challenged, or shared by others. In general, there are four boundaries on managerial power.

---

[35]*Shelley v. Kraemer,* 331 U.S. 803; *McGhee v. Sipes,* 331 U.S. 804; *Brown v. Board of Education of Topeka, Kansas,* 349 U.S. 294. Restrictive covenants are private agreements, usually in deeds, prohibiting the sale of property to racial or ethnic minorities. They were widely used to maintain segregation in residential housing before the aforementioned Supreme Court decisions.

1 *Governments* at all levels and in all countries regulate business activity. Although Dow Chemical Co. once considered buying a deserted island which was not part of any sovereign nation (we are not sure how serious the consideration was), it decided that freedom from taxation, regulations, and political interference was ultimately an illusion.

2 *Social interest groups* form a shifting, kaleidoscopic mirror of power trends in society and restrain business through an array of methods such as picketing, product boycotts, and lobbying for restrictive legislation. Prominent in this century have been labor, environmental, civil rights, religious, consumer, and public interest groups.

3 *Social values* are expressed in civil and criminal law, public opinion, literature, the press, and television. They also are internalized by managers in the education process in schools, churches, training programs, and life experience. Social values include religious, philosophical, and ethical norms, which define imperatives such as duty, justice, taste, manners, and piety.

4 *Economic stakeholders* include stockholders, employees, competitors (represented by market forces), suppliers, and communities where a corporation has significant presence. A range of actions is open to these groups when corporate power is exercised by management in a way that jeopardizes their economic interests.

Because of the existence of these four boundaries in a pluralistic society, any exercise of business power that affects many interests will elicit countervailing pressures and restrictions from many quarters. Observe that in critical areas such as pollution, minority hiring, and consumer product safety, the discretion of managers is hemmed in by all four of these power boundaries. A decision with little societal impact will, however, create few counterpressures. Chances are good that management can unilaterally decide what color to paint the buildings at a plumbing fixture plant. Figure 3-1 illustrates the existence and operation of boundaries on managerial discretion. Just as in the solar system, the planets move freely within but cannot escape their gravitational fields; so, too, major corporations in American society remain in orbits determined by the powers of plural interests. The pluralist argument poses a direct challenge to those who decry economic concentration and to elite theorists. If it is correct, no matter how power is concentrated and irrespective of the existence of a plutocracy, corporate power cannot for long abuse the public interest. A pluralistic society simply does not permit sustained irresponsibility.

In a moment of certitude, Professor Domhoff has written, ''Corporate leaders can invest money where and when they choose; expand, close, or move their factories and offices at a moment's notice; and hire, promote, and fire employees as they see fit.''[36] In a large corporation subject to market discipline, labor agreements, and federal antidiscrimination laws, perhaps no statement could be further from reality.

[36]Domhoff, *op. cit., Who Rules America Now? A View for the 1980s,* p. 77.

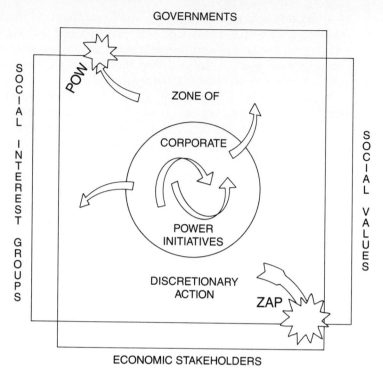

FIGURE 3-1 Boundaries of managerial power.

Some observers believe that a growing profusion of interest groups (or stakeholders) may be draining the vitality of the business institution. Mancur Olson, for one, argued in *The Rise and Decline of Nations* that the longer societies are politically stable, the more numerous groups become.[37] And the more groups develop and achieve their objectives, the more they promote their members' well-being to the detriment of economic efficiency. Union wage demands and government regulatory programs, for instance, increase the welfare of particular groups in society but may simultaneously raise production costs. Group success, says Olson, undercuts economic success. And Peter Drucker warns of "the political disease of single-interest pluralism," a disease characterized by groups that represent a cause such as nuclear disarmament or tobacco crop subsidies and are unwilling to compromise.[38] The strength of such groups lies in their narrow focus, which can command the strong allegiance of an interested minority of peace activists or tobacco farmers. These groups do not promote a conception of the general good, only their single interest. As stakeholders of corporations, such groups may suc-

[37]New Haven: Yale University Press, 1982.
[38]Peter F. Drucker, *The New Realities*, New York: Harper & Row, 1989, chap. 7, "The New Pluralisms."

ceed in selfish redirection of economic enterprise. If Olson and Drucker are correct, there is today a danger that corporations will be co-opted by narrow interests.[39] But the flaw is not the result of elite dominance; rather, it is the result of excessive pluralism.

BUSINESS LEGITIMACY

Legitimacy is the rightful possession of power. Over the ages, legitimacy has been conferred by many doctrines. In primitive times, supreme power was often a matter of *de facto* brute force. In monarchies, the "divine right of kings" legitimated the rule of families presumed to have descended from a deity. Among certain African tribes, as soon as an old king grew ill, his successor clubbed him to death and received his departing soul. The new ruler got legitimacy from this presumed transmigration.[40] In representative democracies such as the United States, the legitimacy of elected officials' exercise of power stems from sanction by the majority and adherence to rules of government, as represented in the Constitution and prevailing popular opinion.

Fundamentally, the source of power conferred upon corporations has been the authority granted by society over the ownership of property. Society has accepted laws, beliefs, and customs associated with the exercise of power over possessed property. Today the grounds of legitimacy for corporate power are shifting. The impact of corporations on their social and physical environments has become too great for the exercise of managerial power to be justified by the legal right of property ownership alone. The conception of the marketplace as a sphere of activity where an impersonal mechanism would hold power accountable is a slim fiction for critics.

Pollster Daniel Yankelovich has argued that there are three basic types of legitimacy or underlying support for the business system and the exercise of power by corporate managers.[41] An examination of these three areas of support provides a conceptual underpinning upon which a more sophisticated understanding of business's legitimacy can be based. The first area of which Yankelovich speaks is *ideological* legitimacy, or support for the rules of the economic game. He indicates that there is widespread support for basic principles of capitalism, such as private property. The second is *functional* legitimacy, or support for the performance and products of business. Here again, most Americans seem to accept the performance levels of enterprise, although the consumer movement has raised levels of public criticism of business's output, and some ambivalence exists in the public mind. Third is

[39]Olson's theory has been subjected to empirical testing and the results are mixed. For a review of the pertinent literature and an example of testing which does not support the theory, see Virginia Gray and David Lowery, "Interest Group Politics and Economic Growth in the United States," *American Political Science Review*, March 1988.

[40]Sir James G. Frazier, *The Golden Bough: A Study in Magic and Religion*, New York: Macmillan, 1922, pp. 308–330.

[41]In Albert T. Sommers, ed., *The Free Society and Planning*, New York: The Conference Board, 1975.

moral legitimacy, or public trust and confidence in the motives and morality of managers. It is here that polls show the business community suffering. People have confidence in the fundamentals of the business system, but they lack assurance that these fundamentals are being observed for the public welfare. They support the profit system but perceive "profiteering" to be what is actually taking place.

Does asset concentration and the existence of a business elite threaten the legitimacy of business power? Not in any fundamental sense. Inevitably, concentration of power arouses public suspicion. But the application of democratic controls over corporate power satisfies the public need for security.

CONCLUDING OBSERVATIONS

In this chapter we have examined two basic theories of business power. One is the dominance theory, which holds that inadequately restrained economic power is concentrated in large corporations dominated by a wealthy elite. The second is the pluralist theory, which holds that corporate power is encircled by multiple restraining forces in an open society. These positions have been debated for many years and both contain insights. As long as corporate power is generally accountable to democratic controls, society will continue to accord it legitimacy.

Construction of the Central Pacific

The term "robber baron" refers to a group of manipulative entrepreneurs who pursued controversial business careers between the Civil War and the early twentieth century. The best-known members of this semipiratical cohort include Andrew Carnegie, Jay Gould, J. P. Morgan, and John D. Rockefeller. These men, prominent in American history books, represent hundreds of others who together constituted a distinct element of unprincipled behavior within the business community of the time.

They began their careers after the outbreak of the Civil War, when political and economic dislocations weakened the settled fabric of national commerce. The war opened the door to unscrupulous promoters, war profiteers, and government war contractors in league with corrupt politicians. The patterns of gaining favoritism by bribing politicians learned at this time were carried over to economic activity after the end of the war. From the 1860s onward, the robber barons also availed themselves of economic opportunities in the developing western territories. Historians believe that the dislocations of the war coupled with a vast increase in the geographic scope of economic activity created a climate in which established norms of business ethics crumbled under the onslaught of ruthless competitors.[42]

The robber barons were buttressed in their actions by values of the time, which extolled the virtues of ruthless competition. Particularly popular were the works of Herbert Spencer (1820–1903), an English philosopher who popularized the doctrine called Social Darwinism. Spencer's philosophy provided a moral basis for the accumulation of large fortunes through economic operations which, in the words of historian Henry Demarest Lloyd, made "the Black Flag the emblem of success on the high seas of human inter-

[42]Chester McArthur Destler, "Entrepreneurial Leadership among the 'Robber Barons': A Trial Balance," *Journal of Economic History*, 1946, vol. 6, supplement.

change." Spencer argued that life was a continuing process of adaptation to a harsh external environment. Businessmen were engaged in a competitive struggle for survival in which the fittest survived. The strongest competitors benefited the human race by their survival and prosperity. This idea enabled the robber barons to justify any effective business tactic, no matter how harsh or cruel, as contributing to a positive end result in the evolutionary process. The widespread acceptance of Herbert Spencer's doctrines made predatory behavior seem acceptable. Mothers proudly pointed to the actions of Gould, Rockefeller, and their ilk as examples worthy of emulation by their children. In the following quotation, John D. Rockefeller, speaking in a Sunday school address, is a convincing exponent of this brand of competition:

> The growth of a large business is merely a survival of the fittest....The American Beauty rose can be produced in the splendor and fragrance which bring cheer to its beholder only by sacrificing the early buds which grow up around it. This is not an evil tendency in business. It is merely the working out of a law of nature and a law of God.[43]

The construction of the Central Pacific Railroad is one of many examples of the infamous commercial activities of the time. Matthew Josephson, a left-wing historian and author of a widely read book entitled *The Robber Barons* (1934), describes the actions of three shop owners in California named Collis Huntington, Mark Hopkins, and Leland Stanford. In 1860 the three combined with a gold miner named Charles Crocker to form a group called the Pacific Associates. The four raised $200,000, which Huntington carried to Washington in a trunk in 1861 and handed out liberally to congressmen and senators in pursuit of a federal charter for a railroad in California. After spending all the money, Huntington came home with the charter and promises of land grants and federal financial support for the fledgling railroad construction project.

In 1863, after Leland Stanford became California's governor, the Central Pacific was able to invoke the power of state government. In May of that year, elections were held in San Francisco for a $3 million bond issue to finance further construction of the railway. Leaving nothing to chance, Leland's brother, Philip Stanford, arrived at the polls in a buggy filled with bags of gold pieces and tossed them liberally into the outstretched hands of the crowd. The bond issue passed.

Later, the Central Pacific raised funds by demanding bond subscriptions from towns through which the roadbed was to pass and by threatening to build elsewhere and cut towns off from "progress." In 1868, for instance, the Pacific Associates extracted 5 percent of the assessed valuation of all of Los Angeles County as the price for connecting the residents there with a rail line to the East. Such a levy was not unusual. In the meantime, Huntington attended to government relations in Washington by spending $200,000 to $500,000 during each legislative session to secure political favors.

---

[43]Richard Hofstadter, "The Pervasive Influence of Social Darwinism," in *The Robber Barons: Saints or Sinners?* Thomas B. Brewer, ed., New York: Holt, Rinehart and Winston, 1970, p. 37.

Construction of the Central Pacific proceeded, utilizing the backbreaking labor of up to 10,000 Chinese workers who were paid $1 a day. Many did not survive the job. The four Pacific Associates received a total of $79 million in bonds, government subsidies, and investor cash during construction of the railroad. Experts have estimated that almost half this amount was in excess of that needed for legitimate construction costs and made its way into the pockets of the four principals. The railroad, however, was built and in operation.

There existed a substantial number in the society of that time who frowned upon dishonest behavior in business. Among them were clergymen and populist protestors. For this group, the lawbreaking and corner-cutting of the Pacific Associates and other corrupt entrepreneurs were sinful blows to the public interest. Today, the actions of the Pacific Associates would lead to the resignation of public officials, fines by regulatory agencies, possible criminal prosecution of corporate executives, and a public hue and cry. But that is today. We must re-create the social atmosphere of another era to fully understand the Pacific Associates.

The robber barons learned to manipulate the corporate form to their advantage. They committed a hundredfold minor larcenies. They corruptly elicited government subsidy for their activities. And despite their paeans to the beauty of Darwinian competition, they replaced it with monopoly. But these observations do not cement a case against them. In fact, there may be much to be said for them. They burst upon the scene at a time of great ferment, when the economy was expansive and the nation was characterized in part by the raw wildness of the frontier spirit. They were well adapted to this turbulent atmosphere and far removed from the fastidious practices of the pre-Civil War Eastern business establishment. And their accomplishments were enormous. In the words of an economic historian:

> Whatever their amoralities and ruthlessness, they helped to lead American business into the stage of full capitalism, creating gigantic organizations capable of servicing the entire continent or several sections at least. They led in extending the corporation into new and important fields of enterprise, in employing hired executives for routine administration and specialized tasks, and in reserving to themselves exclusively entrepreneurial functions of planning, high strategy, and risk taking.[44]

Seen this way, the robber barons contributed substantially to the foundations of the robust industrial economy that followed their era. In a utilitarian sense, an argument can be made that the benefits accruing to society from their businesses exceed the damage to the social fabric resulting from their bribes, deceits, and manipulations.

Would more honest business activity have fostered similar economic development? What would have happened if legal and cultural restraints had controlled the predations of the robber barons? These questions cannot be answered definitively. The historical record shows that law and social standards were too weak to force the robber barons into more ethical channels.

[44]Destler, *op. cit.*, pp. 34–35.

Some scholars have argued that an amount of corruption existing during expansive periods in developing societies is desirable. If there exists in such societies a "functional corruption," which departs from ethical ideals but permits fluid, rapid growth by easing barriers that stem from rules, niceties, and rigid laws, then economic development may be faster. One student of social and economic development, Samuel Huntington, has argued that such "functional corruption" serves the public interest at the same time as it promotes selfish gain. He writes:

> Corruption may be one way of surmounting traditional laws or bureaucratic regulations which hamper economic expansion. In the United States during the 1870s and 1880s, corruption of state legislatures and city councils by railroad, utility, and industrial corporations undoubtedly speeded the growth of the American economy. . . . A society which is relatively uncorrupt—a traditional society for instance where traditional norms are still powerful—may find a certain amount of corruption a welcome lubricant easing the path to modernization. A developed traditional society may be improved—or at least modernized—by a little corruption.[45]

Today we have largely abandoned doctrines of Social Darwinism in favor of new managerial ideologies that redefine the meaning of competition and social responsibility. This changed philosophical backdrop makes today's business environment hostile to wholesale corruption. In addition, generations of scandals and rising public expectations for business behavior have elevated ethical norms far above what they were during the days of the Pacific Associates. Some corruption in business may be inevitable, but it is less likely to be regarded as functional. Today, however, we have the difficult task of looking back more than a century to pass judgment on these robber barons and to clarify their morally ambiguous actions.

QUESTIONS

1 Compare the benefits of the robber barons' activities to their costs. From a utilitarian standpoint, can their actions be justified by arguing that benefits exceeded costs?
2 Do you believe that "functional corruption" can be useful in a developing society? In a developed society? Or is honest commercial activity always preferable?
3 What forces in today's pluralistic society would prevent the robber-baron type of exploitation?

[45]Samuel Huntington, *Political Order in Changing Societies*, New Haven: Yale University Press, 1968, pp. 68–69.

4

Critics of Business

Sisters of Loretto

The Loretto Literary and Benevolent Institution is an order of Roman Catholic nuns that exemplifies shareholder activism by church groups. The Sisters of Loretto began their activism in 1976 by buying eighty-one shares of Blue Diamond Coal Co. for $19,500. They were intent on pressuring the management of this Kentucky company to improve mine safety, following a highly publicized accident. Since then the Sisters have sponsored numerous shareholder resolutions to make corporations more socially responsible. In 1978, for example, the Sisters' sponsorship of a resolution led Gulf Oil Co. to adopt a policy prohibiting payment of further political contributions in South Korea.

There are about 600 Sisters in the order, 300 of whom are retired. Their primary mission as an order is child and adult education, but they also take active interest in working for social justice in the cities where their houses are located. Even if only one sister feels strongly that she is informed about an issue, perceives an injustice, and is willing to work on it, the others in the order will show solidarity.

Like other Roman Catholic orders, the Sisters of Loretto own stock. They have set up an eight-member Investment Committee composed of representatives from houses around the country. The committee meets to make decisions about buying and selling stock and voting the shares at annual meetings. Sometimes the Sisters sell the stock of a company from which they do not care to profit. At other times, they buy shares of a company so that they can bring shareholder resolutions against management as part of a campaign of influence. In recent proxy seasons, the Sisters have sponsored or cosponsored, with other church groups, an average of six to eight socially responsible shareholder resolutions.

A frequent target of the Sisters is General Dynamics Corporation, headquartered in St. Louis. General Dynamics is the nation's largest defense contractor. Its major contracts include the F-16 Falcon jet fighter, the Tomahawk cruise missile, fuselages for KC-10 tanker/cargo aircraft, Stinger and Viper shoulder-fired anti-aircraft missiles, Sparrow air-to-air missiles, Trident missile submarines, ships for the U.S. Navy, and M1 main battle tanks. With the exception of 1987, the Sisters have brought at least one resolution opposed by management to a vote of the stockholders every year beginning in 1983. In that year, they joined with three other Roman Catholic orders asking the company to withdraw its bid for a contract to manufacture major cruise missile components and asking that workers on cruise missile programs be retrained for other occupations. Together, these groups had 740 shares, or one ten-thousandth of 1 percent of General Dynamics 55.4 million outstanding shares. Only 1 percent of General Dynamics' shareholders voted with the Sisters, but subsequent resolutions in later years have received up to 10 percent of the vote.

The Sisters interpret Catholic theology to hold the production of nuclear weapons and their delivery systems as unethical. They believe that papal teachings and Biblical text condemn the manufacture of such potentially destructive force. They also believe that the money and resources pouring into the arms race could be used more constructively to combat poverty around the world.

At General Dynamics, John McGuire, the corporate secretary, regards the Sisters as well-intentioned but misguided. McGuire is a thoughtful Catholic, with three brothers who are priests. He argues that prevailing Church theology permits production of nuclear weapons for use in deterring a catastrophic event such as a third world war. He believes that the Sisters are errant in their interpretation of Church doctrine and mistaken in trying to impose their antiweapons views on the corporation. In addition, he believes that it is not proper for them to buy an infinitesimal share of General Dynamics stock and use the shareholder resolution machinery in pursuit of values that are so divergent from those of the company and other shareholders. The company tries to fend off the resolutions if it can. When, in 1986, the Sisters sought to file a resolution requesting that the General Dynamics board have more members with expertise in marketing civilian products, the company filed a detailed, fifty-page report with the Securities and Exchange Commission accusing the Sisters of harassing it and disputing the legitimacy of the filing under SEC rules. As a result, the SEC disallowed the filing. But the Sisters persisted. In 1988, they joined three other church groups to sponsor a resolution asking the company to describe its plans to attract more civilian work at any factory where over 30 percent of the work was on defense contracts. The resolution got only a 4 percent vote; when repeated in 1989 it got only 2.4 percent.

Corporations today are attacked by a wide spectrum of stakeholders. The story of the low-grade quarrel between the Sisters and General Dynamics is but one of thousands that could be told. It illustrates the difficulty of conflict resolution when corporations confront visionary critics.

In this chapter, we examine criticism of business through history, discuss underlying causes of antibusiness feeling, illuminate the objectives of critics, and give examples of specific complaints and management responses.

HISTORICAL TRENDS IN PUBLIC ATTITUDES TOWARD BUSINESS

Throughout recorded history and across cultures, merchants and businesses have been regarded with suspicion. Here, we put this phenomenon in summary relief.

THE ANCIENT AND MEDIEVAL WORLDS

In early civilizations such as ancient Egypt and Mesopotamia, the Inca and Aztec societies, Confucianist China, and the Hinduized kingdoms of ancient Southeast Asia, the merchant was ranked relatively low on the traditional scale of values.[1] These early societies had a tripartite hierarchy, with rulers at the top, followed by farmers, who made up the great mass of citizens. In the lowest rank were merchants, who were typically regarded as indecent. Perhaps this was because their sharp business practices and temporizing ethics diverged from the more altruistic mores of family and tribal relations developed during generations of recently eclipsed hunter-gatherer society.

Sages of classical civilization encoded the idea that wealth was associated with greed and corruption. The basis for this belief was the view that human wants are insatiable. The acquisition of wealth frees individuals from certain restraints and leaves them free to pursue selfish desires which may be immoral. In the utopian society described in *The Republic,* for example, Plato prohibited the possession of private property to the highest ruling class for fear of corruption and the rise of tyrants. The rulers were, in addition, forbidden even to touch gold or silver.[2] In his *Politics*, Aristotle argued that retail activity for the purpose of monetary gain—as opposed to simply acquiring necessary commodities—is a "perverted or unsound" activity.[3] He also described the lending of money for interest as a "hateful" activity.[4] Likewise, the Stoic philosophers of ancient Rome, such as Epictetus and Marcus Aurelius, taught that the truly rich person was in possession of inner peace rather than capital or property.[5] These thinkers looked down on merchants of their day as materialists who, in pursuit of wealth, sacrificed the opportunity to develop character. Needless to say, this did not deter these merchants from accumulating fortunes and neglecting the study of ideals.

[1]James L. Peacock, "Ethics, Economics and Society in an Evolutionary Perspective," in Ivan Hill, ed., *The Ethical Basis of Economic Freedom*, Chapel Hill, North Carolina: American Viewpoint, 1976.

[2]Trans. F. M. Cornford, New York: Oxford University Press, 1945, see pp. 155–168.

[3]Trans. Ernest Barker. New York: Oxford University Press, 1962, p. 27. Originally written c. 335 B.C.

[4]*Ibid.*, p. 29.

[5]"Asked, 'Who is the rich man?' Epictetus replied, 'He who is content.'" *The Golden Sayings of Epictetus*, trans. Hastings Crossley in Charles W. Eliot, ed., *Plato, Epictetus, Marcus Aurelius*, Danbury, Connecticut: Grolier, 1980, p. 179.

During the Middle Ages, the prevailing theological doctrines of the Roman Catholic Church made the populace intolerant of profit making. Lending money for interest was condemned as sinful. Merchants were exhorted by religious doctrine to charge a "just price" for their wares, a price that was just adequate to maintain them in the social station to which they were born. The concept of a just price stands in contrast to the modern practice of market pricing in which price is determined by supply and demand. But today we hear echoes of medieval theology when consumers complain that high prices for a product are unjust, unfair, or unethical.

Cynicism about wealth and profit making continued during the Renaissance. For example, Montesquieu wrote of a typical progression "from riches to corruption" and Rousseau of a "dissolution of morals [as] the necessary consequence of luxury."[6] Later, as the industrial revolution progressed, new variants of this cynicism emerged. With the rise of large working classes, charges of worker exploitation by wealthy factory owners emerged. With development of mass consumer markets came criticism of products and marketing techniques. As this brief historical survey shows, harsh opinions of business have existed in every age.

ATTITUDINAL TRENDS IN UNITED STATES HISTORY

Opinion polls measuring public attitudes toward business were not introduced until the 1930s. But much higher levels of public confidence in business existed during the early years of our nation than exist now. Historians record generally positive feelings toward entrepreneurs, companies, and the business system until the growth of giant trusts in the latter half of the nineteenth century.

The earliest colonies were formed by English trading companies operated by private individuals for profit. In some instances the motive for colonization was to avoid religious persecution, but the backers of the Pilgrims, for instance, hoped to make a profit. The commercial spirit manifested itself in different ways in colonial America, but it was dominant in most walks of life. The farmer was not a peasant bound to the soil with a pattern of life dictated by custom. Although his way of life was different from that of the retail merchant in the town, they both engaged in buying and selling to make a profit. As the farmer accumulated wealth, he built and ran grain mills and in other ways employed his capital exactly like a merchant. Merchants of great wealth could rise to top status in colonial society in part because there was no tradition of a landed or hereditary aristocracy in the United States, as there was in Europe.

By 1850, America was a predominantly rural, agrarian society of small, local businesses. But explosive industrial growth rapidly reshaped it, creating

---

[6]Montesquieu, *Considerations on the Causes of the Greatness of the Romans and Their Decline,* trans. David Lowenthal, New York: Free Press, p. 29, and Jean-Jacques Rousseau, *Discourse on the Arts and Sciences,* trans. G. D. H. Cole, New York: E. P. Dutton and Co., 1950, p. 163. These quotes and an exposition of the wealth-corruption thesis are from Phillip C. Chapman, "Stress in Political Theory," *Ethics,* October 1969, p. 41.

some very bad social problems in the process. Cities grew as farmers left the land and immigrants swelled slum populations. Most cities were run by corrupt political machines which failed to ameliorate their parlous conditions. Simultaneously, companies in many industries grew into huge national monopolies. These changes were the raw material of two movements critical of big business.

The first was the *populist movement*, a farmers' protest movement, which began in the 1870s and led to formation of a new political party, the People's party, and its ultimate defeat in 1896. Here is how the movement started. Soon after the Civil War, farmers began to suffer from a persistent drop in crop prices. Falling prices were caused mainly by overproduction due to the efficiencies of new farming machinery and by new transportation methods that brought Midwestern farmers into competition with foreign farmers. At the time, farmers did not understand these factors and blamed their distress on railroad companies, the largest and most visibly corrupt businesses of that day, which frequently overcharged farmers when hauling crops, and on "plutocrats" such as J. P. Morgan and others in the Eastern banking community, who controlled finance and industry and sometimes foreclosed on their farms. In a typical tirade, Mary Lease, speaking on behalf of the Minnesota Alliance ticket in 1890, complained:

> Wall Street owns the country. It is no longer a government of the people, by the people and for the people, but a government of Wall Street and for Wall Street. The great common people of this country are slaves, and monopoly is the master. The West and South are bound and prostrate before the manufacturing East.[7]

To solve agrarian ills, the populists advocated government ownership of railroads, abandonment of the gold standard, and measures to control the influence of big business in politics, including direct election of U.S. senators.

Despite the populist critique, historian Louis Galambos believes that there existed a great reservoir of respect for and confidence in business until the late 1880s.[8] Thereafter, analysis of newspaper and magazine editorials shows hostility toward large trusts mounting rapidly. Soon the populists succeeded in electing many state and local officials who enacted laws to regulate the railroads and provided the political groundswell behind creation of the Interstate Commerce Commission in 1887 to regulate railroads. Despite efforts, populists were never able to forge a national coalition with labor organizations. The movement died in 1896 with the decisive defeat of William Jennings Bryan, the People's party candidate for president, but it had created a language and rationale for criticism of big companies at a time when industrialization was straining the social fabric. Populists blamed the unintended,

---

[7]In John D. Hicks, *The Populist Revolt*, Minneapolis: University of Minnesota Press, 1931, p. 160.

[8]Louis Galambos, *The Public Image of Big Business in America, 1880–1940*, Baltimore: Johns Hopkins University Press, 1975, chap. 3. Galambos examined 8,976 items related to big business that were printed in eleven newspapers and journals between 1879 and 1940 using content analysis to reconstruct a rough measure of public opinion among influential groups in the population.

THE WONDERFUL WIZARD OF OZ

The Wizard of Oz is known as a book for children.[9] But it has another dimension. It was written by a writer of children's books, Lyman Frank Baum (1856–1919), in 1900 as an allegory of the populist dream, and it satirizes the evils of an industrial society run by a moneyed elite of bankers and industrialists. The word "Oz" is the abbreviation for ounce, a measure of gold. It and the Yellow Brick Road allude to the hated gold standard. The characters all represent major groups in society. Dorothy represents the common man. The Scarecrow is the farmer. The Tin Woodman is industrial labor. His rusted condition recalls the closing of factories in the depression years of the 1890s and his lack of a heart reminds readers that factories dehu-manized workers. The Cowardly Lion is William Jennings Bryan, the defeated People's party candidate, whom Baum regarded as lacking sufficient courage. The Wicked Witch of the East was intended by Baum to parody the capitalist elite. She kept the munchkins, or "little people," in servitude. At the end of the Yellow Brick Road lay the Emerald City, which was Washington, D.C. When the group arrived, it was met by the Wizard, who stood for the president of the United States. At the end Dorothy melted the Wicked Witch of the East, the Wizard flew off in a balloon, the Scarecrow became ruler of Oz, and the Tin Woodman took charge of the East. This ending was the unrealized populist dream.

adverse consequences of industrialization on bigness, Wall Street, and a bloated American "plutocracy" of wealthy, greedy business magnates. Because industrialization continued, this legacy endured long after the populists faltered.

The second movement was the *progressive movement*, a broader social reform movement lasting from about 1900 until the end of World War I in 1916. It was a movement of great moral indignation about problems created by industrialization and it incorporated the urban middle class as well as farmers. Although a short-lived Progressive party was formed and unsuccessfully nominated Theodore Roosevelt for president in 1912, both the Democratic and Republican parties had powerful, dominant progressive wings. Unlike populism, progressivism was a mainstream political doctrine. Like populism, it was at root an effort to cure social ills by controlling perceived abuses of big business.

Because of broad popular support, progressives were far more effective than populists in their reform efforts, and during their era a reform tide washed over business. Progressives broke up trusts and monopolies, made federal campaign contributions by corporations illegal, imposed federal regulation on consumer products, restricted child labor, started a corporate income tax and inheritance taxes, and regulated safety conditions in factories. "Turn the waters of pure public spirit into the corrupt pools of private interests," wrote Ernest Crosby, editor of *Cosmopolitan Magazine*, "and wash the

[9]First published in 1900 under the title *The Wonderful Wizard of Oz*, Chicago: Reilly & Britten Co., 1915. Eventually, there were fourteen Oz books, and Oz Reading Societies were formed where different Oz books owned by members were read aloud. The classic interpretation of symbolism in *The Wizard of Oz* is Henry W. Littlefield, "The Wizard of Oz: Parable on Populism," *American Quarterly*, Spring 1964.

CAPITALISM

Art Young, a radical cartoonist of the Progressive era, had an impish ability to highlight the excesses of the industrial age. This cartoon, typical of many at that time drawn by Young and others, first appeared in 1912. (*Source:* Art Young. *The Best of Art Young*, New York: Vanguard Press, 1936, p. 89.)

offensive accumulations away.''[10] Progressivism further refined the antibusiness lexicon of the populists and carried their legacy into the twentieth century.

The era was marked by a high level of antibusiness sentiment in the population. Also, it was during these years that the public developed a more im-

[10]''The Man with the Hose,'' August 1906, p. 341.

personal view of the corporation. Previously, big trusts were associated with famous founders such as Andrew Carnegie, John D. Rockefeller, Jay Gould, Samuel Huntington, or Cornelius Vanderbilt. But, according to opinion historian Louis Galambos, as corporations grew in size people began to regard them as impersonal bureaucracies—a tendency that continues today.[11]

After the triumph of progressive reforms, there was a period of high public confidence in big business during the prosperous, expansive 1920s. This rosy era ended abruptly with the stock market crash of 1929 and business once again came under sustained attack. During the 1920s, the idea had been advanced that business knew how to achieve a continuing prosperity, and it was widely accepted. The depression of the 1930s proved this view wrong and, in addition, brought to light much ineptness, criminal negligence, and outright fraud on the part of prominent and previously respected business executives. There was a popular feeling that the economic collapse would not have occurred if business managers had been more capable. Criticism of business was intensified by the callous-appearing reaction of the conservative business community, which believed that government should not intervene to relieve human misery caused by economic collapse.

As criticism of business grew, the old lexicon of populism and progressivism reemerged. In the Senate, for example, Huey Long, a colorful populist Democrat from Louisiana, claimed to be the advocate of the poor against the rich and rose to condemn a "ruling plutocratic class" controlled by the "fortune-holding elements of Morgan, Mellon, and Rockefeller."[12] In 1934, Long introduced a plan to redistribute wealth which would annually tax large fortunes and corporate assets and redistribute the money by guaranteeing every family a gift of $5,000 and an annual income of $2,500.[13] To promote his plan, Long established a Share Our Wealth Society which attracted over five million members in 1935, but he was assassinated before its enactment and the milder reforms of President Franklin D. Roosevelt's New Deal proved sufficient to placate industry critics.

During World War II support for business rebounded. Industry wrapped itself in patriotism, and its high output of war materiel proved essential to Allied victory. As a result, business was seen as the "arsenal of democracy," not as a bloated plutocracy. In a postwar poll only 10 percent of the population believed that where "big business activity" was concerned "the bad effects outweighed the good."[14] This renascence of respect lasted into the 1960s before the populist seed sprouted once again.

[11]*Ibid.*, p. 181–183.

[12]*Congressional Record*, 73 Cong., 2nd Session, p. 6081, speech of April 5, 1934.

[13]The Share Our Wealth Society was first introduced on nationwide radio in February 1934. Long never clarified the exact nature of taxation. The plan focused on taxing individual fortunes annually to gradually reduce them. It would logically have been necessary to tax corporate assets when individual fortunes were being used to control them. For more on the plan see T. Harry Williams, *Huey Long*, New York: Knopf, 1970, pp. 692–704.

[14]Burton R. Fisher and Stephen B. Withey, *Big Business as the People See It*, Ann Arbor, Michigan: University of Michigan Microfilms, December 1951, p. xiii.

RECENT ANTIBUSINESS SENTIMENT

Strong public support for business collapsed in the mid-1960s. It was a time of unrest. Strong social movements attacked basic institutions for their failure to solve major problems. Government, labor, the military, churches, higher education, medicine, the press, and, of course, business all suffered diminished public confidence. Here are examples of polls that reflect the extraordinary negative trend in public attitudes toward business.

• In 1968, 70 percent agreed that business tries to strike a fair balance between profits and the public interest. By 1970 the figure had declined to 33 percent, and in 1976 it had plummeted to 15 percent. This was a drop of 55 points in ten years.[15]

• Two polls, the first in 1966 and the second in 1979, showed that the percentage of Americans expressing a "great deal of confidence" in the leaders of major companies declined from 55 percent to 19 percent.[16]

• Between 1965 and 1977 the average favorability ratings for eight industries fell from 68 percent to 36 percent. Approval of 22 large companies declined from an average rating of 74 percent in 1965 to 48 percent in 1975.[17]

Scholars who studied the plummeting polls theorized that the period of turmoil in American society in the 1960s created a "confidence gap," or a gap between public expectations about how institutions *should* perform and public perceptions of how they actually *did* perform. This gap has persisted for over twenty years. In fact, some poll results show a continuing downtrend in support for big business extending through the 1980s. In Gallup polls the number of Americans expressing "a great deal" or "quite a lot" of confidence in big business has fell from 31 percent in 1985 to 25 percent in 1988.[18] A 1989 Harris poll found that 69 percent believe business has "too much power over too many aspects of American life," and 47 percent believe companies would harm the environment to make a profit.[19]

FACTORS UNDERLYING NEGATIVE ATTITUDES TOWARD BUSINESS

Although the trend today is toward somewhat more positive feelings about business, much criticism still circulates. What causes critical attitudes to persist? Negative attitudes toward business result in part from current events, trends, and values. In addition, public antipathy has complex historical, cul-

---

[15]Seymour M. Lipset and William Schneider, "How's Business? What the Public Thinks," *Public Opinion*, July–August 1978.

[16]Philip Shaver, "The Public Distrust," *Psychology Today*, October 1980.

[17]Seymour M. Lipset and William Schneider, *The Confidence Gap*, New York: Free Press, 1983, p. 31.

[18]*Gallup Report*, "Confidence in Institutions—Trend," no. 288, September 1989, p. 21. See also Seymour M. Lipset and William Schneider, "The Confidence Gap During the Reagan Years, 1981–1987," *Political Science Quarterly*, Spring 1987, p. 11.

[19] "The Public Is Willing to Take Business On," *Business Week,* May 20, 1989, p. 29.

tural, and psychological roots. Here we list and explain some significant forces underlying business-directed opprobrium.

TRADITIONAL AMERICAN ANTIPATHY TO CENTRALIZED POWER

Deeply fixed in the bedrock belief system of American political culture is the fear of concentrated power. Sources of this fear were the experiences of revolutionary America with an imperious England and the acceptance in the United States of the political theories of the English philosopher John Locke, set forth in his *Treatise on Civil Government* (1691).[20] One of the matters Locke was most concerned with was the accountability of power, particularly centralized, governmental power. He elevated the concept of popular sovereignty, or the right of majorities to influence powerful institutions such as legislatures and executives. Hence, with the growth of unprecedentedly large and powerful economic entities that affect the everyday lives of most Americans, the Lockean ideology of antibigness and harnessing of central authority has been applied to big business. Americans fear the self-interested motivations of executives and regard large corporations as remote, impersonal entities that cannot be trusted.

A Gallup poll of 1941 showed 59 percent of a nationwide sample agreeing that "there is too much power in the hands of a few rich men and large corporations in the United States."[21] Since 1959 Opinion Research Corporation has asked whether the public agrees that there is "too much power concentrated in the hands of a few large companies for the good of the nation," and the percentage of those affirming rose from 53 percent in 1959 to 73 percent in 1985.[22]

CONSPIRACY THEORIES

Over and over in American history it has been alleged that some group (and the list includes such diverse groups as city women, European monarchs, immigrants, Jews, blacks, Communists, Masons, Darwinians, munitions manufacturers, international bankers, oil companies, Wall Streeters, and others), acting in secret for its own self-interest, is out to do the public in. This mindset goes back to the first years of the colonies, when colonists feared papal conspiracies to undermine the Protestant nations of the New World.

The percentage of people in the population who believe in conspiracies is not always small. In February 1974, for instance, a Gallup poll revealed that

---

[20]John Locke, *The Second Treatise of Government*, Thomas P. Reardon, ed., Indianapolis: Bobbs-Merril, 1952. Originally published in 1691.

[21]George H. Gallup, ed., *The Gallup Poll: Public Opinion 1935–1971*, 3 vols., New York: Random House, 1972, vol. I, p. 277.

[22]Seymour M. Lipset and William Schneider, *The Confidence Gap: Business, Labor, and Government in the Public Mind*, New York: Free Press, 1983, p. 30, and Lipset and Schneider, "The Confidence Gap During the Reagan Years, 1981–1987," *Political Science Quarterly*, Spring 1987, p. 12. The polls actually rose to a high of 76 percent in 1981.

25 percent of Americans held oil companies responsible for the creation of the energy crisis existing at that time.[23] One month later, Opinion Research discovered that 43 percent of the population believed that the energy shortage was "contrived" by the oil companies to exploit the public.[24] As late as January 1985, 67 percent of the public felt that "the oil companies are just waiting for a chance to create another oil shortage so they can increase their prices again like they did in the 1970s."[25]

The persistence of such conspiracy theories makes big business the object of continued cynicism among certain elements of the population. Such theories are difficult to combat, because the circular logic of those who believe them is airtight. Because conspiracies are alleged to be secret and hidden, they cannot be scientifically observed, tested, or disproved. In this way, say conspiracy theorists, the actions of business leaders can be reduced to furtive manipulations that the public should fear.

For a small number of individuals, conspiracy beliefs are a manifestation of paranoid traits. These people overuse the defense mechanism of projection and endow the actions of leaders in business and government with motivations and goals such as greed, prejudice, or a cruel drive for power that would be unacceptable in themselves. For a larger number of conspiracy believers, however, such theories have a more straightforward appeal. They provide simple explanations for complex events and relieve the mind of strenuous thought.

NEGATIVE RUMORS ABOUT BUSINESS

Rumors, springing as they do from irrational thoughts, ignorance, fear, and incomplete impressions, are a phenomenon related to conspiracy theories. Some have been very costly to business. In the 1940s, for example, the first king-sized menthol cigarette, called Spud, failed in the market due to a groundless rumor that a leper worked in the factory where it was made.[26] In the 1970s, a widespread rumor held that McDonald's hamburgers contained worm meat. This rumor depressed company earnings—particularly in southern outlets—and led to a massive advertising campaign focused on the theme that McDonald's hamburger meat was 100 percent pure beef. Early in the 1980s, Procter & Gamble was hit by two related rumors. In 1980, a tale circulated that the picture of a moon on the Procter & Gamble logo meant that the company had been acquired by the Unification Church of Reverend Sun Myung Moon. In 1981, another story sprang up that the logo, which contains thirteen stars to symbolize the original thirteen American colonies, was a

---

[23]*Gallup Opinion Index*, February 1974, no. 104.

[24]Clarence H. Danhof and James C. Worthy, eds., *Crisis in Confidence II: Corporate America*, Proceedings of the Second Annual Intersession Public Affairs Colloquium, Springfield, Ill.: Sangamon State University, 1975, p. 39.

[25]Edward Byers and Thomas B. Fitzpatrick, "Americans and the Oil Companies: Tentative Tolerance in a Time of Plenty," *Public Opinion*, December/January 1986, p. 44.

[26]Robert Levy, "Tilting at the Rumor Mill," *Dun's Review*, July 1981.

symbol of the Antichrist and implied that the firm was in thrall to Satan. It was even said that an executive of the corporation appeared on a television talk show admitting corporate contributions to satanic cults. None of this was correct, but the rumors were hurtful. Some fundamentalist Christian groups boycotted Procter & Gamble products. Employees were verbally assaulted by irate store owners and shoppers desiring to repel the satanic horde personally. Procter & Gamble fought back by mailing to ministers around the country testimonials from Rev. Billy Graham, Rev. Jerry Falwell, Cardinal Joseph Bernardin, and others, debunking the rumor personally. It also set up a toll-free line to explain the logo to callers, distributed press releases and booklets, and ultimately brought twelve lawsuits against purveyors of the rumor who could be located. These actions failed to arrest its spread. In 1985, the company dropped the logo from its packaging (while retaining it on corporate stationery and on buildings). Still, the rumor would not die. In 1986, Procter & Gamble brought a $1 million libel suit against a mobile-home park newsletter (circulation 140) in San Jose, California, for reprinting the rumor. But it kept circulating. On July 6, 1989, a letter from Sandy M. of Decatur, Ill., appeared in Ann Lander's nationally syndicated column saying that stories were circulating that the head of Procter & Gamble had appeared on "Donahue" bragging he had "sold his soul to Satan in exchange for financial success" and boasting that "the symbol of Satan is carried on all Procter & Gamble products." Ann Landers replied that "there isn't a shred of truth in it," but the rumor may resurface.

Courtesy of The Procter & Gamble Company.

Rumors are thought to proliferate in periods of social stress, economic hardship, and wartime. According to Frederick Koenig, a rumor expert who serves as a consultant to major corporations fighting them:

> Some people see rumors as a way of structuring or understanding reality. A man who is unemployed and just barely scraping by might well be inclined to believe a rumor—even a false one—about a big company's product being contaminated. It somehow makes him feel better to see the corporate giant in trouble. He reasons that his best efforts get him nowhere, so the firm must be cutting corners to be successful. By striking out at a big company and clouding its reputation, he works off some of his aggression.[27]

[27]Frederick Koenig, "Today's Conditions Make U.S. 'Ripe for the Rumor Mill,'" *U.S. News & World Report*, December 6, 1982, p. 42. See also Koenig's book, *Rumor in the Marketplace*, Dover, Massachusetts: Auburn House, 1985.

HAVE YOU HEARD ANY OF THESE?

The following are some rumors that in recent years have circulated widely enough to have been mentioned in print. We are not aware of any truth in them.

- A woman was bitten by a poisonous Asian snake that had hatched from an egg in a pile of coats at a K Mart store. Her arm had to be amputated.
- Tobacco companies will redeem cigarette wrappers saved by smokers to purchase seeing-eye dogs for the blind.
- The oil companies have purchased from an inventor a carburetor that gets 100 miles per gallon. They are hiding it in a warehouse and paying hush money to the inventor.
- Bubble Yum, a children's chewing gum distributed by Squibb, contains spider eggs.
- Pop Rocks, a carbonated candy made by General Foods, can explode in children's stomachs when consumed with a carbonated beverage.

- Flickering Hallmark candles cause lead poisoning.
- A woman who took out some Kentucky Fried Chicken in a box and ate it in the dark found that it tasted terrible. Later, in the light, she discovered the tail of a rat in the box.
- A man drinking Coca-Cola from a bottle found a roach inside.
- Green M&Ms, made by the Mars Company, are an aphrodisiac.
- The Palestine Liberation Organization covertly presides over a multibillion dollar investment empire.
- Manufacturers of cosmetics are secretly using material from aborted human fetuses in their products and listing the ingredient as "collagen."
- Corona Extra, a Mexican beer imported by Barton Beers of Chicago, is contaminated with urine.

There is an element of mystery in rumors. It is unclear how they start, and they seem often to die as quickly as they begin. Their function for the American psyche is obscure, and there is little a manager who presides over a powerful and highly visible corporate entity can do to prevent either rumor or conspiracy theories from developing. When they do develop, depending on their nature, some companies choose to fight, and others find it convenient not to comment.

THE DYNAMICS OF GROUP POWER

Throughout American history, groups have formed during periods of tension to assert new viewpoints. The 1960s witnessed the rise of four powerful types of groups that saw their grievances rooted in existing arrangements of power and authority. These were environmental, public interest/consumer, civil rights, and anti-Vietnam War groups. Their successful attempts to combat existing arrangements paralleled those of earlier movements such as populism, unionism, and temperance.

The very force and success of demands made by these new, organized elements created a climate in which it became legitimate to criticize big business as representative of the status quo and blame it for some of society's ills. Americans traditionally have placed a high value on a pressure group system that countervails the perceived concentration of power in big business.

THE TENSION BETWEEN CAPITALISM AND DEMOCRACY

There is a natural, built-in tension between capitalistic economies and democratic governments because they embody equally legitimate but competing value systems. Capitalistic values include those of economic efficiency, the allocation of resources through an impersonal market mechanism, decentralization of decision making, and self-interest as a major personal motivating force. The democratic political system is marked by popular sovereignty, political equality, and majority rule. Society continuously seeks to balance and reconcile these competing value systems and is molded by the ways in which the systems are reconciled.

In the capitalism-democracy processes, business interests are continuously attacked. This attack happens because democracies have leftward centers of gravity and the logic of participation leads to inclusion of more and more have-nots in the electoral and policy processes. Stable democracies have an inherent leftward drive, and left-wing parties win support with measures that increase the relative power and security of the lower strata. In this process, politicians and political parties appeal to the masses by attacking wealth and privilege.

Conflict between capitalism and democracy produces strains and tensions that must be mitigated by a central authority. A prominent political scientist, E. E. Schattschneider, noted years ago that "the function of democracy has been to provide the public with a second power system, an alternative power system which can be used to counterbalance the economic power."[28] This observation still rings true. One fact of recent history, however, is that the public is cynical about government as well as business. There is an enduring fear that power abuse derives from government-business collusion. Polls in the 1970s and 1980s have shown that over 60 percent of the public feels the government in Washington, D.C., is "run by a few big interests."[29]

GENUINE ABUSES IN THE BUSINESS SYSTEM

The media daily reveal unethical or illegal behavior in business. Front-page incidents, such as the recent scandals in the savings and loan industry and the futures exchange, do not occur frequently, but other types of wrongdoing such as income tax evasion, fines for pollution, minor price fixing arrangements, illegal campaign contributions, corporate spying, and overcharges for auto repair are epidemic. Thus, when a really heinous corporate

[28]*The Semi-Sovereign People,* New York: Holt, Rinehart and Winston, 1960, p. 121.
[29]See, for example, Sommers, *op. cit.,* for a poll showing that the percentage saying that "government is pretty much run by a few big interests looking out for themselves" rose from 29 percent in 1964 to 69 percent in 1980, p. 5. A 1975 poll by the People's Bicentennial Commission found that 59 percent "believed major corporations tended to dominate and determine the actions of public officials in Washington," *Los Angeles Times,* August 31, 1975.

crime comes to light, as for instance when the officers of Film Recovery Systems, Inc., in Chicago were found to have knowingly exposed immigrant workers to lethal cyanide fumes resulting in one death, many in the public are willing to regard it as typical business behavior.

OPERATION OF THE BUSINESS CYCLE

The recurrence of recession and depression in American history has ensured periodic concern about the role of economic institutions and their performance and relationship to government. Panics in the nineteenth century led to a public rage focused on the financial community. The stock market scandals of the 1930s associated with the 1929 market crash tainted business for years. Opinion polls show that people rate economic problems among the most important problems. Polls also show that people may blame business for their economic ills. Lipset and Schneider correlated surveys of confidence in institutional leadership between 1966 and 1980 with rates of unemployment and inflation and found that as unemployment and inflation rose, confidence in the leadership of major companies and other institutions declined.[30] Historically, economic fluctuation also has been shown to detonate and give expression to underlying trends such as fear of power and belief in business conspiracy.[31]

THE EXISTENCE OF RISING EXPECTATIONS

The phenomenon of rising expectations is a familiar refrain that implies that there is a gap between expectations and realities in a society accustomed to rapid progress. The affluence created by industrial development has raised standards of living, but it has also created beliefs that people are entitled to numerous rights and possessions. People want safe products, guaranteed jobs, unlimited supplies of inexpensive gasoline, free schooling, four-day work weeks, guaranteed jobs, and other desiderata. Many such expectations are unrealistic. When they are not met, business is often blamed.

THE PROCESS OF ECONOMIC SOCIALIZATION IN CHILDREN

Babies are not born with preconceived notions of appropriate economic arrangements. Rather, cultural values, including attitudes toward business, are imparted through a gradual learning process known as *socialization*. This process, as it relates to the learning of economic arrangements, is little studied, but there is evidence that children begin to develop cynical attitudes toward business as early as the third grade.[32] Cynicism about business is transmitted

[30]*The Confidence Gap, op. cit.,* p. 62.
[31]W. W. Rostow, "Business Cycles, Harvests, and Politics," *Journal of Economic History,* November 1941.
[32]Lee G. Cooper and John F. Steiner, "Attitudes Towards Business Progress Report," paper series no. 8. Los Angeles, University of California at Los Angeles, Graduate School of Management, November 1976.

through contact with parents, peers, teachers, and media material of all kinds.

Cynicism in children is deeply instilled by recurring historical cycles of scandals involving people in business, such as those during the populist, progressive, 1930s depression, Watergate, and Contragate periods. These scandals also reinforce and increase adult cynicism.

PUBLIC IGNORANCE OF THE BUSINESS SYSTEM

A perennial complaint of defenders of business is that critics and the public at large are uninformed about basic business facts. It is argued that if critics better understood the rudiments of the system, there would be less public mistrust. Intuitively, it makes sense to think that perception of fact influences opinion. A study of American adults by DuPont, designed to measure knowledge and understanding of economic principles and the workings of American business, reported: "The amount people know about economics is correlated with their attitudes toward business. The more information they have, the more likely people are to look with favor on business institutions."[33] In a classic experiment, the Advertising Council sponsored a national economic education campaign between 1976 and 1978. During this period over nine million copies of a book on business economics were distributed, and magazine and newspaper ads were used to promote knowledge of economics. The result? Follow-up surveys showed no improvement in the public's knowledge of basic facts, and there was no improvement in the respondent's attitudes toward business. The campaign was a failure. Postmortems have speculated that a person's social and employment status are much more significant determinants of positive or negative attitudes toward business than is factual economic knowledge and, therefore, that ignorance of the facts is not primarily responsible for negative attitudes toward business.[34]

THE IMAGE OF BUSINESS IN THE MEDIA

Values are both shaped and reflected by depictions of business in journalism and the arts. The image of business in both is often critical.

A long-standing adversarial relationship exists between business and journalists representing the print and broadcast media. In the United States there are roughly 9,200 newspapers, 10,800 magazines, 9,200 radio stations, and 1,100 television stations.[35] Corporations desire to see positive images conveyed through them. The job of editors, reporters, and producers, on the

---

[33]DuPont De Nemours & Company. Survey conducted for the Business Roundtable by the Corporate Marketing Research Section, 1976.

[34]Karen F. A. Fox and Bobby J. Calder, "The Right Kind of Business Advocacy," *Business Horizons*, January–February 1985.

[35]H. Frazier Moore and Frank B. Kalupa, *Public Relations: Principles, Cases, and Problems*, Homewood, Illinois: Richard D. Irwin, 1985.

other hand, is to seek out and publish accurate information in a way that attracts audiences. The result of this difference of mission is that self-interested companies sometimes accuse the news media of distortion, bias, simplification, and omission in business reporting. Journalists, in turn, complain of uncooperativeness. Reporters complain of executives "unavailable" for comment, failure to return phone calls, terse news releases, and overprotective public relations offices that shield top managers from the press. Three other basic factors underlie the friction between journalism and business.

First, many business and economic stories are complex, yet strong forces in the media work against in-depth, sophisticated reporting. Television journalists are usually generalists, not specialists in business affairs. They face short deadlines for stories, and unless the story is a blockbuster, news program editors can rarely give it more than ninety seconds. Television news, owing to the visual nature of its presentation, tends to emphasize colorful, emotional, visually exciting, and dramatic stories involving conflict, but not all or even the most important business news fits these criteria. One recent study of corporate crime reporting over a ten-year period concluded that television news, because of its drive for visual drama, emphasized corporate crime and malfeasance more than printed news.[36] Anecdotal evidence bears this out. Herbert Schmertz, who headed media relations at Mobil, says that: "When a TV journalist wants to interview me, I generally assume...either the story he's working on is hostile to me or my company, or else he wants to use me to attack somebody else. When a print reporter calls, I make no such assumptions."[37] The dynamics of print journalism are less restricting. The most sophisticated daily newspapers, such as the *New York Times* and the *Washington Post*, have specialist business reporters and may devote many pages to a story to achieve depth reporting, although their deadlines are also short. They also have op-ed pages which invite the expression of different views. Weekly news magazines have longer deadlines and are able to do more research on stories.

Second, surveys have shown that journalists have different values than business executives. For example, journalists tend to be liberals and Democrats, whereas executives are the reverse. They have lower income and different educational backgrounds than the managers they cover, and they tend to have different public policy preferences.[38] These differences are grounds for speculation that journalists may put an indirect, liberal spin in their stories. Of course, large media corporations frequently own the news organizations that employ journalists. General Electric, for instance, acquired a major

---

[36]Donna Randall, "The Portrayal of Business Malfeasance in the Elite and General Public Media," *Social Science Quarterly*, June 1987.

[37]*Good-bye to the Low Profile*, Boston: Little, Brown and Company, 1986, p. 99.

[38]For surveys, see Stanley Rothman and S. Robert Lichter, "Media and Business Elites: Two Classes in Conflict," *The Public Interest*, Fall 1982; William Schneider and I. A. Lewis, "Views on the News," *Public Opinion*, August/September 1985; David Shaw, "Public and Press—Two Viewpoints," *Los Angeles Times*, August 11, 1985; and S. Robert Lichter, Stanley Rothman, and Linda S. Lichter, *The Media Elite*, Bethesda, Maryland: Adler & Adler, 1986.

network, CBS, when it merged with RCA. Such ownership ties may raise delicate issues. One scholar of the media describes the chilling effect of the elusive hand of ownership this way.

> Most owners and editors no longer brutalize the news with the heavy hand dramatized in movies like "Citizen Kane".... More common is something more subtle, more professionally respectable, and, in some respects, more effective: the power to treat some subjects accurately but briefly, to treat other subjects accurately but in depth, or in the conventional options every medium has of taking its own initiatives, carefully avoiding some subjects and enthusiastically pursuing others.[39]

A third factor underlying friction between business and journalism is the tradition of muckraking in the profession. This tradition began during the Progressive era after 1902 when a group of moralistic writers published exposes of business greed and corruption in emergent, mass-circulation magazines. Ida M. Tarbell, for instance, began her famous two-volume *History of the Standard Oil Company* as a series of articles in *McClure's* beginning in 1903.[40] Other writers skewered trusts in meat packing, insurance, railroading, tobacco, banking, and life insurance. Basic to the writings of the muckrakers was faith in democracy as an ethical ideal. They felt that big trusts controlled by a small number of businessmen should be subject to the discipline of majority rule. Their writings agitated the public to demand reforms and underlay the righteous mood of the Progressive era. Today's journalists carry on this tradition and work to ferret out excesses of business power and greed. The best contemporary muckrakers win Pulitzer Prizes; the rest pester management with their investigations and expose countless small corruptions. Most people turn to television and printed publications as inexpensive, accessible sources of information. But how much do they move public opinion; how influential are they? A recent study analyzed the impact of ten influence sources on public opinion about eighty prominent issues over a fifteen-year period. The researchers concluded that public opinion on most policy issues was quite stable, but when it did change network commentators, through their interpretation of news events, were more influential than other actors. Television news accounted for more than 50 percent of opinion change.[41] Interest groups, including business corporations, frequently had a negative effect on opinion; that is, the public viewed them as self-interested and moved away from their position.

What about the image of business in literature? In 1988 Tom Wolfe's novel, *The Bonfire of the Vanities*, rose to the top of the *New York Times* best-

[39]Ben Bagdikian, "The Media Brokers: Concentration and Ownership of the Press," *Multinational Monitor*, September 1987, p. 10. Bagdikian documents growing concentration of ownership of media outlets and argues that "large media corporations are the primary shapers of American public opinion" (p. 9).

[40]*The History of the Standard Oil Company*, Gloucester, MA: Peter Smith, 1963, 2 vols. Originally published in 1904. For more discussion of the muckrakers see Louis Filler, *The Muckrakers*, University Park, PA: Pennsylvania State University Press, 1968.

[41]Benjamin I. Page, Robert Y. Shapiro, and Glenn R. Dempsey, "What Moves Public Opinion?" *American Political Science Review*, March 1987, p. 38. See also Robert M. Entman, "How the Media Affect What People Think: An Information Processing Approach," *Journal of Politics*, May 1989.

seller list.[42] It is the tale of a rich Wall Street bond trader named Sherman McCoy, who lives in a Park Avenue apartment and thinks of himself as a "Master of the Universe," after the fantasy theme of the children's plastic action toys by the same name. Wolfe depicts Sherman McCoy's business life as frivolous and empty of enduring values, and, as the plot unfolds, his pretensions of superiority are destroyed by little people, the street punks of New York, working-stiff police detectives, and corrupt politicians. It is a novel the populists would have loved.

Wolfe's sneering look at business is squarely within a long tradition in American literature. While the image of business in American literature reflects a mixture of attitudes among novelists, it is often negative. Literary historian Emily Stipes Watts argues that businesspeople and their values have been systematically derided by American novelists from the colonial period to the modern era. The height of criticism, she says, came in the 1930s, when socialist writers set upon the capitalist system. But, she notes, "most businessmen depicted in post-1945 serious literature are still characterized as greedy, unethical, and immoral (or amoral)."[43] Watts' view, that business is treated with scorn and contempt, may be an oversimplification. A second literary historian, who studied 450 novels with business themes or characters, concludes that American novelists have admired virtues such as hard work, achievement, and integrity. These traits, however, were often seen to be at odds with the norms of business life.[44] And a third analyst argues that the novelist stands for the individual in the struggle against self, society, and corporation, and not against commerce per se.[45]

Much popular literature, of course, has championed business values. In the latter half of the nineteenth century popular novels by Horatio Alger painted a virtuous picture of business for millions who read them. Alger, says one critic, "was the man who put free and untrammeled competition on the side of the angels, and kept it there until well into the next century."[46] Another critic recalls the inspiration of Tugboat Annie, a fictional character in the *Saturday Evening Post*, "who could succeed in business without sacrificing courage, strength, integrity, or compassion."[47]

[42]New York: Farrar, Straus, Giroux, 1987.

[43]*The Businessman in American Literature*. Athens: University of Georgia Press, 1982, p. 150. For additional analysis of how the image of business is reflected in popular literature see Benjamin DeMott, "Reading Fiction to the Bottom Line," *Harvard Business Review*, May–June 1989.

[44]Howard P. Smith, "Novelists and Businessmen: Schizophrenia in the Complex Society," *Journal of Contemporary Business*, Autumn, 1976. See also Wilson C. McWilliams and Henry A. Plotkin, "The Historic Reputation of American Business," *Journal of Contemporary Business*, Autumn, 1976.

[45]Robert P. Falk, "From Poor Richard to the Man in the Gray Flannel Suit: A Literary Portrait of the Businessman," *California Management Review*, Fall 1958.

[46]Steward H. Holbrook, *Lost Men of American History*, New York: Macmillan, 1948, p. 237. A typical Horatio Alger novel is *Ragged Dick*, New York: Collier Books, 1962. It was his first and was originally published in 1867.

[47]Charles Sonnichsen, "Review of *The Businessman in American Literature*," *Business History Review*, Summer 1983, p. 277. Robert Coles, who teaches a course at Harvard University entitled "The Business World: Moral and Social Inquiry Through Fiction," gives his reading list of "morally energetic" novels in "Storyteller's Ethics," *Harvard Business Review*, March–April 1987.

The image of business on entertainment television and in film is, like that in literature, often negative. In 1981, a conservative media watchdog, the Media Institute, studied 200 prime-time television programs on the three major networks and found that two-thirds of business executives were portrayed in a negative light, as greedy criminals, that roughly half of all business activity depicted was illegal, and that in nine out of ten cases where people in business performed positive acts, they were acts of personal do-goodism and had no widespread social impact.[48]

Should we worry that Americans will develop antibusiness attitudes when they watch villains such as J. R. Ewing on "Dallas" and Alexis Carrington on "Dynasty"? Some do. Opinion researcher Robert Lichter has argued that "there is a lot of general evidence that people do tend to fuzz the boundaries between reality and television entertainment."[49] Others do not. Business columnist James Flanigan writes: "To say that enjoying a good villain like J. R. leads to antibusiness sentiments is like saying that reading Milton's 'Paradise Lost' leads to devil worship."[50] Recently a TV critic attracted attention by proposing a weekly series based on the work of a venture capitalist. Producers felt the scripts would be too cerebral and slow for the average viewer, but some titles were suggested, including "Miami Vice President," "The Bionic Business Man," "Merger, She Wrote," "Wall Street Blues," and "Late Night with Alan Greenspan."[51]

An additional source of negative stereotypes about business is cartoons. The wellspring of humor in business cartoons is often a not-so-veiled allusion to greed or mistreatment of society for profit. In recent years, the *New Yorker* magazine—a prestigious outlet for the work of the nation's leading cartoonists—has printed many such cartoons. That they are a source of mirth for the magazine's readers is perhaps confirmation of deep public cynicism about business. The two cartoons reprinted on page 95 are representative.

CURRENT CRITICISM OF AMERICAN BUSINESS

The list of criticisms of business is virtually endless and growing. But the fundamental criticism is that people in business frequently place profit before enduring social values such as truth, justice, virtue, love, and artistic merit. The profit motive is perceived to be less noble than humanitarian motives because it is seen as selfish. Beyond this, other basic criticisms are:

1 Business activity has a corrosive effect on culture. For example, advertising undermines values such as thrift and encourages extreme materialism.

2 Business exploits and dehumanizes workers.

[48]Leonard J. Theberge, ed., *Crooks, Conmen and Clowns: Businessmen in TV Entertainment*, Washington, D.C.: Media Institute, 1981.

[49]In Barbara Basler, "'Bad Guys' Wear Pin Stripes," *New York Times*, January 29, 1987, p. 31.

[50]"The Public, Not the Media, Is the Final Judge of Business," *Los Angeles Times*, October 26, 1983.

[51]In Michael O. Eisner, "The Business People and Television: A Distorted View," *Vital Speeches*, August 15, 1988, p. 666. The television critic who suggested the new TV series was Ben Stein.

"I'll be all right. I was suddenly overcome by a wave of compassion for the poor."
Source: *The New Yorker,* 2/4/85. Drawing by Dana Fradon; © 1985 The New Yorker Magazine, Inc.

"Where there's smoke, there's money."
Source: *The New Yorker,* 4/1/85, p. 45. Drawing by Joe Mirachi; © 1985 The New Yorker Magazine, Inc.

3 Business cheats and harms consumers.

4 Business has inordinate power to influence government and undermines the public interest.

The multinational corporation is subject to these criticisms plus others, such as exploitation of underdeveloped host countries, syphoning off profits and depleting capital in host countries, exporting jobs from the United States, and disrespecting local customs.

This list by no means exhausts the themes in attacks on business. The nature of these attacks and the prescriptions for eliminating perceived ills differ among critics. To oversimplify, there are five basic groups of critics.

ACTIVIST REFORMERS

This group, which includes well-known personalities such as consumer advocate Ralph Nader and genetic engineering critic Jeremy Rifkin, accepts the basic institutional framework of contemporary society but actively presses for reforms in the way business and other institutions operate. They set forth specific solutions for the ills they see. Nader, for example, fought high insurance rates by sponsoring a successful 1988 California ballot initiative called Proposition 103, which required auto and home insurers to roll back their rates.

Activists may be galvanized by personal situations. Lois Gibbs, a housewife living near the Love Canal dumpsite in Niagara Falls, New York, became the leader of nearby families and later started a nationwide crusade to make business dispose of toxic wastes more safely. Phil Sokolof, president of an Omaha metal parts company, had a heart attack and wrote letters to cookie and cereal manufacturers asking them to take high-fat coconut oil out of their products. When they failed to respond he ran full-page newspaper ads which pictured Hydrox cookies, Cracklin' Oat Bran cereal, and other products under the words, "The Poisoning of America." Within months large firms such as Kellogg Co. dropped coconut oil.

Most activism comes not from lone wolves, but from organized groups. Every sector of stakeholders in the corporate social environment—consumer, labor, environmental, civil rights, religious—has a warrior class. There are many examples of such groups at the international, national, state, and local levels. The Infant Formula Action Coalition (INFACT), composed of a worldwide network consumer groups, forced Nestle to alter its infant formula marketing after a seven-year boycott and since 1986 has conducted a similar boycott against General Electric to pressure it out of the nuclear weapons business. Ralph Nader heads a consortium of activist groups in Washington, D.C., with a 1989 budget of $5 million, including a network of public interest research groups which lobby politicians at the state and local levels.

Activists use a wide range of tactics to oppose corporations. Commonplace, low-key pressure tactics include behind-the-scenes negotiation, letter writing, public speaking, lobbying legislatures, research, editorial writing, and sponsorship of shareholder's resolutions at companys' annual meetings. But more can be done. Some groups utilize the lawsuit as a weapon. The National Resources Defense Council, for example, has championed environmental causes primarily by working in the courts. Others organize boycotts. Today there are as many as 100 product boycotts at any given time. Most are sponsored by labor unions, and the AFL-CIO maintains a "Don't Buy" list for members, but many are started by single-issue groups. Successful boycotts are difficult because a large number of committed consumers must participate, generally over a long time, before a company is financially hurt. Picketing, demonstrations, and civil disobedience are used to attract media attention and disrupt the normal business of a corporation. Opponents of some intensive animal agriculture techniques have, for example, broken into farms and stolen farm animals to "liberate" them.

The heavy artillery of corporate activists in recent years has been a provocative campaign of confrontation known as the "corporate campaign." The corporate campaign is the brainchild of labor activist Ray Rogers. Rogers, who finds inspiration in the words and deeds of the abrasive 1960s radical Saul Alinsky, honed the tactics of the corporate campaign in a 17-year-long successful effort to force the J. P. Stevens textile conglomerate to enter into a union contract. Subsequent corporate campaigns have been used mainly by organized labor against recalcitrant managements. They involve a variety of irritating tactics, including:

• Developing coalitions of community and church groups to pressure a corporation's lending institutions, insurers, and other supporters, such as retailers of the firm's products. One church group in Pittsburgh put dead fish in safety deposit boxes at the Mellon National Bank on a Friday afternoon as part of a campaign against USX Corporation for closing steel plants in the area. On Monday morning, the bankers had a malodorous incentive to reexamine their financial ties with USX.

• Directly confronting officers and directors of a company by picketing their homes, demonstrating at their children's schools, and interrupting services at their churches.

• Appearing at shareholder meetings to introduce resolutions, ask questions, and make views known to other shareholders.

• Suing the corporation and individual officers for a variety of trumped up offenses such as racketeering or breach of fiduciary duty.

• Employing more commonplace pressure tactics such as press releases, letter-writing campaigns, public speaking, editorials, picketing, boycotting, and the like.

The demeanor of activists ranges from polite to execrable. Their demands may be reasonable, but often there is a wide gulf between their ideal visions of corporate ethics and actual corporate behavior. Leadership may attack a caricature of evil business behavior to mobilize a following, but this attack makes dialogue and compromise difficult.

LIBERAL INTELLECTUALS

This group is composed of intellectuals who scrutinize business and take up the pen rather than the sword of activism to point out blemishes. Their writings are in the tradition of muckraking that grew up during the Progressive era. They see problems of racism, income inequality, sexism, social alienation, abuse of power, and environmental damage as mistakes or ineptitudes that are separate and distinct from an overall system worth preserving. Included in this group are academics such as sociologist William H. Whyte, Jr., author of *The Organization Man*, a 1956 book arguing that big organizations produced undesirable conformity in their members, and economist John Kenneth Galbraith, whose multiple works over twenty years lament the growing power of business and advocate greater government control.[52] Vance Packard, author of *The Waste Makers*, a 1960 book accusing business of encouraging frivolous, unnecessary consumption, and Rachael Carson, author of *Silent Spring*, a 1962 book on the dangers of pesticides, are examples of social critics who have influenced the public to demand corporate reform.[53]

This intellectual tradition is continuously renewed. Orville Schell's 1978 book, *Modern Meat*, raised public awareness of the dangers of antibiotics and hormones used in raising animals.[54] Jim Mason and Peter Singer created a debate about factory farming techniques in their 1980 book, *Animal Factories*, which made an ethical and philosophical case for the existence of farm animals' rights.[55] In 1986, America's Catholic bishops released "Economic Justice for All: A Pastoral Letter on Catholic Social Teaching and the U.S. Economy," which argued that our economic system was not responsive to the poor.[56] The document suggested moral and theological principles for redirecting policy, including the guideline that managers should evaluate corporate strategy based on how it affected those Americans who are least well-to-do.

MARXISTS

Marxist critics reject current institutional structures and demand replacement with a collectivist state. Unlike reform-oriented critics, this group finds the faults of capitalism rooted in the free market and private capital and demands abolition of these basic institutions.

Marxists remain true to the philosophical and economical theories of their intellectual progenitor, Karl Marx. Much more common today, however, are neo-Marxists, who represent revisionist schools of Marx's thought. Marxist and neo-Marxist scholars have made significant inroads in a number of

---

[52]Whyte, New York: Simon & Schuster, 1956. For Galbraith see, for example, *The Affluent Society*, Boston: Houghton Mifflin, 1958, or *The New Industrial State*, Boston: Houghton Mifflin, 1967.

[53]Packard, New York: McKay, 1960. Carson, Boston: Houghton Mifflin, 1962.

[54]*Modern Meat: Antibiotics, Hormones, and the Pharmaceutical Farm*, New York: Vintage, 1985.

[55]New York: Crown, 1980.

[56]National Conference of Catholic Bishops, Washington, D.C.: United States Catholic Conference, Inc., 1986.

academic disciplines such as economics, history, political science, and sociology, and in the mid-1980s there were about 12,000 faculty members of Marxist-oriented academic societies and two dozen Marxist journals.[57]

Marxists attack traditional scholarly theories for failing to comprehend the abusive aspects of current economic arrangements. Orthodox views of the market, they say, fail to reveal how capitalist institutions depend on worker exploitation, imperialist expansion overseas, resource waste, racial and sexual discrimination, income inequality, militarism, and other evils. A center for Marxist thought is the Institute for Policy Studies in Washington, D.C., which funds research and publications that attack business from a socialist perspective. Marxist thinkers have been influential in many antibusiness groups, but they have rarely advocated violence and their influence is waning. The overthrow of Marxist governments in Eastern Europe in 1989 and 1990 and the visible deficiencies of the economic system in the Soviet Union have blunted their critique.[58]

RADICAL NON-MARXISTS

On an intellectual plane, radical non-Marxist critics demand restructuring of the American system, but do not agree on what should be done, or how. Much antiestablishment criticism is aging now and has an empty, ethereal tone. Charles A. Reich, a professor of law, achieved great notoriety in 1970, for example, with publication of *The Greening of America*.[59] In this book, he condemned the corporate state for stifling individual expression and advocated spontaneous mass conversion to a new lifestyle and liberated mode of thinking called "Consciousness III." He called this new consciousness "the greatest secret in America." It still is.

The last two decades have also seen the appearance of a school of thought that would radically restructure economic goals and institutions by limiting or stopping growth. Critics in this school have emerged with concern for dwindling resources and expanding populations. Economist E. F. Schumacher, for example, wrote *Small Is Beautiful*, in which he set forth conservation lessons drawn from Buddhism and urged a new society in which people lived in harmony with nature instead of dominating and destroying it.[60] The method for conversion to the new society is rejection of economic growth as a goal.

One idea current with radical groups is the idea of "economic conversion," or switching defense plants to consumer goods production. Another program for the radical restructuring of some business activity is found on the agenda of the radical environmental group Earth First! This group is best known for its protests against logging in the Pacific Northwest and tree-

---

[57]David Brock, "Combating Those Campus Marxists," *Wall Street Journal*, December 12, 1985.
[58]For more on the failure of socialism see Irving Howe, *Socialism and America*, New York: Harcourt Brace Jovanovich, 1985, and Zbigniew Brzezinski, *The Grand Failure*, New York: Charles Scribner's Sons, 1989.
[59]New York: Random House.
[60]New York: Harper & Row.

spiking. But it also has a more expansive agenda calling for restoration of huge tracts of wilderness by removing roads, dams, power lines, and other human artifacts. This desire to turn back the clock of industrialization, which is based on a new philosophy of equality in the man-nature relationship, places Earth First! in conflict with much corporate activity.

REACTIONARIES

Reactionary critics assail the business community for responding to liberal critics, going too far in the direction of nonmarket activities, or undertaking political and moral stands in conflict with conservative ideals. Economist Milton Friedman is a leader of the group that flays business for departing from traditional economic roles in social projects that do not maximize profits and for accepting an enlarged role of government in providing incentives and regulations for business. The *laissez faire* orthodoxy of this group is influential with the conservative element of the business community. We feel that it is not fair to call them critics in the ordinary sense, but because their ideas often challenge prevailing practice, these conservative thinkers logically may be included here.

A variety of conservative activists exist. For example, a fundamentalist minister from Mississippi, Rev. Donald Wildman, masterminded an antipornography campaign in 1986 that pressured Southland Corp. to stop newsstand sales of *Playboy* and *Penthouse*. In 1989, Wildman threatened a Christian boycott of Pepsi unless PepsiCo Inc. dropped a $10 million contract with pop singer Madonna. Wildman and his supporters objected to "a pop star who goes around in her concerts with sex oozing out, wearing a cross" being held up as a role model in Pepsi commercials.[61] Wildman's group, the National Federation for Decency, records every prime-time network program and pressures advertisers away from programs that violate Christian values.

In 1985, a group known as the "Washington wives" formed the Parents' Music Resource Center in Washington, D.C., to combat pornography in rock music. They included Susan Baker, wife of Secretary of State James Baker; Nancy Thurmond, wife of Senator Strom Thurmond (R-S.C.); and Tipper Gore, wife of Senator Albert Gore (D-Tenn.). Through a formidable media campaign which included appearing on talk shows, writing magazine articles, giving interviews, mailing literature, and publishing a book, the women created widespread debate on sexually explicit, violent song lyrics.[62] The group advocated a voluntary record industry program to place warning labels on "porn rock" records. Ultimately, the Recording Industry Association of America adopted such a program. Movements such as these show that although most critics of big business are liberal or radical, some business behavior affronts conservative values also.

[61]In an interview with Don Winbush, "Bringing Satan to Hell," *Time*, June 19, 1989, p. 54.
[62]The book is by Tipper Gore, *Raising PG Kinds in an X Rated Society*, Nashville, TN: Abingdon Press, 1987. It was published in paperback by Bantam in 1988.

ACTIVIST CRITICS WHO ARE CORPORATE SHAREHOLDERS

Two brothers, John and Lewis Gilbert, pioneered the art of shareholder activism in the 1930s. The Gilbert brothers have attended thousands of corporate annual meetings to question officers about such delicate matters as their salaries. In 1942, the Securities and Exchange Commission adopted Rule 14a-8, which required corporations to include on proxy statements resolutions suggested by stockholders about important business matters. At the time of the annual meeting, when corporate business is conducted, all stockholders may vote on these resolutions. If they receive a majority of voting shares, they are binding on management. In the 1970s, shareholder resolutions became popular with social activists, especially church groups, as a means of pressing demands for socially responsible corporate action. The Gilberts have filed a large number of them also.

The first use of the proxy mechanism for a socially responsible shareholder resolution occurred in 1970, when a nonprofit public interest group, Campaign GM, qualified two resolutions for a vote in the General Motors Corp. annual meeting. The first, a resolution to expand the GM board of directors by adding public interest representatives, received 2.44 percent of votes cast; the second, a resolution to establish a committee of shareholders on social responsibility, got 2.73 percent of the vote. Although GM management fought with the SEC to keep the resolutions off its proxy statement and opposed them at the annual meeting, within a year GM established a public policy committee on its board of directors and appointed a black minister, the Reverend Leon Sullivan, to the board. Hence, Campaign GM achieved notable impact even though its resolutions got only a tiny fraction of the vote.

Activist critics observed the results of Campaign GM, and soon social responsibility resolutions were common at annual meetings of big corporations. By 1972, a total of thirty-seven were voted on, and the number swelled to 213 in 1976 before levelling off at 100 to 125 in the early 1980s.

The movement was spurred on by the publication in 1972 of a book, *The Ethical Investor*, in which the authors developed a rationale for shareholder activism called the Kew Gardens principle (named after the location in New York City of an infamous incident in which a young woman named Kitty Genovese was repeatedly stabbed before onlookers who refused involvement).[63] According to this principle, there are four criteria which, when met, create a moral imperative for shareholder action. First, a *need* for corrective action exists when corporate activity causes injury. Second, *proximity* exists if a person or group becomes a stockholder of an irresponsible corporation. Third, *capability* to help resolve a problem is created when a shareholder has available the proxy mechanism to force discussion of social issues. And fourth, the element of *last resort* arises when social pressure and other methods exclusive of shareholder activism have been tried and failed. When these

[63]John G. Simon, Charles W. Powers, and Jon P. Gunnemann. New Haven: Yale University Press.

conditions are met, shareholders have an ethical duty, according to the authors of *The Ethical Investor*, to file resolutions.

THE GROWTH OF SHAREHOLDER ACTIVISM

Resolutions were filed by individuals, universities, labor unions, and church groups such as the Sisters of Loretto. Frequent topics were restricting corporate activity in South Africa, nuclear weapons manufacturing, nuclear power, plant closings, marketing infant formula and drug sales in the Third World, energy conservation, affirmative action, and environmental pollution. A few conservative critics filed resolutions to restrict trade with communist countries and to prohibit charitable contributions by companies. Most resolutions received only a few percent of the vote and none passed. Each year the bulk of resolutions were filed by Church groups angry with American corporations doing business in South Africa. The resolutions failed to carry, but the groups attracted considerable attention.

In the mid-1980s, the movement was temporarily slowed by changes in the law making it harder for resolutions to qualify for a vote by shareholders. Until 1984, shareholders with only a few shares were permitted to file resolutions, and many stockholders with as few as one or several shares of a companies' stock originated them. Yet the practice of shareholder democracy forced management to print their statements on proxy material sent to all shareholders. And any resolution that got more than 3 percent in the voting was eligible for inclusion on the proxy statement again the next year. In 1983, 73 percent of the resolutions received 3 percent or more of the vote.

But in January 1984, in response to the lobbying of corporations which saw the resolutions as a nuisance, the SEC changed proxy eligibility rules to require that any shareholder advancing a resolution must have held at least $1,000 worth of stock or 1 percent of outstanding shares for a year. It also required a defeated proposal to achieve 5 percent of the vote to be eligible for balloting the next year, 8 percent for the following year, and 10 percent for the year after that. This change in the law cut the number of resolutions voted on roughly in half in 1984 and 1985, but soon the number started growing again until by 1989, 176 resolutions were voted on.

HOW EFFECTIVE ARE SHAREHOLDER PROPOSALS?

In the early years of their use, effectiveness was often limited by poor phraseology, ignorance of corporate operations, and hostility toward management. However, "ethical investors" are becoming more sophisticated and have growing influence.

No resolution opposed by management has received a majority vote. But the proxy machinery is still valuable as a publicity platform, and resolutions put management on the defensive. Because giant institutional investors with billions of dollars in equities, such as the New York City pension funds, have begun to vote for and even to propose resolutions, the average vote in favor has risen from 5.2 percent in 1983 to 11.3 percent in 1989. In the 1970s, it was rare for resolutions to get as much as 10 percent of the vote, but by the mid-1980s some were getting over 20 percent, and in 1989 a resolution at the US Air annual meeting for secret proxy ballots got 45.2 percent.

Resolutions need not pass, of course, to influence management. Each year many are withdrawn after negotiations. To illustrate, in 1985 Colgate-Palmolive acquired a 50 percent interest in a firm which marketed "Darkie Tooth Paste." The toothpaste, sold only in Asia, came in a package printed with a grinning, blackface caricature of Al Jolson in a top hat. For several years church groups, which found the package an offensive racial stereotype, pressured Colgate to change it. Colgate responded that consumers in Hong Kong, Malaysia, Singapore, Taiwan, and Thailand, where it was sold, were not offended. In 1987, a shareholder resolution sponsored by three church groups (including the Sisters of Loretto) requesting that the name "Darkie" be changed was withdrawn when Colgate-Palmolive agreed "to eliminate any offensive implications." Because Colgate-Palmolive's joint venture partner was reluctant to change, this took two years, but in 1989 the name was changed to "Darlie Tooth Paste" and the black face became a white one.

CONCLUSION: THE FUNCTION OF CRITICISM

In this chapter we have shown that negative attitudes toward business have been common throughout history. In the United States, the rise of big business after 1850 brought with it waves of public criticism.

This criticism is not all bad. The tension and conflict among business, government, and the public that results from ongoing processes of demand and accommodation are vital to societal well-being. Even forces that provoke cynicism are part of a robust and useful process that leads to healthy reexamination of major social institutions. It is not necessarily a benediction to have an abundance of internal harmony. Machiavelli argued that the quarrels between the senate and the people of Rome resulted in laws that were beneficial to the maintenance of liberty and that greater domestic tranquillity would have enfeebled that great state. Public antipathy and resistance to corporate power are a source of stress that may lead to constructive change of the kind that Thomas Jefferson implied when he argued: "A little rebellion now and then is a good thing, and as necessary in the political world as storms in the physical."

Operation Push Negotiates with Corporations

We are tired of you white folks, you racists and you bigots mistreating us. We are tired of paying you to deny us the right to even exist....We mean business, white folks. We ain't gonna shoot you all, we are going to hit you where it hurts most ... in the pocketbook.

—Charles Evers,
April 9, 1969, Port Gibson, Mississippi

Late in 1980, the Coca-Cola Co. was approached by the Reverend Jesse Jackson and other representatives of Operation PUSH (People United to Serve Humanity), a Chicago civil rights organization founded and headed by Jackson. Armed with marketing surveys showing that blacks spent millions annually for Coca-Cola brand soft drinks, the PUSH delegation informed management that the company needed to do more for economic welfare in the black community.

Specifically, Jackson and PUSH demanded that Coca-Cola franchise forty Coca-Cola syrup wholesale operations to black entrepreneurs in the next ten years; sell five of its 550 bottling companies to blacks within five years; hire a black advertising agency for one soft drink brand; increase deposits and loan activity with black-owned banks; double current levels of advertising in black media; and endow chairs at black colleges.

The official Coca-Cola position has always been that the company was enthusiastic about negotiations to improve its relations with the black community. But insiders say there was resentment. Early in the negotiations, Jackson angered Coke management with a newspaper column that suggested that the company was excluding black participation. Later, Coca-Cola offended Jackson when it dispatched a black vice president to negotiate with him. Jackson angrily demanded a meeting with Donald R. Keough, Coca-

Cola's president and chief operating officer, stating that he had "talked to popes and presidents" and wanted the highest authority.[64]

By summer 1981, talks had stalled, and when PUSH held its annual convention in July, Jackson announced a "withdrawal of enthusiasm" from Coca-Cola among black consumers. He accompanied his exhortation with a catchy slogan: "Don't choke on Coke." Throughout the country, black ministers encouraged their congregations to boycott Coke products, and PUSH activists spread the word. Within three weeks, Coca-Cola agreed to a "moral covenant." Although Coca-Cola states the boycott had no effect, PUSH later pointed to a 14.2 percent rise in fourth-quarter earnings in 1981, which would not have taken place if the "withdrawal of enthusiasm" had still been in force. The PUSH-Coke "trade agreement" was sealed with a handshake between Jackson and Keough. It is not legally enforceable, although Coke is encouraged to honor the agreement by the threat of renewed boycott. Under the final terms of agreement, Coke agreed to do the following:

• Set up thirty-two new black wholesale distributors of Coca-Cola syrup over the next year and provide special training for them.
• Set up a venture capital unit to make $1.8 million in low-interest loans to black entrepreneurs in the beverage industry.
• Establish a pool of black investors qualified to buy Coca-Cola bottling franchises if any became available for sale.
• Undertake an affirmative action program to boost blacks from 5 percent of management positions to 12.5 percent and to fill 100 blue-collar jobs with blacks.
• Search for and hire a black to serve on the corporate board.
• Assign a Coca-Cola brand and an $8 million contract to a black advertising agency.
• Increase to $5 million deposits and borrowing from black banks.
• Donate $250,000 in the next year to black charities.

Prior to the agreement, Coca-Cola was generally regarded as progressive with respect to civil rights, but none of its 550 bottlers was black-owned, only two of 4,000 authorized distributors were black, the company spent only $50,000 a year advertising in black media, and it had only about $250,000 in deposit and loan activity with minority banks. The overall PUSH-Coke package was worth an estimated $34 million to the black community.

When the agreement was announced, there was a mild white backlash. Coke's management received many letters criticizing the company for giving in to the pressure. A group called the National Association for the Advancement of White People threatened a reactionary boycott, but it never materialized.

Despite the mild backlash, PUSH reached similar agreements with five other large corporations—with a total value of $1.8 billion in economic benefits to the black community—in the two years following the Coca-Cola

---

[64]Johnnie L. Roberts, "Threatening Boycotts, Jesse Jackson's PUSH Wins Gains for Blacks," *Wall Street Journal,* July 21, 1982.

agreement. The PUSH message proved so powerful that even when a major corporation—Anheuser-Busch—tried to resist, it was forced into an agreement.

JESSE JACKSON CREATES OPERATION PUSH

To understand Operation PUSH, it is essential to understand its creator, the indomitable Jesse Jackson. Jackson was born in Greenville, South Carolina. He enrolled at the University of Illinois, but he soon left to attend North Carolina Agricultural and Technical State University, stating that the Illinois football coaches would not accept a black quarterback. At North Carolina A & T, Jackson quarterbacked the team, was student body president, and became active in the civil rights movement. After graduation, he entered Chicago Theological Seminary and in 1968 was ordained a Baptist minister.

By this time, Jackson was active in the national civil rights movement and was recognized by Martin Luther King as a potential leader. In 1966 King appointed Jackson head of Operation Breadbasket in Chicago. Operation Breadbasket was a Southern Christian Leadership Conference (SCLC) program started to promote the economic welfare of Chicago's black community. It was as head of Operation Breadbasket that Jackson honed the ideas and practiced on a small scale the tactics that later resulted in multimillion dollar agreements with major corporations. Jackson targeted grocery stores in Chicago's slum areas and pressured them to hire more blacks and reserve shelf space for black products such as Mumbo barbeque sauce and Sparkle floor wax. His confrontational, crusading style met with the approval of the black community in Chicago, but it created friction between Jackson and Reverend Ralph David Abernathy, who had assumed the mantle of leadership of the national civil rights movement after Martin Luther King's assassination in 1968.

Jackson challenged Abernathy's authority as president of the SCLC by operating independently and directing attention toward himself. In 1968, for example, Abernathy organized a Poor People's Campaign and led thousands of the poor to Washington, D.C., where they created a tent city on the Washington Monument Mall. After the protest was well under way, Jackson went to the tent city, declared himself "mayor," and then left shortly thereafter. Questions arose about the sharing of funds between Operation Breadbasket in Chicago and the parent SCLC organization, and ultimately the friction led Abernathy to suspend Jackson from SCLC for sixty days in 1971. Jackson then founded Operation PUSH on Christmas Day 1971, during a rally at the Metropolitan Theater in Chicago's black community.

PUSH RISES TO NATIONAL PROMINENCE

In its early years, Operation PUSH pressured white merchants in Chicago to show greater economic and social responsibility toward the black community. If merchants hired too few blacks or sold shoddy products at high prices, Operation PUSH spread the word through the black community not to patronize their stores. A few modest agreements were reached with such corporations as General Foods, Schlitz, Avon Products, Millers Brewery, A & P Stores, and regional units of Coca-Cola. For example, after meetings with Jackson in 1975, Burger King Corp. of Miami announced that it would underwrite a $4,000 breakfast at the Seventh Annual PUSH Expo in Chicago, set up a $6,000 scholarship fund for minority college students, and most important, organize a national Burger King/PUSH Day on which Burger King restaurants serving black communities would contribute 10 percent of sales to PUSH (ultimately $19,000 was raised).[65]

Early in the 1980s, however, Jackson had become the most popular civil rights leader with blacks. A *Jet* magazine poll in 1980 showed him to be number one. And his economic programs came into full bloom. The Coca-Cola trade agreement came first in 1981 and was the model for similar agreements with five other large corporations. The first to follow the Coke agreement was a $61 million trade agreement with Heublein, a large distiller and food products firm with many brand names popular among blacks, including Kentucky Fried Chicken, Smirnoff vodkas, Italian Swiss Colony wine, and A-1 Steak Sauce. Heublein offered to make 122 Kentucky Fried Chicken outlets available to black entrepreneurs and agreed to a multimillion dollar package of expenditures with black-owned banks, insurance companies, advertising agencies, and suppliers. Next came Seven Up, a subsidiary of Philip Morris, which agreed to a similar $51 million package. Burger King USA agreed to a whopping $500 million package. And the Southland Corporation—a large retailer with consumer brands such as Adohr Farms, 7-Eleven, and Chief Auto Parts stores—agreed to a $600 million package.

The next target, however, was resistant. In the summer of 1982, Jackson approached Anheuser-Busch Companies of St. Louis—makers of a number of popular beer brands, including Budweiser, Natural Light, Michelob, and Busch. Unlike some of the other companies approached by PUSH, Anheuser-Busch had an exemplary affirmative action record that was respected in the St. Louis black community. Although black consumers were only 10 percent of Anheuser-Busch's market, 18 percent of its 14,000 employees were black and Hispanic, including 9.6 percent of officers and directors, 7.8 percent of professionals, and 18 percent of technicians. Anheuser-Busch had deposits and loans of $10 million with minority banks, had two blacks on its board of directors, bought $18 million of products a year from minority suppliers, and annually spent $7 million advertising in minority media. True, there were only one black and three Hispanics out of almost 950 distributors, but the company planned to make $5 million in loans to help blacks buy distributorships in the future (Ross, 1982).

Anheuser-Busch's management felt that its level of performance on minority affairs was exemplary and that its accomplishments compared favorably to the negotiated goals of the other five companies with which Jackson had

[65]J. B. Strenski, "How to Communicate with Minorities," *Public Relations Journal*, July 1976.

moral covenants. August A. Busch III, the company's chairman, refused to meet with Jackson; therefore, Jackson proclaimed a black consumer boycott of Anheuser-Busch's beer brands. PUSH activists and black leaders publicized the boycott and Jackson's slogan, "Bud's a dud." The boycott was particularly effective in Chicago where, for example, the owner of a liquor store on the South Side brought out cases of Budweiser while a crowd opened the cans and drained them on the sidewalk. A PUSH official wrote:

> So far, of the corporations we have approached, only Anheuser-Busch has shown the disrespect and arrogance to refuse to negotiate an agreement with the Black Community. As a result PUSH has urged all fair-minded people to withdraw their support from Budweiser, Michelob and other products of this company until Anheuser-Busch is prepared to negotiate a "fair share" agreement as other corporations have done. The record of this corporation is insulting to the Black Community. It substitutes their own definition of charity for a relationship of mutual respect and parity. This is unacceptable and we will continue to boycott this company until a change is effected.[66]

There was much support for Anheuser-Busch in the St. Louis black community, and Jackson angered black business leaders there during a speech when he urged black companies to pay $500 each to join Operation PUSH. Jackson implied that those who joined would be the firms that benefited from the economic bonanza when the trade agreement with Anheuser-Busch was signed. Jackson said, "You've got to pay to play." Black leaders rebelled at such arm twisting. The St. Louis *Sentinel*, a black-owned newspaper, ran editorials critical of Jackson and suggested that he was a "charlatan," defrauding the black community. Jackson sued the *Sentinel* for libel but dropped the matter shortly thereafter.

Anheuser-Busch claimed the boycott was not affecting sales, but PUSH received internal company memos showing otherwise. Eventually the company caved in and reached a trade agreement with Jackson. The boycott was hurting the company financially, and management was afraid that a protracted national conflict with PUSH would permanently sour relations with the black community.

PUSH PHILOSOPHY AND ORGANIZATION

Operation PUSH was founded to achieve material equality for the black community through activism. It is defined in official literature as a "social change" organization, not a civil rights organization.[67] Whereas civil rights organizations seek equal rights, Operation PUSH was founded to move a step beyond this and achieve real economic equality for America's 31 million blacks. "PUSH," says one policy statement, "is helping to point the way and

---

[66]J. H. O'Dell, "PUSH—A Force for Social Change and Spiritual Renewal," in *Black America: A People Whose Time Has Come*, Chicago: Operation PUSH and Fashion Places Magazine, 1983.
[67]Operation PUSH, *The Challenge to Reinvest in America: 18th Annual National Convention*, 1989, p. 9.

push the nation beyond economic and political liberalism—White benevolence; to self-determination—Black liberation."[68]

In 1984, Jesse Jackson resigned as president of PUSH when his presidential campaign took him away from its day-to-day activities. Today PUSH is one of eight organizations headed by Jackson.[69] But using the title of Founder, he retains close ties and a leadership role in its activities.

The organizational philosophy of PUSH is an extension of Jesse Jackson's belief that widespread racism causes economic and social injustice. Jackson believes that American blacks are analogous to an underdeveloped third world nation within a developed nation and that white corporate leadership is similar to a colonial elite that exploits people in the territory it occupies. Jackson favors strict enforcement of civil rights laws, but feels that blacks are entitled to more than the legal minimum. Instead of receiving larger government doles, they should receive economic benefits from corporations proportional to their investment. To Jackson, investment means consumer spending. Hence, the black investment in a corporation is measured as the proportion of its products they purchase.

This novel definition of investment means this. If blacks are 25 percent of a corporation's customers, they should, according to Jackson, be 25 percent of its personnel, drive 25 percent of its trucks and be 25 percent of its suppliers, contractors, bankers, insurers, and franchisees. Because corporations don't live up to this implicit obligation, economic justice for blacks can be achieved only through explicit trade arrangements. Blacks' fair share of corporate spending is a percentage equal to the percentage of the corporate product or service purchased by blacks, not the spending resulting from adherence to federal affirmative action laws. Federal regulations are an important beginning for economic justice, but are only minimums.

"Trade, not aid," is a frequent Jackson battle cry. Blacks spend $250 billion a year as consumers, making them the ninth largest market in the world if compared to national consumer markets. Yet the economic benefits of this spending power primarily accrue to the white community. Black businesses remain small. Among the top 100 black-owned businesses, not one is large enough to appear on the *Fortune* 500. Many are auto dealerships. Although blacks are 12 percent of Americans, all black firms combined have sales of less than $21 billion—less than nine-tenths of 1 percent of all business sales.[70] The major consumer product firms in America continue to be white-dominated.

---

[68] *Ibid.*, p. 9.

[69]The other seven are the PUSH Foundation (a fundraising arm of Operation PUSH), the National Rainbow Coalition Inc. (a political group), Keep Hope Alive (a federal political action committee), the Citizenship Education Fund (a voter registration group), the 1984 and 1988 Jesse Jackson for President Committees (which are still technically active because their debts are still being paid), and Jacqueline Inc. (a corporation which handles Jackson's engagements and royalties). See Tom Sherwood, "PUSHing and Rainbowing and Keeping Hope Alive," *Washington Post National Weekly Edition*, November 6–12, 1989, p. 14.

[70]George E. Riddick, "Year 2000: Future Promise or Future Pathology," *Operation PUSH Magazine*, Winter 1989, p. 63.

To illustrate, although black Americans spend over $2.5 billion each year on tobacco, there are no black-owned tobacco companies; although blacks spend over $30 billion annually on autos, only two-tenths of 1 percent of dealerships are owned by blacks. Because of such inequities, Jesse Jackson has made statements such as the following.

> Corporate America must renegotiate its relationship with Black America, changing that relationship from one of economic concubinage to a true marriage in which our convergent interests and legitimate needs are mutually respected and protected. A deliberate shift must be made, through negotiation, from the patently unfair and myopic policy which advocates that Corporate America sell to Black America, but does not in return buy from Black America. In its stead must be institutionalized a system of nonrestrictive trade reciprocity within which corporate America will gain expanded market opportunities and increased profits, and Black America will achieve economic development and trade parity.[71]

The PUSH philosophy fits into the nonviolent tradition of social protest represented by Thoreau, Gandhi, and Martin Luther King, Jr. It builds on the civil rights campaigns of the 1940s and 1950s which encouraged conformity to the slogan, "Don't buy where you can't work." So rather than calling for violent protest to achieve "silver rights" for black America, Jackson relies on a nonviolent but potent weapon—the black consumer boycott. Boycotts brought Coca-Cola and Anheuser-Busch to their knees, and the threat of a boycott lurks in the background of all Operation PUSH negotiations. Once a "moral convenant" is reached, the same boycott threat ensures that the corporation honors its terms.

The economic boycott has been viewed by blacks as a legitimate weapon since early in the civil rights movement. Until 1982, the boycott had been under a legal cloud because of a long-standing, unresolved case in which white merchants in Claiborne County, Mississippi, sued the National Association for the Advancement of Colored People (NAACP) for damages resulting from a boycott in 1966. When Jackson first began negotiations with Coca-Cola in 1980, the legal status of a black boycott was clouded, and Jackson had to use the euphemistic phrase "withdrawal of enthusiasm" when he implemented economic sanctions. But in 1982, in *NAACP et al. v. Claiborne Hardware Co. et al.*, a unanimous Supreme Court ruled that the black boycott in Mississippi was a legitimate exercise of First Amendment rights, including freedom of assembly, freedom of speech, and the right to petition for redress of grievances. Hence, when Jackson warred against Anheuser-Busch in 1982, he was less restrained in directly calling for a boycott.

PUSH boycotts must be taken seriously. There are forty-six PUSH chapters in twenty-six states, and in addition, PUSH has set up a National Selective Patronage Council composed of local black leaders who spread boycott news through PTOs, labor unions, fraternities, and other groups. PUSH also sponsors a weekly rally in Chicago, featuring the PUSH gospel choir and sermons by Jesse Jackson or visiting black evangelists. The rally is carried on

---

[71]In Operation PUSH, "PUSH International Trade Bureau," *1986 Operation PUSH Souvenir Journal,* Chicago: Operation PUSH, 1986, p. 85.

radio and is held on Saturday mornings, because Saturday is the biggest shopping day of the week. It has been held every Saturday, without exception, for eighteen years and is attended by 300 to 2,000 people, depending on the speaker and theme.

In addition, PUSH has the support of black churches and ministers across the country. The National Baptist Convention U.S.A., in which Jackson was ordained a minister in 1968, is the nation's largest black denomination, with 5.5 million members in 26,000 churches. Traditionally, social activism has been more deeply rooted in black clergy than white clergy. Many blacks have deep respect for the social and political views of ministers, and ministers are willing to spread boycott news. PUSH claims that it is not a church, but it has an intimate relationship with the black religious community. This relationship is an underlying source of strength and legitimacy. There is a Religious Affairs Department in the PUSH organization that maintains liaisons with black church leadership across America. And the PUSH negotiation team that tackles large corporations is headed by clergy. The following is an exerpt from the "Position Statement for the PUSH Religious Affairs Department."

> The negotiations led by the ministers represent the means by which we demand accountability of major corporations and industries in America's private sector where Black Americans this year will spend a minimum of $200 billion.
>
> The expenditures, for the most part, constitute an "invisible investment" of $478 million each day: an investment upon which there have been few if any returns. Indeed, when we contemplate the fact that we receive so little in return (less than 6 percent by some authoritative estimates) we recognize the "trade deficit" between Black and Corporate America as one of the most blatant examples of man's violation of his fellow man. It is a sin in its most hideous form.[72]

PUSH is popular with the black business community. The PUSH International Trade Bureau, described in a PUSH publication as "the nucleus of a black American Common Market," has a board of directors of twenty-five black business executives and 550 member firms and individuals. Membership in the PUSH International Trade Bureau, as stated on an application form, "is open to black-owned corporations and black executives of non-black corporations that would like to be members in order to enhance their corporation's trade relations with black America." Members pay $500 to join and receive certain benefits. PUSH keeps a "match-up file" so that when trade agreements are reached, member black companies can be recommended to participate in the new largess.

WHAT PUSH HAS ACHIEVED

Twenty years after its founding, PUSH is pursuing economic justice for blacks with undiminished zeal. Over the years it claims to have negotiated fair share agreements worth more than $5 billion to blacks. In recent years PUSH has conducted a number of boycotts, including a Christmas boycott of

[72]"Position Statement for the PUSH Religious Affairs Department," in *Ibid.*, p. 121.

Cabbage Patch Dolls made in South Africa and a boycott of Revlon Inc. cosmetics following a disparaging remark by one of its top executives about black-owned competitors. In 1989, PUSH negotiated a fair share agreement with Ford Motor Company. In it, Ford agreed to spend $2.5 billion with black-owned companies between 1989 and 1994, establish seventy-five new black dealerships by March 1990, and maintain a work force with 16 percent black employees. At a press conference with white Ford executives at Ford, Jesse Jackson stated:

> Productive power with maximum profits as the only criteria for development would destroy the market from which companies make their profits. Money and wealth in a healthy economy—like blood in a healthy body—need a circular flow.[73]

The agenda of Operation PUSH, as set by Jackson, is expansive. In addition to pursuing fair share agreements with white-owned corporations, the PUSH platform includes the demand that black investments in pension funds be used to rebuild inner cities and the cessation of redlining in minority neighborhoods by banks.[74] In addition, Jackson has personally advocated a national program in which 10 percent of all government contracts be reserved for minorities. In 1989, he called upon the federal government to pay monetary reparations to black Americans because their ancestors were slaves, but this has not become part of the PUSH policy agenda.[75]

While some items on the PUSH policy agenda are radical for this time, its successes with fair share agreements have legitimized this form of assault on white corporate privilege. Now other groups negotiate them as well. The NAACP, for example, has negotiated forty such agreements. The success of PUSH and other groups sets a precedent for national consumer boycotts to punish corporations whose social performance falls below the expectations of an interest group. Blacks, environmentalists, Christians, animal rights activists, or other groups whose members have great purchasing power have been given an example. If group expectations differ from or exceed the corporate performance standards stipulated by law (as is the case with PUSH), then boycott tactics may force new, extralegal performance standards on corporations. A precedent is set for seeking social goals through economic sanctions against companies, rather than through political pressures on government.[76] Corporations may be held hostage to interest group demands. This is the PUSH message. Some managers would like to ignore it.

---

[73]Quoted in Howard Manly, "Ford and PUSH Sign $2.5 Billion Deal," *Black Enterprise*, March 1989, p. 18.

[74]For statements of the PUSH agenda see Jesse L. Jackson, "Convention Welcome," *Operation PUSH Magazine*, Summer 1989, p. 30, and a message from PUSH's National Executive Director, Rev. Tyrone Crider, "Economic Empowerment: The Challenge of This Decade," *Operation PUSH Magazine*, January/February 1990, p. 8.

[75]Eric Harrison, "Economics Is Key Element as Black Leaders Set Goals," *Los Angeles Times*, April 24, 1989.

[76]Boycotting is actually a common tactic, and at any given time 100 or more boycotts by human rights, peace, labor, environmental, religions, and animal rights groups are in progress. This proliferation has been referred to as a form of grass roots democracy called the "boycott movement." See "On Boycotting," *National Boycott News*, Spring/Summer 1989, p. 11.

QUESTIONS

1 Are the tactics of Operation PUSH, specifically the use of boycotts to divert corporate spending to blacks, unwarranted extortion or a constructive solution to social problems in the black community?

2 Is management correct to make concessions to Jackson, even where corporate equal opportunity programs are in compliance with the law or, as in the case of Anheuser-Busch, exemplary? Or should a brave company try to sit out a boycott and break Jackson's string of successes?

3 Would it be salutary for society if other pressure groups organized consumer boycotts to achieve their social goals? What would happen if the tactic was frequently used? What other groups have large enough memberships to mobilize national consumer boycotts? What factors underly a successful boycott?

4 What companies and industries are likely targets for PUSH now? How should corporations that are potential targets prepare for demands by PUSH and other groups?

PART
TWO

Business Social Responsibilities

CHAPTER
5

The Social Responsibilities of Business

Medical history records that the first organ transplant, that of a kidney, was performed in a Boston hospital in 1954. Today organ transplantation is commonplace. But medical technology has outstripped public awareness. The gap between medical needs for organ transplants—such as heart, liver, kidney, pancreas, and cornea—and organ donations led Dow Chemical U.S.A. in 1984 to launch the Dow Take Initiative Program on transplantation. The program is designed "to improve the quality of life," says Dow, by conducting a national, public educational campaign to encourage more donations of organs. This is a continuing multimillion dollar social activity of the company.

The program launched by Dow is wide-ranging—from its own employees, to other corporations, state and municipal governments, and foreign countries. For example, Dow encourages its 26,000 employees to learn about organ donations through articles in company newsletters and employee chairperson guideline kits. A program entitled "Make a Miracle, America," solicits private sector support of organ/tissue donations by encouraging other corporations to initiate employee donor awareness programs.

In 1986 Dow commissioned a nationwide Gallup poll on public attitudes toward organ transplantation and donation. It found that 50 percent of Americans who had heard of transplants were willing to donate their organs after death, but only 20 percent had completed a donor card, and only 26 percent had talked with their families. It showed that blacks were only half as likely to donate organs as whites. And another finding was that 63 percent of the respondents felt it appropriate for a doctor or nurse to initiate discussion of organ donation with family members upon the death of a loved one.[1]

[1]Gallup Organization, *The U.S. Public's Attitudes toward Organ Transplants/Organ Donation,* Princeton, N.J.: The Gallup Organization, April 1986.

Based on these findings, Dow took several actions. First, it expanded its efforts to educate the public by, for example, having millions of Boy Scouts distribute literature and posters across the country. Second, because kidney failure is more frequent among blacks than any other racial group, and because more people wait for kidneys than for any other organ, Dow developed a program to educate blacks about the need for organ donation. Clive O. Callender, a black physician at Howard University in Washington, D.C., undertook interviews to discover why blacks were less likely to donate and found a variety of reasons, including lack of information, religious fears and superstition, distrust of medicine, and a preference for donating organs only to other blacks.[2] Dow sponsored trips by Callender to Detroit, Chicago, Los Angeles, Philadelphia, and New York—all cities with large black populations—where he made speeches and had media interviews.

And third, because many people were willing to be approached about donation at the time of a loved one's death, and because 60 to 80 percent of those approached agreed to donations, Dow used its lobbying force to promote legislation which makes it mandatory for hospitals to approach relatives of accident victims to ask for organ donations. By 1987, thirty states had passed such laws, and behind-the-scenes prodding from Dow lobbyists was important in gaining political support for the measures in many states.

To reach another critically important segment of the population, Dow started a program in 1988 to provide department of motor vehicle offices in Ohio and Virginia with comprehensive instructional program handbooks, brochures, buttons, posters, videotapes, and tabletop displays, to train employees how to inform drivers about their options.

This programs has been honored with many awards, including a Presidential Citation and a special award from the Department of Health and Human Services. These awards attest to the significance of the program in substantially increasing organ donations.

A notable aspect of the program is that it is unrelated to any of Dow's commercial interests. In the words of Robert Charlton, former director of the program, "We wanted to insure that the program could not be dismissed because there was a commercial gain for the company involved."[3]

The Dow program is a stellar example of corporate responsibility, but it is only one of thousands of such programs, some big, some small, some expensive, some not. In this chapter, we describe other examples of corporate social programs and explore the conceptual and theoretical nature of corporate responsibility as it has evolved in the United States. No one has "the answers" about what should be done, when, how, or by whom. This is, therefore, an exploratory examination of the theory and concepts of social responsibility, what managers are thinking about the issue, and a few guidelines for action.

---

[2]Dow Chemical Company, "Statistics on Blacks' Attitudes toward Organ Donation Reveal Need for More Black Donors," *TIP Sheet,* Autumn 1986.
[3]Robert W. Charlton, Interview with John F. Steiner, November 3, 1986.

CHANGING CONCEPTUAL AND MANAGERIAL VIEWS ON BUSINESS SOCIAL RESPONSIBILITIES

The theoretical academic concepts of business social responsibilities, and what business has done about social obligations, have changed significantly over our history. We present here a brief review of this evolution.

BUSINESS SOCIAL RESPONSIBILITIES IN CLASSICAL ECONOMIC THEORY

In the classical economic view, a business is acting in a socially responsible fashion if it strives to utilize the resources at its disposal as efficiently as possible in producing the goods and services that society wants at prices consumers are willing to pay. If this is done well, say classical theorists, profits are maximized more or less continuously and firms carry out their major responsibilities to society. This concept led most people in business, as well as theoretical economists, to conclude that the sole objective of business was to maximize profits while operating, of course, within the law.

This easily understood goal, derived from Adam Smith's *Wealth of Nations*,[4] was never sought in business practice without reservations. Even Adam Smith voiced a surprising number of exceptions to his principle for social reasons.[5] Throughout our history, business and business people have modified the strict profit maximization principle to address social concerns, not much at first, but more and more as our history unfolded.

THE PERIOD WHEN PHILANTHROPY WAS DOMINANT

In colonial times, the prevailing social concerns of people in business, if they had any, were expressed in charitable giving. This concept was considerably expanded later in the nineteenth century even by those business leaders known for their predation in the market place. For example, during his lifetime John D. Rockefeller gave more than $550 million and endowed the Rockefeller Foundation. Andrew Carnegie, author of a famous article entitled "The Disgrace of Dying Rich," gave away $350 million during his lifetime to social causes, built 2,509 public libraries, and gave thousands of organs to American churches.

Such largess came from individuals personally, not from their companies. Carnegie said that it was the duty of a man of wealth "...to consider all surplus revenues...as trust funds which he is called upon to administer."[6] For most people in business, however, profit maximization remained the sole goal.

---

[4]Adam Smith, *An Inquiry into the Nature and Causes of the Wealth of Nations* (1776), reprint, New York: Modern Library, 1967.

[5]Jacob Viner, "Adam Smith and Laissez-Faire," *Journal of Political Economy,* April 1927.

[6]Andrew Carnegie, *The Gospel of Wealth*, Edward C. Kirkland, ed., Cambridge: Harvard University Press, 1962, p. 25. First published in 1901.

THREE VIEWS OF SOCIAL RESPONSIBILITY IN THE EARLY TWENTIETH CENTURY

During the first three decades of the twentieth century, three themes were used by business and other opinion leaders in expressing social responsibilities of business. First, managers are trustees of various interests focused on the company. Second, managers have an obligation to balance the interests of the main constituents of a company. Third, people in business are responsible for service to society.

One of the first expositors of the trustee idea was President Arthur T. Hadley of Yale University. He said that the president of a large corporation "...is a trustee for the stockholders and creditors of his corporation. In a less obvious but equally important sense he is a trustee on behalf of the public."[7] He argued that if corporations were to stay in power they had better be sensitive to public criticism and order their ethics accordingly or the public would regulate them.

In the 1920s, prominent business leaders expressed the idea that they were more than agents of the owners of the companies they managed. They were, they said, coordinators who reconciled the competing claims of different constituents of their enterprises. They were responsible for balancing competing claims in the long-run interests of the company.

The word "service" was frequently used by business leaders in the early twentieth century as shorthand for a growing sense of responsibility to improve the relationships between business and society. The word meant different things to different leaders, but it encompassed a range of concepts of a company's social responsibilities. Behind the word "service" was the belief that the seamier consequences of industrialization should be moderated by social actions benefiting the community.

These three interrelated ideas—trusteeship, balancing of interests, and service—became accepted by more and more business leaders. One illustrative spokesman for and practitioner of these views was General Robert E. Wood, who led Sears, Roebuck and Company from 1924 to 1954. He believed that a large corporation was more than an economic institution; it was a social and political one as well. In the Sears *Annual Report* for 1936 he wrote:

> In these days of changing social, economic, and political values, it seems worthwhile...to render an account of your management's stewardship, not merely from the viewpoint of financial reports but also along the lines of those general broad social responsibilities which cannot be presented mathematically and yet are of prime importance.

He outlined the ways in which Sears was discharging its responsibilities to what he said were the chief constituencies of the company—customers, the public, employees, sources of merchandise supply, and stockholders.[8]

---

[7]Morrel Heald, *The Social Responsibility of Business: Company and Community, 1900–1960*, Cleveland: The Press of Case Western Reserve University, 1970, p. 29.

[8]James C. Worthy, *Shaping an American Institution: Robert E. Wood and Sears, Roebuck*, Urbana, Illinois: University of Illinois Press, 1984, p. 173.

In speaking about constituents, General Wood repeatedly put the stockholder last "not because he is least important," he said, "but because, in the larger sense, he cannot obtain his full measure of reward unless he has satisfied customers and satisfied employees."[9] He also asserted and acted on the belief, said James C. Worthy, who served as a vice president at Sears for many years under General Wood, that "the management of every business should preserve the balance of the interests of each [constituent]."[10]

General Wood repeatedly lectured his managers on the need to be good citizens in the communities in which they operated. To him, good citizenship meant much more than participating in community affairs and contributing to local charities. He believed that Sears should strengthen the economic base of the areas it served by helping to revive declining industries, reducing unemployment, bringing new industries into the community, and strengthening those that were there.

General Wood was building on a tradition begun by Julius Rosenwald, one of the founders of Sears. In 1912 he offered to contribute $1,000 to any county that would employ an agricultural expert to advise farmers on how to be more efficient. In two years he made grants to 110 counties. These grants led to the Smith-Lever Act of 1914, which set up the county-agent system that has become such an important part of national agricultural policy.

TODAY'S THRUST OF SOCIAL CONCERN TO IMPROVE QUALITY OF LIFE

Today, all these views prevail among business managers as to the meaning of social responsibility. It should be noted parenthetically that managers generally prefer terms other than "social responsibility" because to them these words connote a fixed obligation with unclear commitments. To them the obligation is flexible and varied among companies, and the degree of commitment expected of them is fuzzy. They prefer synonyms like "social concern," "social programs," "social challenge," "community interest," "social commitment," or "public programs." A distinguishing feature of today's concept of social responsibility among business people, in contrast with the past, is the thrust in the direction of improving quality of life. Another important difference between today's managerial commitment and that of the past is the degree to which social responsibilities have been institutionalized into the decision-making processes in corporations. This aspect of the evolution of social concerns of business is treated in detail in the next chapter.

THE SCOPE OF SOCIAL PROGRAMS

The range of social programs assumed by business has expanded from the simple colonial idea that philanthropy was enough, to the acceptance by

[9]*Ibid.*, p. 63.
[10]*Ibid.*, p. 64.

business of virtually any program of social importance. The span includes programs for education, health, employee training, housing, urban renewal, community improvements, pollution abatement, conservation, day-care centers for working mothers, and many others. In any one of these areas, and others, the programs that different businesses have implemented range in the hundreds.

To illustrate just a few types of social programs, we note first that many corporations have their own foundations that give money and equipment for specific purposes ranging from education to health. G. D. Searle, a pharmaceutical company subsidiary of Monsanto, is marking its 100th anniversary by offering heart disease drugs free to poor patients. Merck & Co. has given away millions of dollars worth of a drug to fight the world's leading cause of blindness. Sixteen of the nation's largest corporations have opened their own private school for pupils aged two to nine in the Lowndale area of Chicago. The area is an unexcelled example of our worst urban ills. The Corporate Community School, as it is called, is designed to be a research laboratory to show that children raised in poverty and in drug- and crime-plagued urban communities can learn as well as suburban children.[11] Business leaders have organized the Corporate Responsibility Group of Greater Chicago to "enhance awareness of corporate social responsibility issues," through seminars, prominent speakers, and other community activities. General Electric has a number of educational programs including special classes in a new public school in New York's Spanish Harlem. A few of the company's employees track special students in the school and help them into prestigious universities.[12]

BROAD CONCEPTUAL DEFINITIONS OF SOCIAL RESPONSIBILITIES

While efficient use of resources to make a profit is widely recognized today as a primal responsibility and goal of business, there has developed a view by most managers and academicians that total social responsibilities are broader in concept. Many efforts to encapsulate this new, expanded definition of social responsibility in a few words have been made; almost every author in this field has tried. Here are a few examples from academicians:

- The businessman's decisions and actions taken for reasons at least partially beyond the firm's direct economic or technical interest.[13]
- Obligations to pursue those policies, to make those decisions, or to follow those lines of action which are desirable in terms of the objectives and values of our society.[14]

[11]Larry Green, "Firms Hope Own School Earns an A," *Los Angeles Times*, November 24, 1988.

[12]For other business programs in the education field see Nancy J. Perry, "The Education Crisis: What Business Can Do," *Fortune*, July 4, 1988.

[13]Keith Davis, "Can Business Afford to Ignore Social Responsibilities?" *California Management Review*, Spring 1960, p. 70.

[14]Howard R. Bowen, *Social Responsibilities of the Businessman*, New York: Harper & Brothers, 1953, p. 6.

• The intelligent and objective concern for the welfare of society that restrains individual and corporate behavior from ultimately destructive activities, no matter how immediately profitable, and leads in the direction of positive contributions to human betterment, variously as the latter may be defined.[15]

Business leaders also have tried their hand at definitions. For example, the Committee for Economic Development (CED), an old organization of prominent business leaders throughout the nation, issued a milestone statement in 1971 which boldly stated that "business functions by public consent, and its basic purpose is to serve constructively the needs of society—to the satisfaction of society."[16] Society today, said the report, has broadened its expectations of business into what may be described as "three concentric circles of responsibilities:"

The *inner circle* includes the clear-cut basic responsibilities for the efficient execution of the economic function—products, jobs, and economic growth.

The *intermediate circle* encompasses responsibility to exercise this economic function with a sensitive awareness of changing social values and priorities: for example, with respect to environmental conservation; hiring and relations with employees; and more rigorous expectations of customers for information, fair treatment, and protection from injury.

The *outer circle* outlines newly emerging and still amorphous responsibilities that business should assume to become more broadly involved in actively improving the social environment.[17]

Classical ideology focused solely on the first circle. The new view, of course, is that managerial responsibilities go much beyond this point. But this does not mean diminished profits. On the contrary, say top executives in larger corporations, it is in the self-interest of corporations to assume social responsibilities.

The drafting committee of the CED had great difficulty in getting the report accepted by the CED Policy Committee, but eventually it succeeded. At the time, the average manager did not accept the concepts in the report fully or enthusiastically. In the years that followed, however, more and more managers, particularly of larger corporations, embraced the basic ideas in the report.

In a *Statement on Corporate Responsibility* the Business Roundtable said that the pursuit of profit and assumption of social responsibilities were compatible:

Economic responsibility is by no means incompatible with other corporate responsibilities in society. In contemporary society all corporate responsibilities are so interrelated that they should not and cannot be separated....

[15]Kenneth R. Andrews, *The Concept of Corporate Strategy*, Homewood, Illinois: Dow Jones-Irwin, Inc., 1971, p. 120.

[16]Committee for Economic Development, *Social Responsibilities of Business Corporations*, New York: CED, 1971, p. 11.

[17]*Ibid.*, p. 15.

A corporation's responsibilities include how the whole business is conducted every day. It must be a thoughtful institution which rises above the bottom line to consider the impact of its actions on all, from shareholders to the society at large. Its business activities must make social sense just as its social activities must make business sense.[18]

It is noteworthy that the CED report says that while a company is socially responsible when it operates efficiently, it also has other broader social obligations. The Business Roundtable statement says these two responsibilities are compatible. Most academicians would agree. The academic definitions noted above assume this and emphasize also the need, sometimes, to undertake social responsibilities even though they may reduce profits, temporarily at least, but not necessarily in the long run. But all would agree there are limits, a subject to which we return later in the chapter.

A COMPREHENSIVE VIEW OF BUSINESS SOCIAL RESPONSIBILITIES

Figure 5-1 summarizes and makes clear several important points. First, when business responds to the economics of the marketplace by efficiently and effectively using resources, it is being socially responsible. Second, there are many social programs that business undertakes that are mandated by the government. Also, social programs are undertaken in response to demands of various stakeholders, such as contractual arrangements made in negotiations with labor unions. Third are programs undertaken voluntarily and without pressure. These programs are pursued in response to changing social values and priorities.

Figure 5-1 shows the magnitude of three main types of social responsibilities in the totality of decision making in an enterprise. These proportions are our estimates of the situation in the United States today. The magnitudes will differ among companies and in the same company from time to time. Yet the diagram serves in an elementary way to reveal several significant points. First, the bulk of social responsibilities assumed by business relates to the traditional economic function and mandated programs. Second, the voluntary area is small relative to the total. However, it is of very great significance to business as well as to society, for reasons to be discussed later.

Within the voluntary area are zones of action. First are programs that might be called "legal plus." These are actions that go beyond present legislation and are considered to be socially responsible, such as employee safety, antipollution measures, or minority hiring and promotion programs. Second are programs about which there is a national consensus, such as contributing to local charities or to education. Third is an area about which there is no consensus. For instance, many church groups condemn defense contractors for manufacturing nuclear weapons components and suggest that cessation would be socially responsible. Others, however, disagree and would regard voluntary foreswearing of defense contracts as irresponsible.

[18]Business Roundtable, *Statement on Corporate Responsibility*, New York: The Business Roundtable, October 1981, pp. 12, 14.

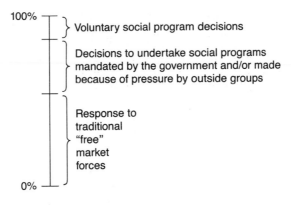

100% — Voluntary social program decisions

Decisions to undertake social programs mandated by the government and/or made because of pressure by outside groups

Response to traditional "free" market forces

0%

TOTAL BUSINESS
DECISIONS

FIGURE 5-1 Principal types of business social responsibilities and their magnitudes in company operations.

A drawing comparable to Figure 5-1 made one hundred or even twenty-five years ago would show substantially different magnitudes. The bulk of business decisions in the nineteenth century were in the lower area. The rapid growth of decisions in the top areas is a product of recent events, as will be explained throughout this book. The voluntary, even though small, is much larger today than in the past.

THE DOMINANT STAKEHOLDERS

Managers generally agree they owe primary responsibilities to four groups who may be called the dominant stakeholders. They are customers, employees, communities, and stockholders. Managers often express their responsibilities to these groups in corporate statements of philosophy or, as they are also called, missions or credos. In the accompanying box is shown the credo of Johnson & Johnson. It is typical of many companies.

However, as pointed out in Chapter 1, there are many other stakeholders, some of whom may from time to time become dominant. For example, when a firm is heavily in debt the financial community and creditors may take front and center positions. Certainly, managers themselves may be considered dominant stakeholders, although they undoubtedly believe it is not fitting to say so publicly. For a very large corporation there are many other stakeholders whose demands not even the largest corporations can completely meet. So each company is forced to set priorities to determine where, within its limited resources, it should meet legitimate demands.

DISAGREEMENT ABOUT DEFINITIONS OF SOCIAL RESPONSIBILITIES

The definitions of business social responsibilities discussed above are by no means universally accepted. In both the business and academic worlds,

Our Credo

We believe our first responsibility is to the doctors, nurses and patients,
to mothers and fathers and all others who use our products and services.
In meeting their needs everything we do must be of high quality.
We must constantly strive to reduce our costs
in order to maintain reasonable prices.
Customers' orders must be serviced promptly and accurately.
Our suppliers and distributors must have an opportunity
to make a fair profit.

We are responsible to our employees,
the men and women who work with us throughout the world.
Everyone must be considered as an individual.
We must respect their dignity and recognize their merit.
They must have a sense of security in their jobs.
Compensation must be fair and adequate,
and working conditions clean, orderly and safe.
We must be mindful of ways to help our employees fulfill
their family responsibilities.
Employees must feel free to make suggestions and complaints.
There must be equal opportunity for employment, development
and advancement for those qualified.
We must provide competent management,
and their actions must be just and ethical.

We are responsible to the communities in which we live and work
and to the world community as well.
We must be good citizens—support good works and charities
and bear our fair share of taxes.
We must encourage civic improvements and better health and education.
We must maintain in good order
the property we are privileged to use,
protecting the environment and natural resources.

Our final responsibility is to our stockholders.
Business must make a sound profit.
We must experiment with new ideas.
Research must be carried on, innovative programs developed
and mistakes paid for.
New equipment must be purchased, new facilities provided
and new products launched.
Reserves must be created to provide for adverse times.
When we operate according to these principles,
the stockholders should realize a fair return.

Johnson & Johnson

highly respected individuals take diametrically opposed views about the social responsibilities of business. We turn now to the pros and cons of this disagreement.

THE CASE FOR BUSINESS ASSUMPTION OF SOCIAL RESPONSIBILITIES

There is no one core idea in the argument that business has social responsibilities. Fundamentally, there seem to be three major core ideas, not mutually exclusive: Corporations are creatures of society and should respond to societal demands; the long-run self-interests of business are best served when business assumes social responsibilities; and it is one means to reduce or avoid government regulation and public criticism.

SOCIETY EXPECTS BUSINESS TO ASSUME SOCIAL RESPONSIBILITIES

The argument is that corporations are creatures sanctioned by society, and when society's expectations about their functioning change, so should the corporation's actions. Many business leaders accept this argument and express it in different ways. David A. Koch, president of Graco, Inc., puts it this way: "The people allowed us to set up corporations. If, as businessmen, we are not responsible to the people, the people won't allow our franchises to exist"[19] Gerhard Bleichen, while chairman of the board of the John Hancock Mutual Life Insurance Company, said, "[I]t never occurred to me that there was a time when American business was at liberty to operate in conflict with the interests of society."[20]

A manager operates within a set of cultural norms and restraints. These are certainly economic but also legal, political, social, and technical. They are powerful, and the manager knows instinctively that as they change, corporate decisions must conform. Sethi argues that there exists a "legitimacy gap" between the response of business to nonmarket social forces and societal expectations of what business should be doing.[21] If this gap grows too large, the corporation will be brought to heel. In truth, many managers accept the idea that because society expects them to assume social responsibilities, they must try to do so. If not, the argument runs, either society will force them to do so through laws, or society may no longer permit them to exist. In either case, it is in the enlightened self-interest of a company to react to society's wishes. History confirms that an institution with power that is not used in conformity to society's desires will lose that power.

[19]Brian S. Moskal, "The Minneapolis Story: A Primer on Social Concern," *Industry Week*, August 10, 1981, p. 60.

[20]Gerhard D. Bleichen, "The Social Equation in Corporate Responsibility," Speech at the Boston University Law School Centennial, 1972.

[21]S. Prakash Sethi, "A Conceptual Framework for Environmental Analysis of Social Issues and Evaluation of Business Response Patterns," *Academy of Management Review*, January 1979, p. 65.

LONG-RUN SELF-INTEREST OF BUSINESS

The Committee for Economic Development report mentioned above concluded, "It is in the enlightened self-interest of corporations to promote the public welfare in a positive way."[22] The statement continued, "Indeed, the corporate interest broadly defined by management can support involvement in helping to solve virtually any social problem, because people who have a good environment, education, and opportunity make better employees, customers, and neighbors for business than those who are poor, ignorant, and oppressed."[23] The continuing belief of business leaders in this notion is affirmed in a *Statement on Corporate Responsibility* by the Business Roundtable. "Business and society have a symbiotic relationship. The long-term viability of the corporation depends upon its responsibility to the society of which it is a part. And the well-being of society depends upon profitable and responsible business enterprises."[24]

It would profit business little to ignore social problems. In the long run, deteriorating cities, consumer dissatisfaction, employee mistrust, harsh government regulations, inflation, rising crime levels, pollution, and poverty are the components of economic stagnation, not corporate welfare. Corporations cannot escape their attachment to and dependence on the social cohesion of American society. The fates of both corporation and society are inextricably linked in the long run.

AVOIDANCE OF GOVERNMENT REGULATION

Since the 1960s, as the reader is well aware, government regulation of business has expanded greatly. Business leaders, sensitive to this intrusion, feel that voluntary amelioration of social ills through social responsibility programs is preferable to government regulation that makes action mandatory. A survey of 116 CEOs in 1984 showed that 71 percent agreed that "if business is more socially responsible, it will discourage additional regulation of the economic system by government."[25] If new regulations are inevitable, business may be denied participation in hammering out the rules if it volunteers its services only after its stubborn resistance to change has been overcome by public pressure. If managers avoid government regulation by responding to social demands, they are likely to reduce their costs, since regulation in general is more expensive than social programs likely to be pursued by business. They will also retain their flexibility and freedom in making decisions and in meeting competition. They restrain concentration of power in government and thereby advance their own relative power.

---

[22]Committee for Economic Development, *op. cit.*, p. 25.
[23]*Ibid.*, p. 26.
[24]*Ibid.*, p. 12.
[25]Robert Ford and Frank McLaughlin, "Perceptions of Socially Responsible Activities and Attitudes: A Comparison of Business School Deans and Corporate Chief Executives," *Academy of Management Journal*, September 1984, p. 670.

EXECUTIVES ARE CONCERNED CITIZENS

Like everyone else, people in business wear a number of hats. As citizens, they see the need for social action. As executives, they may have the power to accept the challenge and do something. Most of what executives do in the social arena may be in reaction to societal pressures and justified in their minds on the grounds of self-interest. Yet, as concerned citizens, many executives welcome the opportunity, however they justify it, to participate in the development of a better world.

A few top corporate executives are remembered for leading their firms to stellar social performances over the years. For example, Robert Anderson, founder and chairman of ARCO, made ARCO unparalleled in the oil industry in its environmental concern and had the courage to break with other business leaders in the 1970s by advocating stringent auto emission controls. William Norris, founder and CEO of Control Data Corporation, was a visionary in promoting corporate applications of computer technology to the solution of social problems. J.C. Penney, founder of the J.C. Penney Company, wrote a code of ethics in 1913 that still guides the company today.

These are a few stars (and perhaps there are conspicuous reprobates who should better remain anonymous on these pages). But often, as Kenneth R. Andrews points out, "corporate executives of the caliber, integrity, intelligence, and humanity required to run substantial companies cannot be expected to confine themselves to their narrow economic activity and to ignore its social consequences."[26] They may derive much pleasure from being socially responsible. The feelings of Thornton Bradshaw were revealed, for instance, when, as president of ARCO, he wrote:

> ...should Atlantic Richfield spend a certain amount of money each year to operate a playground track and field program, the ARCO Jesse Owens Games, because it brings unwonted opportunity and pleasure to thousands of kids, many underprivileged, and perhaps disposes local officials kindly toward our Company? We think a youngster's joy makes the whole thing worthwhile, though I admit the notion is arguable.[27]

THE CASE AGAINST BUSINESS ASSUMPTION OF SOCIAL RESPONSIBILITIES

No worthy argument can be made that business may act irresponsibly without penalty. But one strongly held view, as we have said, is that business is *most* responsible when it operates efficiently to make profits, not when it goes out on a limb to solve social problems. James Russell Lowell caught the essence of this argument in the following rhyme:

[26]Kenneth R. Andrews, *op. cit.*, p. 133.
[27]Thornton Bradshaw, "Temporary Shield Could Aid U.S.," *Los Angeles Times*, December 1, 1985, p. 3.

> Not a deed would he do
>   Not a word would he utter
> Till he weighed its relation
>   To plain bread and better.

There are several variations on this theme.

CONTRARY TO THE BASIC FUNCTIONS OF BUSINESS

The core of the strongest arguments against business assumption of any responsibilities other than to produce goods and services efficiently and to make as much money as possible for stockholders is that business is an economic institution and economic values should be the sole determinant of performance. This is called the classical view because it hews closely to the dictates of classical economic theory. A pertinacious exponent of this view is Nobel laureate Milton Friedman, a respected economist who makes this clear statement on the side of the classicists:

> There is one and only one social responsibility of business—to use its resources and engage in activities designed to increase its profits so long as it stays within the rules of the game, which is to say, engages in open and free competition, without deception or fraud....Few trends could so thoroughly undermine the very foundations of our free society as the acceptance by corporate officials of a social responsibility other than to make as much money for their stockholders as possible. This is a fundamentally subversive doctrine.[28]

Friedman argues that in a free-enterprise, private-property system, a manager is an employee of the owners of the business and is directly responsible to them. Because stockholders want to make as much profit as possible, the manager's sole objective should be to try to do this. If a manager spends stockholder money in the public interest, he or she is spending it without stockholders' approval and perhaps in ways they would oppose. Similarly, if the cost of social action is passed on to consumers in higher prices, the manager is spending their money. This "taxation without representation," says Friedman, should be rejected.[29] Furthermore, if the price on the market for a product does not truly reflect the relative costs of producing it, but includes costs for social action, the allocative mechanism of the marketplace is distorted. The rigors of the market will endanger the competitive position of any firm that adds to its costs by assuming social responsibilities.

SOCIAL RESPONSIBILITY WILL WEAKEN OUR FREEDOMS

Milton Friedman believes that management actions to solve social problems lead to inefficient use of resources and also threaten political freedoms. He

---

[28]Milton Friedman, *Capitalism and Freedom,* Chicago: University of Chicago Press, 1962, p. 133. For a recent affirmation of this position see "Freedom and Philanthropy: An Interview with Milton Friedman," *Business and Society Review,* Fall 1989, no. 71.

[29]Milton Friedman, "The Social Responsibility of Business Is to Increase Its Profits," *New York Times Magazine,* September 13, 1970.

argues that the doctrine of social responsibility means acceptance of the socialist view that political mechanisms rather than market mechanisms are the appropriate way to allocate scarce resources to alternative uses. A manager undertaking activities in the public realm is performing social and political functions and becomes, in effect, a civil servant. The result is that managers will come under growing public scrutiny and eventually may be elected or appointed to reflect public attitudes. This would constitute a dangerous fusion of political and economic power, which ought properly to be kept separate.

Capitalism, with its market mechanism, fragments economic power and separates it from central government control. This system preserves political liberties by keeping power out of the hands of those who would violate human rights to enforce their vision of betterment. Friedman believes that history vindicates this view: "I know of no example in time or place of a society that has been marked by a large measure of political freedom, and that has not also used something comparable to a free market to organize the bulk of economic activity."[30]

The conclusion, for those who subscribe to this view, is that economic and political freedom are linked, and we should not threaten economic freedom by encouraging diversion of capital to social programs run by business. Once again, efficiency is equated with responsibility.

WE DO NOT WANT BUSINESS VALUES TO DOMINATE US

Theodore Levitt supports the classical view because he fears domination of business values.

> But at the rate we are going, there is more than a contingent probability that, with all its resounding good intentions, business statesmanship may create the corporate equivalent of the unitary state. Its proliferating employee welfare programs, its serpentine involvement in community, government, charitable, and educational affairs, its prodigious currying of political and public favor through hundreds of peripheral preoccupations, all these well-intended but insidious contrivances are greasing the rails for our collective descent into a social order that would be as repugnant to the corporations themselves as to their critics. The danger is that all these things will turn the corporation into a twentieth-century equivalent of the medieval Church. The corporation would eventually invest itself with all-embracing duties, obligations, and finally powers—ministering to the whole man and molding him and society in the image of the corporation's narrow ambitions and its essentially unsocial needs.[31]

Levitt's fear is that the values of the more prominent business managers will dominate the values of society. He does not want social values determined in this way. In the past, societies suffered in which values were determined by

[30]Milton Friedman, 1962, *op. cit.*, p. 9. See also Friedrich A. Hayek, *The Road to Serfdom*, Chicago: University of Chicago Press, 1944.
[31]Theodore Levitt, "The Dangers of Social Responsibility," *Harvard Business Review*, September–October, 1958, p. 44.

one major institution, whether it was the church, the military, business, or something else. This concern is echoed by Irving Shapiro, former DuPont executive, who says that, "Unless they are careful, executives can get sucked into controversial areas where they don't have any particular competence, and in extreme cases their efforts to help could amount to unwarranted meddling."[32]

GOVERNMENT, NOT BUSINESS, SHOULD SOLVE SOCIAL PROBLEMS

The foregoing are arguments generally advanced by conservatives. However, liberal and radical thinkers as well often oppose business's assumption of social responsibilities. For example, the view is advanced that government, not business, should take the lead in solving social problems. What is needed, they assert, is not more socially responsible companies but a more responsive government. More regulation of business is preferable to permitting corporations to decide what is in the public interest. It is also argued that business assumption of social responsibility is a means of lulling a gullible public to sleep, while an exploitative elite preserves its power. Some radical activists conclude that the assumption of social responsibilities by business is merely a Band-Aid for dealing with social problems. What is needed, they say, is a major change in our socioeconomic system. In sum, those opposed to the assumption by business of social responsibilities cover a spectrum from the most conservative to the most radical.

AN ASSESSMENT OF THE ARGUMENTS

Critics of the conservative view point out that the classical thinkers want corporations to do something they cannot do, and that is to ignore societal demands on them. The "rules of the game" really have changed for business. Friedman's position is that managers ought to optimize stockholder wealth so long as they stay within the rules of the game. He explains that the rules of the game refer to economic considerations. This simple market model of business response to its environment is obsolete, especially for larger corporations, if it ever really was an accurate description of reality. A more explanatory model is the business ecology model (see Chapter 1), which shows business responding to an overall societal environment, not simply to its markets, as is the case with the market capitalism model. Because stakeholders are numerous, politically powerful, and organized, corporate managers must consider the social impact of their decisions on these stakeholders. If the words "rules of the game" are modernized, there may not be much difference between the Friedman view and that of those who argue for social responsibilities.

Those who argue that the assumption of social responsibilities will lead to society's being dominated by business values very much overstate the trend.

[32]Francis W. Steckmest, ed., *Corporate Performance: The Key to Public Trust*, New York: McGraw-Hill, 1982, p. 152.

In the aggregate, as noted in Figure 5-1, the total is very small. Business is so far from going to extremes that this assumption is equivalent to forecasting that a leaky faucet will bring on the Johnstown flood.

The same can be said for the view that if business pursues social responsibilities, the end will be performance measurement on political rather than economic scales. This would, say the conservatives, lead to economic inefficiency. If business were measured only on political standards, there is little doubt that economic efficiency would suffer, but business is not now and will not likely in the future be so measured.

Some opponents of social responsibility say that profit maximization is essential for achieving economic efficiency in a free-market economy. But as Nobel laureate and professor of economics Kenneth Arrow points out:

> There are two types of situations in which the simple rule of maximizing profits is socially inefficient: the case in which costs are not paid for, as in pollution, and the case in which the seller has considerably more knowledge about his product than the buyer, particularly with regard to safety. In these situations it is clearly desirable to have some idea of social responsibility, that is, to experience an obligation, whether ethical, moral, or legal.[33]

The proponents of social responsibilities are saying that society is not substituting one set of expectations for another. Rather it is broadening the standards by means of which corporate performance is to be judged. But obviously what is meant by this differs from person to person. On the one hand, there are those who seem to believe that a business enterprise really has responsibilities that may require actions that have no direct bearing on profits. On the other hand, some feel that business has a responsibility to find profit opportunities in solving social problems, but no obligation to do more than that.

There are some people who assert that the new views about social responsibilities represent nothing more than a modification of the old profit-maximizing goal of business. In the past the emphasis of business was on maximizing short-run profit, but now a shift has taken place to put a greater emphasis on maximizing long-range profit. The basis for the shift is that managers see many things happening in the environment today that will affect future profits, and they feel they must take action to optimize long-range profits, even though it reduces short-term profits.

In considering this position, it is important to understand the meaning of "profit maximization." To the economist, this is a precise concept that can be measured quantitatively. It means that a firm will attempt to increase its output so long as the marginal revenue from the last item produced is greater than the marginal cost of that item. At that point where marginal cost equals marginal revenue, the firm will receive its maximum profit. This concept is found in all elementary economics textbooks; it means literally that a firm that seeks to maximize profits in this sense will not make any decision

---

[33]Kenneth Arrow, "Social Responsibility and Economic Efficiency," *Public Policy*, Fall 1973, p. 309.

that will prevent it from getting the highest possible profit for its stock-holders.

The economist's strict concept of profit maximization is not an acceptable operational goal for today's larger corporations—assuming they could achieve such a goal, which they rarely can. Much more appropriate is a concept of required and rising profits—or those needed to satisfy the many claims made on the enterprise, including the level necessary to meet the satisfactions of managers from participating in the resolution of social problems, improving the quality of life of employees, and making this a better society. A company that can reach the level of profits required to balance properly the interests focused on its operations is in a position to take social actions. A company not in so favored a position may be unable to assume them.

We conclude with one final argument, that business action in the social realm will distort democratic processes by permitting a small elite of corporate managers to exercise their powers over society and preserve their selfish profit goals. This Marxist specter is completely at odds with reality. Rather than business dictating which actions to undertake, as the Marxists imply, business must respond to strong pressures from all quarters in society and satisfy strongly felt demands. Corporations cannot win with Marxists. If they have no social responsibility programs, they are profit-mongers. If they have social programs, they are conspiring to dominate the situation in their own interests.

ASSESSING MANAGERIAL MOTIVES

What about the motives of corporations and corporate leaders? How should we evaluate statements and actions of social responsibility framed in gradiose terms when clearly corporations and managers may be acting in self-interest? Suspicion of managerial motives is longstanding. In 1909, for example, Coleman du Pont, president of Du Pont, made a remarkable offer to build a new 103-mile superhighway from Wilmington to Dover in Delaware, the state where Du Pont is headquartered. Political opponents in the state legislature, aware that Coleman du Pont had political ambitions, at first rejected the offer, fearing he would gain votes from this grandstand play. Farmers along the planned right-of-way responded to du Pont's generosity by raising the price of their land. The determined du Pont, however, overcame opposition and built the highway, U.S. Highway 13, which became the most modern in the country at the time. In 1924, the highway was given free of charge to the state of Delaware.[34]

Firms may act responsibly when under great pressure. In 1984, for example, William K. Coors, the chairman of Adolph Coors Company, was quoted in the *Rocky Mountain News* on a number of remarks widely construed as racist (although he later sued the newspaper for libel, saying that the reporter had taken his remarks out of context). These *faux pas*, including the comment

[34]Leonard Mosley, *Blood Relations: The Rise and Fall of the du Ponts of Delaware*, New York: Atheneum, 1980, p. 262.

that blacks "lack the intellectual capacity to succeed," were quoted nationally and added fire to ongoing boycotts of the company by black, Hispanic, and labor groups. With sales dropping in states like California and Texas, Coors signed pacts with minority groups and agreed to use more minority suppliers, hire more minorities, and spend millions supporting minority causes. Coors has kept the bargain and gone beyond, even sponsoring rodeos in honor of black cowboys in frontier days and publishing salutes to outstanding Hispanic athletes. In 1985, a year after the pacts were signed, Coors sales were up 14 percent, mostly due to the return of minority beer drinkers.[35]

Must corporations be entirely altruistic to be truly responsible, or should these examples cause cynicism? In the *Foundations of the Metaphysics of Morals,* philosopher Immanuel Kant developed a perfectionist test of intentions. The test of ethical action was, according to Kant, acting from a "good will" that was good in itself, independent of consequences achieved. Human actions could be divided into "moral" actions that truly proceeded from a good will and "prudential" actions that accorded with truly moral actions but were taken out of self-interest. The sometimes self-interested actions of corporations do not meet the strict Kantian test, but perhaps they are helpful, and it is appropriate for a capitalist society that morality and self-interest find felicitious combination.

SOCIAL AND ECONOMIC PERFORMANCE: ARE THEY RELATED?

Is there a reward for virtue? Are social responsible companies more profitable than those that are not? Does their stock perform better? Are they better managed? It would be nice to answer yes to these questions. Unfortunately, after a large number of studies by scholars during the past fifteen years, no clear answer is available.

One study examined a wide range of other research which related corporate social performance to economic performance over an extended period of time, 1972 to 1985. The reviewers of these studies found that "[a]lthough many studies concluded that a relationship existed, those studies that appeared to be most methodologically sound did not reach that conclusion."[36] The authors then conducted their own in-depth analysis of the relationship and said that their study "has not been able to corroborate the claims of either advocates or critics as to the value social responsibility may have for industrial organizations."[37]

In another, later study, some correlations were found between social responsibility and financial performance, but the study concluded that the measurement problems were so formidable as to cloud the creditability of the results. Indeed, they suggested that future scholars may find it more fruitful

[35]Janet Simons, "Coors Turns Boycotters into Buyers," *Advertising Age,* February 27, 1986.
[36]Kenneth E. Alpperle, Archie B. Carroll, and John D. Hatfield, "An Empirical Examination of the Relationship Between Corporate Social Responsibility and Profitability," *Academy of Management Journal,* June 1985, pp. 460–461.
[37]*Ibid.,* p. 462.

to study how financial performance influences social responsibility, not the reverse.[38]

These conclusions are not particularly surprising, because researchers have extraordinary problems in drawing convincing relationships between the assumption of corporate social responsibilities and economic performance. To begin with, social responsibilities can, as we have seen, be described in different ways. Furthermore, responsibilities vary with factors such as a firm's location, size, profitability, strategy, management philosophy, products, important stakeholders, and'so forth. Which social responsibilities should be correlated? How uniform is the implementation of these responsibilities among companies studied? Anyway, when social responsibilities are defined, how can they be measured quantitatively for research purposes? Then, which economic measures will be used? It is much easier to quantify economic measures (such as profit, return on assets, or stock price), but another major problem intrudes. How can a researcher be convincing in relating social responsibility to economic measures? After all, all sorts of forces influence economic results of a company's operations, and socially responsible actions may have very little impact.

One other point should be mentioned. A company that is financially prosperous may assume social responsibilities that it would not otherwise accept. On the other hand, a company that is doing poorly may cut back on its social programs. Nevertheless, as noted above, many managers believe that the proper assumption of social responsibilities will be in the company's long-run economic interests.

SOCIALLY RESPONSIBLE INVESTING

Although a positive relationship between corporate social responsibility and financial performance has not been substantiated, a growing number of investors in mutual and other investment funds are attracted to those with portfolios of socially responsible companies. The record of these funds is mixed. In some years, some funds do better than the Standard and Poors index of stock prices and others do not. One study comparing a five-year span between four of the major socially oriented funds and all mutual funds showed that one fund did better (by a small margin) but the others did not, several by wide margins.[39]

It seems fair to conclude that, over time, the socially oriented funds are not likely to do any better or worse than typical funds. But they offer a needed service for a growing number of "ethical investors" who want to make investments that support their social views.

Funds that screen for social responsibilities are growing in numbers and portfolio value. However, they are so small that they exert no pressure on corporations that offend their values.

---

[38]Jean B. McGuire, Alison Sundgren, and Thomas Schneewels, "Corporate Social Responsibility and Firm Financial Performance," *Academy of Management Journal*, December 1988, p. 869.
[39]Jill Rachlin, "A Question of Principle: Can Do-gooders Do Well?" *U.S. News and World Report*, January 26, 1987.

PRESSURES ON INSTITUTIONAL INVESTORS

Institutional investors who act as trustees of state, city, and union pension funds and of college endowments own almost half of publicly traded stock and the majority of shares of large companies such as IBM. Managers of these institutional funds are sometimes pressured by activist groups to use their portfolio purchasing and divestiture policy to force corporations to be socially responsive. The principal concerns behind these pressures are multitudinous. Institutional managers have been asked to liquidate investments in corporations operating in South Africa, major defense contractors, nuclear weapons, component manufacturers, tobacco companies, chemical companies, drug companies, infant formula manufacturers, companies perceived as antiunion, and other firms that have somehow offended a politically active segment of society.

Usually, large institutional investors resist such pressures and prefer to invest for maximum financial return, arguing that it is a fiduciary duty to institutional clients to do so. But occasionally, enough political pressure is created to force a change in investment policy. Since 1983, for instance, a number of states and municipalities have passed resolutions requiring disinvestment of holdings in American firms doing business in South Africa.

A number of difficult questions arise when such political pressure is exerted. For example, how can a portfolio manager decide which companies should be favored and which avoided? IBM, for instance, has long been condemned by activist groups for selling computers to the South African government. Yet IBM also ranks high on many lists of the most socially responsible companies.

Activist disinvestment groups seek to substitute social and political objectives for prevailing policies of maximum return. They attempt to control institutional capital for their own social ends. Of course, once a precedent is established for buying or selling stocks for social reasons, a case can be made for avoiding investment in virtually any company. A political or social disinvestment standard could expose an institutional investor to huge financial losses, including brokerage fees, opportunity costs, or worse. So far there has been little apparent adverse impact on either the performance of institutional investors or corporations from divestment of securities for social reasons.

To date, only a few institutional investors have divested securities for social reasons, and that has been for specific purposes, such as doing business in South Africa. There has been no general policy of any of the large institutional investors to buy or sell securities on the basis of what a company does in the area of social responsibility. But they are becoming more active in pressuring managements of companies in which they have large stock holdings to take specific actions which they favor. This is a subject we discuss at length in Chapter 19 on corporate governance. If they choose to do so, they can exert significant impact on a corporation's management and stock price. In the final analysis, there is no reason why managers of investment portfolios ought not exert pressures on companies in which they invest. However, the pressures ought to be in the interests of the constituents of the investment manager, as they see their interests. This means, of course, maintaining and improving the financial position of the investment portfolio.

BUSINESS AND MAJOR SOCIAL PROBLEMS

BUSINESS IS NOT SOLELY RESPONSIBLE FOR SOLVING SOCIAL PROBLEMS

Business is a predominant instrumentality in society for dealing with major social problems, but it is not the institution of sole or last responsibility. It is government that has the central role in dealing with such problems. Business has incentives for working on these problems, as noted previously. It has great talents that it can exert, such as the development of new equipment to reduce pollution of various types or the free contribution of managerial knowledge to government agencies. A central issue in dealing with social problems concerns the extent to which government should provide incentives for business to become involved in solving social problems when it does not appear to business to be profitable to do so. It also must be pointed out that other institutions in society, such as universities, labor unions, and religious institutions, and people themselves, individually and in groups, can make valuable contributions to overcoming major social problems.

SOCIAL RESPONSIBILITY AND THE COSTS OF DOING BUSINESS

Will not the socially responsible company be put at a competitive disadvantage? If it goes too far, the answer is yes. However, a great many social responsibilities can be pursued without substantial costs to an enterprise—for example, improving due process within the company, encouraging managers to lend their knowledge in resolving local community as well as national problems, and locating plants in underprivileged areas. Many social responsibilities are consistent with making profits. Some may be costly, such as not closing a marginal plant in a community dependent upon it, making large capital equipment expenditures to reduce pollution, and giving heavily to the community for beautification.

HOW MUCH SOCIAL COST SHOULD BUSINESS BEAR?

Social costs are the total costs of business activity, including immediate costs of production plus all other costs. For instance, a factory dumping pollutants into a clear stream incurs two kinds of costs. One is the cost of its operation; the other is the cost that results from changes in the stream's ecology—perhaps human and animal disease, perhaps the destruction of natural beauty. To the extent that business does not bear these external costs, they must be borne by others.

These "other costs" include a spectrum of elements. They may involve direct and indirect losses to third persons, such as reduced real estate values from nearby factory noise. They include human damage in the form of disease, accident, unemployment, disturbance of social relationships, and changes in the lifestyle of groups. They may include defaced landscapes, ugly buildings, or traffic congestion. Some costs are incurred immediately; others may take a long time to be felt. Some costs can be measured in dollars, such as the price for cleaning up a polluted stream. Others, such as the impairment of health resulting from air pollution, cannot be gauged in quantitative terms. Indeed, the determination of many social costs depends upon the value society attaches to a particular impact and its relationships to the benefits of social change.

Capitalism has been called "an economy of unpaid costs." This means that a large part of the actual costs of production are not counted as business expenses but are shifted to and borne by third persons or by the community as a whole. As society has become more complex, there has been a rise in the unpaid costs of business. Earlier in our history, these costs generally were considered to be implicit by-products of economic life, and regarded as the short-run price to be paid for the higher economic efficiency and long-run social advantage resulting from the operation of the economic system. Eventually, laws were passed to force business to meet unpaid costs where injury to third parties could be reasonably determined. The political history of the United States increasingly has reflected popular unwillingness to bear the social costs of economic development without help from government. Throughout this history, business pressure groups have sought to avoid the assumption of social costs that had been transferred to others.

In considering business responsibility for social costs, it should be remembered that business also creates social value. Important benefits accrue to society through business's activities. A business, for instance, may introduce an innovation that will cut the costs of making a particular product. Assuming no other significant cost than that of production, the result is a net gain in social value. A company may erect a beautiful building, tastefully landscaped. Or it may contribute to advancing knowledge. Theoretically, a business firm should in the long run cover all costs of production and should profit from the social benefits it creates. This attitude suggests that in the long run, social costs should be borne by those responsible for creating them, or those who bear them should be compensated. It also suggests that a firm should be compensated in accordance with its contribution to social benefit. Unfortunately, in only a comparatively few instances can such cause-and-effect relationships be isolated and measured. More often, the determinants cannot be identified or quantified.

CRITERIA FOR DETERMINING THE SOCIAL RESPONSIBILITIES OF BUSINESS

There is no magic touchstone or standard for determining social responsibilities. Because the concept is not expressed in concrete, legal, or axiomatic terms, managers must be thoughtful about responsible corporate behavior.

What might be a few major overall guides to business's assumption of social responsibilities? We suggest the following.

First, there is no formula for all businesses or any one business. Each firm must decide for itself. Business can take action, but it is not compelled to do so except when law and custom determine otherwise. The first social responsibility of each business is to think carefully before acting about what it thinks its social responsibilities are. In deciding what it should be doing, a company must consider many factors. For example, included would be its financial position, the values and interests of its managers and employees, its exposure to public scrutiny and legal requirements, the priorities for being successful in the business in which it is engaged, and, very important, what the many interests outside the company expect of it. This would include not only broad general social expectations but also expectations of individual stakeholders.

Second, business must be considered to be predominantly an economic institution with a strong profit motive. Business should not be used to meet noneconomic objectives of society in a major way without financial incentives. As the Business Roundtable says in its *Statement on Corporate Responsibility:* "If a corporation is not profitable in the long run, there is no way that it can fulfill any responsibilities to society. If the bottom line is a minus, there is no plus for society."[40] It is of paramount importance that no action be taken to erode the profit motive in American business ideology. The fundamental justification for this view is supported by Will and Ariel Durant, who looked over the broad sweep of history they so assiduously chronicled and concluded that "the experience of the past leaves little doubt that every economic system must sooner or later rely upon some form of the profit motive to stir individuals and groups to productivity. Substitutes like slavery, police supervision, or ideological enthusiasm prove too unproductive, too expensive, or too transient."[41] We must continue to judge business performance primarily on the basis of economic criteria.

Third, business should be expected to take the long view and perform socially responsible actions that might temporarily lessen net profits but that are consistent with profit interests of the company in the long run. Clearly, the long-range self-interest of business lies in correcting such problems as unemployment, civil disorders, environmental pollution, and crime.

Fourth, an individual business has social responsibilities, says Keith Davis, commensurate with its social powers.[42] That power and responsibility go hand in hand is an idea as old as civilization itself. This can be only a rough guide to action, but it can be a useful one. For instance, company A is the major employer in a town, and company B is an employer of only 5 percent of the people in the town. Both companies are planning to move. It would seem that, other things being equal, company A should give more thought to its social responsibilities in moving than should company B. Hav-

---

[40]Business Roundtable, *op. cit.*, p. 5.

[41]Will Durant and Ariel Durant, *The Lessons of History*, New York: Simon & Schuster, 1968, p. 54.

[42]Keith Davis, *op. cit.*

ing said this, however, we still do not know to what extent considerations of social responsibility should alter the decision of company A.

Companies also, Davis says, have "socio-human responsibilities." Considering a business as only an economic institution may lead to the conclusion that it has some responsibilities concerned with the economic costs of unemployment, but not with the erosion of human dignity or social disorganization that accompanies unemployment. A business may be concerned with increasing creative capability in individuals to improve productivity, but not with attempting to help workers get more self-fulfillment from their jobs. Davis says that this is wrong because business deals with the whole person in a whole social structure. Furthermore, managers have socio-human power, that is, power over the quality of a person's life. As such, they have socio-human responsibilities commensurate with that power. Again, this equation yields no sure answers in any situation, but it should help.

Fifth, and closely associated with the preceding point, is the matter of company size and type. As a firm grows larger, it influences more and more people. Society then takes a greater interest in what it does, and the company in turn thinks more carefully about its responsibilities. As corporations acquire more power over people, there is pressure for them to install policies, rules, and actions so that individuals are less likely to be treated unjustly or without due process. The social responsibilities of the smallest entrepreneur-owner business are not many, but there are some. For example, a very small business in an urban slum has a social responsibility not to raise prices arbitrarily or to sell defective goods as first quality.

Social responsibilities differ with respect to types of company. A company involved in the mass production of a competitively priced product is in a very different position with respect to the feelings and personal interests of employees in leading the good life at work from, say, a technically oriented and highly profitable laboratory staffed by Ph.Ds. A mining company is in a different position with respect to employee safety from, say, a small real estate office.

Sixth, an individual business should choose only those social responsibilities it can best manage. Traditionally, business does a better job when the task entails a minimum of political involvement, does not get directly into the democratic political processes, deals with a physical problem that can be quantified and measured, and is one in which it has experience.

Seventh, business should be obliged to internalize more of its external costs. In the past, businesses were excused from bearing such costs of production as air and water pollution, scarring hillsides in the search for coal, and defacing natural beauty because society held the economic output of business to be of higher priority. Today priorities are shifting, and business is expected to bear more social costs.

War Toys

The wolf also shall dwell with the lamb, and the leopard shall lie down with the kid; and the calf and the young lion and the fatling together; and a little child shall lead them.

—Isaiah 11:6

"We need reinforcements, folks...here's the supply...General, you have to realize that you'll be held responsible...we need more support...General, sir, I have to get in there...but I want...Fire—over there....The others are coming, hey, you: stay there...over there, they are attacking again....Fire...it's burning...hurry up, another tank...God, it's heavy....Quick, away with the jeep...alarm, faster, alarm...fire, come on....Hey, you, handle the flak....The Americans are running short of men...no more men, gee..."

—Thomas, an 11-year-old German child,
playing with tanks and soldiers in his room[43]

Today's toy store is a miniature arsenal. It contains playthings fashioned in the image of every manner of past, present, and future weapon. In a tour of the aisles, a child can see pistols, rifles, artillery, bows and arrows, knives, warships, warplanes, military "action figures," war strategy games, laser weapons, and armed star cruisers.

War toys are not unique to modern America. They are—like balls, blocks, tops, and dolls—ageless and found in all cultures. In primitive societies children pretended that sticks were spears and practiced war games. Archeologists have found toy soldiers in excavations of ancient Greek and Roman dwellings. During the Middle Ages, young princes were trained in the art of generalship by advisers using war toys. A famous 1516 woodcut by Hans Burkmair, entitled "Games of the Young Emperor Maximilian," shows the young boy-ruler and his royal entourage firing a cannon, stringing a longbow, shooting a bird off a branch with a crossbow, and jousting with miniature figures of mounted knights placed on a table.

[43]Quoted in Christian Buettner, "War Toys or the Organization of Hostility," *International Journal of Early Childhood*, vol. 13, no. 1, 1981, p. 104.

TOYS AND CULTURAL VALUES

Cultural values are learned during play. Toys and the way they are used reflect the influence of the larger, adult society. They may, for instance, mirror a nation's concept of a hero. In ancient Rome, children played games with toy chariots and emulated great heroes of the races. Nearly 2,000 years later, children of American democracy lionized the common soldier by playing with Hasbro Corporation's popular "G.I. Joe" action figures after World War II.

Toys and games may also be influenced by the values and events of a historical period. The board game "Monopoly" was invented by an unemployed engineer to help fill idle days. It was a big hit when introduced in 1934 because, as one toy analyst writes, the unemployed "loved playing tycoon, and men who were homeless needed to build dream castles."[44] One era with a pronounced and lingering impact on toyland is that of the American Wild West. During the 1870s and 1880s, the epic adventures of cowboys and Indians thrilled readers around the world. Children in America and Europe played with six-shooters and tomahawks. The fad became a permanent theme in children's games, partly because fascinating Western events occurred just when the toy industry developed the technology to mass produce toys at affordable prices. For example, the mechanical cap gun, which was invented in 1859, was at first made by hand and affordable only by wealthy families. But with the advent of standardized, mass produced parts the price dropped and they became widely affordable. The allure of the Wild West for children the world over helped give birth to the modern consumer market for toys.

Today, the proliferation and mass advertising of toys of all kinds, including war toys, is a reflection of our society's materialistic, consumption-oriented values. The U.S. toy market is the world's largest. Over 800 toy manufacturers make an estimated 150,000 products for sale in 140,000 retail outlets. Five companies—Hasbro, Inc.; Mattel, Inc.; Tonka Corp.; Galoob; and Nintendo of America—dominate the market, with just under 50 percent of domestic toy sales. And the market is growing. In 1989, domestic toy sales were $13 billion, up from just over $4 billion in 1976.[45]

Social trends outside the toy industry underlie continuing sales growth. The number of children between the ages of 4 and 15 grew 10 percent annually during the 1980s, and continued growth is predicted. Parents have growing incomes, and the average sum spent on toys for each child rose from $100 a year in 1980 to $203 in 1990. A growing number of remarriages multiply the number of parents and grandparents for some children, further increasing toy sales. And longer life expectancy promises that grandparents will have more time to spoil grandchildren.

Other factors pushing up toy sales have come from within the industry. Discount retail chains, such as Toys "R" Us (where one of every five toy dol-

---

[44]Marvin Kaye, *A Toy Is Born*, New York: Stein and Day, 1973, p. 41.
[45]Joseph Pereira, "Ghosts of Yules Past Haunt the Toy Shelves, Gottahaves' Are Gone," *Wall Street Journal*, December 12, 1989.

lars in the United States spent), have brought discount merchandising trends to the toy industry and have changed toys from a largely seasonal sales item to a year-round staple.[46] This growth of toy discounters has, for example, forced big department stores that formerly set up toy departments only just before Christmas to keep a toy department all year. Otherwise, customers turn away permanently to discounters.

Toy manufacturers have, of course, zealously promoted their products in this fertile demographic and retailing climate. They spend up to $25 million to introduce new products, advertise heavily, and create and sell television cartoon series based on characters in their toy lines. These TV series have provoked enormous criticism because they blur the distinction between programming and advertising. The trend toward children's programs based on toy products began in 1984, when the Federal Communications Commission (FCC) dropped standards limiting commercial minutes on programs directed at children. Elimination of these guidelines was part of the deregulatory effort of the Reagan administration, which felt that overcommercialization should be controlled by the marketplace rather than by government officials. With the end of FCC restrictions, the commercialization of children's television grew. Under FCC rules, commercials had been limited to 9.5 minutes per hour on weekends and 12 minutes on weekdays, but soon stations were running over 16 minutes per hour. Criticism arose about excessive exposure for products such as war toys, sugary cereals, junk food emporiums such as McDonald's, and toll lines such as the Slime Line and the Freddy Pumpkin Horror Story Line. In addition, the shows themselves became ads for products, and critics argued that commercialization was driving out the educational thrust of children's TV. Between 1985 and 1987, seventy-five new TV programs were based on toys, including animated shows for G.I. Joe, The Transformers, Robo Force, and other action figures.[47] Such programs not only blurred the distinction between programming and advertising, but they contained frequent violence. In fact, most of the twenty top selling toys in 1988 were based on television programs, and about half these programs had violent themes.[48] Violence, according to one study, is rising. It found that the number of violent acts in children's programming rose from 18.6 per hour in 1980 to 26.4 in 1989 (compared to a steady five or six per hour in adult

---

[46]Faye Rice, "Superelf Plans for Xma$," *Fortune*, September 11, 1989, p. 151.

[47]Hearings Before the Committee on Energy and Commerce, House of Representatives, *Commercialization of Children's Television*, September 15, 1987. Remarks of Peggy Charon, President, Action for Children's Television, pp. 23–24. For an in-depth look at the growth of "program-length commercials" for children see Dale Kunkel, "From a Raised Eyebrow to a Turned Back: The FCC and Children's Product-Related Programming," *Journal of Communication*, Autumn 1988, pp. 90–108. For more criticism of the phenomenon see Rene Riley, "War Toys 'R' Us," *Business and Society Review*, Winter 1988, pp. 48–51.

[48]Hearing before the Committee on Commerce, Science, and Transportation, United States Senate, 100 Cong., 1st Sess., *Children's TV Act of 1989*. Statement of Dr. Francis Palumbo, American Academy of Pediatrics, p. 90. A Children's Television Act of 1988 was passed in 1988 but vetoed by President Reagan. It and the 1989 proposal limited ads to 10.5 minutes per hour on weekends and 12 minutes on weekdays.

shows).[49] It is, of course, characteristic of American culture that watching violence is found entertaining.

Not all parties are critical of directions in children's programming. Toy makers and advertisers argue that they fulfill a market demand or they would not be so popular and, in any case, restriction of programming of any kind is abhorrent as a violation of free speech in broadcasting. Others simply have faith in kids. An editorial writer for a news magazine recently noted:

> Does anyone now recall the great comic book scare of the late Forties and Fifties? Many a great mind of that era feared that children were being corrupted by the gross-me-out crudities of the first generation of mass-marketed comic books...
>
> Yet somehow, a generation weaned on *Mad* magazine grew up with its own critical faculties sufficiently intact to deplore the culture of its children. This suggests an enduring and perhaps inevitable cycle. I, for one, would be loath to put a stop to it. It makes for such an amusing spectacle. Almost as amusing as seeing Wile E. Coyote get crushed.[50]

Finally, of course, the use of war objects as playthings may reflect the martial values of society. German children learned war games at school until the end of World War I. Later, German parents of the post-World War II generation tried to deemphasize war toys and inculcate antimilitaristic values in their children. In a study involving European children, children from Austria, which has a strong military tradition, more often chose war toys over such playthings as animals and dolls than did children from Holland, which has a history of antimilitarism.[51] In 1979, Sweden, another country with a strong antimilitarist tradition, banned the sale of war toys. Underlying pacifist values are similarly reflected in Swedish TV programming, which has virtually no Westerns or crime/action series and where the use of violence to attract audiences is prohibited. In 1986, Finland followed Sweden's lead. A voluntary agreement between the government and toy manufacturers ended the manufacture, import, or sale of war toys. Norway has a similar voluntary pact.

ATTACKS ON TOYS

Toy makers have been criticized through the ages—sometimes unfairly. In 1746, Jumping Jacks, the most popular toy in France, were banned because officials believed pregnant women who looked at their spindly limbs would give birth to deformed babies.[52] Toys are geared to cultural values; when those values come under attack, so do toys that reflect them. In the United States, many toy product lines have recently come under attack because of underlying changes in social values.

[49]Noted in Shawn Pogatchnik, "Kids' TV Gets More Violent, Study Finds," *Los Angeles Times*, January 26, 1990.
[50]Richard Starr, *Insight*, May 23, 1988, p. 64.
[51]Buettner, *op. cit.*, p. 107.
[52]Marvin Kaye, *A Toy Is Born*, New York: Stein and Day, 1973, p. 167.

Toys that perpetuate racial and ethnic stereotypes are no longer appropriate, due to pressure from minority critics and widespread acceptance of principles of equality. For years, toy manufacturers perpetuated racist images. Most toys mirrored white society. For instance, although a few black dolls were marketed, they were invariably slaves or minstrels, never authority figures. Writing in the *Journal of Black Psychology*, Doris Y. Wilkinson points out, "Creators of stereotyped Black toys have translated and incorporated the ideology, attitudes, and customs of a race-conscious social order," and this has been a "propaganda strategy that supported at the level of play the stigmatization of African-American males,"[53] The damage of such stereotypes may be significant. In the mid-1960s, a psychiatrist studying black children's self-images placed both black and white dolls in front of black children. The children invariably preferred to play with white dolls.[54] Similarly, Kathleen and James McGinnis, authors of *Parenting for Peace and Justice*, criticize the toy industry for stereotyping Native Americans as warlike. They note that "packages of little plastic cowboys and Indians always have the Indians with rifles or tomahawks."[55]

Feminists have accused toy manufacturers of perpetuating harmful sex-role stereotypes. Much criticism has been focused on Mattel's Barbie doll, one of the most successful mass appeal toys in history. In the early 1960s, Barbie and her male companion, a "dream date" named Ken, were marketed along with fashions and accessories. Both were white. Barbie's outfits reinforced traditional feminine roles such as "Friday Night Date," "Career Girl," "Dinner at 8," and "Sophisticated Lady." Ken's outfits reflected masculine roles such as "Dreamboat," "Campus Hero," and "Ski Champion." Feminists complained. Barbie was also accused of fostering the acquisitive instinct in little girls, who learned to manipulate their parents into getting more clothes and accessories for Barbie. Critics alleged this behavior might carry into adult life; women who had played with Barbie might pressure their husbands to buy things for them. Some found Barbie even more sinister. In 1966, Dr. Alan F. Leveton, director of the Pediatrics Mental Health Unit at the University of California Medical Center in San Francisco, said:

> We are seeing children who are excited and disturbed by dolls like Barbie and her friends. . . . Boys are being seen at the clinic who use Barbie for sexual stimulation, a fact which might trouble the same parents who are scandalized by comic books and pinball machines, were it not for the fact that Barbie masquerades as a child's toy. Both boys and girls are introduced to a precocious, joyless sexuality, to fan-

---

[53]Doris Y. Wilkinson, "Play Objects as Tools of Propaganda: Characterizations of the African-American Male," *Journal of Black Psychology*, August 1980, p. 11. Children of all races react selectively to gender-based toys; see for example Yvonne M. Caldera, Aletha C. Huston, and Marion O'Brien, "Social Interactions and Play Patterns of Parents and Toddlers with Feminine, Masculine, and Neutral Toys," *Child Development*, February 1989.

[54]Kaye, *op. cit.*, p. 82.

[55]Kathleen McGinnis and James McGinnis, *Parenting for Peace and Justice*, Maryknoll, New York: Orbis Books, 1983, p. 63.

tasies of seduction and to conspicuous consumption. This reflects and perpetuates a disturbing trend in our culture, which has serious mental-health complications.[56]

Barbie survived criticism and celebrated her thirtieth anniversary in 1989 as the nation's second most popular toy (behind the Nintendo Entertainment System). Because of criticism over the years, Barbie has taken on non-traditional occupations such as astronaut, and there are black, Latina, and Asian Barbies.

In the 1960s and 1970s, the toy industry, like other industries, was attacked by consumer advocates. Toys were criticized for shoddy construction. Toy ads were said to exploit naive children and subvert parental authority. Toy companies stood accused of creating desires for tasteless merchandise such as bouncing eyeballs and ghoulish monsters. In 1971, a crusading critic named Edward M. Swartz pained toyland with a viciously critical book entitled *Toys That Don't Care*. Swartz meticulously sullied toys with electrical hazards, sharp points, or sharp edges; toys that shot dangerous projectiles; toys that were too loud; toys that glamorized drug use; toys that were toxic if ingested; and toys that were flammable or blew up. The toy industry, in short, shared the avalanche of ill will felt by other industries in the era of emergent consumerism. These criticisms strengthened the market niche for sturdy, sensible, educational toys. Other market niches have been filled by small companies that make toys representing social values important to specific market segments. For instance, a growing number of religious toys, such as Grace the Pro-Life Doll and Heroes of the Kingdom action figures from biblical times, are made by small companies that cater to fundamentalist Christians. Olmec Corp. markets a line of black, Hispanic, and Asian action figures which are advertised in magazines such as *Essence*. As a socially responsible gesture, Mattel markets a line of disabled dolls, Hal's Pals, and donates the proceeds to charities for disabled children.

PSYCHOLOGICAL EFFECTS OF WAR TOYS

A recurrent criticism of toy sellers is that they encourage and glorify violence by selling toy guns and other war equipment. The criticism stems from timeless parental concern that war toys sold to impressionable boys aged three to ten (girls rarely play with them) (1) increase aggressive behavior; (2) embody the idea that conflict resolution through violent physical force is acceptable; (3) encourage development of militaristic attitudes in successive generations; (4) desensitize children to the brutality of killing and destruction; (5) foster the development of black and white, good guy–bad guy perceptions of conflict; and (6) legitimize hunting animals for sport. War toy manufacturers and sellers, say the critics, must bear moral responsibility for psychological damage in children and for the subsequent damage to peoples and nations that results from the predispositions to violence in adults who grew up with war toys.

[56]*National Peace Education Bulletin*, vol. 2, no. 3., February 1966, p. 1.

Lines of action figures such as G.I. Joe, Masters of the Universe, and Marshall BraveStarr have attracted additional criticism. Action figures usually come with elaborate prepackaged legends or stories that tell children about the figures' personalities, backgrounds, and friendly or unfriendly dispositions. This theme-giving reduces the child's opportunity to create a play fantasy. Children wind up imitating a theme marketed by toy manufacturers rather than inventing a play script of their own.

War play itself (if not all war toys) is defended by some developmental psychologists, who argue that children naturally have aggressive instincts and that play warfare is a cathartic outlet. To appreciate this argument it is necessary to understand the nature of child's play. Play serves important functions. Through play, children increase their knowledge of the world and learn to solve problems. They learn about society—its social roles, sex roles,

Two examples of popular action figures. In 1987 the G.I. Joe® line was the best-selling toy in the United States. (Random House photo by Stacey Pleasant.)

and values—and experiment with adult behaviors to develop competence. In addition, children release energy and develop strength, coordination, logical reasoning, and abstract reasoning through play. Thus, war play, like play with other themes, can further developmental needs. As two professors of education recently noted: "In war play, children can work on their understanding of the boundaries between pretend and reality, build basic cognitive concepts, develop a beginning understanding of political and moral ideas, and even learn about cooperation and the needs of others."[57]

War play is universal among children of varying cultures. In the 1930s, anthropologists observing a primitive African society, the Tale, found young boys playfully shooting barbless arrows. It was theorized that they were preparing for adult responsibilities, which included hunting with deadly poisoned arrows.[58] Play fighting is a common rehearsal for adult life among the young of animal species, and human young may be genetically predisposed as well. Male children in industrial societies seem inevitably to engage in play fighting as a rehearsal for adult life. Consider the experience of one German mother who tried to instill pacifist values in her children—an experience common in all cultures.

> Our children listened carefully and appeared to have understood what we were trying to teach them. But gradually and evidently independently of our endeavors their armoury in the play-room multiplied. We did not buy the plastic monsters of the Western or war kind for them, but they themselves took care of this "increase of power" with their spending money and swapping, just to roam the streets and playgrounds in hordes, fully weaponed and wildly gesticulating—being sheriffs, TV detective heroes, cowboys, or gang leaders...how little they understand of the non-violence we were trying to explain to them all those years.[59]

Nobody knows exactly why children develop a taste for guns and battle toys. Peer group pressure is a frequently cited factor. The appeal of active, adventurous play themes is another. Other explanations offered by psychologists are that the gun holds attraction as a phallic symbol, that young boys wish to multiply their power by using weapons, that war toys are intrinsically interesting gadgets, and that they symbolize problematic issues such as evil and death, which the child must learn to handle emotionally. A less subtle explanation, of course, is that the child is imitating violence in the adult world.

Does play with war toys make children more aggressive? A small body of experimental research on children between the ages of four and eight years uniformly indicates that it does. Four studies have measured aggressive and antisocial behavior in children who have just played with war toys and in

[57]Nancy Carlsson-Paige and Diane E. Levin, *Who's Calling the Shots: How to Respond Effectively to Children's Fascination with War Play and War Toys*, Philadelphia: New Society Publishers, 1990, p. 31.
[58]Robert E. Schell and Elizabeth Hall, *Developmental Psychology Today*, 4th ed., New York: Random House, 1983.
[59]Buettner, *op. cit.*, pp. 104–105.

children who have played with neutral toys such as farm animals, dolls, or coloring books. The studies all show increased levels of "inappropriate" aggression and antisocial behavior among children who have just played with war toys.[60] These results are contrary to the so-called catharsis hypothesis, which is that children playing games with war toys drain their aggression and are less aggressive afterward. The studies do not make clear how long the aggressive aftereffects of war play last. It is, of course, a nightmarish research problem to prove that playing with tanks and guns as a child causes the development of violence-prone, criminal, or militaristic attitudes in an adult. No experimental research projects address this idea. Among some who deal with children on a daily basis, however, there is an intuitive feeling that war toys engender aggressive behavior. For this reason, "Most preschools have rules that say children can't bring war toys to school because when they do it escalates fighting, kicking, and biting—behavior that is intended to inflict physical and psychological pain."[61]

The toy industry defends war toys. Toy manufacturers claim that toys teach lessons about patriotism, forces of good and evil, and the nature of war—all unalterable elements of adult life. Toy makers operate in a very competitive market, and there is perennial demand for war toys. Stiff competition ensures that some manufacturers will fill demand even if others voluntarily give up war-toy revenue. One critic scoffs at this defense, saying: "No one argues that a drug pusher is a wholly innocent third party providing a neutral service; so also, if the country is addicted to war and violence, we cannot rationally view the toy industry's role as simply one of catering impersonally to this addiction."[62] Says Stewart Sims, formerly an Ideal Toys executive, "[I]t is not a toy company's role to create an artificial society, one that doesn't exist. Because if we did that, we would be superimposing our own values on the world."[63] Another spokesperson for the toy industry says bluntly: "Playthings correspond to what's going on in society."[64]

---

[60]Seymour Feshbach, "The Catharsis Hypothesis and Some Consequences of Interaction with Aggressive and Neutral Play Objects, "The Effects of Exposure to Toys Conducive to Violence," *Journal of Personality,* June 1956; Alicia Mendoza, unpublished doctoral dissertation, University of Miami, 1972; Charles W. Turner and Diane Goldsmith, "Effects of Toy Guns and Airplanes on Children's Anti-Social Free Play Behavior," *Journal of Experimental Child Psychology,* April 1976; and Christine N. Wolf, "The Effects of Aggressive Toys on Aggressive Behavior in Children," unpublished doctoral dissertation, University of Montana, 1976. A large body of literature also strongly supports the conclusion that watching violent cartoons or television programs increases aggression and conflict with peers among children. A recent study which contains a bibliography is Joyce Sprafkin and Kenneth D. Gadow, "The Immediate Impact of Aggressive Cartoons on Emotionally Disturbed and Learning Disabled Children," *Journal of Genetic Psychology,* March 1988.

[61]John Dreyfuss, "The Word War over Realistic Toy Guns Is Getting Hotter," *Los Angeles Times,* December 19, 1986.

[62]Swartz, *op. cit.,* p. 71.

[63]Tim Shorrock, "The Corporate Santa," *Multinational Monitor,* December 1983, p. 14.

[64]Penny Richman, quoted in Cynthia Kooi, "War Toy Invasion Grows Despite Boycott," *Advertising Age,* March 3, 1986.

CHANGING VALUES AND WAR TOYS

Attitudes toward war toys have varied over time in the United States. A few protests were organized during World War I. Despite the level of global carnage in World War II, that conflict did not elicit attacks on toy makers (with the exception of a few angry parents who destroyed toys imported from Germany). A wartime pamphlet on child rearing published by the Child Study Association even supported war play. "Boys have always played games that gave release to their war-like feelings," it said, adding that "a certain amount of such play is needed by most normal young males at any time."[65]

After 1945, demand for war toys grew steadily. Some companies, such as Lone Star Products and Parris Manufacturing, specialized in making guns for children. There is evidence that parental attitudes toward war toys were lenient well into the 1960s. A 1963 survey of nursery school classes at Pacific Oaks University in Pasadena, California, indicated that 90 percent of teachers and students, 84 percent of mothers, and 79 percent of fathers agreed that "children should be allowed to use guns." Only eleven mothers and fathers out of 139 surveyed felt that children should "never be allowed to use guns."[66] G.I. Joe, a foot-high doll introduced by Hasbro Industries in 1964, sold well in the marketing environment of a victorious, patriotic nation pursuing an expansionist foreign policy based on military alliances.

But later in the decade a confluence of historical forces altered American attitudes toward war toys. The assassinations of John F. Kennedy, Martin Luther King, and Robert Kennedy—combined with widespread crime and racial violence—fostered negative feelings about guns. Guns, and handguns in particular, were seen as a major culprit behind domestic violence. Further, the dismal, prolonged military involvement in Vietnam soured public attitudes toward war. Changed public attitudes pulled the rug from under gun and war toy sales. Toy stores such as F. A. O. Schwartz adopted policies of not carrying such merchandise. Later, chains such as Sears, Marshall Field & Co., and K Mart Corp. followed suit. Hasbro "furloughed" the G.I. Joe product line in 1976 when orders virtually ceased.

But times changed. By the late 1970s, the market for toy guns returned. Analysts attributed a sales rise of 32 percent in 1979 to fading memories of Vietnam and several hit Western films. Between 1980 and 1985, sales of guns and other war toys skyrocketed from $100 million to over $1 billion, the increase in consumption being attributed to the popular martial dimension of the Reagan administration. Toy companies were quick to exploit growing demand. Hasbro, for example, brought back the G.I. Joe product line in 1982 as a "Mobile Strike Force Team," modeled on the rapid deployment force concept that was emergent in the strategic thinking of the U.S. armed services. G.I. Joe's assignment became that of stopping a mad terrorist named Cobra

---

[65]Child Study Association of America, *Children in Wartime: Parent's Questions*, New York: Child Study Association of America, 1942, p. 9.

[66]Mio Polifroni, "Attitudes towards Children's Gun Play at Nursery School," unpublished manuscript, Pasadena, California: March 22, 1964. Mimeographed.

from dominating the world, a play theme that paralleled the evil empire theme in President Reagan's early speeches. Other companies cashed in on the trend also. Lionel Corp. made a "Commando Assault" train set. Coleco Industries marketed Rambo toys with a line that included bicycle horns shaped like hand grenades. War toys sold well throughout the 1980s. Each year, for example, G.I. Joe was among the ten best-selling toys, and by 1989 over 300 million G.I. Joe action figures, tanks, planes, and other accessories had been sold for revenues of $1.2 billion.[67]

ORGANIZED RESISTANCE TO WAR TOYS

Although the popularity of war toys remains high, there is resistance. Since Christmas 1985, there has been an international war toy boycott. Hundreds of groups have been involved, including antiwar groups such as the New England War Resister's League, groups against violence such as Action for Children's Television, and ad hoc citizens' groups such as the War Toy Disarmament Project in Vermont. Such groups have used petitions, letter writing, boycotts, lobbying, and various publicity efforts such as toy trade-ins, where toy guns are swapped for teddy bears. One group in Canada has tried to cut war toy sales by purchasing large quantities of war toys just before Christmas and then returning them in January for a refund. Another prints stickers which its members surreptitiously place on toys in retails stores. One reads: "Think before you buy. This is a war toy. Playing with it increases the tendency toward anger & violence in children. Is this what you *really* want for your child?" The greatest impact of antiwar toy groups, however, has been in passing laws prohibiting the sale of realistic-looking toy guns in several large cities and the state of California.

Criticism of war toys and the sometimes violent cartoon programs which sell them are a signal to the toy industry that parents are deeply concerned about the psychological impact of these products on children. Many parents must make a difficult choice. Should they deny war toys to children, thereby creating the allure of forbidden fruit? Or should they allow their offspring to arm themselves and thereby conform to playground trends? Toy manufacturers are determined to give parents this choice.

QUESTIONS

1 Do you favor banning war toys? Given the state of competition in the toy industry, will voluntary restraints serve to make fewer objectionable toys available? What guidelines for industry would you suggest?
2 Visit a toy store. Are there any war toys in it that offend you as a consumer or parent? Which ones?
3 Do toy companies have an ethical responsibility not to sell war toys? What measure of responsibility do parents have if children use them?

[67]Joseph Pereira, "After 25 Years, Toy Maker Enjoys Fortune of Soldier," *Wall Street Journal*, February 6, 1989, p. 1.

4 Do you think that war toys inflict psychological harm on children? Why or why not? Is televised violence an equal or greater cause of violent behavior in children?

5 Should the toy industry have anticipated the charges of critics over the past twenty-five years? How can the industry examine changes in its environment today to anticipate future criticism and prepare for it with socially responsible marketing and strategy?

6 What changing values in society today portend changed attitudes toward either war toys or other kinds of toys tomorrow?

CHAPTER
6

Institutionalizing Social Concerns in Business

The Hewlett-Packard Company (HP) is a major designer and manufacturer of more than 10,000 products and systems in computers, calculators, test equipment, medical equipment, and scientific instrumentation. In 1989 it ranked as the 33rd largest industrial corporation in the United States, with total sales of $11.9 billion and net earnings of $829 million. Slightly less than half of its business is generated outside the United States. The company employs 84,000 people.

It is corporate policy at HP "to honor our obligations to society by being an economic, intellectual, and social asset to each nation and each community in which we operate." This purpose has been institutionalized through philanthropic and employee-volunteer programs. HP is among the top half-dozen largest philanthropic donors among industrial corporations, with a total of about $50 million each year. The largest part of the company's grants program is in equipment.

The company's executive committee and foundation set broad policies for the grants program. The grants are implemented through a network of committees and individual employee initiatives at all levels in the corporation. There are four main categories of programs at HP.

Community grants are made to service agencies (e.g., health, arts, and other services) located in the immediate neighborhoods of the divisions of the company. Each division makes its own decisions about such grants through a Community Contributions Committee, in which employee membership rotates periodically. Both cash and equipment grants are made.

National grants contribute to the development of science, engineering, technology, and medicine. Programs include equipment grants to education; engineering and computer-science faculty development and faculty loan programs; science- and engineering-oriented affirmative action contributions; philanthropic underwritings of university high-technology centers; and cash and equipment grants to nationally active, nonacademic organizations in the arts and human service fields when creative bridges between the sciences and the humanities can be built. Various committees at company headquarters and in the divisions share in making decisions about these grants.

A third set of programs matches employees' philanthropic cash donations. HP matches (one to one) employee gifts to such organizations as United Way and universities. It matches three to one employee gifts of equipment to both public and private educational institutions.

Finally, HP makes direct equipment contributions and cash awards in countries in which it does business and where such donations are permitted.

Some of the financing for these programs comes from the HP foundation, and some of it is included in the annual budgets of the divisions of the company as operating expenses, not philanthropy. Most of HP's grants are to education. Indeed, HP ranks in the top three or four companies in the nation in the size of its contributions to education. In addition to equipment and cash donations, the HP programs include many voluntary employee contributions. Employees get involved with schools and colleges after a grant is made. This involvement takes many forms, such as helping teachers in the use of the equipment donated, serving on curriculum committees, and teaching. HP encourages other organizations to become involved in community-support programs. For example, the American Electronics Association recently funded a $6 million program to aid doctoral engineering candidates, following a program started by HP.

It should be added that David Packard and William Hewlett, the two founders of HP, have for years been active philanthropists. Together they have given tens of millions of dollars to educational institutions and other organizations.

Hewlett-Packard is one of many companies to show its social concern actively. In the 1970s, corporations began weaving a bright thread of social concern into the conservative tapestry of existing policy and strategy. In the late 1970s, larger corporations had formalized a variety of programs to inject social concerns in decision making. This trend has continued, and today more and more firms have institutionalized the social point of view. This chapter is concerned with important aspects of this institutionalization.

It is virtually meaningless for a company to profess being socially responsible without taking specific measures to make the policy operational. A policy of social responsibility must be institutionalized if it is to be effective. This chapter explains what institutionalization means and how corporations do it.

PATTERNS OF CORPORATE SOCIAL RESPONSES

As explained in the last chapter, the perspective of social responsibilities held by people in business evolved through a number of phases. Individual companies, of course, could and did agree or disagree with broadly held philosophical views. Today, we believe that strategies of individual companies can be classified into six dominant categories. First is *rejection*. In this stance, a company denies any obligation to engage in any responsibilities beyond obeying the law and operating economically and efficiently.

Second is the *adversary* strategy. In this stance a firm fights to avoid having to take social actions but will, under severe pressure, grudgingly give in. A good example is the battle waged by Firestone Tire & Rubber to avoid recall of its ill-starred Firestone 500 steel belted radial tires. Over a six-year period in the 1970s, the excessive failure rate of these tires led to at least thirty-four deaths, sixty injuries, and hundreds of accidents. Firestone resisted early efforts by the National Highway Traffic Safety Administration to force remedial action and ultimately had to conduct two huge recall campaigns.

Third is *defense*. In this strategy, a corporation may make token moves to satisfy demands that it assume more social responsibilities than it deems appropriate. Another aspect of this strategy is to publicize social actions taken by a company in order to ward off increasing demands for undertaking further social programs. Finally, a company may be criticized for a social program and defend itself publicly. Mobil Corporation, for example, was criticized for contributing to public action committees. It ran advertisements in newspapers around the country pointing out that the company was outraged by false accusations that this was spending shareholders' money to exert undue pressure on the workings of democratic government.

Fourth is *accommodation*. In this strategy, a firm reconciles its policies with public demands to take social actions of one kind or another. There are many nuances of this strategy. A company may, for instance, have some reluctance to pursue social programs, but does so in response to social pressures. Or a company may modify a specific social program to respond to public criticisms of the way the company is currently pursuing that program. A company might, for instance, decide to change day-care center programs, advertising that irritates some constituents, or aid to public education which may be perceived as self-interest.

Fifth is *proaction*, or the making of an anticipatory response designed to prevent criticism. For example, Monsanto Co. responded to public fear of chemicals and strict new medical and environmental tests used by government agencies by setting up a "devil's chemicals project" to examine existing products for trace contaminants of dangerous chemicals such as dioxin. It is company policy at Monsanto to assess formally possible hazards of a new substance or material at multiple stages of research and development. More companies today are creating, testing, and redesigning products to meet changing social demands.

Sixth is *management with a social conscience*. With this strategy, a company fully embraces social responsibility and formulates specific social programs that are implemented throughout the company. Many managers and companies historically adopted such a strategy. Outstanding, for example, are J. C.

Penney, Cyrus McCormick of the Harvester Company, and General Robert E. Wood of Sears, Roebuck and Company.[1]

The social programs of most companies, especially the larger ones, display an implementation of each of these strategies. Since no company can meet all the social demands made upon it without threatening bankruptcy, there are many instances where the company must say "No, this is not our responsibility." A company may be most generous in its philanthropy and reject a demand that it guarantee lifetime employment for its employees. A company may feel obliged to accede to one social pressure and not another. This is true with respect to social programs that it can voluntarily accept or reject. It is not true, of course, with respect to social programs mandated by the government.

We believe that in the years to come, the current era will be seen as one in which corporations, especially the larger ones, became increasingly anticipatory in their response to social concerns and sought actively to influence public debates about important matters affecting business. We believe also that this era will be seen as one in which businesses institutionalized more and more social programs in their operations.

EXPOSURE INFLUENCES SOCIAL PROGRAM STRATEGY

Robert Miles, in his book *Managing the Corporate Social Environment*, points out that a company's exposure to the social environment may influence its responses to social change.[2] There are four dimensions to the phenomenon of exposure.

First is product mix. If the general public, for example, considers a product to be a necessity rather than a luxury, the exposure of a company to social reactions escalates. If the product is a necessity, a company producing it must be much more concerned about such matters as availability, affordability, reliability, and safety. The product "becomes affected with a public interest." If the product or process by which it is produced involves potential hazards that might affect public health or safety, the exposure becomes that much greater.

A second dimension is customer mix. If a product is a consumer good it tends to be more exposed to social concerns than an industrial or commercial product. The producer of a diamond drill made to perform a highly specialized task in the aerospace industry, for example, is exposed to much less threat than, say, a manufacturer of an automobile. In the latter case, disgruntled consumers not only may threaten a company with a liability suit if the car does not perform as advertised, but may also ask the government to force the firm to recall the car to fix a defect.

A third dimension is geographic mix. Generally, a company selling a con-

[1] For many other examples, see Morrel Heald, *The Social Responsibility of Business: Company and Community, 1900–1960,* Cleveland: The Press of Case Western Reserve, 1970.

[2] Robert H. Miles, *Managing the Corporate Social Environment: A Grounded Theory,* Englewood Cliffs, New Jersey: Prentice-Hall, Inc., 1987.

sumer necessity in an urban area is more exposed than when the product is distributed in a rural area. One reason is that regulators in urban areas tend to be more sophisticated, have access to more information, and are better organized. Also, concentrations of consumer groups in urban settings create a greater mass of pressure than scattered consumers in rural areas. However, rural areas still have political clout in legislative bodies.

A fourth dimension is company size. Generally, other things being equal, a large company is more exposed to consumer concerns than are small companies.

WHAT DOES INSTITUTIONALIZATION MEAN?

From a societal view, as well as from the view of top managers who accept the idea of social responsibilities for their firms, it is desirable to have the social point of view institutionalized. This means that once a top social policy has been formulated, its implementation becomes a part of the day-to-day, routine decision-making processes throughout the company. Managers consider it in their decision making without continuous surveillance by higher-level managers. When an activity is not institutionalized, it is likely to be periodic, separate from the critical activities of the business, easily forgotten by busy managers, and perhaps controversial.

It is important to recall from the last chapter three types of social action programs. First are the programs pursued because of legislation, such as equal opportunity or worker safety. In this category also are programs undertaken because of contractual arrangements with labor unions, such as those concerning equitable hiring, promoting, and firing of employees. The second category includes company social programs that top management decides voluntarily to undertake. Included here would be programs initiated by managers in the organization without pressure from inside or outside. Also included would be programs undertaken as a result of pressures from groups inside or outside. In the third category are social programs undertaken by managers throughout an organization on a voluntary basis and not dictated by higher-level managers.

If a company is to avoid legal penalties for noncompliance, it must, in the case of the first class of actions, establish policies, plans, procedures, control mechanisms, and incentives to ensure that goals are achieved in conformance with law and contract. In this way, the social program is entwined in the decision-making processes of the company, from top to bottom. If this is not done and if top management does not continuously survey activities, lower-level managers may sabotage the program if they find themselves in opposition to it on value, economic, or other grounds.

Similarly, actions of the second type may not be undertaken in organizations even when policy has been announced, in the absence of implementation procedures, rewards, and penalties. The problem here is somewhat different, however, because here the motivating force results from greater top-management interest and not from any legal compulsion. Lower-level managers not in complete sympathy with the program may be more difficult to persuade than when legal sanctions are involved. This is especially true, as noted below, if social goals and manager-financial goals are in conflict.

Finally, it is even more difficult for top managers to get lower-level managers to act in the third category if they are not disposed to do so. There is a world of difference between lofty top management rhetoric at high levels of abstraction—"Olympian megathoughts," as one manager put it—and specific actions on the front lines of lower-level managers.

Because of such considerations, most companies begin the pursuit of voluntary social programs gradually and only slowly develop full-scale programs by means of which they become institutionalized in the decision-making process. Before we examine this transition, it is worthwhile to comment further about why there is resistance to institutionalizing social programs in many companies.

REALITIES IN INJECTING VOLUNTARY SOCIAL ACTION INTO THE DECISION-MAKING PROCESS

Chief executives of companies are thought to have extraordinary power to get things done in their enterprises. When asked about their power, however, they begin talking about how little power they have. President John Kennedy used to comment frequently to visitors: "I agree with you, but I cannot speak for the State Department." What he meant was that even with all the power at his command, he found it difficult to move the State Department to act as he wanted it to act. Much the same problem exists for the chief executive of a large company.

Every organization has a culture. It is composed of the styles and behavior of managers and other personnel; shared values of people in the organization ("the way we do things around here"); the policies and strategies of the organization; the skills and capabilities of personnel, from managers to workers; the composition and functioning of staffs; the structure of organizational units, such as divisions and departments; and the systems which bind operations together, such as the accounting, budgeting, and informational systems.

Top executives have an important hand in the design and operation of such a total system, but they also must operate within the culture. The power of chief executives is restrained because they know that if they force a significant change in the culture, the results may not be entirely what they want. There are serious risks in trying to change a culture quickly. This does not mean that chief executives do not have power. They do. It means that wise managers exercise their power very carefully and, if possible, gradually and with the concurrence of others in the company.

If the complex culture of a corporation has not taken social concerns into consideration in decision-making processes, the decision of top management to do so may seriously conflict with traditional ways of doing things in that company. The gap between top management's concept of needed social responsiveness and the traditional managerial processes may be broad and difficult to bridge.

There are many barriers to the implementation of social policy. Robert Ackerman, when a professor at the Harvard Business School, found that the social institutionalization of companies he studied ran into three major difficulties. First, managers believed that the separation of corporate and division responsibilities was upset. Second, the planning and control systems were inadequate to assure compliance with policy. Third, the executive performance, evaluation, and reward systems did not recognize performance in terms of social concerns.[3] There are many other sources of resistance. For example, a traditional response of many managers, when faced with pressures to do something new, is to deal with the matter in an ad hoc, fire-fighting mode on the assumption that the issue is temporary and will go away. Or managers may file any directives to take social action until such time as it is clear top management means business. Another form of resistance is to deal with such new pressures through a typical public relations effort. Some managers may hold strongly to a classical managerial ideology and have deep reservations about the responsibility of a corporation to undertake social programs not required by law. Such managers may only sluggishly comply with top management directives to undertake social programs. This by no means exhausts the list of barriers to implementing social programs, but it does illustrate grave potential problems which may exist.

A CONCEPTUAL MODEL FOR IMPLEMENTING SOCIAL STRATEGIES

The model in Figure 6-1 shows that the process of institutionalization moves through a series of phases or steps. The process begins with a growing concern of top management about a social matter that may have significant impact on the company. Top management also may wish to deal with a social issue even though it may not have a direct and important impact on the firm's operations. This is a problem-identification phase.

A second phase takes place when top management makes a commitment to action. This immediately requires the formulation of strategies and policies which are to be used in implementing the program. In this phase, of course, the issue to be addressed becomes better defined.

In a third phase, policies and plans are developed in detail through continuous dialogue among top managers, division managers, and staffs.

In a fourth phase, tactical plans are translated into specific procedures and rules and become part of the daily decision-making routine of operating personnel. This administrative learning experience should serve to eliminate problems and assure smooth implementation of company policy and plans.

In a fifth phase, the system is working satisfactorily and the strategies and policies are fully implemented.

[3] Robert Ackerman, *The Social Challenge to Business*, Cambridge, Massachusetts: Harvard University Press, 1975.

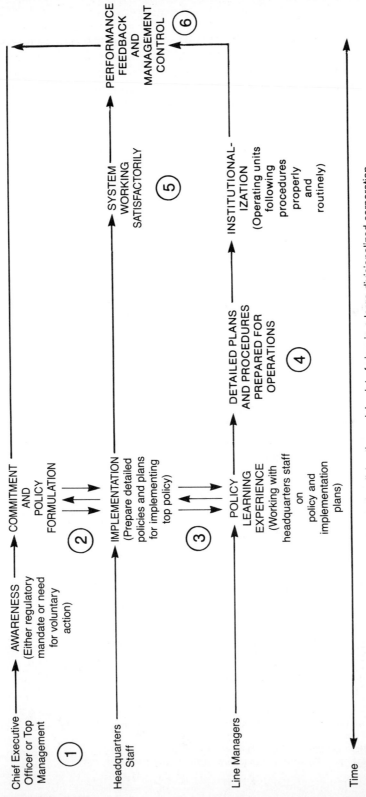

FIGURE 6-1 A conceptual model of the process of institutionalizing the social point of view in a large divisionalized corporation.

A final step is management control and performance feedback. To assure proper implementation it is necessary to employ a full range of managerial surveillance and control systems. Included would be reports to management of performance so that corrective action can be taken if needed.

As suggested by the above discussion of barriers to institutionalization, it may be necessary for the company to change the corporate culture, reorganize, or alter various systems, such as performance rewards. This can be and is done, where necessary, through the same steps noted above. If a corporation must implement a government mandated social program, that too will be institutionalized through the same conceptual steps.

This is, of course, a highly simplified model of what actually happens in a company. In the real world, this process can take years to complete satisfactorily. Two studies that made a thorough analysis of the process concluded that it took an average of eight years for the programs they studied.[4] This seems too long, but consider the time it often actually takes to overcome many barriers. It may take some time, for example, for a company to develop an effective program if it concerns a government regulation that is not clear, not fully understood, or conflicting with other actions of a company. If it is necessary for top management to change important elements of the company's culture, for example, that can be very time consuming. If organizational changes are needed, that, too, takes time to perfect. Considering the experience of the past ten years with social programs, however, the institutionalizing process should not take as long today in the typical company. Less complex social programs and those that can easily be accommodated within the usual operational systems of a company need not take much time to implement. Some, such as philanthropic programs, may be implemented virtually at once when a decision is made.

SELECTED MANAGERIAL ISSUES IN MAKING SOCIAL PROGRAMS OPERATIONAL

As we have pointed out, the institutionalization process involves all important aspects of corporate management. Space does not permit examination of all the programs that a company employs in institutionalizing social programs, and so we focus only on the most significant ones.

FORMULATING SOCIAL POLICY AND STRATEGY

The basic philosophy and frame of reference of the top management in a corporation are of importance in formulating social policy. This philosophy is generally expressed in the formulation of a company's statement of mission or in its creed. Most of our large corporations include in such statements strong objectives about social concerns. We noted Hewlett-Packard's statement at the beginning of this chapter and Johnson & Johnson's credo in the

---

[4] Edwin A. Murray, Jr., "The Social Response Process in Commercial Banks: An Empirical Investigation," *Academy of Management Review*, July 1976, and Ackerman, *op. cit.*

last chapter. Most major corporations have similar policy statements. For instance, General Motors managers carry with them a 3- by 5-inch card entitled "General Motors Guiding Principles." There are eleven principles, and the final one is: "We will participate in all societies in which we do business as a responsible and ethical citizen, dedicated to continuing social and economic progress."

TOP MANAGEMENT LEADERSHIP

When taken seriously, such policies are powerful forces in assuring that decision making will reflect social concerns throughout an organization. If top management does not express and show by action its commitment to such policies, there will be indifferent or no implementation of them in the organization. This is not an easy responsibility to discharge, for reasons noted previously. It requires constant attention and leadership by top managers, beginning with the chief executive officer. It requires, in addition, attuning the corporate culture to social concerns, making the necessary organizational changes, training and selecting managers for social concerns, relating performance measurement and reward systems to social concerns, and developing informational flows that reflect social concerns in the community and corporate actions.

CHANGING THE CORPORATE CULTURE

Institutionalizing social concerns in decision-making processes may require important alterations in the corporate culture. The CEO must take the lead in this effort. It may involve changes in all of the elements of a corporate culture that were identified above. This difficult task can be and has been done very successfully.

Donald R. Stephenson, Director of Corporate Communications at Dow Chemical Canada, Inc., describes how he and his staff went about "changing the attitudes of a lot of hard-nosed, profit-oriented management people."[5] Stephenson believed that top-level Dow managers, such as former chairman Carl Gerstacker, had socially enlightened attitudes but that these attitudes had not yet seized the hearts and minds of middle management. He and his staff put together several hundred copies of a book intriguingly entitled *Dow's Secret Weapons*, which was a collection of elevating quotations from speeches by important Dow executives and prominent scholars on subjects such as profits, relations with external groups, corporate objectives, and people development. The preface stated that the material in the book represented Dow operating philosophy.

Rather than distribute this publication widely, Stephenson planted copies with a few sympathetic managers and let word leak out that copies of the book were available, but only on request. "Lo and behold," said Stephenson,

---

[5] Donald R. Stephenson, "Crisis Situations: Opportunities in Work Clothes," *Vital Speeches*, March 1, 1983, p. 319.

"Dow's Secret Weapons became over many months a prized acquisition among hundreds of managers, its contents used in many a presentation, and the philosophies employed in hundreds of ways right down to the grass roots."[6] This is an interesting story, and undoubtedly the book had a significant influence in changing attitudes at Dow. However, much more in a company's culture may be required to alter attitudes and ways of doing things. Changing attitudes is central to making modifications throughout the culture, but it is not enough in itself. Other elements of the culture may also need to be modified.

ORGANIZATION CHANGE

Top management may decide that it is necessary to make structural changes in the company. For example, a company that is seriously concerned with social affairs may add to the board one or more directors with a broad social point of view. This is not a suggestion that such directors "represent" society but that they bring the societal view to the top decision-making level of the company.

As early as 1970, General Motors Corporation created the Public Policy Committee composed of five outside members of the GM board. The committee has no direct power, but it has been highly influential in getting social programs under way at GM. Many other companies have comparable board committees, including Ford Motor Company, IBM, Kimberly Clark, and Philip Morris.

Many companies have found it necessary to centralize the administration of social programs, particularly government programs. Generally the location is in a staff. These staffs may serve only to make policy recommendations to top management. Some prescribe detailed procedures for the divisions to follow. Creating the most effective structure and lines of authority involves, of course, organizational change.

Corporate activities associated with social programs may be spread among a number of functional and operational areas. For example, many activities concerning social programs may be undertaken in the office of public affairs. The well-developed public-affairs function encompasses the following areas: government relations, community relations, social forecasting and planning activities, corporate communications, and public-issues management. These activities deal with only one phase of the institutionalization process. They vary widely from company to company and from time to time in the same company. They also complement as well as conflict with work of other groups. Resolving such conflicts may necessitate many organizational changes.

MANAGERIAL SELECTION AND REWARDS

In interviews with top executives, the point was frequently made to the senior author that among other traditional requirements for promotion, man-

[6] *Ibid.*, p. 319.

agers must have some sensitivity to sociopolitical forces.[7] But the socially sensitive manager must be supported by an appropriate evaluation and reward system. Middle managers in corporations typically are evaluated and rewarded on the basis of short-range financial performance. Under such conditions, it is difficult to convince them that long-range trends or social concerns are relevant to job success. In addition, middle managers are at a different stage in their life cycle from top managers; they relate differently to family and community responsibilities and are perhaps more concerned than senior managers with personal career goals as opposed to broad organizational goals.

This being the case, compliance with social policy may take a back seat to achievement of quarterly goals. Some companies deal with the short-term performance myopia of middle management by making social performance part of the reward structure. For example, nonfinancial objectives may be set for minority hiring, government relations, and community involvement. Objectives are specific enough that performance can be measured. A proportion of incentive pay (say 50 percent) is given for good performance in meeting these objectives. Nonfinancial objectives differ according to the manager's job, but in the case of a plant manager, they might be heavily weighted toward environmental protection and health and safety goals. If social actions involve out-of-pocket costs, a manager's profit objectives should be adjusted accordingly.

MANAGERIAL TRAINING PROGRAMS

Companies make available to managers a variety of training programs. Rogene Buchholz surveyed companies about their educational programs with environmental or public policy content and found many different programs, including: sending managers to university seminars, conferences, and institutes that deal with public-policy matters; sending managers to advanced management programs, in which public-policy material constitutes part of the content; scheduling management retreats and seminars, some of which deal with public-policy issues; involving employees in the creation of social programs for the company; assigning employees to the company's charitable-foundation advisory committee; and inviting university faculty to speak before management groups about public issues.[8]

ENVIRONMENTAL ASSESSMENTS (EAs)

All companies evaluate their environments both formally and informally. In the larger corporations there is typically a staff or staffs to analyze rigorously the environments of concern to the company. There are four major environmental areas that are analyzed. They are, as described in Chapter 2, the eco-

---

[7] George A. Steiner, *The New CEO*, New York: Macmillan, 1983.
[8] Rogene A. Buchholz, "Education for Public Issues Management: Key Insights from a Survey of Top Practioners," *Public Affairs Review*, 1982, vol. III.

nomic, the technical, the social, and the political. Years ago, companies analyzed only their economic environment. Later, the technical environment became part of the evaluation process as managers became aware of the impact of technology developments on their affairs. More recently, corporations have added the social and political environments to their environmental evaluations as these areas became of increasing significance in the functioning of their companies. Today these total environmental analyses, especially in the larger corporations, become basic premises in the strategic planning processes. This means they are fundamental in the development of company policies, strategies, tactical operating plans, and decision making generally.

Figure 6-2 is a conceptual model of the place of environmental analyses in corporate decision making. The model refers to analyses of the four major environmental areas noted above, but our comments are directed primarily to social environmental analyses. Since we have discussed the content of the block on the left of the chart, we move to organizational responsibility for making environmental analyses.

FIGURE 6-2   Environmental analysis model.

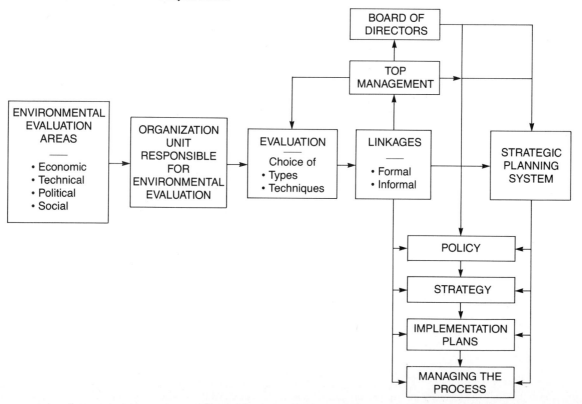

WHO MAKES THE EVALUATIONS?

Economic and technical evaluations typically are made in corporate planning units or special staff units, such as the office of the chief economist or the office of the chief scientist. Only the largest corporations have such special staffs. When a corporation evaluates the social and political environment, the public affairs department often is responsible. The typical public affairs office is deeply involved in identifying public issues for corporate attention; setting priorities for dealing with these issues; providing forecasts of social and political trends to corporate planning staff, divisions, and departments; and reviewing corporate and division plans for sensitivity to emerging social and political trends.[9] A few of our largest companies have special staffs to make these analyses.[10]

SOCIAL AND POLITICAL EVALUATION TYPES AND TECHNIQUES

The social and political evaluation of the environment proceeds, of course, from specifications of the type of evaluation to be made and techniques to be employed. Here we identify two major types: macro and functional. The latter focuses on a specific current task or future concern about a product or service of an operating unit. For example, the analysis might focus on how changing social attitudes of consumers will affect the sale, design, price, etc., of a particular product. The macro focus is concerned with broader topics, such as emerging issues that may have an impact on company strategy. These issues include the changing attitudes of people in organizations, women's rights, demands for more federal regulations of advertising, or business ethics.

The palette of analytical techniques that can be employed is large. Techniques range from purely intuitive to comprehensive, systematic, and interdisciplinary. We shall return shortly to a brief examination of the methods typically used in business in making these analyses.

COMMUNICATING RESULTS

Next in the model are linkages, the connections between the results of the analysis and managerial thinking and planning. In the chart are identified two types of linkage, formal and informal. Formal linkages are prescribed procedures for the passage and use of information. They might, for example, be incorporated as a systematic ingredient in a formal strategic planning process, or they might be a specified periodic reporting to top management. The informal linkages, as the name implies, are more casual, ad hoc passages of

[9] Public Affairs Research Group, *Public Affairs Offices and Their Functions: Summary of Survey Responses,* Boston: School of Management, Boston University, 1981.
[10] R. T. Lenz and J. L. Engledow, "Environmental Analysis Units and Strategic Decision-Making: Field Study of Selected 'Leading Edge' Corporations," *Strategic Management Journal,* January–February 1986.

information, such as communications with either top management or the corporate planning staff in informal meetings.

The chart shows that there is a linkage between top management, including the board of directors, and the strategic planning system. This linkage can take many forms, such as the establishment of policy and strategy for action in the social-political area, or discussions that may influence planning in the company. The chart also shows that top management may, in the absence of a well-formulated strategic planning process, directly establish policy and strategy for implementation.

THE STRATEGIC PLANNING SYSTEM

In most large companies, there is some type of formal strategic planning system. Formal strategic planning is, in essence, the systematic identification of opportunities and threats that lie in the future environment (external and internal) which, in combination with other relevant data (e.g., company strengths and weaknesses), provides a basis for a company's making better current decisions to exploit the perceived opportunities and to avoid the threats. It is an orderly process which, to simplify, sets forth basic objectives to be achieved, strategies and policies needed to reach the objectives, and tactical plans to make sure that strategies are properly implemented. It is a structure of plans. The structure and linkage among plans vary from company to company and from time to time in the same company. Formal strategic planning enables companies to respond in an organized way to increasingly complex market and social forces and to do so in a way that is in keeping with internal resources and managerial philosophy. When social issues are part of strategic thinking in the planning process, social responsiveness tends to be included in corporate strategy, policy, and decision making.

IMPLEMENTING SOCIAL POLICIES AND STRATEGIES

We need not dwell on the remainder of our model. We have already emphasized the fact that policy and strategy (formulated either in the planning process or in an ad hoc manner) really are useless without proper implementation.

THE MULTIPLE PURPOSES OF SOCIAL ENVIRONMENTAL ANALYSES

These analyses have many different but important purposes. As a result, there is much experimentation in the processes employed in making them, organizational arrangements for evaluating and using them, and flows of information about the evaluations. Some of the important uses of these evaluations are as follows:

• They provide mind-stretching exercises for managers and staff. This is an educational purpose but also may help to assure that managers focus on environmental matters continuously rather than sporadically, systematically rather than randomly. Some top managers believe it is their responsibility to speak out on major issues of the day. Environmental analyses provide for such managers an identification of issues to be addressed.

• They identify major threats and opportunities so that risks can be contained, crises avoided, and opportunities exploited. In this way, they are basic assumptions to aid in the formulation of company policy and strategy.

• They help managers set priorities for the development of policies and strategies.

• They also provide, of course, a context within which policies and strategies can be evaluated.

THE SCOPE AND METHODOLOGY OF ENVIRONMENTAL ANALYSES

We noted above the difference between the macro and micro, or functional, focus. Scope may also differ in breadth of analysis. Some studies may be made for a comparatively narrow range of subjects, such as demand for a specific product, consumer preferences, or interest rates. Other studies may cover the four main areas in a total comprehensive environmental analysis. The time frame also ranges from the few years ahead to well into the twenty-first century. Both the scope and time frame heavily depend on the purposes of the study.

Evaluations may be done on an irregular, regular, or continuous basis. The range of methodology used is very wide. For economic and technical analysis, for example, many qualitative and quantitative computer-based methods may be used. For analyses in which the major focus is sociopolitical and the range far into the future, the most widely used method by far is the intuitive search. The next most widely employed method is scenario construction. Other widely used techniques are systematic qualitative search, Delphi, trend analysis, cross-impact analysis, and impact/probability matrix. Any two or all of these techniques often are used in the preparation of a comprehensive scenario. Before discussing each of these methods, we should mention that nomenclature in this area varies widely, among both academicians and practitioners. For example, scenarios have been referred to as futures research, futures explorations, alternative futures, survey research, scanning, exploratory planning, and environmental forecast, among others.

Intuitive Search   This technique is used by all managers who concern themselves with the changing environment. It involves a random, unsystematic, qualitative search for information, by means of which the manager comes to conclusions about forces in the environment of concern to him or her and the company. The selection of information and its evaluation are based upon experience, judgment, insight, and "feel." When done by experienced managers who continuously survey the evolving environment, it is more powerful than any other technique.

Scenarios Scenarios are credible descriptions of the future based upon careful analysis of complex, interacting social, economic, political, and technological forces. They are not predictions of the future but disciplined and structured judgments of future possibilities. They set forth fundamental projections about anticipated trends and their outcomes. They are also designed to fit a particular set of needs of managers.

Scenarios with a social focus include the General Electric Company's formerly ongoing project for evaluating changing social values that might have affected the company in the 1980s and beyond. Another scenario was the result of the Environmental Protection Agency's commissioning the Stanford Research Institute to prepare alternative futures up to the year 2000 that would be useful in developing environmental policy planning. The Shell Oil Company recently completed a scenario concerning public, worker, and plant community attitudes toward carcinogens and cancer risks. For a number of years, this company has had a sophisticated environmental analysis program.[11]

Systematic Qualitative Search Sears, Roebuck & Co. used systematic qualitative searches to provide information for its managers. The staff assigned to make the EA maintained well over 100 categories for classifying information that bore on the company's future. The categories included population changes, income distribution, values and lifestyles, public attitudes toward corporations, employee privacy, agricultural productivity, and government regulations. The accumulation of information started with printed matter. Added to this were interviews with academic experts and knowledgeable people in business, government, and professional associations. Periodically all this information was analyzed and conclusions were drawn about major trends that were of significance to Sears managers in their decision making.

Delphi The Delphi technique is a way to distill expert opinion into a vision of the future. It works this way. A group of experts is selected, and each person is asked to express individually an opinion about the probability of a future event or events in his or her area of expertise. These projections are then shared with the other experts. Each expert then makes a prediction in a second round of statements. After several more rounds, advocates of the technique agree that the likely result is a convergence of expert opinion on the most likely predictions of a future event or situation. Originated by the Rand Corporation in the 1950s, this technique has enjoyed much popularity and success among such corporations as Du Pont, Scott Paper, AT&T, Lever Brothers, and Montana Power Company.

Trend Analysis Trend analysis is a technique to study how events may affect or move one or more trends. For example, if recent trends have shown

[11] Rene D. Zentner, "How to Evaluate the Present and Future Corporate Environment," *The Journal of Business Strategy,* Spring 1981.

a steady rise in public demands for removing carcinogens from the atmosphere, a trend analysis will study those forces which may accentuate the trends in the future, reduce the force of public demands, or continue present trends.

Cross-Impact Analysis Cross-impact analysis is a method to structure the study of how events affect each other. Because events are interelated in time, and some events do not occur unless others do (or do not), a technique such as this is used to study the relationships among events. A matrix is used to facilitate analysis. Events to be studied are listed in the vertical column, and those which will be affected by a particular event are listed horizontally. For example, assume that on the left side of the matrix, the event is "the invention of an automobile engine that will get 100 miles for every gallon of fuel." If the time horizon is 1995, a probability for the happening of this event is calculated at, say, 0.8. This calculation then is used to make a probability calculation for items listed horizontally, such as the chance that "the United States will import over 50 percent of its total consumption of oil"; "the price per barrel of crude oil will be over $20"; and "utilities will switch from gas and coal to oil." Sophisticated cross-impact models may have dozens of items for which probabilities are calculated.

PROBABILITY/IMPACT MATRIX

In this technique, events foreseen for the future are analyzed in terms of their probability and potential impact on the company. The matrix used is shown in Figure 6-3. This is a straightforward but really powerful tool. If an evaluation places an issue, likely occurrence, or trend in the upper left corner of

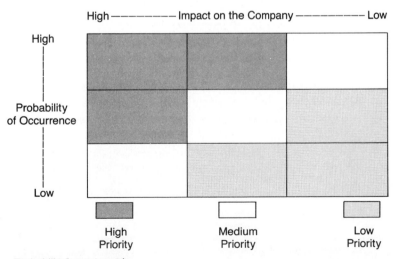

FIGURE 6-3   Probability/impact matrix.

the matrix, it should be a matter of concern to a company. If, on the other hand, an event is judged to fall in the lower righthand corner, it will be given a low priority for action. Forces falling in the medium priority areas raise questions about what action, if any, should be taken. The General Electric Company used a matrix like this for a number of years with significant results.[12]

ISSUES MANAGEMENT

The phrase "issues management" embraces a process that identifies environmental issues for management attention. There is no consensus about the definition of issues management. There is consensus, however, about one thing: it is not an issue that is managed but a company's response to it.

Issues management may be defined very narrowly by a manager as the identification of a few selected social issues which he or she is interested in tracking. The purposes may range from getting general background information to deal with local interest groups, to providing specific data for making decisions about redesigning products and improving their marketing.

Issues management may be defined broadly as the entire process of identifying a wide range of environmental issues, formulating company policy to deal with them, and implementing that policy. This process was described at length above in this chapter.

A definition of issues management resting between these two extreme views is more generally accepted. As defined in most of the literature on the subject and as practiced by business, issues management is concerned with the identification of *social* and *political* issues of importance to a company, and the formulation of appropriate company policy and procedures to deal with them. Not only has the literature on this subject grown rapidly,[13] but enough business practitioners of issues management were found in 1982 to begin a new society, the Issues Management Association.

The range, purposes, evaluation techniques, and implementation of issues management programs vary much among companies. Here are a few different approaches.

Issues management in larger corporations takes place in many organizational units with varying degrees of coordination. A chief executive, for instance, may have a special staff to identify issues for her or his purposes. For example, Reginald Jones, former CEO of General Electric, used a small staff

---

[12] For a discussion of the methodology used by General Electric see George A. and John F. Steiner, *Business, Government and Society*, 4th ed., New York: Random House, 1985, pp. 279–282.

[13] See for example Robert L. Heath, *Strategic Issues Management*, San Francisco: Josey-Bass Publishers, 1988; Steven L. Wartick, "How Issues Management Contributes to Corporate Performance," *Business Horizons*, Spring 1988; James E. Dutton and Edward Ottensmeyer, "Strategic Issues Management Systems: Forms, Functions, and Contexts," *Academy of Management Review*, April 1987; Robert L. Heath and Richard Alan Nelson, *Issues Management: Corporate Policymaking in an Information Society*, Beverly Hills: Sage Publications, 1986; and Steven L. Wartick and Robert E. Rude, "Issues Management: Corporate Fad or Function?" *California Management Review*, Fall 1986.

to identify and evaluate issues which he personally addressed in public speeches and meetings with congressional leaders and the President of the United States.

In a sense, all corporate executives are issues managers, or ought to be. Some manage marketing issues, some financial issues, some personal issues, some government regulatory issues, and so on. All managers should identify issues of particular concern to them and prepare fitting responses.

Typically, in most companies the systematic and continuous review of environmental issues takes place in such departments as Strategic Planning, Public Affairs, Government Relations, Human Resources, and Corporate Communications. Generally, the more comprehensive and longer-term evaluations are made in strategic planning departments. Social and political short-range analysis is associated more with other departments noted above.

There is no uniformity among companies in the methodology used to identify and respond to issues. Nor is there uniformity in the types of issues examined. Much depends upon interests of top managers and the linkages with other organizations in the firm.

We should note what issues management, as that phrase is generally used, is not. It is not crisis or catastrophe management. Crisis and catastrophe management deals with future events which would have great potential impact on the company if they occurred. Nor is it strategic management, as defined in Chapter 1, or strategic planning, as defined earlier in this chapter. Both are much broader in scope and purpose. Issues management, however, can and often is incorporated in both strategic planning and strategic management.[14]

The many unpleasant surprises hitting managers in the recent past—unprecedented public pressure to act on behalf of interest groups, massive increases in government regulations, and changes in the tax laws—have taught them that they cannot afford to stand idly by and not seek to understand, influence, or adapt to important social and political issues.

Issues management has various purposes among different companies, but fundamentally they are to allay tensions between the firm and society, avoid expensive surprises in the environment, cope with social change through proaction instead of isolation and resistance, and engage in meaningful participation in the creation of public policy. It is unlikely that a large, highly visible firm can comfortably exist today without an issues management program of some type.

INSTITUTIONALIZATION OF CORPORATE PHILANTHROPY

Philanthropy means the giving of money, time, products, or services to help the needy or to support institutions working to better human welfare; it is a synonym for charity. Corporations engage in philanthropy. A legacy of

---

[14] Stephen L. Wartick, "Getting the Most from Issues Management," *Strategic Planning Management*, vol. 6, no. 6, 1989. This article briefly traces the history of issues management and contrasts it with strategic planning.

America's colonial ties was the transplantation from England of the notion that part of the role of an enlightened businessperson was to make charitable contributions. As they grew, large corporations also began giving money to various causes and, over the years, this giving has become more organized and sustained. Hence, one way that social responsiveness is institutionalized in companies is through philanthropic programs.

THE LEGALITY OF CORPORATE PHILANTHROPY

During the nineteenth century and into the twentieth, courts of law held that a corporation existed only to provide profits for distribution to stockholders. Corporate giving was identified as an *ultra vires* act and therefore illegal. The first major break in this thesis came in the Revenue Act of 1935, when Congress made it possible for corporations to deduct from taxable earnings their charitable contributions, up to 5 percent of net profits before taxes. This was raised to 10 percent by the Economic Recovery Act of 1981. Most states now also have such legislation. The legal requirements that directors of corporations must exercise sound business judgment and act in a fiduciary capacity to corporate interests are not relaxed, however.

The legality of using corporate funds for purposes other than clearly charitable giving under the Revenue Act, however, continued to be very doubtful. This restraint was removed in 1953 by the *A. P. Smith* case, in which the Supreme Court refused to review a decision of the highest court in New Jersey. The board of directors of the A. P. Smith Company, manufacturers of machinery and equipment for water and gas industries, gave Princeton University $1,500 as a contribution toward its general maintenance. Questioned by the stockholders, the corporation sought a declatory judgment asking that its action be sustained. The New Jersey Supreme Court, in affirming a lower court decision, said:

> The contribution here in question is toward a cause which is intimately tied into the preservation of American business and the American way of life. Such giving may be called an incidental power, but when it is considered in its essential character, it may well be regarded as a major, though unwritten, corporate power. It is even more than that. In the Court's view of the case, it amounts to a solemn duty.[15]

WHY GIVE?

As pointed out in the last chapter and chronicled by many historians, businesspeople and their companies have a long history of philanthropy. There are many reasons which for convenience we attribute to social responsibility. But that is an umbrella for a cluster of motives. In a survey of top corporate managers, the following were given as reasons for making contributions (in descending order of numbers of executives identifying motives):

[15] *A. P. Smith Manufacturing Company v. Barlow et al.*, 26 N. J. Super. 106 (1953), 98 Atl.— (1982).

- Practice good corporate citizenship.
- Protect and improve environment in which to live, work, and do business.
- Benefit company employees in communities in which they live.
- Public relations value. Enhance company image.
- Preserve a pluralistic society by maintaining choices between government and private sector alternatives.
- Interests of directors or senior officers in particular causes.
- Pressure from business peers, customers, and/or suppliers.
- Practice altruism with little or no direct or indirect company self-interest.
- Increase the pool of trained manpower or untrained manpower or access to minority recruiting.[16]

Most corporate officers view philanthropy as enlightened self-interest. C. C. Gavin, Jr., when chairman of Exxon, expressed the thought succinctly yet precisely in these words: "Business does best in communities that are healthy, alive and secure. To stay in business, we have to make a profit. To succeed in business, we have to share some of that profit for the public good."[17] His company, as noted in Chapter 1, is one of the largest philanthropic donors in the United States.

PHILANTHROPIC ALLOCATIONS

Overall corporate giving rose from $2.4 billion in 1980 to $4 billion in 1987, a large sum. Still, it is far less than the charitable contributions of individuals, who gave over $70 billion in 1987. In fact, corporate charity is only about 5 percent of all charitable giving in the country each year. Business contributions cannot be expected to offset cuts in social programs stemming from deep federal budget cuts. In 1987, the corporate charitable-contributions pie was divided as follows: education, 36.8 percent; health and human services, 27.2 percent; civic and community activities, 14.2 percent; culture and art, 10.8 percent; and all other, 11 percent.[18] In addition, as noted previously, corporations contribute the time of their employees and various products and services.

In most corporations, the process of making charitable contributions is managed by public affairs or public relations departments. A small number of companies have established separate foundations to make gifts. Often the contribution process is not very systematic. A single staff person may control the contributions budget. Individuals, groups, and causes may submit proposals for corporate funding to this staff person, who may make donation

---

[16] James F. Harris and Anne Klepper, *Corporate Philanthropic Public Service Activities,* New York: The Conference Board, 1981.

[17] C. C. Gavin, Jr., "Exxon Chairman Urges More Formal Corporate Giving Programs," *Management Review,* April 1982, p. 34.

[18] Linda Cardillo Platzer and Maureen Nevin Duffy, *Survey of Corporate Contributions, 1989 Edition,* New York: The Conference Board, Inc., 1989.

decisions in conjunction with a contributions committee. There may be few criteria for giving and little follow-up to see how the donation has been used.

RELATING PHILANTHROPY TO THE BOTTOM LINE

As demands on corporations mount, the requests are facing more rigorous analysis on merit and benefits to the donor. There are many ways in which charity may profit a company, but none so direct as when marketing activities are combined with social programs. In recent years, a small number of firms have experimentally linked charity with product sales, while many others have watched with interest to gauge public reaction. For example, General Foods tried to attract the attention of mothers by donating 10 cents to Mothers Against Drunk Driving for every Tang coupon redeemed. General Foods also donated 50 cents to the maintenance of national park trails for every Post Natural Raisin Bran boxtop mailed in because it perceived a connection between this cause and the psychological profile of targeted buyers.

A pioneer in cause-related marketing is American Express, which for years has mixed philanthropy with its mainstream credit-card business. In 1983, it began a program of trimonthly donations to the Atlanta Arts Council based on the frequency and type of card used in the Atlanta area. It contributed 5 cents for each card transaction, $2 for each new card issued, and $5 each time travel arrangements exceeding $500 were made with the card. In a similar campaign, the company raised a $1.7 million contribution to the restoration of the Statue of Liberty. Another campaign, called "Project Hometown America," raised money for local organizations throughout the country which had demonstrated an "innovative approach to solving a pressing local human problem."

Marketing campaigns such as these must be carefully presented to the public. People may see them either as a method for carrying out corporate social obligations or as a crass marketing tool. What, for example, would be the public reaction to a brewery that contributed $1 to a rehabilitation center for alcoholic teenagers with each six-pack sold?

If cause-related marketing programs are generally successful, corporations may tend to support social programs that lend themselves to sales campaigns. These programs, picked from an array of contenders, may or may not be the most worthy. Such innovations illustrate that social responsibility can be tied to competitive, profit-oriented behavior. But so far, these programs have not made much money, because the expense of advertising them usually exceeds the revenue they generate.

There are many other ways to tie charity to the bottom line.[19] A company may sponsor special events in the community, such as sports, concerts, festivals, art shows, and educational events. Highly visible gifts to a museum or

---

[19] Timothy S. Mescan and Donn J. Tilson, "Corporate Philanthropy: A Strategic Approach to the Bottom-Line," *California Management Review*, Winter 1987.

educational institution, for example, are forms of promotion which enhance the image of a company.

From time to time business leaders have organized to bring about major improvements in the communities in which they live. This has occurred in such cities as Boston, Philadelphia, Los Angeles, and Pittsburgh. Turn now to what happened in Cleveland.

HOW CLEVELAND'S BUSINESS EXECUTIVES REVIVED THE CITY

In the late 1970s and early 1980s, the city of Cleveland was a basket case. Its political, economic, and social framework was falling apart. Its mayors in this period were inept and incompetent. City services were a shambles and its bonds were in default. Its economy was in distress as it saw its heavy industries—automobile parts, steel, and iron ore—decline sharply. Unemployment, which was 4.7 percent in 1978, reached 11.3 percent in 1983, and labor-management relations were angry. The inner city areas were seething with discontent and suffered the scars of wild rioting in the late 1960s.

E. Mandell de Windt, the now retired CEO of Eaton Corp., began to organize business executives to do something about the situation. The business community had for years been active in supporting the city. The focus, however, was on the art museum, the Cleveland orchestra, and charities. It was not on a broad range of civic affairs. This was changed with the creation of several groups of business executives. Cleveland Tomorrow was formed in 1982 by a group of fifty CEOs to concentrate on the broad range of civic problems. The concern of the group with the town's labor relations led to the establishment of the Work in Northeast Ohio Council. Meanwhile, the Greater Cleveland Roundtable was formed to foster better labor-management relations. It was composed of CEOs, heads of labor unions, and political leaders.

As a result of the activities of these groups and the spirit which they stimulated throughout the city, Cleveland today is a vibrant and thriving city. One of the first things done by the Cleveland Tomorrow group was to induce the then-Lieutenant Governor George Voinovich to run for mayor. He ran and won, and changed the political climate. Voinovich got ninety executives to help him improve the administration of the city. This group, with the help of management consultants, made over 650 proposals for reform, ranging from a new financial system to contracting out some city services. Voinovich adopted about 500 of the suggestions, thereby saving the city millions of dollars and strengthening city administration.

Cleveland Tomorrow spurred business to stay in Cleveland instead of leave, as a few did, and to reenergize plans to modernize and expand. In this effort it mobilized the resources of local universities and colleges. In 1984, the group set up a $30 million venture capital fund. It sparked the development of a cooperative self-help program among small businesses. Labor-management relations improved significantly and the unemployment rate fell to around 5.5 percent, the national rate.

The construction of housing for the poor has expanded and the downtown area of the city has been transformed. Funds have been allocated to help disaffected students and hiring preference is given by companies to graduates of Cleveland high schools, to keep students in school.[20]

CORPORATE SOCIAL REPORTING AND THE SOCIAL AUDIT

In the early 1970s, considerable pressure was put on corporations to make and publicize social audits. The movement represented an acceptance of the idea that corporations were accountable to the public for their social activities and programs.

The business social audit is a report of social performance, in contrast to the financial audit, which is concerned with economic performance. There are two fundamentally different types of social audits. One is required by the government. A large corporation, for example, must report to the government about many programs, such as tests of flammable textiles (FTC), performance in meeting pollution standards (EPA), and minority employment (EEOC). The second type of audit is for programs voluntarily undertaken by a company. Virtually all audits of voluntary programs are of the inventory type, that is, a general description of what a company has done.

Many corporations add a section to their annual report to stockholders that discusses their social programs. Some publish separate reports. These range from public relations statements to thoroughly researched, illuminating reports. A good example of the latter is the annual report of the General Motors Corporation, entitled *Report on Progress in Areas of Public Concern.*

A study of 284 corporations (mostly larger companies) in 1973 showed that 76 percent said that they had made a social audit.[21] Since then, pressure on corporations to make social audits has declined. Part of the reason is that government regulation and reporting requirements have led to increased corporate disclosure of the social actions that concern the public.

Many corporations today continue to prepare and disseminate periodic reports on their voluntarily assumed social programs. But the reports usually are not complete and, with few exceptions, seem to be more cosmetic than accountability reports. The idea, however, is not dead. It has surfaced periodically ever since it was first proposed in the 1940s. It is likely that some time in the future, public pressure will again build for it.[22]

---

[20] This is based upon Myron Magnet, "How Business Bosses Saved a Sick City," *Fortune,* March 27, 1989.

[21] John J. Corson and George A. Steiner, *Measuring Business's Social Performance: The Corporate Social Audit,* New York: Committee for Economic Development, 1974.

[22] For two recent studies on the subject see Richard E. Wokutch and Liam Fahey, "A Value Explicit Approach for Evaluating Corporate Social Performance," *Journal of Accounting and Public Policy,* Fall 1986; and Gregory D. Upah and Richard E. Wokutch, "Assessing Social Impacts of New Products: An Attempt to Operationalize the Macromarketing Concept," *Journal of Public Policy & Marketing,* vol. 4, pp. 166–178.

CONCLUDING COMMENT

The demands that corporations, especially the larger ones, continue to expand their efforts to help society achieve its economic and social objectives are strong, growing, and not likely to diminish. To meet these demands in an appropriate fashion, corporations will continue to perfect the institutionalization of the social point of view in their decision-making processes.

The Union Carbide Corporation and Bhopal: A Case Study of Management Responsibility

On December 3, 1984, operations went awry at a Union Carbide pesticide plant in Bhopal, India. Rapidly, a sequence of safety procedures and devices failed. Fugitive, lethal vapors crossed the plant boundaries, killing 2,347 and seriously injuring 30,000 to 40,000 more.

The gas leak has been called the worst industrial disaster ever. It created enormous pressures on the Indian government and the management of Union Carbide. Industry critics were galvanized. "Like Auschwitz and Hiroshima," said one, "the catastrophe at Bhopal is a manifestation of something fundamentally wrong in our stewardship of the earth."[23]

UNION CARBIDE BEFORE BHOPAL

In 1984, the year of the tragic events in Bhopal, Union Carbide was the nation's thirty-fifth-largest industrial corporation. The giant firm, founded in 1886, had grown from a small dry-cell battery company into the nation's third-largest chemical producer, with a net profit of $199 million on $9.5 billion in sales. It employed 98,366 "Carbiders" at 500 facilities in thirty-seven countries, and foreign sales were 31 percent of total sales. The company had a variety of product lines, including petrochemicals, industrial gases, welding equipment, and popular consumer products such as Prestone antifreeze, Eveready batteries, Glad bags, and Simoniz wax.

Although the third-largest U.S. chemical producer, Carbide ranked only sixteenth in profitability. Its petrochemical sales were 28 percent of total sales in 1984 but only 23 percent of operating profits; Carbide, a low-cost producer of petrochemicals such as ethylene, had been slow to divert its resources to more profitable business lines. To make matters worse, the entire chemical

[23] David Weir, *The Bhopal Syndrome*, San Francisco: Sierra Club Books, 1987, p. xii.

industry was in a three-year slump. And new Saudi Arabian petrochemical plants were scheduled to come on-line in 1985 and 1986. Chemical companies worldwide faced formidable competition from those Saudi plants, which had access to low-cost crude oil, the primary raw material in petrochemical production. In anticipation of Saudi production, chemical manufacturers the world over were reducing capacity. Hence, by 1984, Carbide's strategy was to emphasize growth segments in its other operating divisions.

Union Carbide had a reputation as a socially and environmentally concerned company; a 1983 *Fortune* magazine survey ranked Carbide in the upper half of the chemical industry for environmental responsibility. In 1977, Carbide added Russell E. Train, former head of the EPA, to its board of directors and, shortly thereafter, set up a corporate department of health, safety, and environmental affairs.

UNION CARBIDE'S BHOPAL PLANT

Union Carbide first incorporated in India in 1934 to make batteries. It operates through an Indian subsidiary in which it owns a 50.9 percent majority interest, and Indian investors own a 49.1 percent minority interest. Among Indian investors, the Indian government predominates; it owns roughly half the 49.1 percent minority interest. This jointly owned subsidiary, named Union Carbide India Ltd. (UCIL), trades its shares on the Bombay Stock Exchange and is operated entirely by Indians. In 1984, UCIL had fourteen plants and 9,000 employees, including 120 at the Bhopal plant in central India. Although UCIL contributed less than 2 percent to Carbide's revenues, it was the fifteenth-largest in sales among all Indian companies in 1984. Most of its revenues came from sales of Eveready batteries.

Union Carbide elected to build a pesticide plant in Bhopal in 1969. At that time, there was a growing demand in India and throughout Asia for pesticides, due to the burgeoning "green revolution," a type of planned agriculture that requires intensive use of pesticides and fertilizers in the cultivation of special strains of food crops such as wheat, rice, and corn. Although pesticides may be misused and pose some risk, they also have great social value. Without pesticides, damage to crops, losses in food storage, and toxic mold growth in food supplies would cause the loss of many lives from starvation and food poisoning in developing countries such as India. It has been estimated that pesticide use increases India's annual crop yield by about 10 percent—enough to feed roughly 70 million people. In India, about half the nation's population of 750 million lives below a minimum caloric intake established as a poverty line by the government. An overall assessment of mortality risk would conclude that an Indian citizen is far more likely to die of starvation than of pesticide poisoning or a Bhopal-type disaster.

In the early 1970s, the small Bhopal plant formulated pesticides from chemical ingredients imported to the site. The plant was encouraged by the government of the city of Bhopal and the state of Madhya Pradesh with tax incentives. In 1975, however, UCIL was pressured by the Indian government to stop importing chemical ingredients. The company proposed, therefore, to manufacture methyl isocyanate (MIC) at the plant rather than ship it in from Carbide facilities outside the country. This was a fateful decision.

Methyl isocyanate, CH_3NCO, is a colorless liquid with a sharp odor. At the Bhopal plant it was used as an intermediate chemical in pesticide manufacture. It was not the final product. Rather, MIC molecules were created and then pumped into a vessel to react with other synthetic organic chemicals. The reaction process created uniquely shaped molecules that interfere with the natural chemistry of insect nervous systems and thus act as chemical weapons within pests. The two pesticides made by an MIC reaction process at Bhopal, with the trade names Sevin and Temik, are carbamate pesticides that disable a critical enzyme in the nervous systems of pests, leading to convulsions and deaths.

In 1975, Carbide received a permit from the Ministry of Industry in New Delhi to build a methyl isocyanate unit at the Bhopal plant. Two months prior to approval of this permit, the city of Bhopal enacted a development plan that required relocation of dangerous industries to an industrial zone fifteen miles outside the city. Pursuant to the plan, M. N. Buch, the Bhopal city administrator, tried to relocate the UCIL pesticide plant and convert the site to use for housing and light commercial activity. This effort failed for reasons that are unclear, and Buch was shortly thereafter transferred to forestry duties elsewhere.

Between 1975 and 1980, the MIC unit was constructed from a design package provided by Union Carbide's engineering group in the United States. Detailed design work was done by an Indian subsidiary of a British firm. The unit was built by local labor using Indian equipment and materials. The reason for such heavy Indian involvement with the plant was an Indian law, the Foreign Exchange Regulation Act of 1973, which requires foreign multinationals to share technology and use Indian resources.

In 1980, the project was finished, and the MIC unit began operation. During construction, large, unplanned slums and shantytowns called *jhuggis* had grown up near the plant, peopled mainly by manual laborers and unemployed people seeking work. Of course, the plant had become far more dangerous, for it now manufactured the basic chemical ingredients of pesticides rather than simply making them from shipped-in ingredients. One step in the manufacture of MIC, for example, involves the production of phosgene, the lethal "mustard gas" used in World War I. The slum dwellers outside the plant had little knowledge of its dangers. It was simplistically understood that its product was a kind of mysterious yet benevolent elixir that helped plants grow.

In 1981, a phosgene gas leak at the Bhopal plant killed one worker, and a crusading Indian journalist wrote a series of articles about the plant and its potential dangers to the population. No one took any action. In 1982, a second phosgene leak forced temporary evacuation of some surrounding slum areas. Also in 1982, a safety survey of the plant by three Carbide engineers from the United States cited approximately fifty safety defects, most of them minor, and noted "no situation involving imminent danger or requiring immediate correction."[24] Subsequently, all suggested changes in safety systems and procedures were made (except one troublesome valve outside the accident area). Worker safety and environmental inspections of the plant were carried out by the Department of Labor in Madhya Pradesh. The agency had only fifteen factory inspectors to cover 8,000 plants and had a record of lax enforcement.[25] This was typical of the generally low commitment to pollution control in India by regulators at all levels.

A recent downturn in the Indian economy and stiff competition from other pesticide firms marketing new, less expensive products soon caused the Bhopal plant to lose money for three years in a row. As revenues fell, its budgets were cut, and it was necessary to defer some maintenance, lessen the rigor of training programs, and lay off some workers. At the time of the accident, the MIC unit was operating with a reduced crew of six workers per shift rather than the normal twelve—a condition some process-design engineers thought unsafe.

UNION CARBIDE'S RELATIONSHIP WITH THE BHOPAL PLANT

The Bhopal pesticide plant fit into the Union Carbide management hierarchy as depicted in the organization chart in Exhibit 6-1. Although some Americans had staffed the plant and had conducted safety inspections in its early years, Carbide turned the plant completely over to Indian personnel after 1982. It did so under Indian government pressure to increase national self-sufficiency. Plant safety inspections after 1982 were the responsibility of the Indian subsidiary, UCIL. At the time of the accident, therefore, line responsibility for the day-to-day operations and safety of the plant rested with the plant manager, an Indian employee of UCIL. The plant operated with a great deal of autonomy. But Union Carbide had majority ownership of UCIL and, in addition, was represented by five members on the UCIL board of directors, four from Union Carbide Eastern, Inc., and the fifth from the international headquarters group. The Bhopal plant was also in close contact with the management of Union Carbide Agricultural Products Company, Inc., which was Carbide's arm for the production and marketing of pesticides.

Top management at Union Carbide's Danbury, Connecticut, headquarters received monthly reports from the Bhopal plant and approved major financial, maintenance, and personnel decisions. Carbide engineers also provided UCIL and the Bhopal plant with the processing manual on MIC that was supposed to guide plant operations.

In the reporting relationship, Union Carbide's top management in Connecticut had ultimate, formal responsibility for the operation of the Bhopal plant. Shortly after the accident, Chairman Warren M. Anderson stated in

[24] L. A. Kail, J. M. Poulson, and C. S. Tyson, *Operational Safety Survey, CO/MIC/Sevin Units, Union Carbide India Ltd., Bhopal Plant,* South Charleston, West Virginia: Union Carbide Corporation, July 28, 1982, p. 1.

[25] Sheila Jasanoff, "Managing India's Environment," *Environment,* October 1986, p. 33.

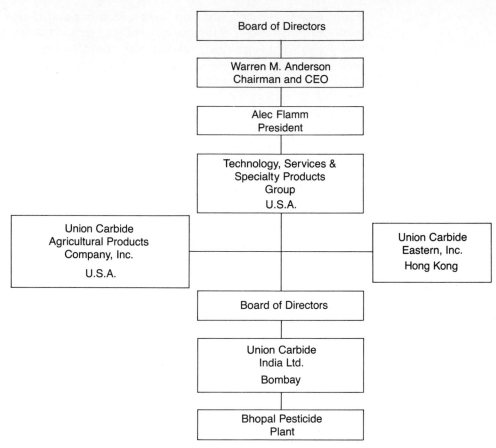

EXHIBIT 6-1   Union Carbide's organization structure as related to the Bhopal plant.

interviews that Carbide accepted "moral responsibility" for the tragedy. Nevertheless, the Bhopal plant was but one of hundreds of sites worldwide in which the company had an equity interest. For this reason, and because of the vast physical distances separating the two sites, Carbide's U.S. management team delegated considerable authority over operations to UCIL's management team on the spot. The exact nature of this shared authority remains unclear, since the gas victims' claims have never come to trial.

THE GAS LEAK

On the evening of December 2, storage tank 610, one of three storage tanks at the MIC unit, was filled with 11,290 gallons of MIC. The tank, which had a capacity of 15,000 gallons, was a partly buried, stainless steel, pressurized vessel. The purpose of Tank 610 was to store large batches of MIC. MIC was produced elsewhere at the plant and routed through pipes into Tank 610. At an appropriate time, operators in a control room would open and close valves to move one-ton batches of MIC through a transfer pipe to the area where pesticides were made.[26] The MIC would then be converted to Sevin (or Temik).

At about 9:30 p.m., a supervisor ordered R. Khan, an operator in the MIC complex, to unclog four filter valves near the MIC production area by washing them out with water. Khan connected a water hose to the piping above the clogged valves, but neglected to insert a slip blind above the point of water entry. A slip blind is a simple device that seals lines to prevent water leakage into adjacent pipes. Khan's omission violated instructions in the MIC processing manual, the technical manual which sets forth procedure established by the chemical engineers who set up the plant.

Either because of this careless washing procedure or the introduction of water elsewhere, 120 to 240 gallons of water entered Tank 610, initiating a powerful exothermic (heat building) reaction. Initially, operators were unaware that the reaction was proceeding that night. At 10:30 p.m., tank pressure was logged at 2 pounds per square inch. Then, at 10:45, a new shift came on duty. At 11:30 p.m., a new operator in the MIC control room noticed that the pressure in Tank 610 was 10 pounds per square inch, but was unconcerned because this was within tolerable limits, the gauges were often wrong, and he did not read the log to discover that pressure was five times greater than it had been one hour earlier.

As the reaction continued, the temperature in Tank 610 rose. Unfortunately, the refrigeration units that cooled the tanks had been shut down for five months as an economy measure. Had the tanks been refrigerated, as the MIC processing manual required, the heat buildup from the reaction with the water might have taken place over several days instead of several hours.

As pressure built in the tank, a leak developed. At about 11:30, workers smelled MIC, and their eyes watered. At 11:45, one operator spotted a small, yellowish drip of MIC from some high piping and informed his supervisor. The supervisor suggested fixing the leak after a tea break scheduled for 12:15 a.m. on December 3.

At 12:40, the tea break ended. But by this time a gauge in the control room showed that the pressure in Tank 610 was 40 pounds per square inch. It rose in a short time to 55 pounds per square inch, the top of the scale. A glance at the tank temperature gauge brought more bad news: the MIC was vaporizing at 77° F, 36° higher than the safety limit specified in the MIC processing manual. After reading the gauges, an operator ran out to look at Tank 610. He felt heat radiating from the tank and heard the concrete over it cracking. Within

---

[26] Some other companies used a different production process to make carbamate pesticides in which MIC was manufactured in small amounts and then immediately reacted to produce the pesticide. The advantage? Storage of large batches of MIC was unnecessary. After the accident, Carbide was criticized for using a production process that required storage of tens of thousands of gallons of MIC for long periods. Some process chemists thought it particularly inappropriate to use the method in a less developed country lacking experience with high-risk production technologies.

seconds, a pressure-release valve opened, and a white cloud of deadly MIC vapor shot into the atmosphere with a high-decibel screech.

Operators back in the control room turned a switch to activate the vent gas scrubber, a safety device designed to neutralize any escaped toxic gases from the MIC unit by circulating them through a caustic soda solution. The scrubber, however, failed to operate because it was down for maintenance. Subsequent investigation established that even if the scrubber had been on-line, it was not designed to handle the temperature and pressure reached by the MIC in the tank and would have been quickly overwhelmed. A flare tower designed to burn off toxic gases before they escaped into the atmosphere was also off-line; it had been disassembled for maintenance, and an elbow joint was missing. Another emergency measure, the transferring of MIC from Tank 610 to one of two other storage tanks, was impossible, because both of those tanks were full or nearly so. This situation also violated procedure in the MIC processing manual, which called for leaving one tank empty as a safety measure.

EXHIBIT 6-2   The tank storage area and safety equipment in Bhopal. Unfortunately, the refrigeration unit was off, and the vent gas scrubber, flare tower, and water spray failed to prevent disaster. The service drop in the lower left corner is a possible source of the water that caused the reaction. (Courtesy of Union Carbide.)

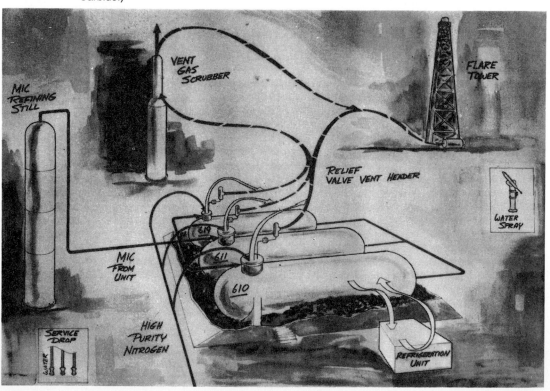

At about 1:00 a.m., an operator turned on an alarm to warn workers of danger from escaping gas. The plant superintendent, who had arrived in the control room, directed that a water spray be turned on the escaping MIC vapor to knock it down, but this had little effect. At this time, most workers in the plant ran in panic, ignoring four parked buses, which they were supposed to drive through the surrounding area to begin evacuation of residents. Only two workers stayed in the MIC control room. They shared the only available oxygen mask when the room filled with MIC vapor. Finally, at about 2:30 a.m., the pressure in the tank dropped, the leaking safety valve resealed, and the MIC leak stopped.

Over a two-hour period, roughly 10,000 gallons or about 90 percent of the MIC in Tank 610, vaporized and blew out in a white cloud. The cloud spread for miles across the sleeping city. That night the wind was calm, the temperature about 60°, and the heavy chemical mist lingered just above the ground. The gas attacked people in the streets and seeped into their homes. Those who panicked and ran into the night air suffered higher doses of toxic vapor. Because MIC is so reactive with water, simply breathing through a wet cloth would have saved many lives. But people lacked this simple knowledge. Animals died. Trees were stripped of leaves. Crowds of Bhopal residents fled the city. As the poisonous cloud enveloped victims, MIC reacted with water in their eyes. This reaction created heat which burned corneal cells, rendering them opaque. Residents with cloudy, burning eyes staggered into aid stations, permanently or temporarily blind.

Many victims suffered shortness of breath, coughing fits, inflammation of the respiratory tract, and chemical pneumonia. In the lungs, MIC molecules reacted with moist tissues, causing chemical burns. Fluid oozed from seared lung tissue and pooled, a condition called pulmonary edema, and many victims literally drowned in their own secretions. When they did not suffocate from edema, chemical burns destroyed cells that facilitate the exchange of gases in breathing and the clearing of foreign matter from the lungs. In survivors, the burned tissue eventually healed over with a tough protein substance called fibrin, which created areas of pulmonary fibrosis that diminished breathing capacity.

There is no known antidote for MIC exposure. Treatment consisted of administration of oxygen, mechanical ventilation of the lungs, the use of diuretics to maintain fluid balance, and the short-term use of steroids to decrease lung inflammation. Unfortunately, many residents of the slums around the plant were already in poor health from living in poverty and suffered from malnutrition, tuberculosis, and a variety of infections. These chronic conditions worsened the effects of MIC injury.

How many died at Bhopal? The Indian government issued 1,450 death certificates, but many families built funeral pyres without consulting local authorities. The local police department estimated 1,900 deaths. Bhopal's mayor said 3,000. Other Indian officials suggested a toll as high as 7,000 to 10,000. Finally, in November 1986, the Indian government established an official death toll of 2,347. About 200,000 of Bhopal's roughly 700,000 residents were exposed to the gas, and the government estimates that 30,000 to 40,000 were seriously injured.[27] Victims continue to die in hospitals from gas-related injuries long after exposure, and visitors to Bhopal describe sounds of coughing and wheezing wherever people congregate.

UNION CARBIDE REACTS

Unprecedented management problems faced Warren M. Anderson, age sixty-three, chairman and CEO of Union Carbide. Awakened early in the morning on Monday, December 3, he rushed to Carbide's Danbury, Connecticut, headquarters and learned of the rising death toll. In the early morning hours, when the extent of the disaster was evident, an emergency meeting of a senior management committee was held. The committee sent emergency medical supplies, respirators, oxygen (Carbide products), and an American doctor with extensive knowledge of MIC to Bhopal.

The next day, Tuesday, December 4, Carbide dispatched a team of technical experts to examine the plant. Production of MIC was halted immediately at Carbide's plant in Institute, West Virginia. Staff members were pulled from other duties to work in corporate communications and return phone calls. On Thursday, Anderson himself departed for India. He went both as a symbol of top-level commitment and as an on-the-scene crisis manager. Only two phone lines into Bhopal were working, and it was difficult to get information in Danbury about events there. Upon arriving in Bhopal, Anderson was arrested, charged with criminal negligence, briefly detained in the guest house at the Bhopal plant, flown to New Delhi, and then asked to leave the country.

With worldwide attention focused on Bhopal, Carbide held daily press conferences. It released copies of the 1982 safety inspection of the Bhopal plant. Anderson made two videotapes telling employees to bear up, and 500 copies of each were dispatched to plants around the world. Christmas parties were canceled. Flags at Carbide facilities were flown at half-mast. All of Carbide's nearly 100,000 employees observed a moment of silence for the victims. Many employees contributed to a relief fund. Carbide gave $1 million to an emergency relief fund and offered to turn its guest house in Bhopal into an orphanage. Months later, Carbide offered another $5 million to the state of Madhya Pradesh, but the money was refused because Indian politicians thought they would appear to be in collusion with the company. The political

---

[27] Many Bhopal residents have reported injuries other than to the respiratory tract and eyes, including ulcers, colitis, memory loss, hysteria, and birth defects. See Mark Fineman, "Bhopal—Death Won't Leave City," *Los Angeles Times,* March 13, 1989. But there is no evidence that MIC had other target organs and animal tests show minimal or no effects on fertility, reproduction, and immune defense mechanisms. See, for example, Ernest E. McConnell *et. al.,* "Toxicity of Methyl Isocyanate," *Environmental Science and Technology,* vol. 21, no. 2, 1987. Hence, reports of excessive numbers of birth defects among Bhopal residents are suspect. Psychological problems such as depression are common and evidence suggests that MIC impairment of the lungs is not reversible. Death and injury tolls continued to mount after 1984. In 1989, the Indian government published an official death toll of 3,415 and said 60,000 living victims were seriously impaired.

climate was so hostile that anything associated with Carbide was reviled. Later, when the government discovered that Union Carbide had set up a training school for the unemployed in Bhopal, the facility was bulldozed.

In the days following the disaster, Anderson assumed responsibility for management problems related to Bhopal. Alec Flamm, president and chief operating officer of Carbide, assumed responsibility for normal business operations. A five-member board of directors' committee, chaired by former EPA head Russell E. Train, was set up to oversee Bhopal-related actions.

Investor confidence in Carbide was shaken. Carbide's stock fell from about $49 at the time of the disaster to a low of $32.75. As lawsuits were filed on behalf of the victims, with a potential payout exceeding Carbide's net worth, Standard & Poor's, a rater of securities, lowered Carbide's debt rating, an action that made it more difficult and costly for the company to raise money. Anderson, as spokesperson for Carbide, had to undertake the delicate task of assuring investors that the company would continue to make profits while appearing not to show callous disregard for the human tragedy in Bhopal.

CARBIDE FIGHTS LAWSUITS AND A TAKEOVER BID

No sooner had the MIC vapor cleared than American attorneys arrived in Bhopal seeking litigants for damage claims against Union Carbide. They walked the streets signing up plaintiffs. Some confused gas victims signed up with more than one attorney. Just four days after the gas leak the first suit was filed in a U.S. court; soon cases seeking $50 billion in damages for 200,000 Indians were filed against Carbide.

But soon after these filings the Indian Parliament passed a law giving the Indian government the exclusive right to represent victims.[28] A week later India filed a suit in the United States. Union Carbide offered $350 million to settle existing claims (an offer rejected by the Indian government) and brought a motion to have the cases heard in India. Both Indian and American lawyers claiming to represent victims opposed the motion, knowing that wrongful death awards in India were small compared to those in the U.S.[29] In May 1985, a federal court ruled that the cases should be heard in India rather than in the U.S., noting that "to retain the litigation in [the U.S.]...would be yet another example of imperialism, another situation in which an established sovereign inflicted its rules, its standards and values on

[28] Indian Parliament Act No. 21 of 1985, *entered into force* Feb. 20, 1985, GAZETTE OF INDIA (EXTRAORDINARY), pt. 2, sec. 2, March 29, 1985.

[29] Indian courts rarely awarded more than $10,000 for a wrongful death, and families of Indians killed by buses usually received $100–$200. By contrast, in U.S. courts there have been hundreds of awards exceeding $1 million. James Flanigan, "Bhopal a Hard Lesson in Value of Safety Rules," *Los Angeles Times*, February 15, 1989. There had never been a wrongful death judgment in India greater than $40,000. R. Clayton Trotter, Susan G. Day, and Amy E. Love, "Bhopal, India and Union Carbide: The Second Tragedy," *Journal of Business Ethics*, June 1989, p. 447.

a developing nation."[30] This was a victory for Carbide and a defeat for American lawyers, who could not carry their cases to India in defiance of the government.

In September 1986, the Indian government filed a $3.3 billion civil suit against Carbide in the Indian court system. The suit alleged that Carbide, while engaged in the hazardous act of making pesticides, had breached duties to (a) protect the environment, (b) protect human life, (c) utilize effective safety practices, and (d) disclose the full risks of the Bhopal plant. The suit was brought only against Union Carbide Corporation, U.S.A., not against Union Carbide India Ltd., the Indian subsidiary. It was based on a novel "theory of multinational enterprise liability." The traditional law of parent corporation responsibility holds that except in cases where the affairs of parent and subsidiary are so commingled as to be indistinguishable, the parent cannot be held liable for acts of a subsidiary. But the Indian government's brief held that "key management personnel of multinationals exercise a closely-held power which is neither restricted by national boundaries nor effectively controlled by international law;" hence, for justice to be done, the parent firm must be held responsible for acts of the subsidiary.[31] In addition to the civil suit, Carbide's chairman, Warren Anderson, and several other executives were charged with homicide in Bhopal Criminal Court. However, no attempt to arrest them has ever been made. Carbide's lawyers believe the Bhopal court has no jurisdiction over them and that the charges were a pressure tactic.

In addition to its legal battle, Carbide had to fight for its independence when in August 1985 GAF Corporation started to buy Carbide shares for a possible takeover bid. In December, this takeover effort materialized. In a month-long war of wills, Carbide successfully repelled GAF, but only at the cost of taking on enormous new debt to buy back 55 percent of its outstanding shares. In 1986, after the takeover battle, Carbide's debt-to-capitalization ratio exceeded 80 percent. This huge debt load had to be reduced, because interest payments were crippling. So in 1986, Carbide sold $3.5 billion of assets, including its most popular consumer brands—Eveready batteries, Glad bags, and Prestone antifreeze. The company also sold more than a dozen other businesses and restructured into three tightly focused business groups—chemicals and plastics, industrial gases, and carbon products. It had become a smaller, weaker company.

---

[30] *In re Union Carbide Corporation Gas Plant Disaster*, 634 F.Supp. 867. This opinion was upheld on appeal to the U.S. Court of Appeals, Second Circuit, on January 14, 1987. The appeals court did, however, strike several procedural conditions imposed on Union Carbide related to discovery, parallel jurisdiction, and satisfaction of eventual judgment. Left intact was an order that Union Carbide wave defenses based on the statute of limitations. Nos. 86-7517, 86-7589, 86-7637. In October 1987 the U.S. Supreme Court, without comment, let the judgment stand.

[31] Quoted in Robert A. Butler, "Claims Against a Parent Corporation from the Perspective of In-House Counsel," paper presented to the Practicing Law Institute Program on "Responsibility of the Corporate Parent for Activities of a Subsidiary," New York, June 10, 1988, pp. 2–3.

INVESTIGATIONS INTO THE CAUSE OF THE MIC LEAK

In the days following the disaster there was worldwide interest in pinning down the precise cause of the gas leak. A team of reporters from the *New York Times* visited Bhopal and interviewed plant workers. Their six-week investigation led to publication of lengthy newspaper accounts which concluded that the accident was caused by a large volume of water entering Tank 610 and reacting with the MIC.[32] The water entered because the operator who had washed out piping earlier in the evening violated procedure and failed to use a slip blind. So water from the hose simply backed up and eventually flowed about 400 feet into the MIC storage tank. The *Times* account was widely accepted as authoritative, and this theory, called the "water washing theory," gained wide currency. Media audiences found it a plausible explanation that satisfied their curiosity.

Immediately after the accident, Union Carbide also rushed a team of investigators to Bhopal, including scientists, chemical engineers, attorneys, and accident investigation experts from the independent consulting firm of Arthur D. Little. But the team was severely hampered by lack of cooperation from Indian authorities, who were under political pressure from anti-Carbide protest groups and anti-American public feeling in the wake of the tragedy. It was denied access to plant records and blocked from interviews with workers by the Indian Central Bureau of Investigation, which was conducting a criminal inquiry into the incident. In accident investigation, early debriefing of witnesses is critical because memories of minor detail fade and stories tend to alter and harden over time.[33] But Carbide was denied this advantage and was unable, in the short run, to counter the image of inept management and blundering projected in the *New York Times* stories.

The Carbide investigative team was, however, given access to Tank 610 and took core samples from the bottom residue. These samples were sent to the U.S., where over 500 experimental chemical reactions were undertaken to explain their chemical composition. In March 1985, Union Carbide finally released its first report of the accident. The short, twenty-five page Carbide report concluded that the accident had been caused by the entry of water into the tank, but did not accept the water washing theory. It stated that "the source of the water is unknown" but focused attention on the possibility of entry through misconnection of a water line at a utility station near the tank.[34]

Utility stations (or "service drops," as they are sometimes called) are located throughout chemical plants and provide needed services. Typically,

---

[32] Stuart Diamond, "The Bhopal Disaster: How It Happened," *New York Times*, January 28, 1985; Thomas J. Lueck, "Carbide Says Inquiry Showed Errors But Is Incomplete," *New York Times*, January 28, 1985; Stuart Diamond, "The Disaster in Bhopal: Workers Recall Horror," *New York Times*, January 30, 1985; and Robert Reinhold, "Disaster in Bhopal: Where Does Blame Lie?" *New York Times*, January 31, 1985.

[33] Ted S. Ferry, *Modern Accident Investigation and Analysis*, 2nd ed., New York: John Wiley & Sons, 1988, p. 32.

[34] *Bhopal Methyl Isocyanate Incident Investigation Team Report*, Danbury, Connecticut: Union Carbide Corporation, March 1985, p. i.

they contain headers for compressed air, water, nitrogen, and steam—all essential for chemical plant operation. At the utility station near Tank 610, the nitrogen and water lines are located together (see the lower left-hand corner of Exhibit 2). The Carbide investigation team hypothesized that if a worker had deliberately or accidentally connected piping leading to Tank 610 with the water line at the service drop, the resulting flow could have released an amount of water sufficient to cause the reaction. Carbide investigators rejected the water washing hypothesis for several reasons. The piping system was designed to prevent water contamination. Valves between the piping being washed and Tank 610 were found closed after the accident. And the amount of water contamination required to create the reaction—1,000 to 2,000 pounds—was too great to be explained by valve leakage.

The Carbide report contradicted the water washing theory, but within nine months an investigation sponsored by the Indian government embraced it once again. This study, made by Indian scientists and engineers, stated that the entry of water into Tank 610 was the cause of the accident and that water had gotten into the tank as a result of improper water washing procedure.[35]

There matters stood until December 1985, when a U.S. court ordered the Indian government to give Carbide access to plant records and the names of workers. This order corrected an unfairness in the litigation process in which the government of India was suing Carbide, yet also barred Carbide from access to critical evidence that might prove its innocence. Carbide renewed its investigation, sending a team of interviewers to India to seek out and interview plant workers. Over seventy interviews, plus careful examination of plant records and physical evidence, led the investigators to conclude that the cause of the gas leak was sabotage by a disgruntled employee who intentionally hooked up a water hose to Tank 610.

Here is the sequence of events on the night of December 2–3 that Carbide set forth. At 10:20 p.m. the pressure gauge on Tank 610 read 2 pounds per square inch. This meant that no water had yet entered the tank and no reaction had begun. At 10:45 the regularly scheduled shift change occurred. Shift changes take half an hour and the MIC storage area would have been deserted. At this time an operator who had been angry for several days about his failure to get a promotion stole into the area. He unscrewed the local pressure indicator gauge on Tank 610, hooked up a rubber water hose, and turned the water on. Five minutes would have sufficed to do this. Carbide claims to know the name of this person, but has never revealed it.

Why did he do it? Carbide speculates that his intention was simply to ruin the MIC batch in the tank. It is doubtful that this worker realized how toxic MIC vapor was or intended any loss of life. The interviews had revealed that the workers thought of MIC chiefly as a lachrymator, or a chemical that pro-

---

[35] *Report on Scientific Studies on the Release Factors Related to Bhopal Toxic Gas Leakage.* Bombay: Indian Council of Scientific and Industrial Research, December 1985. The report suggested another possible route for water entry into Tank 610, backflow from the vent gas scrubber. As evidence, the report cited high concentrations of sodium in the residue of Tank 610, which would indicate that water had mixed with the caustic soda in the scrubber prior to entry.

duces tearing; they did not regard it as a lethal hazard. Indeed, there had been no prior experience with fatalities from release of vaporized MIC and, after the venting of Tank 610 into the air, operators in the MIC control room felt some relief. They believed the threat had passed and informed town authorities there was no danger to life.

A few minutes after midnight, MIC operators noted a strong pressure rise in Tank 610. Walking to the tank, they found the hose connected and removed it, then informed their supervisors. The supervisors tried to prevent a catastrophic pressure rise by draining water from Tank 610. Between 12:15 a.m. and 12:30 a.m., just minutes before the major gas release, they transferred about one metric ton of MIC from Tank 610 to a holding tank in the Sevin manufacturing area. Water is heavier than MIC and the transfer was accomplished through a drain in the bottom of Tank 610; thus, the supervisors hoped to remove the water. They failed. At 12:45 a.m. the gas leak occurred.

Union Carbide investigators had physical evidence to support this scenario. After the accident, the local pressure gauge hole on Tank 610 was still open and no plug had been inserted as would have been normal if it was removed for normal maintenance. When written records for the MIC unit were examined, a crude drawing of the hose connection was found on the back of one page from that night's log book. Also, operators outside the MIC unit told the investigation team that MIC operators had told them about the hose connection that night.

Log entries in the MIC unit had been falsified, causing the Carbide team to conclude that the operators engaged in a crude cover-up. The major falsification was an attempt to hide the transfer of MIC from Tank 610 to the Sevin production area. The operators on duty that night made clumsy efforts to show that the transfer had come from Tank 611 instead and had been done more than an hour earlier, before the shift change. But the entries were out of chronological sequence and in the handwriting of operators who did not come on until the night shift. Further, analysis of the contents of the MIC transferred into the Sevin area showed it to be contaminated with reaction byproducts. The MIC in Tank 611, from which the operators claimed to have made the transfer, was found to be on-specification and untainted. The transfer had to have come from Tank 610.

Why did the supervisors and operators attempt a cover-up? One Carbide investigator has written this explanation.

> Not knowing if the attempted transfer had exacerbated the incident, or whether they could have otherwise prevented it, or whether they would be blamed for not having notified plant management earlier, those involved decided on a cover-up. They altered logs that morning and thereafter to disguise their involvement. As is not uncommon in many such incidents, the reflexive tendency to cover up simply took over.[36]

[36] Ashok S. Kalelkar, "Investigation of Large-Magnitude Incidents: Bhopal as a Case Study," paper presented at The Institution of Chemical Engineers Conference on Preventing Major Chemical Accidents, London, England, May 1988, p. 27.

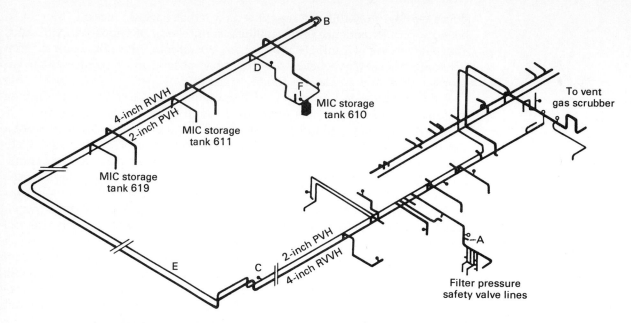

According to water-washing theory of Indian government, water was introduced through a hose into bleeder A at filter pressure safety valve lines. As hose kept running, water proceeded through leaking valve in that area and rose up into the relief valve vent header line (RVVH). It took a turn at the jumper line, B, and moved into the process vent header line (PVH), filling it in the reverse direction all the way to the slip blind, C. When PVH was completely filled, water rose at line D and proceeded into MIC storage tank 610. On Feb. 8, 1985, two months after the leak, India's Central Bureau of Investigation drilled a hole in the PVH line at point E to drain any water left in the line. No water emerged. Carbide says this fact alone disproves the water-washing theory. The fact that various valves in the pathway to the tank were closed also disproves the theory, according to Carbide. Carbide espouses an alternate theory: The company says it has proof that water was introduced by a "disgruntled employee" who removed pressure gauge F, attached a hose to the open piping, and ran water into the MIC tank. Gas then escaped through a rupture disk and proceeded through the RVVH and out the vent gas scrubber.

EXHIBIT 6-3   Two theories clash on water entry into MIC tank. (*Source:* Wil Lepkowski, "Union Carbide Presses Bhopal Sabotage Theory," *Chemical & Engineering News*, July 4, 1988, p. 10.)

This theory of deliberate sabotage became the centerpiece of Carbide's legal defense. The Indian government made no public comment, but Srinivason Varadarajan, lead investigator in the 1985 study by the Indian Council of Scientific and Industrial Research, commented: "We have other evidence showing the likelihood that water came in by the water washing. I don't think we'll have any difficulty showing it."[37] And some observers noted that the sabotage theory failed to mitigate management responsibility for equipment failures and procedures inadequate to contain the MIC reaction.

[37] Wil Lepkowski, "Union Carbide Presses Bhopal Sabotage Theory," *Chemical & Engineering News*, July 4, 1988, p. 11.

A SETTLEMENT IS REACHED

At last, on February 14, 1989, a settlement was reached. Carbide agreed to pay $470 million. In return, India dropped all pending lawsuits and indemnified Carbide and its officers against any further legal action. Carbide's insurers paid approximately $200 million. The *Washington Post* estimated that Carbide had also paid over $100 million in legal fees since 1984.[38] Carbide was pleased with the settlement. It was affordable and required only a $0.50 per share charge against 1988 profits of $5.31 a share. The case was a festering political sore for Indian Prime Minister Rajiv Gandhi, who feared that opposition candidates in the next general election would pillory him for his failure to force Carbide into paying restitution. Thus, the Indian government was anxious to settle.

Victims' groups such as the Bhopal Poison Gas Struggle Front were immediately upset. Some estimated the needs of Bhopal victims in the billions of dollars, and many Indians had demanded a harsher punishment for the American company. Shortly after the settlement was announced, victims of the gas leak gathered outside UCIL Offices in New Delhi shouting "Killer Carbide, quit India." About 50 stormed the offices, breaking windows and furniture. In parliament opponents of Prime Minister Gandhi walked out upon learning of the settlement, and his party was later defeated at the polls. Several legal challenges to the settlement were made, but by early 1990 most had been rejected by the Indian Supreme Court.[39]

Because the case has not come to trial, the water washing theory and the sabotage theory have never clashed in a legal forum. The world does not know which would be more persuasive to a jury.

QUESTIONS

1 Who is responsible for the Bhopal accident? How should blame be apportioned among the parties involved, including Union Carbide Corporation senior management, UCIL managers, workers at the MIC unit in Bhopal, government in India that issued permits and provided incentives for the plant, slum dwellers who moved near the plant in illegal settlements, Indian environmental and safety inspectors, and others?

2 What principles of ethics and responsibility are applicable to the actions of the parties in question?

3 How well did the legal system work? Do you agree with the decision to try the lawsuits in India? Were victims fairly compensated? Was Carbide sufficiently punished?

4 Did Union Carbide handle the crisis well? No company has ever been faced with a similar situation. How would you grade Carbide's performance?

[38] Malcolm Gladwell, "Bhopal's Final Chapter," *Washington Post National Weekly Edition*, February 20–26, 1989.
[39] See Stephen J. Adler, "India's Justices Uphold Bhopal Settlement," *Wall Street Journal*, January 2, 1990, and Richard Koenig and Stephen J. Adler, "Experts Doubt India's Ability to Push Carbide," *Wall Street Journal*, January 23, 1990.

Business Ethics

CHAPTER
7

Ethics in the Business System

Beech-Nut
Nutrition Corp.

The Beech-Nut Nutrition Corp., headquartered in Pennsylvania, manufactures baby foods. In 1977, it began buying large amounts of apple concentrate from Universal Juice Inc., a Brooklyn, New York, wholesaler. This concentrate was used to make Beech-Nut Apple Juice, sold in small jars, each labeled "100% FRUIT JUICE" and "NO SUGAR ADDED," as part of a line of about 100 baby foods.

Bottled apple juice is made by mixing various apple concentrates to achieve desired flavoring. These concentrates, which are processed apples dehydrated to one-seventh their original bulk, may be frozen and stored for later use. The manufacturer adds water and pasteurization to make "natural" apple juice with a long shelf life. Beech-Nut added no artificial ingredients during reconstitution. The production of a "natural" product was critical for two reasons. First, consumer attraction to "natural" foods was strong, and Beech-Nut had adopted a competitive strategy of emphasizing "natural" ingredients. Second, consumer perception of purity and integrity are especially valuable assets in the baby food industry, because parents are exceptionally demanding about infant nutrition.

Soon, chemists in Beech-Nut's nutrition lab suspected that the concentrate was not pure. For one thing, it cost 20 percent less than the market rate. A possible reason was that Universal Juice was mixing refined sugars and flavoring in the concentrate instead of more costly real apples. For another, when Beech-Nut chemists complained of coloration or pH problems, the supplier corrected them immediately—something that would be difficult with real batches of apple concentrate. There is no conclusive chemical test that can prove adulteration by added sugars, but Beech-Nut ran sugar profile tests that strongly suggested adulteration with corn syrup, beet sugar, or cane sugar. These results led Beech-Nut chemists to visit the Universal Juice plant one day, but they were not allowed to see the concentrate manufacturing process.

Jerome LiCari, a Beech-Nut chemist, spoke to managers about the suspected adulteration and on numerous occasions urged changing suppliers. In 1981, he sent a memo to senior executives stating the existence of "a tremendous amount of circumstantial evidence" which constituted "a grave case against the current supplier."[1] The response: LiCari was criticized in a performance evaluation for not being a team player. The vice president in charge of manufacturing gave him the nickname "Chicken Little." A meeting with Beech-Nut's president produced no action. LiCari soon resigned from the company.

In fact, Beech-Nut *was* buying adulterated concentrate; there was little or no apple juice in a typical batch. It was sugar water, the fraudulent product of a nationwide network of shady brokers, wholesalers, shippers, and ingredient makers dealing in phony concentrate. This criminal group grossed millions annually, and Beech-Nut was its biggest customer.

Rumors spread in the industry about suspicious concentrate. Other manufacturers, including Beech-Nut competitors Gerber Products Co. and H. J. Heinz Co., cut off suppliers when they could not prove the purity of their products. Beech-Nut was less demanding. At Beech-Nut, the burden of proof was on company chemists to prove adulteration, not on the supplier to prove purity. But in 1982, a detective hired by the Processed Apples Institute, a trade group, gathered evidence that the concentrate was adulterated. He informed Beech-Nut in June, and the company finally cancelled its contracts with Universal Juice.

Beech-Nut continued, however, to sell its inventory. Through the summer and into the fall of 1982, it pushed distribution of its apple juice with promotions and deep dealer discounts. When the Food and Drug Administration (FDA) requested records, Beech-Nut refused to comply because of a loophole in the law which deprives the FDA of the power to subpoena records. When the FDA tested apple juice on store shelves and identified specific adulterated lots by number, Beech-Nut destroyed them so they could not be submitted for FDA tests. When the New York State Agricultural Department threatened seizure of remaining inventory in a New York warehouse, Beech-Nut brought in six trucks and overnight removed 26,000 cases to neighboring New Jersey. Beech-Nut finally ordered a recall in October, but its inventory of 700,000 cases of apple juice had been reduced to just 20,000.

The FDA, angered by Beech-Nut's defiance, requested that the Department of Justice prosecute the company and two top executives. As a result, in 1987 the company was fined $2 million. In 1988, its president and vice president of operations resigned and were sentenced to one year in jail and fines of $100,000 after conviction on hundreds of felony counts of conspiracy to defraud consumers. The conviction was, however, overturned on a jurisdictional technicality in 1989. It may be retried. The ultimate cost to the com-

---

[1]*Consumer Reports*, "Bad Apples: In the Executive Suite," May 1989, p. 295.

pany in fines, legal fees, lost market share, cancelled government contracts, and settlement of class action lawsuits by defrauded retailers and consumers is estimated at $25 million.

Why did Beech-Nut continue to purchase adulterated concentrate and later ship mislabeled apple juice? There are two reasons. First, top management was under urgent financial pressures. Beech-Nut had been purchased from Squibb Corp. in 1973 and its sole products were baby foods. Its competitors in the processed baby food industry, Gerber and Heinz, had the advantage of diversified product lines. Between 1973 and 1979, Beech-Nut lost money, and in 1979 it was sold and became a subsidiary of the Nestlé S.A., the international food conglomerate. President Niels Hoyvald had promised Nestlé that Beech-Nut would turn a profit by 1982. Buying the questionable concentrate saved the company $1.3 million in ingredient costs over a five-year period. Revenue from the apple juice was $60 million, roughly one-third of Beech-Nut's baby food sales.[2]

And second, a pervasive climate of rationalization existed. In court, Hoyvald defended himself by arguing that no chemical analysis of the concentrate had ever proved beyond the shadow of doubt that it was adulterated. He also rationalized that the sugar water they were selling posed no health risks. Readers may guess that an unspoken excuse was that the evil of deception was justified by the benefit of maintaining corporate financial health.

The Beech-Nut scandal teaches two important lessons. First, the unvarnished motivation was greed, illustrating the centrality of temptation in much corporate wrongdoing. Second, government regulation could not prevent it in incipient stages, illustrating the importance of ethical restraint as a control on corporate action. In this chapter and the next we discuss the practice of ethics in our business system, showing how ethical principles that guide business conduct originated, how they are observed and breached, and how they may be inculcated within companies and individuals to prevent disreputable behavior. In our discussion we are mindful of but not made reticent by Mark Twain's admonition: "To be good is noble. To tell people how to be good is even nobler, and much less trouble."

WHAT ARE BUSINESS ETHICS?

Ethics is the study of what is good and bad, right and wrong, and just and unjust. Business ethics, therefore, is the study of good and bad, right and wrong, and just and unjust actions in business. The material used in the study of ethics is a mass of principles, rules, values, and thoughts concerned with what conduct *ought* to be. The application of this material to business activity is an art involving judgment about the motivations behind an act and its consequences. This judgment, based on principles and standards of ethical conduct stemming from religious and philosophical thinking, cultural

[2]Cost and revenue estimates are in Stephen Kindel, "Bad Apple for Baby," *Financial World*, June 27, 1989, p. 48.

values, legal codes, and human conscience, determines whether an action is ethical or not.

Discussions of ethical issues in business frequently emphasize refractory and unclear situations, perhaps to show drama and novelty. Although all managers face ethical conflicts and difficult problems, the vast majority of ethical problems in business yield to resolution through the application of clear guidelines. The Eighth Commandment, for example, prohibits stealing from another and clearly makes practices ranging from theft of a competitor's trade secrets to taking a screwdriver home from work unethical. A misleading or lying advertisement violates a general rule of the Western business world that the seller of a product should not purposely deceive the buyer about its price or quality. This general understanding stems from the Mosaic law, the Code of Hammurabi, Roman law, and other sources and is part of a general ethic favoring truth that has remained unchanged for at least 3,000 years.[3] Beech-Nut, for example, violated this general rule when it labeled sugar water as "natural" apple juice.

In general, ethical traditions that apply to business favor truth-telling, honesty, protection of human and animal life and rights, respect for law, and operation in accord with policies adopted by society to achieve justice for citizens. Some of these touchstones go back thousands of years. Other ethical standards, such as the principle that a corporation is responsible for the health and safety of its workers, have emerged quite recently. In keeping with this long ethical heritage, most business actions can be clearly shown to be ethical or unethical; it may be difficult to eliminate some unethical behavior, such as the illegal activity of organized criminals, but knowing the rightness or wrongness of actions is not difficult in the majority of cases. This is not to say, of course, that universal clarity exists. Ethical problems may easily arise and persist. The definition of kickbacks, for instance, is blurred in currently popular airline frequent-flyer programs. Managers traveling at corporate expense may earn free trips and reduced fares by repeatedly flying on one airline. Frequent-flyer awards are given to the individuals who fly, not the companies that pay for tickets. Thus, after regularly spending their employer's money with a single supplier, these managers are given a free flight in return. Some companies have asked airlines to report frequent-flyer awards given to their employees, but the airlines have refused.

In addition, major ethical quandaries exist that are neither easily resolved nor trivial in their consequences. These include moral debates over questions such as the production of nuclear weapons, the payment of bribes to get foreign business, and the use of intensive husbandry techniques to raise food animals. Although numerous ethical standards apply to these situations, there are conflicts among them that prevent easy resolution. The point remains, however, that the novelty or gravity of ethical issues should not obscure the existence of clear ethical guidelines for most business behavior.

[3]See George C. S. Benson, *Business Ethics in America*, Lexington, Massachusetts: D. C. Heath, 1982, p. xvi.

TWO THEORIES OF BUSINESS ETHICS

There is an old debate, present both in the business community and in the literature of business ethics, about whether ethics in business may be more permissive than general societal or personal ethics.

One view is that commercial activity is amoral and that actions should be based solely on consideration of economic self-interest. This *theory of amorality* saw its apex of popularity during the nineteenth century, when doctrines of Social Darwinism and laissez-faire economics were popular. Indeed, some blue-chip corporations that developed during the period when "survival of the fittest" was a prevailing business ideology must admit to a checkered past. For example, John D. Rockefeller, founder of the Standard Oil Trust, spied on competitors by bribing their employees, gave kickbacks to railroads, blew up a widow's oil refinery when she refused to sell out, and lied to a congressional committee.[4] In 1903, Henry Ford started Ford Motor Company with $28,000 from eleven investors. They supplied the money and he the technical expertise. In 1919, Ford appointed his son president of FMC and planted a rumor that he was going into partnership with Harvey Firestone to build a new car to compete with Ford. This new car would allegedly sell for $100 less than the $460 Model T. Another rumor started by Ford was that he was planning to sell his shares of Ford Motor stock to General Motors. The eleven stockholders, alarmed by the false rumors, sold their stock back to Henry Ford at bargain prices, making Ford Motor Company entirely family-owned—the point of this carefully constructed artifice.[5]

Throughout a long period of our history, the question of ethics was neglected in business or was not a subject of doubt because of the popular notion that business and personal ethics existed in separate compartments. Dan Drew, a builder of churches and the founder of Drew Theological Seminary, typified the compartmentalization of business decision making in the nineteenth century in these words:

> Sentiment is all right up in the part of the city where your home is. But downtown, no. Down there the dog that snaps the quickest gets the bone. Friendship is very nice for a Sunday afternoon when you're sitting around the dinner table with your relations, talking about the sermon that morning. But nine o'clock Monday morning; notions should be brushed aside like cobwebs from a machine. I never took any stock in a man who mixed up business with anything else. He can go into other things outside of business hours, but when he's in the office, he ought not to have a relation in the world—and least of all a poor relation.[6]

---

[4]These are the accusations of historian Matthew Josephson in *The Robber Barons: The Great American Capitalists: 1861–1901*, New York: Harcourt, Brace & World, 1934. They are generally confirmed by other historians, but for a more definitive and sympathetic look at Rockefeller see Allan Nevins' two-volume *Study in Power: John D. Rockefeller*, New York: Charles Scribner's Sons, 1954.

[5]John D. Dahlinger, *The Secret Life of Henry Ford*, New York: Bobbs-Merrill, 1978, p. 124.

[6]Robert Bartels, ed., *Ethics in Business*, Columbus, Ohio: Bureau of Business Research, College of Commerce and Administration, Ohio State University, 1963, p. 35.

Capacity for the nobler feelings is in most natures a very tender plant, easily killed, not only by hostile influences, but by mere want of sustenance; and in the majority of young persons it speedily dies away if the occupations to which their position in life has devoted them, and the society into which it has thrown them, are not favourable to keeping that higher capacity in exercise.

John Stuart Mill, Utilitarianism (1863).

Classical economists often have supported the theory of amorality when arguing that the common good is best achieved by the individual pursuit of self-interest and profits by those in business, rather than by activity based on conscious moral purpose. Morality, they say, will emerge from the overall workings of the market and not from individual do-goodism. This comforting argument may mitigate the guilt of a manager who undertakes ethically questionable actions. Religious codes of ethical behavior do this when they make reference to evil spirits, fate, or original sin, all of which have the effect of absolving individuals from some measure of blame and sheltering them from the full force of guilt. Similarly, the competitive pressures of the market system provide release from the burden of guilt and justification for behavior that would be condemned in private life. And so Daniel Haughton, chairman of Lockheed, found it permissible to pay $38 million in bribes in the 1970s to save jobs in the United States and profit stockholders and management. Since foreign competitors were willing to make these questionable payments, the market ethic permitted their payment. As one management scholar has argued, the "core values" of business—economic growth, power, the drive for profits, rational calculation of gain, pragmatism, and loyalty to the spirit of capitalist ideology—incline business to raw-edged ethics that are "perhaps no part of the intention of the individual businessperson caught in the system's toils."[7]

A second major ethical orientation is that it is possible to harmonize high levels of personal ethics with the demands of business life. This is the *theory of moral unity,* which holds that business actions can be judged by the general ethical standards of society, not by a special set of more permissive ethical standards. Only one basic ethical standard exists.

Indeed, many in business have been ethically pure. An example is James Cash Penney. Although we now remember Penney for the successful construction of a chain of retail outlets, his first enterprise was a butcher shop. As a young man, Penney went to Denver and, finding notice of a shop for sale, wired his mother for $300 (his life savings) and purchased it. The departing butcher advised that Penney's success would depend heavily on trade from a nearby hotel. "To keep the hotel for a customer," the butcher explained, "all you have to do is buy the chef a bottle of whiskey a week." Penney regularly made the gift, and business was good, but gradually the opinion of his father, who reviled alcohol, preyed more and more on his

[7]William C. Frederick, "Corporate Social Responsibility in the Reagan Era and Beyond," *California Management Review,* Spring 1983, p. 147.

mind. He resolved not to make profits in such a manner, stopped giving the bribe, and at the age of twenty-three was flat broke when the shop failed. Penney later started the Golden Rule Department Store in Denver and argued that his principles of honesty contributed to his ultimate success. A number of companies, such as J. C. Penney's, have successfully operated on religious principles and high moral standards, and their example counterbalances the gamesmanship ethos.

To those who adhere to the theory of moral unity, the market is not an excusing condition for misconduct. Philosopher Armin Konrad dismisses the right of managers to exist in "ethical sanctuaries," arguing that all professionals, including doctors, lawyers, educators, and public administrators, are faced with ethical conflicts. But there are no grounds for avoiding these conflicts and the ethical judgment necessary to resolve them with high standards simply because one is a business manager. People in business are a part of society and must be sensitive to the ethical rights of others and meet human obligations.[8] Nor is business analogous to a game. Rather, it is a vital social institution. People's lives depend on it. To compare business to a poker game with special rules, insulated from generally applicable ethical principles, is to trivialize an essential institution and way of life.[9]

According to the theory of moral unity, people act in organizations as individuals and citizens, not as cogs in an impersonal machine. The strong precedent set by the military tribunal at Nuremberg, which tried Nazis for war crimes, indicates that Western society expects members of organizations to follow the dictates of their conscience and reject forced implementation of unethical policies. Just as no Nazi war criminal argued successfully that he was forced to follow an order in an impersonal military chain of command, so no business manager may claim to be the helpless prisoner of competitive forces or organizational loyalties that crush free will and justify unethical actions.

We are left with the intriguing question: Do any factors excuse unethical business behavior? The answer is yes. Essentially, the factors that diminish responsibility for ethical behavior in business are the same as those that diminish ethical responsibility in other areas of life. Perhaps no explication of these factors in the last two thousand years has improved much on that given by Aristotle in *The Nicomachean Ethics*.

According to Aristotle, ethical behavior is a state involving voluntary choice, and only unethical actions that are involuntary can be excused. The two factors that may lead to involuntary behavior are *ignorance* and *incapacity* to perform an action. A person may be ignorant of facts or the consequences of an act. For example, a manager may manufacture a product according to a chemical formula unknowingly stolen by subordinates who kept their espionage secret. Later, despite conscientious testing and regulatory oversight,

[8]Armin Richard Konrad, "Business Managers and Moral Sanctuaries," *Journal of Business Ethics,* August 1982.

[9]Norman C. Gillespie, "The Business of Ethics," *University of Michigan Business Review*, November 1975.

the chemical product proves harmful to consumers. In both these cases, involuntary ignorance diminishes ethical wrongdoing. (Naturally, negligence in getting facts increases culpability, as does failure to have an interest in acquiring knowledge of relevant ethical principles.) Incapacity arises from circumstances that render actions involuntary. Circumstances leading to incapacity arise when: (1) a course of action may impose unrealistically high costs—for example, an automobile manufacturer cannot be expected to prevent all traffic deaths since the costs of a perfectly safe vehicle in materials, design, and production are staggering; (2) there may be no power to influence an outcome—for example, a manager of an oil company doing business in the Middle East cannot end national frictions or religious differences; (3) no alternative exists—for example, the continued use of asbestos is inevitable despite the human health costs; and (4) external force may compel action—for example, a manager may pay excessive and unjust taxes in a foreign country because a corrupt ruler demands them.

Aristotle cautions, however, that "[t]here are some things such that a man cannot be compelled to do them—that he must sooner die than do, though he suffer the most dreadful fate."[10] Unlike cases of ignorance, cases of unethical behavior involving circumstantial coercion are never completely involuntary, since a manager can always voluntarily refuse to comply with an external force. Was Cy Osborne, an executive vice president of General Motors in the 1960s whose son suffered irreversible brain damage in a Corvair accident, compelled by GM's ethic of managerial team play to permit sales of an unsafe car? Executives and scholars who argue that the market is a force majeure that overrides individual values give too little credit to the strength of human will.

ETHICAL PRACTICE IN BUSINESS

Opinion polls show that the American public perceives high levels of unethical behavior in business. Several recent surveys exemplify this. In one, 55 percent of the public thought that most corporate executives were dishonest.[11] In another, 49 percent felt that white-collar crime was "very common" in business.[12] In a third, 69 percent felt that "most" or "many" employees take home tools and office supplies from work.[13] These opinions are typical of survey findings over the past twenty years. Is public perception accurate?

Unfortunately, ethical behavior in business is not subject to an accurate, aggregate measure. It may, however, be analyzed at four levels. First is the level of the *business system*, which is concerned with the total impact of busi-

[10]*The Nicomachean Ethics,* translated by J. A. K. Thompson, New York: Penguin Books, 1953, p. 122. Originally written c. 334–323 B.C.

[11]Adam Clymber, "Low Marks for Executive Honesty," *New York Times,* June 9, 1985.

[12]Stewart Jackson and Harris Collingwood, "*Business Week*/Harris Poll: Is an Antibusiness Backlash Building?" *Business Week,* July 20, 1987.

[13]A Roper Organization Poll reported in Merrill McLoughlin, "A Nation of Liars," *U.S. News & World Report,* February 23, 1987, p. 57.

ness activity on society. Historically, industrial activity has been supported as having beneficial effects that far outweigh costs. But ethical questions exist. In a pastoral letter, the U.S. Catholic Bishop's Conference has stated that the economy operates unjustly, failing to meet the needs of poor people. Environmentalists say that industrial pollution violates an ethical duty to preserve nonhuman life. The use of fossil fuel to power industrial processes, especially since 1850, has increased the concentration of carbon dioxide in the atmosphere and raises questions about our duties to future generations which may live in a warmer climate as a result.

Second, ethics may be examined at the *industry* level. In a recent survey, 87 percent of corporate directors and officers felt that ethical standards differed among industries. They ranked commercial banking; utilities; and drugs, pharmaceuticals, and cosmetics as the most ethical.[14] There are, of course, enduring, systemic ethical problems in other industries. The defense industry, for example, has long been tarnished by fraudulent billings, kickbacks to purchasing agents from subcontractors, and bid rigging. These pervasive, longstanding breaches have existed since the Revolutionary War, and historians record a flagrant peak during the Civil War. They are related to industry dynamics. Competition is limited where the government grants monopolies on specific weapons. The existence of a single buyer, the government, encourages cozy familiarity. The size of contracts is huge, and getting one may double or triple revenues for years, encouraging bribery and deceptive bidding. Eradicating impropriety has proved difficult. In 1986, after glaring scandals, the Department of Defense required thirty-nine major defense contractors to sign an agreement known as the Defense Industry Initiative, which required extensive ethical education of employees and the establishment of policies conducive to ethical behavior. Yet in 1988, thirty-four of the thirty-nine became the targets of a total of 200 government investigations. In the same year a total of 1,028 companies were banned from defense contracts for ethical breaches.[15]

Other industries, such as prescription drug manufacturing, savings and loan, and futures trading, have, of course, been touched by pervasive scandal in recent years, and as with the defense industry, structural factors are partly to blame. The misbehavior in these industries pales, of course, in comparison to the ethical burden placed on the business system by drug cartels and organized crime which, in addition to their illegal activities, infiltrate legitimate industries.

Third, *companies* differ in ethical practice. A number of firms, for instance Levi Strauss, Merck and Co., and Johnson & Johnson, are consistently noted for high ethics and have institutionalized a concern for ethics in their operating policies. Critics frequently cite some other companies as unethical. It is difficult to conclude that a large corporation is unethical, because misbehavior mentioned in the press is often counterbalanced by socially responsible

[14]Touche Ross, *Ethics in American Business: A Special Report,* Chicago, Illinois: Touche Ross & Co., 1988, p. 69.
[15]Robert Wrubel, "Addicted to Fraud?" *Financial World,* June 27, 1989, p. 58.

actions that receive no publicity. Still, many companies have been labeled as having less ethical operating climates. In some large companies, at some times, aggressive competition may shade into unethical behavior. There are, of course, many examples of smaller companies operated toward criminal ends, such as Sunshine State Bank, the Miami bank taken over by drug smugglers and used for money laundering.

Last is the *individual* level of ethical behavior. Conspicuously unethical managers are regularly uncovered, their misdeeds publicized. Yet the unmasking of bad executives probably exaggerates the ethical problem for the public. For every Aldo Gucci (former chairman of Gucci Shops, Inc.) who pleads guilty to evading $7 million in income taxes, thousands of top executives honestly report earnings. For every corrupt Wall Street investment banker, such as Dennis B. Levine, who got $12.6 million in profits from illegal insider trading deals, there are thousands of brokers who trade legally. Conspicuous breaches of ethics should not be mistaken as indicative of the level of ethical practice in the business system as a whole. Since the 1960s, however, the widespread use of surveys has illuminated the sanctum of individual ethics.

EVERYDAY ETHICAL PRACTICE

What is individual ethical practice like at mundane operational levels of business where millions of employees toil each day? Although measurement of everyday ethical practice is handicapped by conflicting standards of measurement and the difficulty of determining the difference between what people actually believe and what they say they believe, survey results are remarkably consistent. We emphasize here two important findings.

First, significant unethical behavior exists. One survey, for example, reported that 18 percent of business executives polled had been approached by suppliers for kickbacks, 10 percent had been asked by their bosses to do something illegal, and 47 percent had fired one or more subordinates for unethical behavior.[16] Another survey reported that 33 percent of employees admitted to calling in sick when they were not, 18 percent padded expense accounts, and 22 percent felt that some circumstances justified stealing from an employer.[17] A 1988 survey of office workers found that 41 percent believed the largest gap between what they wanted at work and what they actually experienced was in "management that is honest, upright, and ethical in its dealing with employees and the community."[18]

---

[16]Roger Ricklefs, "Public Gives Executives Low Marks for Honesty and Ethical Standards," *Wall Street Journal*, November 2, 1983.

[17]Susan McBee, "Morality: The State of American Values," *U.S. News & World Report*, December 9, 1985, p. 52.

[18]This was a Louis Harris and Associates survey reported in Michael R. Kagay, "Workers Want to Help in Decisions," *New York Times*, June 14, 1988.

Second, surveys taken over three decades show lessening conflict between business ethics and personal ethics. Two large-scale surveys of readers in the *Harvard Business Review*, the first in 1961 and the second, and update of the first, in 1976, reveal less conflict.[19] When asked whether they had ever had a conflict between their roles as a profit-oriented manager and as an ethical person, 76 percent in 1961 said they had. In 1976, however, only 57 percent reported such conflicts—a decrease of 19 percent. A third survey, in 1989, found that only 35 percent of managers aged 21–30 faced some pressure to engage in unethical behavior, and the feeling of pressure declined with age. Only 22 percent of managers aged 61–70 felt such pressure.[20]

There have been a number of additional findings in surveys of ethical behavior over the years. A few that are consistent stand out. The general public thinks that business ethics are lower than do business managers. The behavior and example of superiors is listed by managers as the most important single influence on ethical or unethical behavior in companies. People in business are cynical, as suggested by survey findings that managers see their companies as more ethical than competitors, and their fellow managers as less ethical than themselves. Younger managers are less ethical than older managers—apparently age and the socialization process increase ethical sensitivity.

In addition, there is persuasive evidence for other observations, although survey data is not yet conclusive. Women in business may be slightly more ethical than men, perhaps because the female gender role, into which they are socialized, emphasizes consideration for others.[21] Unethical behavior may be more predominant in those lacking attachment to a religion.[22] And there are indications that managers are more inclined today to pick ethical choices on survey questionnaires than they were in the 1960s or 1970s.

There are differences in ethical values between managers in the U.S. and other countries. Managers in Europe, Asia, and Latin America are more willing to pay a wide range of bribes than U.S. managers. Japanese employees do not blow the whistle on their companies in the face of wrongdoing; they are restrained by a powerful social norm of loyalty to employers that derives from the strong Confucian ethic of faith toward family and ruler. Some surprising ethical idiosyncracies also exist. For example, a study of Hong Kong

---

[19]Raymond C. Baumhart, "How Ethical Are Businessmen?" July–August 1961, and Steven N. Brenner and Earl A. Molander, "Is the Ethics of Business Changing?" January–February 1977.

[20]Justin G. Longenecker, Joseph A. McKinney, and Carlos W. Moore, "The Generation Gap in Business Ethics," *Business Horizons*, September/October 1989, p. 12.

[21]See, for example, Ishmael P. Akaah, "Differences in Research Ethics Judgments Between Male and Female Marketing Professionals," *Journal of Business Ethics*, May 1989 and Michael Betz, Lenaham O'Connell, and Jon M. Shepard, "Gender Differences in Proclivity for Unethical Behavior," *Journal of Business Ethics*, May 1989. A survey which finds no differences between men and women in the importance of ethics in work life is Ralph A. Mortensen, Jack E. Smith, and Gerald F. Cavanagh, "The Importance of Ethics to Job Performance: An Empirical Investigation of Managers' Perceptions," *Journal of Business Ethics*, April 1989, p. 257.

[22]See Longenecker, *et al., op. cit.*, p. 11.

MEASURING BUSINESS ETHICS

How do researchers measure managerial ethics? One method frequently used is response to a short vignette. These three, from surveys by scholars, are typical.

I

Harry Ruckus, Vice President of Westerly Chemical Company, feels that sending expensive Christmas gifts to customers compromises their position as buyers, and thus is a form of bribery. Yet he knows that this is a common practice among his competitors and that sales are likely to be adversely affected by failure to conform to the traditional practice. He decides to send the gifts.

Approve	_____	1
Somewhat approve	_____	2
Somewhat disapprove	_____	3
Disapprove	_____	4

This vignette was first given to managers in 1964, when their average score was 3.3 (meaning most had answered "somewhat disapprove" and "disapprove"). Repeated over twenty years later in 1987, the score was an identical 3.3.[23]

II

An executive earning $50,000 a year has been padding his expense account by about $2,500 a year.

_____ Unacceptable, regardless of circumstances
_____ Acceptable, if other executives in the company do the same thing
_____ Acceptable, if the executive's superior knows about it and says nothing

When asked in 1961, 86 percent of executives responding found this unacceptable, regardless of circumstances. In 1976 the number rose to 89 percent, and in 1985 it rose further to 98 percent.[24]

III

Rollfast Bicycle Company has been barred from entering the market in a large Asian country by collusive efforts of the local bicycle manufacturers. Rollfast could expect to net $5 million per year from sales if it could penetrate the market. Last week a businessman from the country contacted the management of Rollfast and stated that he could smooth the way for the company to sell in his country for a price of $500,000.

Managers in France, Germany, and the U.S. were asked to indicate what they would do. Answers were placed on a scale ranging from "definitely would not" (0) to "definitely would" (10). The results: French managers were most likely to pay, with a mean score of 6.9, Germans were somewhat less likely to pay with 5.8, and Americans were the least likely at 4.0.[25]

[23]The two studies are John W. Clark, *Religion and the Moral Standards of American Businessmen*, Cincinnati, Ohio: South-Western, 1966, p. 98, and Harold H. Kassarjian and Barbara E. Kahn, "The Ethical Standards of Business Students, Business Professors, and Business People," paper presented at the Western Marketing Educators' Association; San Francisco, California: April 13–15, 1989, Table 3.

[24]The three surveys are Baumhart, *op. cit.*, Brenner and Molander, *op. cit.*, and Scott J. Vitell and Troy A. Festervand, "Business Ethics: Conflicts, Practices and Beliefs of Industrial Executives," *Journal of Business Ethics*, July 1987, p. 118.

[25]Helmut Becker and David J. Fritzsche, "A Comparison of the Ethical Behavior of American, French and German Managers," *Columbia Journal of World Business*, Winter 1987, p. 91.

managers showed that older managers more readily agreed to unethical practices than younger ones, just the reverse of the U.S. situation.[26] On the other hand, foreign managers show a wide range of values similar to those of U.S. managers when confronted with specific situations raising ethical problems. The United States is perceived by managers of many nations as having the highest ethics of any country.

INDIVIDUAL VERSUS CORPORATE ETHICAL RESPONSIBILITY

Can a corporation be held ethically, in addition to legally, responsible for antisocial actions, or is ethical responsibility always vested in the human beings who are its employees? A vigorous debate exists on this question.[27]

One view is that corporations are moral entities and may be held responsible for their behavior. Some corporate decisions are not attributable solely to individuals because the internal decision-making process focuses collective efforts and gives groups a purpose and force greater than that of the component individual wills. Company strategies, policies, controls, and norms harness employees and may create an organization climate in which unethical behavior is tolerated. Agreeing with this idea, John Z. DeLorean, former vice president of General Motors, writes that "the system of American business often produces wrong, immoral, and irresponsible decisions, even though the personal morality of the people running the business is often above reproach."[28] Executives at GM acceded to production of the rear-engined Corvair automobile, knowing that it was dangerously unstable in high-speed turns. "There wasn't a man in top GM management who had anything to do with the Corvair," says DeLorean, "who would purposely build a car that he knew would hurt or kill people."[29] But as good team players, the executives first failed to speak out when its safety was questioned and later sought to suppress information showing the car's deficiencies. A perversely intriguing part of DeLorean's story is the list of relatives of top executives at GM who were killed or injured in Corvair accidents. The human cost of corporate loyalty in this instance was high.

A second view is that ethical responsibility attaches only to individual corporate employees. In this view, two factors are required to establish ethical responsibility. First, an action must cause harm. Second, the action must be accompanied by an intent to act. But there are no corporate actions not attributable to individual members and their intentions. Furthermore, if a corporation were to be held responsible for social crimes, it follows that it could be

---

[26]Gael M. McDonald and Raymond A. Zepp, "Ethical Perceptions of Hong Kong Chinese Business Managers," *Journal of Business Ethics*, November 1988, p. 835. The explanation given is that younger managers are more tightly constricted in their behavior by work group norms than are older managers who have the independence to depart from rigid integrity.

[27]See, for instance, Peter A. French, *Collective and Corporate Responsibility*, New York: Columbia University Press, 1984; Manuel G. Velasquez, "Why Corporations Are Not Morally Responsible for Anything They Do," *Business & Professional Ethics Journal*, Spring 1983; and Jan Garrett, "Unredistributable Corporate Moral Responsibility," *Journal of Business Ethics*, July 1989.

[28]In J. Patrick Wright, *On a Clear Day You Can See General Motors*, New York: Avon, 1979, p. 61.

[29]*Ibid.*, p. 67.

punished and then all its members—including those who were not involved in the mischief—would suffer. It is not possible to punish organization charts, decision structures, or corporate cultures—only human employees.

We conclude that this is a debate between extreme positions. Ethical responsibility for corporate behavior clearly rests with individual managers. It can never be delegated by top executives, who must establish strong information and control systems. But there is no question that an organizational climate of low ethics gathers momentum and undermines the integrity of some employees. Indeed, a number of corporations recognize the power of company culture to reinforce the ethical climate and attempt through management training to create cultures in which profit pressures are not allowed to create ethical conflicts.

IS THERE A REWARD FOR VIRTUE?

Is there a relationship between corporate ethics and corporate profits? When over 1,000 executives, business school deans, and members of Congress were asked if high ethical standards help a company to compete, a large majority, 63 percent, answered yes. A much smaller group, 14 percent, believed that high ethical standards made companies weaker competitors. And another 23 percent said that ethical standards had no effect on competitiveness.[30] Who is correct?

The answer seems to be everyone. The impact of ethics in the marketplace varies with specific circumstances. Sometimes high ethics generate profit. The classic case of this was the immediate recall of Tylenol by Johnson & Johnson, a company which has made exceptional efforts over many years to create an ethical corporate culture for employees. When the threat of cyanide poisoning in Tylenol capsules subsided, Johnson & Johnson's integrity was rewarded by loyal customers who returned to the product. A subsequent survey showed that the public gave the company a ranking of 8 on a 10-point scale of trust, far above the 3.3 given to business in general.[31] Conversely, low ethics may cost a company business. In innumerable instances, fraud and deception have led to bankruptcy and severe financial difficulties. A rollcall of firms landing in dire financial straits due to misbehavior includes Beech-Nut, Manville, A. H. Robins, and a large number of savings and loans. A recent study of 130 big manufacturing firms revealed that companies with records of trade law violations were less profitable than companies which had no record of legal violations.[32] A similar study of securities companies touched by insider trading scandals in 1986 concluded that their stock fell as a result.[33]

[30]Touche Ross, *op. cit.*, p. 69.

[31]Cited in "Clare Discusses Johnson & Johnson Credo," *Ethics Resource Center Report*, Spring 1988, p. 5A.

[32]Richard E. Wokutch and Barbara A. Spencer, "Corporate Saints and Sinners: Philanthropy, Crime, and Organizational Performance," *California Management Review*, Winter 1987.

[33]Khalil M. Torabzadeh, Dan Davidson, and Hamid Assar, "The Effect of the Recent Insider-Trading Scandal on Stock Prices of Securities Firms," *Journal of Business Ethics*, April 1989.

At other times, however, questionable ethics pay off. Concrete contractors fronting for organized crime in New York City have huge profits because legitimate firms are often intimidated from entering bids for major projects. Few honest competitors remain. And David Vogel, a professor at the University of California at Berkely, notes that "for every insider trader who gets caught, one presumes that there are others who live happily ever after."[34]

Finally, there are instances where ethical behavior is unrelated to profit. Helping local communities, contributing to charity, making a safe product, or barring Christmas gifts from suppliers may not increase the efficiency of core business activities which produce profit. Bracing do-goodism often does not contribute to profitability except in an ethereal, impalpable, long-run sense.

In conclusion, the relationship between ethics and profits is highly situational. Examples from life in the business world support any hypothesis. Hence, there is no universal rule, and several possibilities, as described above, exist.[35]

SOURCES OF THE BUSINESS ETHOS

Every manager stands at the center of a web of values connecting interrelated value systems. There, they are influenced by five external repositories of ethical values: genetic inheritance, religion, philosophy, cultural experience, and law. These systems exert varying degrees of control over individuals and in the same individual over time. A common theme, the idea of reciprocity or mutual help, is found in all these value systems. The function of this idea, which is to bind the vast majority of individuals in society into a cooperative whole, is the central purpose of all ethics. In business or in other pursuits, ethics is a mechanism that controls behavior. Its use is more efficient with society's resources than are cruder controls such as police power or economic incentive. Ethical principles are intended to channel individual energy into pursuits that are benign to others and beneficial for society.

GENETIC INHERITANCE

Embedded deeply in our value systems is the accumulation of genetic inheritance. The work of scientists in the field of sociobiology provides evidence that evolutionary forces promoting the survival of groups also generate such traits as cooperation, organizational loyalty, mercy, and the altruism that leads individuals to self-sacrifice for the common good. Such traits, of course, have shaped the development of ethical principles and values in human society.

[34]In "Ethics and Profits Don't Always Go Hand in Hand," *Los Angeles Times*, December 28, 1988. A recent study of auto recalls by two other professors determined that "dubious corporate behavior" in some instances failed to have an adverse impact on stock prices. See Philip Bromiley and Alfred Marcus, "The Deterrent to Dubious Corporate Behavior: Profitability, Probability and Safety Recalls," *Strategic Management Journal*, May–June 1989, p. 248.
[35]For a philosophical discussion of the relationship between ethics and profits see Rogene A. Buchholz, *Fundamental Concepts and Problems in Business Ethics*, Englewood Cliffs, New Jersey: Prentice Hall, 1989, Chapter 2.

According to theoretical models of gene frequency in populations, a genetically based trait of altruism will evolve when the average fitness of all individuals within groups displaying it is greater than the average fitness of all individuals in otherwise comparable groups that do not display it.[36] Sociobiologists point out that altruistic traits have evolved in many lower species, and it is unrealistic to assume that natural selection has not played a part in their development in humans. For example, workers of ant species leave the nest when sick or dying to avoid contaminating it. Honeybees die protecting their hives because their barbed stingers tear apart their viscera when they sting. The soldiers of some termite and ant species place themselves in the most dangerous positions to defend the nest, while workers run inward to avoid harm.[37]

Theoretically, humans have developed similar altruistic behaviors. Major components of the social ethics of business organizations, such as the sanctity of contracts, organizational loyalty, generosity toward coworkers, and the formation of alliances, may be genetically predisposed behaviors that confer advantage in the evolutionary struggle. Individuals who exhibit such behavior are more likely to accrue a biological advantage over rivals because, according to sociobiologist Edward O. Wilson, "The behavior of individual members in particular cultural settings determines their survivorship and reproduction, hence their genetic fitness and the rate at which the gene ensembles spread or decline within the population" (Lumsden and Wilson, 1981). The implication for business is that managerial responses to moral challenges will be shaped and limited by the genetic predispositions of individuals. "The genes," Wilson remarks, "hold culture on a leash."[38]

RELIGION

One of the oldest sources of inspiration for ethical conduct is religion. More than 100,000 different religions exist today and pose a confusing welter of ethical creeds and belief systems to a seeker. But despite doctrinal differences, the major religions, and particularly the Judeo-Christian tradition that is dominant in American life, converge in the belief that ethics are an expression of divine will that reveals to the faithful the nature of right and wrong in business and other areas of life. The great religions are also in agreement on fundamental principles, similar to the building blocks of secular ethical doc-

---

[36]Edward O. Wilson, *The Insect Societies*, Cambridge, Massachusetts: Harvard University Press, 1971, p. 321. For discussion of gene frequency modeling and behavior see S. A. Boorman and P. R. Levitt, "A Frequency-Dependent Natural Selection Model for the Evolution of Social Cooperation Networks," *Proceedings of the National Academy of Sciences, U.S.A.*, Volume 70, No. 1. See also, George Edgin Pugh, *The Biological Origin of Human Values*, New York: Basic Books, 1977; E. O. Wilson, *Sociobiology: The New Synthesis*, Cambridge, Massachusetts: Belknap Press, 1975, Chapter 5, "Group Selection and Altruism;" and Lionel Tiger, *The Manufacture of Evil: Ethics, Evolution, and the Industrial System*, New York: Harper & Row, 1987.

[37]Charles J. Lumsden and Edward O. Wilson, *Genes, Mind, and Culture*, Cambridge, Massachusetts: Harvard University Press, 1981, p. 344.

[38]Edward O. Wilson, *On Human Nature*, Cambridge, Massachusetts: Harvard University Press, 1978, p. 176.

trine. The principle of reciprocity toward one's fellow humans is found, encapsuled in variations of the Golden Rule, in major religions such as Buddhism, Christianity, Judaism, Confucianism, and Hinduism. The great religions preach the necessity for a well-ordered social system and emphasize in their tenets the social responsibility of people to act in such a way as to contribute to the general welfare, or at least not to harm it. Built upon such verities are many other rules of conduct.

In the Judeo-Christian heritage, the Ten Commandments, the Golden Rule, and the Sermon on the Mount have often been mentioned as guides for managers. Donald V. Seibert, former chairman of J. C. Penney Company, Inc., advocates daily Bible reading for executives and says that two books are particularly relevant to business. "Proverbs," he writes, "is replete with references to the proper approach to business transactions, such as 'A wicked man earns deceptive wages, but one who sows righteousness gets a sure reward' [11:18]. And Jesus's teachings and parables in Matthew have enough practical wisdom in them to provide a blueprint for almost an entire working experience."[39]

A survey of executives by Daniel Harris shows that Seibert is not alone in his feelings. In it, 86 percent agreed that the use of Christian resources such as prayer, scripture reading, meditation, and church worship sharpen their judgment and sharpen moral imagination and the sense of obligation to others.[40] And an estimated 7,000 Christian-based U.S. firms, mostly smaller companies, try to operate on biblical principles.[41] The founders of the motel chain Days Inns of America, Inc., for example, consciously adopted a Christian-based strategy of not serving alcohol, giving away Bibles, and catering to families. Until the chain was sold by the founding family, four full-time, roving chaplains were available to help employees. A Christian fast-food chain based in Atlanta, Chick-fil-A Inc., refuses to open on Sunday, a policy which has excluded it from some desirable mall locations.

There is, of course, no firm proof for the validity of religious ethics; acceptance and belief are acts of faith. For this reason they are not embraced by all; many in business are doubters who question the existence of a Divine Will. Chester Barnard, for instance, a management scholar and former president of New Jersey Bell, has, along with others, questioned the applicability of spiritual guides to business conduct. To him they "seemed to have...little application or relevance to the moral problems of the world of affairs."[42] Barnard argued that biblical injunctions were the product of simple rural and agrarian societies characterized by the nomadic life of lambs and shepherds

[39]Donald V. Seibert and William Proctor, *The Ethical Executive*, New York: Simon & Schuster, 1984, pp. 119–20.

[40]"Religious Models for Ethical Managerial Decision Making," paper presented to the Western Academy of Management, Monterey, California, April 1981, pp. 10–11.

[41]This is the estimate of the Fellowship of Companies for Christ International, noted in Roger Ricklefs, "Christian-Based Firms Find Following Principles Pays," *Wall Street Journal*, December 8, 1989.

[42]Chester I. Barnard, "Elementary Conditions of Business Morals," *California Management Review*, Fall 1958, p. 3.

described in the Bible. In this society simple personal relations dominated and the Judeo-Christian ethic that developed to regulate these situations could hardly furnish complete rules for activities such as international trade, where people were too numerous and remote to have reality as individuals. He also lamented that Christian ethics were too perfectionist, since they set up ideals that could not be attained in concrete business situations in which failure to live up to an abstract ideal did not necessarily mean immorality. Thus, although many in business find strong guidance and great comfort in religious teachings, others, like Barnard, find them substantially irrelevant.

Other management scholars, however, have shown the relevance of the Judeo-Christian tradition. Williams and Houck write that although the Bible has few, if any, ethical prescriptions directly applicable to modern corporate life, it is an inspirational wellspring of models, analogues, and stories that can increase ethical sensitivity and teach important lessons.[43] The story of the rich man and Lazarus (Luke 16:19–31), for instance, teaches concern for the poor and challenges the Christian business manager to improve the living conditions of the less privileged. The parable of the prodigal son (Luke 15:11–32) sets out an image of an unconditionally merciful father—a model applicable to ethical conflicts in the superior-subordinate relationships in large corporations.

While some in business doubt the efficacy of religious values, they are a source of inspiration to most and, in any case, they are a repository of some of the most enduring and humane values in Western civilization, along with, if we agree with Bertrand Russell, some of the harshest. Writes Russell: "I do not myself feel that any person who is really profoundly humane can believe in everlasting punishment."[44]

PHILOSOPHICAL SYSTEMS

The Western manager looks back on over two thousand years of philosophical inquiry into ethics. This rich, complex, classical tradition is the source of a variety of widely embraced notions about what is ethical in business. Every age has added new ideas to this tradition, but it would be a mistake to regard the history of ethical philosophy as a single debate which, over the centuries, has matured to bear the fruit of growing ethical wisdom and clear, precise standards of conduct. Even after two millennia, there remains considerable dispute among ethical thinkers about the nature of right action. If anything, standards of ethical behavior were arguably clearer for ancient Greek civilization than for twentieth-century Americans.

In a brief circumambulation of milestones in ethical thinking, we turn first to the Greek philosophers. Greek ethics, from Homeric times onward, were

---

[43]See Oliver F. Williams and John W. Houck, *Full Value: Cases in Christian Business Ethics,* New York: Harper and Row, 1978, and Oliver F. Williams and John W. Houck, eds., *The Judeo-Christian Vision and the Modern Corporation,* Notre Dame: University of Notre Dame Press, 1982. Another management scholar who derives practical guidance from biblical passages is R. Henry Migliore in *Common Sense Management: A Biblical Perspective,* Tulsa: Honor Books, 1988.

[44]Bertrand Russell, *Why I Am Not a Christian,* New York: Simon & Schuster, 1957, p. 17.

embodied in the discharge of duties related to social roles such as shepherd, warrior, merchant, citizen, or king. Expectations of the occupants of these roles were clearer than in contemporary America, where social roles such as those of business manager or employee are more vague, overlapping, and marked by conflict.[45] Socrates (469–399 B.C.) asserted that virtue and ethical behavior were associated with wisdom and taught that insight into life would naturally lead to right conduct. He also initiated the idea that men should respond to a moral law higher than man's law, an idea that protestors have used to demand supralegal behavior from modern corporations. Plato (428–348 B.C.), the gifted student of Socrates, carried his doctrine of virtue as knowledge further by elaborating the theory that absolute justice exists independently of individuals and that its nature can be discovered by intellectual effort. In *The Republic*, Plato set up a fifty-year program to train rulers to rule in harmony with the ideal of Justice.[46] Plato's most apt pupil, Aristotle, spelled out virtues of character in *The Nicomachean Ethics* and advocated the study to develop knowledge of ethical behavior.[47] A lasting contribution of Aristotle is the Doctrine of the Mean (or Golden Mean), which is that people can achieve the good life and happiness by developing virtues of moderation. To illustrate, courage was the mean between cowardice and rashness, modesty the mean between shyness and shamelessness.

The Stoic school of ethics, which spans four centuries from the death of Alexander to the rise of Christianity, furthered the trend toward character development in Greek ethics. Epictetus (A.D. 50–100), for instance, taught that virtue was found solely within and should be valued for its own sake, arguing that virtue was a greater reward than external riches or outward success.

In business, the ethical legacy of the Greeks remains as a conviction that virtues such as truth telling, charity, obedience to the law, good citizenship, justice, courage, friendship, and the correct use of power are important. An unethical manager may still try to trade integrity for profit, of course, and sacrifice character for business success. We condemn this, in part, due to the teachings of the Greeks.

Moral philosophy after the rise of Christianity was dominated by the influence of the great Catholic theologians St. Augustine (354–430) and St. Thomas Aquinas (1226–1274). Both extolled the need for right relations between man and God and asserted the primacy of religion over philosophy. The function of worldly activity was to prepare the soul for the kingdom of heaven. The Christian religion was the source of ethical expectations based on faith in God and the wisdom of God, as revealed in specific rules such as the Ten Commandments and other injunctions found in the Old Testament—for example, those for the ethical treatment of the poor in Psalms 9 and 12.[48]

---

[45] Alasdair MacIntyre, *After Virtue: A Study in Moral Theory*, South Bend, Indiana: University of Notre Dame Press, 1981, p. 115.

[46] Trans. F. M. Cornford, New York: Oxford University Press, 1945 (reprinted).

[47] *Op. cit.*

[48] Benson, *op. cit.*, p. 51.

With the Enlightenment came a decline in the religious domination of ethical thinking. Secular philosophers such as Baruch Spinoza (1634–1677) tried to demonstrate ethical principles logically rather than ordain them by reference to God's will. Immanuel Kant (1724–1804) tried to find universal and objective ethical rules in logic.

Another milestone came when Jeremy Bentham (1748–1832) developed a utilitarian system as a guide to ethics. Bentham observed that "nature has placed mankind under the governance of two sovereign masters, pain and pleasure," and that the ethical worth of an act was the extent to which it produced the greatest increment of pleasure over pain. The legitimacy of majority rule in the United States rests in part on Bentham's theory of utility as refined later by J. S. Mill (1808–1873). Utilitarianism also has sanctified industrial development by legitimizing the notion that economic development brings benefit to the overwhelming majority; thus the pain and dislocation it brings to a few may be ethically permitted.

Other philosophers of the era, such as John Locke (1632–1704), developed and refined doctrines of human rights, leaving an ethical legacy supporting belief in the inalienable rights of human beings, including the right to pursue life, liberty, and happiness, and the right to freedom from tyranny. Our leaders, including business leaders, continue to be restrained by these beliefs.

A "realistic" school of ethics also developed alongside the "idealistic" thinking of Spinoza, Kant, and the Utilitarians. The "realists" believed that nature was dominated by a mixture of good and evil and, therefore, that human relations were naturally marked by the same. Machiavelli (1467–1526) argued that important ends justified expedient means. Herbert Spencer (1820–1903) wrote prolifically of a harsh ethic based on the evolutionary process where the good is that which survives, and the bad that which fails. Friedrich Nietzsche (1844–1900) rejected the ideals of earlier ethics, saying they were prescriptions of the timid, designed to fetter the actions of great men whose irresistible power and will was regarded as dangerous by the common herd of ordinary mortals.

Nietzsche believed in the existence of a "master morality" in which great men made their own moral rules according to their convenience and without respect for the general good of the average person. In reaction to this "master morality" the mass of ordinary people developed a "slave morality" that shackled the great men. For example, according to Nietzsche the great mass of ordinary men celebrated the Christian virtue of turning the other cheek because they did not have the power to revenge themselves on great men. He felt that prominent theories of the day were recipes for timidity and once said of utilitarianism that it made him want to vomit.[49]

At the turn of the century, G. E. Moore founded a new school of ethics (the emotivist school) by espousing the doctrine that all ethical judgments are nothing but expressions of personal preference and cannot be objectively

---

[49]His exact words were: "...'the general welfare' is no ideal, no goal, no remotely intelligible concept, but only an emetic..." In *Beyond Good and Evil*, New York: Vintage Books, 1966 (originally published in 1886), p. 157.

proven right or wrong or shown as contrary to divine will. This rejection of both religion and principle has not, however, stopped the philosophical debate about ethics in our century. Managers continue to seek religious guidance for their actions and philosophers seek to build new ethical principles appropriate to the age.

The legacy of more than 2,000 years of recorded ethical debate is such that no single approach or principle is proven superior to others as a guide to right conduct in business. The wise student of business ethics will examine managerial behavior from a number of perspectives and make judgments only with humility that is born of the knowledge that there is centuries-old disagreement about moral standards.

CULTURAL EXPERIENCE

Culture may be defined as a set of traditional values, rules, or standards transmitted between generations and acted upon to produce behavior that falls within acceptable limits. These rules and standards always play an important part in determining values because individuals stabilize beliefs by anchoring their conduct in the culture of the group. Civilization itself is a cumulative cultural experience in which people have passed through three distinct stages of moral codification.[50] These stages correspond to changing economic and social arrangements in human history.

For millions of generations in the *hunting stage* of human development, ethics were adapted to conditions in which our ancestors had to be ready to fight, face brutal foes, and suffer hostile forces of nature. Under such circumstances a premium was placed on pugnacity, appetite, greed, and sexual readiness, since it was often the strongest who survived. Trade ethics in early civilizations were probably deceitful and dishonest by our standards, and economic transactions were frequently conducted by brute force and violence.

Civilization passed into an *agricultural stage* approximately 10,000 years ago, beginning a time when industriousness was more important than ferocity, thrift paid greater dividends than violence, monogamy became the prevailing sexual custom because of the relatively equal numbers of the sexes, and peace came to be valued over wars, which destroyed crops and animals. These new values were codified into ethical systems by the philosophers discussed in the previous section. Hence, great ethical philosophies that guide educated managers today are products of the agricultural revolution. Included would be the ethical teachings of the church which provide the reward for good conduct—salvation and everlasting peace.

Two centuries ago, society entered an *industrial stage* of cultural experience, and ethical systems once more began evolving to reflect the changing physical, cultural, institutional, and intellectual environment. Large factories and corporations, population growth, capitalist and socialist economic doctrines, and new technologies have all assaulted the ethical standards of the

[50]Will Durant and Ariel Durant, *The Lessons of History*, New York: Simon & Schuster, 1968.

agricultural stage. Industrialism has not yet created a distinct ethic, but it has created tensions with old ethical systems based on the values of agricultural societies. It does this by changing values related to what is good and bad. For example, the copious outpouring of material goods from factories has encouraged materialism and consumption at the expense of older virtues such as moderation and thrift. Many of the most difficult ethical problems faced by managers arise from changing cultural experience. Corporate social responsibilities, for instance, are occasioned by widespread, negative, unintended impacts of industrialization. The presence of computers raises new issues of privacy rights unlike those debated in agricultural days when biblical injunctions were written. Accumulating scientific evidence showing environmental damage from industrial processes is new in this century and creates the need for new ethical guidelines to protect nature.

Because managers run an industrial apparatus creating portentous ethical problems, they are on the cutting edge of cultural experience. The tensions they create and wrestle with make business more ethically complex than ever in our history. A cartoon in the *New Yorker* once depicted a cluster of managers sitting around a conference table. They all looked perplexed and confused, and the boss talked into the intercom to his secretary. "Miss Jones," he said, "will you please send someone in here who can tell right from wrong!" The boss had a point.

THE LEGAL SYSTEM

The law is a codification of customs, ideas, beliefs, and ethical standards that society wishes to preserve and enforce. As social views about what is right and wrong change and crystallize, they are reflected in new laws or the abandonment and neglect of old ones. A major cause of higher ethical standards in business is the addition of laws to prevent violations of what society considers to be proper. Of course, the law does not establish all standards of ethics for society. Law simply cannot blanket all areas of conduct, and this is even more true today than in the past. Law is a reactive institution, and the enactment of new statutes always lags behind the opportunity for business to take advantage of developing situations.

Nevertheless, over the past twenty years, a "legal explosion" of new government regulations, stricter product liability doctrines, consumer and stockholder lawsuits, changes in tort law, and new criminal statutes has forced corporations to comply with rising standards of ethical behavior. More of the corporation's activities are subject to legal control. Both civil and criminal liability of executives and corporations have expanded.[51]

[51]The expanding scope of federal criminal statutes, for instance, is illustrated by passage of the Insider Trading Sanctions Act of 1984, the Corporate Crime Control Act of 1984, and the False Claims Act amendments of 1986. A related development is the frequent application of the Racketeer Influenced and Corrupt Organizations Act (RICO) of 1970 by U.S. attorneys against corporations and corporate white-collar offenders. These and other statutes set stiff guidelines for fines and prison terms.

There are a number of administrative and legal weapons for getting corporate compliance with the law. Two main methods for sanctioning illegal corporate acts are fines and prosecution of individual managers. Neither is unflawed as a device for controlling corporate crime.

Fines may be levied to take away ill-gotten gains. Often, they include punitive payments designed to punish wrongful behavior. The Criminal Fine Enforcement Act of 1984, for instance, authorizes fines of up to $500,000 for each felony count on which a corporation is convicted and for every misdemeanor resulting in a death.[52] In cases of fraud, corporations may also be fined an amount twice the gross gain of their illegal activities and be forced to pay restitution to victims.

Fines often do not hurt large firms. A few years ago, General Electric pleaded guilty to defrauding the federal government of $800,000 on a Minuteman missile contract. A manager in a Minuteman plant and his subordinates had falsified worker time cards, fraudulently billing the government for work unrelated to the Minuteman contract. GE agreed to reimburse the government for the $800,000 and was fined an additional $1,040,000. The fine created slight adverse publicity and damaged the manager's career, but it was financially insignificant. To GE it was the equivalent of a $25 fine for a person with a $50,000 annual income.

Courts hesitate to impose truly damaging fines because their burden would fall partly on innocent bystanders—shareholders, workers, suppliers, and others who had no knowledge of or control over the corporation's deviant behavior, but whose livelihood depended on its benefactions. Fines that are fixed in dollar amounts in civil and criminal statutes often do not hurt large corporations. Fines could be assessed in proportion to a firm's assets or revenues—as is sometimes done in European countries—but it might not be equitable to fine one firm twenty times more than another for the same transgression. Also, fines play no direct role in strengthening the weak organizational controls or corrupt corporate cultures that permit illegal behavior.

A second legal weapon for sanctioning corporate crime is the prosecution of individual managers. In the past, judges have been reluctant to sentence managers to jail terms for fraud, embezzlement, polluting the environment, or breaking health and safety laws. Managers ordinarily do not violently endanger society, may not have the motive or opportunity to repeat a crime, and would further crowd prisons. Investigating corporate crimes also is difficult for prosecuting attorneys, who are faced with a mass of highly technical corporate documents to review, a network of complex organizational relationships to sort out, and the conflicting priority of violent street crime to compete for their resources. Corporations ordinarily are defended by highly competent defense lawyers; the states' case ordinarily is championed by underfunded, less experienced attorneys. For these reasons, U.S. and state

---

[52]P.L. 98-596. See Daniel A. Reznick, "The New Criminal Fine Enforcement Act of 1984," *Corporate Criminal Liability Reporter* (Spring 1987), p. 35.

attorneys with limited resources for prosecution find it easier to justify simple indictments for street criminals and shy away from the complex corporation cases.

Nevertheless, some highly publicized cases against executives who have violated criminal statutes have led to prison terms. In a landmark 1985 conviction, three managers of Film Recovery Systems, a Chicago firm that recovered silver from used photographic film, were sentenced to 25 years in prison when an employee died after exposure to uncontrolled cyanide fumes from a vat used in the extraction process. The three were convicted after an investigation revealed that they had known of the dangers but had failed to inform employees or install air filtering in the plant. Incidentally, a month after the death, the Occupational Safety and Health Administration inspected the plant and imposed fines of only $4,855 for twenty safety violations.[53]

Courts have also imposed lengthy sentences for criminal fraud. Some landmarks are the 1985 conviction of Jacob F. Butcher, a Tennessee banker, to twenty years in prison after pleading guilty to charges that he fraudulently used funds and caused the failure of eight banks he controlled; the 1986 conviction of Jeffrey Levitt, who caused the failure of two Maryland savings and loans he owned through fraudulent real estate schemes and was sentenced to thirty years in prison, fined $12,000, and required to forfeit $10 million in personal property; and the 1989 sentencing of Barry J. Minkow, the twenty-three-year-old multimillionaire owner of ZZZZ Best Co., a carpet-cleaning company built on fraud and money laundering, to twenty-five years and restitution of $26 million. These sentences are atypically long; most white collar criminals who go to prison receive a few years at most. The insider trading scandals on Wall Street in the mid-1980s, for example, led to prison terms for only ten traders, with sentences ranging from thirty days to four years.

Other methods for punishing corporate crime exist. One guideline for applying them is that they should not cripple or render inefficient legitimate corporate activity. Courts have appointed directors to preside over organizational changes designed to enforce better behavior. They have also required advertisements and speeches to publicize wrongdoing. Some corporations have paid their fines to community service projects, and executives have been ordered to do charity work. In 1988, Victor Posner, a corporate raider who once controlled forty companies, was convicted of income tax evasion. A federal judge in Miami sentenced him to pay back taxes and fines totaling $4 million. Posner was also required to invest $3 million of his own money and spend a minimum of 5,000 hours, averaging twenty hours a week, creating and implementing a project to help the homeless. In addition, he was required to spend five hours a week working at a Miami mission for the homeless operated by the Brothers of the Good Shepherd. "He will be serv-

---

[53]This fine was later halved. See Note, "Getting Away with Murder: Federal OSHA Preemption of State Criminal Prosecutions for Industrial Accidents," *Harvard Law Review*, vol. 101, 1987, p. 535. The company itself was convicted of manslaughter and reckless conduct by the state of Illinois. It was fined $24,000 in 1985.

ing food for the street people," Brother Paul Johnson told a *Wall Street Journal* reporter: "It may be a blessing in his life."[54]

THE ROLE OF INDIVIDUAL PSYCHODYNAMICS

Some managers are unethical and others scrupulously honest. Ethical values are displayed through the prism of individual personality, so the process of personality development explains in part why ethical propensities differ.

Sigmund Freud (1856–1939) explained human personality as consisting of three parts. The *id* is the source of primitive, aggressive impulses. The *ego* shapes and directs these impulses in conformity with the realities of the outer world. And the *superego* both provides an ideal image of the self and incorporates a conscience to police behavior.[55] The conscience part of the superego incorporates parental discipline about the rightness and wrongness of particular actions. According to developmental psychologists, the child, being in a helpless and dependent state, must satisfy parental authority. On an elemental level, pleasing the parents is a matter of survival to the child and so the child is receptive to parental moral teaching and begins to incorporate ethics at an early age.

The conscience is largely formed in childhood and in adulthood is an internal reservoir of parental authority with the power to mete out psychological reward and punishment. The power of the conscience to do this is believed to be derived from an internal diversion of part of the primitive destructive effect of the id. Incidentally, a vivid proof of the presence of the conscience is the polygraph, or lie detector. Changes in respiration, pulse rate, and skin chemistry are the measurable effects of the action of the conscience when a person violates the built-in parental prohibition against lying.

The tremendous force of the conscience in ethical affairs may be illustrated in the fate of Eli M. Black, chairman of United Brands Co., who leaped to his death from the forty-fourth floor of the Pan American building in Manhattan in 1975, shortly before *Wall Street Journal* reporters discovered that United Brands had paid a number of overseas bribes. Black was the son of a rabbi and was shaken, according to friends, when a director of the company, who was not supposed to know about the payments, raised a question about them. We may speculate that the seeds of Black's destruction were planted in his conscience and that, in making foreign payoffs, Black turned his internal police state against himself as an implacable foe. On a more mundane level, work itself is a powerful source of appeasement for the pressures of the conscience. Through work an individual may achieve worthy goals of the conscience through punctuality, productivity, and honesty.[56] The need of some

---

[54]Jose de Cordoba, "Posner Is Sentenced to Set Up Program for the Homeless," *Wall Street Journal*, February 16, 1988.

[55]Sigmund Freud, *New Introductory Lectures on Psychoanalysis*, New York: Norton, 1933.

[56]Harry Levinson, *Executive*, Cambridge, Massachusetts: Harvard University Press, 1981.

workers to do high-quality work represents the desire to meet the stern dictates of the conscience.

The way in which a manager perceives and utilizes ethical principles available in society is also a function of the dynamics of personality development. Various abnormal developments in personality are associated with the pathological application of ethics. For example, demands for moral perfection may be neurotic if they are based on the need to be superior to others rather than on a healthy desire to improve oneself. Emphasis on justice may be a camouflage for vindictiveness and sadistic tendencies based on the neurotic need to redress childhood humiliations and assert neurotic superiority.[57] The tyranny of the superego in obsessive-compulsive personalities often leads to the development of a harsh and unyielding moral judgment, which the person directs against both self and others. The obsessive-compulsive neurotic may spend a lifetime trying to live up to impossibly high moral ideals rather than unleash the anxiety that would come from failure to be perfect.[58]

Psychopathic insincerity and lying are common traits in impulsive personality types and stem from flawed development of the conscience. The psychopath is typically an "operator" who is ethical when necessary or in self-interest, but who does not feel pangs of conscience for behaving unethically. A person with paranoid tendencies may erroneously perceive conspiracies among colleagues or company management and employ rigorous ethical standards to condemn these allegedly harmful, though entirely fictitious, schemes. Many "wheeler-dealers" in the business community may in reality be among the 3 to 10 percent of the population suffering from mood disorders, such as manic depression.[59] At the height of elation, a manic may be so euphoric as to feel immune from ethical considerations. Psychotic individuals are out of touch with reality and may engage in violent and unethical behavior because they are unable to understand the consequences of their actions.

Research suggests that the ability to use moral reasoning may also develop in stages and differ among individuals. Lawrence Kohlberg, an educational psychologist, demonstrated through twenty years of following the lives of seventy-five American boys (now men) that there are six sequential stages of moral development. The child moves from complete reliance on external rules and standards to states of increasing reliance on internal controls as follows: (1) avoidance of breaking rules in order to avert punishment, (2) obedience to ethical standards to satisfy self-centered needs and to elicit reciprocity from others, (3) subordination of self-interest to group interest to please others and gain their approval, (4) respect for the law and authority as necessary to preserve the social system, (5) flexible interpretation of legal authority as balanced with the rights of individuals, and (6) principled reasoning with ethical concepts of personal choice. Most individuals in Kohlberg's study attained stages four and five by adulthood, but only a few progressed

[57]Karen Horney, *Neurosis and Human Growth*, New York: Norton, 1950.
[58]David Shapiro, *Neurotic Styles*, New York: Basic Books, 1965, p. 41.
[59]Ronald R. Fieve, *Moodswing*, New York: Bantam Books, 1975, p. 27.

to stage six.[60] If Kohlberg's theory is correct, business managers respond differently to common problems of business ethics depending on their level of moral development.

In conclusion, the ethical implications of personality are a significant part of corporate life. Ethical behavior is an integral part of all human behavior, and, to the extent that personality development imposes burdens of abnormality, anger, anxiety, fear, self-doubt, and neurotic needs, individual ethics may be altered to facilitate the personality integration activities of the ego. Some managers are therefore unethical and others scrupulously honest because of internal impulses as well as external constraints.

MANAGING ETHICS AT THE CORPORATE LEVEL

In the past, most corporations were managed in keeping with the assumption that ethics is a matter of individual conscience. A few pioneers made formal efforts to manage company-wide ethics. In 1913, James Cash Penney, founder of J. C. Penney Company, formalized a conduct code for employees. In 1945, Robert Wood Johnson, president of Johnson & Johnson, wrote "An Industrial Credo" spelling out fair relationships with customers, employees, communities, and stockholders. Today, both of these companies have strong corporate cultures supporting high ethics. In each, the rudimentary ethics policies of yesteryear evolved into more formal programs to insure ethical behavior. Recently, many other companies have set up ethics programs to develop similarly strong ethical cultures. Ethics programs are a comprehensive set of interrelated policies designed to sensitize employees to ethical issues, prevent scandal, and promote decorous relationships in the organization and with the public. They require interventions in the basic management functions—leading, planning, staffing, organizing, and controlling—to insure that ethical behavior becomes an organizational priority. Without a management system to handle ethics issues, ethical behavior remains largely a matter of individual conscience, and the organization is less able to prevent lapses.

THE GENERAL DYNAMICS PROGRAM

An example of a comprehensive ethics program is one adopted by General Dynamics Corp. In May 1985, Navy Secretary John Lehman suspended Navy contracts with General Dynamics worth over $1 billion, citing as one reason a "pervasive corporate attitude" inappropriate to the public trust. The company had been caught in a series of unethical and illegal acts. Managers were shifting expenses from fixed-price contracts to contracts that permitted cost overruns. The company had given numerous, expensive gifts to Admiral Hyman Rickover and his wife. Executives charged country club dues to military contracts, and Chairman David Lewis billed the government for his

[60]Lawrence Kohlberg, "State and Sequence: The Cognitive Developmental Approach to Socialization," in *Handbook of Socialization Theory and Research*, D. A. Gosline, ed., Chicago: Rand-McNally, 1969.

flights from company headquarters in St. Louis to his farm in Georgia. The condition for lifting the suspension of General Dynamics from Pentagon contracts was a fine of $676,000 for the gifts, cancellation of $22 million in overcharges, and the installation of a strict ethics program.

The ethics program set up by General Dynamics is far-reaching. A twenty-page booklet, *General Dynamics Standards of Business Ethics and Conduct*, or *Standards* for short, was written and distributed to all employees.[61] Distribution began when Chairman Stanley C. Pace handed it to all persons reporting to him. In turn, these managers distributed the booklet in person to their subordinates, and so forth until the ethics code reached the lowest organizational levels. The *Standards* instruct employees to "observe a basic code of conduct in the workplace," and define applicable conduct in the areas of conflict of interest; selling/marketing; pricing, billing and contracting; time card reporting; supplier and consultant relations; quality/testing; expense reports; bribery, kickbacks, and illegal payments; security of secret information; political contributions; environmental protection; and obeying laws in foreign countries. Specific policies are very strict. A draconian policy on giving and accepting gifts or entertainment prohibits employees from accepting even trivia like calendars or pens from subcontractors. When military personnel visit General Dynamics facilities, they must pay 25 cents for each cup of coffee they drink.[62] The Board of Directors set up a Committee on Corporate Responsibility to review implementation of the ethics program. And a top executive group composed of leaders in functional areas was also formed to give advice on implementation. A professor from the University of Chicago was hired to direct the ethics program. Reporting to him are thirty-four Ethics Program Directors in separate General Dynamics facilities.

To familiarize employees with the ethics program, General Dynamics began a massive training effort. It started with a workshop for the chairman and top executives in 1986, and within a year all 103,000 employees had attended. Workshops are led by managers rather than outside consultants. Employee time was often charged to government contracts. By 1989, approximately 12,000 new employees a year underwent training near the time of hiring. New employees are also required to sign a card acknowledging their receipt and understanding of the *Standards*. Over 60,000 suppliers and subcontractors have received the booklet and are asked to abide by its provisions.

General Dynamics opened up new communications channels to air ethical concerns. All managers are expected to receive subordinates who approach them with ethics inquiries and are charged with "maintaining a workplace environment that encourages frank and open communication, free of the fear of reprisal, concerning the upholding of the Standards."[63] Annual bonus

---

[61]*General Dynamics Standards of Business Ethics Conduct*, St. Louis: General Dynamics Corp., August 1985.

[62]Ford S. Worthy, "Mr Clean Charts a New Course at General Dynamics," *Fortune*, April 28, 1986, p. 74.

[63]*General Dynamics Standards of Business Ethics Conduct*, Second Edition, St. Louis: General Dynamics Corp., October 1987, p. 7.

awards are based in part on how the ethical dimension of work is managed. The company has set up twenty-nine ethics hotlines, special numbers answered by the ethics directors, which employees or suppliers can call to ask questions, seek advice, or allege wrongdoing. Callers can remain anonymous if they wish. After business hours, hotline numbers are connected to answering machines in locked rooms or compartments so that confidential messages are received twenty-four hours a day.

In 1987, 3,197 calls came in through the hotlines and 25 percent of callers preferred to remain anonymous even though the company has adopted a no reprisal policy. Despite efforts to allay fears, a survey of employees showed that 32 percent fear reprisal for use of the hotline. Procedures have been established for classifying allegations of wrongdoing based on their seriousness and for subsequent investigation.

When violations of the *Standards* are discovered, company policy makes punishment mandatory. Regulations stipulate that punishment should meet two tests. First, it should take mitigating and aggravating circumstances into consideration. Second, it should be evenhanded; all people should be treated equally in similar situations. As a result of employee allegations and internal investigations, 205 sanctions were imposed in 1987, including 27 discharges. The most frequent problem area was time card reporting.[64]

The ongoing program is supported in many ways. Each year the ethics program is reviewed by the internal auditors as well as the board of directors. An annual report of the program is written by the corporate ethics program director and a separate report is sent to the Department of Defense. In 1987, a second, updated edition of the *Standards* booklet was written and distributed to every employee. The company paper, *General Dynamics World,* carries stories about the program. Posters advertising hotline numbers are put up. Most employees like the program; to wit, 70 percent in the aforementioned survey thought the hotline was a good idea. But others dissent. Some believe that ethics is a personal matter and find corporate guidelines condescending. Others see the hotline as a management conspiracy to encourage employees to "snitch." Some have tried to extract favors in return for signing the acknowledgment card they receive with the *Standards* booklet. Overall, however, the response is positive.

GUIDELINES FOR MANAGING ETHICS PROGRAMS

The General Dynamics approach exemplifies a state-of-the-art effort to create an ethical corporate culture. These critical elements of an ethics program may be derived from it and from the experiences of other companies.

Top Management Leadership   The chief executive officer should initiate the ethics program and make clear statements about the importance of legal and ethical behavior. A vivid illustration of how this can be accomplished is

[64]Statistics related to the General Dynamics program are from General Dynamics, *The General Dynamics Ethics Program Update,* St. Louis: General Dynamics Corp., October 1988, pp. 12–19.

offered by the actions of Robert Cushman, CEO of the Norton Company, an abrasives manufacturer with plants in twenty-seven countries. After introducing a strong ethics code in 1976, Cushman presented it at a conference for his international managers. A vice president in attendance that day remembers how he was challenged.

> During a panel discussion, some of the key Europeans were particularly animated in objecting to the code's stringent rules on certain kinds of payments which were standard in their countries. Cushman acknowledged their differences of opinion openly and then reiterated what "the Company" expected them to do. He was decidedly unapologetic about taking an authoritarian stance: "I've had to live by certain rules, and so do you." [Some were] taken aback by Cushman's words, but found the session to be a real eye opener about just how strongly top management meant the code to be enforced.[65]

Codes of Ethics   Codes of ethics have become popular—over 90 percent of *Fortune* 500 companies have one, and roughly half adopted them in the last decade.[66] Many codes were spurred by foreign payoff scandals in the 1970s. Scandals in other industries, such as defense, and increasing public concern about business ethics have led to a crescendo of code writing in the 1980s. Companies without a code risked appearing indifferent to ethics. Codes vary from long formulations, such as IBM's thirty-two page *Business Conduct Guidelines*, to succinct credos which in one or two pages express a general philosophy for managing conflicts. The short two-and-one-half page statement of ethics of the Koppers Company states that management accepts the teachings of the great religions in regard to moral and ethical conduct and cannot improve upon them. One of the simplest codes on record was that of the Sampsonite Company, which used to issue to its sales force small marbles with the Golden Rule printed on them.

The longer codes tend to be legalistic and authoritarian, combining exhortations to be ethical with listings of prohibited behaviors. Broad ethics codes are often supplemented by more detailed operational policies on such things as accepting gifts or discounts from suppliers. Developing a code is an occasion for members of a firm to think through ethical conflicts and duties. When Security Pacific Bank developed a code in the 1980s, it enlisted seventy volunteers among senior managers to meet in groups discussing ethical dilemmas. Their dialogues identified central needs that the bank's "Credo" eventually addressed.

Changes in Organization Structure   General Dynamics anchored responsibility for its ethics program in committees at the board of directors and senior management level. It put individual ethics program directors in major locations and involved all functional areas and the internal auditing staff in code enforcement. Hotlines were set up to establish new communications

---

[65]This story is related by Laura L. Nash, "The Norton Company's Ethics Program," in Business Roundtable, *Corporate Ethics...op. cit.,* p. 120.

[66]See Ronald E. Berenbeim, *Corporate Ethics,* New York: The Conference Board, 1987, p. 14.

channels between work locations and hierarchical levels. Opening multiple upward channels facilitates the ventilation of allegations, since many employees fear speaking to their immediate supervisors.

Training Sessions At General Dynamics, workers went to half-day workshops where they learned about the ethics program, watched two video tapes, and discussed case studies. Other companies do it differently. At Citicorp, among other activities, attenders in ethics workshops play a game called Work Ethic. Players draw cards printed with brief ethical dilemmas and multiple choice answers. At Allied Chemical, managers submit anonymously written cases based on personal experience prior to attending two-day retreats on business ethics. They are then discussed by the group. The basic function of training is to inform workers about the program and to sensitize them to common ethical issues.

Enforcement A number of mechanisms are used to force compliance with ethics policies. At General Mills, employees must sign annual compliance affidavits. Ethical performance may be tied to compensation. At Boeing, managers are aware that a scandal in their plant or program will lead to a severe reduction in pay—even if they are not involved. At Dow Corning, internal auditors conduct face-to-face ethical audits lasting from four to six hours and including questions such as: "Are there any examples of business that Dow Corning has lost because of our refusal to provide 'gifts' or other incentives to government officials at our customers' facilities?" and "Which specific Dow Corning policies conflict with local practices?"[67] Of course, violators of the code must be dealt with. Their treatment enters the folklore of the organization and conveys whether top management is really serious or whether it winks when violations occur.

There are many other steps which can be taken to implement ethics programs. Some companies use ombudsmen to resolve disputes. Others survey employees to understand their ethical problems. Many try to recruit ethical employees. The important thing is that ethics programs require a set of reinforcing actions tailored to individual companies. If such actions are taken, a strong, ethical culture should emerge over time.

CONCLUSION

Breaches of business ethics are a perennial problem. They may be traced to individual misbehavior, permissive industry or company climates, and even, perhaps, to the characteristics of the business system itself. Guidelines for ethical behavior come from religion, philosophy, law, and cultural heritage. Interpretation of these sources is an art, not an exact science, and in Chapter 8 we discuss how ethical decisions are made and why they are so difficult.

[67]Patrick E. Murphy, "Creating Ethical Corporate Structures," *Sloan Management Review*, Winter 1989, p. 84.

A. H. Robins Co. and the Dalkon Shield

This is the story of a venerable and proud company brought to its knees by a dime-sized contraceptive device. The company, A. H. Robins, grew from an apothecary shop started in 1866 by a pharmacist named Albert Hartley Robins into a prosperous multinational with $700 million in sales and 6,100 employees in 1985. Were it not for the firm's persistence in selling the Dalkon Shield intrauterine device in the face of clear evidence of its dangers, Robins might today be flourishing. But during the 1970s, Robins' management lost its way. Oblivious to signals of danger, it opened itself to lawsuits, government restrictions, public criticism, hostile investigative reporters, and a bidding war by competitors trying to acquire its assets. In 1985, Robins was forced to seek protection under Chapter 11 of the bankruptcy laws to escape costly lawsuits.

In December 1989, after four years of legal maneuvering, the company emerged from bankruptcy. Its assets and product lines—Chapstick lip balm, Robitussin and Dimetapp cold medications, and a variety of prescription drugs—were intact. And the bankruptcy years had been profitable ones. However, it was immediately acquired by American Home Products Corp., which erased its identity by integrating Robins' various parts into AHP subsidiaries. The end of Robins as an independent entity parallels the fate of at least twenty women who died of Shield-related complications. But many surviving women believe that this retribution is inadequate. The story begins with some background on intrauterine devices.

INTRAUTERINE DEVICES

An intrauterine device (IUD) is simply a foreign object placed in the uterus to lower fertility. No one is sure exactly how it works. In their heyday they came in a variety of shapes and sizes. There were rings, spirals, loops, bows, T-shapes, and contorted forms that defy description. Some released copper or progesterone slowly into the body to enhance contraceptive effect. All these permutations were attempts at greater contraceptive effectiveness in a process not yet fully understood. Much study of how IUDs work has been undertaken. It is thought that they function by stimulating cellular actions which cause fertilized eggs to be rejected by the endometrium or womb lining so that embryos cannot implant and receive nourishment from the mother's body. The question remains as to whether IUDs are contraceptives or abortifacients.

One of the earliest uses of IUD technology was by ancient desert nomads, who placed stones in the uteri of their camels to prevent pregnancy from occurring during prolonged marches.[68] IUDs were not much used in humans until the late nineteenth century, and the first real medical experimentation came in the 1920s. They continued to languish until the 1960s when, simultaneously, new designs incorporating flexible plastics became available and women, aware of the drawbacks of birth-control pills, sought alternatives.

For women who could not tolerate the pill, remember to take it, or feel comfortable with its risks, IUDs were an attractive alternative. Once inserted in the uterus in a minor procedure done at the doctor's office, the IUD generally requires no further attention. Its contraceptive effects end promptly with removal. Adverse side effects risked in IUD use include abdominal pain, cramps, bleeding, and heavy menstruation. IUDs also pose a risk of pelvic inflammatory disease, a dangerous infection by bacteria associated with the foreign object in the uterus that spreads throughout the reproductive system and body. IUDs occasionally perforate the uterine wall as well.

DEVELOPMENT OF THE DALKON SHIELD

The Dalkon Shield was invented in the late 1960s by Hugh J. Davis, M.D., an assistant professor of obstetrics and gynecology at the Johns Hopkins University School of Medicine. To sell the new IUD, he and two partners, an electrical engineer named Irwin Lerner and an attorney named Robert Cohn, formed the Dalkon Corporation. The word Dalkon was derived from combinations of the three partners' names. The device was called a shield because its shape was similar to a policeman's badge.

Although Davis originally patented the IUD in 1967, Lerner tinkered with it and added ten fin-like projections around the sides so that it would stay more firmly in the uterus. In 1968 this altered design was patented, and Lerner the electrical engineer, rather than Davis the physician, was listed on the patent application as sole inventor. In Davis' mind this renunciation of patent right apparently freed him to use medical research facilities at Johns Hopkins University to study the Shield's efficacy, even though he owned 35 percent of the Dalkon Corporation, which sold the Shield—a clear conflict of interest.[69]

---

[68]David A. Edelman, Gary S. Berger, and Louis G. Keith, *Intrauterine Devices and Their Complications*, Boston: G. K. Hall, 1979.

[69]Morton Mintz, *At Any Cost: Corporate Greed, Women, and the Dalkon Shield*, New York: Pantheon, 1985, Chapter 1.

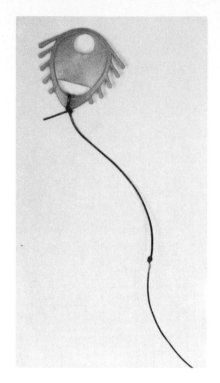

The Dalkon Shield was made of plastic. Side projections anchored the device in the uterus; the tail string extended into the vagina, and women and their doctors could check the position of the device. (Courtesy of Planned Parenthood of New York City, Inc. Random House photo by Stacey Pleasant.)

Davis conducted a clinical study to show that the Shield was safe and effective. In February 1970, he published an article in the *American Journal of Obstetrics and Gynecology* containing data on 640 users.[70] It showed a pregnancy rate of only 1.1 percent, lower than the 1.4 percent rate typical for birth-control pills. Davis noted no serious side effects from the Shield, and, of course, failed to note his financial interest in the product.

In 1971 Davis also published a book, *Intrauterine Devices for Contraception*, in which he compared the Dalkon Shield to other IUDs and concluded that it was superior. Later, both this book and the article were criticized as highly misleading by other medical researchers. For example, in his study of women fitted with Shields, Davis had followed his subjects for only five and one-half months. This was insufficient time to show the typical pregnancy rate among Shield wearers of over 5 percent or to observe the predictable development of pelvic infections. Moreover, he failed to follow up on women who dropped out of the study, the very women most likely to have become pregnant or to have had complications.

The Dalkon Shield began to sell based on this foundation of trumped-up medical evidence. It came on the market at a time when sexual mores were loosening and when many women were having second thoughts about birth-control pills because of recent congressional hearings regarding their adverse

[70]"The Shield Intrauterine Device," February 1, 1970.

side effects and risks. To increase sales, Davis and his partners tried to find a major pharmaceutical firm that would market the device nationally. This is how A. H. Robins entered the picture.

A. H. ROBINS CO. BUYS RIGHTS TO SELL THE SHIELD

Early in 1970, Robins, which was looking for an entry into the booming market for birth-control devices, purchased rights to the Dalkon Shield. In those days, the Food and Drug Administration (FDA) required no premarket testing of medical devices such as IUDs, and so Robins could enter the market immediately. It did so without conducting any research on the device to confirm its safety or effectiveness.

Robins began an aggressive campaign to market the Shield to doctors around the country through a sales force of several hundred that had been trained in a special sales pitch about the device. The sales force was pressured to meet quotas, as the following 1971 telegram from one division sales manager to his sales force shows:

> Northern Division will not be humiliated by a lack of Dalkon sales. If you have not sold at least 25 packages of eight, then you are instructed to call me. Be prepared to give me your call-back figures. No excuses or hedging will be tolerated, or look for another occupation.[71]

Ads in medical journals were another part of the marketing campaign. They emphasized that the Shield had been "anatomically engineered" to fit the uterus. They billed the Shield as a logical choice for women who were not good candidates for the pill, including young women inexperienced with birth control, those with adverse reactions to the pill, those in mass programs at birth-control clinics, and those too disorganized women who couldn't follow the daily regimen. Some of the ads in 1971 and 1972 featured a chart showing low pregnancy rates in four studies—two of which, including the earlier study by Davis, had been done by physicians with a financial interest in sales of the Shield and the other two were poorly designed.

By 1971, the Shield—which cost $.25 to make but was sold to doctors for $4.35—was outselling all other IUDs. Eventually it grabbed a 40 percent market share; 2.9 million were sold in the United States. Part of the reason for the Shield's success was that the company took the unusual step of marketing the IUD to general practitioners (GPs) as well as to obstetricians and gynecologists. The latter were the usual market for IUDs because of their specialized knowledge, but Robins chose to market the Shield to GPs in order to reach the majority of women who consulted only their family doctors about birth control. Some members of the Robins Medical Advisory Board cautioned against this move, but to little effect.[72]

[71]Mintz, *op. cit.*, p. 67.
[72]*Ibid.*, p. 71.

STORM CLOUDS GATHER

For several years the Shield was the hottest selling device in an expansive IUD market. Each year between 1970 and 1974, over one million new women chose to be fitted with an IUD. But as customers multiplied, problems arose. Doctors reported large numbers of pregnancies among Shield users, including a higher than normal number of ectopic (extrauterine) pregnancies requiring surgery. Other women required surgery to remove IUDs that had penetrated the uterine lining. Many suffered infections of the reproductive system and abdominal area triggered by bacterial contamination of the womb related to IUD use. These women required X-rays, antibiotics, blood transfusions, and at times major surgery to remove diseased organs. Women who became pregnant with IUDs in place frequently miscarried in the second trimester or lost their babies when bacterial infections required septic abortions. Many surgeries and miscarriages left women sterile, turning the allegedly carefree method of birth control into an involuntary nightmare.

Although these complications were associated with all IUDs, the Dalkon Shield ultimately proved to be far more risky than its competitors. One reason was the design of its tail string. The Shield, like other IUDs, had a short string dropping from it into the vagina so that women and their doctors could check the position of the IUD and make sure it was properly sited. This was an important safety measure, since a lost IUD might perforate the uterus and enter the abdomen. But the tail string on the Shield, unlike those of competing devices, was made of interwoven fibers and acted like a wick that drew bacteria from the vagina up the microscopic paths between the fibers into the womb; this "wicking" was the cause of an unusually high rate of pelvic inflammatory disease among women wearing the Shield. Studies by Robins employees demonstrated the dangers inherent in this tail-string design, and several employees in the factory where Robins manufactured the Shield suggested switching to a monofilament tail string to obviate the problem. An alternative string was sought and found, but it cost 6.1 cents per device compared to the older string's cost of .63 cents per unit. No change was ever made. And the Robins employees never pursued the matter outside the company.

In 1973, a subcommittee of the House Government Operations Committee held hearings on the need to give the FDA authority to regulate intrauterine devices. At these hearings, doctors and FDA officials testified about problems caused by the Shield. But at this time, the problems beginning to appear had not been documented systematically, and Jack Freund, vice president for research and development at Robins, rebutted the critics with information from company studies. Here is an excerpt from his extensive testimony.

We have sponsored ten prospective clinical studies of the product totaling 1,703 insertions, designed for individual patient exposure periods of at least twenty-four months. At a sixteen months data cutoff date, involving 11,728 women-months of use, statistical analysis—life table method—of data from these studies reveals the following rates per 100 women: pregnancy, 1.6; expulsion, 2.9; medical removal,

13.2; and continuation, 76.9. There was one uterine perforation reported in this group of patients. . . .

Since we acquired the Dalkon Shield, and after an estimated 1.8 million insertions, we have received approximately 400 voluntary reports of problems associated with use of the shield. In general, these have been of the nature associated with other IUDs.[73]

But by early 1974, studies had appeared showing pregnancy rates among Shield wearers as high as 10 percent. Stories of Shield complications appeared in medical journals. Robins reacted to accumulating criticism by calling a one-day conference in February to bring together experts on IUDs to discuss the situation. As a result of this conference, Robins sent letters to approximately 120,000 physicians advising them of the reported septic abortions and deaths and recommending removal of the Shield in patients who became pregnant or termination of pregnancy if the Shield could not be removed.

Still, evidence mounted that the Shield was more dangerous than other IUDs. In May, the Center for Disease Control in Atlanta released a study linking the Shield to 73 percent of IUD hospitalizations among women who had never born children and showing that the overall risk of IUD-related disease requiring hospitalization was twice as high for the Shield as for all other IUD brands combined. Shortly thereafter, an Arizona doctor published an article discussing five IUD-related deaths from septic midtrimester abortions and noted that four of the women had been wearing Dalkon Shields. The article included these observations:

The greatest concern is the rather insidious yet rapid manner in which these patients become ill. In three of the five noted maternal deaths, the first symptoms, which were disarmingly innocuous in and of themselves, occurred within 31 to 72 hours of death from sepsis and the sequelae of sepsis. It appears that the infection becomes generalized at about the same time as or before there are any localizing signs, and therefore the margin of safety that time ordinarily provides in treating such infections is not present. One wonders if there may be something about the design of the shield-type device that allows vascular dissemination of infection that might otherwise be locally contained.[74]

Shortly after publication of this article, the FDA recommended to Robins that the Shield be withdrawn from the market. In June, Robins voluntarily withdrew it from further sales but did not recall supplies in the distribution system and did not suggest that women already wearing it have it removed. After further study, however, the FDA decided to allow Robins to remarket the Shield if it conducted a registration and record-keeping program with doctors and if it switched to a monofilament tail string. This decision was made only in the face of considerable dissension within the agency but was

[73]In *Regulation of Medical Devices: Intrauterine Contraceptive Devices*, Hearings before a subcommittee of the Committee on Government Operations, House of Representatives, 93rd Congress, First Session, June 12, 1973, pp. 304–305.
[74]C. D. Christian, "Maternal Deaths Associated with an Intrauterine Device," *American Journal of Obstetrics and Gynecology*, June 15, 1974, p. 433.

rationalized as a step toward accumulating definitive proof of the Shield's performance.

The Shield was never remarketed. Robins decided against further sales because of the bad publicity it had received. But the FDA decision permitting remarketing left Robins in the favorable position of having permission from this watchdog of the public health to market the Shield. Also, the Shield was withdrawn before full information about its dangers could be acquired by the FDA-mandated record keeping program. Sales of the Shield in eighty foreign countries continued until late 1975. Many were sold in less developed countries, where the dangers of pelvic inflammatory disease were greater than in the United States, because hospitalization and a course of antibiotics were not routinely available.

LAWSUITS AND BANKRUPTCY

Exact figures for the injuries suffered by American women are not available, but the Dalkon Shield has been called "the Bhopal of the woman's health movement."[75] Robins' own estimate is that 4 percent of women using it were injured. Twenty deaths are recorded. Tens of thousands suffered infections. Roughly 110,000 had unexpected pregnancies, and of these 60 percent miscarried—248 in dangerous septic abortions.[76] Because of Shield-related infections and scarring, many users became sterile. Others found intercourse—indeed any physical activity—painful. Because of these incapacities, failed marriages are common among Shield victims.

Beginning in the early 1970s, injured women sued Robins. At first, there was a trickle of cases, and the company strenuously opposed them. Victims generally filed product liability claims that Robins was negligent in marketing a hazardous product and that its advertising for the Shield fraudulently warranted safety. In court, Robins' attorneys argued that the Shield was as safe as other IUDs, that the FDA permitted its marketing, and that top management was uninformed of excessive pregnancy rates or unusual risks. Robins had not been negligent; rather, it had been reasonably prudent and had acted in line with industry standards for marketing pharmaceuticals. These products often pose risks which cannot be discovered in advance of widespread public use. When injured women took the witness stand, Robins' attorneys subjected them to questions about the number of partners and type of sex the women had experienced, the level of hygiene they achieved, and whether they used devices or objects during sex. Faced with public humiliation about these intimate matters, many women declined to litigate.

Most early cases were settled out of court, but some went to trial. The first came in 1975 and resulted in an $85,000 jury award, of which $75,000 was punitive damages. Punitive damages are, of course, awarded to punish defendants for aggravated or outrageous acts of misconduct and are intended

---

[75]By attorney Sybil Shainwald, quoted in Catherine Breslin, "Day of Reckoning," *Ms.*, June 1989, p. 46.

[76]These figures are cited in Mintz, *op. cit.*, pp. 2–7.

to deter others from similar behavior. The cost of jury awards and settlements soon escalated. A landmark case was the suit of Carrie Palmer, wife of a physician and mother, who had been fitted with a Shield in 1973 because she wanted to postpone having more children for several years. Only seven months after insertion she got pregnant. In her fourth month she became violently ill with flu-like symptoms. Admitted to the hospital, she suffered a spontaneous septic abortion due to uterine infection. Soon, she went into septic shock due to massive infection. Her blood pressure fell and natural blood clotting ability was impaired. To save her life a total hysterectomy was performed. Thereafter, Palmer suffered chronic health problems. In 1979, a Colorado jury awarded her $600,000 in compensatory and $6.2 million in punitive damages.[77]

In 1983 twenty-one Shield cases in Minnesota were assigned to a blunt-speaking district judge named Miles Lord. Lord came to believe that Robins was using a variety of corner-cutting legal tactics to delay lawsuits, that it was outrageously wrong in refusing to recall Shields still implanted in women, and that its officers were avoiding personal responsibility for fraudulent actions by disclaiming knowledge of the devices' dangers. Finally, when Robins in 1984 hired a Minneapolis law firm employing Lord's son, the judge realized that he could no longer preside over Shield cases without conflict of interest. In an unusual move, he drafted a statement directed at Robins management, and as a condition in the out-of-court settlement of several Shield cases, he required three top Robins executives to appear in his courtroom.

On the morning of February 29, 1984, he read the following statement to E. Claiborne Robins, Jr., president and CEO, William Forrest, vice president and general counsel, and Carl D. Lunsford, senior vice president for research and development. The statement was designed to shame these men and sear the responsibility they bore into their consciences so that they could never again disavow knowing the Shield's hazards.

> "I did not know." "It was not me." "Look elsewhere." Time and time again, each of you has used this kind of argument in refusing to acknowledge your responsibility....
>
> Gentlemen, the results of these activities and attitudes on your part have been catastrophic. Today as you sit here attempting once more to extricate yourselves from the legal consequences of your acts, none of you has faced up to the fact that more than 9,000 women have made claims that they gave up part of their womanhood so that your company might prosper. It is alleged that others gave their lives so you might so prosper. And there stand behind them legions more who have been injured but who have not sought relief in the courts of this land.
>
> If one poor young man were, by some act of his—without authority or consent—to inflict such damage upon one woman, he would be jailed for a good portion of the rest of his life. And yet your company without warning to women invaded their bodies by the millions and caused them injuries by the thousands.

---

[77]Robins appealed this decision citing eighty-one procedural and constitutional claims, but it was unsuccessful. See *Palmer v. A. H. Robins Co.*, 648 P.2d 187 (Colo. 1984).

And when the time came for these women to make their claims against your company, you attacked their characters.

Mr. Robins, Mr. Forrest, Dr. Lunsford: You have not been rehabilitated. Under your direction, your company has in fact continued to allow women, tens of thousands of women, to wear this device—a deadly depth charge in their wombs, ready to explode at any time....The only conceivable reasons you have not recalled this product are that it would hurt your balance sheet and alert women who already have been harmed that you may be liable for their injuries. You have taken the bottom line as your guiding beacon, and the low road as your route. This is corporate irresponsibility at its meanest...

Please in the name of humanity, lift your eyes above the bottom line.[78]

At about this time, the pleas of ignorance made by Robins' executives were further discredited. Attorneys for the injured women acquired internal company memoranda showing that the dangers of the Shield had been reported to management. During a deposition on one Shield case, a former A. H. Robins attorney broke a long silence, revealing that he and several others had destroyed documents on the wicking tendencies of the Shield by burning them in a furnace. The documents had been destroyed in 1975 on the orders of William Forrest, vice president and general counsel of Robins. Unknown to Forrest, however, some papers were squirreled away by the attorney, who later left the company and decided to tell the story to salve his conscience. This information entered Shield trials. Robins executives still denied their culpability. But now they were less credible.

Awards continued to rise, and by late 1984 Robins had paid out over $300 million in Shield cases. The decision was finally made to recall the Shield, and in October 1984, ten years after marketing of the Shield ended, Robins took out television and print ads to recall it from an estimated 80,000 women.

The avalanche of lawsuits became overwhelming. By the summer of 1985, Robins and its insurer Aetna Casualty and Surety Company had paid $517 million for twenty-five trial judgments (out of forty cases which went to trial) and 9,238 settlements. Its legal costs were over $107 million. And no end was in sight because 5,100 lawsuits were pending and nearly 400 new suits were filed each month. There was considerable recruiting of Shield victims by lawyers. One Ohio lawyer got 106 cases as a result of advertising, resulting in a disciplinary proceeding against him.[79] Lawyers were, naturally, taking the cases on a contingency fee basis, and generally took 40–52 percent of awards and settlements. The size of jury awards was rising too. In a 1985 Wichita, Kansas, trial, a woman who had undergone a total hysterectomy due to Shield use was awarded a record $9.2 million, including $7.5 million in punitive damages.

At this point, E. Claiborne Robins, Jr., decided to seek protection under the bankruptcy laws to, in his words, "protect the company's economic vitality

---

[78]Quoted in Morton Mintz, "A Crime Against Women: A. H. Robins and the Dalkon Shield," *Multinational Monitor*, January 16, 1986, pp. 6–7.

[79]See *Zauderer v. Office of Disciplinary Counsel of the Supreme Court of Ohio*, 471 U.S. 626, 105 S. Ct. 2265 (1985).

must, under the conditions of the reorganization plan, contribute $5 million to the Dalkon Shield Trust Fund.

One angry woman injured by the Shield said: "The Robinses are getting carried out of the courtroom on silk pillows, when they should have a suitcase in hand, bound for federal prison."[86] She made a point. Unlike the Manville Corporation Chapter 11 bankruptcy case, where common shareholders lost most of their equity in reorganization, Robins' common shareholders were rewarded. Furthermore, if sales of Robins' products hold up, American Home Products will be able to pay off all Shield claims up to the $2.475 billion cap out of operating profits in seven years.[87] Payments are deductible from taxable income, a factor that accelerates debt reduction.

Victims, of course, continue to suffer. Says Constance Miller, treasurer of the International Dalkon Shield Victims Education Association: "Every day I talk to desperate women all over the country, some who are still economically devastated and severely disabled, some who are just now finding out they're injured."[88]

QUESTIONS

1 Why did A. H. Robins continue to sell the Dalkon Shield for as long as it did? Why did it not recall it until 1984?
2 Was the conduct of A. H. Robins or its managers unethical? Which specific actions were unethical and why?
3 If the Dalkon Shield story is stained by unethical behavior, is this behavior best explained as arising from individual conduct? Or is it best explained as a corporate crime arising from the structure, policies, and culture of Robins in interaction with its business environment?
4 Does an adequate balance exist between the harm that Robins did and the penalties it and its executives are paying today and will continue to pay in the future?
5 What is the proper way to punish a corporation such as A. H. Robins and the individuals in it?

---

[86]Quoted in Breslin, *op. cit.*, p. 51.
[87]This estimate is based on calculations made by Sanofi S.A. when it was bidding for Robins in 1988. See Frank J. Comes, Thane Peterson, and Tom Ichniowski, "Will A. H. Robins Acquire a French Accent?" *Business Week*, January 18, 1988, p. 25.
[88]Quoted in Breslin, *op. cit.*, p. 48.

CHAPTER

8

Making Ethical Decisions in Business

JCPenney

Ethical decisions are sometimes difficult. Here is how one company tries to help its employees.

In 1913, James Cash Penney met with a group of his partners in a Salt Lake City hotel room to create a distinctive set of principles upon which to run a fledgling business named the Golden Rule Store Company. The result of this meeting was a short set of statements they called "The Penney Idea," and the final principle was this: "To test our every policy, method and act in this wise: 'Does it square with what is right and just?'" As the Golden Rule Store Company metamorphosed into the giant modern-day retailer we know as J. C. Penney Company, Inc., the seed of an ethics policy contained in that final principle also grew.

As the years passed, many internal policy statements were written about such matters as accepting gifts, entertaining suppliers, and using proprietary information. Since 1986, however, the major elements of these disconnected policy statements have been condensed into a seventeen-page "Statement of Ethics," which is distributed to all employees. The ethics code contained in the "Statement of Ethics" is divided into three parts. Part I deals with "Compliance with Law," Part II is on "Conflicts of Interest," and Part III is on "Preservation of Company Assets."

A unique, didactic feature of the code is the illustration of provisions with short cases. Analysis accompanying these cases exemplifies correct interpretation to employees reading the code. Here is a sample of three cases that help explain conflict-of-interest situations involving competing companies. In these examples, note that the word "associate" is used to refer to Penney's employees.

THE OFFICIAL J. C. PENNEY POLICY STATEMENT

Each Associate of the Company shall avoid any activity, interest or relationship with non-Company persons or entities which would create, or might appear to others to create, a conflict with the interests of the Company.

EXAMPLE A

A newly employed Associate has worked for a major competitor of the Company, and during the course of that previous employment has acquired shares of stock which amount to a very small percentage of the outstanding stock of the competitor. A question has arisen as to whether ownership of that stock will constitute a conflict of interest.

Analysis of Example A Ownership of stock in a competitor will not be deemed a conflict of interest if both of the following conditions exist: (a) the stock is publicly traded, and (b) the amount owned by the Associate and his or her "relatives" (as defined in this booklet) does not exceed one-tenth of 1 percent of the amount outstanding.

EXAMPLE B

A Company store manager proposes to buy a substantial number of shares of stock of a corporation formed to operate a women's apparel shop. The shop will be located in a shopping center which also contains a Penney store and will carry similar merchandise.

Analysis of Example B A conflict of interest would exist. The apparel shop is a competitor because of its location and because of the merchandise it carries. In addition, the proposed purchase of stock by the Associate does not meet the guidelines described in the Analysis of Example A above.

EXAMPLE C

A general merchandise manager sells casualty and life insurance for a major insurance company on a part-time basis (i.e., after work and on weekends).

Analysis of Example C A conflict of interest may exist. Part-time work for an insurance company may be deemed to be a conflict of interest because the Company sells life and casualty insurance through its Financial Services division. Accordingly an Associate should notify his or her department head or superior of the activity. The Associate's department head, in conjunction with the Director of Insurance, will determine whether the Associate's activity is competitive with any Company insurance operations and, accordingly, whether a conflict of interest exists.

Each Penney employee, upon receipt of the code, is required to sign an attached Certificate of Compliance, which states in part: "I am in compliance and will continue to comply, with the policies set forth in the booklet. . . ." If there is doubt about compliance, the individual is instructed to approach his or her unit manager or department head to ask advice. Under three conditions an employee is, however, instructed to go directly to the General Counsel at headquarters in New York City. These urgent exceptions are cases that (1) threaten the overall integrity of the company, (2) raise the possibility of major financial loss or criminal penalty, and (3) endanger human life.

At the end of the "Statement of Business Ethics," employees are given notice that "failure to comply with the principles described in this booklet, including the disclosure requirements, may result in termination of employment."

This chapter suggests guidelines for making decisions about ethical issues for people in business faced with practical problems and for students discussing cases and issues in the business-government-society area. Value decisions cannot be programmed like production and inventory control decisions, but an ethics decision is, after all, still a decision, and helpful guidelines exist.

PRINCIPLES OF ETHICAL CONDUCT

Over the centuries, attempts have been made to discover rules that lead to perfectly just actions. Plato thought he had found the right method of moral decision making when he described an intuitive leap of revelation that would take place after years of study and character development in a utopian society. St. Augustine suggested that virtue came from an interior illumination that was a gift of God. St. Thomas relied on painstaking research of Scripture to reveal the true path, and a sense of complete certainty pervades his massive, twenty-three-volume *Summa Theologica*, in which moral questions are examined. Recent efforts to find a methodology for business decisions regarding ethics have been less mystical and elaborate. They are described in the following sections.

We begin, however, with a compendium of ethical principles—some ancient, some modern—that are alternative decision rules for managers. We list them alphabetically. These principles are a distillation of two thousand years of ethical thought. To the extent that they offer ideas for resolving ethical dilemmas, they are not vague abstractions, but useful, living guides to conduct.[1]

THE CATEGORICAL IMPERATIVE

The categorical imperative (meaning, literally, a command that admits no exception) is a guide for ethical behavior set forth by the German philosopher Immanuel Kant in his *Foundations of the Metaphysics of Morals*, a tract pub-

---

[1]Studies of managers show that they are guided by some, but not all, of these principles. See Phillip V. Lewis, "Ethical Principles for Decision Makers: A Longitudinal Survey," *Journal of Business Ethics*, April 1989.

lished in 1785. In Kant's words: "Act only according to that maxim by which you can at the same time will that it should become a universal law."[2]

In other words, one should not adopt principles of action unless they can, without inconsistency, be adopted by everyone else. Using this guideline, a manager faced with a moral choice must act in a way that he or she believes is right and just for any person in a similar situation. Each action should be judged by asking: "Could this act be turned into a universal code of behavior?" This quick test of universalizability has achieved great popularity.

Kant was an extreme perfectionist in his personal life. He walked the same route each day at the same time, appearing at places along the route so punctually that neighbors set their clocks by him. Before leaving his house, he attached strings to the top of his socks and connected them to a spring apparatus held by his belt. As he walked, the contraption would pull the slack out of his socks. To no one's surprise, his ethical philosophies are perfectionist also. He emphasized, for example, the importance of a person's motives. Most modern ethical theories stress instead the consequences of an action in evaluating whether or not it is right. If Kant were in a corporation today, he would argue that it is less meritorious to hire minorities to avoid lawsuits than it is to hire minorities because you believe your duty is to treat fellow humans with fairness and justice. How would you know this is your duty? The categorical imperative is the principle that reveals universal ethical law and your duty is to follow this law.

THE CONVENTIONALIST ETHIC

This is the view that business is analagous to a game and special, lower ethics are permissible. In business, people may act to further their self-interest so long as they do not violate the law. This ethic, which has a long history, was popularized some years ago by Albert Z. Carr in his book, *Business as a Game*.[3] "If an executive allows himself to be torn between a decision based on business considerations and one based on his private ethical code," wrote Carr, "he exposes himself to a grave psychological strain."[4]

Business may be regarded as a game, such as poker, in which the rules are different from those we adopt in personal life. Assuming game ethics, managers are allowed to bluff (a euphemism for lie) and to take advantage of all legal opportunities and widespread practices or customs. Carr used two examples to illustrate situations where game ethics were permissible. In the first, an out-of-work salesman with a good employment record feared discrimination due to his age—fifty-eight. He dyed his hair and stated on his resume that he was forty-five. In the second, a job applicant was asked to check off magazines that he read and felt justified in not placing check marks by *Playboy, The Nation,* or *The New Republic.* Even though he read them, he

[2]Immanuel Kant, *Foundations of the Metaphysics of Morals,* trans. Lewis White Beck. Indianapolis: Bobbs-Merrill, 1969, p. 44.
[3]New York: New American Library, 1968.
[4]"Is Business Bluffing Ethical?" *Harvard Business Review,* January-February 1968, p. 149.

feared being labeled controversial or politically extreme. He checked conservative magazines such as *Reader's Digest*.[5]

The conventionalist ethic has been criticized by those who make no distinction between private ethics and business ethics. They argue that industrial activity defines the life chances of millions and is not a game to be taken lightly. As a principle, the conventionalist ethic provides no way to elevate business practice. It is a thin justification for deceptive behavior in business situations.

THE DISCLOSURE RULE

This rule has been popular in recent years and is found in many company ethics codes. Here is the way it is stated in IBM's *Business Conduct Guidelines*: "Ask yourself: If the full glare of examination by associates, friends, even family were to focus on your decision, would you remain comfortable with it? If you think you would, it probably is the right decision."[6]

When faced with an ethical dilemma, a manager asks how it would feel to explain the decision to a wide audience. Sometimes newspaper readers or television viewers are substituted for acquaintances as the disclosure audience.

This rule screens out base motivations such as greed and jealousy, which are unacceptable if disclosed, but does not always provide guidance for ethical dilemmas in which strong arguments can be made for several alternatives. Also, an action that sounds acceptable if disclosed may not always be the most ethical.

THE DOCTRINE OF THE MEAN

This ethic, set forth by Aristotle in *The Nicomachean Ethics* and sometimes called the "Golden Mean," due to subsequent but un-Aristotelian embellishment, calls for virtue through moderation. Right actions are located between extreme behaviors, which represent excess on the one hand and deficiency on the other. When faced with a decision, a decision maker first identifies the ethical virtue involved (such as truthfulness) and then seeks the mean or moderate course of action between an excess of that virtue (boastfulness) and a deficiency of it (understatement). Likewise, according to Aristotle, modesty is the mean between shyness and shamelessness. The Doctrine of the Mean is today little recognized and mostly of historical interest, although the notion of moderation as a virtue lives on.

At its root, the Doctrine of the Mean is platitudinous. To observe it is simply to act conservatively in a situation and not to act in an extreme way. The moderate course and specific virtues such as honesty, however, are defined only in terms of what they are not.

[5]*Op. cit., Business As a Game*, p. 142.
[6]International Business Machines Corp., *Business Conduct Guidelines*, Armonk, New York: IBM, undated, p. 6.

THE GOLDEN RULE

A universal ideal found in every great world religion, the Golden Rule has been a popular guide for ethical decisions for centuries. Simply put, it is: "Do unto others as you would have them do unto you." It includes not knowingly doing harm to others. A manager trying to solve an ethical problem places himself or herself in the position of another party affected by the decision and tries to determine what action is most fair to that person.

A problem with the Golden Rule is that people's ethical values differ, and decision makers may err in assuming that their preferences coincide with others'. It is primarily a perfectionist rule for interpersonal relations. It is sometimes hard to apply in corporations where the interests of individuals are subordinated to the needs of the firm and where competitive activities demand selfish behavior. Marketing strategies, for example, do not treat competitors with kindness, but are based on self-interest.

THE INTUITION ETHIC

This ethic, as defined by philosophers such as G. E. Moore in his *Principia Ethica* (1903), holds that what is Good is undefinable.[7] Rather, it is simply understood. That is, people are endowed with a kind of moral sense by which they can apprehend right and wrong. The solution to moral problems lies simply in what you feel or understand to be right in a given situation. You have a "gut feeling" or "fly by the seat of your pants."

This approach is subjective. No standard of validation outside the individual exists. Self-interest may be confused with ethical insight. Worse, intuition may fail to give clear answers. It is nevertheless correct that most managers rely on *intuitive* reasoning to resolve ethical dilemmas rather than on *principled* reasoning, which requires a disciplined thought process and the application of abstract principles.

THE MARKET ETHIC

This principle was sanctioned in the world of commerce by Adam Smith in his *Wealth of Nations.* Implicit in Smith's description of a market economy is the idea that selfish actions in the marketplace are virtuous because they contribute to efficient operation of the economy. This efficient operation is, in turn, responsible for the higher goods of prosperity and the optimum use of resources. Decision makers may take selfish actions and be motivated by personal gain in their business dealings. They should ask whether their actions in the market further financial self-interest. If so, the actions are ethical.

This form of ethical guidance is applicable only in market situations. It is not useful in interpersonal relations and, therefore, is not a universal principle. Also, there are areas of market behavior where society has determined

---

[7] New York: Cambridge University Press, 1948 (reprint).

that the broad social good or public interest is not furthered by selfish market behavior. The antitrust statutes are a prime example of legislated ethics here.

THE MEANS-ENDS ETHIC

This principle is age-old, although it is often associated with the Italian political philosopher Niccolò Machiavelli. In *The Prince* (1513), Machiavelli wrote that worthwhile ends justify efficient means, that when ends are of overriding importance or virtue, unscrupulous means may be employed to reach them.[8] When confronted with a decision involving an ethically questionable course of action, a decision maker should ask whether some overall good— such as the survival of a country or business—justifies cornercutting. This was the thinking of John D. Rockefeller during the period when his Standard Oil trust carried out a triumphant strategy of horizontal integration at the refinery level, choking competitors and requiring employees to undertake ruthless predations that surely chilled the hearts of some. Late in his life, Rockefeller argued that only by smashing his competitors and controlling refining capacity could he tidy up the oil industry and rescue it from the chaotic price fluctuations that marked its infancy in the 1860s.[9] He may have been correct.

By accepting the validity of the ends-justify-the-means principle, however, a manager concedes the highest virtue and accepts the necessity of ethical compromise. In some situations, of course, means may be as important or more important than ends. For example, protecting the privacy rights of workers and retaining employee trust may be far more important than catching a drug abuser or petty thief at work by hidden video surveillance. The end of catching deviant workers may not justify the use of any means available to gather evidence.

THE MIGHT-EQUALS-RIGHT ETHIC

This ethic defines justice as the interest of the stronger. It is represented by Friedrich Nietzsche's "master-morality," Marx's theories of the dominance of the ruling class, and in the practiced ethics of drug cartels. The rationale for some competitive strategies and marketing tactics shades into this thinking. What is ethical is what an individual or company has the strength and power to accomplish. When faced with an ethical decision, individuals using this ethic seize what advantage they are strong enough to take without regard for lofty sentiments.

In the 1860s, Ben Holladay, owner of the Overland Stage Line, perfected a competitive strategy based on this thinking. He entered new routes with low-ball coach fares and subsidized his stages with profits from monopoly

[8]T. G. Bergin, ed., New York: Appleton-Century-Crofts, 1947. Written in 1513 and first published in 1532.

[9]Allan Nevins, *Study in Power: John D. Rockefeller*, vol. II, New York: Charles Scribner's Sons, 1953, p. 433.

service elsewhere until local competitors went bankrupt. In 1863, a small stage line between Denver and Central City in Colorado, for example, was charging $6 per run. Holladay put a lavish new-model stage, a Concord Coach with a leather interior, on the line and charged only $2. The competing line soon folded, whereupon Holladay replaced the new Concord Coach with primitive stages resembling freight wagons and raised the fare to $12.

The weakness of the might-equals-right ethic lies in its confusion of ethics with force or physical power. Yielding to such force or power is not the same as acting from ethical duty. An ethical principle that can be invalidated by its foundation (e.g., physical force) is not a consistent, logical, or valid principle. The might-equals-right ethic is not seen as legitimate in civilized settings. Observance of it invites retaliation and condemnation, and it is not to be used for long-term advantage. Seizure by power violates established rules of cooperation and reciprocity on which societies are based, and the social fabric would be torn apart by widespread use of this principle. Holladay, incidentally, sold the Overland Stage Line to Wells, Fargo & Company in 1866 when he sensed that railroads were about to end the dominance of stages in transportation west of the Mississippi. He started a railroad, which failed, and died an alcoholic in 1887.

THE ORGANIZATION ETHIC

This is an old principle for resolving ethical questions with increased applicability in modern times. This is an age of large-scale organizations. Simply put, this dictum states; "Be loyal to the organization." It is functional for the endurance of large organizations. Many people have a deep sense of loyalty to an organization that far transcends their self-interest. We have seen people jeopardize their health and work excessively long hours without pay, contrary to their selfish interests, because of their loyalty to their task and/or company.

There are similar personal loyalties that one individual has to another—such as the loyalties of a subordinate to a supervisor—when they are acting in their official capacities. Frequently, these loyalties are in conflict with the ethical standards one applies when acting as an individual. For instance, the general manager of a division of a large company withheld information from central headquarters about impending disastrous financial troubles. Several of his subordinates, who were men of high moral character and who had close connections with headquarters managers, did not inform headquarters of the problems, principally because of strong personal loyalty to their superior officer.

In practice, the organization ethic implies that the wills and needs of individuals should be subordinated to the greater good of the organization (be it church, state, business, military, or university). An individual should ask whether actions are consistent with organizational goals and do what is good for the organization.

The weakness of this principle is that service to the organization is a tempting way to rationalize behavior that would be unethical for the individual. The Nuremberg trials highlighted the dangerous tendencies of obedience and jaundiced obligation. In some cases, the greatest virtue may result when individuals are served by organizations rather than subservient to them.

THE PRACTICAL IMPERATIVE

In addition to the categorical imperative, a second and related imperative or universal ethical command suggested by Immanuel Kant, in the *Foundations of the Metaphysics of Morals*, is "Act so that you treat humanity, whether in your own person or in that of another, always as an end and never as a means only."[10] Simply translated, this principle admonishes a manager to treat other persons as ends in themselves and not means to ends or objects of manipulation. Each person, by his or her very existence as a rational, thinking being, is entitled to be treated in this fashion. No person should manipulate others for selfish ends. A manager may comply with this dictum by using the "reversibility" test, asking if he or she would change places with the person affected by the contemplated policy or action.

The practical imperative has two flaws. First, in large organizations the achievement of collective goals often requires the abridgment of individual rights. Generals may send soldiers to die, and corporate presidents may move managers around the world and make them work away from their families. And second, in modern society, people may deal with each other in terms of representative roles rather than as individuals. Thus, a plant manager may pressure and manipulate corporate top management for a bigger annual budget without engaging the people involved as individual personalities. Or a company may adopt a behavior-modification program to motivate workers and use positive reinforcement to alter behavior solely as a means to increase productivity. Within American business culture, such practices are not seen as necessarily unethical.

THE PRINCIPLE OF EQUAL FREEDOM

This principle was set forth by the philosopher Herbert Spencer in his 1850 book, *Social Statics*. "Every man may claim the fullest liberty to exercise his faculties," said Spencer, "compatible with the possession of like liberty by every other man."[11] Thus, a person has the right to freedom of action unless such action deprives another person of a proper freedom. Spencer believed that this was the first principle of ethical action in society. He thought it essential to protect individual liberty from infringement by others; his deep faith that human progress was based on such free action was unshakable.

In applying this principle, a decision maker asks if a contemplated action will restrict others from actions that they have a legitimate right to under-

[10]*Op. cit.*, p. 54.
[11]New York: Robert Schalkenbach Foundation, 1970 (reprint).

take. This principle is quite popular today. One version is, "Your right to swing your fist ends where my nose begins."

One problem with this principle is that it does not provide a tie breaker for situations in which two rights or interests conflict. Such situations require invocation of an additional principle to decide which right or freedom is more important. Another difficulty is that some ethically permissible management decisions may circumscribe the rights of some for the benefit of others. For example, all employees have broad privacy rights, but management may abridge them when it hires undercover detectives to investigate thefts.

THE PROPORTIONALITY ETHIC

Proportionality, a concept incubated in medieval Catholic theology, is an ethical doctrine designed to evaluate actions which have both good and evil consequences. For example, the manufacture of small-caliber, short-barreled, low-priced handguns which are irreverently called Saturday Night Specials has a dual impact on society. It makes cheap, easily concealable weapons available to criminals. But it also creates a supply of inexpensive self-defense weapons for poor people in high crime areas who cannot afford large-caliber, expensive handguns costing as much as $500. In this and similar cases, where a manager's action results in an important good effect but also entails an inevitable harmful effect, the concept of proportionality may be appropriately applied.

A classic formulation is that of Thomas M. Garrett, a Jesuit priest who wrote about business ethics. Garrett developed a "principle of proportionality" which stated that managers are ethically responsible for their actions in situations where both good and evil effects might occur. And they are ethically permitted to risk predictable, but unwilled, negative impacts on people or society (for example, innocent people being shot by handguns) if they carefully consider and balance five factors. First, according to Garrett, managers must assess the type of good and evil involved, distinguishing between major and minor forms. Second, they should calculate the urgency of the situation. Would, for example, the firm go out of business unless stockholder dividends were cut? Third, they must assess the probability that both good and evil effects will occur. If good effects are certain and risks of serious harm are small or remote, the situation is favorable. Fourth, the intensity of influence over effects must be considered. In assessing handgun injuries, for instance, manufacturers might assume that criminal action was an intervening force over which they had little control. And finally, the availability of alternative methods must be considered. If, for instance, an advertisement subtly encourages product misuse, a more ethical action might be to change the ad. Garrett believed that an overall assessment which took all these factors into consideration would bring out fully the ethical dimension in any decision.[12]

A simpler ethical principle derived from the concept of proportionality is

---

[12]*Business Ethics:* New York: Appleton-Century-Crofts, 1966, p. 8.

the "principle of double effect." It states that in a situation from which both good and evil consequences are bound to result, a manager will act ethically if: (1) the good effects outweigh the evil, (2) the manager's intention is to achieve the good effects, and (3) examination reveals that no better alternative is available.

These are complex principles, involving a wide range of considerations. Their complexity is a strength if it forces fuller consideration of relevant factors. Proportionality may be used disingenuously to justify harmful acts. What kind of otherwise questionable acts, for instance, may a failing firm take that are justified by the "proportionate reason" of the impending evil of bankruptcy?

THE PROFESSIONAL ETHIC

In an age of specialization and education in complex skills, this ethic has gained importance. In simple form, it holds that you should do only that which can be explained before a committee of your peers.

This ethic is applied by doctors, engineers, architects, college professors, lawyers, and business executives in resolving the special problems of their professions and fields of interest. It is similar to and an application of the disclosure ethic discussed previously.

Professional people have strongly internalized ethical codes that guide their actions. Many of these ethical standards are deep-seated. For instance, we are convinced that the high standards of most engineers in the aerospace industry would prevent them from making a cheap lawn mower. They are so used to working with exceedingly close tolerances and high quality that they could not bring themselves to the task. The acceptance of lower standards would be morally repugnant to them.

The professional ethic is not a universal principle because it does not apply to conflicts outside special or esoteric settings. In addition, most of the so-called special problems of the professions are really amenable to the application of broader ethical principles.

THE REVELATION ETHIC

This ethic has ageless appeal to the religious. Through prayer or other contact with transcendent beings and forces, answers are given to individual minds. A priest, or manager, may pray for guidance and find that God has provided an answer. This ethic is close to the intuition ethic, but in the latter divine presence is unnecessary.

Many people, of course, are not deeply religious and would be suspicious of this method and reluctant to trust it. The kind of ethical truth derived from godly inspiration is incompatible with more pragmatic ethical standards. No compromise is possible when you have been inculcated with perfect virtue. Also, insight based on revelation has sometimes led to cruel actions. In 1989, Ayatollah Ruhollah Khomeini, the spiritual leader of Islamic fundamentalists in Iran, sentenced to death Salman Rushdie, author of a book, *The Satanic Verses,* which irreverently retold legends of the Prophet Muhammad.[13] Soon Rushdie was forced into hiding by an Iranian bounty of $5.2 million if he was killed by an Iranian and $2 million if killed by a non-Iranian. To the consternation of the publisher, Viking Press, martyrdom was promised for execution of any party involved in publication or sale of the book. Some bookstores removed the book from their shelves.

Discussion of revelation raises a theological problem of long standing which may be phrased as a question. If God is omnipotent, how can His will fail to be realized, whether we do right or wrong?

THE RIGHTS ETHIC

The rights ethic encompasses the notion that people have fundamental rights. Rights are entitlements to something. Ethical persons recognize the duty to protect the exercise of these rights in others. Fundamental human rights may be abridged only for compelling reasons of benefit to society. These rights generally include freedom of speech, freedom of conscience, the right to own property, the right to life, and the right to be honestly informed. Other rights may be established in laws or contracts and differ from fundamental ethical rights.

In applying the rights ethic, a decision maker evaluates intended actions based on whether they deprive any party affected by the decision of a right that must be respected. For example, management should not permit operation of an unsafe machine because workers would be deprived of the right to a safe workplace. This right is based on the natural right to protection from harm by the actions of others and is underscored by legal rights established in the Occupational Safety and Health Act. If some risk in operating a machine is unavoidable, workers have the right to be informed with an accurate risk assessment.

Theories of rights emphasize and protect individual freedoms. They are properly used to protect individuals from exploitation but may be misused to excuse selfish demands. In a broad sense, rights theories have encouraged the development of exaggerated entitlements in American society. An additional observation about this ethic is that rights are not absolute, and at times it is hard to define their limits. For example, every person has a right to life, but in modern society corporations daily expose people to risk of death by releasing carcinogens into the environment. To make the right to life absolute would require cessation of much industrial activity (for example, petroleum refining).

THE THEORY OF JUSTICE

Ethical theories of justice define the nature of fairness in corporate relationships. Justice requires: (1) that the benefits and burdens of company life be

[13]New York: Viking Press, 1989.

distributed according to impartial criteria, (2) that rewards and punishments be meted out evenhandedly, and (3) that laws, rules, and administrative procedures apply equally to each employee and organizational unit.

A contemporary moral philosopher, John Rawls, has developed a widely discussed set of principles for a just society. In *A Theory of Justice* Rawls speculates that rational persons situated behind a hypothetical "veil of ignorance" and not knowing their place in a society (i.e., their social status, class position, economic fortune, intelligence, appearance, or the like) but knowing general facts about human society (such as political, economic, sociological, and psychological theory) would choose two rules to ensure fairness in any society they created. First, "each person is to have an equal right to the most extensive basic liberty compatible with a similar liberty for others," and second, "social and economic inequalities are to be arranged so that they are both (a) reasonably expected to be to everyone's advantage, and (b) attached to positions and offices open to all."[14] The lofty generalizations in Rawl's theory are best used in analysis of broad social questions, but they may inspire business decisions.

The impartiality and equal treatment called for in the theory of justice are resplendent in theory, but their operational meaning is difficult to pin down. Most rules give advantage to one group more than another. It should be noted that competing conceptions of justice exist. Rawls bases justice on distribution of social goods according to need, but others have based theories of justice on other fundamental concepts such as the legitimate acquisition of property[15] and the unity of mankind.[16]

THE UTILITARIAN PRINCIPLE

This principle is so named because it was espoused as a method of determining right and wrong by philosophers of the English utilitarian school such as Jeremy Bentham and John Stuart Mill. It is simply expressed as "the greatest good for the greatest number."

In making a decision with this principle in mind, one must determine whether the harm in an action is outweighed by the good. If the action maximizes benefit, then it is the optimum course to take among alternatives that provide less benefit. Individuals and other decision makers should try to maximize pleasure and reduce pain, not simply for themselves, but for every party affected by their decision. Utilitarianism facilitates the comparison of the ethical consequences of various alternatives in a decision. It is a popular, widely used principle. Cost-benefit and risk-benefit studies embody the spirit of the utilitarian principle.

The importance of utilitarianism in justifying much industrial activity can-

[14]Cambridge, Massachusetts: Harvard University Press, 1971, pp. 60–71.
[15]Robert Nozick, *Anarchy, State, and Utopia*, New York: Basic Books, 1974.
[16]Plato, *The Republic*, trans. F. M. Cornford, New York: Oxford University Press, 1945 (reprint), p. 55.

not be overestimated. Since the 1850s, this doctrine has been used to verify that the social benefits of manufacturing and commerce are greater than attendant social costs. Yet is has important weaknesses. First, because decisions are to be made for the greatest good of all, utilitarianism may lead to decisions that permit the abridgment of human rights, even the right to life, for the greater good of a larger group. And second, it provides no criterion for measuring levels of goodness. Thus, the exact definition of the "greatest good" is a matter of opinion.[17]

THE USE OF PRINCIPLED ETHICAL REASONING

There are a wide variety of methods for making ethical decisions. Some managers are relatively insensitive to ethical issues. Others may notice ethical problems and make decisions using simple ethical criteria such as: be honest, help others, avoid harm, tell the truth, be fair, and respect the life and property of others. There is great wisdom in such basic admonitions. The application of ethical principles such as those in the foregoing section, however, enhances the manager's skill for resolving complex ethical issues. There are two reasons. First, common-sense ethical wisdom may be derived from these broader ethical principles. For example, the categorical imperative dictates that individuals tell the truth, because truthtelling can be made universal, unlike lying, the universalization of which would cause chaos. Second, the application of ethical principles to ethically complex decisions encourages stringent standards and forces consideration of issues that might otherwise remain hidden. A cashier pockets twenty dollar bills from the register at the end of the day. The person's supervisor strongly feels that stealing is wrong and fires the cashier. Ethical common sense is all that is needed in this situation. But consider the following situation.

> Richard Tarnovich, the night plant manager for Western Electroplating Company, recently revealed to coworkers that he was proud to be a member of the American Communist party. Some of the employees on the night shift have found it more difficult to cooperate with him and accept his authority since this disclosure. Tarnovich has tried to perform his job without confrontation, but a series of minor social abrasions have occurred between him and other workers on the shift. Absenteeism has risen, the rejection rate on completed jobs has increased by 5 percent, and there have been two minor injuries in the past month traceable to inattentiveness of machine operators. Earl Mizushima, the assistant night manager, is popular with the workers and well trained. He has hinted he is anxious for advancement. Should Richard Tarnovich be moved from his position?

An ethically insensitive manager might perceive this case solely as a problem of productivity, see Tarnovich as a drag on efficiency, and remove him

---

[17]A famous essay, "Utilitarianism," by John Stuart Mill, deals directly and brilliantly with these and other criticisms and should be read by critics. It is reprinted in Mary Warnock, ed., *Utilitarianism and Other Writings*, New York: New American Library, 1962.

> You are sailing to Rome (you tell me) to obtain the post of Governor of Cnossus. You are not content to stay at home with the honours you had before; you want something on a larger scale, and more conspicuous. But when did you ever undertake a voyage for the purpose of reviewing your own principles and getting rid of any of them that proved unsound?
>
> *Source*: Epictetus, *The Discourses* (c. A.D. 120).

from the position. But let us apply three important ethical principles to the case: utilitarianism, rights, and justice.

From a utilitarian standpoint, management must calculate which course of action would result in the greatest net benefit for the plant and all its workers. In this situation it might be reasonable to decide that removing Tarnovich would increase productivity and build morale among many workers while hurting only one person, Tarnovich.

From the standpoint of the rights ethic, however, employers must consider the idea that employees have the right to freedom of conscience and political belief. In American society, workers are free to hold unpopular political and philosophical views in their private lives. Although Tarnovich has brought his communist affiliation into the workplace by telling others about it, there is no evidence that his politics is part of his management style or that he has been argumentative.

From the standpoint of justice, corporations are required to promote fair, evenhanded treatment of employees. If management allows other workers to be Republicans, environmentalists, or Ku Klux Klan members off the job, the same permission must be granted to Tarnovich the communist.

Readers may make up their own minds about this case. If the productivity problem is substantial, management must intervene. But when ethical concerns about employee rights and equitable treatment are carefully weighed, management may consider alternatives to removing Tarnovich, including mediation by an ombudsman, counseling, or removing one or more workers for insubordination to Tarnovich. At some point, however, management may need to invoke the utilitarian argument and remove Tarnovich if his supervision becomes ineffective and low productivity endangers the general welfare of the company. The rights of one individual cannot, in this instance, jeopardize the benefits many others derive from the company.

This case is typical of incidents discussed in ethics training programs. It illustrates the application of three important and mutually reinforcing principles in a decision-making technique that is popular in the literature of business ethics.[18]

---

[18]See, for example, Gerald F. Cavanagh, *American Business Values*, 3rd. ed., Englewood Cliffs, New Jersey: Prentice-Hall, 1990, pp. 194–199. A derivative, formal technique for making ethical decisions is set forth by Archie Carroll in *Business & Society: Ethics & Stakeholder Management*, Cincinnati, Ohio: South-Western, 1989, p. 128.

PRACTICAL SUGGESTIONS FOR MAKING ETHICAL DECISIONS

Individuals in business can take a number of steps to see and resolve ethical problems.

First, learn to think in principled terms, and use concepts like universalizability, reversibility, utility, equity, and other ethical guidelines suggested by the list of principles earlier in this chapter. These principles are powerful decision criteria that enhance the capacity to discover or create ethical alternatives. Use a principle that is meaningful to you. As the famous anthropologist Sir James Frazer remarked: "Once the harbor lights have been passed and the ship is out of stormy waters, it matters little whether the pilot steered by a jack-o-lantern or the stars."

Second, consider some simple decision tactics that help to illuminate moral choices. The ethical philosopher Bertrand Russell advocated imaginary conversations with a hypothetical opponent as an antidote for dogmatic certitude. Have a conversation or debate with an intelligent person who takes a different viewpoint or who has additional insights. Seek out a more experienced, ethically sensitive person in the organization to be your ethical adviser. This variant of a mentor relationship is of great value in revealing the ethical climate of your company and industry. Alternatively, write an essay in favor of a position and then a second opposed to it. Write a case study in the third person about your situation. Try to apply ethical principles in answer to obvious questions raised by the case.

More than 200 years ago, a balance sheet of pros and cons was proposed as an approach to decision making by Benjamin Franklin in a letter to a scientist friend in England. Since that time, numerous decision makers have used a balance sheet approach. One of the best known is Richard Nixon, who as President was fond of writing down pros and cons in columns on a yellow legal pad and then crossing out roughly equal considerations until a preponderance was left on one side or the other.

The balance sheet has advantages. First, it organizes information. Studies have shown that the human brain can simultaneously grapple only with between five and nine bits of information. Because many decisions, including moral ones, involve more considerations than this, a balance sheet may prevent chaotic and random thinking. Second, the use of such a procedure forces decision makers to make entries in a number of relevant categories, and new or unconscious considerations may be brought to light. One disadvantage of the balance sheet approach in making moral decisions is that utilitarian considerations may be weighed equally with even the most fundamental moral principles.

Another useful method of applying principles is to draw them out in the form of questions a manager might ask when contemplating a decision. This is known as the "critical questions approach." John Leys surveyed the systems of the great philosophers and derived thirty-six critical questions for the decision maker.[19] The following are a few examples: What are the authorita-

[19]In *Ethics for Policy Decisions*, Englewood Cliffs, New Jersey: Prentice-Hall, 1952.

tive rules and precedents, the agreements, and accepted practices? If there is a conflict of principles, can you find a more abstract statement, a "third principle," that will reconcile the conflicting principles? What is not within our power? What are the undesirable extremes in human dispositions? A shorter set of leading questions, suggested by Laura Nash, is based on traditional philosophical frameworks but designed to avoid the very abstract level of reasoning characteristic of broad principles. This list of twelve questions is shown in Table 8-1.

Third, sort out ethical priorities early, before problems arise. If you do so, you will get the full benefits of considering alternatives when you are not under stress. Clear ethics reduce stress by reducing temptation, deflating your conscience as a source of pain or anxiety, and eliminating conflicts of interest in your decision making. When doing the ethical thing is not the most profitable financially, for instance, it helps to decide in advance that you will put ethics before tainted profits.

Fourth, commit yourself publicly on ethical issues. Examine your work environment, and locate potential ethical conflicts. Then tell others of your opposition to padding expense accounts, stealing supplies from the company, discriminating against minorities, price fixing, or harming nature. They will be less tempted to approach you with corrupting intentions, and your public commitment will force you to maintain your integrity or risk shame.

Fifth, set a good personal example for employees. This is one of the basic managerial functions. An ethical manager can create a morally uplifting work environment. An unethical manager may make money, but he or she and the organization pay the price—and the price is one's integrity. Employees who see unethical competitive behavior, for instance, may wonder when their superiors will turn their antisocial predilections inward and focus on them. This behavior has the potential for creating morale and loyalty problems.

TABLE 8-1   TWELVE QUESTIONS FOR EXAMINING THE ETHICS OF A BUSINESS DECISION

1. Have you defined the problem accurately?
2. How would you define the problem if you stood on the other side of the fence?
3. How did this situation occur in the first place?
4. To whom and to what do you give your loyalty as a person and as a member of the corporation?
5. What is your intention in making this decision?
6. How does this intention compare with the probable results?
7. Whom could your decision or action injure?
8. Can you discuss the problem with the affected parties before you make your decision?
9. Are you confident that your position will be as valid over a long period of time as it seems now?
10. Could you disclose without qualm your decision or action to your boss, your CEO, the board of directors, your family, society as a whole?
11. What is the symbolic potential of your action if understood? If misunderstood?
12. Under what conditions would you allow exceptions to your stand?

Sixth, note and resist the ethical temptations to which you are most prone. Aristotle, in *The Nicomachean Ethics*, advised:

> We must notice the errors into which we ourselves are liable to fall (because we all have different natural tendencies—we shall find out what ours are from the pleasure and pain that they give us), and we must drag ourselves in the contrary direction; for we shall arrive at the mean by pressing well away from our failing—just like somebody straightening a warped piece of wood.[20]

Hence, examine your personal traits. Are you marked by greed, prejudice, sadism, cowardice, insensitivity? Work to overcome these, just as the ancient Greeks worked to develop character. Ethical behavior is conditioned by practice. You learn more about it by working hard.

Seventh, cultivate your sympathies and charity toward others. The question, "What is ethical?" is one on which well-intentioned people may differ. As Marcus Aurelius wrote: "When thou art offended at any man's fault, forthwith turn to thyself and reflect in what like manner thou dost err thyself; for example, in thinking that money is a good thing, or pleasure, or a bit of reputation, and the like."[21] Reasonable managers differ with respect to the rightness of factory closings, genetic testing of workers, leveraged buyouts, and other nettlesome ethical questions. We should neither be overly indulgent nor wholly stern and unforgiving because of pride in high standards.

Eighth, translate your thoughts into action—display courage. Knowing and doing are, of course, different. It is often easier to reach a valid ethical judgment than to act on it, especially lower in the organizational ranks. When you are sure that you are ethically right, you may be called upon to risk revenue for your company or jeopardize your job by standing firm.

Finally, remember that ethical perfection is illusory. We live in a complicated, baffling civilization with a profusion of rules, obligations, and duties. No manager can perfectly resolve all the conflicts that arise. There is an old story, perhaps apocryphal, about the inauguration of James Canfield as president of Ohio State University. With him on the inaugural platform was Charles W. Eliot, president of Harvard University for twenty years and a senior statesman in the ranks of academic leadership. After receiving the mace of office, Canfield sat next to Eliot, who leaned over and whispered, "Now son, you are president, and your faculty will call you a liar." "Surely," said Canfield, "your faculty have not accused you of lying, Dr. Eliot." Replied Eliot, "Not only that, son, they've proved it!"

WHY ETHICAL DECISIONS ARE DIFFICULT

Why are ethical problems refractory even in the presence of principles and methods to guide resolution? In this section we list ten reasons.

First, managers confront a distinction between facts and values when

---

[20]*Op. cit.*, p. 109.
[21]*The Meditations of Marcus Aurelius Antoninus*, trans. George Long, Danbury, Connecticut: Grolier Enterprises, 1980 (reprint), p. 281. Originally published circa A.D. 180.

making ethical decisions. Facts are statements about what *is*, and we can observe and confirm them. Values, on the other hand, are views individuals hold independently of facts. For example, in 1989, Burroughs Wellcome Co., a British firm, was accused of overcharging for azidothymidine (AZT), the drug that slows replication of the AIDS virus. The wholesale price of a capsule which cost $0.30 to $0.50 to manufacture was $1.50. Its retail price was $1.60 to $1.80. The company had never released a profit figure for AZT, but also never denied making a profit on it. AZT is one of the most expensive prescription drugs on the U.S. market and for those on a regimen of twelve pills a day the annual cost was nearly $8,000. Was Burroughs Wellcome exploiting desparate AIDS patients or was it entitled to retrieve AZT's high cost of research and development and earn a profit above that? The answer to this question involves a value judgment. Facts, such as prices, do not logically dictate values. What *is* never fully defines what *ought* to be. Therefore, when people in business ask what is ethical in a given situation, even a full description of the facts involved cannot automatically dictate a just answer.

Second, it is often the case that good and evil exist simultaneously, in tandem, and interlocked. Two examples illustrate this enigmatic probability. Nestlé's sales of infant formula in less developed countries such as Kenya and Zambia led to infant deaths as mothers mixed the powdered food with contaminated local water and their babies died of dysentery. But evidence also shows that sales of formula have led to the saving of other infants' lives when the mother is not available, the infant won't breastfeed, or dietary supplementation is indicated. The mixture of good and bad effects is likewise present in the use of Paraquat, perhaps the most effective herbicide in existence. The availability of Paraquat, manufactured by Imperial Chemical Industries in England and Chevron Chemical Company in America, may significantly increase crop yields, but the chemical is also highly toxic to humans, and its application—inevitably untutored at times, especially in less developed countries—has led to a number of illnesses and deaths. (A newspaper headline even read: "NYMPHO GETS LIFE FOR KILLING HUBBY WITH PARAQUAT GRAVY.")[22]

Third, knowledge of consequences is limited. Many ethical theories, for instance the utilitarian theory of the greatest good for the greatest number, assume that the consequences of a decision are knowable. But the impact of business policy is uncertain in a complex world. In 1977, for example, General Motors substituted Chevrolet engines in Pontiacs, Oldsmobiles, and Buicks, with a policy that extended an old industry practice of parts switching to entire engines. The intention of the policy was to achieve the salutary effect of making more large block engines available over a wider range of automobiles to satisfy consumer demand. Unpredictably (for General Motors), consumers looked on the engine switching as an attempt to manipulate buyers and rob owners of status—an ethical implication perhaps entirely at odds with corporate motivations.

---

[22]David Shaw, "Murdoch: Press Loves to Hate Him," *Los Angeles Times*, May 25, 1983.

Fourth, the existence of multiple corporate constituencies exposes management to competing and conflicting ethical claims. Customers, stockholders, workers, government agencies, and various pressure groups such as environmentalists and feminists are among the most important judges of managerial behavior. To illustrate, tobacco firms find themselves in a crossfire of competing ethical claims. Tobacco farmers, representing more than 275,000 farming families, give ethical priority to maintenance of the tobacco economy in southern states. Stockholders urge the priority of profits and growth through cigarette sales. The Surgeon General's office and the medical establishment condemn harmful health effects of smoking. Hence, managers must weigh competing ethical doctrines, and a balancing process is sometimes reflected in corporate strategy. Since 1967, for example, the proliferation of "safer" low-tar cigarettes has brought those brands from a 2 percent share of the domestic market to over 40 percent, as the tobacco companies have reacted to safety concerns in their market environment. But simultaneously, these firms have sought to expand their sales in less developed countries, where few people had discretionary income for cigarettes until the 1980s. The tobacco companies take advantage of lax restrictions on marketing in these countries and sometimes do not include health warnings. As these markets develop, smoking-related illnesses have risen. Many third-world governments encourage investment by tobacco firms; it provides sorely needed economic benefits.

Fifth, antagonistic wills frequently use incompatible ethical arguments to justify their intentions. Often, then, the ethical stand of a corporation is based on entirely different premises from the ethical stand of critics or constituent groups. Many members of the Animal Liberation Front believe that animals are entitled to rights similar to those enjoyed by humans, including the right to life. The group recently raided a northern California turkey farm, causing $12,000 in damage and freeing about 100 turkeys, which were taken to "safe homes." Later, members broke into a Delaware poultry farm, taking twenty-five hens and drawing an analogy between Nazi death camps and factory farms in the scrawled message they left behind: "ANIMAL AUSCHWITZ." Poultry growers, on the other hand, accept the utilitarian argument that raising food animals brings benefits to society greater than the harm of animal suffering. A publicist for the industry stated that the group's viewpoint was "an insult to victims of the Holocaust."[23]

Sixth, ethical standards are variable; they may change with time and place. In the 1950s, American corporations overseas routinely made payoffs to foreign officials, but managers had to curtail this practice after public expectations changed and a new law, the Foreign Corrupt Practices Act of 1977, prohibited most such expenditures. Certain bribes and payments are accepted practice in Asian, African, and Latin American countries but are not regarded as ethical in the United States. Doing business with close friends and family is standard practice in the Arab world, but in the United States or Western

[23]Quoted in Kevin Thompson, "Meat Is Murder?" *Meat and Poultry*, September 1987, p. 39.

Europe the same actions are often regarded as constituting a conflict of interest. Even circumstances peculiar to a single corporation may modify the possibility of virtuous conduct. For instance, if a firm is going bankrupt, it may force workers to accept reduced pay and poorer working conditions or be granted more ethical latitude if it actively recruits a competitor's employee or fails to hire minorities. Right conduct is an elusive goal and the application of standards and principles an art.

Seventh, ethical behavior is molded from the clay of human imperfection. Even well-intentioned managers may be mistaken in their ethical judgment. Evidence exists, of course, that not all managers are even well-intentioned. Perhaps the nadir of comic wrongdoing was reached by Robert B. Beasley, a Firestone Tire and Rubber Company executive who, when placed in charge of Firestone's $12.6-million slush fund for illegal payments and campaign contributions, embezzled more than $500,000 from it. (He was discovered and received a four-year jail sentence. Firestone pleaded guilty to IRS tax avoidance charges on the slush-fund money.) When faced with temptation or pressure for profit performance, otherwise honest managers may compromise their standards.

Eighth, existing ethical standards and principles are not always adequate to resolve conflicts. To be sure, most situations, particularly those involving simple honesty, truth telling, trade secrets, or following pertinent laws, are clear. For instance, at the turn of the century, Du Pont employed a chief mechanic, George Seitz, who was sent to rival firms, applied for jobs under an assumed name, and once hired, collected information about manufacturing processes, customers, and the companies' strengths and weaknesses. When Seitz reported back to top Du Pont executives, Du Pont used his information to undercut its rivals by stealing customers and then offering to buy a company at a bargain rate.[24] Premeditated corporate behavior such as this is clearly unethical. It violates high-level ethical abstractions such as the Golden Rule and the categorical imperative and contradicts more specific prohibitions in the Western tradition against lying and conflict of interest.

However, when conflicts between and among ethical standards arise, as they may in other cases, the application of principles at any level is not a guarantee of resolution because much latitude for specific application exists. A person and a corporation should, for example, obey the law. But an American corporation operating in the legal structure of racial separation in South Africa faces the ethical dilemma of violating ethical standards on human equality set out in the United Nations "Universal Declaration of Human Rights," and the spirit of American civil rights laws when obeying South African laws enforcing white supremacy. No principles exist to replace human judgment in such cases.

Ninth, the twentieth century presents managers with newly emerged problems of ethics that embody more than traditional concerns such as hon-

---

[24]Leonard Mosely, *Blood Relations: The Rise and Fall of the du Ponts of Delaware*, New York: Atheneum, 1980, p. 209.

esty, charity, and modesty. Although such qualities are still basic, vexing new problems have arisen. For example, modern ethical theory has not yet developed a principle for weighing human life against economic factors in a decision. Cancer studies may predict that workers or nearby residents exposed to plant emissions will become ill in small numbers far in the future. How should this information be balanced against costs of emission regulation, inflationary impact, capital investment reduction, or loss of jobs and economic benefits from forced plant closings?

Other examples of tough new ethical problems exist. Computer technology is a prolific source of them. Data banks on individuals have led to the rethinking of privacy rights. Software for monitoring computer terminal workers such as airline reservationists and data clerks at insurance companies has raised related questions about invasiveness. The automated teller machine (ATM), a computerized device, has simultaneously made banking more convenient and more dangerous. Banks have been forced to reexamine their responsibility for the safety of customers who use ATMs. By using a computerized gas chromatograph to chemically analyze a perfume's contents, entrepreneurs have for the first time been able to make nearly exact copies of expensive, established designer perfumes such as Ralph Lauren's Polo and Calvin Klein's Obsession. Because a scent cannot be trademarked like a brand name, the imitations are legal and can be sold cheaply enough to undercut the established brand and capitalize on the extensive advertising that built the foundation of its popularity. Of course, product imitation is an ancient problem. But here the technology has outpaced legal remedy and ethical consensus.

Finally, the growth of large-scale organizations in the twentieth century gives new significance to ethical problems such as committee decision making that masks individual responsibility, organizational loyalty versus loyalty to the public interest, and preferential hiring of affirmative action candidates. These are ethical complexities peculiar to large organizations that managers must deal with.

CONCLUDING COMMENT

There are many paths to ethical behavior. Few business executives fully appreciate the repertoire of ethical principles available to help resolve problems of business ethics. It may also be true that when they do resolve such problems, they intuitively use principles corresponding to some of those mentioned in this chapter. We believe that by studying the principles and guidelines presented here, a person can become more sensitive to the presence of ethical issues. And, having become more sensitive, he or she will likely become more resolute in correcting deficiencies. In addition, we think that these principles and guidelines are invaluable for application to ethical issues that arise in the case studies in this book. We encourage students to frequently refer to this chapter for ideas and conceptual tools.

An Application of Ethical Principles

The situations described below raise ethical conflicts for some readers. If you believe that an ethical problem exists in an incident, be specific in stating its nature. Then try to use principled reasoning to resolve the conflict by applying one or more of the ethical principles in the chapter.

1 Homeowners near an airport want to end commercial flights into the airport because of noise. As airport manager, you leak to the press some long-buried "contingency plans" for runway expansion without emphasizing that no expansion is likely. You hope that the complaining residents will be satisfied to negotiate a compromise that leaves the airport open to commercial flights but precludes expansion. Is this an ethical method of negotiation?

2 You operate a small, specialty metals business. An inexperienced customer calls with an order for a rare alloy. The customer has no idea what your costs are and what a reasonable price is for this alloy. Six other customers buy this alloy at a standard price. Should you add a little more to the price for this customer? Why or why not?

3 You have been offered a promotion to the position of project manager for a new-car development project at General Motors. The car is code-named the Screaming Demon. Careful marketing surveys show a continuing market for a fast, small car about the size of the Volkswagen GTI or Mitsubishi Mirage. The car is to be powered by a large-displacement, turbocharged engine and will have acceleration and top speeds rivaling those of the Chevrolet Corvette.

The car must sell for $9,000 to $11,500, and this will put severe constraints on engineering and materials costs. It will be a spartan automobile, with a harsh ride and few amenities, but it is to be marketed to the sixteen to twenty-five age group of drivers as a hot rod with a speed image. Ads being sketched by agencies competing for the account emphasize performance and handling and associate ownership of the automobile with adventurous young-adult lifestyles. Will you accept leadership of this project?

4 Six employees in the Grand Star Insurance Company work in the same room. Three are smokers who smoke freely during the day. Three are non-smokers who are irritated by the smoke. The nonsmokers recently approached the office manager and complained. "We have a right to protect our health from the dangers of sidestream smoke," one argued. When the office manager discussed the problem with the smokers, they argued that they had a right to smoke because no company or city ordinance prohibited it and because they had been hired by the company as smokers years ago and should not be required to give up their habit now. What ethical principle(s) might be applied to resolve this conflict?

5 You are asked by a potential employer to take a psychological profile test. A sample segment includes these items.

	Yes	No	Can't Say
It is difficult to sleep at night.			
I worry about sexual matters.			
Sometimes my hands feel disjointed from my body.			
I sometimes smell strange odors.			
I enjoyed dancing classes in junior high school.			
Not all of my friends really like me.			
Work is often a source of stress.			

Because you have read that it is best to fit into a "normal" range and pattern of behavior, and because it is your hunch that the personnel office will weed out unusual personalities, you try to guess which answers are most appropriate for a conservative or average response and write them in. Is this ethical?

6 You are the president of a company that manufactures chain saws. A chain saw is a dangerous but necessary tool. Each year some workers are injured while using your saws and the saws made by your competitors. You comply with all pertinent federal safety standards. But there are expensive design alterations you could incorporate into your product that would prevent some injuries. These alterations would raise production costs considerably in a very competitive industry. It is probable your competitors would not follow suit. Are you ethically remiss if you do not change your design?

7 When two vice presidents of American Can objected to the sale of two subsidiary companies, Chairman William Woodside promptly named them each as president of one of the companies and divested. Does this action raise ethical questions?

8 As a new middle-management employee for a corporation that owns a number of pear orchards, one day you see migrant workers mixing quantities of amitraz, an insecticide used on pears, in preparation for spraying. You recall that early in 1986 the Environmental Protection Agency canceled registration of amitraz after laboratory tests showed it to pose a risk of producing tumors in human tissue. After this action, amitraz was removed from the market and its application banned unless a special permit was issued. When you inquire about its use, you are told that the company had stored a large quantity of amitraz, that it is not a problem to use it because the EPA is overcautious, and that nobody in the company ever makes waves about mi-

nor noncompliance with stupid government regulations anyway because the firm's safety record is excellent. Would you take further action?

9 As president of an accounting firm in a large city, you were prepared to promote one of your vice presidents to the position of senior vice president. Your decision was based on a record of outstanding performance by this person over the eight years she has been with the firm. A new personnel director recently insisted on implementing a policy of resumé checks for hirees and current employees receiving promotions who had not been through such checks. Unfortunately, it was discovered that although the vice president claimed to have an M.B.A. from the University of Michigan, a check revealed that she dropped out before completing her last twenty units of course work. No other discrepancies exist. Would you proceed with the promotion, retain the vice president but not promote her, or fire her?

10 Entrepreneur Tommy Galambos, a fifty-year-old former eyeglasses manufacturer, spent a year researching state and municipal laws before starting his new business. He now owns sixteen "dogcycles" which daily fan out from a Van Nuys, California, garage to sell hot dogs in the San Fernando Valley. The dogcycles are used Cushman three-wheel motor scooters driven by college students and others who make up to $80 a day. Dogcycle drivers park their carts in public parking spaces on busy streets such as Ventura Boulevard and Van Nuys Boulevard, put change in the parking meters, raise umbrellas over their rolling restaurants, and wait for customers.

The drivers prefer to park in front of restaurants and storefront hot dog stands, where they can lure customers away. Police have received complaints from chains such as Hamburger Hamlet and from smaller operations such as The Wienery, a hot dog stand on Ventura Boulevard in Woodland Hills. There is no legal recourse for the land-bound establishments. In California food carts are permitted to sell non-prepackaged meals by a 1985 state law. Each dogcycle is designed to meet applicable state laws. The law specifies, for example, that carts must use steam rather than an open flame to heat food. Each dogcycle has a propane-burning steam table. To comply with state health regulations each also has a small refrigerator, water tanks, and a hand-washing basin with hot and cold running water.

Although restaurant owners have no legal recourse, this has not stopped them from confronting the rolling hot dog wagons. Several altercations have required police intervention. Do the dogcycles raise any ethical issues? What are they and how should they be resolved?

11 When Admiral Thomas Westfall took command of the Portsmouth Naval Shipyard, theft of supplies was thought to be endemic. It was a standing joke that homes in the area were painted gray with paint stolen from the Navy. Admiral Westfall issued an order that rules related to supply practices and forbidding theft would be strictly enforced. Within a few days, two career petty officers were apprehended carrying a piece of Plexiglass worth $25 out of the base. Westfall immediately fired both of them and also a civilian storeroom clerk with thirty years service. The clerk lost both his job and his pension. According to Westfall; "The fact that I did it made a lot of honest citizens real quick." Did the Admiral act ethically?

12 Sam, Sally, and Hector have been laid off from middle-management positions. Sam and Hector are deeply upset by their misfortune. They are nervous, inarticulate, and docile at an exit meeting in the personnel department and accept the severance package offered by the company (consisting of two weeks pay and continuation of health benefits for two weeks) without questioning its provisions. Sally, on the other hand, manifests her anxiety about job loss by becoming angry. In the exit meeting she complains about the inadequacy of the severance package, threatens a lawsuit, and tries to negotiate more compensation. She receives an extra week of pay that the others do not get. Has the company been fair in its treatment of these employees?

13 In the past five years seven department-store sales employees in a large retailing corporation have been fired and prosecuted for stealing from daily cash register receipts. They received sentences of community service followed by a term of probation. All acquired a criminal record.

A senior vice president of the same firm was caught diverting $68,000 from corporate accounts into fourteen personal bank accounts. He was allowed to resign quietly after repaying the corporation and was not prosecuted. This action was taken after much discussion by senior management. The senior vice president was prominent in civic affairs. His prosecution would have been newsworthy, and the corporation did not want to invite extensive negative publicity. After considering the ethical implications do you concur with the corporation's decision to permit a resignation of this nature?

Catholic Social Teaching and the U.S. Economy*

On November 13, 1986, the more than 300 Roman Catholic bishops of the United States assembled at their annual meeting in Washington, D.C., culminating a six-year process by voting approval of a landmark document on the moral dimensions of the U.S. economy. Entitled "Economic Justice for All: Catholic Social Teaching and the U.S. Economy," the pastoral letter invited American Catholics to reflect on the human and ethical dimensions of economic life and to fashion a more just society for the poor and the powerless.[25]

The bishops intend the letter not only to provide guidance for Roman Catholics but also to help shape new public policy for the United States. The hope was that the document would foster a "renewed public moral vision." There is no question but that if the letter were the guiding force today, our economy would have a whole new look. The pastoral letter challenged many common assumptions about economic life in the United States and placed the Catholic Church in the vanguard of social activism. Many, including a number of people in the business community, have been critical of the church's involving itself in economic matters.

CATHOLIC SOCIAL TEACHING

The point of the bishops' statement was to remind people that the U.S. economy is still far from where it might be. There are too many able-bodied people who cannot find work, and a disproportionate number of those are minorities and women. There are too many who slip through the safety net, going without adequate food, housing, and medical care. The plight of peo-

*By Oliver F. Williams, C.S.C.
[25]This case includes some material previously published: See O. Williams, "The Church and Social Activism: A Catholic Perspective," *Saint Louis University Public Law Review* 5: 439–450; and O. Williams, "Bishops Challenge Facilities to Act with Hope, Realism," *Health Progress* 66(1): 29–31, 1985.

ple in developing countries is also a central concern. So many in the U.S. live so well that it is easy to forget about those who are barely getting along.

The tradition of the Roman Catholic Church is that although the gospel message offers a vision of the sort of person one ought to become and the sort of communities one ought to try to form, this biblical vision requires human reason as well as the help of the social sciences to become concrete. The structures, institutions, and policies that ought to guide society are a product of disciplined reflection on the biblical vision. Thus, the church has a long tradition of social teaching stated in encyclicals (pastoral letters written by the Pope as the chief shepherd of the church), bishops' pastoral letters, and the writings of theologians. The object of this social teaching is not to advocate either capitalism or socialism but to point out where existing economic systems are failing to meet crucial human needs and aspirations.

Catholic social teaching begins with the conviction that human nature is flawed, following on its doctrine of original sin, but that human freedom responding to God's grace can overcome the selfishness that destroys community. People need others to grow and develop, and there is a natural, God-given tendency to come together in various groups—families, churches, trade unions, businesses, professional associations, and so on. Society is simply the sum total of all the various groupings. The role of the state is to facilitate cooperation among the natural groupings of society. Legislation is always enacted with an eye to the "common good," a term used frequently in Catholic social teaching to refer to the total environment—cultural, social, religious, political, and economic—required for the living of a humane life. Legislation is envisioned as evoking the cooperative dimension of the person and as fostering an environment in which the basic goodness of the person might flourish.

Although Catholic social teaching would never endorse any one particular country's economic arrangements, it has repeatedly stressed that the role of the state is to serve society. Thus, for example, in Pope John Paul II's 1981 encyclical, *On Human Work,* there is a vigorous defense of the workers' right to form unions. While this right is guaranteed by law in many nations, it is still far from universal. For example, in socialist China, the state is identified with society, and hence the government controls all dimensions of life and leaves little space for freedoms taken for granted in most of the Western world. This pervasive control is clearly not in accord with Catholic ideals.

The sort of society envisioned by Catholic social teaching is one in which private property is respected. Following the medieval scholar Thomas Aquinas, the church assumes that private property enables the human development intended by the Creator. Yet the teaching has always insisted that private property has a social dimension that requires that owners consider the common good in the use of property. This vision of society assumes that some people will have more material goods than others but that the affluent will provide for the less fortunate, either through the channels of public policy or other appropriate groups of society. The emphasis is always on respect for the human dignity of the poor, even in their unfortunate situation. The ideal is to structure society so that all those who are able might provide for themselves and their families by freely employing their talents. Although Catholic social teaching has never formally endorsed the mixed economy of the United States, there clearly are not many countries that have approached the ideal so closely as has the United States.

ESCALATING ACTIVISM

This social vision of the sort of world toward which Christians should be working has been stated and restated any number of times in papal encyclicals and other church documents in the twentieth century. How does one account for the rather sudden activist movement in the U.S. Catholic Church in the last fifteen years? Countless shareholder resolutions have been initiated by Roman Catholic religious orders in the last decade. Boycotts have been endorsed by high church officials. The bishop of El Paso, in 1973, requested the more than 250 U.S. bishops to support the boycott of all Farah products to aid the Mexican-American workers in their struggle with the firm. There have been pastoral letters from the bishops of the United States, first on nuclear ethics and now on the economy. What is happening in the church, and where is it likely to lead? It may be helpful to explore some of the social causes for this increasingly activist role as well as some of the theological reasons.

"PEOPLE PERSONS"

Bishop James Malone, the president of the National Conference of Catholic Bishops of the United States during the process of writing the letter on the economy, has long been an influential member of the assembly, and in many ways his pastoral experience has been similar to that of his brother bishops. Malone, as bishop of Youngstown, Ohio, has seen the dismantling of the steel industry and all its attendant problems. Unemployment, alcoholism, divorce, and child abuse all have been chronic in his diocese in recent years. Malone has often stated that there must be a more humane way to phase out an industry. It seemed as though people did not count. Many bishops today have had much pastoral experience and, unlike their predecessors, who were often chosen for their skills in raising money, building schools, and so on, this new breed of leaders are "people persons." They have been deeply touched by the problems of the poorest and the least advantaged in their midst, and many in their communities want the bishops to take action.

Whereas twenty years ago the U.S. bishops would not have been inclined to address social problems with a pastoral letter directly challenging public policy, the presence of a small but vocal minority sometimes called the "Catholic left" in the Catholic community has added a new dynamic to the dialogue. Often critical of the hierarchy on a number of issues, the Catholic left had its roots among the many who participated in the civil rights demonstrations. Following Martin Luther King, Jr., from Selma to Montgomery, then joining the anti-Vietnam War movement, many came to realize that they could change social structures that were unjust. Philip and Daniel Berrigan, leaders in the anti-Vietnam War protest, became great heroes to many young Catholics, and the influence of these two clerics in the U.S. church cannot be neglected.

UPWARD MOBILITY

Another factor that must be considered is the rapid upward mobility of many Catholics in the United States. Past generations of Catholics were largely blue-collar people, but today Catholics are more influential in business, government, and the wider society. The focus of encyclicals was formerly on the need for political and economic rights for lower-class Catholics. Now that Catholics have much more power and wealth, there is a shift in concern in church teaching to the plight of developing countries and the poorest of the poor in the global economy. It would have made little sense to tell Catholics of the United States in 1891 to change social structures, for these newcomers to America were still on the outside looking in. Now that many wield power, their church challenges them to exercise their stewardship well.

SOCIAL DIMENSIONS

Although the Catholic Church traditionally has stressed both the individual and the social aspects of human life, the social dimension has been increasingly emphasized in the last twenty-five years. The Gospels call not only for a change of heart but also for a change in social structures. There has been a renewed awareness that God's intentions for humankind concern not only matters of personal attitudes and conduct (for example, on sexuality), but also how the community is organized—the social, political, cultural, and economic dimensions of society. The overarching theme is that all people ought to have the opportunity to lead a humane life.

Although church documents always note that there will be no heaven on earth, since the late 1960s, Church teaching has stressed that Christians must be concerned with making the world a better place, especially for the least advantaged around the globe. This emphasis began with the teaching of Pope John XXIII but was fully developed under his successor, Pope Paul VI. The Second Vatican Council document, *The Church in the Modern World*, provides the full-blown rationale for the social mission of the church.

The present pope, John Paul II, continues to focus on the church's ministry to the person enmeshed in social and political structures but has repeatedly found it necessary to accent the fact that Christ can never be understood as a political revolutionary. Although especially concerned that the poor somehow be enabled to find a place in the mainstream of society, John Paul II has spent considerable effort differentiating authentic Catholic theology from a brand of theology with Marxist overtones that has a popular appeal in certain areas of Latin America. In that he comes from Poland, the pope is not naive to the stifling of society that results when the state imposes a single version of acceptable truth. Under Soviet domination, the Polish church has only recently begun to enjoy adequate freedom, and the rights of the people continue to be a cause of unrest. In addition, Marxist notions of an inevitable class struggle go against the grain of Christian thought. "The struggle is always for justice, not against others."

THE VISION IN CONTEXT

The U.S. bishops decided in November 1980, following the counsel of papal teaching, to write a pastoral letter on the economy that would bring Catholic social teaching in dialogue with the particular situation of the United States (paragraph 26[†]). After listening to theologians, major religious leaders of all faiths, economists, business and government leaders, and a host of others, and after receiving critical comments on three drafts of the document, the bishops finally issued the fourth and final version in November 1986.

There was some discussion among the bishops writing the document on whether it should include only the principles and moral vision of religious social teaching or whether some specific application of the principles in the form of policy recommendations should also be stated. Realizing that policy recommendations to reform the economy involve prudential judgments and therefore do not share the same kind of authority as moral principles, the bishops nevertheless decided to include some specific policy suggestions. At the least, these would indicate a direction and perhaps would stimulate debate on what a more humane economy might entail. It may be helpful to consider first a brief summary of the vision and principles and then an outline of the policy recommendations included in the letter.

The bishops' letter formulated a vision from biblical and theological grounds and was rooted in "its vision of the transcendent worth—the sacredness—of human beings" (paragraph 28). Recognizing that human dignity can only flourish in community, the pastoral draws on a rich biblical tradition to elaborate the essential social dimension of the person. In fidelity to scripture, the poor and the powerless are never to be forgotten. "The dignity of the human person, realized in community with others, is the criterion against which all aspects of economic life must be measured" (paragraph 28). "The fundamental moral criterion for all economic decisions, policies and institutions is this: They must be at the service of all people, especially the poor" (paragraph 24). This vision is developed with the biblical motifs of *creation, covenant*, and *community*.

By exploring these three biblical motifs, the document reminds Christians of the sort of people they ought to become and of the sort of communities they ought to form. For Christians, the Bible ought to have a decisive influence on their overall vision of life, their attitudes, convictions, and inten-

---

[†]All paragraph references are to "Economic Justice for All: Catholic Social Teaching and the U.S. Economy."

tions. Creation stories remind us of the gift-like character of life and the mandate to be faithful stewards of *God's* world. Using human talents and ingenuity, people are indeed called to continue God's creative work by building a more humane world. "Men and women are also to share in the creative activity of God....They can justly consider that by their labor they are unfolding the Creator's work" (paragraph 32).

As the ancient Hebrews fleeing Egypt came together in solidarity during their exodus and finally formalized their community in the covenant, so too those living today under the new covenant should be known for their community and solidarity. Because of this bond, the Christian community ought to be a model of concern for the less fortunate.

In the biblical vision, the justice of a community is demonstrated by its treatment of the powerless in society—the widow, the orphan, the poor, and the stranger. The poor in early Christianity were seen as the special concern of God. Following the 1979 statement at Puebla, Mexico, by the assembled Latin American bishops and the speeches of John Paul II, the pastoral focused on "the preferential option for the poor." The document detailed three challenges that follow from this option for the poor:

1 It posed a prophetic mandate to speak for those who have no one to speak for them, to be a defender of the defenseless, who in biblical terms are the poor.

2 It also demanded a compassionate vision that enables the church to see things from the side of the poor and powerless and to assess lifestyle, policies, and social institutions in terms of their impact on the poor.

3 Finally, and most radically, it called for an emptying of self, both individually and corporately, that allows the church to experience the power of God in the midst of poverty and powerlessness.

A GUIDING ASSUMPTION

Underpinning the pastoral letter is the idea that today the notion of the "rights" of an individual must be expanded to include not only civil and political rights, but also economic rights.

The concept of a right is embedded in the very founding of these United States. The Declaration of Independence and the Bill of Rights enumerate a long list of entitlements or rights. These legal rights of U.S. citizens, such as "life, liberty, and the pursuit of happiness," are correlated with a duty others have toward the individual. For example, to the framers of the Declaration of Independence, the right to life meant that a person had the right not to be killed and that the government had the duty to protect this entitlement. In the eighteenth century, the concept of a right was understood to circumscribe an area in which others had a duty *not* to interfere. The role of government was to insure that a person's free speech, privacy, property, and other rights were protected from undue interference. Today these civil rights are discussed in the philosophic literature as "negative rights"; that is, they point to the duty another has of *not* interfering. Although it is surely a significant accomplishment that a whole range of negative rights are guaranteed for so many today, a body of literature has developed in the twentieth century arguing for "positive rights." Positive rights are taken to be those entitlements a person has by virtue of being human. It is these rights which were championed by the bishops in their pastoral on the economy.

The concept of a positive right implies that someone or some institution in society has the *positive* duty to provide for whatever is necessary to pursue the interest in question. For example, today when one speaks of the "right to life," in contrast to the eighteenth-century understanding of the right not to be killed, what is generally meant is that a person has a right to the minimum necessities of life. The United Nations 1948 "Universal Declaration of Human Rights" lists a whole array of positive rights that are taken to be entitlements for all by virtue of being a person: the right to work, to just and favorable conditions of work, to protection against unemployment, to rest and leisure, including reasonable limitation of working hours and periodic holidays with pay, and so on.

The pastoral letter reminded the reader that Pope John XXIII, in the encyclical *Peace on Earth*, enumerated the rights that are the minimal conditions for a just economy, such things as the right to food, clothing, shelter, jobs, basic education, and medical care, as well as the right to security in the event of sickness and the rights of property ownership. However, the bishops recognized that there was no consensus yet in the United States that all of these really are rights that ought to be guaranteed nor how one might actually guarantee them. To help form this consensus was one of the major purposes of the pastoral. It must begin with the formation of a new cultural consensus that *all people really do have rights in the economic sphere* and that society has a moral obligation to take the necessary steps to insure that no one among us is hungry, homeless, unemployed, or otherwise denied what is necessary for living with dignity.

Four principles to guide policies in all economic institutions were suggested in the document.

1 The fulfillment of the basic needs of the poor is of the highest priority.

2 Increasing active participation in economic life by those who are presently excluded or vulnerable is a high social priority.

3 The investment of wealth, talent, and human energy should be especially directed to benefit those who are poor or economically insecure.

4 Economic and social policies as well as the organization of the work world should be continually evaluated in light of their impact on the strength and stability of family life.

POLICY RECOMMENDATIONS

Chapter 3 of the pastoral letter focused on four economic issues in the light of the religious vision and ethical principles discussed in the first two chapters.

The issues—employment, poverty, food and agriculture, and the U.S. role in the global economy—are not intended to exhaust the concerns of Catholic social teaching, but they do lend themselves to specific applications of Catholic moral principles. Thus new policies are advocated for reaching full employment, for eradicating U.S. poverty, for preserving family farms and discouraging agribusiness from dominating agricultural resources, and for aiding developing nations.

Chapter 3 of the five-chapter letter comprises 167 paragraphs, more than 45 percent of the document. Here is one of the specific recommendations under the section on employment:

> We recommend increased support for direct job creation programs targeted on the long-term unemployed and those with special needs. Such programs can take the form of direct public service employment and also of public subsidies for employment in the private sector. Both approaches would provide for those with low skills less expensively and with less inflation than would general stimulation of the economy. The cost of providing jobs must also be balanced against the savings realized by the government through decreased welfare and unemployment insurance expenditures and increased revenues from the taxes paid by the newly employed (paragraph 162).

Chapter 4 intended to move beyond particular policy recommendations and offers "a long-term and more fundamental response" to the challenge of achieving economic justice for all. It suggested new forms of cooperation and partnership to replace the adversarial relationships that so often dominate the major actors in society. The chapter considered four areas: cooperation within firms and industries; local and regional cooperation; partnership in the development of national policies; and cooperation at the international level.

Chapter 5 concluded the letter with reflections on the church as a model of economic justice and on the importance of the notion of vocation in the world today. "Through their competency and by their activity, lay men and women have the vocation to bring the light of the Gospel to economic affairs so that the world may be filled with the spirit of Christ and may more effectively attain its destiny in justice, in love and in peace" (paragraph 332). The letter is indeed hopeful that together people can fashion a world that is both more humane and more virtuous.

THE PROBLEMS AND POSSIBILITIES OF CHURCH SOCIAL ACTIVISM

The particular recommendation of the pastoral stated above on job creation programs was sharply attacked by the *Wall Street Journal* as "simply poor policy." The *Journal*'s criticism points up the dilemma of trying to be specific in a church document. Joseph A. Califano, Jr., Secretary of Health, Education, and Welfare from 1977 to 1979, commenting on the first draft of the letter, highlighted the dilemma.

> When the bishops move to what they call "policy applications," they sound more like one of the great society legislative messages I helped draft for Lyndon Johnson

than a group of clerics calling attention to the moral, religious, and ethical dimensions of the society they are trying to reshape. Here the bishops bring much of the criticism on themselves....My concern is that by dipping its toes too deeply in the waters of detailed federal programs, the bishops' message may be drowned.[26]

Although the bishops were careful to point out in their "Policy Applications" section that the moral authority of applications is much less than that of universal moral principles, Califano offered a telling criticism. In the judgment of many, the bishops were simply in over their heads in discussing concrete policies. But the document stimulated intense debate and, one hopes, will result in generally raising awareness of the moral dimension of economic decisions. This, to be sure, would be no small achievement.

Edward L. Hennessy, Jr., chairman of Allied Corporation, offered a penetrating critique of the bishops' economic ethics:

> It seems to be that intelligent discussion of the pastoral's recommendations requires that we put a price on them. Then, the bishops and everyone else can make a judgment about whether the cost might merely inconvenience the well-to-do, or whether it might reduce incentive, lessen the capital investment which creates jobs, slow the economy and seriously interfere with the goals of balancing the budget, cutting interest rates and making the United States competitive again with foreign producers.
>
> No one I know questions the need to provide adequate social services for the poor in our society. But the Pastoral letter, in its apparent determination to redistribute a significant part of our society's wealth, risks damaging the most productive economic system yet devised. It is a risk the bishops of the American church should, I think, hesitate to take.[27]

Is Hennessy correct in his judgment? There is nothing near a consensus on the issues in question. When the bishops speak in the area of medical or sexual ethics, they have a long tradition to draw from. The problem is that there is not an established body of literature or a tradition of economic ethics that is commonly accepted by the relevant academic and professional communities.

TOWARD THE FUTURE

It may be that the social-activist movement is only a phase in the church life as it moves toward a genuine ministry to managers of our public and private institutions. In the Catholic Church, the ministry had focused on laborers in the workplace because almost all Catholics were blue-collar workers. Today the children and grandchildren of those blue-collar people are running corporate America, often without any guidance or support from their churches. Business executives are often treated by their churches as either robber barons—with open hostility—or as rich benefactors—with undue deference.

---

[26]"The Prophets and the Profiters," *America*, January 12, 1985, p. 6.
[27]"A Pastoral for the Poor, Not the Economy," *America*, January 12, 1985, p. 17.

The churches are trying to relate to managers as people, people who often have substantial power and influence to shape communities and lives and who need the support of their religious community.

One suggestion for a new role for church pastors highlights a central point in the pastoral letter.

> Every pastor has employers and potential employers in his congregation. Many congregations will also include planners, academics, professionals of all kinds, union members, government employees, bankers, entrepreneurs, managers, merchants—a variety of people with ideas and experience—who, if brought together for discussion and action, could create jobs. Pastors can convene them for discussion and motivate them for action.[28]

While this is only one example of ministry to the business community, it may be a start of a new and challenging relationship between managers and pastors.

QUESTIONS

1 Peter M. Flanigan, director of the Council of International Economic Policy under President Nixon, is critical of the pastoral letter. In particular, he objects to the suggestion that our society can guarantee to all citizens "economic rights" in the same way as they are guaranteed civil and political rights. "The proposed guaranteed right to a job forces the government to do something that is not normally within its competence and that experience teaches it can do only with a loss of productivity or of freedom or of both."[29] Comment.

2 A *Fortune* editor commenting on the second draft noted "that the bishops keep contradicting themselves.... At one point, the bishops emphasize the importance of productivity; at another they groan about technology that displaces jobs. They make affirmative noises about the importance of entrepreneurs but then turn around and say that investment should be designed primarily to benefit the poor. (You think that's what they're trying to do in Silicon Valley, fellows?)"[30] Comment.

3 James Tobin, professor of economics at Yale University and Nobel laureate in 1981, offered this judgment on the bishop's letter. "The values expressed in the pastoral letter are presented as derived from Catholic theology. I, a non-Catholic and indeed an unrepentant "secular humanist," find them of universal appeal, striking responsive chords among persons of all religious faiths and of none. The ethics of equity and equality are very American, just as much as the ethics of individuals heard so exclusively today. The two are married in general adherence to the principal of equality of opportunity."[31] Comment.

4 A *New York Times* editorial (November 18, 1986) expressed a judgment.

> Mr. Buchanan [Patrick Buchanan, Reagan White House communications director] expressed hope that "the bishops recognize that the greatest enemy of material poverty in human history has been the free enterprise system of the United States." The bishops do

---

[28]William J. Byron, S.J., "Pastors Implementing the Economic Pastoral," *The Priest*, November 1988, p. 4.

[29]"The Pastoral and the Letter," *America*, January 12, 1985, p. 13.

[30]Daniel Seligman, "Continuing Fog," *Fortune*, November 11, 1985, p. 150.

[31]"Unemployment, Poverty, and Economic Policy," *America*, May 4, 1985, p. 359.

not dispute that. They would challenge the complacent theory that economic growth alone can solve poverty and unemployment. They also question the easy thought that private charity will suffice.

The bishops remind those in the government and the public willing to hear what many people would like to forget: that we are measured by the condition of the least of our brethren.[32]

Do you agree with the *Times?* Why or why not?

5 Some have suggested that religious critics, such as the Catholic bishops in their pastoral letter, are capitalism's best friend. Explain.

---

[32]"Infallibly Poor," *New York Times*, November 18, 1986, p. A30.

FOUR

Business and Government

CHAPTER
9

The Government-Business Relationship: An Overview

The Supreme Court of the United States has throughout our history played a decisive role in governmental regulation of business. In the following two cases the court slammed shut the door of federal regulation and then in a complete flip-flop reversed itself and opened the flood gates of regulation. Among the regulatory agencies launched in the Roosevelt Administration to combat the deep economic depression of the 1930s was the National Recovery Administration (NRA). It was the most ambitious peacetime experiment in industrial controls ever attempted in this country.

The heart of the NRA regulatory process lay in "codes of fair competition." The codes provided, among other things, for a minimum scale of weekly wages, maximum hours of work, collective bargaining by labor unions, prohibitions against employing child labor, an agreement not to raise prices beyond that justified by payroll increases, and a refusal to deal with all nonsigners of the agreement. Details of the first code agreements were hammered out by business trade associations and organized labor. Each code pertained to a designated industry. When government officials approved a code, it became the law of the land. Several million employers operated under codes and the public was encouraged to boycott those employers who did not display an emblem of the "Blue Eagle" which denoted acceptance of the industry code applicable to them.

A SICK CHICKEN GROUNDS THE MIGHTY BLUE EAGLE

The Schechter Poultry Corporation, a New York City firm, fell under the NRA's Live Poultry Code which included the standard provisions and a few others, such as prohibitions against selling tubercular chickens. Schechter slaughtered chickens and resold them to local retail dealers and butchers.

The government charged the company with violating several provisions of the Live Poultry Code, including the sale of sick chickens, the minimum wage, and maximum work hours.

The company argued that the NIRA (National Industrial Recovery Act), which created the NRA, was unconstitutional. A long history of Supreme Court cases, said the company, concluded that the right of the government to regulate business under the Commerce Clause of the Constitution (Article 1, Sec. 8) did not extend to local manufacturing and processing operations such as those of the Schechter Corporation.

The government argued that 96 percent of the poultry sold in New York City came from out of state and that activities of Schechter substantially affected the stream of interstate commerce and therefore fell within the powers granted to the government by the Commerce Clause to regulate interstate commerce. The government pointed to a history of Supreme Court decisions which stopped state regulations of local activities when they directly affected interstate commerce. The NIRA was therefore, said the government, constitutional.

THE COURT'S DECISION

In a unanimous decision, the Supreme Court declared the NIRA unconstitutional (*Schechter v. U.S.*, 1935).[1] First, said the Court, the Act put too few restrictions on the President and granted him "virtually unfettered" power to prescribe codes throughout industry. This, said the Court, is "an unconstitutional delegation of legislative power."

Second, said the Court, "Neither the slaughtering nor sales by defendant were transactions in interstate commerce." "...[A]fter the (poultry) has arrived and has become comingled with the mass of property within the State and is there held solely for local disposition and use" the flow of commerce stops. "The poultry has come to a permanent rest within the State." Thus, the Commerce Clause cannot apply to the defendant and the NRA codes are unconstitutional. As usual, the Court left a loophole. It said that the Commerce Clause could reach an essentially local or intrastate activity which had "direct" effects upon interstate commerce. In this instance, however, the effect was indirect and "...such transactions remain within the domain of State power." To conclude otherwise, said the Court, "there would be virtually no limit to the Federal power, and for all practical purposes we should have a completely centralized government."[2]

IMPORTANCE OF THE DECISION

The *Schechter* decision was a devastating blow to the regulatory, relief, and reform program of President Roosevelt. So incensed was he that following

[1]*Schechter Poultry Corp. v. United States*, 225 U.S. 495 (1935).
[2]For an excellent discussion of this and the following *Jones and Laughlin* case, see Richard C. Cortner, *The Jones & Laughlin Case*, New York: Knopf, 1970.

his second-term inauguration in 1937 he sent to the Congress his famous "Court-Packing Plan." This was a proposal to reorganize the nation's judicial system. Among its recommendations was a proposal to expand the Supreme Court by six new members, something that could be done constitutionally with congressional approval. The idea, of course, was to permit him to pick judges who would be more liberal interpreters of constitutional powers granted to the federal government. This plan created a national furor and was never implemented.

THE COURT REVERSES ITSELF

Under powers granted by Congress in the National Labor Relations Act of 1935, the National Labor Relations Board (NLRB) ordered the Jones and Laughlin Steel Corporation to cease and desist engaging in unfair labor practices. The corporation said the Board had no powers to make such demands and the issue went to the Supreme Court for resolution in *NLRB v. Jones and Laughlin Steel Corp.*[3]

At the time, Jones and Laughlin was the fourth largest steel company in the country. It employed 22,000 workers, of which 10,000 were in the Aliquippa plant in Pennsylvania, the target of the NLRB's suit.

Jones and Laughlin had a long history of strife with labor unions, a battle which was exascerbated by deep depression in the steel industry and huge financial losses. The NLRB pointed to a long list of unfair labor practices in the Aliquippa plant, including firing union labor leaders on grounds of trivial violation of company rules and the refusal of the company to recognize the rights of workers to organize and bargain collectively.

Jones and Laughlin argued that its operations in the plant consisted entirely of production, a local activity that the Court in previous cases had said was not interstate commerce. The claim of the NLRB that it had the power to regulate interstate commerce under the Commerce Clause of the Constitution was, therefore, invalid.

The NLRB argued that the plant was a focal point or throat through which an ever-recurring stream or flow of interstate commerce passed. Therefore, a strike in the Aliquippa plant, which was threatening, would have a direct, substantial, and immediate impact upon interstate commerce. Since the federal government could regulate interstate commerce, it clearly had the power, said the NLRB, to prohibit Aliquippa managers from engaging in unfair labor practices.

THE DECISION

Four days after President Roosevelt submitted his court-packing plan to Congress, the Supreme Court began hearings in this case and four others which tested the constitutionality of the National Labor Relations Act and, of

---

[3]*National Labor Relations Board v. Jones & Laughlin Steel Corp.* 201 U.S. 1 (1937).

course, the powers of the NLRB. In April 1937, the Court, by a 5 to 4 vote, concluded that the NLRB was acting upon legitimate constitutional authority. The Court found that obstruction to interstate commerce was within congressional power under the Commerce Clause, and it had the right to delegate that power to the executive branch in the National Labor Relations Act. A strike or work disruption at the Aliquippa plant would produce such an obstruction.

Congress cannot be held powerless to regulate, said the Court, "when industries organize themselves on a national scale, making their relation to interstate commerce the dominant factor in their activities...." (In later decisions this doctrine was applied by the Court to a cannery that shipped only a third of its output to other states and a power company that sold an insignificant part of its current across state lines.) Furthermore, said the Court, the right of employees to organize was a "fundamental right" equal to that of employers to organize their businesses.

SIGNIFICANCE OF THE DECISION

The complete reversal of the *Jones and Laughlin* decision from the *Schecter* case opened wide the door for federal regulation of individual businesses. It was, with other contemporary cases, one of the most important legal foundations supporting the flood of federal regulation that has been enacted since then. It illustrates also that the Supreme Court's interpretation of the Constitution reflects changes in its environment.

This chapter provides a framework for understanding why government regulates business and the evolution of regulations over time. We discuss how this has led to what we call the Second Managerial Revolution. We mean by this that government regulations today have changed significantly the ways in which managers view their responsibilities, make decisions, and run their companies. We conclude the chapter with an evaluation of the Reagan administration's strategy to promote regulatory relief and reform, and current demands for further regulation.

LEGAL BASIS OF GOVERNMENT ACTION TOWARD BUSINESS

The impact of government on business derives from laws applied by individuals in the executive branches of governments or tested in courts of law. These laws and their implementation are, in turn, based upon legal powers given to governments and the administrators of government programs. The fundamental basis for this tower of regulations is the Constitution of the United States.

In the Constitution, most of the economic powers exercised by the federal government are contained in Article 1, Section 8. This section gives Congress the power to levy and collect taxes; to pay debts and provide for common defense and general welfare; to borrow money; to regulate commerce; to establish bankruptcy laws; to coin money and regulate its value; to fix standards of weights and measures; to stop counterfeiting; to establish post offices and post roads; to promote science and useful arts by granting patents and exclusive rights over writings and discoveries; to punish piracies; to exercise exclusive legislation over the geographical seat of government, military establishments, and other lands owned by the government; and "to make all laws which shall be necessary and proper for carrying into execution these foregoing powers, and all other powers vested by this Constitution in the government of the United States, or in any department or officer thereof." A reasonable interpretation of such grants of authority permits the national government in today's economy to do just about anything that is likely to pass through congressional law-making machinery.

The federal government is delegated powers from the states. State governments retain those powers not explicitly or implicitly granted to the federal government or taken by it. States, therefore, may do whatever they choose as long as they are not prevented from doing so by the Constitution or the federal government. Local governments are created by and vested with powers by the states. The more important powers exercised by state and local governments over business enterprises concern powers to incorporate businesses, power to levy and collect taxes, and the police power. The first needs no elaboration. The power to tax has been used not only to raise revenue, but also to regulate and promote business. The police powers enable states to prevent fraud, ensure adequate service at reasonable rates, protect employees from employer exploitation, maintain competition, restrict competition, fix prices of commodities, establish standards for processing food and drugs, establish standards for safety in mines and factories, and in many other ways regulate and promote business.

THE SCOPE OF GOVERNMENT RELATIONS WITH BUSINESS

The federal government, the focus of this chapter, is massively involved with the business community. The following overview illustrates the breadth and depth of the relationship between government and business.

Government prescribes rules of the game. Government prescribes broad rules of business behavior within which individuals are comparatively free to act in conformity with their self-interest. Typical rules of the game concern competitive behavior, labor-management relations, the sale of securities, advertising, business incorporation, and safety regulations concerning automobiles. The regulations vary in the extent to which they restrain an individual business, but they serve to establish the "rules for playing the game."

Government is a major purchaser of the output of business. Out of a prospective GNP in calendar 1990 of $5.4 trillion, federal, state, and local governments are expected to purchase $1.1 trillion or 19.9 percent. The federal government is expected to purchase $409 billion of this total. Government purchases range from paper clips to space vehicles. Many companies, and some very large ones, sell their entire output to government. Few companies do not directly or indirectly benefit from government procurement.

REGULATING THE HAMBURGER

The ordinary hamburger is the subject of 41,000 federal and state regulations. They spring from 200 laws and 111,000 precedent-setting court cases.

A sampling of the laws governing the hamburger that you buy at the corner sandwich stand or in a fancy restaurant follows:

Bun—enriched bun must contain at least 1.8 milligrams of thiamine, 1.1 milligrams of riboflavin, and at least 8 but not more than 12.5 milligrams of iron.

Content—must be fresh or frozen chopped beef and not contain added water, binders, or extenders.

Growth promoters—use of growth-stimulating drugs must end two weeks before slaughter.

Pickle—slices must be between ⅛ and ⅜ inches thick.

Tomato—must be mature but not overripe or soft.

Cheese—must contain at least 50 percent milk fat and, if made with milk that is not pasteurized, must be cured for 60 or more days at a temperature of at least 35 degrees Fahrenheit.

Inspections—as many as six inspections under Federal Meat Inspection Act can occur as meat is checked before and after slaughter and at boning, grinding, fabrication, and packaging stages.

Mayonnaise—may be seasoned or flavored as long as the substances do not color it to look like egg yolk.

Ketchup—to be considered Grade A fancy, it must flow no more than 9 centimeters in 30 seconds at 69 degrees Fahrenheit.

Lettuce—must be fresh, not soft, overgrown, burst, or "ribby."

Fat—no more than 30 percent fat content.

Pesticides—no more than 5 parts of the pesticide DDT per million parts of fat in the meat

Source: Excerpted and adapted from *U.S. News & World Report*, February 11, 1980, p. 64. Copyright © 1980, U.S. News & World Report.

The government uses its contracting power to get business to do things the government wants. Businesses that want government contracts must subcontract to minority businesses, pay prevailing minimum wages, comply with safety and sanitary work regulations, refrain from discrimination in hiring, and meet government pollution standards. Government contracting agencies by law must prefer domestic to foreign products (Buy American Act), ship all military and at least one-half of foreign aid goods in United States vessels (Cargo Preference Act), purchase all brooms and similar items from nonprofit agencies for the blind (Blind-Made Goods Act), and purchase only United States-made buses (1969 Defense Authorization Act). It is a case of "no compliance, no contract."

Government promotes and subsidizes business. The government has a complex and powerful network of programs to aid business. Promotion ranges from tariff protections to loans, guarantees of loans, maintenance of high levels of economic activity, and direct subsidies. It is, of course, in the interest of government to ensure growing and vigorous business activity, but the ways in which government promotes business vary enormously and sometimes are highly controversial. For instance, tax incentives to stimulate business to make capital investments are controversial, but training military pilots who subsequently are hired by airlines is not. Both are promotional and worth calculable dollars and cents to the business concerned.

Promotion, of course, is not limited to money, but includes favorable legislation and administrative action. For instance, rights given by government to operate a TV station may be extremely valuable. Because the successful promotion of the interests of one group sets a precedent for others, government promotion of business activity steadily expands despite the strong pleading of many business leaders for reduced government expenditures and more limited government.

Government owns vast quantities of productive equipment and wealth. The government is an important producer of goods and services, often in direct competition with private business. It produces goods and services such as rubber, high-octane gasoline, ammunition, guns, ships, atomic energy, postal services, weather-reporting services, and dams. The federal government owns vast stockpiles of raw materials and productive equipment, which it often lends to private industry. It also owns most of the land in many western states.

Government is an architect of economic growth. It has assumed responsibility for achieving an acceptable rate of stable economic growth, as set forth in the Employment Act of 1946. This policy benefits business by reducing economic uncertainty and making long-range planning more feasible. In the past few decades, we have had relative economic stability compared with the unexpected economic crises experienced in the century prior to World War II.

Government protects interests in society against business exploitation. For instance, many laws protect the interests of investors, customers, employees, and the competitors of a business.

Government directly manages large areas of private business. The word "manage" here means that government dictates a certain amount of decision making. It does not mean that the government is the manager in the way a chief executive of a company manages. In the sense meant here, the government manages important parts of industries through regulation, supervisory surveillance, and joint decision making.

Government is the repositor of the social conscience and redistributes resources to meet social ends. Government increasingly redirects resources by transfer payments, research and development expenditures, tax incentives, and subsidies. These traditional means have expanded in recent years. The government also exerts moral pressure on business to act in conformity with generally accepted social goals.

This overview of the multiple ways in which government affects managerial decision-making is only an introduction. It scarcely suggests the massive and complex impact of government relationships with business. Throughout this book, various aspects of this interconnection will be explored in detail.

UNDERLYING REASONS FOR GOVERNMENT REGULATION OF THE PRIVATE SECTOR

Federal justifications for regulating the private sector can be divided into two groupings: when flaws appear in the market place that produce undesirable consequences; and where adequate social, political, and other reasons for government regulation exist. Regulations until recent years were introduced mostly in response to flaws in the market mechanism; in recent years regulations increasingly have been introduced for broad social reasons.

FLAWS IN THE MARKET

The competitive market, when functioning properly, yields the "best" answer to the questions of what should be produced, when, and how the product will be distributed. When functioning perfectly, the market mechanism determines how society's resources can be used most efficiently in producing the goods and services that people want. This competitive model has high appeal in democratic societies because with it social welfare can be advanced without central government control.

Although highly efficient, the free-market competitive model is not flawless. Some of the more important market failures that have justified government action are as follows.

Natural Monopoly   When a firm can supply the entire market for a good or service more cheaply than any combination of smaller firms, it is said to have a natural monopoly. Under such circumstances competition would be wasteful of resources. Typical examples are, of course, public utilities. Unregulated natural monopolies have a tendency to produce insufficient output to meet demand so as to extract a higher price than would exist if competition prevailed. As a result, government traditionally has regulated utilities to determine what they may charge, to establish a minimum quality of service, and to determine the size of profit that is permissible.

Natural Resource Regulation   Exploitation of a natural resource can result in monopolistic practices that should be regulated. For example, the total volume of oil that can be produced in a single field is a function of the number of wells drilled and the rate of pumping. Too many wells and too rapid pumping reduce the field pressure and the quantity of recoverable oil. That should be avoided. Government allocation of limited wavelengths in the electromagnetic spectrum is another example of natural resource regulation.

Destructive Competition   Destructive competition can take many forms, but the classic illustration is an industry with heavy fixed costs, comparatively unable to use fixed capital for multiple purposes, and in which the introduction of new productive capacity is slow in meeting new demands. Railroads are a classic illustration of an industry that, when unregulated, falls into cutthroat competition and rates fall below marginal incremental costs.

Externalities   Externalities are costs of production that are borne, not by the enterprise that causes them, but by society. A classic illustration is pollution. One steel mill that tries to eliminate air and water pollution will go bankrupt if other mills do not install antipollution equipment. The principle applies to industrial safety practices, health hazards, and jet noise, to give just a few examples.

Inadequate Information   Competitive markets operate more efficiently when everyone associated with them has enough information to make informed choices. To the extent that such information is not available, government finds justification for regulating the knowledge in question. This category covers a very wide range of information, including information for consumers about product quality, warranty, content, and so on; information to workers about work hazards; disclosure of financial information for investors; disclosure of costs of capital to investors; and so on.

SOCIAL, POLITICAL, AND OTHER REASONS FOR REGULATION

During the past several decades there have been a number of structural and value changes taking place in our society that have resulted in increasing pressure on government to interfere in the market mechanism. Here are a few.

Quality-of-Life Demands   Pressures on government and business to meet new quality-of-life demands are significant causes of new government regulations. Clean air, clear water, and toxic waste disposal are examples.

Concern for Individuals   Concern for individuals has always been a cause of federal regulation. The very first Congress of the United States passed legislation to help poor and indigent sailors. Help to individuals has expanded to include programs for safe working conditions, better and safer products for consumers, eliminating discrimination in employment, and providing better health care.

Business Abuses   Unethical and immoral actions of business are, of course, a subject for regulations that aim to prevent their occurrence.

Equality   New definitions of equality give rise to new entitlements, which in turn result in government regulations to provide them; e.g., equal opportunity.

Resolution of National Problems   For more than 200 years, the United States has been a nation, and since around the turn of the century, we have been a national economy. But not until recently have we become a national society in the sense that shocks felt in one part of the country are immediately felt in every other part. As our nation became a national economy, the federal government took on increased responsibilities in resolving the problems that accompanied its development, such as the regulation of railroads, of banking, and of aviation. These are still problems of a "national society," but more and more the "national society" evidences quality-of-life problems, such as pollution, which demand national solutions.

Regulation to Benefit Special Groups   It is possible for regulations to be passed largely as a result of special group pressures on the legislative process to pass measures in their own selfish interests. The expressed justification for such legislation, however, is based not on that objective but on more lofty goals. Nevertheless, a good bit of regulation does protect the interests of special groups, such as manufacturers of steel and producers of peanuts.

Conservation of Resources   Federal regulations seek to conserve our natural resources, such as agricultural land, pristine forests, lakes and mountains, clean air, and endangered species.

Other Social and Political Causes of Regulation   Federal regulations also spring from national security requirements, resolving group conflicts, and alleviating risks of groups and individuals. Many government regulations before World War II attempted to reduce risks of groups and individuals from economic hazards. Today much regulation attempts to reduce other risks, such as physical harm from pollution or working conditions.

BUSINESS SOMETIMES SEEKS GOVERNMENT REGULATION

It is true that people in business, generally, loudly protest new government regulations. Yet business people often seek government help on their behalf. There are many reasons for this paradox.

Frequently it is a different group that seeks help from the one that rejects a regulation. But sometimes, the same group cries against one regulation but asks for a different one to help their business.[4]

Many of the reasons for regulation given above often prompt business people to seek government regulatory help. In mind, for example, are protection from unfair competition, controlling monopoly power, lowering interest rates, guaranteeing loans, or, as in the case of farmers, subsidizing income. On occasion, business people have sought federal regulations to prevent chaos in their activities. This has been the case with respect to setting standards for products, for example.

CHANGING HISTORICAL PATTERNS OF GOVERNMENT-BUSINESS REGULATORY RELATIONSHIPS

In our history, there have been four primary peacetime waves of government regulatory action affecting business (see Figure 9-1). Government regulatory activity historically has come in sudden bursts, or "waves." It has moved in

[4]For an interesting account of this phenomenon see Dan I. Worrell and Edmund R. Gray, "Uncle Remus Meets Regulatory Reform: The Brier-Patch Phenomenon," *Business Horizons*, July–August 1985.

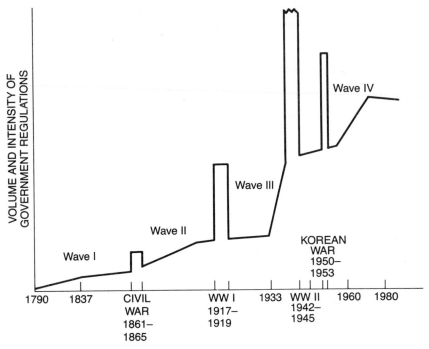

FIGURE 9-1   Historical waves of government regulation of business.

a ratchet-like pattern. Each wave has been triggered by the rise of popular demand for government to solve particular problems. After each burst of activity, the rate of new regulation has leveled off or declined. Except after wartime, the declines have been minimal. Generally, each new wave has brought more regulatory activities than existed previously; the exception has been the controls imposed during wartime, most of which were lifted following the end of hostilities. Here are some highlights of each wave.

THE FIRST WAVE

This wave of government regulation took place from 1790 to 1837. During this period, government regulations were predominantly promotional for business. The government gave vast financial subsidies and huge grants of land (to be sold) to private interests for the building of turnpikes, canals, and railroads. Through these actions the federal government facilitated the building of a much-needed infrastructure.

During this period a major legal foundation for business was laid in the *Dartmouth College* case (1819). The New Hampshire legislature amended the charter of Dartmouth College, a private institution, to make it a public institution. The Supreme Court ruled that state legislatures could not impair a contract, and the charter "is a contract, the obligation of which cannot be impaired without violating the constitution of the United States."[5] The corporate form thereby gained freedom from arbitarary post-facto legislative interference.

THE SECOND WAVE

This wave of government regulation took place during the late nineteenth and early twentieth centures. The progressive movement, as described in Chapter 4, led to state laws regulating railroads. The Supreme Court said these laws were constitutional in *Munn v. Illinois* (1877) and declared that "When private property is devoted to a public use, it is subject to public regulation."[6] It becomes "affected with a public interest." This case provided a new foundation for broad regulation of industry. It supported the creation of the Interstate Commerce Commission in 1887 to control railroads, the Sherman Antitrust Act in 1890, the Food and Drug Act and the Meat Inspection Act of 1905, and other major pieces of legislation. In contrast to the first wave, the thrust of new laws was to curb the abuses of an ebullent, aggressive, and often irresponsible business world.

There were, however, some positive developments for business. The Supreme Court ruled in the Santa Clara case in 1886 that corporations are cloaked in the mantle of the Fourteenth Amendment to the Constitution.[7] This amendment had been passed in 1868 to protect blacks and forbade states to abridge the privileges and immunities of citizens; to deprive any person of life, liberty, or property without due process of law; or to deny to any person within its jurisdiction the equal protection of the laws. The Court ruled that a corporation is a person and that therefore the benefits of the amendment extended to it. In effect, states could regulate corporations, but the regulations had to be developed through accepted legal procedures and be nondiscriminatory as compared with those covering individual citizens. This armor proved to be highly protective to business in the legal jungles of regulation.

Efforts by federal, state, and local governments to introduce social reforms, such as permitting workers to strike and improving working conditions, met with repeated rebuffs by the Supreme Court. For example, the state of New York attempted to reduce the hours of work in bakeries to ten a day. But this attempt, said the court in *Lockner v. New York* in 1905, was an unreasonable, unnecessary, arbitrary, illegal, and "meddlesome interference with the rights of the individual" and contrary to the Fourteenth Amendment.[8]

THE THIRD WAVE

This wave of regulation was brought about by the Great Depression of the 1930s, one of the most severe human and economic catastrophes ever to strike

---

[5]*Dartmouth College v. Woodward,* 4 Wheaton 519 (1819).
[6]*Munn v. Illinois* (1877), 297, 299, 317.
[7]*Southern Clara County v. Southern Pac. Ry.* 118 U.S. 394 (1886).
[8]*Lockner v. New York,* 198 U.S. 45 (1905).

the American people. In combating this crisis, the federal government assumed an entirely new role in economic life and in its relationship with business.

The statistics of this depression starkly reveal the extraordinary tragedy. For instance, GNP dropped (in current dollars) from $103.1 billion in 1929 to $58 billion in 1932. Industrial production was almost halved between these two dates. Durable goods production in 1932 was one-third the 1929 level. Steel production in 1932 was at 20 percent of capacity. The unemployment rate rose in 1933 to 25 percent of the labor force. Thousands of businesses and farmers went bankrupt, and millions of investors lost their life savings.

The New Deal of Franklin D. Roosevelt broke new regulatory ground. The federal government for the first time assumed responsibility for stimulating business activity out of an economic depression. The federal government undertook to correct a wide range of abuses in the economic machinery of the nation, particularly in business, and amassed more far-reaching laws to this end in a shorter period of time than ever before or since. For the first time it assumed responsibility on a large scale for relieving the distress of businesspeople, farmers, workers, homeowners, consumers, investors, and other groups caused by adverse economic events.

THE FOURTH WAVE

A groundswell of interest in improving the quality of life in the 1960s and 1970s led to the fourth wave of government regulations. The result was the development of new controls that involved government ever more deeply in managerial decision making, enormously increased the volume of regulation, and tightened government's control over business—precisely the topics that make up the subject of much of this book. Figure 9-2 illustrates how government regulatory agencies are involved in decision-making in every major functional and operational area of a typical large corporation.

WAR BLIPS

As Figure 9-1 shows, wars have brought sudden increases in government controls. During the Civil War, there was very little control over production and prices, but the North created the National Banking System to help finance the war, and this had lasting impact on our financial system. World War I witnessed the introduction of substantial controls over industry, but the war ended before the controls began to "bite." The federal government exercized complete control over the economic system during World War II and to a lesser extent, but still substantial, during the Korean War. After both wars the wartime controls were completely abandoned.

THE SECOND MANAGERIAL REVOLUTION

The fourth wave of regulations has brought about a virtual revolution in the way our corporations are now managed. We contrast it with the first mana-

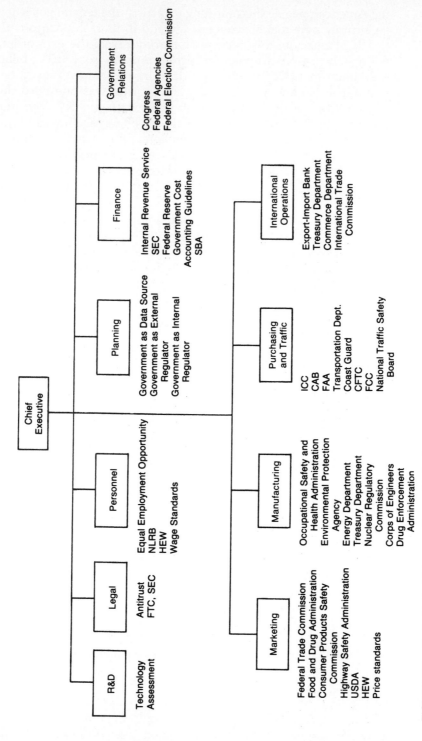

FIGURE 9-2 Typical industrial corporation and federal government relations (*see Table 9-1 for agency titles*). (*Source:* Murray L. Weidenbaum, *Business, Government, and the Public*, 2nd ed., p. 375. © 1981. Copyright. Reprinted by permission of Prentice-Hall, Inc., Englewood Cliffs, New Jersey.)

gerial revolution, when the old entrepreneurial class of managers was replaced by corporate professional managers. This change took place over a long period of time but gained public attention in the classic study by Berle and Means called *The Modern Corporation and Private Property,* published in 1932.[9] The second managerial revolution is characterized by a massive transfer of power from the managerial class to a new class of public servants in the federal, state, and local governments armed with authority to make decisions heretofore reserved for managers in privately owned and operated businesses.

TRADITIONAL INDUSTRY VERSUS FUNCTIONAL REGULATION

This fourth wave of regulation follows a "new model" of regulation which contrasts with the "old model." The new model is functional regulation, in contrast to the old industry regulation. As shown in Figure 9-3, the old style of regulation was and still is concerned with one industry, such as railroads, airlines, drugs, and so on. The main focus of this model is huge industry segments of the economy. In contrast, the functional regulations cut across industrial lines and concentrate on one function in a company rather than the organization as a whole.

The principal purposes of the older type regulations (of agencies such as ICC, FTC, and FCC) (see Table 9-1 for agency titles) were to prevent monopoly; to increase competition; to establish uniform standards of safety, security, communications, and financial practice; and to prevent abuses of managerial practices. The newer regulations are principally to improve the quality of life by securing cleaner air and clearer water, protecting consumers from shoddy products, assuring more information to consumers, preventing discrimination in the workplace, and so on.

Older agency policies and regulations generally applied to entire companies in an industry. The newer agencies apply specific rules to specific business functions to implement their policies. For example, automobile seat belt rules established by NHTSA are directed at design engineers, OSHA worker safety rules are focused on safety engineers, and the EEOC sets standards for hiring and discharging workers. In this respect, regulators of these agencies are concerned with their particular functional area and not the total profitability of the company. Indeed, in pursuit of their mandate they not only ignore but may insist on regulations which adversely affect profits. This is in contrast to older regulators who, like the ICC, were more concerned about a whole company and industry.

These are broad generalizations to make a point. In fact, many regulatory agencies of government are mixtures of both models. The SEC, for example, regulates the securities industry but also sets rules concerning content of financial statements prepared by corporations, and how securities will be

---

[9]Adolf A. Berle, Jr., and Gardiner C. Means, *The Modern Corporation and Private Property,* New York: Macmillan, 1932.

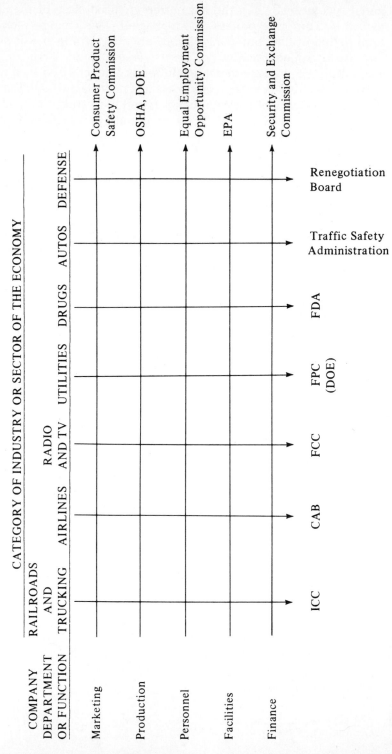

FIGURE 9-3   Comparison of the older and the newer regulatory models (*see Table 9-1 for agency titles*). (*Source:* Murray L. Weidenbaum, *Business, Government, and the Public*, p. 14. Copyright © 1977. Reprinted by permission of Prentice-Hall, Inc., Englewood Cliffs, New Jersey.)

TABLE 9-1 MAJOR FEDERAL REGULATORY AGENCIES CLASSIFIED BY DOMINANT ORIENTATION

Agency	Date established
Predominantly Industry	
Interstate Commerce Commission (ICC)	1887
Food and Drug Administration (FDA)	1906
Federal Reserve Board (FRB)	1913
Federal Trade Commission (FTC)	1914
Federal Home Loan Bank Board (FHLBB)	1932
Federal Deposit Insurance Corporation (FDIC)	1933
Federal Communications Commission (FCC)	1934
Federal Aviation Administration (FAA)	1958
Federal Maritime Commission (FMC)	1961
Nuclear Regulatory Commission (NRC)	1975
Federal Energy Regulatory Commission (FERC)	1977
Predominantly Functional	
Securities and Exchange Commission (SEC)	1934
National Labor Relations Board (NLRB)	1935
Equal Employment Opportunity Commission (EEOC)	1964
Environmental Protection Agency (EPA)	1970
National Highway Traffic Safety Administration (NHTSA)	1970
Occupational Safety and Health Administration (OSHA)	1971
Consumer Product Safety Commission (CPSC)	1972
Mine Safety and Health Administration (MSHA)	1977

traded. The FTC, an older agency, is concerned with assuring fair competition but also specifies in detail rules for a company's advertising.

As late as the 1950s, aside from World War II, the federal government assumed major regulatory responsibility in only four areas: antitrust, financial institutions, transportation, and communications. Today, as illustrated in Figure 9-2, at least one federal agency regulates something in virtually every business activity.

IMPACT OF NEWER REGULATIONS ON MANAGERIAL DECISION MAKING

The patterns of newer regulations make government officials active managerial partners with business executives. Government has always been a partner with business, but has never been so directly active in the management of an enterprise as it is today. It is involved from the highest corporate managers, through the specific ways in which products are made and distributed, to what takes place between producer and customer after products are sold. Many business managers today in fact act as agents of the government without being under contract. The chairman of General Motors Corporation lamented: "Government today has something to say about how we design our products, how we build them, how we test them, how we warrant them, how we repair them, the compensation we pay our employees, and even the prices we may charge our customers."[10]

Regulations have pushed companies toward a greater degree of centralization of decision making in areas subject to compliance or review. Larger companies particularly have found it necessary to centralize so as to prevent different divisions from interpreting government regulations in various ways. Most pronounced are laws with respect to equal opportunity employment, pollution controls, worker safety, cost accounting standards, advertising, warranties, and consumer protections. Implementation of regulations still continues to take place in divisions and decentralized units of a company, but company policy and review is centralized.

THE VOLUME OF REGULATORY LEGISLATION

The sheer volume of regulations has an impact on management even though there is no good measure of the impact. Reliable current data of volume are difficult to get, but there are indicative measures. For example, one U.S. Senate study made some years ago showed that at that time the *Code of Federal Regulations*, which contains general and permanent regulations of federal agencies, filled a fifteen-foot-long shelf with 60,000 pages of fine print. Another survey counted 9,800 forms sent out by federal departments and agencies with 556 million responses each year.[11]

A more up-to-date index of volume is pages in the *Federal Register*, a fine-print publication that sets forth proposed and new regulations of federal departments and agencies. After hitting a peak of some 17,500 pages in 1944, there was a drop to about 10,000 pages. A slow increase to 1970 brought the yearly total to about the wartime peak. Then a tidal wave of regulations hit a level of about 87,000 pages in 1980. During the Reagan administration there was a sharp drop to around 50,000, a level comparable to 1975.

It must be noted that when considering the volume of regulations affecting business, there should be added state and local government regulations. There is no good measure of volume here, but it is very large.

Of course, there are large variations among firms as to the regulations applicable to them. Automobile and steel producers probably are subject to more regulations than is a maker of soft drinks. Large companies, too, generally are subject to more regulations than smaller ones.

The present volume of government regulations of business is so large that no corporation can faithfully comply with all the laws and regulations to which it is subject. Commenting on this point, Walter Wriston, then CEO of Citibank, said:

> What worries me is that General Motors and Citibank have a fighting chance of obeying all the new regulatory laws because we have the staff and the big-time lawyers to do so. But most small businesspeople do not. They cannot even find out

---

[10]Ted Orme, "Washington Report," *Motor Trend*, September 1977.
[11]Congressional Quarterly, Inc., *Regulation: Process and Politics*, Washington, D.C.: Congressional Quarterly, Inc., 1982.

what the law is. There are, for example, 1,200 interpretations by the Federal Reserve staff of the Truth in Lending Act. Now, 90 percent of the more than 14,000 commercial banks in this country have fewer than 100 employees. If you gave every staff member those regulations and started them reading, they wouldn't be finished by next year.[12]

COSTS AND BENEFITS OF COMPLYING WITH REGULATIONS

There are no adequate measures of the monetary costs to business of complying with regulations, but a few numbers are illuminating. The Federal Paperwork Commission, formed to study the cost of paperwork, calculated that the cost borne by industry is approximately $25 to $32 billion per year. The ten largest firms in the United States are estimated to have spent between $10 and $12 billion on paperwork, an average of more than $1 billion each, and to have filled out more than 10 billion sheets of paper a year.[13] A rigorous study was made by Arthur Andersen & Company for the Business Roundtable of incremental costs to forty-eight large companies in complying with six federal agency programs. The study concluded that incremental costs amounted to $2.6 billion. Incremental costs were defined as only those that the companies would not have borne in the absence of regulation. The six programs were those of the EPA, EEO, OSHA, DOE (Department of Energy), ERISA (Employee Retirement Income Security Act), and the FTC. The $2.6 billion incremental cost was equal to 43 percent of what the forty-eight companies spent on research and development and to 16 percent of net income.[14]

These studies were made several years ago but are probably within the ranges of current figures. Again, of course, the costs vary greatly from company to company.

There are many other costs to regulations, but figures are not available concerning them. In mind are costs associated with manufacturing and distribution of products, costs that necessitate higher product prices and erosion of a firm's foreign competitive position, costs of management time diverted from other company business, and costs related to changing business-government power relationships. Offsetting costs, however, are significant benefits of government regulations.

Government's impact on business is not necessarily negative. It very often is munificently positive. No government action in economic life is wholly negative or wholly positive. Restraint for one person or business may mean freedom for another. One function of government is to implement the wishes of the people about the kind of freedom that shall be restrained in order to advance another.

Business could not operate and society could not prosper without certain types of regulations. Regulations have protected and subsidized business in-

---

[12]Quoted in *Time*, May 1, 1978, p. 44.

[13]U.S. Commission on Federal Paperwork, *Final Summary Report*, Washington, D.C., 1977.

[14]Arthur Andersen & Co., *Cost of Government Regulation Study for the Business Roundtable*, New York: Arthur Andersen, 1979. See also Michael E. Simon, "Government Regulation: Adding up the Cost," *Journal of Contemporary Business*, vol. 9, no. 1980.

terests as well as consumer and general-public interests. Regulation has helped society achieve economic and social goals. It has helped improve the position of minorities, achieve cleaner air, hold business accountable, prevent abuses of the market mechanism, prevent monopoly, reduce industrial accidents, and so on. The pluses of government regulation are many.

The issue today is not the justification for a particular type of regulation (government finds legal, social, and political justification for virtually any type of regulation it chooses to employ), but the choice of regulatory methods and the sheer volume and cost of the regulation.

Much more will be said throughout this book about the cost/benefit equation of government regulation. Before discussing other aspects of regulations, we turn to an overview of how regulations evolve in the federal government.

THE REGULATORY LIFE CYCLE

The government regulatory life cycle begins with the *emergence of an issue.* A problem such as air pollution may have existed for many years, but until public attention is focused on the matter, government action is nonexistent or negligible. Activists, interest groups, and media attention bring the issue to public attention. Second is the *formulation of a government policy.* In this stage, the issue is debated, hearings before Congress are held, pressure groups are formed to lobby legislators, alternative solutions are proposed, and, finally, a bill is formulated and funding provided for its implementation. The pressure groups try to exert influence in every step from here on, including, on occasion, the legal review of the courts. The third stage is the *implementation of the legislation.* The agency (or agencies) responsible for implementation develops and enforces specific regulations spelled out in the legislation and/or developed to implement the broad policy directives in the legislation. These regulations are circulated, business's actions are monitored and, when necessary, informal or formal corrective actions are taken. The next step is *modification of the regulation.* Following experience with the regulation, it may be appropriate for the regulatory agency or the Congress to amend the basic legislation. Then follows a state of relaxation when public attention moves to higher priorities and government surveillance is relaxed. Finally, for a few regulations, the problem originally addressed may be solved, or new circumstances may give rise to different alternatives, as happened with airline deregulation. In either case, *deregulation* is the final stage in the life cycle. Figure 9-4 shows this process in a little more detail, but still oversimplified.

ACHIEVEMENT OF RECENT FEDERAL REGULATIONS

THE REAGAN ADMINISTRATION'S STRATEGY FOR REGULATORY RELIEF

President Reagan promised in his campaign of 1980 to roll back twenty years of federal regulatory buildup. Almost immediately on taking office, he announced (on January 20, 1981) his creation of a Task Force on Regulatory Re-

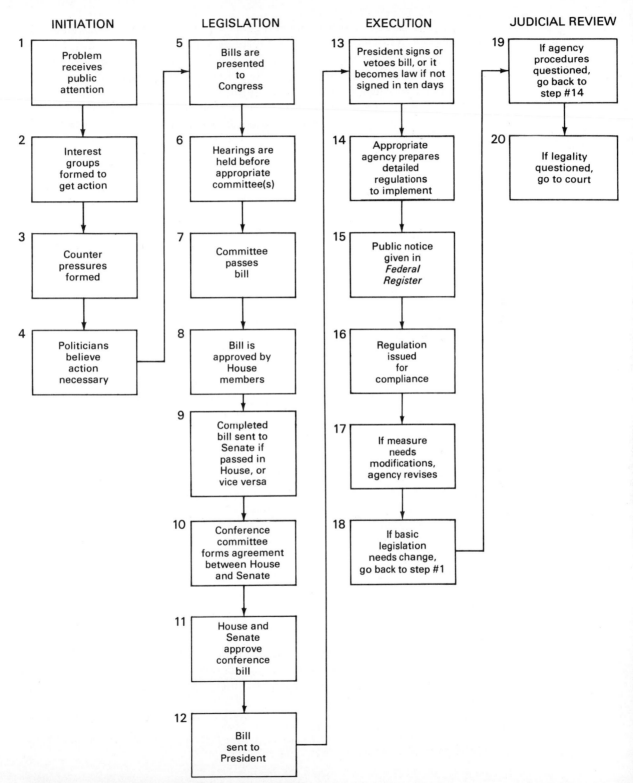

FIGURE 9-4   Major steps in development of a regulation.

lief. Vice President Bush was named chairman and other members were cabinet officers. At the same time, the President set up the Office of Information and Regulatory Affairs (OIRA) in the Office of Management and Budget (OMB) with strong powers over review of regulations in conjunction with the Vice President's task force. Both institutions were given muscle in Executive Order 12291 to review and evaluate old as well as new proposals for regulations. Regulations had to pass a number of tests, among which was this requirement: "Regulatory action shall not be undertaken unless the potential benefits to society from the regulation outweigh the potential costs to society."

These policies and programs were buttressed with the appointments to cabinet and subcabinet level posts of like-minded individuals—those who were dedicated, as the President was, to reducing the burden of government regulations, including the deregulation of some industries. A number of the new appointees were drawn from regulated industries and could hardly have been expected to deal harshly with their own industries when the prevailing ideology in Washington at that time was to free industry from all unnecessary burdens. What was unnecessary was defined broadly.

A final part of the administration's strategy was to reduce sharply budgets of regulatory agencies, which necessitated a reduction of regulatory employees and, in consequence, less surveillance of how laws were implemented. The first budgets of the Reagan administration sharply reduced expenditures of the regulatory agencies. Budgets were increased later so that their expenditures in fiscal year 1988, after adjustment for inflation, were at $8.5 billion, only a little over the 1980 budgets.[15] However, regulatory staff dropped by about 14 percent over these years.

AN ASSESSMENT OF THE SUCCESS OF THESE STRATEGIES AND GOALS

The Presidential Task Force on Regulatory Relief issued a final report in 1983 and turned its business over to other agencies. It claimed that the result of the Reagan strategies was the modification of hundreds of old regulations and the failure of hundreds of new proposals to be enacted. It claimed that its efforts would save more than $150 billion in private sector and state and local funds over the next decade. The Task Force pointed with pride to the fact that there had been put in place a "credible, effective, and even-handed Executive oversight mechanism, centered in OMB, for the review and coordination of new regulations."[16]

There were some notable deregulations of industries. Building on the initiatives of the Ford and Carter administrations, the Reagan administration deregulated railroads and trucking. Airline deregulation, accomplished in

---

[15]P. N. Tramontozzi and K. W. Chilton, *U.S. Regulatory Agencies under Reagan 1980–1988*, St. Louis: Center for the Study of American Business, 1988.

[16]George Bush, Statement by Vice President George Bush and Fact Sheet, Washington, D.C.: The White House, August 11, 1983.

the Carter administration, was continued with the abolition of the Civilian Aeronautics Board, in December 1984. The administration deregulated natural gas, financial institutions, parts of the communications industry, oil pipelines and intercity buses. Not in all instances, of course, was the deregulation total.

The Reagan administration claimed other successes. White House review of regulations was an innovation in the regulatory process of great importance. So was the strong focus on government-wide use of cost-benefit analysis. The appointment of regulatory relief–minded cabinet and agency officials resulted in a sharp slowdown in launching new regulations. It also resulted in a strong reluctance of many agencies to implement vigorously many old regulations. There was also in the Reagan administration a significant drop in stopping mergers and acquisitions which previously would have been declared contrary to the antitrust laws. This is a matter discussed in the next chapter.

Critics of the administration's policies and programs point to a number of important deficiencies. One was the failure of the administration to get Congress to change statutes that would make regulation more efficient and effective. For example, the strict provisions of some regulations (such as the unattainable goals specified in the Clean Water Act of eliminating the discharge of all pollutants and making all lakes and streams fishable and swimmable) needed modification. The strategy of seeking regulatory relief and reform through management of the process did, indeed, bring short-term successes. But critics insist, and correctly, that if there is to be any permanent improvement in regulations, there must be changes in the basic statutory legislation.[17]

For example, the use of cost-benefit analysis to determine whether regulations would be issued was a keystone of the Reagan administration's strategy. But basic legislation placed roadblocks in the way of the application of this principle, a matter which only changes in the statutes could correct. Yet the administration did not seek such changes in the Congress. For example, the Toxic Substances Control Act *requires* the EPA to consider cost-benefit factors in applying the law. The Clean Air Act *permits* the EPA to consider cost-benefit analysis. The Delaney Amendments to basic FDA legislation implicitly *forbid* cost-benefit analysis. The same is true with the Endangered Species Act.

In a milestone case on June 17, 1981, the U.S. Supreme Court dealt a critical blow to cost-benefit analysis where the enabling legislation casts doubt about its applicability. OSHA decided to use cost-benefit analysis in setting cotton-dust standards for worker health. Justice William J. Brennan, Jr., writing for the majority in a five-to-three decision, said that economic and technical feasibility constitute the only limits on OSHA's power to lay down worker health and safety standards. He said:

[17]Marshall R. Goodman and Margaret T. Wrightson, *Managing Regulatory Reform: The Reagan Strategy and Its Impact*, New York: Praeger, 1987.

Congress itself defined the basic relationship between costs and benefits, by placing the "benefit" of worker health above all other considerations save those making attainment of this "benefit" unachievable.[18]

Justice Brennan noted that some regulations required cost-benefit analysis, but not those promulgated by OSHA. He also said that only Congress could amend the law to require OSHA to conduct cost-benefit analyses of its health standards. Subsequent court decisions have reaffirmed this principle: that whatever the consideration given to costs and benefits, an agency cannot substitute its judgment for rules laid down by the Congress in legislation.

The administration's deemphasis of regulations drew fire from the Congress and interested groups.[19] Longer-range consequences of staff cuts are still being manifest in revelations, for example, about oversight failure in the savings and loan industry, and mismanagement and staff deficiencies in the Housing and Urban Development Administration. *Business Week* lamented in 1988 that the SEC staff is so overworked and hobbled by a skimpy budget for staff that it risks losing control of Wall Street.[20] Critics assert that shortfalls in staff funding during the Reagan administration compromised the ability of virtually every regulatory agency to fulfill its responsibilities. This devitalization of staff occurred at the same time demands on the public service have been escallating.[21] The malady has persisted in the Bush administration.

GROWING DEMANDS FOR NEW REGULATIONS

There is no lack of ideas for new government regulations, but most of them do not become law. Today, however, there are problems of such severity that rising demands for action will justifiably bring new regulations. For example, trends toward global warming, disposal of nuclear and other toxic wastes, and the introduction of new genetically engineered microbes, plants, and animal strains demand regulation. American companies have watched their costs for employee health and medical benefits rise to the point where they are exerting pressure on the government, along with other groups, to introduce a national health plan. They want to get these costs off their balance sheets. One of the results of the Reagan administration regulatory laissez-faire policy was to dump the problems onto the states. They began to address the problems neglected by federal regulatory authorities, and introduced their own regulations. There is a growing chorus by business executives for a renewal of federal intervention to set uniform standards in a number of ar-

---

[18]*American Textile Manufacturers Institute v. Donovan and National Cotton Council*, 101 Sup. Ct. 2478, June 17, 1981.

[19]For evaluations of the administration's regulatory and relief policies and programs see Gregory A. Deneke and David J. Lemak, eds., *Regulatory Reform Reconsidered*, Boulder, Colorado: Westview Press, 1985.

[20]Tim Smart and David Zigas, "Watchdog Woes: Up against It at the SEC," *Business Week*, October 10, 1988.

[21]See, for example, Mark L. Goldstein, "Hollow Government," *Government Executive*, October 1989.

eas. This would avoid their having to deal with fifty different sets of regulations. For example, pesticide manufacturers and trade groups have asked Congress to amend the Federal Insecticide, Fungicide and Rodenticide Act to preempt states from getting involved in pesticide residues in food. Manufacturers want uniform product liability laws. Automobile companies have asked the Federal Trade Commission to overturn procedures required in forty-four states under so-called lemon laws. Insurance, food processing, oil, and pharmaceutical companies seek more uniform laws concerning their areas of activity.[22] Whether this all will lead to the fifth wave of regulation remains to be seen.

THE MIXED ECONOMY

Government regulation of business has evolved to the point today that in principle virtually no aspect of business and overall economic activity is closed to government action. Despite this comparative open door to intervention, the remarkable fact about the American economy is not how much of economic life the government controls but how much it does not. Although the federal government directly controls or indirectly influences economic activity to a significant degree, the economy is in no way centrally administered or controlled.

The great bulk of goods and services are produced by individual business firms whose resources are not owned or managed by government. Millions of individual proprietors, consumers, and workers, corporations, labor unions, and farm cooperatives are relatively free to choose from among alternative courses of action. These groups and individuals determine in large degree how scarce resources are used. Although it is true that some of these decisions are made within a framework of rules laid down by government, people are rather free to pursue their economic interests as they see fit. Ours is a mixed economy in which individuals enjoy much economic freedom, in which the free market mechanism is still a powerful allocator of resources, but in which governments, especially the federal government, exercise pervasive and strong controls.

---

[22]W. John Moore, "Dear Feds—Help!" *National Journal*, July 9, 1988.

The Savings and Loan Bailout

On his very first day in the Oval Office, President Bush faced a financial crisis in the savings and loan (S&L) industry. He made a decision to deal forthrightly and quickly with a problem which had long been a festering sore that the previous administration had consistently failed to address. He sent a proposal to Congress to deal with the situation, and in August 1989 he received a bill, which he promptly signed, to bail out failing S&Ls at a cost of $166 billion. This was the largest corporate welfare program in our history.

This bill is the result of an extraordinary failure of deregulation policy. How and why did this disaster take place? This is the question addressed in this case.

ORIGIN AND EARLY HISTORY OF S&LS

S&Ls originated in Great Britain and entered the United States in the 1830s. They have played an historic role in this country as the main source of funding for home mortgages.

Historically, S&Ls accepted funds from depositors who became shareholders and who presumably left their capital in the firm for a long period of time. With these long-term funds the S&Ls made long-term mortgage loans. Savings banks accepted short-term savings but did not make such loans. Commercial banks accepted short-term deposits and eschewed long-term loans. Thus, S&Ls virtually had the mortgage market to themselves. In the Great Depression of the 1930s, however, depositors of these three institutions withdrew their funds. Massive failures were registered in these institutions. About 2,000 S&Ls failed and millions of people lost their savings.

To save as many thrifts as possible, the Federal Home Loan Bank System was created to provide liquidity for them. There were a number of other major pieces of legislation at the time to provide relief to and reform of the entire banking system. The Federal Home Loan Bank Board (FHLBB) was created to supervise the new system and was given the right to charter and regulate federal S&Ls. States also could charter S&Ls and the legislation creating the FHLBB authorized it to regulate them. To protect future depositors from loss, the Federal Savings and Loan Insurance Corporation (FSLIC) was created in 1934 to accumulate a fund called the Federal Insurance Reserve to insure depositors against loss if their S&L failed. The Federal Deposit Insurance Corporation (FDIC) was established at the same time to insure deposits of commercial banks. This system operated well until the 1960s, when problems in the S&Ls began to appear.

DEREGULATION AND DISASTER

Rising Interest Rates Reduced S&L Profits   From 1933 to 1962, Regulation Q of the Federal Reserve Board fixed at 3 percent the rate of interest that commercial banks could pay depositors, and many banks paid less. S&Ls were not restricted and paid from ½ to 2 percent more to attract funds. S&Ls then made mortgage loans at fixed rates of interest for up to twenty or twenty-five years. The interest rates were generally from 2½ to 3 percent over the rate paid for savings deposits and provided, therefore, a comfortable profit margin for the S&Ls.

From the end of World War II to the mid-1960s, interest rates were relatively stable, and since mortgages were of high quality there were virtually no S&L failures. In the mid-1960s, a few failures were reported primarily in Illinois and Nevada, due principally to poor management. Then interest rates began to rise and squeeze S&L profit margins. To help the S&Ls, Regulation Q was modified to put a ceiling on deposit interest rates of both S&Ls and commercial banks. The ceiling on commercial banks held at 3 percent, but S&Ls could pay ¼ to ½ percent more. This assured them access to funds and a profit. However, as interest rates continued to rise, the ceilings could not be sustained and Regulation Q was abolished.

The payment of higher interest rates on deposits raised costs and cut profits since the income of the S&Ls was derived from mortgages which had been made at low rates of interest. Net income as a percent of net worth hit a high of 15.0 in 1955 and declined, with ups and downs, through the 1970s, dropping to 2.4 percent in 1980.[23]

The weakened financial position of the thrifts resulted in a decline in funds available for mortgages, and S&L failures threatened to bankrupt the FSLIC. It was believed at the time that a free market would correct these conditions, and pressure for deregulation escalated.

Expanding the Lending Powers of S&Ls   The first major move toward deregulation was the enactment in 1980 of the Depository Institutions Deregulation and Monetary Control Act (DIDMC). This Act phased out interest rate ceilings for both banks and thrifts and allowed the thrifts to diversify into many areas hitherto forbidden, such as offering checking accounts.

In 1975, the state of California permitted state-chartered thrifts to offer for the first time adjustable rate mortgages. The FHLBB followed by authorizing

---

[23]Ned Eichler, *The Thrift Debacle*, Berkeley, California: University of California Press, 1989.

federal-chartered banks to do the same thing in 1981. The theory was that if S&Ls could make loans whose interest rates fluctuated with changes in the general interest rates, their profit margins would be protected as interest rates rose.

Such measures did not stop the flow of red ink, and in 1981 and 1982 the thrift industry suffered its greatest losses. The industry lost over $4.6 billion in 1981 and over $4.1 billion in 1982.

In the face of such losses, the Congress in 1982 passed the Garn-St. Germain Depository Institutions Act, which provided a statutory basis for the FHLBB to expand significantly the investment opportunities for S&Ls. For example, S&Ls were permitted to make commercial real estate loans up to 40 percent of assets, and could provide 100 percent financing of appraised value. Consumer loans up to 30 percent of assets were also permitted. These were unprecedented expansions of S&L powers and, as we will see shortly, opened the door wide for all sorts of abuses.

The Garn-St. Germain bill encouraged states to continue expanding powers of state-chartered thrifts. Some of them proceeded to go further than the federal-chartered thrifts. For example, there were no limits placed on the ability of Texas chartered thrifts to make loans on oil and gas proven reserves, to invest in real estate, to finance unsecured loans, or to invest in corporate securities. There were limits, however, to the aggregate loans which could be made to one borrower, but they were high. States with the most liberal regulations were Arizona, California, Florida, and Texas. But other states loosened considerably control over S&Ls.[24]

Erosion of Net Worth Requirements   Net worth is the equity which owners have in an enterprise and is a cushion for absorbing losses that might be incurred. Of great importance, too, is the fact that the higher the equity owners have in a business the more likely they are to manage or watch others manage so as to preserve and increase their capital. In the case of S&Ls, the less equity owners have in the firm the greater the risks they may be willing to take. The reason is that if the investments turn out successfully they profit, and if the investments fail the government picks up the cost of paying the depositors. Deregulation encouraged excessive risk-taking because the industry became for the S&L owner a "heads-I-win-tails-you-lose" game.

Originally, S&Ls were required to have a net worth (the difference between asset value and liabilities) of 5 percent as a buffer for losses. If this reserve was insufficient to pay depositors of failed S&Ls, then the FSLIC would foot the bill. The S&Ls pressured the Congress to reduce this requirement from 5 to 4 percent and the FHLBB asked authority to vary it between 3 and 6 percent for individual companies. This authority was granted in the DIDMC Act of 1980, and by December 1981 the FHLBB had reduced the statutory net worth requirement to 3 percent.

---

[24]Norman Strunk and Fred Case, *Where Deregulation Went Wrong: A Look at the Causes Behind Savings and Loan Failures in the 1980s,* Chicago: United States League of Savings Institutions, 1988.

The American Bankers Association asserted that "[t]he dismantling of net worth requirements during the 1972–82 period was the single most important factor contributing to the wave of S&L failures after 1982."[25] This is an exaggeration, as we shall see, but it did reinforce the incentives for entrepreneurial high-rollers to enter the business, since they could do so with very little capital and great profit potential.

Raising the Level of Insured Deposits   In the meantime, a series of actions by Congress increased the level of insured deposits. Originally, the FSLIC insured deposits up to $5,000. The level rose to $10,000 in 1950, to $20,000 in 1969, to $40,000 in 1974, and to $100,000 in 1980, where it remains. This expanding coverage, of course, encouraged deposits and also increased the potential liability of the FSLIC.

Accounting Flexibility   When losses mounted and eroded net worth of many thrifts in 1981, the FHLBB introduced new accounting rules to help S&Ls stay statistically within the rules. For example, when thrifts were merged under the supervision of the FHLBB they were permitted to use good will as part of their assets in calculating net worth. Good will, of course, had no tangible value and could not be used to cushion losses. Thrifts also were permitted to defer losses on loans to show better profits. Such accounting changes were called Regulatory Accounting Principles (RAPs). They contrasted with Generally Accepted Accounting Principles (GAAPs) which were much more rigorous. The RAPs helped failing S&Ls to stay out of technical insolvency.

Weakening Federal Controls of S&L Operations   Deregulation was reflected not only in basic statutory legislation but also in federal control over S&L operations. Under the powers given to the FHLBB, Richard T. Pratt, chairman of the board from 1981 through 1983, widened S&L powers to the limit and at the same time loosened federal regulations pertaining to and surveillance of S&L operations. He was a strong advocate of unshackling financial institutions and letting the market operate freely, so he removed as many restraints as possible from the ability of thrifts to operate freely.[26] The result was freedom for thrift managers to freewheel and also for thrift regulators to relax supervision over S&Ls. We will return to this subject shortly.

DISASTER

The result of this chain of events was disaster. Aggregate S&L profits plummeted, S&Ls went bankrupt in large numbers, and the FSLIC had exhausted its

---

[25]The FSLIC Oversight Committee of the American Bankers Association, "Savings and Loan Association Regulatory Reform: Action Recommendations and Historical Perspective," A Report Submitted to Subcommittee on Financial Institutions Supervision, Regulation and Insurance of the Committee on Banking, Finance and Urban Affairs, House of Representatives, U.S. Congress, Hearings March 16, 21, 22, 1989.

[26]Strunk and Case, *op. cit.*

available funds to reimburse depositors of the failed companies.

There were two waves of thrift failures. The first was from 1981 to 1984. It was caused by the interest rate spread between the cost of funds and the revenues which thrifts received from low-interest mortgages. The second was from 1985 to 1988 and was primarily caused by problems of mismanagement and fraud within the individual S&Ls. Net operating income of the thrift industry fell during these two waves to a loss in 1987 of $7.8 billion and $12.1 billion in 1988.

At the beginning of 1989, there were three major classes of S&Ls: first were the well-managed and financially sound organizations; second were the marginal firms that might slip into insolvency; and third were the hopelessly insolvent firms, called by some people "the living dead." There were 921 firms in the first classification, with $921 billion in assets. In the second were 302 firms with $316 billion in assets, and in the third group were 364 associations with assets of $114 billion. In 1989, 325 S&Ls failed.

FAILURES OF GOVERNMENT SUPERVISION

There are many causes of the debacle. No single one can explain the S&L's failures, but the shortcomings of government regulation rank high in importance.

One would expect that with the extent of the deregulation of the thrifts set forth above, controls over their operations would tighten. But just the reverse happened; they loosened. This laxness began at the very top of the surveillance pyramid with the Bank Board chairman's laissez-faire philosophy about regulating the S&Ls, and extended throughout the organization.

The FHLBB staff of examiners was far too small for the job it had to do, and it was also not directed to function as changed conditions in the industry required. Examiners were essentially "fact finders." They sought only to determine whether an S&L was in specific compliance with a regulation. They were not trained as financial analysts to audit the financial soundness of an S&L.[27] The regulatory staff increased in the 1970s but declined in the 1980s. Furthermore, salaries were lower than in competing financial institutions and the best regulators left. Edwin Gray, who succeeded Pratt, tried to get more examiners but was denied funds by the Office of Management and Budget.

The FHLBB supervisors were excessively cautious in taking quick and tough actions about important irregularities in the S&Ls. Many reasons were given to explain this flaw in the supervisory process. For example, the dual role of the FHLBB as a promoter of the thrift institutions and also as a regulator created a conflict leading to indecision. But of major importance was the prevailing inclination in the Reagan administration to soften the impact of federal regulations. As noted previously, this philosophy was strongly asserted under Chairman Pratt. Political influence, exerted by the Congress and state politicians, was powerful in restraining regulators. It was called "regulatory forbearance."

[27]*Ibid*, pp. 147–148.

POLITICAL INFLUENCE OVER REGULATORS

Widespread accusations of congressional influence on S&L regulators have been aired for years. For example, in 1986, when FHLBB chairman Gray was seeking funding authority for the FSLIC (whose funds were seriously depleted as a result of S&L failures), House of Representatives Speaker James Wright used his power over the fate of the bill to force Gray to relieve a bank examiner who had stopped Westwood Savings and Loan in California from making a loan to one of Wright's friends. Gray later said: "The speaker used his power and influence to bring about behavioral changes in a regulator. It was an abuse of power and improper. I felt he was putting us through hoops to do his bidding."[28] Wright resigned the speakership in 1989 partly because of his long exertion of influence in the S&L industry.

Another illustration of congressional influence concerns five senators who accepted substantial campaign contributions from Charles H. Keating Jr., owner of Lincoln Savings & Loan. Senators Alan Cranston (Democrat, California); Dennis DeConcini (Democrat, Arizona); John Glenn (Democrat, Ohio); John McCain (Republican, Arizona); and Donald W. Riegle Jr. (Democrat, Michigan) collectively received $1.3 million in campaign contributions from Keating. Keating has been well known for making generous campaign contributions to politicians in both the Congress and state legislatures.

At a press conference in April 1987, when his contributions to these senators and their actions in his behalf came to light, Keating commented on his political influence. He said: "One question, among the many raised in recent weeks, had to do with whether my financial support in any way influenced several political figures to take up my cause. I want to say in the most forceful way I can: I certainly hope so."[29]

On April 2, 1987, Gray underwent the first of two lobbying sessions with these senators. The senators asked Gray to withdraw a new regulation that would have required Lincoln Savings and other S&Ls to devote more of their loans to traditional home mortgages and less to speculative investment. Keating strongly opposed this regulation because he wanted to put Lincoln Savings' money in advanced development schemes. On April 9, a second meeting was arranged by the senators with three examiners from the FHLBB's San Francisco office who had given a poor appraisal of Lincoln Savings. The examiners said they were making a recommendation for Lincoln Savings' receivership or conservatorship. Again the senators sought to restrain the regulators.[30]

Shortly thereafter, Gray resigned and M. Danny Wall became chairman of the FHLBB in July 1987. Despite examiner reports of the financial problems of Lincoln Savings, it was two years before Wall closed the S&L. As a conse-

[28]Stephen Pizzo, Mary Fricker, and Paul Muolo, *Inside Job*, New York: McGraw-Hill, 1989, pp. 213, 288.

[29]Quoted in Ralph Frammolino and Paul Jacobs, "Vast Investment in State Politics by Keating Told," *Los Angeles Times*, November 28, 1989.

[30]For an extended discussion of these meetings see Pizzo, Fricker, and Muolo, *op. cit.*; and James Rink Adams, *The Big Fix*, New York: John Wiley, 1990.

quence, observers claim that the cost to the taxpayer doubled to a staggering loss of $2 billion, the largest in S&L history.

These episodes raise extremely serious questions about congressional ethical standards and the politics of the regulatory process. An important question, to which we shall never get a certain answer, is just how much pressure is exerted on the regulatory process by politicians. A very difficult question to answer is how far a politician should go in intervening in the regulatory process for a constituent. Some people called the Lincoln Savings fiasco "legalized bribery." But most politicians, including the five senators, certainly would not trade their votes for financial gain. Politicians say, however, that they have a responsibility to respond to constituent complaints about what they perceive to be unnecessary government actions. A question arises, however, as to the line between simple inquiries to the executive branch and pressure on regulators to take specific actions, especially those contrary to the judgment of regulators.

The plight of the five senators raises another question of importance, namely the necessity for politicians to seek substantial funding to finance expensive reelection campaigns. One wonders whether the senators would have become as involved in Lincoln Savings' problems if their campaign financing had come solely from public sources or small private donations.

Lobbyists for the S&L industry have swarmed over federal and state legislators as well as regulators. Joseph A. Grundfest, Commissioner of the Securities and Exchange Commission, flayed the U.S. League of Savings Institutions (a powerful voice of the S&L industry) for its lobbying activities in a speech before the League members. He quoted with approval a letter from Warren Buffett to the League in which he resigned as a member because of what he called "disgraceful" lobbying.[31] He also said that the League "has mastered the art of agency capture," and added that few regulatory bodies such as the FHLBB have been subject to influence as great as that by the League. It is noteworthy, also, that as the thrift industry's troubles have mounted, Political Action Committee (PAC) donations to key congressmen have increased. For example, Fernand St. Germain, former Chairman of the House Banking Committee, a co-author of a very generous bill to expand S&L investment authority, received $149,200 in PAC funds.[32]

BROKERED DEPOSITS

In less than four years, real estate businessman Edwin T. McBirney parlayed Sunbet Savings in Texas from an obsure $90 million S&L into a financial empire of $3.2 billion. A number of other institutions grew in the same proportion. One of the reasons was that the FHLBB in March 1982 repealed all re-

---

[31]Joseph A. Grundfest, "Responsibility and Regulation," speech delivered to the U.S. League of Savings Institutions, Hyatt Regency Hotel, Washington, D.C., June 26, 1989.

[32]Brooks Jackson, "As Thrift Industry's Troubles and Losses Mounted, Its PAC's Donations to Key Congressmen Surged," *The Wall Street Journal*, February 7, 1989.

strictions on S&Ls accepting deposits from brokers. This relaxation opened the doors to virtually unlimited financing which, in turn, attracted the buccaneers who saw a means of making fortunes with little risk. This is how it worked.

Deposit brokers dealt with billions of dollars of funds from pension systems, insurance companies, institutional investors and rich people throughout the world. They searched the nation continuously for S&Ls that paid the highest deposit interest rates and then purchased $100,000 certificates of deposits with their investors' funds. The fluidity of these deposits lured S&Ls to pay higher and higher rates of interest to attract them. Some brokers bought certificates of deposit from S&Ls and accumulated them in a package. Then they sold shares in the fund to investors for $100,000 or less.

A small S&L anywhere in the United States could attract such funds from anywhere in the nation to build its assets and profits. Thus, for example, an entrepreneur could start or buy a thrift for, say, $2,000,000, get brokered deposits of $400,000,000 and loan that to a developer for a new construction project. The S&L could then record a profit of, say, $20,000,000 in fees. This process could readily be continued and would show the S&L growing very profitably.

This sort of financial legerdemain could and did go on until adverse economic conditions, mismanagement, and fraud bankrupted many S&Ls.

MISMANAGEMENT, FRAUD, AND INADEQUATE INTERNAL CONTROLS

It is difficult to restrain outrage at the mismanagement, fraud, and lack of internal controls in the S&Ls that is costing taxpayers so much. The General Accounting Office (GAO) examined twenty-six failed S&Ls which accounted for the bulk of the losses as of September 30, 1987, and found widespread abuses.[33]

Fraud and Insider Abuses In March 1988, the FHLBB reported to Congress that fraud and insider abuse was the most pernicious of all factors leading to the insolvency of many thrift institutions. Its definition of fraud and insider abuse covered a long laundry list of actions. Included was not only poor financial judgment but immoral, unethical, improper, illegal, and in some cases criminal actions. For example, trading on insider information; self-dealing; milking institutions for personal advantage; making high-risk speculative investments in the hope of personal gain; paying exorbitant dividends as the institution approaches insolvency; having the institution pay for personal vacations, parties, automobiles, and so on; excessive consulting fees; maintaining fraudulent records to hide deficits; and reporting fictitious profits.

[33]Frederick D. Wolf, "Failed Thrifts," Statement before the Subcommittee on Criminal Justice, Committee on the Judiciary, House of Representatives, U.S. Congress, March 22, 1989, p. 8.

Every one of these abuses, and many others, was discovered by the GAO among the twenty-six failed S&Ls. Such practices should have been caught and corrected by examiners but were not. In hindsight, and it should have been recognized in foresight, the widening of investment powers of thrifts attracted not only entrepreneurs who took risks up to or a little beyond the law, but financial pirates who used the permissive control atmosphere to feed their greed by egregious, immoral, and fraudulent transactions. Too many high rollers saw the thrifts as their own personal piggy bank. Keating and his family received $34 million in three years from Lincoln Savings. Loans were made to friends in the knowledge that they never would be repaid. Schemes abounded to siphon funds from complex transactions into personal bank accounts.

The Bank Board finally began attacking fraud vigorously, and in 1987 over 6,000 cases were referred to the Department of Justice for criminal prosecution. This compared with 434 referrals in 1985. Since this time, hundreds of lawyers have been added to government payrolls to prosecute wrongdoing in the S&Ls.

Inadequate Board Supervision and Dominance by One or More Individuals The GAO study revealed that in 73 percent of the twenty-six cases, this situation led to circumvention of policies or internal controls; unsafe and unsound practices such as poor quality loans; lending to one person far above the legal limits; and domination of the board of directors. In one case, members of the board said they thought the former chairman could run his business as he pleased, since he owned it. He did, and the thrift lost $1.3 billion, which had to be assumed by the FSLIC.

The management failures recorded here are clear evidence that S&L boards of directors did not direct. Directors have a fiduciary responsibility to stockholders which includes, of course, responsibility for maintaining the financial integrity of the organization. Directors in many failed thrifts not only did not direct; they often were personally involved in abusing the powers granted to them.

Transactions Not Made in the S&Ls' Best Interests This mismanagement was reported in almost all of the cases. Transactions often personally benefitted directors, officers, and other related parties. For example, thrifts are not supposed to buy property from a director or officer unless the FLHBB approves. This rule was violated in 81 percent of the thrift failures in the study. Also, in many cases the thrift chairman bought and sold properties and, contrary to regulations, accepted huge fees for the transaction. In one case, the FHLBB informed an officer that he could not accept a fee for a loan transaction he had arranged. Review of the records later showed that he went ahead anyway and received a $1 million fee.

Abuses in Loan Applications and Appraisals In 92 percent of the thrift failures, there was inadequate credit analysis of a borrower's ability to repay a loan. Regulators found shoddy appraisals and noncompliance with loan terms. In some cases, thrifts received no appraisals of property value at all but went ahead anyway and made a loan on the property. Appraisals were often made at the borrower's request and, of course, can be suspected of being too high. Indeed, some appraisals were found to be virtually criminally overoptimistic, yet loans were made on that basis. Because of such appraisals, some borrowers invested nothing in the property on which the loan was granted.

Noncompliance with Loan Terms   Loans were made and the money was used for purposes not in the terms of the loan. For instance, a developer received $2 million to be used only for land acquisition but spent $1.8 million for other purposes.

Excessive Compensation and Expenditures   In one case, the regulators told a thrift that a bonus of $800,000 (one third of the thrift's earnings) paid to an officer/director was excessive. In response, management paid the individual $350,000 to relinquish his right to future bonuses and increased his salary from $100,000 to $250,000! Extravagant expenditures included trips abroad, lavish parties, expensive art works, and so on.

The chairman of Sunbelt Savings in Texas undoubtedly felt he had free rein to use his S&L money as he saw fit. For two parties in two years, he spent $1.3 million of the firm's money. His S&L had a fleet of seven airplanes. Its investment portfolio included eighty-four Rolls-Royces which it bought from an Indian guru in Oregon. Some of the cars were decorated with peacocks and geese in flight. It was not unusual for the management to make a $100 million loan, take a quick $5 million fee, and wind up with only $5 million of the total loan when the borrower defaulted.[34]

High-Risk Land Loans   Land development and construction loans often were excessively risky. There were limits on the extent to which such loans could be made that were constantly violated. Thrifts often put up all the money on highly risky ventures that were launched with overoptimistic forecasts of potential profits. Sometimes the S&L agreed to receive profits in compensation for the loan, and it turned out there were none.

Loans to Borrowers Exceeded Legal Limits   Prudent financial management spreads risk by not making large loans to one individual. There were specific rules governing the limits of loans to one individual, but the GAO survey found that they were ignored in 88 percent of the failed thrifts.

Recordkeeping Was Often Deplorable   In some cases, the examiners found S&L records so poor that they could not tell the true financial conditions of the thrift. In some instances records were incomplete, and in others they were completely inaccurate.

[34]Thomas Moore, "The Bust of '89," *U.S. News and World Report,* January 23, 1989.

Transactions Recorded in a Deceptive Manner Some records were fixed to hide violations of regulations. For example, maintaining a level of net worth prescribed by the FHLBB is an important financial rule that some thrifts violated and hid by "cooking the books." In some cases, records were doctored to cover fraudulent actions.

CHANGING ECONOMIC ENVIRONMENTS

Interest rate changes have had an important impact on S&L profits, as we have already noted. The general economic recession in 1982, together with high interest rates, wrecked many S&Ls. The collapse of oil prices in the 1980s had a devastating impact on thrifts in Texas. Not only had they made large loans to energy-related businesses, but the drop in oil prices devastated the economy of that state. Thrifts that had large loans in real estate and agriculture suffered. While economic conditions in the late 1980s were not as important in thrift failures as the mismanagement of the thrifts, they did play a significant part in the failure of many.

COMPETITION FROM OTHER FINANCIAL INSTITUTIONS

Competition in mortgage lending has mounted in recent years from banks, mortgage bankers, and other intermediaries. The S&Ls, which for a long period of our history were virtually the sole mortgage lenders, originated only 30 percent of home mortgages in 1986. This was down from 43 percent in 1979 and is expected to decline further. In addition, competition for deposit funds has been strong, especially from money market funds, junk bonds, and commercial banks.

SALVAGING THE S&LS

President Bush signed the Financial Institutions Reform, Recovery and Enforcement Act (FIRREA) on August 9, 1989. This legislation altered fundamentally the structural and operational framework of banking institutions. It authorized $166 billion to salvage the thrift industry.

The law sought to do four major things: (1) ease the large financial deficit of the FSLIC; (2) reconstruct the regulatory framework of the thrift industry; (3) make the thrift industry operate more like the commercial banking industry; and (4) give the federal banking agencies the strong powers over financial institutions that they need and have sought for a number of years. The act is a massive and complex document, so here we can present but a few highlights. Also, many of its provisions are still unclear, and some remain for detailed clarification by the agencies involved.[35]

---

[35]For a description of what the act contains see McKenna, Conner & Cuneo, "An Analysis of the Financial Institutions Reform, Recovery and Enforcement Act of 1989," New York: Pandick, Inc., 1989; and Gibson, Dunn & Crutcher, "Analysis of the Financial Institutions Reform, Recovery, and Enforcement Act of 1989," Washington, D.C.: Gibson, Dunn & Crutcher, August 25, 1989.

Structural Changes   The FSLIC was dissolved and the Federal Deposit Insurance Corporation (FDIC), which was the guarantor of all banks deposits, became the insurer of both S&L and bank deposits. The total of both institutions was $3 trillion! Within sixty days after the act was signed, the FHLBB was abolished and its chartering and supervisory authority was transferred to a new Office of Thrift Supervision (OTS), which was placed under the authority of the Secretary of the Treasury. The OTS and the FDIC jointly supervise and regulate savings associations, both federally and state chartered. The Resolution Trust Corporation (RTC) was formed to assume sole responsibility for selling the assets of failed S&Ls. An RTC Oversight Board was established to develop goals and strategies for the RTC, approve RTC's financing requests and review its performance. The RTC is to use the FDIC staff to discharge its responsibilities and will be terminated no later than December 31, 1996.

The Bank Holding Company Act of 1956 was amended to permit bank holding companies to acquire healthy savings associations. Heretofore, banks could acquire only insolvent thrifts. This is a fundamental change in the authority of banks and will permit them to acquire healthy thrift institutions throughout the United States. This not only will allow banks to expand their operations in the residential lending market but will also further erode the difference between the S&Ls and commercial banks. This provision will undoubtedly lead to an acquisition and merger spree and will result in a substantial decline in the numbers of S&Ls. It will help make banks look more like S&Ls, and with their present powers the S&Ls will look more like commercial banks. It will become harder to distinguish between them.

Operational Rules for S&Ls   The act imposed new restrictions on thrifts and legislated tougher standards. Commercial banks have had stiffer operational standards than S&Ls, and many will now apply to the S&Ls. Following is a brief sampler of the new regulations.

- Net worth requirements are higher for the thrifts, gradually approaching those of the commercial banks.
- The method of calculating net worth is stricter.
- Accounting and disclosure standards to be used are comparable to those of the banks.
- The Director of OTC can prohibit growth of any association not meeting prescribed capital standards.
- Limits are lower on loans made to one borrower.
- Limits are tightened on loans to officers and/or directors of associations.
- Limits are placed on the ability of associations to acquire and control subsidiaries.
- Limits are placed on loans for commercial real estate.
- Qualified thrift investments are carefully specified and must equal or

exceed 70 percent of total portfolios of investments. This is above the current 60 percent requirement, a level often ignored by failing thrifts.

• The ability of S&Ls to buy corporate bonds is limited. Some types of low-quality bonds, such as "junk bonds," are prohibited, and S&Ls now holding them must divest them within five years.

Regulations such as these, and there are many more, should correct many of the weaknesses of S&L portfolio management. Critics argue, however, that the restrictions do not go far enough in assuring safer portfolios. They want S&Ls to have less freedom to make commercial and real estate development loans.

Observers are worried, also, about the administrative jumble created by the act. A dozen departments and agencies are assigned roles in the bailout, reconstituting a regulatory structure that has been in place for more than fifty years. The bureaucrats are already feuding over mismatched computers, changing industry standards and their own salaries.[36]

Particularly worrisome is the responsibility of the RTC to dispose of roughly $300 billion in failed S&L assets. This is a gigantic undertaking which the government currently is not in a position to deal with expeditiously and efficiently.

Finally, the act probably does not provide enough money for the bailout. FDIC Chairman L. William Seidman informed the Congress in November 1989 that he had identified an additional 223 troubled S&Ls and that he might need another $50 to $100 billion. Since Seidman's testimony, estimates of the bailout costs have escalated. For example, the GAO in June 1990 calculated that the cost will be $325 billion at a minimum over the next 30 years. This figure includes interest payments of $133 billion on government borrowings. Cost could reach $500 billion, said the GAO, in the event interest rates rise and/or an economic recession occurs.

CONCLUDING COMMENT

The failures in the thrift industry clearly are the result of regulatory mismanagement during the Reagan administration. Deregulation of the industry accelerated in tandem with flaccid supervision both in government agencies and within individual thrift institutions. The Congress not only passed regulations, approved by the administration, which significantly relaxed government controls, but also actively tried to influence regulators to further relax their surveillance. Within a framework where thrift owners had little or no liability for losses, but unlimited opportunities for profits, and where the government insured depositors from loss, a prescription for disaster was obvious. Adverse economic conditions merely quickened and exascerbated this predictable end. While current legislation to bail out the thrift industry respects the guarantee against loss given to depositors, and strengthens controls over the thrift industry, it is not enough to prevent another disaster.

---

[36]Paulette Thomas, "Thrift Bailout, Lacking a Chief and Floundering as Officials Feud, Slows and Grows More Costly," *The Wall Street Journal*, October 11, 1989.

Fred Balderson, professor at the Haas School of Business, University of California Berkeley, makes the point this way:

> . . . the financial system is itself undergoing continuing changes through globalization, interpenetration of markets, and technological advances. These advances give rise to numerous new products and a continually more rapid pace of transaction-processing and informational support for financial decisions. Thus, there are ever-growing needs for sophistication in regulatory oversight . . . the current bailout is a step forward, but it is no guarantee, as it stands, against a recurrence of serious trouble.[37]

QUESTIONS

1 It has been said that the S&L industry was, so far as the owners were concerned, a "heads-I-win-tails-you-lose" proposition. Explain it and its consequences.
2 In what ways was the federal government responsible for the S&L debacle?
3 In what ways were failed S&Ls poorly managed?
4 How does the FIRREA propose correcting the S&L crisis?
5 What ethical and moral conclusions do you draw from this case?
6 What political issues stand out in your mind from this case?
7 Does the failure of deregulation policy described in this case mean that the government should stop deregulation? Explain your position.

---

[37]Frederick E. Balderson, "The S&L Bailout: A Policy Review," Working Paper No. 89-163, Center for Real Estate and Urban Economics, University of California at Berkeley, June 1989, p. 22.

Reforming the Regulatory System

Advanced Genetic Sciences, Inc. (AGS) was a small company located in Oakland, California. In 1988, it was acquired by DNA Plant Technology Corporation, now the world's largest independent agricultural biotechnology company. The AGS story illustrates new issues in federal regulation as well as in law, ethics, agronomy, and environment. Founded in 1979, AGS, a high-technology company, applied advanced biological techniques to develop new products for the agricultural and food-processing markets.

AGS came to public attention when the Environmental Protection Agency (EPA) lifted a ban on the company to conduct outdoor tests of a frost-blocking bacteria called Frostban. In November 1985, AGS got approval from the National Institutes of Health (NIH) to be the first company legally authorized to conduct these tests on strawberry plants near Monterey, California. The Monterey County supervisors quickly passed an ordinance banning the experiment for a year. In the meantime, a disgruntled employee of AGS told the EPA that the company had conducted an outdoor experiment with the organism contrary to EPA rules. The EPA promptly rescinded the approval granted by NIH and fined the company $20,000.[1]

Steven Lindow, a scientist at the University of California, Berkeley, whose research was partly supported by grants from AGS, sought and received permission from the EPA to conduct an experiment on potatoes in November 1984 that would use the same technology as that of AGS. Roadblocks imme-

---

[1]In April 1984, a Cabinet Council Working Group on Biotechnology was formed to coordinate government regulations in this area, because many government agencies were involved. The three principal agencies are the United States Department of Agriculture, the Food and Drug Administration, and the Environmental Protection Agency (EPA). The council allocated, for regulatory purposes, biotechnology areas among these agencies and gave the EPA authority over AGS testing.

diately were placed in his way. The people in Monterey County, where Lindow's experiments were to take place, strongly objected to the tests. They were joined by four activist groups that filed suit in the U.S. District Court of the District of Columbia to block the tests. Judge John Sirica granted the injunction.[2] In May 1986, after almost three years of legal struggles, Lindow was granted permission by the EPA to conduct his outdoor experiments. The next month, AGS got permission to test outdoors.

AGS and Lindow are engaged in genetic engineering, a branch of biotechnology. According to the Office of Technology Assessment, biotechnology includes any technique "that uses living organisms (or parts of organisms) to make or modify products, to improve plants and animals, or to develop microorganisms for specific uses." Biotechnology is an old science. For example, the fermentation process in making wine uses microorganisms to convert sugar into alcohol. What is new and dramatic in the field today is the ability of scientists to alter the structure of cells to affect the growth characteristics of microorganisms. These alterations promise a new class of products as exciting as those based upon the microelectronic computer chip that ushered in the information revolution. New medicines to cure human and animal diseases, new seeds that will grow disease-resistant and larger plants, new insecticides to kill bugs, new products to produce larger and healthier animals in a shorter period of time, cheaper and more nutritious foods, and new enzymes to absorb toxic wastes are but a few of the possibilities.

The federal government has had a powerful role in funding the biomedical and other fundamental research in biology, biochemistry, and genetics that has formed the basis for the new biotechnology. The NIH, the National Science Foundation, and the Department of Defense have sponsored basic research that lies at the foundation of the new biotechnology.

The first genetics firm founded for commercial purposes was Genentech, Inc., in 1977. Growth of private commercial firms was slow until the Supreme Court ruled in 1980 that microorganisms could be patented under existing law.[3] General Electric became the first company to get such a patent. After that, the creation of new companies to do research in the field was explosive.

Very simply, AGS has genetically modified a bacterium that ordinarily causes frost to form on plants when the temperature is below 32 degrees Fahrenheit. In greenhouse tests, AGS's product reduced the point at which frost forms to about 23 degrees Fahrenheit. It is estimated that this product, if successful in outdoor testing, will save over $1 billion annually in crop damage.

But, as we have noted, this new technology has generated a storm of controversy. Jeremy Rifkin, the head of Washington-based Foundation for Economic Trends, is representative of those who are opposed to its use. He says that this new technology will introduce "thousands of genetically engineered

---

[2] *Foundation for Economic Trends v. Heckler,* (587 F.Supp. 753 D.D.C.), 1984.
[3] *Diamond v. Chakrabarty,* 100 Sup. Ct. 2204, 1980.

microbes, plants, and animal strains...to our ecosystem, every year, all over the world." The introduction of genetically modified organisms into the atmosphere, he argues, could well eclipse by an order of magnitude the damage that has been caused by the release of petrochemical products into the world's ecosystems.[4]

The federal government and scientists disagree with this position. Following the initial ban on AGS outdoor testing, the EPA assigned an audit team to evaluate AGS's experiments. The team concluded that AGS was conducting its experiments according to accepted laboratory practices and that it was not likely that outdoor experiments would produce any adverse effects. Upon the basis of this report, EPA granted AGS permission to test.

The social fire that singed AGS taught that company and other biotechnology companies a lesson. Monsanto, for example, made careful preparations before field testing an altered gene in tomato plants at an Illinois farm. The company consulted with local governments, took out newspaper ads to inform the public, brought truckloads of farmers and community members to its St. Louis headquarters for a barbecue, and sent its scientists to farming communities to explain the world of biotechnology. It apparently worked well. While the climate for field experiments has much improved since the ASG incident, it still is hostile and must be handled very wisely.

Serious problems lie in government regulation. It is estimated that there will be 8,000 biotech patent applications waiting to be processed in the Patent and Trademark Office at the end of 1989. Currently it takes from 2.5 to 4 years to process an application. This is much too long in a rapidly developing technology. Companies complain that before a patent is processed a new improvement may be invented, but it cannot easily be pursued because it would require a new application to the Patent Office. There are fears that unless the application-approval process can be speeded, U.S. firms may lose out to foreign competitors who also are deeply committed to biotechnology.

One major problem in the Patent Office is hiring enough skilled staff to review the applications. This is partly a budgetary problem but also one of finding and keeping those who have the technical skills necessary for review. In 1989, industry and the Patent Office announced formation of the Biotechnology Institute, headed by a board composed of industry and government members. The purpose of the Institute is to help train new patent examiners and to keep the Patent Office abreast of rapidly developing technology in the field. Unfortunately, this is a long-term solution; current delays in processing applications are likely to continue.

The industry encounters delays in getting the EPA's permission to experiment in the atmosphere. One industry manager claims it takes about two months to prepare a study for the EPA and five to six months for the agency to review it and approve a field test.

[4]"Trouble in the Promised Land: An Interview with Jeremy Rifkin," *Multinational Monitor*, February 28, 1986.

This case illustrates some of the regulatory issues that the new biotechnology raises. Here are other important regulatory issues that must be addressed.

- Is there enough or too much oversight of biotechnology experiments?
- Are new laws needed to deal with this burgeoning field?
- How should regulatory agencies coordinate their actions to avoid impeding progress in the field?
- Do the potential benefits of biotechnology justify the risks that may be incurred? How should risks and benefits be determined? Who is to determine them?
- Are there ethical problems in tampering with genes?
- Are there ethical problems involved when academic scientists team with industry to produce commercial products?

These are extremely difficult questions to answer to the satisfaction of industry, the government, and the general public. The answers that are given, however, will have profound impacts on the quality of life in the United States as well as its economic position in the world.

As demonstrated in the above case and in the last chapter, despite the efforts of the Reagan administration to produce regulatory relief and reform, there remain today significant flaws in the regulatory structure and processes that should be corrected. In this chapter we discuss some of these deficiencies and recommendations for reform. While antitrust laws are part of the regulatory apparatus of government, they stand in a somewhat different category from the types of regulations which were the subject of the last chapter. Here too, however, there have been substantial recent changes that have had an important impact on business. The chapter includes, therefore, discussion of this subject.

STRESS THE COMPARATIVE ADVANTAGE OF GOVERNMENT AND BUSINESS

An effort should always be made to determine whether business or government can best perform an activity that is needed by society. Each has strengths and weaknesses. There clearly are certain activities that government can perform more efficiently than individuals in the private sector. For example, Mobil Corp. recognized that only government can perform these significant functions:

- Only government can set forth national goals and work out the necessary compromises to reconcile conflicting regional and other interests and to recognize the priorities among various energy sources.
- Only government can develop the ground rules under which private industry must work.
- Only government can formulate a national policy on environmental trade-offs that will strike a sensible and workable balance between unacceptable environmental risks and unacceptable economic risks.

• Only government can hammer out the sort of balanced policy that does not permit extremist approaches to environmental protection to delay for years programs toward achievement of national goals on energy.[5]

Government is the superior institution to express common social goals, to establish policies, and to tax for social purposes. But government has grave deficiencies compared with other institutions in performing certain other functions. As we have noted, government action stimulates interest groups. Costs of government management of productive facilities are likely to be higher than those of the private sector because of a requirement for accounting for "the last penny," because equal attention must be given to unimportant and important elements of the activity, because in government personnel loyalty is often more valued than efficiency, and because any activity assumed by government becomes part of a huge bureaucracy with inherent inefficiencies resulting from its size.

Business can avoid these problems more readily than governments can. Even the largest businesses are smaller than governments and therefore enjoy an advantage in flexibility and adaptability. For these reasons, it seems sensible to assign to governments and businesses the production of those goods and services that clearly are their responsibility and that each can produce at the lowest cost, using that word broadly.

RELY MORE ON THE FREE MARKET

Economists, as well as the general public, are strongly in favor of relying more on the free market mechanism. This means not only an inhibition against unnecessary controls, but also more reliance on market incentives in meeting regulatory goals. When the market is functioning ideally, there is no superior mechanism for using scarce resources efficiently to produce the goods and services that society needs at prices people are willing to pay. As noted in Chapter 9, a major responsibility of government is to prevent abuses in the operation of the free market mechanism and to facilitate its operation in the most effective and efficient manner.

Government's functioning with respect to the free market has been a mixed bag. It has stimulated competition by deregulating a number of industries. On the other hand, protectionist legislation for many products, from peanuts to automobiles, has reduced free competition. The desirable condition, of course, is for the government, as in an old song by Johnny Mercer, "to accentuate the positive, eliminate the negative." In our complex society, striking this balance is not easy, but it is a goal toward which we must constantly strive. Some major policies that might be used to achieve this end follow.

[5]Mobil Corporation, "Energy Solutions and Nonstarters: Where a Government Role is Needed: Accent on Achievement," New York: Mobil, 1978.

HARNESS THE POWER OF SELF-INTEREST

The core advantage of free markets in achieving social purposes is basically self-interest, which, fortunately, has been broadened today by the acceptance of voluntary social responsibilities by more and more managers. Charles Schultze, former chairman of the President's Council of Economic Advisers, has evaluated this force as follows: "Harnessing the 'base' motive of material self-interest to promote the common good is perhaps the most important social invention mankind has yet achieved."[6] This is a bit of an exaggeration, yet it does make a valid point. It seems strange, says Schultze, that

> For a society that traditionally has boasted about the economic and social advantages of Adam Smith's invisible hand, ours has been strangely loath to employ the same techniques for collective intervention. Instead of creating incentives so that public goals become private interests, private interests are left unchanged and obedience to the public goals is commanded.[7]

REDUCE COMMAND CONTROLS AND SUBSTITUTE INCENTIVE CONTROLS

Command controls require firms and individuals to meet specific standards or behavior patterns and are enforced by civil and, in some cases, criminal penalties or loss of government contracts. Some controls achieve the regulatory objective directly. For example, automobile manufacturers have had to improve the fuel efficiency of their cars to meet specific standards and thereby have conserved gasoline. Other standards are employed because it is believed that complying with the standard will result in meeting the control objective. OSHA's standards, for instance, are presumed to bring about conditions that will reduce job-related injuries to workers.

Command standards have many weaknesses. For example, they are generally difficult to enforce because they are applied so widely that it is impossible to monitor compliance completely. For example, OSHA cannot inspect all the plants within its authority. Federal and state inspection programs together cover no more than 4 percent of firms to which regulations apply. Since standards are static and the world is dynamic, they must constantly be updated. Such rule making is time-consuming and frequently confusing to those regulated. Standards also can be counterproductive if they deflect efforts from the ultimate objective to compliance with the standards. For example, management may feel that all obligations to patients who use a new drug are fulfilled if the FDA approves the drug's introduction. Or, resources for job safety may be exclusively devoted to meeting OSHA standards without giving careful attention to specific hazards.

---

[6]Charles L. Schultze, *The Public Use of Private Interest,* Washington, D.C.: The Brookings Institution, 1977:18.

[7]*Ibid.,* p. 6.

The use of fixed standards is justified as a regulatory tool when there is a strong causal relationship between the standard and the objective of control *and* when there are no alternatives. Certain health hazards, such as unallowable levels of carcinogenic pollutants in the work environment or nuclear power plant safety standards, are best dealt with by fixed standards.

But for many command controls, alternatives do exist that allow for more individual freedom. Market incentives are alternatives to most command controls. Market incentives impose prices and/or costs upon unwanted outcomes. Companies faced with such costs seek to reduce them in order to remain competitive and thereby move toward achievement of the regulatory objective. Achievement of the objective is, therefore, decentralized. Economic incentives can take many forms, such as taxes, fees, fines, and penalties. The most effective are those that set the cost in relation to the size of the offense and those in which inspection is frequent enough to ensure that companies comply before the inspector arrives.

The present penalty structure generally does not meet these requirements. Penalties for pollution violations, for example, are generally low compared with costs to society. Despite the army of regulators, inspections are usually not frequent enough to ensure general compliance. In too many cases, business is willing to face a potential fine of, say, $1,000 in order to avoid spending far more to be in compliance. OSHA launched a program to exempt construction companies from routine inspections as inducements to the companies to develop their own tough inspection programs. Not many companies asked for relief, and only a few requests were granted. In companies that have developed their own systems, as approved by OSHA, safety records have improved dramatically. Why have so few companies asked for exemption? It is because chances of OSHA inspection are minimal and fines for violations are small compared to the costs of setting up private inspection systems. However, Terrence Scanlon, chairman of the Consumer Product Safety Commission, claimed that the voluntary-agreements program of the agency was working well in more than fifty product areas and that it was saving CPSC a great deal of time and money.

At this stage in our regulatory history it would not be possible to replace command controls with incentive regulations even if there were a consensus to do so. We have built a mountain of detailed regulations, interpretations, court cases, administrative processes, and expectations of command controls, so that only gradual conversion is possible.

PROPOSALS FOR FURTHER DEREGULATION

There has been much deregulation, as noted previously. Still, strong recommendations for more complete or partial deregulation are frequently made. There are many who assert that, with deregulation, resources will be used more efficiently in the public interest.

"Deregulation" is a shorthand word that means two different things. First, it can mean the removal of regulations so that reliance is placed on the free market mechanism. Second, it can mean relaxation or reform of regulations to make the regulations more efficient and effective by reducing costs, increasing the benefits, eliminating nonsense rules, and so on. The first applies to many regulations in the economic area, as noted above. The second applies more to social regulations, such as relaxation of pollution controls. Although much has been accomplished in recent years in both areas, most people believe that much more can be done. For example, further deregulation of natural gas, agriculture marketing orders, and tariff protections would expand free markets and competition.

REPRIVATIZE MUCH GOVERNMENT-OWNED PROPERTY AND SERVICES

Selling or contracting out government-owned and operated production and service facilities to the private sector is called privatization. Reprivatization jokingly has been called "a little yard sale" of excess government assets. But it is much more than that. The argument, of course, is that private enterprise and not the government should be doing things that should be privatized. It is also argued that, for many services, private enterprise can do the work much more efficiently.

People have proposed reprivatizing the Federal Housing Administration, Amtrak, the Naval Petroleum Reserve, federal grazing and timberlands, hydropower and irrigation water systems, airports, the postal service, and weather satellites. Almost all of these proposals have run into congressional fire storms, and very little has been sold. Despite efforts to sell assets, the federal government is actually increasing them. For example, the government has recently acquired tens of billions of dollars of assets under the savings and loan industry bailout.

Some of the federal impetus toward reprivatization also arises from the widespread policy of state and municipal governments to contract out public services to private firms. They contract out vehicle towing, legal services, streetlight operations, solid waste disposal, street repair, hospital operation, ambulance service, data processing, and other services. The claim has been made and substantiated that private enterprise can do these things more cheaply and efficiently than local governments.

But municipal transfers of such activities to the private sector are not without their critics. For instance, it is claimed that reprivatization costs jobs and opens up only lower-paying jobs for those affected. Critics also fear corruption, since it is alleged that ethics in government are higher than in some private businesses.

Each major proposal for reprivatization of federal assets draws its own set of supporters and critics. For the post office, it is said that the federal government could operate as efficiently as private enterprise and with comparable costs were if not for legal requirements to subsidize certain types of mail and congressional authorization of higher wages and benefits for postal workers than for private mail services.

IMPROVE ADMINISTRATION OF THE REGULATORY PROCESS

While many laws are administered efficiently and effectively (e.g., Federal Reserve Board open market operations), others are nothing short of scandalously managed. For example, the nation currently is facing the price of poor management of the Housing and Urban Development Department and the savings and loan industry. Shortcomings in regulatory administration are rooted in many causes. Among the root sources of poor management are lax administration, poorly drafted basic statutory legislation, contradictory laws and regulations, insufficient budgets for proper implementation, fraud, bureaucratic inertia, and incompetent management. Following is a sample of regulatory shortcomings that should be changed.

FLAPDOODLE STANDARDS AND SPECIFICATIONS

One significant dimension of federal regulations is the growth of nonsense regulations. Classic examples are found in early OSHA regulations, many of which now have been expunged. For example, "Exit access is that portion of a means of egress which leads to the entrance to an exit." "When ascending or descending [a ladder], the user should face the ladder." "Jacks which are out of order shall be tagged accordingly, and shall not be used until repairs are made." Such trivia have little to do with the really important causes of industrial accidents and worker illness, which are supposed to occupy the attention of OSHA. Nonsense regulations are not, of course, confined to OSHA. Other regulatory agencies are just as guilty of this shortcoming. For instance, the Charles Hanson Company in Georgia had manufactured Red Fox denims for twenty-eight years. Several years ago, the FTC said that the company could no longer use the name. Why? The denims did not have any red fox fur in them, said the FTC! The Pentagon has drafted eighteen pages of specifications for the traditional holiday fruitcake. For example, candied orange peel must be "thoroughly deragged and processed with sugar and corn syrup to not less than 72 percent soluble solids." Flavoring "shall be pure or artificial vanilla in such quantities that its presence shall be organoleptically detected." Diced candied pineapple must be in quarter-inch chunks, and shortening must have the "stability of not less than 100 hours." Senator Sam Nunn of Georgia has called this the "cost-is-no-object fruitcake."[8] Although many silly rules have been eliminated or modified, many remain.

BUREAUCRATIC SNAFUS

At a different administrative level are snags that entangle effective action. For example, note this fishy story.

---

[8]Michael Weisskopf, "Nutty as a Military Specification," *Washington Post Weekly Edition,* January 6, 1986.

A heavy run of steelhead trout, back to spawn, overcrowded the National Fish Hatchery in Lewiston, Idaho. Someone suggested that the excess trout be given to the Valley Food Bank, a local, private, nonprofit agency that would distribute the fish to needy people. The Interior Department, which operated the hatchery, agreed with this solution.

Unfortunately, someone discovered that Interior had no authority to do this. Therefore, it was proposed that the fish be transferred to the Department of Agriculture. Agriculture was to declare the fish surplus government food and give them to the needy. Unfortunately, existing law said that Agriculture had to deal only with state agencies in distributing surplus foods. Meanwhile, the trout began to die. The food bank offered to buy the fish and dispose of them some other way. The only other way was to declare the fish scrap. Unfortunately, the law said that surplus government foodstuffs classified as scrap had to be identified as "unfit for human consumption."

To untangle this knot, an interested Lewiston resident called a friend in the White House. The state of Idaho was asked to act as middleman in solving the problem. Agriculture lawyers worked with the state in preparing necessary papers to release the fish to the food bank through the state of Idaho. But to distribute the fish, the food bank needed federal approval in declaring that all federal health and safety requirements had been met. Unfortunately, the Department of Commerce, not Agriculture, had to make an inspection to give this approval. This inspection was supposed to cost $3,000, but the White House obtained a waiver for this fee. Red tape was finally cut, and the fish were transferred.[9]

MISMANAGEMENT

Agencies of government are constantly being charged with mismanagement. This accusation can mean many things, from criminal felonies to ineptitude. Here is one example.

For many years, the agencies that have stewardship over the 600 million acres of public land in the West, about 25 percent of the nation's land, have been charged with mismanagement. These agencies, principally the Forest Service in the Department of Agriculture and the Bureau of Land Management in the Department of Interior, have been accused of selling and leasing lands at prices far below fair market value, failing to properly conserve the lands, and ignoring environmental damage in disposing of and using the lands. For example, grazing fees paid by cattle growers are below fair market fees and the government loses money on the program. The government builds roads in remote forests and sells the timber for prices that do not cover the costs of the program. Under antiquated mining laws it is possible, when ore is discovered on public lands, to buy the land at $2.50 to $5.00 an acre. One miner is reported to have bought sixty acres of a scarred and trash-

[9]Adapted from *U.S. News & World Report*, April 4, 1983. Copyright 1983, U.S. News and World Report.

strewn hillside overlooking Phoenix for $2.50 an acre and later to have sold it for $400,000 and an interest in the development built on the land.[10] Aside from old laws which govern land management, it is clearly impossible for the Bureau, with its limited staff, to manage efficiently the vast lands under its jurisdiction.

CONFLICTS AMONG REGULATIONS

The regulatory structure is filled with conflicts. Here are but a few illustrations. The OMB has the power to disapprove new proposals for paperwork when it considers the requirement to be excessive. This power was given to the agency by the Paperwork Reduction Act of 1980. The Supreme Court in one decision, however, denied the agency that right. The case involved a proposed Hazard Communication Standard of OSHA. The Court said OMB had no authority to disapprove this proposal because it "embodied substantive policy decision making entrusted to the other agency (OSHA)."[11]

Antipollution requirements have forced some companies to abandon marginal plants, a policy that conflicts with federal goals of reduced unemployment. Economists have for a long time pointed out that minimum wage legislation increases teenage unemployment, although national policy clearly seeks to reduce unemployment, which is far too high among teenagers. As we shall see in Chapter 12, restrictive trade policies are opposed to a presumed free trade policy of the United States.

DELAYS IN ADMINISTRATIVE DECISION-MAKING

As we have noted, the process of decision making in regulatory agencies is slow. Businesspeople have complained for years about excessive delays in decisions concerning matters vital to them. A few recent cases illustrate the point. In 1982, the federal government settled antitrust suits against AT&T and IBM that had been in process for over a decade. The Dow Chemical Company had plans to build a multimillion-dollar petrochemical complex in northern California, but after two years of effort to gain the required approval for sixty-five permits, it abandoned the effort. A public utility in California today must get clearances from thirty agencies to build a plant, and any one of the agencies can deny the permit. To introduce a new drug in the United States and meet all FDA requirements may take as much as ten years and cost from $50 to $60 million.

---

[10]For two descriptions of the issues, see Emily T. Smith, Vicky Cahan, Randy Welch, and Michael Parks, "This Land Is Whose Land?" *Business Week,* April 24, 1989; and Mark A. Stein and Louis Sahagun, "BLM Woes Spill Onto Public Lands," *The Los Angeles Times,* May 21, 1989.

[11]*United Steelworkers of America v. Pendergrass (USWA III),* 855 F.2d 108 (3rd Cir. 1988), petition for cert. filed. 57 U.S.L.W. 3472 (U.S. Dec. 28, 1988) (No. 88–1075). For an analysis of this decision and the paperwork act, see John V. N. Philip, "The Paperwork Reduction Act in United Steelworkers of America v. Pendergrass: Undue Restrictions and Unrealized Potential," *Columbia Law Review,* May 1989.

MAKE NEEDED CHANGES IN BASIC STATUTORY LEGISLATION

In the past three decades we have had five major comprehensive studies of our regulatory system. They all were headed by prestigious, responsible, and knowledgeable people, such as former President Herbert Hoover. There have been innumerable commissions formed to improve regulatory procedures in individual agencies, such as those seeking to improve the weapons acquisition process of the Department of Defense. In addition are the many studies and recommendations about individual programs by the congressional watchdog, the General Accounting Office. They all have been only marginally successful. There are many reasons for this. One, of course is the extraordinary complexity of the system. But there are many others, such as the inertia which is inherent in entrenched bureaucracy, the difficulty of altering embedded self-interests in particular regulations, and the fact that most of them failed to remedy the basic problems stemming from the legislative statutes.

The regulatory system would function more efficiently if some of the basic legislation were changed to facilitate smoother implementation, avoid fundamental conflicts, and permit agencies to better balance the benefits of regulation with the costs. We have noted a number of instances where such changes would be in the interests of better regulation. The "zero discharge" goal of the Clean Water Act, for example, leads to ineffective regulation because it cannot be met. Basic legislation controlling the Bureau of Land Management needs to be changed to avoid selling off government lands at bargain prices. Laws which prevent the application of cost-benefit analysis, such as the OSHA Act, should be changed in the interests of more rational administration.[12]

OTHER PROPOSALS FOR REFORM

In addition to problems created for regulatory agencies by basic statutory legislation and court decisions, deficiencies in regulating spring from poor management. Many suggestions have been made to improve administration. The strengthening of administrative direction in the Executive Office of the President which took place in the Reagan administration certainly should be continued and possibly tightened. Such control should reduce nonsense regulations and those carrying excessive costs. Ways should be found to give more attention to cost-benefit analysis in approving regulations, despite the many problems in applying this decision-making tool. More will be said about this in Chapter 15. One clear requirement is to increase budgets for regulatory agency staff so as to hire more regulators and higher caliber staff. Criteria for appointment and promotion should be tightened to ensure that highly qual-

---

[12]For other recommendations to change basic legislation, see Murray L. Weidenbaum and Ronald J. Penoyer, *The Next Step in Regulatory Reform: Updating the Statutes*, Center for the Study of American Business, Washington University, St. Louis: 1983; Stephen Breyer, *Regulation and Reform*, Cambridge, Massachusetts: Harvard University Press, 1982; James Q. Wilson, ed., *The Politics of Regulation*, New York: Basic Books, 1980; and Daneke and Lemak, *op. cit.*

ified and competent administrators move into key decision-making posts. Means should be found to make it easier for top managers to discharge incompetent managers and staff.

INNOVATIVE POLITICAL AND JUDICIARY PROPOSALS FOR REFORM

The above regulatory reform proposals follow conventional lines. There are other proposals that are less conventional for reforming the political processes which could improve our regulatory posture. Several of these are presented here.

PASS SUNSET LEGISLATION

There is no orderly procedure for reviewing federal regulatory agencies to determine whether or not important changes should be made in their mandates and operations. During the past few years "sunset" bills have been put before Congress, but to date none has been passed. Sunset legislation would require the President to make recommendations to the Congress for changes in specific regulatory agencies. In a given number of years, say eight or ten, the President would be obliged to report on all major regulatory agencies. If Congress failed to act upon the President's recommendations for a particular agency, the agency's powers would be curtailed or eliminated. In this way, Congress would be forced to act to continue the agency as is, to alter its powers, or to bring about its demise.

Sunset laws have been advocated for years. In 1978, the Senate overwhelmingly passed a sunset bill that set a ten-year reauthorization cycle for most federal programs. But the House did not act on the bill and it died. Since then, enthusiasm for the idea has faded. One important reason is that committee members in both chambers of Congress have become increasingly concerned about the work load they bear and the additional burden that sunset laws would create.

REFORM CONGRESS

Observers of the political scene take the position that a serious recent phenomenon in Congress is the decline of party leadership power and the rise in power of autonomous committee and subcommittee chairpersons. Members of these committees are biased against remedies that harm their constituents, and they have the power to block such initiatives in the Congress.

What is needed is reform in Congress. Specifically, more power needs to be put in the hands of the budget committee, the appropriations committee, the rules committee, and chairpersons of full committees. Also needed is tighter coordination between the President and the legislative process.[13]

---

[13]Clifford M. Hardin, Kenneth A. Shepsle, and Barry R. Weingast, *Public Policy Excesses: Government by Congressional Subcommittee*, St. Louis: Washington University Center for the Study of American Business, September 1982.

PREPARE CONGRESSIONAL COST-BENEFIT ANALYSIS BEFORE LEGISLATION IS PASSED

Although provisions have been made for economic analysis of proposed regulations in the executive branch, there is no program in Congress for making a systematic cost-benefit analysis of new legislation. One of the shortcomings in the development of regulatory legislation is the tendency for Congress to take prompt action in dealing with an urgent problem without considering the costs involved. It is difficult to prepare a convincing cost-benefit analysis of new legislation in a new field, but the thought involved in making it might well prevent ill-conceived regulations.

IMPROVE BUSINESS BEHAVIOR

Progress in reforming government regulation of business will depend somewhat on business behavior. It is important that business, especially the larger companies, assume social responsibilities beyond producing goods and services efficiently. As noted in Chapter 4, business is not held in high esteem in this society, and there are deep antipathies to business, especially the large corporation. History is clear on the point that this attitude makes it much easier to legislate new regulations and rigorously enforce old rules. Better business behavior will modify these patterns in favor of business.

Individual businesses and groups of business people also must act responsibly in lobbying and dealing with regulatory agencies. Lobbies and pressure groups can and do perform many valuable services, but if their selfish interests are pursued at the expense of the public interest, the welfare of the nation is not served. There is no implication in this statement that there is always a conflict between selfish business interests and the public interest. Both can be advanced at the same time. For instance, a tax incentive to industry to buy capital equipment during low economic activity can help individual businesses and advance the general welfare.

OUTLOOK FOR REGULATORY GROWTH AND REFORM

REGULATIONS WILL INCREASE IN VOLUME AND COMPLEXITY

John Maurice Clark, a distinguished economist and a perceptive observer of the changing business-government relationship, observed over fifty years ago:

> The frontiers of control [government of business] are expanding. They are expanding geographically, increasing the importance of national functions as compared with those of local governments.... And they are expanding in the range of things covered and the minuteness of regulation.... Whether one believes government control to be desirable or undesirable, it appears fairly obvious that the increasing interdependence of all parts of the economic system... will force more control in the future than has been attempted in normal times in the past.[14]

The same forecast can be made today. The only uncertainty is the speed with which new regulations are introduced into the system.

[14]J. M. Clark, *Social Control of Business*, New York: McGraw-Hill, 1932.

REFORM SHOULD NOT NEGLECT REGULATORY BENEFITS

But in reforming the regulatory system, we must always bear in mind the benefits of that system. We must not throw out the baby with the dirty bath water. As the Tolchins remind us:

> Regulation is the connective tissue, the price we pay for an industrialized society. It is our major protection against the excesses of technology, whose rapid advances threaten man's genes, privacy, air, water, bloodstream, lifestyle, and virtual existence. It is a guard against the callous entrepreneur, who would have his workers breathe coal dust and cotton dust, who would send children into the mines and factories, who would offer jobs in exchange for health and safety, and leave the victims as public charges in hospitals and on welfare lines.... Regulations provide protection against the avarice of the marketplace, against shoddy products and unscrupulous marketing practices from Wall Street to Main Street. They protect legitimate businessmen from being driven out of business by unscrupulous competitors, and consumers from being victimized by unscrupulous businessmen.[15]

EXTENSIVE REFORM NOT LIKELY

No matter how "obvious" may be the need for a reform in our regulatory system, powerful forces operate to resist change. Among them certainly is the sheer inertia in bureaucracy. In addition, despite all of the clamor for reform, it has a weak political base. One reason for this is that the general population is not excited about reform. Aside from business, the ultimate beneficiaries are generally unaware of their stake in reform. Because the benefits of reform to one person are very small in relation to the costs involved in bringing it about, there is a lack of initiative by individuals except those in business. The result is a coalition of congressional committees, bureaucrats who administer the laws, and interest groups—constituting a political power that resists quick and substantial regulatory reform. There is no comparable opposing political power.[16]

In this light, one should not expect any massive regulatory reform. However, it is not too much to hope that with patience and slow but steady progress in building on the initiatives already taken (for example, civilian aviation deregulation, gradual oil and gas deregulation, pressure for sunset legislation, and so on), the proposals made in this chapter may gradually be accepted in part or in whole.

REFORMING THE ANTITRUST LAWS

Today, the antitrust laws are a prominent feature of every manager's environment, especially those in the large corporations. These laws define acceptable size of companies, the market shares they can enjoy, and the kinds of illegal behavior that can lessen competition. Here we discuss how the application of our antitrust laws has changed substantially in theory and prac-

---

[15]Susan J. Tolchin and Martin Tolchin, *Dismantling America: The Rush to Deregulate*, New York: Oxford University Press, 1983.
[16]Wilson, *Politics of Regulation, op. cit.*

tice in recent years. There are widely contrasting views about the wisdom of these changes which also will be examined.

THE SHERMAN AND CLAYTON ACTS

Our basic antitrust laws are the Sherman Act (passed in 1890) and the Clayton Act (passed in 1914). There have been few amendments to these fundamental laws. But judgments about the legality of various business practices today differ greatly from those of ninety, fifty, or even twenty-five years ago. These changes are partly attributable to changes in the law, but mainly to shifts in Supreme Court decisions.

Background of the Sherman Act   The immediate grounds for the passage of the Sherman Act lay in the rapid development of monopolistic practices following the Civil War. The Standard Oil Trust and its many imitators in the 1880s provoked formidable opposition among small-business owners, farmers, and the general population. This was a period of concentration of economic powers, price fixing, market sharing, and other monopolistic agreements among formerly competing companies. So widespread was the opposition to the monopoly movement that the Sherman Act passed the Senate with but one dissenting vote and passed the House without opposition.

Basic Provisions of the Act   The two most significant sections of the Sherman Act are 1 and 2. Section 1 reads: *"Every contract, combination* in the form of trust or otherwise, or *conspiracy, in restraint of trade* or commerce among the several States, or with foreign nations, *is hereby declared to be illegal"* (italics added). Section 2 says: *"Every person who shall monopolize,* or attempt to monopolize, or combine or conspire with any person or persons, to monopolize any part of the *trade* or commerce among the several States, or with foreign nations, *shall be deemed guilty* of a misdemeanor, and, on conviction thereof, shall be punished by fine" (italics added).

Much has been written about the purpose of the Sherman Act, but one of the best statements was given in a Supreme Court opinion:

> The Sherman Act was designed to be a comprehensive charter of economic liberty aimed at preserving free and unfettered competition as the rule of trade. It rests on the premise that the unrestrained interaction of competitive forces will yield the best allocation of our economic resources, the lowest prices, the highest quality, and the greatest material progress, while at the same time providing an environment conducive to the preservation of our democratic political and social institutions. But even were that premise open to question, the policy unequivocally laid down by the Act is competition.[17]

This legislation did not provide anything new legally, because monopolistic agreements had been held unenforceable under common-law prohibitions of agreements that unreasonably restrained trade. But many states had experienced problems in applying these laws to giant companies doing busi-

---

[17]*U.S. v. Northern Pacific R. R. Co.,* 356 U.S. 1 (1958).

ness in many states. With the Sherman Act, however, these conspiracies now were offenses against the federal government.

Early Supreme Court Decisions   The first decisions of the Supreme Court to interpret antitrust law met with disbelief and dissatisfaction. In the first case brought to the Court, *U.S. v. Knight* (1895), the Court decided that a gigantic sugar refining company, which controlled 98 percent of the market, had not violated the act.[18] This ruling naturally encouraged merger and concentration. The decision was reversed in several celebrated cases, such as *U.S. v. Standard Oil* (1909)[19] and *U.S. v. American Tobacco* (1911).[20] Both of these companies enjoyed about 95 percent of their respective markets and the court declared this percentage contrary to the law. However, the Court also said in passing judgment that there were reasonable and unreasonable restraints of trade and that if other large companies were to use their powers reasonably, they would not run afoul of the law. The Court did not define the meaning of these words, which became known as the "rule of reason."

THE CLAYTON AND FEDERAL TRADE COMMISSION ACTS

Dissatisfaction with these decisions and the legal uncertainties they posed to business led to the passage of the Clayton Act and the Federal Trade Commission Acts of 1914. The Clayton Act sought to identify those monopolistic practices which were prohibited by law. The FTC Acts created an agency to continuously supervise and administer the antitrust laws and to stop "unfair methods of competition in commerce, and unfair or deceptive acts or practices in commerce..." (Section 5 (a) as modified by the Wheeler-Lea Act of 1938).[21]

The Clayton and FTC acts are long and their language is often fuzzy. Section 7 of the Clayton Act, the most important section for the present analysis, is comparatively simple:

> *no corporation* engaged in commerce *shall acquire,* directly or indirectly, the whole or any part of *the stock* or other share capital of another corporation engaged also in commerce *where the effect of such acquisition may be to substantially lessen competition* between the corporation whose stock is so acquired and the corporation making the acquisition *or to restrain such commerce in any section or community or tend to create a monopoly of any line of commerce.* (Italics added.)

Other sections of the Clayton Act spelled out in some detail price discrimination and exclusive dealings that "may...substantially...lessen competition or tend to create a monopoly in any line of commerce...."

---

[18]*U.S. v. E. C. Knight Co.,* 156 U.S. 1 (1895).
[19]*U.S. v. Standard Oil Co.,* 221 U.S. 1 (1909).
[20]*U.S. v. American Tobacco Co.,* 211 U.S. 106 (1911).
[21]The Department of Justice has the authority to enforce the Sherman Act and shares jurisdiction with the FTC in Clayton Act cases. The FTC can issue orders to business enforcing provisions of both acts, but only the Department of Justice can prosecute for criminal violations of the antitrust laws. The Supreme Court, of course, has the final word in interpreting the application of both laws.

SUPREME COURT DECISIONS CONCERNING FIRM SIZE, PRICE FIXING, AND MERGERS

A thumbnail sketch of the history of Supreme Court decisions about firm size, prices, and mergers is useful in understanding present law and the controversies associated with it. It is also a fascinating account of the many ways in which the relationship between business and government has changed.

SHIFTS IN THE LEGALITY OF SIZE AND PRICE FIXING

For decades after the Clayton Act, the Supreme Court continued to apply the "rule of reason" in deciding the legality of companies with high market shares. In 1916, for example, the Court said that it would not destroy a company even though it produced 90 percent of the nation's cans. The reason for this position, said the Court, was that the company "had done nothing of which any competitor or any consumer of cans complains, or anything which strikes a disinterested outsider as unfair or unethical" (*U.S. v. American Can Co.*)[22] In 1920, a steel company that controlled over two-thirds of many steel products was not broken up because "the law does not make mere size an offense or the existence of unexerted power an offense" (*U.S. v. United States Steel Corporation*).[23] In 1927, a company that controlled 64 percent of its market was not held to be in violation of the law (*U.S. v. International Harvester Co.*).[24]

In contrast, in a series of cases going back to 1899, the Court held price fixing to be a per se violation, meaning that no extenuating circumstances could make price fixing legal. For example, in 1927 the Court held, "The power to fix prices, whether reasonably exercised or not, involves power to control the market and to fix arbitrary and unreasonable prices. The reasonable price fixed today may through economic and business changes become the unreasonable price of tomorrow." It did not make any difference, said the Court, whether the agreement to fix price was loose or formal (*U.S. v. Trenton Potteries Co., 1927*).[25]

These two lines of thought encouraged the very thing that the Sherman Act was designed to stop. Because price fixing was illegal but large size was not, firms merged to form huge companies with enough power to monopolize markets. In later cases the Court recognized the irony of this result and extended the rule of reason to price fixing as well as to company size. In 1933, for example, price fixing was held to be legal because the price agreements in question were designed to end injurious competition and to promote a "fair market" (*U.S. v. Appalachian Coals, Inc.*).[26] In 1945 the Court held that a company with 90 percent of the primary aluminum market in this country was a monopoly contrary to the law. The power to fix prices by such a company, said the Court, was inherent in its size (*U.S. v. Aluminum Co. of*

---

[22]*U.S. v. American Can Co.*, 230 Fed. 859 (1916).
[23]*U.S. v. United States Steel Corporation*, 221 U.S. 417 (1920).
[24]*U.S. v. International Harvester Co.*, 247 U.S. 643 (1927).
[25]*U.S. v. Trenton Potteries Co.*, 273 U.S. 392 (1927).
[26]*U.S. v. Appalachian Coals, Inc.*, 288 U.S. 344 (1933).

America).[27] This doctrine was upheld in 1946 in *U.S. v. American Tobacco Company*,[28] and again in 1948 in *U.S. v. Paramount Pictures*.[29] But also in 1948, in *U.S. v. Columbia Steel*[30] the Court seemed to slip back into its more permissive attitude. In this case, a steel company had 51 percent of the rolled-steel or ingot capacity on the Pacific Coast. This share was held not to be unlawful. Size is significant, the Court said, but the steel industry itself is big.

CONGLOMERATES AND THREATS TO COMPETITION

Most of these cases involved mergers (both horizontal and vertical) and the behavior of one or a few companies with large shares of a market. In the late 1950s and 1960s, there was a wave of mergers consummated by conglomerates.[31] This activity receded in the 1970s but picked up again in the 1980s. The legality of the size and behavior of these firms had to be decided by the courts.

In a milestone case, *U.S. v. Brown Shoe Company* (1956),[32] the Supreme Court said that one must look not only at total concentration but concentration in particular markets. Furthermore, combinations were illegal if they posed a *potential* threat to competition. In this case, Brown Shoe, a producer, acquired the G. R. Kinney Company, an independent chain of shoe stores. Together they controlled 2.3 percent of total retail shoe outlets and 1.5 percent of the nation's shoe output. But in some local areas, sales of women's shoes ran as high as 57.7 percent of the local market. In forty-seven cities, the combined share of children's, men's, and women's shoes was a little over 5 percent. The Court said that if it approved this merger, competitors would do the same thing, and this move would encourage the oligopoly Congress sought to avoid. It was therefore important to nip in the bud incipient threats to competition.

In subsequent conglomerate cases, the Court widened the antitrust net. It rejected a merger of a small with a larger company even though the two did

---

[27]*U.S. v. Aluminum Co. of America*, 148 F.2d 416 (1945).
[28]*U.S. v. American Tobacco Co., et al.*, 328 U.S. 781 (1946).
[29]*U.S. v. Paramount Pictures, Inc.*, 334 I.W. 4211 (1937).
[30]*U.S. v. Columbia Steel Co.*, 335 U.S. 495 (1948).
[31]A *horizontal* merger is one that combines the activities of companies within the same industry, such as two steel mills. A *vertical* merger takes place when a company acquires other firms, either back in the production chain, toward raw materials, or forward, toward consumers of final products and services. For example, a merger of a company producing fabricated steel shapes and forms with one iron ore and one building steel bridges is a vertical merger. A *conglomerate* merger is neither horizontal nor vertical and involves two firms that are engaged in unrelated lines of business. A simple illustration would be the merger of a producer of wooden office furniture with a company owning and mining coal.
Conglomerate mergers can, of course, be of different varieties. For example, the acquired companies may be completely unrelated, or they may associate with a basic company purpose. Conglomerates may merge with firms that are not directly competitive, such as those with common production or distribution characteristics, or companies in the same general product line but making sales in different geographic regions.
[32]*U.S. v. Brown Shoe Co., Inc.*, 370 U.S. 294 (1962).

not compete. The reason: the larger company could be a "deep pocket," a "rich parent" that could open up all sorts of possibilities for the small company to undersell or otherwise "ravage the less affluent competition" (*FTC v. Reynolds Metal Company*, 1962).[33] In another case, the Court rejected the merger of a small and a large company because there would exist a clear probability of reciprocal buying that would weaken competition in the industry (*FTC v. Consolidated Foods Corporation*, 1965).[34] Two years later the Court agreed with the argument that even though two companies that wanted to merge were not competitors, the possibility that potential competition in an industry might be inhibited was enough for it to deny the petition to merge (*FTC v. Procter & Gamble*, 1967).[35]

It is true that such theories as incipient threats to competition, "deep pocket," probable reciprocal buying, and potential threats to competition would, if companies acted as the Court said they might, result in injury to competition. These theories seem to be based on the idea that it is better for consumers to forego the efficiencies that could accrue to a merger in order to avoid a hypothetical future injury to competition.

At about the same time, the Court reaffirmed its prohibition of price fixing, excessive domination of a market by large corporations, and any behavior that seemed likely to weaken competition. For example, the Court ruled that no corporation should seek or exercise the power to control the prices in or to exclude others from a market (*U.S. v. Grinnell Corp.*, 1966).[36] It ruled that a dominant company must not engage in any monopolistic restraint, such as cutting off rivals from essential sources of supply (*Zenith Radio Corp. v. Hazeltine Research, Inc.*, 1969).[37] The allocation of exclusive territories to distributors or dealers to exclude competitors was forbidden (*U.S. v. Arnold, Schwinn & Co.*, 1967).[38]

THE SUPREME COURT LOOKS BEYOND MARKET SHARES FOR LEGALITY

Until the 1970s, the Supreme Court measured the legality of mergers in terms of market shares. In 1974, in *United States v. General Dynamics*, the Court generated new thinking about the importance of market concentration. The Court said that the competitive effects of a merger should not rely exclusively on structural tests, but should take into account a much broader range of economic information and business conditions.[39] In this and other cases it said that it was ready to consider the impact of mergers and price fixing on mar-

[33]*FTC v. Reynolds Metal Co.*, (U.S. S. Ct. 1962) 1962 Trade Cases, Par. 70, 741.

[34]*FTC v. Consolidated Foods Corp.* (Gentry Inc.), (U.S. S. Ct. 1967) 1967 Trade Cases, Par. 71, 432.

[35]*FTC v. Procter & Gamble Co.* (U.S. S. Ct. 1967) 1967 Trade Cases, Par. 72 061.

[36]*U.S. v. Grinnell Corp.*, 384 U.S. 563 (1966).

[37]*Zenith Radio Corporation v. Hazeltine Research, Inc.*, 395 U.S. 100 (1969).

[38]*U.S. v. Arnold, Schwinn & Co.*, (U.S. S. Ct., 1967) 1967 Trade Cases, Par. 72, 126.

[39]*U.S. v. General Dynamics Corp.*, 415 U.S. 486 (1974).

kets rather than to decide cases solely on the basis of corporate size, market shares, or industry concentration.[40]

In a later important decision, in the *Montford* case (1986), the Court rejected market share as a sole basis for determining legality. Excell, a wholly-owned subsidiary of Cargill, wanted to acquire Spencer Beef. Excell was the second largest beef packer and Spencer Beef was the third. Montford, the fifth largest packer, wanted to block the merger. It argued that the combined companies would be able to buy cattle at high prices and sell boxed beef at low prices and thereby squeeze Montford's profit margin. The district court agreed with Montford and enjoined the merger.

The case went to the Supreme Court, where a 6-to-2 decision reversed the lower court decision. The Court said that Excell was correct when it argued that any damage resulting from increased competition did not represent antitrust injury. The antitrust laws, held the decision, should not be used to protect a competitor from price competition even if competition was increased by a merger. Furthermore, said the Court, a challenge to a merger must have more concrete evidence than mere speculation about potential price squeezes, predatory pricing, and other anticompetitive activities.[41] It is notable that the district court based its decision on the structure theory and the Supreme Court ruling reflected the performance theory, or as Weston calls it, the theory of dynamic competition.[42]

THE STRUCTURE VERSUS PERFORMANCE THEORIES

Until recently, the Supreme Court, as well as government regulators and academic economists, leaned toward the structure theory in deciding antitrust cases, as supported by most of the scholarly studies on concentration and merger. In the late 1960s, however, an increasing body of impressive evidence emerged that contradicted this view in support of the performance theory.

In 1949, Professor Edward S. Mason argued in a landmark article that public policy toward industrial organizations ought to aim at promoting sound market structures as well as efficient business performance. The market structure and performance tests, he observed, "must be used to complement rather than exclude each other."[43] By *performance* he meant product and process innovation, reductions in costs by various managerial and technical methods that were passed on to consumers in lower prices, suitable capacity in relationship to output, profits not out of line with other industries, and emphasis on product and service rather than excessive advertising expendi-

---

[40]James DeQ. Briggs, "An Overview of Current Law and Policy Relating to Mergers and Acquisitions," *Antitrust Law Journal*, volume 56, issue 3, 1987.

[41]*Cargill, Inc. and Excell Corporation v. Montford of Colorado, Inc.*, 55 L.W. 4027 (1986).

[42]J. Fred Weston, Kwang S. Chung, and Susan Hoag, *Mergers, Restructuring and Corporate Control*, Englewood Cliffs, New Jersey: Prentice-Hall, 1990.

[43]Edward S. Mason, "The Current Status of the Monopoly Problems in the United States," *Harvard Law Review*, June 1949.

tures. Since Mason wrote his article, there has been sharp controversy between those who argue for a structural public policy and those who support a policy based on performance.

The conventional economic wisdom up to recent years and still held by many was that the structure of the marketplace is a reliable index of monopoly power. More precisely, the theory argues that the more concentrated the sales and assets of a few firms in an industry, the greater the monopoly power of those firms. Not only is there substantial concentration today of sales and assets in individual industries but there is high concentration of all corporate assets in the largest companies in the United States. In that everyone is opposed to monopoly, the proper public policy is one that slows down and reverses this trend. If not, in three or four decades we will be dominated by concentrations of economic power in our large corporations.

Excessive concentration of market power, it is argued, gives corporate managers discretionary power to fix market prices, determine which products come to market and in what volume, and make excessive profits. Furthermore, monopoly power has produced price inflation, inefficiencies in production and, of course, a decline in competition.

Structuralists argue that if competitive markets can be created by breaking up concentrations of economic power or by preventing mergers of large firms, individual companies will behave competitively, with economically desirable performance. Therefore, they argue, large concentrations of economic power should be broken up. Antitrust policy will be clearer and more effective if there is some fixed rule based on structure.

This market-concentration doctrine is rebutted by others. Some argue that concentrations of economic power in large companies are due to market forces and not to motivations to monopolize. Large size is a necessary concomitant to a large economy. In certain industries, large companies and concentration are essential because of the heavy capital investment needed to do business. Industries do not become concentrated unless there is a basic economic reason for large-scale operations. Business structure is therefore the result of underlying economic forces.

Many observers see competition rising rather than declining. They see there are many forms of nonprice competition which take place. Smaller firms can specialize and take advantage of any excessive pricing of large companies. High profits of large firms may be associated more with efficiency than the exercise of monopoly power. Product innovation is a major source of competition by large firms because they can afford heavy research and development expenditures that small firms cannot.

In sum, it is the performance and behavior of large firms that should be examined and not simply structure. A market structure composed only of small firms would be quite out of tune with the demands of modern society and would, in addition, bring about economic distortions and inefficiencies.

A few other issues between the market structurists and the business performists may be presented in capsule form. The structurists reject performance because they say there are no clear and acceptable standards for measuring performance. Those who emphasize performance do so because they say there are no suitable standards to measure acceptable structure. Structure is favored because when it is suitable, there will be many competitors, the market will regulate economic activity, and government interference in the market mechanism will be unnecessary. Those who hold to performance point out the extraordinary change that would be required to bring about anything approaching pure competition. Furthermore, if cost advantages of size are prevented, will not the cost to consumers be excessively high? Structurists say it is not performance which is sought, but competition. There is an implicit assumption that if structure is acceptable, there will be better products, improved service, and lower prices. But it is said that mergers and company expansions are necessary to ensure efficiency, which benefits society. It is pointed out that structure can be perfect and performance terrible because market conditions may lead to cutthroat competition. And so the arguments, like a shuttlecock, move back and forth from one position to another. To many observers, both sides make good points.

RESEARCH SUPPORTING THE STRUCTURE AND PERFORMANCE THEORIES

A typical measure of concentration of market power is the ratio of sales of the largest companies to total sales in an industry. These data, of course, vary greatly from industry to industry. It is true that in some industries (mainframe computers, automobiles, and jet engines, for example), the four largest companies account for well over 70 percent of the value of total domestic shipments. In most industries, however, the concentration ratio for the four large companies is under 50 percent. Longitudinal studies show that the concentration ratios for most industries have remained remarkably stable.[44] When world markets are considered, the concentration, however, drops substantially for virtually all major industries. For example, Ford Motor Company had 29 percent of the U. S. truck market in 1988 but only 16.8 percent of the world market.

Earlier studies suggested that high concentration led to excessive profits.[45] However, later studies have shown a lack of correlation between conventional measures of concentration and excessive profits.[46] Contrary to structure theory, new research shows that substantial price flexibility exists in concentrated industries and that price increases during inflationary periods were lower in industries dominated by "super concentrations" than in those less concentrated. Productivity also has risen faster in concentrated than in other industries. Structuralists allege that innovation in concentrated indus-

---

[44]J. Fred Weston, *Concentration and Efficiency: The Other Side of the Monopoly Issue.* Croton-on-Hudson, New York: Hudson Institute, 1978.

[45]John M. Blair, *Economic Concentration: Structure, Behavior and Public Policy*, New York: Harcourt, 1973.

[46]Weston, *Concentration and Efficiency, op. cit.*

tries is less than in nonconcentrated industries, a fact which is difficult to prove but which is challenged by some studies.

Such research findings do not reject completely every assertion by structural theorists. Some concentrations at some time and place may result in excessive profits, price inflexibility, inhibitions to innovation, and so forth. They do conclusively show, however, that for most cases of concentration, structure theory describes the opposite of reality.

SIGNIFICANCE OF CORPORATE DIVISIONALIZATION

One of the very important recent developments partly explains the wide difference between structural and performance theories. It is that major corporations have transformed themselves from one-product to multi-product firms. Between 1949 and 1969, the number of firms with multiple product divisions among our largest 200 companies jumped from 20 to 76 percent of the total.[47] This trend has continued, and now very few of our largest companies have only one product line and one centralized management.

This change is of cardinal significance in antitrust theory. The assumption that our large corporations are huge monolithic enterprises leads to very different conclusions about behavior than the assumption that they are multi-product, decentralized organizations. Huge corporations that are centrally controlled and have one or a few products do tend to suffer from all the classical managerial deficiencies of massive bureaucracies. They may very well behave economically as the structure theorists claim. However, what goes on in the typical divisionalized corporation with many products, even though the corporation is very large, is much different.

A decentralized corporation with major divisions like General Electric, for instance, is divided into so-called strategic business units (SBUs). These units, with only moderate control from company headquarters, have considerable authority to operate as independent businesses. They enter into a competitive market populated heavily by divisions of other conglomerates. This market typically is highly dynamic and volatile. The SBU faces serious competitive threats, such as new products developed by other firms both in and outside the industry; technical advances in products developed by competitors; new substitute products that may render the SBU's products obsolete; and foreign competition. The result, of course, is strong pressure on the SBU to maintain its competitive position.

To stay competitive, the SBU may try to protect itself in many ways. The SBU may differentiate products; expand research to improve the quality and consumer acceptance of present products; invest in new equipment to increase productivity; cut costs by speeding inventory turnover; increase advertising expenditures; lift market share by cutting prices and costs per unit; develop more efficient distribution methods; and stimulate worker participa-

---

[47]Richard P. Rumelt, *Strategy, Structure, and Economic Performance,* Boston: Graduate School of Business Administration, Harvard University, 1974.

tion in the decision-making processes to advance product quality, worker productivity, and morale. All these forces and many others inevitably improve efficiency and benefit consumers. Companies and SBUs that depend upon nothing but the presumed power of their high market share are doomed to lose share and eventually go bankrupt.

Basic in structural theory is the assumption that managers form mergers with other companies to increase their power in the marketplace. Some mergers have been engineered by entrepreneurs molded after the industrial buccaneers of the late nineteenth century. Their motivations range across a wide spectrum—power, the fun of the game, money, and the like. Some have acquired underpriced companies with the hope of selling assets piecemeal for a total financial gain. Some apparently have forced a reluctant takeover target to buy back the acquirer's stock at a premium to end the takeover attempt. Some have acquired companies with large tax write-off carryovers that would help the acquiring company to shelter future profits. Some few may have been motivated solely by an effort to acquire economic power in the marketplace.

But in most recent mergers, the overwhelming drive has been economic efficiency. More specifically, the underlying purposes have included: growth of sales and profits, avoidance of dependence on one product line, stability of sales and earnings over the business cycle, acquisition of needed technology and fuller employment of technological capabilities, reduction of costs by using an underemployed distribution system, entry into foreign markets, acquisition of raw materials, use of excess productive capacity, completion of a product line, taking advantage of tax laws, and a combination of these objectives. Unquestionably, many mergers have been prompted by the fact that it has been less costly (because of comparatively low share prices in the stock market) for one company to acquire another through the purchase of stock than to achieve these objectives through internal growth.

On the other side of the coin, in many instances the acquired company has sought the merger. An aging owner of a company, for example, may wish to retire by selling the firm to another company, a firm may be in financial trouble and need access to cash, or it may be apparent to both companies that joint efforts will more readily achieve mutual economic objectives.

A veritable revolution in management techniques has facilitated the growth of large and prosperous corporations with virtually independent subsidiaries (SBUs). For example, we have learned much about how managers must deal with people in organizations to get the best results. Techniques have been perfected concerning how to identify opportunities in the environment; how to appraise current and future competitive threats; how to manage a portfolio of SBUs with many different products, resource needs, problems, and opportunities; how to develop better communications and information systems; how to automate production lines for greater efficiency; how to minimize manufacturing and distribution costs; and how to optimize the results of research.

The central reality is that most mergers, as well as the increase in size of companies through internal growth, have resulted because managers have had to make sure that their companies, and each SBU or division, are strong in highly competitive markets. Operating efficiency is the key to achieving this result.

DEPARTMENT OF JUSTICE MERGER GUIDELINES

The newer trend in court decisions concerning mergers was paralleled by changing guidelines prepared by the Department of Justice (DOJ) and the FTC. The DOJ guidelines have had the greatest impact. Guidelines were issued in 1982 and 1984. Basically, they codified the thrust of the newer research on mergers and thereby modified the more traditional view that the decisive litmus test of merger legality was market share as measured by sales and/or assets.

To begin with, the traditional concentration measure was changed. In its place is a new measure called the Herfindahl-Hirschman Index (HHI). It employs a formula based on the theory that if one or more firms have a relatively high market share, that is of much greater concern than the shares of the largest four firms in an industry.[48] The guidelines place considerable emphasis on the economic effect of a merger. Factors to be considered are impacts on prices, impact on consumers, ease of entry of new firms, and ease and profitability of collusion. It is assumed that firms will be less likely to attempt to coordinate price increases if collusion is difficult or impossible. Factors to be considered in making this judgment include product differences, frequent quality changes of product, frequent introduction of new products on the market, technological changes, cost differences among suppliers, and so on. In sum, the guidelines espouse a more sophisticated economic evaluation of the anticompetitive potential of a merger than the calculation of market share as measured by sales.

Some observers viewed the guidelines as an abdication of the government's responsibilities in antitrust. Others saw them as a revision of the laws needed to keep pace with economic realities. There is no question that, during the 1980s, the DOJ did not challenge many proposed mergers that heretofore would have been considered contrary to the antitrust laws. On the other hand, there are a number of cases that were brought before the Supreme Court in the past which under the new guidelines would not have been challenged. Among those which were noted previously would be *Brown Shoe* and *Consolidated Foods.*

The DOJ and FTC are accused of being far too lax in antimerger enforcement. This is denied, however. The DOJ claims that it has brought, during the Reagan administration, 425 criminal cases under the Sherman Act compared with 165 such cases brought during the Carter administration. Its total

---

[48]For an explanation of the HHI Index see Weston, *et al., Mergers, op. cit.*

fines exceeded $110 million compared with $54 million.[49] The FTC also claims that it has been diligent and not only blocked more transactions in 1986 than in the past ten years but caused a number of others to be abandoned.[50] Critics discount these assertions.

In the meantime, states have increased their antitrust activities. The Hart-Scott-Rodino Act of 1976, among other provisions, significantly expanded the powers of state attorneys general to institute triple damage antitrust suits. These powers, plus the change in policies of the DOJ and FTC, have stimulated a growing number of suits.

One other reform in the antitrust laws should be noted. It is the National Cooperative Research Act, passed in 1984, which permits manufacturers to engage in cooperative research. This law was passed to permit U.S. companies to form consortia to combat foreign companies that are permitted by their laws to do the same thing. This will be discussed in detail in Chapter 13. At this writing, there are indications that the DOJ will ask the Congress to permit companies in selected manufacturing industries to engage in cooperative manufacturing. Again, this is designed to help U.S. companies in global competition. Such activities heretofore have been outlawed by the antitrust laws.

THE FUTURE OF ANTITRUST REFORM

At this writing (fall 1990) it is not clear what direction antitrust enforcement will take in the Bush administration. There is every indication, however, that there will be much more antitrust activity than in the Reagan administration. For example, James F. Rill, the new Assistant Attorney General, Antitrust Division of the Department of Justice, said "...I believe in the Department's 1984 Merger Guidelines as a sound prescription for merger policy, and I will enforce them." He also commented that "...I wish to underscore the fact that the Department of Justice fully endorses increased penalties for convicted antitrust felons." He said that "...no matter what its guise, cartel behavior constitutes no more than fraud and theft from consumers."[51] In an interview with editors of the *National Journal*, he expressed this attitude about bigness: "I follow the rule of thought that antitrust is not an appropriate vehicle for challenging bigness unless that bigness has or threatens to have an adverse effect on competition. I think that view is in the mainstream of antitrust law."[52]

Janet Steiger, Chairman of the FTC, has asserted that her agency will vigorously increase its antitrust activities. She said that "...we will continue to place our highest priority on investigating those mergers that have the great-

[49]Charles F. Rule, "Interview with Charles F. Rule," *Antitrust Law Journal*, 56, 1987, pp. 261–281.

[50]Daniel Oliver, "Interview with Daniel Oliver," *Antitrust Law Journal*, 56, 1987, pp. 233–257.

[51]James F. Rill, "Antitrust Enforcement: An Agenda for the 1990s," Remarks before the 23rd Annual New England Antitrust Conference, Cambridge, Massachusetts, November 3, 1989.

[52]James F. Rill, "Bush's Antitrust Enforcement Chief...Says He's in the Legal Mainstream," *National Journal*, September 30, 1989, p. 2404.

est likelihood of causing consumer injury."[53] She said that the inaction of the FTC in the past has cost it credibility in its antitrust vigilance and she is committed to changing that perception.

No one knows precisely what the Supreme Court will decide in particular antitrust cases. There is a strong predisposition of justices to follow precedent. But, as we have seen, the Court has modified significantly the doctrine of years long past. It can be concluded, we believe, that the performance theory of antitrust is likely to continue competing with the structure theory for some time to come.

---

[53]Janet Steiger, "Agenda for the Federal Trade Commission," Remarks before the 23rd New England Antitrust Conference, Cambridge, Massachusetts, November 3, 1989.

Airline Deregulation*

After forty years of regulation of the airline industry, President Jimmy Carter, responding to a climate of opinion which supported less government regulation of business, backed an experiment in airline deregulation. With his support, the Airline Deregulation Act (ADA) was passed in 1978.

The ADA, over a six-year transition period, eliminated most federal rules governing the airlines. Although economists and the business community generally welcomed the measure, there was opposition. Some major airlines feared revenue losses from fare wars that might result from an open climate of competition. Small airlines feared predatory pricing practices by larger competitors. Airline unions feared loss of jobs as the result of a shakeout of weaker firms. And small towns worried that airlines would neglect them in favor of more profitable big city routes.

Nevertheless, proponents of the new experiment were optimistic. A major advocate of deregulation was Alfred Kahn, chairman of the Civil Aeronautics Board (CAB), the primary agency regulating the airlines. In a lecture, Kahn spoke of the "fascinating venture in applied economics" that he envisioned:

> During the next several years...I look to a more variegated airline industry structure, in which the traditional rigid geographic and functional boundaries between different carriers and categories become blurred and governmentally protected spheres of influence less distinct, a structure that offers the maximum possible assurance of continuation of the competitive spur and that offers exciting new opportunities for managerial enterprise. And I look for a corresponding and increasingly variegated set of price and service options, competitively offered to passengers and shippers.[54]

*By T. K. Das, Baruch College, City University of New York.

[54]"Deregulation of Air Transportation—Getting From Here to There," in Donald P. Jacobs, ed., *Regulating Business: The Search for an Optimum*, San Francisco: Institute for Contemporary Studies, 1978, p. 59. In 1988 Kahn reviewed the past decade of experience with deregulation and concluded that "airline deregulation has been a success." See Alfred E. Kahn, "I Would Do It Again," *Regulation*, no. 2, 1988, p. 22.

AIRLINE REGULATION AND THE TRANSITION TO DEREGULATION

The Air Commerce Act of 1926 was the first federal legislation regulating the airline industry, but it was confined primarily to safety requirements. It imposed no economic or competitive restrictions on airline managers. In those days successful air carriers were generally those that had airmail contracts with the U.S. Post Office Department. The various airmail statutes and the bidding for the airmail contracts were principal factors governing the growth of the industry until the Civil Aeronautics Act of 1938 was passed.

The 1938 law was wide-ranging. It not only superseded the Air Commerce Act of 1926 and various airmail legislation, but, most important, it introduced regulations, similar to those regulating public utilities, designed to promote economic growth of the airline industry. It also provided for more comprehensive safety regulation.

A regulatory agency, the Civil Aeronautics Board, was set up under the 1938 act to regulate air fares and route entry and exit (oversight of airline safety was mostly in the hands of another agency, the Federal Aviation Administration). Over time, the CAB developed a broad blanket of ever-more-detailed rules regulating airline operations. Managers often found the bureaucratic regulatory processes of the CAB to be slow and confining.

The Airline Deregulation Act provided that the CAB would phase out rule enforcement and cease operations by December 31, 1985. This came to pass. Various residual CAB functions were then relinquished to other federal agencies. Accordingly, remaining authority permitted by law over domestic airline mergers, intercarrier agreements, and interlocking directorates was transferred to the Justice Department. Most other functions, such as the handling of consumer complaints, were shifted to the Department of Transportation. A subsidy program for maintaining service to small communities was phased out at the end of 1985. However, a new subsidy program to guarantee essential service to specific communities continued until 1988.

With implementation of the Airline Deregulation Act, the regulatory environment of the industry changed dramatically. And although it has been over twelve years since deregulation began, the industry remains in a state of transition. Not everyone believes that the transition is moving in the right direction. What follows is an accounting of major changes that occurred when the fetters of federal regulation were first loosened, then lifted completely in many areas of airline operation. This story raises questions about the future of the airlines, how well they serve the public, and how well events bear out the rosy prognostications of free market enthusiasts made at the time of deregulation in 1978.

AUTOMATIC MARKET ENTRY

Prior to deregulation, the CAB had carefully controlled airline routes, permitting flights to and from cities only after a lengthy, complex decision process. To enhance competition among companies, the Airline Deregulation

Act permitted air carriers to choose routes freely. It phased out all restrictions on the choice of cities served as the CAB was divested of its authority to control the number of carriers serving specific markets.

This automatic market entry program was introduced gradually to minimize damaging competition during the transition to a deregulated market. For three years, until the end of 1981, a carrier needed no prior CAB approval to introduce one new route per year. Simultaneously, each carrier had the option of identifying one existing route per year which would be protected from entry by competitors. But, as indicated, all CAB control over domestic route entries ended in December 1981.

The CAB temporarily retained authority to require airlines to provide "essential services" to small communities if it so chose. Otherwise, carriers could stop service to any city simply by notifying the CAB. But, in general, the new law mandated that the CAB place maximum reliance on competition, simplify its formerly complex and time-consuming decisions, and ease restrictions. For instance, the CAB had once imposed "closed door" rules prohibiting airplanes from picking up passengers at intermediate stops on long-distance routes. This protected other airlines operating at these airports from competition, but to consumers it appeared nonsensical. In part, it was inefficient-appearing rules such as this which led to the deregulation movement. Under the new law, however, "closed door" rules and similar restrictions were dropped.

When restrictions were loosened, airlines entered new routes with enthusiasm. Their competitive strategies reflected the increased freedom. New airlines were formed to compete with existing carriers. Fares wars ensued. The airlines developed sophisticated computerized reservation systems to promote their flights with local travel agents and to keep track of daily changes in seat prices which reflected supply and demand in markets served. Major airlines emphasized hubs at regional airports and developed close relationships with the commuter airlines which fed them passengers.

PRICE COMPETITION

With deregulation, airlines were able to use price competition as a competitive strategy. Fare cuts were used to increase market share on established routes, to establish footholds in new markets, to punish weaker competitors, and to encourage feeder airline transfers at major airports. New non-union carriers with lower wages than the major carriers offered discount fares. Quickly, discount fares came to dominate the fare structures of all airlines. In fact, it has been calculated that "between 1978 and 1988, as a result of deregulation, air travelers saved about $100 billion."[55]

IMPACT OF THE NEW COMPETITION ON CONSUMERS

According to Senator Edward Kennedy (D-Mass.), the ADA, "while preserving the government's authority to regulate health and safety, frees airlines

---

[55]Kenneth Labich, "How Airlines Will Look in the 1990s," *Fortune*, January 1, 1990, p. 55.

to do what business is supposed to do—serve customers better for less."[56] This rationale was one of the prime considerations behind the ADA. But whether the consumer has actually gained from the ADA is open to debate. To begin, one analyst addressing this question in 1983 made these observations:

> There has been a great deal of new competition, sharp discounts, wars among trunks in long-haul markets. For the economy-minded traveler willing to take the time to shop around, the situation is probably better, as there is a wider choice of discounted fares, of carriers and aircraft than ever before.[57]

Deregulation also helped bring airline travel within the reach of millions of travelers. The number of domestic passengers rose from 292 million on 14.7 million commercial flights in 1980 to an estimated 392 million passengers on 19.2 million flights in 1986. The Federal Aviation Administration foresees over 650 million passengers and 26.4 million flights in 1997.[58]

The increase in passengers has been accompanied by an increase in the number of written and telephone complaints to the Department of Transportation about the quality of airline service. Two major factors contributing to the deteriorating standard of service are overburdened airports and a strained air traffic control system.[59] With the growth of airline traffic over the years, authorities are finding it increasingly difficult to resolve problems of safety and congestion at airport terminals. Limited capacity at airports has, in many cities, effectively negated the notion of unrestricted market entry. Certain contractual obligations have remained from the days of regulation. For example, majority-in-interest provisions allow the majority of airlines at an airport to veto capital improvements and airport expansion projects. These arrangements may restrict market entry. Given the escalating demand at the busiest airports for gates and ground facilities, it is no surprise that airlines face considerable problems in acquiring slots or the rights to land and take off. Although the number of airline trips nearly doubled between 1977 and 1987, no major new airports were built. By 1990, the federal government had accumulated a $6 billion Aviation Trust Fund from a tax on airline tickets. The purpose of this fund is to finance improvements in the air transport system. But so far, it has not been used.

The increase in air travel combined with static facilities meant more inconvenience for passengers. In a story published in *U.S. News & World Report*, the spokesman for the Dallas-Fort Worth Airport is quoted as saying: "I remember when you were going to fly, you put on a coat and tie and the planes were not crowded—you could travel in class and style. Today, it's like taking a bus."[60] The story also notes that "a bewildering jumble of airline connections, dozens of fares to the same destination, sudden airline bank-

---

[56]Quoted in William N. Leonard, "Airline Deregulation: Grand Design or Gross Debacle?" *Journal of Economic Issues*, vol. 17, 1983, p. 454.
    [57]*Ibid.*, p. 457.
    [58]Jeremy Main, "The Worsening Air Travel Mess," *Fortune*, July 7, 1986, p. 50.
    [59]John Rhea, "Grounded!" *Government Executive*, January 1990.
    [60]"Paying the Price of Cheaper Airline Fares," March 5, 1984, p. 66.

ruptcies, congestion and circuitous routings are just a few of the rough spots passengers must negotiate even before they leave the ground."[61]

Passengers have been further inconvenienced by the increasing trend among most airlines to rely on the "hub-and-spoke" system, whereby a number of flights interconnect at "hub" airports. The main advantage of a highly developed hub-and-spoke operation is that it multiplies the pairs of cities that an airline can service with a given amount of mileage. The percentage of flights originating at hubs has increased considerably since deregulation. The authors of a study of airline deregulation have noted that: "Since a large proportion of city-pair markets cannot support convenient nonstop service, hub-and-spoke operations have proved to be the dominant networking strategy of air carriers since deregulation."[62] Congestion and delays, however, are inevitable with this type of operation. For example, airlines try to make close connections on flights and want to have their flights arrive and depart at popular times. Since facilities are limited, the system does not always work smoothly. Delays tend to snowball during bad weather.

The trend toward hub-and-spoke systems can be traced to the airlines' efforts to service their passengers to their destinations without inter-airline transfers. Usually, the system is justified for markets that do not warrant nonstop service. As one airline executive put it: "It's not part of the hub-and-spoke concept to inconvenience passengers who could go nonstop. But with deregulation, the incentive is there to market hubs in order to hold on to passengers."[63]

After a shaking out period which lasted until the end of the 1980s, service complaints died down somewhat and airlines began to use better service as a competitive strategy. Still, growth in passenger miles and the hub-and-spoke system have permanently changed the ambience of air travel.

MERGERS, ACQUISITIONS, AND CONSOLIDATION IN THE INDUSTRY

With CAB route protection removed, airlines were thrust into an environment of tooth-and-claw competition. Many new airlines were started, but most soon failed. Since 1978, over 200 new and established air carriers have either gone bankrupt or merged with competitors. The result has been the emergence of an oligopolistic industry structure in which a few large airlines dominate. This is not, of course, the structure of many fiercely competing smaller airlines envisioned by deregulation advocates. In 1988, the top five carriers—American, United, Delta, Continental, and Northwest—controlled 69.5 percent of the national market, and the top ten airlines together controlled 92.1 percent.[64] In addition, some airlines dominate the air travel mar-

---

[61]*Ibid.*, p. 66.

[62]Elizabeth E. Bailey, David R. Graham, and Daniel P. Kaplan, *Deregulating the Airlines*, Cambridge, Massachusetts: MIT Press, 1985, p. 196.

[63]Quoted in *Air Transport World*, "Deregulation Has Spawned Dramatic Changes in Airline Marketing," August 1983, p. 27.

[64]Thomas Canning, "Profits Come Home to Roost, But Fleets Are Aging," *Standard & Poor's Industry Surveys*, New York: Standard & Poor's Corporation, May 4, 1989, p. A17. See also Janice Castro, "The Sky Kings Rule the Routes," *Time*, May 15, 1989.

ket in certain cities because they have hubs there and control so many gates that competitors cannot flourish. Since 1977, for example, TWA's share of passengers in St. Louis went from 39 percent to 82 percent; Northwest's share at Minneapolis/St. Paul went from 45 percent to 81 percent; and Piedmont's share at Charlotte, N.C., went from 10 percent to 88 percent.[65]

The fear of consumer advocates is that dominance of major carriers in national and regional markets will eventually bring an end to fare competition. When only a few major airlines dominate passenger travel, their tendency will be to raise prices in concert to increase income and recoup some of the foregone revenues of a decade of price competition. Indeed, in 1989 the industry seemed to bear out this prediction by imposing major rate hikes and eliminating many discounts. The average ticket price early in January 1989 was $413, as compared to $356 a year earlier.[66] And over the course of 1989, ticket prices increased by 25 percent.[67]

Other anticompetitive effects are being felt as well. For example, some have charged that the dominant airlines have cleverly designed their computerized reservation systems so that travel agents are more apt to ticket passengers on their particular airlines' flights, even where such flights are not necessarily more convenient or thrifty. And most small commuter airlines have learned that they cannot survive without a "code sharing" arrangement with one of the major carriers. Code sharing occurs when the commuter's daily flights are listed in the computer system of a major carrier with the same code as the major's flights. Code sharing, in effect, incorporates the tiny commuter into the route system of the trunk carrier. This reduces the independence of the commuter line, because dropping the code sharing arrangement would deprive the small carrier of the advantages of a worldwide reservation network. Of course, many commuter airlines are now wholly or partly owned by larger airlines.

EMPLOYMENT PROTECTION

To gain the support of unions for deregulation, the ADA provided for compensation of up to six months for employees with at least four years service with an air carrier if they lost their jobs, had their wages cut, or were forced to relocate due to increased competition in consequence of deregulation. But very little seems to have been done to implement this employee protection provision in terms of either providing federal subsidies for laid-off workers or ensuring the right of first hire as required under the statute.

According to one analysis, 30,000 airline workers lost their jobs between 1978 and 1982, but none received any benefits, because the necessary rules had yet to be drawn up.[68] The requisite rules were published after consider-

---

[65]*Ibid.*, p. A17.

[66]*Ibid.*, p. A5.

[67]Paul A. Graham, Jr., "Air Transport Industry," *The Value Line Investment Survey*, December 29, 1989, p. 252.

[68]Michael Wines, "Verdict Still Out on Deregulation's Impact on U.S. Air Travel System," *National Journal*, March 6, 1982, p. 409.

able delay by the Carter administration in 1980, but their adoption is believed by many employee union leaders and others to have been blocked by the Reagan administration.[69] Related statistics about the employment situation among airline pilots show that of the 35,000 members of the Air Line Pilots Association, 5,000 were laid off.[70] In addition to layoffs, employees also suffered changes in work rules, the imposition of two-tier wage systems wherein newly hired workers were paid less, and powerful assaults on pilots', machinists', and flight attendants' unions. In 1983, for example, Texas Air Corporation took its Continental Airlines subsidiary into Chapter 11 bankruptcy proceedings, claiming that existing union wage agreements implied imminent bankruptcy and could not be continued. Continental was successfully reorganized as a non-union carrier and returned to the marketplace with a substantially lower cost structure as a result—all the better to compete in the discount fare wars.

SERVICE IN SMALL COMMUNITIES

The fear that deregulation could result in loss of service to small and isolated communities prompted the provision in the ADA which guaranteed "essential air transportation service" for ten years. The CAB was empowered to order any servicing airline to retain "essential" routes, and to facilitate this the agency could subsidize the airlines for losses incurred serving small communities.

Despite these provisions, there have been reports that many small cities have suffered in terms of the quality of air service after deregulation. William Leonard reported that in the first eighteen months of deregulation, seventy-five smaller cities being served by major airlines found this service was replaced by local and commuter airlines with smaller planes.[71] An added inconvenience to passengers was the frequent loss of nonstop flights to larger cities. According to Matthew V. Scocozza, assistant secretary of transportation, the federal government paid airline subsidies of $26 million in 1986, an average of more than $100 per passenger. An assessment of the impact of deregulation on smaller communities in that year is as follows:

> According to Avmark Inc., an aviation management and marketing service, commercial air service was available at the time of deregulation at 523 non-hub cities. Since then, 108 of the cities have been given improved service; 19 have more seats but fewer flights; 96 have more flights but with smaller planes and fewer total seats; and 150 have lost all service.[72]

---

[69]C. V. Glines, "Deregulation: The Bomb That Exploded," *Air Line Pilot*, November 1983, p. 18.

[70]"Airline Financial Woes Prompt Consideration of Industry Regulation," *National Journal*, October 8, 1983, p. 2076.

[71]Leonard, *op. cit.*, p. 17.

[72]Robert E. Dallos, "Debate Still Rages over Deregulation," *Los Angeles Times*, November 2, 1986, p. 21.

SAFETY

The responsibility for ensuring that the safety regulations in the airline industry are carried out remains with the Federal Aviation Administration. Questions have been raised about whether intensified competitive pressures and the entry of a number of new carriers into the airline industry have diluted safety standards.

Competitive pressures may, of course, affect the resources allocated to aircraft maintenence. So also with the deployment and training of mechanics. The situation in this regard is unsatisfactory, according to some observers. One of them, writing in 1988, says this:

> Many carriers have not had sufficient resources to devote to maintenance or new equipment purchases. Since deregulation, the average age of our nation's aircraft fleet has grown 21 percent. More than 2,800 jets are more than sixteen years old—the geriatric jets, as some call them. For every year an aircraft ages, it requires 2 percent more in maintenance expenditure. But during the last six years, capital devoted to maintenance has decreased 30 percent. As the profit margin has shrunk, so has the margin of safety.[73]

Nevertheless, comparative statistics show that there has probably been some decrease in accident rates. In the nine years before deregulation (1970–78), the accident rate was 0.0141 per million miles and 0.584 per 100,000 flight hours. Corresponding figures for the nine post-deregulation years (1979–87) were 0.0065 and 0.266.[74] A safety report put out by the FAA in 1988 concludes that "the total accident rate is slightly lower than the 1978 level, while the fatal accident rate is more than 60 percent lower than the rate recorded ten years ago."[75]

RE-REGULATION?

Some observers are having second thoughts about whether all of the ADA provisions were beneficial to the airline industry, consumers, labor, and smaller cities. A study completed in late 1984 concluded: "After six years of deregulation, it is still not possible to render a final verdict on whether on net balance, deregulation is producing a domestic air transportation system better or worse than what previously existed."[76]

---

[73]P. S. Dempsey, "Deregulation Has Spawned Abuses in Air Transport," *Aviation Week & Space Technology,* 129(21), pp. 147–151.

[74]J. D. Ogur, C. L. Wagner, and M. G. Vita, *The Deregulated Airline Industry: A Review of the Evidence,* Washington, D.C.: Federal Trade Commission, 1988.

[75]Federal Aviation Administration, *Annual Report of the Effect of the Airline Deregulation Act on the Level of Air Safety,* Washington, D.C.: U. S. Department of Transportation, July 1988, p. EX-1.

[76]Melvin A. Brenner, James O. Leet, and Elihu Schott, *Airline Deregulation,* Westport, Connecticut: Eno Foundation for Transportation, 1985, p. xi. When he took office in 1989, Secretary of Transportation Samuel K. Skinner ordered a detailed study of competition in the airline industry. The study was said to conclude that deregulation has had a "net positive effect," but that there were "pockets of concern" to be scrutinized. See Hobart Rowen, "Deregulating Sanity," *Washington Post National Weekly Edition,* December 25–31, 1989, p. 5.

In the early 1990s, this is still a sound assessment; the jury is still out. The situation is this. Mergers continue and market concentration grows. Although pockets of competition exist, starting new airlines is no longer practical, and niche competitors such as Alaska Airlines are struggling to avoid being crushed by the biggest carriers. Most commuters have become satellites in the orbits of the big carriers. After years of deep discounts, air fares are beginning to rise. Passenger miles traveled and the number of flights continue their steady rise, promising continued congestion, delays, and service problems. The airport system is daily becoming more inadequate. All this sounds troublesome, but with consumers travelling more, discount air fares still plentiful, and safety under control, there are rumblings, but no emergent movement to broadly re-regulate the airline industry.

QUESTIONS

1 The ADA of 1978 was passed to unleash competition in the industry and thereby benefit consumers. In your judgment, has the public interest been advanced since passage of the act? Explain what you mean by "the public interest," and defend your position.

2 Are airlines like a typical public utility and, if so, should they be subject to similar economic regulation? Or is the airline industry more similar to a typical service industry and, therefore, merits no more or less government regulation than a service industry?

3 Are you pleased or disturbed by the state of the airline industry in 1990? What are the positive and negative dynamics of the industry? Would you favor reintroduction of federal regulation in any areas? Explain which ones and what type of regulation you believe is called for.

4 What do you think the airline industry will look like in the year 2000?

11

Business in the Political Process

TOSHIBA

In the 1970s, the Soviet Union approached Toshiba Machinery Co., a machine tool manufacturing company in the Toshiba Group, seeking to purchase secret, technically advanced milling machines. Under Japan's Foreign Exchange Control Law, export of such machines to communist countries was forbidden. They can be used to mill ultraquiet propellers, which would render submarines harder to detect. Toshiba rebuffed the Russians, learning later that a French rival had sold to them.

In 1980, the Russians approached Toshiba Machine Co. again. This time its managers changed their minds. Between 1982 and 1983, Toshiba sold eight advanced milling machines worth four billion yen to the Soviets. The firm held clandestine demonstrations for the Russian buyers, exported the machines with fraudulent labels of simpler models to fool export inspectors, and altered normal accounting procedures to spread Russian payments over several quarters and disguise the sizeable income.

In 1987, a whistle-blowing employee made Toshiba's actions known to the Japanese government and a scandal ensued. The president and chairman of parent Toshiba Corp. soon resigned in shame. Americans were furious, since the sale made it harder for U.S. Navy electronic gear to detect Russian subs. Several bills were introduced in Congress. One of them would have banned the sale of all Toshiba products in this country for five years—a loss of roughly $10 billion in revenues.

Toshiba mounted a huge lobbying campaign, hiring four American lobbying firms at a cost estimated as high as $9 million. Lobbyists for these firms included Leonard Garment, former White House aide to Richard Nixon, and James R. Jones, a former Democratic representative from Oklahoma. Toshiba executives lobbied members of Congress, as did Japanese government officials and diplomats. One theme of the lobbying campaign was that banning

Toshiba products would cost 100,000 U.S. jobs. Toshiba also recruited American companies that used its products, including AT&T, General Electric, and IBM, to pressure Congress. These companies argued that Toshiba semiconductors were vital to the defense effort. At the time there was a worldwide shortage of megabyte DRAMs and Toshiba was a leading producer.

The lobbying campaign was effective. In the end, a watered-down sanctions bill was passed banning only U.S. government purchases of Toshiba products for three years after December 1988. Its provisions are riddled with exemptions and loopholes. The stiffest provision bans sales of Toshiba household electronics goods on U.S. military bases. But they will still be available in stores, and private firms can purchase from Toshiba.

The Toshiba lobbying campaign illustrates the new political power of foreign investors such as the Japanese. It also hints at the increasing complexity of influence networks in Washington, D.C. In this chapter we will explain how the political activity of corporations has changed recently to accommodate new realities of national politics.

BUSINESS AND THE AMERICAN POLITICAL SYSTEM

Throughout American history, business has sought and exercised political power in a government that is extraordinarily open to influence. This power, whether used for good or ill, is exercised on constitutional terrain created by the Founding Fathers 200 years ago. The Constitution, as elaborated by judicial interpretation over the years, establishes the structure of government and broad rules of political activity. Its formal provisions, in turn, predispose a certain pragmatic, freewheeling political culture that is manifest in day-to-day political life.

The First Amendment protects the right of business to organize and press its agenda on government. There, in elegantly archaic language, is stated the right "to petition the government for redress of grievances." The First Amendment also protects rights of free speech, freedom of the press, and freedom of assembly—all critical in applying political pressure to government. Without these guarantees, the letter-writing campaigns, speeches, newspaper editorials, and advocacy advertisements that business orchestrates to influence government might be threatened. Imagine how undesirably different our system would be if the public, excited by "windfall profits" in some industry, pressured Congress to restrict the lobbying rights of those companies to press for tax breaks.

The corporate right to free political expression was challenged in a case where the First National Bank of Boston conducted a political advertising campaign in opposition to a graduated personal income tax proposed in a state referendum. The Massachusetts attorney general, Francis X. Bellotti, challenged the legitimacy of the bank's expenditure, arguing that the tax matter did not materially affect the bank's welfare and was a wasteful use of the equity of bank shareholders, who might disagree with the bank's position. In addition, Massachusetts had a law prohibiting corporate spending to influence such referendum campaigns. The Supreme Court, in *First National Bank of Boston v. Bellotti* (1978), upheld the bank's right to make a political statement and affirmed that business has the right, protected by the First Amendment, to be politically outspoken on issues only indirectly affecting corporate operations.[1] This decision has sanctioned growing corporate political activism in recent years.

The Constitution also creates a specific, formal structure of government, a structure that reflects the Founders' fears of concentrated power. It sets up a federal system in which important powers are given to both the states and the federal government. State governments, in turn, share some of their powers, such as the power of taxation, with cities. In an effort to further diffuse power, the Constitution establishes a system of separation of powers, whereby the three branches of the federal government—the legislative, executive, and judicial—each have checks and balances over each other. The states mimic these power-sharing arrangements in their governments.

This system is open. It has many points of access, and it invites business and other special interests to attempt influence. Because no single, central authority exists, significant government action requires widespread cooperation among levels and branches of government that share power. The system also is particularly vulnerable to blockage and delay. Because actions of significance require the combined authority of several elements in the political arena, special interests can block action by getting a favorable hearing at only one juncture. To get action, on the other hand, an interest like business must successfully pressure many actors in the political equation. Thus there has developed a practical political culture in the American system in which interests are willing to bargain, compromise, and form temporary alliances to achieve their goals rather than stand firm on rigid, ideological positions.

Though not ordained in the Constitution, the preeminence of business interests in the political pressure equation has been an enduring fact of life in American government. The Founders who drafted the Constitution were an economic elite. John Jay and Robert Morris, for example, were among the wealthiest men in the colonies, and it should come as no surprise that the government arrangements they fabricated are conductive to influence by economic interests. Although the long shadow of business influence often is called oppressive, there is a germ of fairness in business' frequent dominion over government. As Gerald Keim has noted, "the employees, shareholders, and their spouses of the 1,000 largest corporations in the U.S. number over 50 million people."[2] Numbers like this make the corporate community more than a narrow and privileged population segment seeking selfish gain.

[1]438 U.S. 907.
[2]Gerald D. Keim, "New Directions for Corporate Political Strategy," *Sloan Management Review*, Spring 1984, p. 53.

THE POLITICAL ARENA OF YESTERYEAR

Historically, business interests were accorded a warm reception in the halls of government. Business has had credibility in government because it was perceived as pleading for and against measures to help or hurt the economy. Unlike some European countries, there was no socialist opposition to dilute the legitimacy of capitalism or challenge the laissez-faire tradition. In years past, a widely used tactic was the application of behind-the-scenes pressure by business leaders or their agents on key officials and political kingpins. Sometimes, of course, business manipulated government corruptly, with gifts and favors. Under these advantageous conditions most corporations lobbied through trade associations, made campaign contributions, and occasionally contacted government officials for favors. This style of political activism worked through the 1950s, the era when Dwight D. Eisenhower was a pro-business President with an administration dominated by political appointees from business, when public opinion polls still showed high support for business, when a pro-business conservative coalition of Southern Democrats and Republicans in Congress ensured legislative support, and when government regulation was a fraction of what it is now. Soon, however, changing political winds forced business into more aggressive and sophisticated forms of political intervention.

During the 1960s and 1970s, national politics were dominated by a liberal reform agenda. The public demanded that business be bridled with massive new regulatory programs and that government itself be made more openly democratic and responsive. Many factors converged during this period to encourage more corporate political activity.[3] Growing regulation was one. Executives felt that, for the first time, control over day-to-day operations was slipping away to government regulators. The Equal Employment Opportunity Commission dictated who could be hired. The Occupational Safety and Health Administration intervened directly in factories. The Environmental Protection Agency required expensive alchemy. Other new agencies bit into corporate decision making elsewhere.

Two other changes in the corporate political environment were also important: first, antagonistic public interest groups had mobilized, and second, changes in the political system diffused power in a Congress that was becoming increasingly independent of presidential power.

THE RISE OF PUBLIC INTEREST GROUPS

During the 1960s, the climate of pressure politics changed with the rise of new groups set up to pursue ideological causes, single interests, and the

---

[3]The political dynamics of this period are analyzed at length by David Vogel in *Fluctuating Fortunes: The Political Power of Business in America*, New York: Basic Books, 1989. Vogel indicates that the period of business vulnerability to legislative reverses was between 1966 to 1977, and argues that the following changes in the political environment put corporations on the defensive: (1) public perception that economic prosperity would continue and business could afford more social investment, (2) a downturn in support for business in opinion polls, (3) the rise of public interest groups, and (4) the growth of a "new class" of educated, middle-class professionals who favored more regulation of business. See Chapters 3–6.

"public interest." These groups purported to speak for consumers, taxpayers, and previously underrepresented citizen interests. One scholar at the time defined a public interest group as "one that seeks a collective good, the achievement of which will not selectively and materially benefit the membership or activists of the organization."[4] Thomas Sowell, a leading conservative intellectual, offers a more cynical definition, calling them simply "politically organized liberals."[5] In fact, most public-interest/environmental/ reform groups appeal to a liberal constituency; many oppose business, labor, and government agencies. In the late 1970s, a study of lobbyists from eighty-three such groups showed that 74 percent placed themselves from liberal to radical on the political spectrum, and only 10 percent called themselves conservative.[6] A similar survey of Common Cause members found that a huge majority, 89 percent, felt that "big business has too much influence on how the country is run."[7]

Citizen lobbies enjoy certain advantages. Many are associated with dramatic, emotional, or popular issues and have easy access to the mass media. Another source of strength is general public sympathy for reform causes, which permits these groups to identify with the lofty ideal of the public interest in opposition to the so-called special interests of business and labor. Although one of six jobs in the economy is related to the auto industry, and the oil companies have more than 14 million stockholders, both industries are regarded as special interests when compared with public interest lobbies—no matter how small the membership or interest in the latter might be.

Some of these groups, however, are large-membership groups with considerable resources. Two of biggest and best known are Common Cause and Ralph Nader's Public Citizen, Inc. with 280,000 and 50,000 dues-paying members respectively. The Consumer Federation of America is an umbrella organization for more than 200 consumer groups. The environmental lobby is also a formidable force in Washington, led by groups such as the Sierra Club, the National Wildlife Federation, and the National Audubon Society, which have several hundred thousand members.

Hundreds of other groups exist that affect the fortunes of business. A wide array of single-interest groups, such as the National Council of Senior Citizens, Zero Population Growth, the Fund for Animals, the National Organization for Women, and the National Abortion Rights Action League, are a few examples. These groups are generally small in comparison to industry groups, but any one of them may be a formidable adversary if business activity touches on the narrow public policy domain which is its focus.

From the inception of the public interest movement in the mid-1960s until about 1977, the political atmosphere was congenial to the citizen's groups' agenda of corporate reform. But by the end of the 1970s, the public increasingly saw regulation as inefficient, costly to consumers, and partly responsi-

---

[4]In *Lobbying for the People*, Princeton: Princeton University Press, 1977, p. 7.
[5]Quoted by Peter Brimelow in "A Man Alone," *Forbes*, August 24, 1987, p. 44.
[6]Berry, *op. cit.*, p. 94.
[7]In Ann Cooper, "Middleman Mail," *National Journal*, September 14, 1985, p. 2062.

ble for the inability of American firms to compete with foreign firms. Public interest groups found their popular mandate to push sweeping reforms weakened, but they did not fade away. They remain as an institutionalized counterpoint to business. The Consumer Federation of America, for example, dropped its legislative drive for a mighty Consumer Protection Agency and narrowed its focus. Between 1987 and 1990, it pushed six new banking laws through Congress to benefit consumers by, for example, capping interest rates on adjustable rate mortgages and limiting holds on checks deposited by consumers in banks. These laws create modest new consumer rights, but they are not sweeping reforms.

The desire to enact broader reforms lives on, awaiting an era of renewed public agitation for control of business power. Recently a Ralph Nader lieutenant said this:

> I don't know of anyone who's changed *less* in a quarter of a century than Ralph. He has a belief system he sees the world through, and it's largely the same. Is monopoly more efficient now than it was twenty-five years ago? Is politics less corrupt? Is there a case to be made *for* pollution?[8]

DIFFUSION OF POWER IN GOVERNMENT

A second change in the climate of politics, in addition to new groups, has been the diffusion and decentralization of power in Washington, D.C. This began with reforms in Congress.

Traditionally, both the House and Senate were run autocratically by a small number of party leaders and powerful committee chairs. Many of these chairs were Democrats from southern states, who had great longevity in Congress due to the vagaries of southern party politics. The stubborn resistance of these deeply entrenched southerners in Congress to popular, overdue civil rights legislation led to public dissatisfaction with the seniority system. The system was dismantled in the early 1970s by an uprising of junior members of Congress, who passed a series of procedural reforms stripping committee chairs of traditional prerogatives such as automatic reappointment and the right to assign subcommittee chairmanships. This revolution, largely complete by 1974, democratized Congress by taking power from a few hands and giving a measure of it to many. After 1974, subcommittees could hold hearings on any subject that they wished, developed large staffs, and often became small fiefdoms of independent action.

At the same time, changes outside Congress further undermined the influence of party leaders. One change was the rise of political action committees (PACs) formed by interest groups and corporations to contribute campaign money. Previously, Senate and House members who were loyal to the party hierarchy could count on substantial campaign contributions from the

---

[8]Mark Green, quoted in Thomas A. Stewart, ''The Resurrection of Ralph Nader,'' *Fortune*, May 22, 1989, p. 116. For more on public interest lobbies see Kelley Griffin, *Ralph Nader Presents More Action for a Change*, New York: Dembner Books, 1987, and Michael Pertschuk, *Giant Killers*, New York: W. W. Norton, 1986.

Republican and Democratic parties. Under this regime, party affiliation was the single most accurate predictor of congressional roll call voting. After 1974, however, special interest PACs began contributing such large amounts of money that legislators developed greater loyalty to them than to their parties. And why not? In 1982, for instance, oil company PACs alone gave more to Democratic congressmen than did the Democratic National Committee.[9]

A second factor eroding party authority is television, which has to some extent replaced the parties as the middleman between the public and their representatives. Telegenic politicians attract national audiences by speaking on emotional issues. Both houses of Congress have video production crews and editing facilities. Members can produce daily video spots about their activities and send them through uplinks on Capitol Hill to satellites and thence to TV stations in their home districts throughout America. They are designed to fit into evening news programs and TV stations may run them intact. Television has had other impacts. For example, the cost of TV spots has led to skyrocketing campaign costs, which have, in turn, increased the reliance of House and Senate members on PAC money.[10]

Several other trends have also diminished party power. Both Senate and House members use the franking privilege to send out computerized mailings independently of party endorsement. They have much larger staffs than in previous years to service constituents and make friends with voters. In the electorate at large there has been a decline of party voting. Many voters today identify only weakly with the parties. They increasingly split their ballots and use decision cues other than party labels. Another blow to the party system came when Congress became increasingly assertive against the presidency following Watergate. The president, who is titular leader of his party, is now less able to command members of that party in Congress. One sign of Congress' new autonomy was the creation of a Congressional Budget Office in 1974 to evaluate economic data independently of the executive branch and to avoid reliance on figures produced by the president's economic advisors.

The significance of these centrifugal forces is that centralized authority in the federal government has declined. When the old seniority system was intact, rank and file members of Congress generally got ahead by quietly kowtowing to the few leaders who could assign or withhold favors and party support. If business interest could influence this small handful of House and Senate powerbrokers, they had no meaningful opposition. But with the demise of the seniority system, business lobbyists had to contact nearly every member of a committee or subcommittee to get support for a measure, rather than just the chair. No longer could party leaders exercise as much control over floor votes.

Government today, in addition to being more decentralized, is increasingly complex. One root cause is the expansion of regulation. New regula-

---

[9]Gregg Easterbrook, "What's Wrong with Congress?" *The Atlantic Monthly*, December 1984.

[10]Between 1974 and 1986, the average cost of a campaign by an incumbent in the House rose from $56,539 to $334,222. In the Senate the rise was from $555,714 to $3,303,518. Hedrick Smith, *The Power Game*, New York: Ballantine Books, 1988, p. 155.

tory agencies, each with authority over discrete areas of business activity, further fragment government power even as it swells. Another cause is the presence of more interest groups in Washington, D.C., than ever before. These groups mobilized as government became more active and intrusive, effecting the fortunes of new segments of society. Many have a narrow policy focus. The expansion of group activity has begotten a vast, extragovernmental lobbying industry composed of law, public relations, and government relations firms plus consultants on every aspect of the influence process such as grass roots campaigning and computerized mailing. The interaction between this lobbying industry and official government is timeless, but more byzantine and inscrutable today.

CURRENT TRENDS IN THE BUSINESS-GOVERNMENT POLITICAL EQUATION

In the early 1990s, an assessment of the political activity of business would stress four basic points.

First, corporations are much more active in politics today than in past eras. They speak out on more issues because more government activities have an impact. Top executives are more knowledgeable about politics and lobby actively. Many large corporations have political outposts and staffs in Washington, D.C. Small businesses are more active also.

Second, the political activities of business are sophisticated. Corporations are adopting coordinated strategies for political contributions, establishing elaborate programs to analyze issues, using computerized mailings to mobilize public support, training managers to watch political trends, and hiring influential Washington insiders to work on a parallel course with company lobbyists. Business today is by a large margin the most complex interest sector in Washington politics.

Third, business today is opposed by a formidable proliferation of citizens' groups and other interest groups that promote a single idea or narrow cause. Many have an anti-business bias. They are well organized opponents, capable of using their own sophisticated and tenacious influence techniques. These groups have replaced organized labor as the primary adversaries of economic interests.

And fourth, despite occasional setbacks, business is consistently effective in its pressure tactics. In part this is because no other sector can match its resources and organization. Even combined, the constellation of groups representing labor, consumers, civil rights, the environment, and various public-interest or single-issue groups cannot match the financial and organizational resources of the business community. Of course, victory is never assured. From 1984 to 1986, when the Reagan administration sought to overhaul the tax code, corporations large and small lobbied energetically to preserve favored tax subsidies. But in the end corporate taxes were raised, and the battle for tax breaks was lost by many powerful industries. The reasons included a division in the business community over whether to support tax reform; support by a popular, conservative, Republican president for a new tax code; and strong public support for lower individual tax rates and higher corporate rates.

BUSINESS INTEREST ORGANIZATIONS

There are literally thousands of groups that represent business. What follows is a summary of this universe. We begin by briefly describing six well-known organizations that broadly represent business.

The Chamber of Commerce, founded in 1912, is today the largest business outpost in Washington, D.C. It represents a federation of 2,800 local and state chapters, 1,350 trade associations, and 180,000 companies. The primary work of the Chamber is to influence Congress on legislative issues of national impact. Because Chamber membership is so large and diverse, it cannot lobby strenuously on policy issues that divide opinion in the business community. Over time, it has been predictably antiregulation, antitax, and antilabor.

The National Association of Manufacturers is an older group, founded in 1895, and currently boasting a membership of 13,600 companies. The NAM was originally formed to promote foreign trade, but it gradually assumed the role of a counterweight to the rising influence of labor earlier in this century. In the early 1960s, the NAM was a low-key organization which held only two membership meetings and a dinner each year. But today it runs a state-of-the-art lobbying campaign with a staff of 208, including about forty registered lobbyists to carry its largely conservative message to Congress and federal agencies.

Both the Chamber and the NAM are composed mainly of small companies—85 percent of the Chamber's members are companies with fewer than 100 employees, and 75 percent of the NAM's members have fewer than 500. Although the boards of directors of both groups are dominated by executives of large companies, their memberships include many small and medium-sized firms. This fact makes them slow in reacting to political issues and sometimes unable to strongly support the positions taken by the largest corporations. Hence, several powerful organizations have developed to represent the views of the big-business elite.

The oldest of these is the Business Council, which was founded in 1933 when President Roosevelt asked to have organized a group of top-echelon business executives with whom New Deal administrators could exchange views about key economic issues. Originally, the council was attached in an advisory capacity to the Department of Commerce, but in 1962 it declared its independence from government (in part because of growing curiosity and suspicion about its quasi-governmental status). Today, the council continues to act as an advisory body that links big business and government. It expresses views in a low-key manner and does not lobby directly. The membership is limited to sixty-five chief executives of the largest corporations, and an effort is made to represent geographic regions and major industry groups. The members are organized into a small number of liaison committees that connect with different government departments. Here is where influence is exercised. Twice a year, the full membership meets, and periodic briefings are held so that members may hear and question high government officials.

A second group representing the interests of big business is the Committee for Economic Development. The CED is directed by 200 trustees, most of whom are corporate chief executive officers. The CED does not lobby government directly. Rather, subcommittees composed of trustees and assisted by staff develop written policy statements on important issues. These are published and may attract much attention.

The Business Roundtable is a group of 200 CEOs of the largest corporations in America. Unlike the Business Council and the CED, however, the Roundtable is not low-key; it is the lobbying arm of big business. The Roundtable includes CEOs of companies such as Exxon, General Motors, Mobil, General Electric, Texaco, Ford, IBM, Sears, Citibank, Bank of America, and Prudential. It takes action on a limited number of issues each year. Member CEOs divide into task forces on legislative issues; individuals selected as lead members of these task forces are expected to lobby personally for Roundtable goals. In recent years, a primary objective has been legislation restricting hostile takeovers.

The American Business Conference is a lobby group started in 1980 to represent medium-sized, high-growth firms. Its membership is limited to 100 CEOs of corporations that have grown 15 percent annually, averaged over the previous five years, and have revenues between $25 million and $1 billion. Member companies represent a wide spectrum of manufacturing and service activities and include, for instance, MCI Communications Corp., Arthur Andersen & Co., and Dunkin' Donuts, Inc. Most members, however, are in fast-expanding, high-technology industries that create new jobs and do not pollute heavily.

In addition to these six overarching organizations, more than 3,900 trade associations represent companies grouped by industry. Virtually every industry has its own association. To illustrate, there are the American Beekeeping Federation, the American Insurance Association, the American Paper Institute, the Association of Japanese Textile Importers, the Frozen Onion Rings Packers' Council, the Institute of Pharmaceutical Manufacturers, the American Federation of Retail Kosher Butchers, and the Peanut Butter Manufacturers' Association.

Trade associations lobby for the interests of the industries they represent, and some have formidable resources. The American Iron and Steel Institute, for example, has a membership of 2,600 companies and a budget of over $10 million a year. The National Association of Realtors has had the richest business-related political action committee (PAC) in recent elections, and other trade association PACs are among the largest because corporate PACs contribute to them as well as directly to candidates. Some trade associations capitalize on strengths peculiar to their industry. The Motion Picture Association of America capitalizes on the glamour of Hollywood with a private theater in Washington, D.C., in which invited Senators and Representatives view films prior to public release. The International Ice Cream Association throws a huge ice cream party in a courtyard of the Russell Senate Office Building each year. Hundreds of members of Congress and their staffs come for free ice cream cones; a rival lobbyist assesses the event this way: "For that one event, they get more good feeling on Capitol Hill than most groups that spend a lot more money do lobbying day to day."[11] Much trade association lobbying, however, is not fancy. The Fertilizer Institute, a group representing chemical and agricultural corporations, finds strength in directness. A staff member in the House describes their lobbyists this way.

> They pick out little issues, sink their goddamn teeth into them, and they are relentless. They sit in everybody's office until they talk to them, and bang the shit out of you until they get what they want...They're up there making their case day after day after day...They just wear out their shoe leather.[12]

Business organizations and trade associations gain strength when they are united, but there is frequent disunity. Continuous skirmishes occur, for example, between truckers and railroads, manufacturers and distributors, bankers and borrowers, and raw material producers and end-product manufacturers. The International Ice Cream Association has fought for years against federal price subsidies on milk, which are backed by the National Milk Federation. Large corporations have recently pushed legislation to make hostile takeovers more difficult, in opposition to Wall Street investment bankers protecting a lucrative industry.

LABOR UNIONS IN POLITICS

Labor unions are, of course, an important player in the political arena, and they frequently oppose business. A dominant motivation in pursuing corporate political action is to counterbalance what is perceived to be a politically powerful labor union movement. For years the strength of NAM, for instance, was in business' hatred for regulation and fear of union power. Many executives see in union political activity the capability to elect politicans favoring the labor point of view. They believe that union strength not only will result in legislation that curtails their managerial prerogatives and reduces their profits, but will undermine the very foundations of the traditional business system. In this light, business has supported those associations that help combat union political strength.

Labor unions have considerable political strength, but in recent years they have faced effective opposition from business, limited access to Republican presidents, givebacks at the bargaining table forced by intense international competition and deregulation, and a turn of the screw in management phi-

---

[11]Burt Solomon, "Measuring Clout," *National Journal*, July 4, 1987, p. 1706.
[12]Quoted in Solomon, *op. cit.*, p. 1708.

losophy favoring Japanese-style worker-management harmony. The ranks of labor are no longer expanding as fast as is the hourly work force. Late in the 1970s, labor suffered critical political setbacks when business forces defeated two priority issues—common site picketing in 1977 and revision of laws protecting union organizing in 1978. Members of Congress, long in awe of labor power, learned that they could defy the AFL-CIO and survive politically. By the late 1980s, however, labor had won a number of important legislative victories, including a law banning most polygraph testing of workers and a law mandating sixty days' notice of plant closings. Unions remain influential, even if they lack the strength of bygone days when the unionized work force was larger. One critical factor in their continued influence is PAC spending. Led by the International Brotherhood of Teamsters PAC, a half-dozen union PACs are among the largest givers to federal candidates.

THE GOVERNMENT RELATIONS PROCESS

There are two basic areas of business involvement in politics. The first is government relations, or lobbying, in which business influences the formulation, implementation, enforcement, and adjudication of policy by contacting government officials. The second is the electoral process, in which business contributes to political campaigns at all levels of government. Naturally, these areas are interrelated.

LOBBYING BY BUSINESS

A lobby may be broadly defined as the point of access of a corporation, trade association, or other interest group to a part of government. A lobbyist is the individual who represents an interest. This is a mildly pejorative term, because although lobbying is more open today than in the past, it is still sometimes seen in a negative light. Therefore lobbyists may refer to themselves as legislative advocates, government or public relations consultants, or lawyers.

There are more lobbyists today than ever before. There were 5,500 lobbyists in Washington in 1989, registered under the Federal Regulation of Lobbying Act of 1946, twice as many as in the mid-1970s. Many lobbyists do not register, however, because of a loophole in that act, and estimates place the real number of lobbyists in Washington at closer to 25,000.

Most lobbying at the federal level, including business lobbying, is done in the legislative and executive branches. Many bills passed by Congress, such as tax, trade, and appropriations laws, have a direct impact on earnings. Legislation today is complex; some bills are hundreds of pages long. The change of a few words or the insertion of a special exception for a company can be worth millions of dollars. For example, lobbyists for Warner-Lambert Co. got a special insert in a 1988 trade bill extending patent protection for three and a half years on a cholesterol-reducing drug. This extension prevents competition by foreign firms and is worth an estimated $100 million to the company. Administrative agencies in the executive branch also draw lobbyists seeking to influence the application of regulations. The Supreme Court is less a target of influence because judges insulate themselves from special interests.

Although business lobbyists have been condemned for pleading selfish interests, overriding a legitimate "public interest," and engaging in corrupt practices, the predominant viewpoint among students of American politics is that lobbyists are basically honest and perform valuable functions. Specifically, lobbyists provide legislators with useful technical information about bills and also give them politically relevant information about how constituents and affected interests feel about policy. These functions are extremely valuable to busy legislators who do not always have staffs to make such investigations themselves. Every industry has special quirks and problems, of which industry lobbyists have special knowledge. Says former Representative Bob S. Bergland:

> Lobbyists perform a useful function. For example, I served on two committees of the House, but there were dozens of bills on the floor from committees [of] which I was not a member. I oftentimes would not know how they would affect my district. I would call lobbyists and ask them. If they level with you it's terribly important.[13]

It is possible, naturally, for a lobbyist to mislead an elected official or committee staff members with biased information. But this is counterproductive in the Washington game because the lobbyist who lacks integrity loses access to the very people he or she earns a living from influencing. Congressmen shut out lobbyists who mislead them. Effective lobbyists are prepared to present and discuss opposition views.

HOW BUSINESS LOBBIES GOVERNMENT

Business uses many lobbying techniques. A time-tested technique is talk and discussion with an important government contact. Lobbyists telephone, visit, and dine with people who can help. They also attend committee meetings in the House and Senate. In some cases they stand in the hall outside and confer with members who come out of the meeting. These hallways are sometimes called "Gucci Gulch," in reference to the footwear popular among lobbyists. Lobbyists also sit in committee rooms, and it is common practice for them to catch a representative's eye and give a thumbs up or thumbs down signal as various provisions come to a vote.

Direct contact with legislators, however critical, occupies only a minor portion of the typical corporate lobbyist's day. They are too busy to be available often or for long meetings. So about 90 percent of contact time with government officials is spent with committee staff members on Capitol Hill, staff in

---

[13]Myron Struck, "Deaver Probe Revives Doubts about 'Revolving Door' Ethics," *Insight,* June 9, 1986, p. 17.

administrative agencies, or in preparing technical documents. Lobbyists attend parties on the Washington social circuit, including fundraisers. They also like to serve on steering committees for political campaigns for the obvious advantage it gives them in working with the elected official later on. Corporations and trade associations also sponsor charity events, seminars, and speaking engagements for members of Congress. For example, each year corporations sponsor the Senators' Ski Cup, a four-day skiing weekend in Park City, Utah. In 1988, thirty corporations, including American Express, Delta Airlines, and Mountain Bell, bought $3,000 to $10,000 tickets for government relations specialists to attend and mingle with senators at receptions, meals, and on the slopes. Through this corporate sponsorship, the expenses of ten senators and their families were paid and $120,000 was raised for the Primary Children's Medical Center.[14]

About 700 firms now have offices in Washington, compared with less than 200 in the late 1960s. These Washington offices, housing corporate government relations staffs, are set up mainly by big companies. Although a few smaller firms have them, they are expensive, and small businesses tend to rely on trade associations, hired lawyers, or public relations consultants. One of the most sophisticated Washington offices is that of General Electric, which has a staff of 120. It is divided into separate organizational units specializing in lobbying efforts for aircraft engines, aerospace radar, electronics, flight simulators and weapons systems, nuclear power plants, the Export-Import Bank, and the regulation of CAT scanners. There is also a separate unit that lobbies on company-wide issues, such as taxes, labor law, and environmental regulation. In the latter unit, one lobbyist specializes in contacting Republicans; another works on Democrats. A third person coordinates GE's activities with other business groups.

Many corporations employ their own lobbyists. If they don't, and increasingly even if they do, they may hire Washington public relations, consulting, law, and lobbying firms to press their cases. The most prominent of these firms employ former administrative officials, former legislators, and knowledgeable insiders of both political parties to offer a potent mix of access, influence, and advice. An example is Black, Manafort, Stone & Kelly, which represents Bethlehem Steel, Johnson & Johnson, the Air Transport Association, and Donald Trump, among others. Among other services, it develops strategy for congressional campaigns, runs the campaigns, and then lobbies the elected officials for its business clients after the election. In 1988, one of the firm's partners ran the Republican nominating convention in New Orleans, and two others served as top strategists in the Bush campaign. Subsequently, the firm lobbied the Bush administration on behalf of a broad range of clients. The type of insider influence bought in this way often is very effective. For example, shortly after his election, President Bush extended import restrictions on foreign steel, a step sought by Bethlehem Steel, a Black, Manafort, Stone & Kelly client.

---

[14]This is one of a number of such annual charity events. See Viveca Novak, "Sweet Charity," *Common Cause,* January/February 1989.

This has raised ethical questions.[15] But the firm's partners reject insinuations of conflict of interest, saying that two separate organizational elements within the firm handle electioneering and lobbying. Most corporations simply cannot duplicate this kind of influence network in a Washington office, and so many retain a prestigious "hired gun."

Corporations also increasingly use the services of lobbying firms to mastermind an array of political techniques, many of them highly specialized and technically sophisticated. There is growing reliance on these techniques to conduct what are called grass-roots campaigns, or efforts to influence public opinion in such a way that people pressure government officials for action. A "full-service" public relations firm develops media kits full of information about a company or issue and sends them to newspapers and television stations around the country. These kits may contain articles that small-town newspaper editors can turn into editorials. The firm may maintain a list of reporters who specialize in covering the industry, may write op-ed page pieces for top company executives to send to newspapers, and may develop advocacy advertisements or TV commercials. The firm may conduct public-opinion polls and send out letters to the constituents of elected officials that encourage them to write to Congress in favor of or against pending legislation of interest to the corporate client.

Mass mail and Mailgram campaigns are frequently generated by influence seekers in Washington, although their effectiveness in influencing officials is not proven. Yet when a House or Senate member receives half a million identical postcards, it is an indication that people support a position. Such mass mail can be generated in a variety of ways, including calls from phone banks, mailings with preprinted cards to send to the elected official, or newspaper ads suggesting that people write. Firms such as Matt Reese and Associates use computerized polling and census data to pinpoint people in specific neighborhoods who, because of their education, income, and opinions, belong to one of forty "lifestyle clusters" that make them likely supporters of a business cause.

All such grass-roots campaigns are designed to show an elected official that voters hold an opinion in an industry's favor. Corporations rely increasingly on them in conjunction with less visible insider efforts. For example, the American Bankers Association (ABA) asks senators and representatives which bankers they respect in their districts. When particular bills are contested, the ABA then informs these key bankers of its position and encourages them to transmit their views. At present, the ABA has 1,200 "contact" bankers. The Chamber of Commerce uses a computer in its Washington headquarters to locate and mail information to business managers around the country and encourage them to contact their representatives. Through its various publications and "action calls," the Chamber may ultimately reach

---

[15]See, for example, Thomas B. Edsall, "In Position to Play," *Washington Post National Weekly Edition*, August 21–27, 1989; Jill Abramson, "Despite Role in HUD Scandal, Lobbying Firm of Black Manafort Rides High with Its Clients," *Wall Street Journal*, August 4, 1989; Anna Cifelli Isgro, "Pricey Lobbyists Who Do It All," *Fortune*, July 20, 1987. See also "Law Firms Vie for 'Influence Industry' Clout by Cultivating Ties to Presidential Candidates," *Wall Street Journal*, August 31, 1988, and John W. Moore, "A Law Firm's Path to High Visibility," *National Journal*, June 17, 1989, about the firm Sidley & Austin.

up to 7 million business sympathizers, who have been known to besiege Congress with cards, letters, telegrams, and phone calls.

Forming coalitions is another tactic that business groups sometimes use to increase their strength. Members of Congress are unlikely to support the demands of one pressure group if it means alienating several others. Forming a united front enhances lobbying power. When the semiconductor industry, a relatively small industry, sought government protection from unfair trade practices by Japanese competitors, it was rebuffed by politicians because big buyers of semiconductor chips such as IBM feared higher prices and opposed it. But when the Semiconductor Industry Association created a coalition of companies and trade associations representing both manufacturers and buyers of chips to lobby for action against the Japanese, it got helpful legislation and trade action in the executive branch.[16]

POLITICAL ISSUES MANAGEMENT

Companies with high political exposure frequently employ a government relations staff to scan the political environment and report on developments. This function may be housed in the public affairs or public relations departments, or it may be separate. Wherever located, the staff typically sets up a program to manage political issues that has the following steps.

• Monitor the environment. Staff members listen to the media, cultivate professional, corporate, and trade-association contacts, and watch government. They look for information about issues of current consequence and for emerging issues that will be important to the company in three to five years. Congressional staff members frequently push along new issues to get attention as do challengers for political office, and these sources can be closely monitored.

• Develop a portfolio of issues. A company typically locates fifty to 100 issues of importance and may follow them as they develop. There should be a separate file for each. Issues may be organized around company functions, such as personnel, finance, marketing, and international operations, or may be classified along various product lines. There may be a division among federal, state, and local issues.

• Analyze issues and select a small number of critical ones. There are a smaller number of major issues that the company should try to manage in its favor. These issues should be extensively analyzed by the government-relations staff or a committee. Monsanto, for example, has an Issue Identification Committee, which selects a dozen issues for closer attention out of over 100 suggested by staff.[17] These issues are then given more careful written analysis and sent to a second committee of top executives, which further narrows the list to the five most critical issues.

---

[16]The story of the political strategy of the semiconductor industry is told in detail by David B. Yoffie in "How an Industry Builds Political Advantage," *Harvard Business Review*, May–June 1988.

[17]Joseph T. Nolan, "Political Surfing When Issues Break," *Harvard Business Review*, January–February 1985.

- Take action. Once firms have identified major issues, they should take concrete action to manage them. At Monsanto, the top executives' committee assigns each of the five critical issues to one of its members, who must develop an action plan for dealing with it, complete with periodic goals and progress reporting. Action may be taken through trade associations, hired lobbyists, or company personnel.

Thus far, we have discussed only the government-relations aspect of business political involvement. However, another significant area of involvement is that of campaign contributions. We turn now to that area.

THE CORPORATE ROLE IN ELECTORAL POLITICS

In the first presidential campaign, George Washington spent no money and little time getting elected. Since then, the length and cost of political campaigns for federal offices—president, vice president, senator, and representative—have soared. In 1988, total campaign expenditures were about $500 million. This is a large sum, but should be kept in perspective. It is less than the cost of a B-2 bomber, one-tenth the cost of an aircraft carrier, and less than the annual advertising budgets of large consumer product companies such as Coca Cola, Procter & Gamble, or Philip Morris.

Since the rise of political campaigns, corporations and business interests have given money in many ways. Throughout the nineteenth century, companies made direct contributions from their treasuries to candidates, a practice which reached its zenith in William McKinley's campaigns. The election of 1896 matched the pro-business, Republican McKinley against the radical populist William Jennings Bryan. Bryan, a great spellbinder on the stump, scared the eastern financial community by advocating the silver standard, a radical and unwelcome change in the currency system. Marcus Hanna, campaign manager for McKinley, capitalized on this fear. He systematically assessed 0.25 percent of the assets of each bank from the trembling financiers and raised about $3.5 million.[18] This doubled the amount raised in previous elections and was sufficient to elect McKinley. In 1900, Bryan opposed McKinley again, this time on a platform attacking trusts. So Hanna assessed giant trusts such as Standard Oil and U.S. Steel, based on their assets. A new record sum was raised, and McKinley won by an even larger margin. Hanna believed his system had elevated the ethics of campaign finance above the borderline bribery and petty extortion which had long characterized it, but progressive reformers sought to derail the business juggernaut. In 1907, they passed the Tillman Act to prohibit banks and corporations from making direct contributions to federal candidates, and this is still the law today.

The American political culture is based on democratic ideals. Huge campaign contributions by business strain popular belief in a rough equality among interest groups. The Tillman Act was the first of many efforts to pro-

---

[18]See Herbert Croly, *Marcus Alonzo Hanna: His Life and Work,* New York: MacMillan, 1912, p. 220. A grateful McKinley engineered the appointment of Hanna to the U.S. Senate.

tect the electoral system from lopsided contributions by business interests. But money, and especially corporate money, plays an essential role in funding elections. Money is a resource that may be converted to power. Candidates use it to reach and persuade the ultimate power-holders—the voters. Contributors use it to buy access, influence, and favors. Because money is elemental in electoral politics, new sources and methods of giving arise whenever federal laws limit unsuitable contribution methods.

The Tillman Act, a well-intended reform, was quickly and continuously circumvented. Companies found numerous indirect ways to funnel money into elections. These included giving salary bonuses to managers for use as campaign contributions, loaning money to candidates and then forgiving the loans, paying for expensive postage-stamp-size ads in political party booklets, loaning employees to campaigns, and providing free services such as air travel or rental cars. Also, since individual contributions were not limited by the Tillman Act, wealthy donors stepped in. In 1972, for instance, Richard Scaife, an heir to the Mellon family fortune, gave $990,000 to the Nixon campaign.

During the early 1970s, campaign reform again became a national issue, due to large and secretive cash contributions revealed in the Watergate scandals, and Congress passed the Federal Election Campaign Act (FECA) of 1971 (and five amending acts between 1974 and 1984). It was intended to curb the influence of wealthy contributors by placing ceilings on contributions, providing for more public disclosure of contributions, and creating the Federal Election Commission (FEC) to oversee enforcement.

The Federal Election Campaign Act, which is current law, attempts to limit contributions from wealthy contributors and special interests by restricting individuals to donations of $1,000 per election per candidate, $5,000 per year to PACs, $20,000 per year to national political party committees, and $25,000 per year total to all sources (Figure 11-1). Direct contributions from corporations remain illegal. The law is, of course, applicable only to federal elections. State and local laws vary widely and sometimes permit unlimited individual contributions and direct corporate contributions. Despite its promise, the Federal Election Campaign Act, as amended, has failed to control large corporate, special interest, and individual contributions as intended. Part of the reason is that the Federal Election Commission created to enforce the law is a moribund watchdog practicing generally weak enforcement.[19] But more fundamentally, corporations have discovered ways to circumvent the law, ranging from questionably legal to disingenuous to straightforward. Their

---

[19]The FEC is a six member commission composed of three Democrats and three Republicans. It has the power to issue advisory opinions on election law or to bring suit in federal courts seeking fines and corrective action in case of violations. In practice, the Commission divides 3-3 in votes on major loopholes that benefit one party or the other in campaigning. It has, for example, refused to take action restricting the raising and use of soft money (explained later in this chapter). Often, its enforcement actions focus on more minor matters. For example, in 1989 it fined the Citizen's Party, a political committee, $10,000 for failing to file four reports (*FEC* v. *Citizens Party*, 87-CU-1577). In another action, the wife of a New York congressional candidate was fined $100 for temporarily putting $10,000 of campaign receipts in her personal bank account (*FEC* v. *Committee to Elect Bennie O. Batts*, No. 87-5789 GLG).

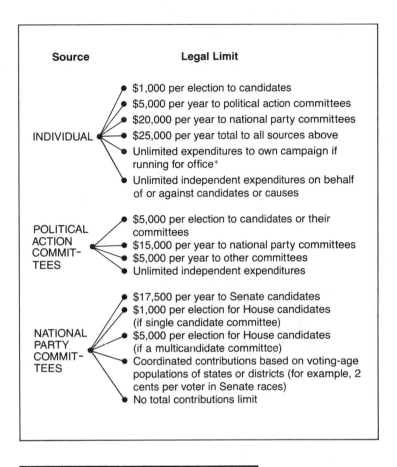

FIGURE 11-1   Federal campaign contribution and expenditure limits.

machinations parallel those that followed the reforms of the Tillman Act of 1907 and have been as effective. What follows is a discussion of some of the ways corporations now funnel money to politicians and government officials. Primarily this is done through PACs, but there are some other ways also.

POLITICAL ACTION COMMITTEES

When Congress limited individual contributions, it left open a loophole permitting organizations to establish political action committees (PACs), or committees composed of organization members who receive money from other members and contribute it to candidates. Corporations had never formed PACs, although union PACs were common. Corporate PACs were not explicitly permitted by the new election laws, but since individual contributions

TABLE 11-1   THE GROWTH OF CORPORATE PACS

	Actual number	Yearly increase (or decrease)	Percentage increase (or decrease)
1974	89	—	—
1975	139	50	56
1976	433	294	211
1977	550	117	27
1978	784	234	43
1979	948	164	20
1980	1,204	256	27
1981	1,327	123	10
1982	1,415	88	7
1983	1,536	121	9
1984	1,682	146	10
1985	1,687	5	0.3
1986	1,809	122	7
1987	1,906	97	6
1988	2,008	102	5
1989	1,796	(212)	(11)

Source: Federal Election Commission press releases, August 19, 1985, April 9, 1989, and January 17, 1990.

were limited by the FECA their advantages became evident. By 1974, eighty-nine companies had formed PACs, and in 1975, the FEC issued an advisory opinion allowing Sun Oil to establish a PAC to raise money for candidates through solicitation of management personnel. This ruling removed doubt about the legality of corporate PACs and, as Table 11-1 shows, more and more companies formed them.

HOW PACS WORK

To set up a PAC, a corporation must follow legal guidelines. The corporate PAC must, for example, divide those eligible for solicitation into two groups. Group I, or stockholders, executive employees, administrative employees, and their families, may be solicited as often as desired. Solicitations may be in person or through the mail and may even involve monthly payroll deductions. Many corporations suggest appropriate contribution levels based on a percentage of salary scales, usually about ¼ to 1 percent of annual salary. Group II, or hourly paid employees and their families, may be solicited only twice a year by a corporate PAC, and then only by mail to the home. Labor union PACs, conversely, may solicit their membership as frequently as desired and have the "twice a year" option to solicit management and stockholders by home mail.

A PAC may contribute $5,000 per election to candidates and their committees, $15,000 a year to national party committees, and $5,000 per year to other committees. (See Figure 11-1.) A geographically decentralized corporation may set up numerous PACs at division headquarters around the country, but their contributions may not put the corporation as a whole over these spending limits. PACs are not allowed to contribute to presidential general elections in which candidates receive public financing. However, there are no upper limits to total PAC contributions each year, and there is no limit to so-called independent expenditures that are undertaken on behalf of candidates without their request, cooperation, or knowledge. Thus, the PAC may buy TV or radio spots promoting a candidate so long as members of the candidate's campaign do not approve, coordinate, or request the help. Such unlimited independent expenditures are permitted by a 1976 Supreme Court decision, *Buckley v. Valeo*, which established that they are a form of free speech protected by the First Amendment.[20] Through independent expenditures, therefore, PACs may exceed the dollar limits for contributions to candidates.

Corporations may, and typically do, pay the administrative costs of PACs, but all money collected for contributions must be kept in a "separate segregated fund" to which the corporation cannot legally donate one cent (because of the prohibition since 1907 of direct corporate campaign contributions). The money collected by a PAC is disbursed to candidates based on decisions made by PAC officers, who are corporate employees.

PACs adopt various contribution strategies. Many contribute modest amounts to a large number of candidates who are incumbents or are likely to be elected so that the company can have access later on to a large number of elected officials. These PACs often play both sides by contributing to opposing candidates running for the same office. Other PACs make fewer and larger contributions that reward past political favors. A few PACs are more ideological and contribute to, say, conservative Republicans, thereby hoping to expand or reinforce that element in Congress. PACs frequently coordinate their contributions with company lobbyists. Acceptance of PAC contributions implies a willingness to support the PAC position. Some lobbyists contend that a donation merely entitles the PAC to access. Access, of course, is an important strength, since opposing interests which do not make PAC contributions may not have it. But taking PAC money can create a political debt. The etiquette of legislator-lobbyist relations requires that its collection be discreet. Former Senator Tom Eagleton (D-MS) explains.

> I've never had...a guy come into this office or over the phone say, "Tom, such-and-such vote's coming up next week. You remember I gave X in your last campaign, and I'm certainly expecting you to vote that way." I've never had anything that direct, blunt, or obscene. However, let's change the phraseology to this: "Tom, this is so-and-so. You know next week an important vote's coming up on such-and-such. I just want to remind you, Tom, I feel very strongly about that issue.

[20]424 U.S. 1. Recently, the Michigan Chamber of Commerce challenged state and federal laws prohibiting independent expenditures from corporate funds (instead of from segregated PAC funds). But in a 6-3 decision the Supreme Court held that restrictions on the use of corporate money in politics and any resulting diminution of First Amendment free speech rights were justified by the danger that corporate wealth flowing freely into elections would corrupt politicians. See *Austin* v. *Michigan Chamber of Commerce*, 58 LW 4371 (1990).

Okay, my friend, good to hear from you." Now, a senator receives "gentle" calls of that sort.[21]

Although Congress imposed the aforementioned limits on PAC contributions, two practices have developed that challenge the spirit of the law. The first is *bundling*. It is legal for any individual (even a non-employee) to contribute to a corporate PAC and to earmark the contribution, or stipulate which candidate is to receive it. The PAC then acts as a conduit for these earmarked funds, which do not count against its lawful contribution limits. Bundling is used to pass on a collection of checks "bundled" together and given to a politician. In 1985 ALIGNPAC, an insurance industry PAC, bundled checks worth $170,000 from industry executives and gave them to Sen. Bob Packwood (R-OR).[22] This was $165,000 more than ALIGNPAC's legal contribution limit for non-earmarked money. Packwood was chair of the Senate Finance Committee, which was considering tax changes on insurance matters.

A second development is *targeting*, which takes place when contributions by multiple PACs are coordinated. Targeting is practiced by groups of PACs in a specific industry, which focus their contributions on key legislators on committees that oversee industry matters. The Business-Industry Political Action Committee (BIPAC) coordinates giving by PACs in many different industries. BIPAC issues ratings of how legislators vote which are used by a network of pro-business PACs in making contributions. Bundling and targeting make senators and representatives increasingly dependent on single-interest groups with PACs for reelection.

At the end of 1988, there were 4,828 PACs, including 2,008 corporate PACs, 401 union PACs, and 848 trade association and other membership group PACs.[23] With the growth of PACs has come dramatic growth in spending. In 1974, PACs gave $12.5 million to congressional candidates: in 1984, $104 million, an 830 percent increase; and in 1988, $172.4 million, of which $56.3 million came from business PACs.

SOFT MONEY CONTRIBUTIONS

Another channel for business money entering politics is contributions to state and local political party committees. Such contributions are called "soft money," a phrase invented by the media. An amendment to the Federal

---

[21]Quoted in Smith, *op. cit.*, p. 255. For an extensive roundup of views of some former members of Congress on the subjects of giving and indebtedness, see Philip M. Stern, *The Best Congress Money Can Buy*, New York: Pantheon Books, 1988, Chapter 5. See also Brooks Jackson, *Honest Graft: Big Money and the American Political Process*, New York: Knopf, 1988.

[22]ALIGNPAC stands for Associated Life Insurance Group National Policyholders Advisory Committee.

[23]Federal Election Commission, "Distribution of PACs by Total Contributions," *FEC Record*, vol. 15, no. 8, August 1989, p. 7. For analysis of historical PAC spending patterns, see Theodore J. Eismeier and Philip H. Pollock III, *Business, Money, and the Rise of Corporate PACs in American Elections*, New York: Quorum Books, 1988.

Election Campaign Act in 1979 permitted unlimited expenditures by state and local parties on "party building" activities such as voter registration drives, compiling lists of voters, yard signs, bumper stickers, and literature. Shortly, the national political parties began to collect contributions from companies and large donors earmarked for state and local parties. All such contributions are unregulated by federal law because they are contributions to state and local parties and are regulated only by state and local laws. Therefore, federal contributions limits do not apply.

In 1988, 375 individuals gave donations of $100,000 or more as each of the national parties raised about $20 million in soft money. Corporations also contributed directly. For example, Atlantic Richfield Co., Occidental Petroleum Corp., Paine Webber Group Inc., PepsiCo Co., Revlon, and RJR Nabisco gave over $100,000 to the Republican National Committee.[24] Since these contributions were to state and local parties, they did not violate the Tillman Act. Soft money is used to make "hard money," or money raised under federal contribution limits, go further. In some activities it is also mixed with hard money, being allocated by formulas for activities that benefit federal and state and local candidates. If, for example, a brochure for congressional candidates also mentions state and local candidates, some soft money may be allocated for its printing. Naturally, parties have found innumerable ways to use soft money in place of hard money. The Federal Election Commission has not regulated soft money contributions because federal law does not require reporting them, but it has issued rules defining reasonable accounting methods when soft and hard dollars are mixed. Soft money has become a means by which unlimited individual contributions and direct corporate contributions can once more affect the fortunes of federal candidates, albeit indirectly.

HONORARIUMS

Companies, trade associations, and PACs can pay a fee, or honorarium, to members of Congress for brief speeches. Honorariums used to be paid by civic groups or colleges for lengthy speeches by political leaders. In recent years, though, honorariums have been used by lobbyists to channel money to legislators. A typical situation is one in which the member of Congress appears at a breakfast attended by executives and lobbyists from a corporation. The member is on a subcommittee considering a bill of importance to the corporation. During breakfast, the member speaks briefly, fields questions, and is paid $2,000. In April 1987, for example, the Oshkosh Truck Corp. put on such a breakfast for five members of the House Armed Services Committee. The members spoke on "the outlook for the defense budget" for five minutes and then listened to speakers from the company. Each was paid $2,000. Later that day, the Armed Service Committee voted funds to pur-

---

[24]Charles R. Babcock, "Some Hard Numbers on Soft Money," *Washington Post National Weekly Edition*, November 28–December 4, 1988, p. 15.

chase 4,737 Oshkosh ammunition transports. This was 3,849 more of the 10-ton vehicles than the U.S. Army had requested.[25] All told, members of the Armed Services Committees in both houses received honorariums of $520,000 from defense contractors in 1987.[26] And honorarium receipts totaling $10 million were disclosed by all House and Senate members in that year.[27]

Until Congress passed reform legislation, representatives could keep up to 30 percent of their salaries in honorariums ($25,885 in 1989) and senators could keep 40 percent ($34,992 in 1989). If they earned more than that sum, and many did, they could contribute the remainder to charities in their home district. Rep. Dick Cheney (R-WY), for instance, retained $25,350 in honorariums and gave away another $54,000 in donations to ninety-seven Wyoming charities in 1987. The top honorarium earner in the Senate in 1987, Bob Dole (R-KS), earned $106,500 and directed that much of the surplus be donated to his Dole Foundation, which distributed it to charities for the disabled.[28] In 1989, Congress changed the rules slightly. In the House, members were forbidden to accept honorariums as personal income. But to compensate for this financial loss, they voted a 33 percent pay increase giving them higher salaries by 1991 than they would have had if they made the maximum in honorariums under the old rules. And honorariums earned could still be donated to non-profit groups and charities in the home district. In the Senate, members voted a ten percent pay increase and reduced the limit on personal income from honorariums by a dollar amount equal to the pay raise.

Honorariums as payments for speeches are fictions; they are used by industry lobbyists to get support. Members of Congress defend these speeches and the meetings at which they take place as helpful in learning about industries their votes affect. But a candid industry lobbyist recently said: "If your committee is regulating an industry and you're getting your $30,000 in honoraria from that industry, it doesn't take a rocket scientist to figure out that there obviously is a connection between the giving of the money to that member and hoping that money will influence the member when he's considering your issues."[29]

MORE ROUTES FOR INDUSTRY MONEY TO ENTER POLITICS

There are additional methods for funneling industry money into politics. Corporations help finance the national nominating conventions of the par-

[25]Tim Carrington, "Oshkosh Truck Paid Lawmakers Prior to Vote," *Wall Street Journal*, June 13, 1988.

[26]Bill Whalen, "With a Salary Study Comes the Honorarium Furor Again," *Insight*, December 19, 1988, p. 21.

[27]Brooks Jackson, "U.S. Lawmakers' Take from Honorariums Hits $10 Million a Year," *Wall Street Journal*, November 1, 1988, p. 1.

[28]Viveca Novak, "Sweet Charity," *Common Cause Magazine*, January/February 1989, p. 21.

[29]Quoted anonymously in Whalen, *op. cit.*, p. 21.

ties. In 1988, for example, Atlantic Richfield donated $100,000 to the Republican convention to pay for chairs and lighting. General Motors loaned cars from local dealerships to VIPs at the conventions of both parties. FEC rulings have sanctioned such expenditures. Central among the transgressions of House rules that led to the resignation of Speaker Jim Wright (D-TX) in 1989 were ethically questionable payments and services from corporations. To circumvent the limit on honorarium income, trade associations and companies bought multiple copies of his autobiography, netting Wright royalties. He also accepted free rides on corporate jets when traveling back to his home district in Texas. Congressman Tony Coelho (D-CA) resigned in 1989 after accepting an insider tip and a loan on the purchase of junk bonds from Columbia Savings & Loan Association.

Some corporate giving is plainly illegal. Periodically, for instance, it comes to light that companies have given employees salary increases to turn into campaign contributions.[30] Joseph Hill, an executive of Unisys Corporation, over a period of years received money from the company with the understanding that it would be contributed to political candidates. In January 1989, Hill pleaded guilty in federal court to making contributions in the name of another. Recipients were required to return the money to Unisys.[31]

All these methods of inserting money into politics may be used in concert and add up to an unknown but large total. Corporations are spending money to change grass roots opinion, hire lobbyists, fund campaigns, finance legislators' favorite charities, support state and local political parties, pay honorariums to lawmakers, and contribute in myriad other ways. Washington, D.C., is awash in money spent to buy influence.

CONCLUSION: ASSESSING THE ROLE OF CORPORATE MONEY IN POLITICS

In America there is a historic public apprehension that business interests, through lobbying, electioneering, campaign contributions, and cronyism in Washington, will not only dominate but also corrupt the political system. Some corruption inevitably exists in the innumerable influential efforts of business, but the real issue is whether business power, legally exercised, is too great by some measure.

Critics argue that corporate money creates unwholesome obligations to special interest in Congress. PAC contributions, honorariums, and other money favors, they say, are blatant efforts to buy votes; they are investments from which donors expect a return. This is often correct. Sometimes, how-

[30]See, for example, Los Angeles Times, "Campaign Contributions, Falsified Expense Claims Disclosed by Unisys," August 7, 1988; Claudia Luther, "Video Entrepreneur Pleads Guilty to Campaign Donations Conspiracy," Los Angeles Times, August 3, 1988; and Byron Harris, "A PAC of Lies: The Commodore Savings Case," Wall Street Journal, June 18, 1989.

[31]Congressman Richard Ray and his committee, for example, had to return $1,000 received from Hill's personal bank account in May 1988. See FEC Advisory Opinion 1989–5, FEC Record, July 1989, p. 4.

ever, personal views, party positions, opposition lobbies, and constituent pressures also are powerful factors in voting decisions.

Critics argue that through the use of PACs, soft money contributions and other contribution methods, corporations are circumventing at least the spirit of election laws. The situation today, however, is typical of past eras. If PACs and other conduits were not channeling corporate money into the system, history teaches that it would enter from another direction. Political money is like water in a stream; dammed up in one place, it flows around and over in another. The problem faced by reformers is that the Supreme Court has equated free speech, guaranteed by the Constitution, with spending money to support candidates and political views. Reformers must find a way to restrict corporate expenditure without restricting the expression of ideas and political support—a tough task.[32]

It has been argued that business lobbying manifests an unfair imbalance between monied special interests and other legitimate interests. Important interests, such as those of poor people, small farmers, and minorities, are underrepresented in the policy process as a result. We note that this imbalance has existed throughout American history and is not attributable to specific abuses such as PAC bundling so much as to the general responsiveness of the system to pressure reinforced by money. If public financing reforms were enacted tomorrow, the system would inevitably remain attuned primarily to the needs of special-interest lobbyists.

In sum, it may be said that money flowing through the political system poses problems, but these are generic problems that also existed in past individual and corporate contribution patterns. The eroded campaign finance reforms of the 1970s have given advantages to special interests, but overall the present contribution system may be cleaner and more open than in the past because of new disclosure requirements. When electoral and lobbying laws are changed by new reforms and PACs or honorariums or soft money are banned, new incarnations of worrisome special-interest giving will probably float out of the wings and onto political center stage.

The challenge for American society is to balance the free exercise of political freedoms granted to corporations in the First Amendment against the compelling social interest in maintaining an open marketplace of political ideas free from unwarranted tyranny by monied interests. So far, our society has been successful in maintaining a rough balance. When, in the past, business power has appeared to be excessive and inadequately counterbalanced, an aroused public has called for reform. If, in the future, corporate political influence should appear to be inadequately checked, it is likely that the wheel of reform will turn again.

---

[32]For a discussion of basic reforms see the *Congressional Digest*, "Election Campaign Financing," August-September 1988. In June 1989, President Bush submitted a proposal for campaign finance reform to Congress which would ban business, labor, and trade association PACs (see Christopher Madison, "Ethics As Usual?" *National Journal*, July 8, 1989). Common Cause has a detailed agenda for reform set forth in its booklet *The Common Cause Agenda*, Washington, D.C., October 28, 1988.

PANPAC and the Senate Candidate

Jonathan Conrad, Republican candidate for the United States Senate, paced nervously back and forth in his dimly lit, downstairs study. His campaign for high office in a southern state would draw to a close in less than two weeks with the general election, but the most difficult decision of the campaign, indeed of his career, loomed before him. Now, with the house nearly darkened, his wife and two children in bed, Conrad discovered that the repose and detached reflection he had promised himself were not forthcoming.

Conrad, a native son and prominent big-city banker in his state, had been a reluctant candidate. Although he had served on the city council in his home town for four years, been elected to the State Assembly for a term, and spent an additional year as chairman of the state's Republican Central Committee, his reputation as a fair and reliable politician stemmed partly from lack of ambition for higher office. He earned a yearly salary of $120,000 as president of Midland City Bank. This was supplemented by income from several businesses in town that he owned and by the earnings of bank shares in his name. He led a gentleman's life and valued the time he was able to spend away from politics with his family.

Several years ago, however, state leaders became concerned about the growing influence of Alvin "Big Toe" Weaver. Weaver had captured the sentimental attachment of the voters in a race for a seat in the House of Representatives by touring his district in shoes with holes in the front to dramatize the plight of poor sharecroppers who would be displaced from their land by construction of a dam. Weaver, a Democrat, had so skillfully exploited this issue in speeches filled with purple oratory that he was elected by a margin of almost two to one.

The landslide fed Weaver's ambition, and during three terms in the House of Representatives he curried the favor of party professionals and placed cohorts on party committees across the state. Two years ago, when Joshua Ironwright, the popular Democratic senior senator from the state, announced his retirement at age eighty-one, the dominance of the so-called Weaver machine in Democratic party politics assured Weaver's nomination for the seat.

In anticipation of the forthcoming election, Weaver had spent more time at home than in Washington during the last year and a half, crisscrossing the state with a proposal to cut unemployment in the state's huge pool of unskilled labor. In speech after speech, Weaver proposed a three-step plan, which he referred to as "a new Bill of Rights for the working man." Step 1 would require all major corporations operating in the state to reinvest capital gains from state operations in programs for training and hiring the unemployed. Step 2 called for each business that employed more than twenty-five workers to hire an additional labor force of not less than 5 percent of the total number of workers. Step 3 provided for the establishment of a "citizen overseer body" to enforce reinvestment and the hiring of minority workers.

Business leaders, including Conrad, had opposed this plan by calling it unworkable, inefficient, and probably unconstitutional, but Weaver persisted in its advocacy, and his charismatic appeal met with success. A statewide polling organization determined that as a result of Weaver's canvassing, 55 percent of the voters approved the plan, 30 percent disapproved, and 15 percent were undecided.

Approximately a year ago, however, doubts about Weaver began to grow—even among Democrats. He launched a bitter attack against businesspeople, educators, and politicians who opposed the plan by branding them bigots and exploiters. The issue, already hotly debated, developed racial overtones. It was then that a bipartisan committee of state politicians, businesspeople, and professionals had come to visit Conrad.

Weaver was dangerous, they explained. His ability to incite the base emotions of the population on the race issue was feared. Furthermore, there were unconfirmed but widely circulated rumors that Weaver was mentally unstable. Aides reportedly swore that he had delusions of grandeur and late at night would lock himself behind his office doors and rage at the demons that tormented him. "We have come to you," the committee spokesman explained, "to enlist your service to the state. We want you to oppose Weaver in the upcoming senatorial race because your reputation for fair play and popularity with voters make you the only candidate with which to oppose a demagogue like Alvin Weaver." Conrad had consented, but now he halfwished that he had not.

With the support of all factions of his party and the endorsement of some prominent Democrats, Conrad breezed through the June primary. The first polls of the Conrad-Weaver match-up in early July, however, showed Weaver leading in voter preference with 64 percent and Conrad trailing miserably, with only 28 percent; 8 percent were undecided. With only three months until the general election, the situation seemed bleak.

Conrad chose a staff, set up a headquarters in the capital, and conducted fund-raising campaigns that netted $2.1 million. Throughout the remainder of July and well into August, he conscientiously attended teas and rallies, spoke before large but reserved audiences, and earnestly solicited funds.

Much of the money was allocated for staff expenses and mass mailings. Volunteers went door to door and telephoned voters. Billboard space was purchased to ensure that Jonathan Conrad became a household name. Some radio and television spots were purchased, but emphasis was placed upon reaching "influentials" in the electorate, or community leaders who supposedly could swing others' votes.

This effort produced inadequate results. A poll in the first week of September revealed that Weaver still held a substantial lead, although the margin had narrowed somewhat, to 61 percent for Weaver versus 33 percent for Conrad, with 5 percent undecided. Throughout September, Conrad's attempts to diminish the large gap, although partly successful, lagged behind projections, and it appeared that Weaver's magnetic personality was sufficient in itself to overcome even the most concerted effort and widespread party support. Then it happened.

Weaver and Conrad had shared a platform together at the dedication of a new textile plant. At the conclusion of his speech, Conrad had pivoted to return to his chair when an angry Weaver jumped up and confronted him. With noses barely inches apart, a debate between the two ensued, much to the delight of the roaring crowd. Then, after an angry exchange of words, Weaver spat on Conrad in full view of the audience. This action was greeted with a loud chorus of boos, and Weaver's bodyguards were forced to struggle to lead him to safety.

The incident was widely reported in the press, and the public—its sense of fair play violated—began to listen to what Conrad had to say. His carefully thought-out proposals suddenly gained new support and now, ten days from the November 5 election, the polls showed that he had closed to within 5 percentage points of Weaver. In a meeting with advisers earlier that day, however, there had been a feeling of impotence despite such great gains.

A privately commissioned poll showed that although Conrad had closed to within 5 points of Weaver, the gain capped a leveling off trend, and the rise was not likely to continue without increased effort. It was time for a major media blitz to push Conrad over the top, but not enough money remained. Advisers estimated such a campaign would cost $415,000, but the cost was academic because campaign coffers held only $78,610. It seemed too late for further fund-raising efforts.

After the meeting with his advisers, Conrad returned home, where he soon received a phone call from an excited aide at his campaign headquarters. The aide indicated that PANPAC, a political action committee of the Pacific National Oil Company, had just committed $350,000 to run pro-Conrad messages on radio and television stations around the state. Pacific National was one of the nation's largest oil companies and had several big refineries in the state. The money had not been solicited by either Conrad or members of his staff but had been committed "independently" by PANPAC.

The aide suggested a meeting the next day to plan a new campaign strategy to take advantage of this unexpected windfall. But Conrad told the surprised caller that he was not sure that he would accept the help. Conrad said that he would call back in the morning with a decision that could, if it were negative, be immediately relayed to PANPAC and end the group's effort on his behalf.

QUESTIONS

1 If you were in Conrad's position, what would you do? Why?

2 If Conrad accepts the help and is elected, will he be beholden to the oil company interests when he votes or otherwise exercises his influence as a senator? In all areas of public policy? In some?

3 Are present campaign financing and spending laws adequate to regulate practices that might later lead to subtle forms of political blackmail?

4 Do businesses and people with great wealth have the right to translate their economic power into political influence? Do federal laws properly control them?

5 Should independent expenditures by corporate PACs be curbed?

International Management Issues

12

Multinational Corporations and Government Relationships

"Our market is the world," said Henry J. Heinz when he founded the H. J. Heinz Company over 100 years ago. He began offshore operations when he sold his products in Great Britain. Ever since, the company has expanded its foreign activities. The Heinz company today is a major worldwide provider of processed food products and nutritional services. It now produces more than 3,000 product varieties and does business in over 200 countries. It has 36,200 full-time employees and thousands of part-time seasonal workers. In fiscal 1989, its total sales were $5.8 billion, of which 40 percent came from outside the United States. The company claims that 55 percent of its foreign sales came from products which held the number-one brand in their respective markets.

This is a brief story of the company's strategy in entering emerging countries. It begins in 1980, with a study of the company's future and the world environment. The study reported that 80 percent of the world's population, located in emerging countries, were not exposed to Heinz products. The company decided to do something about that.

HEINZ'S STRATEGIES

The key Heinz strategy has been the use of joint ventures as its entrée to different regions of the emerging-country world. A joint venture offered the firm the twin advantages of facilities and familiarity with a country. Heinz insists that a partner must be a successful private business in a host government having favorable characteristics and policies. It must have natural resources, political stability, acceptable price and tax policies, potential for economic growth, and favorable natural resources. When a partner is found, the company insists on retaining 51 percent ownership. This policy is based upon Heinz's conviction that it must have control to insure the needed quality in its factories and products.

Heinz uses nationals wherever possible, because they understand their countries better than anyone else. This policy, says Anthony J. F. O'Reilly, chairman, president and chief executive officer of the H. J. Heinz Company, is "not just a benediction to local sensitivity: it has major cost implications. Americans overseas are expensive."

One basic managerial policy of the company is to be constantly aware of local conditions. This policy is not only essential to good management, but is also strategic in tailoring products to local circumstances. Furthermore, the company philosophy places a high priority on being a good citizen in the countries in which it does business.

The first two countries in which Heinz implemented its emerging-country strategies were Zimbabwe and the People's Republic of China (RPC). Here is a brief summary of its experience in these two nations.

ZIMBABWE

The first move in Heinz's strategy was made in 1980, when the firm began negotiations with Olivine Industries (OI) in Zimbabwe. OI was a family-owned company manufacturing soaps, candles, edible oils, fats and margarine. Its facilities were extremely sophisticated and used modern technology. The quality of its products was high.

Negotiations began in October 1980 with OI, whose ownership was receptive to the idea of a joint venture. The Zimbabwe government, however, resisted the 51 percent Heinz ownership principle, and also insisted that it should become a participant in the joint venture. These sticking points took a year and a half to resolve. The government finally accepted Heinz's 51 percent principle and Heinz accepted the government as a partner.

In May 1982, the government withdrew a subsidy for raw materials used to make edible oils and refused to permit the joint venture to raise retail prices of oil. These policies, of course, could have bankrupted the venture. It took seven months to resolve this problem. An additional roadblock was caused by Zimbabwe's lack of participation in the Overseas Private Investment Corporation (OPIC). (This is a corporation authorized by the U.S. Congress in 1971 with authority to insure high-risk investments of American companies against war and expropriation in foreign countries). Since Zimbabwe did not participate in OPIC, Heinz could not get insurance. The issue was finally resolved when the government agreed to be bound by United Nations arbitration of disputes. Finally, two years after negotiations began, the joint venture was ready to operate in Africa.

The OI management remains the same today as it was prior to the acquisition. Heinz remains subject to the rules of the host government with respect to lifetime employment and to foreign exchange rules that sometimes delay importing equipment and raw materials. As part of its commitment,

Heinz promised the government assistance in agriculture, food production, training, and new product development. The firm introduced the Michigan pea bean to Zimbabwean soil, and the bean now provides a nutritious product for home consumption and export. Heinz agronomists are helping to produce new strains of tomatoes in the country. The Heinz Foundation has given $200,000 to build a medical clinic and contributed $50,000 for the construction of a hospital.

The joint venture is a success. Not only has it been successful in Zimbabwe, registering sales of $80 million in 1989, but it has provided a base for exporting the product and the establishment of factories in other countries of the region. In 1989, its foreign sales were $15 million, a leap from $1 million when the joint venture began operations.

THE PEOPLE'S REPUBLIC OF CHINA

The China venture began in 1984. In negotiations, Heinz agreed to build a $10 million factory in Guangzhou, China, to produce baby foods. The factory began operations in June 1986. Heinz holds a 60 percent share of the venture and has two partners: the General Corporation of Agriculture, Industry and Commerce (AIC), and the United Food Enterprise (UFE), both government agencies. UFE, a vast agribusiness employing some five million people throughout China, is a cooperative of food manufacturers and distributors under the wing of the Ministry of Light Industry.

Aside from the factory, Heinz promised to establish a program to study the problems of malnutrition among Chinese infants. This work not only was of benefit to China but helped the company to develop instructional materials for mothers and to improve its products to fit local conditions in the country.

Heinz believes that the government wants the company to succeed "as a symbol of the way they (government officials) feel multinationals should participate in the Chinese economy."

CONCLUDING COMMENT

Heinz's emerging-country strategy has been successful financially, and will provide the base for further expansion in emerging countries. The experience of this company demonstrates that a company need not be forced into a Mephistophelean pact with tyranny in an emerging nation. Both multinational companies and host governments can cooperate to the benefit of the peoples of the emerging countries and the companies.[1]

This brief discussion of how a multinational corporation (MNC) has successfully entered new markets is a useful frame of reference for the issues treated in this and the following chapter. While the initial investment of

---

[1]This case was derived principally from Anthony J. F. O'Reilly, "Establishing Successful Joint Ventures in Developing Nations: A CEO's Perspective," *Columbia Journal of World Business,* Spring 1988; remarks by Dr. Anthony J. F. O'Reilly before the Boston Security Analysts Society, March 15, 1989; and *The Heinz Company 1989 Annual Report,* Pittsburgh, Pennsylvania, 1989.

Heinz in emerging countries is not large in terms of its total overseas invest-ment or its total assets, the experience of this company shows clearly what successful foreign operations require by way of managerial strategy.

Following a definition of the nature and role of the MNC, we examine the more significant conflicts that exist between MNCs and host governments, and then the dominant relationships between United States–based MNCs and the federal government. Then, after considering current pressures for protectionism and deviations from free-trade principles, the chapter closes with a discussion of foreign payoffs and the controls required to curb them.

NATURE AND ROLE OF THE MNC

THE MNC DEFINED

There are many definitions of the MNC. We accept one used by the United Nations, that MNCs are "enterprises which own or control production or ser-vice facilities outside the country in which they are used."[2] The MNC is an agency of direct, as opposed to portfolio, investment in foreign countries. It is not always incorporated or private. It can be a cooperative or state-owned entity. Almost every large business organization has some direct or indirect involvement with foreign companies, but only when an enterprise confronts one or more of the problems of designing, producing, marketing, or financ-ing its products or services within and among foreign nations does it become truly multinational. Many MNCs progress through several stages.

1 Exports its products to foreign countries.
2 Establishes sales organizations abroad.
3 Licenses use of its patents and know-how to foreign firms that make and sell its products.
4 Establishes foreign manufacturing facilities.
5 Multinationalizes management from top to bottom.
6 Multinationalizes ownership of corporate stock.
7 Coordinates global operations.

There are probably several hundred thousand U.S. companies in stage 1, many fewer in stages 2 and 3, only five or six thousand in stage 4, and many fewer in stages 5, 6, and 7.

MNCs are divided into two categories—those that operate in countries through subsidiaries that are more or less autonomous (Figure 12-1) and those that operate on a global basis (Figure 12-2). In the former, there is often a separate organization for each nation or group of nations. In the latter, somewhere in the world there is an executive group responsible for integrat-ing and planning for the product line and allocating company resources ac-cordingly. The decisions of (1) what to sell, (2) where to sell, (3) where to

---

[2]United Nations Economic and Social Council, Special Intersessional Committee, *The Impact of Transnational Corporations on the Development Process and on International Relations*, New York, 1975. See also Jack N. Behrman, *Some Patterns in the Rise of Multinational Enterprise*, Chapel Hill, North Carolina: University of North Carolina, 1969.

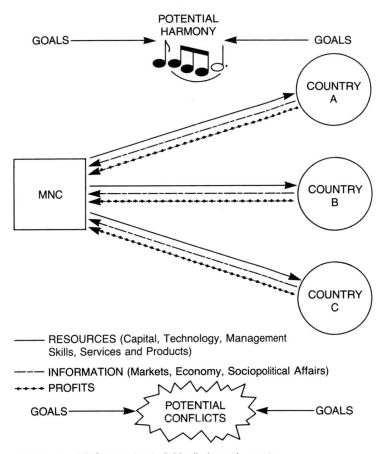

FIGURE 12-1   Model of an MNC operating individually in each country.

manufacture, and (4) where to buy raw materials and components are determined on a worldwide basis. In the one case, competition is national, and in the other it is international. Some writers call such corporations transnational, global, or worldwide. We call them global for our discussion. Sometimes it is difficult to distinguish between companies operating in individual countries through subsidiaries and those coordinating operations worldwide.

CONCEPTUAL OBJECTIVES OF MNCs AND HOST GOVERNMENTS

The fundamental motive of going abroad is, of course, profit. MNCs in stages 1 through 3 seek to profit in obvious ways. The process is more complicated when a company gets to stage 4. Theoretically, in this stage, management would like to manufacture in those countries where it finds the greatest competitive advantage; it would like to buy and sell anywhere in the world to take advantage of the most favorable price to the company; it would

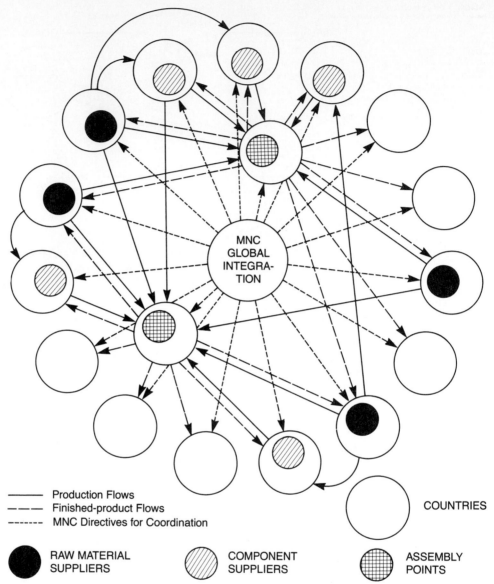

- —————— Production Flows
- — — — Finished-product Flows
- - - - - - - MNC Directives for Coordination

COUNTRIES

RAW MATERIAL SUPPLIERS

COMPONENT SUPPLIERS

ASSEMBLY POINTS

FIGURE 12-2 Model of an MNC coordinating global operations.

like to take advantage throughout the world of changes in labor costs, productivity, trade agreements, and currency fluctuations; and it would like to expand or contract on the basis of worldwide comparative advantages. Its objectives are to obtain a high and rising return on invested capital; achieve rising sales; keep financial risks within reasonable limits in relation to profits; and maintain its technological and other proprietary strengths.

TABLE 12-1 The LARGEST U.S.-BASED MULTINATIONALS

Rank		Company	Products	Export sales		Total sales	Exports as percent of sales	
					Percent change	*Fortune* 500		
1988	1987			$ Millions	1987:88	$ Millions	Rank	Percent Rank
1	1	GENERAL MOTORS, Detroit	Motor vehicles and parts	9,392.0	7.6	121,085.4	1	7.8 41
2	2	FORD MOTOR, Dearborn, Mich.	Motor vehicles and parts	8,822.0	15.9	92,445.6	2	9.5 35
3	3	BOEING, Seattle	Commercial and military aircraft	7,849.0	24.9	16,962.0	19	46.3 1
4	4	GENERAL ELECTRIC, Fairfield, Conn.	Jet engines, generators, medical systems	5,744.0	19.0	49,414.0	5	11.6 29
5	5	INT'L BUSINESS MACHINES, Armonk, N.Y.	Computers and related equipment	4,951.0	24.0	59,681.0	4	8.3 39
6	8	CHRYSLER, Highland Park, Mich.	Motor vehicles and parts	4,343.9	42.3	35,472.7	7	12.2 28
7	6	E.I. DU PONT DE NEMOURS, Wilmington, Del.	Specialty chemicals, energy products	4,196.0	19.0	32,514.0	9	12.9 26
8	7	MCDONNELL DOUGLAS, St. Louis	Commercial and military aircraft	3,471.0	7.0	15,072.0	25	23.0 5
9	10	CATERPILLAR, Peoria, Ill.	Heavy machinery, engines, turbines	2,930.0	33.8	10,435.0	35	28.1 4
10	11	UNITED TECHNOLOGIES, Hartford	Jet engines, helicopters, cooling equipment	2,848.1	37.5	18,087.8	16	15.8 20

Source: Edward Prewitt, "America's Biggest Exporters." *Fortune,* July 17, 1989, p. 51.

This focus on profits does not mean that MNCs reject social responsibilities. MNCs would like to achieve the highest possible level of economic rationality in their decision-making consistent with assuming a reasonable share of social responsibilities. As Edmund T. Pratt, Jr., CEO of Pfizer, Inc., said: "I hope we have a broader sense than just the importance of making a dollar (in our foreign operations)," and added that he thought the basic mission of his company included building world understanding.[3] Illustrations of such programs among MNCs are plentiful. For instance, Pfizer, along with other American-based firms, has helped the Gambian government to develop better health-care systems. Union Carbide has built and equipped a technical college in Zimbabwe. Ford Motor Co., S.A., in a program two decades old, has built 128 schools in Mexico that serve 170,000 children annually.[4]

Who are the big players in the world? The ten largest industrial MNCs in 1988 (measured in terms of total foreign revenues) are shown in Table 12-1 together with the percent of sales received from exports. The largest industrial corporations outside the United States are shown in Table 12-2. Unfortunately, data are not available for the volume of revenues derived from countries outside their home base. It can be concluded, however, that for these corporations the percentages are much higher than those of the U.S. companies. All of these companies have total revenues greater than the gross national products of most of the countries in which they do business. While these companies are the largest MNCs in terms of total sales, there are many smaller companies that depend much more on foreign sales for their profits

[3]Edmund T. Pratt, Jr., "CEO: The Whole Man. Fame versus the Family," interview by David Finn, *Across the Board,* December 1985:35.

[4]Ann McKinstry Micou, "The Invisible Hand at Work in Developing Countries," *Across the Board,* March 1985.

TABLE 12-2 THE LARGEST FOREIGN-BASED MULTINATIONALS.

Rank by sales				Sales	Profits	
1988	1987	Company	Country	$ Millions	$ Millions	Rank
1	1	ROYAL DUTCH/SHELL GROUP	BRITAIN/NETH.	78,381.1	5,238.7	1
2	3	TOYOTA MOTOR	JAPAN	50,789.9	2,314.6	3
3	2	BRITISH PETROLEUM	BRITAIN	46,174.0	2,155.3	4
4	4	IRI	ITALY	45,521.5	921.9	28
5	5	DAIMLER-BENZ	W. GERMANY	41,817.9	953.1	26
6	7	HITACHI	JAPAN	41,330.7	989.0	23
7	9	SIEMENS	W. GERMANY	34,129.4	757.0	39
8	8	FIAT	ITALY	34,039.3	2,324.7	2
9	10	MATSUSHITA ELECTRIC INDUSTRIAL	JAPAN	33,922.5	1,177.2	18
10	6	VOLKSWAGEN	W. GERMANY	33,696.2	420.1	77

Source: "The International 500." *Fortune*, July 31, 1989, p. 291. Copyright © 1989 The Times Inc. Magazine Company. All rights reserved.

and report a higher proportion of their sales from exports. For example, Sun Microsystems, a computer workstation producer, has foreign sales of 42 percent of total sales, mostly in Japan.

Generally speaking, dominant goals of most countries around the world, developed and less developed, would embrace the following: economic growth, full employment of people and resources, raising the skills of workers, price stability, a favorable balance of payments, more equitable distribution of income, a fair share of the profits made by MNCs, improving technology in and productivity of domestic business firms, national hegemony over the economic system, control over national security, social stability, and advancing the quality of life.

MNCs have been and can be of enormous help to governments of the world in their efforts to achieve most of these goals, especially the economic ones. At the same time, however, it is clear that conflicts between the two sets of goals and decision-making processes are inevitable. In recent years, host governments have eased some of their demands, but conflicts still are serious.

COMPLAINTS OF HOST GOVERNMENTS

Host governments have a long list of complaints about the MNCs that operate within their borders. Among them the following are the most frequently heard major complaints.

1 *The Challenge to Nation-State Sovereignty.* Host governments see the power of the MNC as a challenge to their sovereignty. Powers of MNCs vary, of course, but the perception of great power persists even though the total volume of investment in a country is small.

2 *Inequities.* Many complaints about alleged inequities are made. One of the most enduring and persistent is that prices of raw materials extracted from nation-states are falling while prices of imported manufactured goods are rising. This, say foreign countries, creates a growing inequity. Behind this view is the belief that foreign countries that export manufactured goods prevent competition and permit monopolies to raise prices, while competition prevails in raw-material extraction in host countries of MNCs.

3 *MNCs Create Economic and Social Disruption.* Complaints in this area take a variety of directions. MNCs, it is alleged, possess competitive advantages over local entrepreneurs and, as a result, prevent the development of local business skills and capital investment. MNCs are said to create inflationary pressures that host governments cannot control. They misapply and exhaust host natural resources. They also are accused of fundamentally altering the customs, mores, and habits of host countries in ways that are detrimental to social and political stability.

4 *Lack of Concern for Local Conditions.* MNCs are seen as instruments to exploit the host country's natural wealth for the primary benefit of citizens of another country. They are said to be motivated by money and little else. They take the position that "what is good for their company is good for the country," and that, say host governments, is not the case. For instance, Nestlé introduced powdered milk as a baby food into West Africa as an alternative to breast feeding. Infant mortality increased because mothers, in an effort to combat extreme poverty, diluted the milk with water to the point where there was no nutrition. Nestlé made profits, it is said, but babies died.

5 *MNC Imperialism.* Many of the awakening nations look on foreign businesspeople with fear and distrust as the embodiment of an old exploitative colonialism not easily forgotten. It is not difficult for the awakening nations to find current illustrations to support their fears. American investors have taken out of Latin American countries more money than they have invested. This is called economic imperialism by these nations. Many less developed countries (LDCs) feel relegated to the role of supplying raw materials and cheap labor because they are denied the technology to develop into industrialized nations. Their frustrations are leveled at the MNCs that export their raw materials and cheap labor. The sins of the past and allegations of the present cannot easily be erased in the minds of formerly exploited colonies.

6 *Symbol of Frustration and Antipathy.* The LDCs have grievances about their position in the world that have nothing to do with the MNC, but the MNC is a visible target for their anger. For example, there are adverse reactions to the power of the United States, and the MNC is seen as epitomizing that power. Also, many of the LDCs are governed by dictatorships that are naturally antagonistic to the free-market mechanism governing decision making of the MNCs.

These are broad criticisms. They lay a foundation, however, for dozens of specific demands or restrictions that may seriously conflict with the integration strategies of MNCs. For example, local governments and local interests seek to limit repatriation of assets and earnings; they want component parts or raw materials to be purchased from local suppliers; they demand the transfer of new technology to their countries; they require MNCs to appoint local nationals to top-management positions in local operations; they try to limit the company's share of local markets; they insist that the company produce or sell certain products as a condition of entry into local markets; they push export expansion and import reduction; and they want more local employment even at the expense of the company's operating efficiency.

RECENT EASING OF DEMANDS

In the 1970s, criticism of and demands for restraints on MNCs reached a crescendo. Raymond Vernon, a respected scholar of the MNC, wrote in 1977: "Just a few years ago multinational enterprises were busily and profitably occupied in spreading their subsidiaries across the globe. Today the world is awash with actions and proposals that would restrain the multinational enterprise and alter its relations to nation-states"[5] The view that MNCs are exploitative and disruptive persists, and it is fed by such tragic accidents as that at the Union Carbide plant in Bhopal, India. Today, both the criticism and restraints are strong. But they have diminished somewhat during the past decade. For example, many LDCs have discovered that the MNCs can help them expand exports and reduce imports to create a trade surplus with which to help repay their huge debts. One result has been renewed efforts to attract foreign capital, especially from MNCs. The welcome mat has replaced the formerly barred door in many countries, from China to Latin America. Also, says Peter Hanse, executive director of the United Nations Center on Transnational Corporations, "[d]eveloping countries gained a great deal of experience and can meet companies with a great deal more self-confidence than in the early 1970s, when I think they felt overwhelmed."[6]

RESPONSE OF THE MNCs

Naturally, MNC managers and their defenders respond that many of the criticisms of their behavior are only partially true at best and outright untruths at worst. Despite their alleged shortcomings, they say, MNCs significantly help host governments to achieve their national aims. The most frequently expressed claims of how MNCs benefit host nations, in no particular order of priority, are:

- Provide employment.
- Train managers.
- Provide products and services that raise the standard of living.
- Introduce and develop new technical skills.
- Introduce new managerial and organizational techniques.
- Provide greater access to international markets.

[5]Raymond Vernon, *Storm Over the Multinationals: The Real Issues*, Cambridge, Massachusetts: Harvard University Press, 1977, p. 191.
[6]Nicholas D. Kristof, "Multinationals, Once Shunned, Now Welcomed," *New York Times*, May 10, 1985.

- Lift the gross national product.
- Increase productivity.
- Help to build foreign exchange reserves.
- Serve as a point of contact between host country business people and politicians in home country.
- Encourage the development and spin-off of new industries.
- Assume investment risk that might not otherwise be undertaken.
- Mobilize for productive purposes capital that might otherwise go for less productive uses.

MNC managers have their own litany of complaints. Aside from outright expropriation of MNC subsidiaries or the threat of expropriation, MNC managers complain about controls that restrict their prerogatives in making what they consider to be rational managerial decisions over people in the organization, products and production, flows of capital, and profits. They do not like, of course, mandatory disinvestment or limitations on reinvestment of earnings or remittance of profits. They are disturbed at rules that force them to fill quotas for local production, employees, exports, use of output of local producers, or managerial positions. They do not like to be told where to put plants, and they resist restrictions on their importing components for assembly of final products. For example, when the Ford Motor Company wanted to produce automobiles in Spain, the Spanish government set specific restrictions on sales and export volume. Ford's sales volume was limited to 10 percent of the previous year's total automobile market, and export volume had to be equal to at least two-thirds of its entire production in Spain. Also, Ford had to agree not to broaden its model lines without government authorization.[7]

OTHER SOURCES OF CONFLICT WITH MNC GOALS

The above conflicts between MNC goals and those of host governments can be and often are serious. Beyond these, however, MNC managers face many other sources of conflicts with their company goals. For example, U.S. companies face rigorous competition in developed countries like West Germany. Voluntary organizations with sociopolitical objectives are growing in foreign countries in both number and influence. They include consumer, environmental, labor, and religious groups. As demonstrated in the United States, such groups can and do exert considerable influence on corporations. The U.S. government may impose sanctions on a country which will, of course, restrict our exports to that country. Foreign countries may subsidize their own manufacturers and undersell U.S. firms. Customs in foreign lands may

---

[7]Yves L. Doz and C. K. Prahalad, "How MNCs Cope with Host Government Intervention," *Harvard Business Review*, March–April 1980. For further discussion of MNC-host country relationships see Yves L. Doz, "Government Policies and Global Industries," in Michael E. Porter, ed., *Competition in Global Industries*, Boston, Massachusetts: Harvard Business School Press, 1986. Also see Lee A. Tavis, ed., *Multinational Managers and Host Government Interactions*, Notre Dame, Indiana: University of Notre Dame Press, 1988.

adversely affect our exports. In Japan, for example, ma and pa retail outlets work with an intricate network of distributors to favor Japanese-made products over foreign imports. These examples serve to illustrate the complexity of forces with which managers must contend in globalizing their production and distribution.

CODES OF CONDUCT

Pressure for codes of conduct of MNCs operating in LDCs (lesser developed countries) began in the mid-1960s, when it was feared that powerful MNCs would dominate small host governments. Codes were prepared by the United Nations, the International Chamber of Commerce, the Organization for Economic Cooperation and Development (OECD), and others. Rather than repeat the contents of these codes, we have prepared a set of broad guidelines which catches the essence of these codes and a little more.

A PROPOSED CODE FOR MULTINATIONAL COMPANIES

The multinational company shall

- conform to the established policies and the laws of the host country.
- respond affirmatively to the social and economic plans of the host country.
- progressively staff host country operations, including management, with local personnel.
- permit host country nationals to acquire ownership interests in the foreign affiliate of the company or in the parent company.
- refrain from activities that would harm the functioning of the local capital markets.
- supply appropriate information to local authorities about health, safety, and the environmental effects of the company's products.
- provide for the host nation's people a clear statement of the basic mission and policies of the company.
- seriously consider credible complaints and try to eliminate them.
- help LDCs that seek increasing technology transfer to do so by introducing well-known technology or by helping local entrepreneurs to produce products at a profit.
- not make payments to any official of the host country or to any political candidate for public office, except as required by law.

A PROPOSED MINIMUM CODE FOR HOST COUNTRIES

The host country shall

- make explicit its priorities and maintain them with reasonable consistency.
- enact and adhere to fair codes of foreign investment.

- tax and regulate affiliates of foreign-based companies equally with home-based enterprises.
- respect all investment agreements and not make unilateral or retroactive changes in them.
- pay prompt, adequate, and effective compensation to a foreign company whose local properties are nationalized or expropriated.
- make reasonable rules regarding payments of dividends to, and repatriation of capital by, a foreign company.
- establish laws and policies against extortion and enforce them.

These are broad codes of conduct, and if attempts are made to follow them they will reduce conflicts to the advantage of both host governments and MNCs.

THE TOTAL ENVIRONMENT OF MNCs IN HOST COUNTRIES

High on the list of the most important managerial problems of MNC executives are their relations to governments. Dealing with the types of criticism, demands, and controls noted earlier is a difficult task. But this is only part of the environment of the typical MNC. There are many other environmental forces that are of great concern to them. Table 12-3 shows basic elements in four major environments.

Every aspect of all four environments in Table 12-3 presents a challenge, an opportunity, or a threat.

Misjudgment, misinterpretation, or ignorance of any one of many forces can adversely affect a company's foreign operations. For example, a finance manager may get into trouble if he or she does not properly appraise potential exchange instability of a host country's currency. A new plant manager may get into trouble if local workers' values and habits are misread. A plant may be expropriated because of a manager's inadvertent insult to a local government official. David Ricks's book on *Big Business Blunders* is filled with illustrations of problems that companies face in doing business in foreign cultures. He cites, for example, the case of Coca-Cola in China:

> When the Coca-Cola Company was planning its strategy for marketing in China in the 1920s, it wanted to introduce its product with the English pronunciation of "Coca-Cola." A translator developed a group of Chinese characters which, when pronounced, sounded like the product name. These characters were placed on the cola bottles and marketed. Was it any wonder that sales levels were low? The characters actually translated to mean "a wax-flattened mare" or "bite the wax tadpole." Since the product was new, sound was unimportant to the consumers; meaning was vital. Today Coca-Cola is again marketing its cola in China. The new characters used on the bottle translate to "happiness in the mouth." From its first marketing attempts, Coca-Cola learned a valuable lesson in international marketing.[8]

[8]David A. Ricks, *Big Business Blunders: Mistakes in Multinational Marketing*, Homewood, Illinois: Dow Jones-Irwin, 1983.

TABLE 12-3   FOREIGN GOVERNMENT ENVIRONMENTAL FORCES

Economic environment	Political environment
Gross national product	Form of government
Per capita income	Political ideology
Natural resources	Political stability
Inflation	Attitude toward opposition groups
Interest rates	Effectiveness of legal system
Wage and salary levels	Treaties with foreign nationals
Economic crises	Laws affecting business firms
Balance of payments	Foreign policy
Exchange rate volatility	Restrictions on imports/exports
National debt	Quality of government management
Income distribution	State companies
Composition of exports	Corruption (bribery)
	Role of military
	Privileged environment for local competition

Technical environment	Social environment
Skill levels of workers	Customs and mores
Engineering skills	Religious or ethnic splits
Management skills	Riots, demonstrations
Technical competition	Public attitudes toward MNCs
Special technical requirements of country	Demography
Technical capabilities in universities	Class divisions
	Major social concerns of population
	Labor union attitudes

Forces governing operations in some countries are often ambiguous, contradictory, and shifting. The revolution in Iran is a classic illustration. Not only do such conditions complicate the decision-making process of MNCs, but if appraisal of environment is wrong, a company may suffer severe consequences, ranging from nationalization and expropriation to controls that reduce managerial prerogatives, raise costs, and lower profits.

In light of such conditions, MNCs, if they are wise, will make themselves (or have management consulting firms) prepare environmental analyses and forecasts of forces in the countries in which they do business. There is no uniform way to make these analyses. They range from a high-price luncheon with Henry Kissinger to a comprehensive in-depth study of current and future environmental changes relevant to the decisions to be made.

Those persons preparing evaluations must choose for analysis those questions that are most pertinent to the issue to be decided. A question of where to build a new plant requires answers different from those related to international transfer of funds. To illustrate the types of questions to be asked, we note typical questions concerned with political forces.

- Will the present form of government last, and if so, for how long?
- What special political or social problems are important to our company?

- What is the attitude of the government toward foreign investment?
- Is there a threat of nationalization? If so, what?
- What treaties does the country have with the United States that are of interest to us?
- What controls does the government exercise over foreign investment in each major area—production, domestic content, pricing, technology, employment, and the like?
    - Are there clear and modern corporate investment laws?
    - What major problems will exist in dealing with government officials?

Evaluation of economic, technical, and social forces will, of course, raise different questions.

MNC STRATEGIC MANAGEMENT MODELS FOR DEALING WITH HOST GOVERNMENTS

Amir Mahini set forth three conceptual strategic management models as a framework for his interviews with 180 managers in thirteen MNCs. He found that none of the MNCs followed rigorously any of the three models but that aspects of all of the models were found in the MNCs.[9]

In the *ad hoc strategy,* government issues are dealt with when they arise. Firms adopting this strategy have no long-term strategies or policies to deal with issues. Such firms view government issues as unforseeable or exogenous to the firm. When issues arise, the firm satisfactorily deals with some and ignores others. In this strategy, front-line managers may have considerable flexibility in dealing with host government issues. MNCs following this model risk serious losses through unforeseen government actions. They also risk having precedents set which they later may regret.

In the *policy strategy,* a firm establishes a set of specific policies and guidelines to deal with anticipated issues. MNCs with power may use these policies as a basis of negotiation or as a condition for operating in a country. These government-related strategies are derived from and integrated into the overall strategies of the company. They seek to regularize company operations, to diminish the need for negotiations, to reduce conflict, and to assure better coordination of global operations. This strategy has many obvious advantages for the MNC, but also risks locking a firm into specific policies which may need revision as environmental forces change. A tough MNC stand may erode goodwill that it may need if its power for any reason is weakened.

In the *organizational overlay strategy,* a specialized government affairs staff and supplementary units, such as temporary task forces, project teams, and permanent coordinating teams, are established. These teams gather information, monitor government issues, and deal with issues when they arise. This type of organization facilitates the granting of power to foreign subunits to deal with local issues. The whole apparatus assumes that many government

---

[9]Amir Mahani, *Making Decisions in Multinational Corporations: Managing Relations with Sovereign Governments,* New York: John Wiley & Sons, 1988.

issue-areas can be anticipated but that the precise manner in which they appear cannot be prescribed and cannot be dealt with by simple formula. This strategy recognizes that the company must be able to manage effectively the government issues that arise. It also presumes, of course, that something can be done to prevent issues from arising or reduce their seriousness when they do arise. This strategy lies between the first two. MNCs with such a strategy may or may not have sufficient bargaining power to impose their policies on governments.

UNITED STATES MNCs AND THE FEDERAL GOVERNMENT

The special relationships between the MNCs based in the United States and the federal government are diverse, significant, and changing. We discuss a few of these complex relationships.

UNITED STATES FOREIGN RELATIONS

United States foreign policy and business interests always have been intertwined. The U.S. Navy attacked the Barbary pirates in 1801 to stop interference with Yankee shipping, but it may also have been an excuse to secure the presence of the American Navy in the Mediterranean. Our flag has followed our trade. Gunboat diplomacy on behalf of business may have been used years ago, but no more. Today there is a much more sophisticated and intricate relationship among the federal government, MNCs, and foreign host governments in the conduct of foreign policy. This interrelationship does not always serve the selfish interests of business, although that has always been important in the conduct of foreign policy. The federal government has aided business, and business has served the economic and political interests of the United States. In their normal operations, MNCs do support United States foreign policy. They are catalysts for international cooperation by supporting regional integration, building infrastructure, and working with governments to solve mutual problems. They can enhance the national economic influence of both home and host nations by improving skill, technology, international distribution networks, and exports.

A major policy of the United States has been for many decades, and still is, to foster economic progress throughout the world. In furtherance of this policy, the government has viewed the MNC as an essential instrument of strong and healthy global economic progress. Sometimes, in implementing this policy, the goals of MNCs and United States foreign policy conflict. Conflict is particularly likely with respect to export controls, which have become an important instrument of American diplomacy in recent administrations. The basic authority of such bans rests in The Export Administration Act of 1979, subsequently revised in 1985. It permits export controls of two types. First are national-security controls. These place restrictions on exports (especially of high technology) that would make a significant contribution to the military potential of another country and that would be detrimental to the national security of the United States. Second are foreign-policy controls. These are restrictions on exports of goods and technology to further United States diplomatic objectives.

For example, a long list of electronic and computer products and technologies cannot be exported to the Soviet Union for national-security reasons. A classic illustration of export restrictions for diplomatic reasons was President Reagan's order in 1982 prohibiting Dresser Industries, Inc., from shipping machinery needed by the Soviet Union to complete a gas pipeline to Western Europe. United States sanctions have been applied to many countries in recent years—Cuba, Iran, Nicaragua, and South Africa, to name a few. These policies raise a dilemma for this country. How can the government curb some exports in furtherance of national goals without injuring United States companies?

The business community accepts export restrictions for national-security purposes, although questions are raised about the expanding number of prohibited exports. But there is much irritation in the business community about the use of export restraints to achieve diplomatic goals, especially when they conflict with MNC business logic.[10]

There are, of course, many other dimensions to the interrelationships between business and United States foreign policy. They range from export subsidies to broad financial agreements between the United States and other countries of the world to assure financial stability in world markets. There is also a growing recognition that economic strength at home is a fundamental pillar of our national-security posture. This recognition, of course, leads to federal government action to strengthen our economy and help business achieve a stronger competitive position in world markets. Of special interest is foreign trade, to which the remainder of this chapter is devoted.

PROTECTIONISM VERSUS FREE TRADE

From the very beginning of our history we have, on the one hand, maintained a free trade policy but, on the other hand, protected our industries from foreign competition. At no time in the past, however, have protectionist demands been at a higher pitch of urgency than today. Paradoxically, at no time in recent years have greater pressures been brought to bear by our government on foreign governments to lift trade barriers for our companies wanting to do business abroad. This is especially so with Japan.

WHY FREE TRADE?

The case for free trade is comparatively simple. By virtue of climate, labor conditions, raw materials, capital, management, or other considerations, some nations have an advantage over others in the production of particular goods. For instance, Brazil can produce coffee beans at a much lower price

[10]Erik Lindell, "Foreign Policy Export Controls and MNCs," *California Management Review,* Summer 1986.

than the United States. Coffee beans could be grown in hothouses in the United States, but not at a price equal to that which Brazilians can charge and make a profit. But the United States has a distinct advantage over Brazil in producing computers. Resources will be used most efficiently when each country produces that for which it enjoys a cost advantage. Gain will be maximized when each nation specializes in producing those products for which it has the greatest economic edge. This is what economists call the law of comparative advantage. It follows that maximum gain on a worldwide basis will be realized if there are no impediments to trade, if there is free competition in pricing, and if capital flows are unrestricted.

It is not always easy, however, to see just where a nation has a comparative advantage. At the extremes the case is clear, but not at the means. Differences in monetary units, rates of productivity of capital and labor, changes in markets, or elasticities of demand, for instance, obscure the degree of advantage one nation may have over another at any time. Nevertheless, it is argued that free trade will stimulate competition, reward individual initiative, increase productivity, and improve national well-being. It will enlarge job opportunities and produce for consumers a wider variety of goods and services at minimum prices and with higher quality. Free-trade advocates argue that protectionism leads to just the reverse. It stifles competitive activity, dampens individual initiative, costs consumers more in higher prices, and sets off trade wars that result in economic stagnation and depression.

This is the theory. In practice, all nations of the world have erected protective tariffs for one reason or another. We turn now to current protectionist pressures in this country and abroad.

PRESSURES FOR PROTECTIONISM

President Reagan repeatedly asserted by his rhetoric and vetoes of protectionist bills that the United States has a free-trade policy. In response to criticism of our trading partners by protectionists, he said: "We're in the same boat with our trading partners. If one partner shoots a hole in the boat, does it make sense for the other one to shoot another hole in the boat?" But this philosophy is by no means universally accepted in the top levels of our government, nor did Reagan follow it in practice. There are many people, especially in the Congress, who assert that the United States, with its free-trade philosophy, is being "played for a sucker" by other countries that do not have a free-trade philosophy. They subsidize their exports to the United States and bar our products to their markets. "It's time to get tough," these critics assert. President Bush is reported to have said when he was Vice President "No more Mr. Nice Guy," when referring to the issue of free trade versus protectionism. Many bills currently in the Congress reflect strong protectionist pressures in the United States today.

What is behind the protectionist upsurge? One is the wide U.S. trade deficit. Another is the severe loss of markets in many industries to foreign competition, with a subsequent loss of jobs. Another is what many people consider unfair trade practices by our trading partners.

In 1980, the United States enjoyed a small trade surplus, but since then we have incurred huge trade deficits of $125 to $150 billion a year. Many industries have seen their share of the domestic market decline drastically in recent years. For example, in the 1970s, rod and reel makers controlled 80 percent of the domestic market. Today their share is less than 10 percent. The irony is that the basic technical ideas for this equipment originated in this country, but now foreign countries can make the products more cheaply than our own companies. The same thing has happened to a number of other industries.

From 1980 to 1987, the share of domestic markets held by U.S. manufacturers of phonographs fell from 10 to 1 percent, for color television sets from 60 to 10 percent, and for telephones from 88 to 25 percent. Comparable losses of markets have been registered in many other areas: dolls, shoes, luggage, boys' shirts and nightwear, women's blouses, machine tools, motorcycles, and bicycles, to name a few.[11] James E. Olson, the late chairman of AT&T, observed (and he is probably in ballpark range) that 70 percent of all American-made products have intense foreign competition in the United States.[12]

The trade deficit is due more to our lagging exports than to surging imports. Professor Paul W. McCracken reminds us that in 1988, even with a sharp recovery, our exports were only 6.6 percent of U.S. output, compared with 8 percent in 1980. In 1988, our $440 billion in imports followed historical trends. Merchandise imports were a bit over 9 percent of GNP, about the same as in 1980.[13] There are many reasons for this state of affairs which will be discussed in the next chapter. Whatever the causes, there is severe pressure on the federal government to raise tariff barriers here and force foreign governments to free up trade in the belief that such action will reverse these trends.

Protectionist pressures are rooted in widespread beliefs that many countries have unfair trade practices, especially the Japanese. Figure 12-3 shows the results of a poll made in May 1989 on behalf of Times Mirror. But these convictions reflect only one of many deep causes of our trade problems.

For example, some foreign manufacturers have been accused of selling their products here at prices lower than in their home countries, a practice called "dumping." (Japanese microchip manufacturers, for example, were found in March 1986 to be dumping in this country by the Department of Commerce after a prolonged study of the issue.) Foreign governments also have been accused of subsidizing certain industries, such as steel and agriculture, to permit producers to cut their export prices. At the same time, American companies have been complaining loudly that they face a variety of trade barriers when they seek to sell products abroad. We shall examine this question later in the chapter.

---

[11]International Trade Administration, U.S. Department of Commerce.

[12]James E. Olson, "Toward A Global Information Age," in Jerome M. Rosow, ed., *The Global Marketplace*, New York: Facts on File, 1988, p. 99.

[13]Paul M. McCracken, "Why U.S. Exports Are a Casualty," *Wall Street Journal*, March 3, 1989.

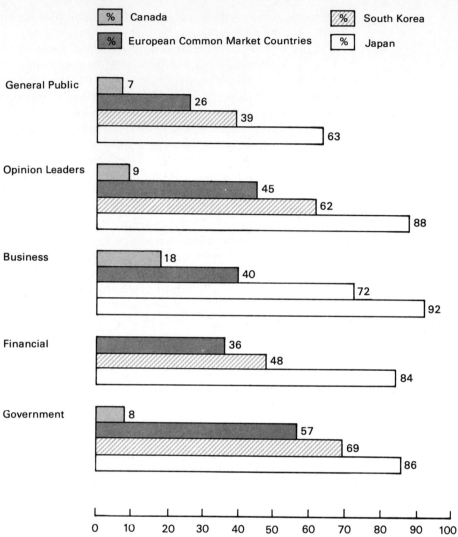

FIGURE 12-3 Percentage who believe countries' trade policies are unfair to the United States. (*Source: Fortune,* July 17, 1981, p.51. Copyright © 1989 The Time Inc. Magazine Company. All rights reserved.)

In 1948, ninety-two trading nations negotiated a multilateral agreement called General Agreement on Tariffs and Trade (GATT). It sought to encourage freer, fairer, and expanded international trade. Under GATT, world trade boomed. By the late 1970s, the world's average tariff on manufactured goods had fallen to around 3 percent. But then many countries, faced with unemployment, stagnant economies, inflation, and overcapacity in major industries, began to encourage more exports and restrict imports. Protectionist sentiment became a worldwide phenomenon.

As explained in more detail in the next chapter, however, many American companies have exhibited serious shortcomings in selling their products abroad. Our productivity has been very low relative to historical standards, and our wage rates have been high. Our capital investment has not kept our manufacturers at the cutting edge of new technology. The result has been high costs and selling prices, exaggerated by a high dollar. Furthermore, many of our managers have not displayed the marketing skills in selling abroad that foreign producers have shown in the United States.

The net result of all of this is an unprecedented trade deficit, demands by business for protection from foreign competitors, and pressure on the federal government to persuade foreign governments to remove their trade barriers on our products.

Dozens of bills have been introduced in Congress in recent years to protect U.S. industry from foreign competition. Few passed, and many of those that did were killed by presidential veto. In July 1988, however, Congress passed the 1988 Omnibus Trade and Competitiveness Act, which was signed by President Reagan. This 1,000 page act is both protectionist and pro-free trade, but is not as restrictive as many people would have liked.

The act contains no major new tariff barriers. It retains current restrictions for the most part, reduces some tariffs, and provides aid for exporters. It also gives the president new authority to deal vigorously with foreign countries which are identified as engaging in unfair trade practices.

The bill eliminates duties on many products for which there is no source in the United States. Also, the administration is given the authority to slash duties as much as 50 percent in its current negotiations on tariffs with other countries. It reinforces the ban on dumping (selling products in the U.S. at prices below costs). The president is required to negotiate with foreign officials to open their markets to U.S. products and is directed to seek more reciprocity in scientific exchanges with other countries. The U.S. Bureau of Standards is encouraged to work on leading-edge technologies such as superconductivity, biotechnology, and advanced composite materials. The bill provides $2 billion to boost exports of agricultural products. Funds are made available to retrain workers who lose their jobs because of plant closings or modernization. It also expands assistance, now in the law, for retraining workers displaced by imports. Various provisions seek to expand information about foreign trade for both governmental and business use. Export controls are dropped for a long list of electronic products which heretofore were denied export licenses for national security reasons. Finally, an important power is given to the president to retaliate against countries accused of unfair trade practices.

Earlier trade laws have given the president authority to impose trade sanctions against countries engaged in unjustifiable trade practices. Section 301 of the Omnibus Trade Act goes much further. It mandates that the president report on countries engaged in "unfair" trade practices and to take action against them if negotiations fail to correct the situation. Pursuant to this act, the president, in May 1989, cited Japan, Brazil, and India, and placed twenty-two other countries on a "watch list." The Japanese have been a special target for retaliation because of their huge trade surpluses, not only with the United States but other nations, and were cited for barriers to imports of U.S. supercomputers, satellites, and lumber. The administration could have named Japan's virtual ban on foreign rice and its limited purchases of many other products made in the United States, such as semiconductors and fiber-optic cable. Under the provisions of the act, the president is required to reach a satisfactory agreement with the cited countries (in this case Japan) within a few months. If agreement is not forthcoming, the administration is empowered to impose punitive 100 percent tariffs on some Japanese imports to the United States. The citation was a shock to the Japanese, but negotiations were satisfactorily concluded and the sanctions were not imposed. Section 301 has teeth in it, but also dangers of retaliation.

FOREIGN OBSTACLES TO U.S. EXPORTS

Foreign obstacles to our exports, both real and perceived, cover a wide spectrum from tariffs, outright bans, import procedures and cumbersome bureaucracies to customs and behavior patterns of people and their institutions. Following are illustrations of some of the barriers that inflame protectionists.

Quotas, or restrictions on the quantity of foreign imports, are a favorite barrier. Japan, for instance, has restrictions on a long list of agricultural products. Selective tariffs impede the flow of many products. France and the United Kingdom, for instance, have tariffs on communications hardware and most grains. "Buy Domestic" restrictions are widespread. Many other types of barriers exist, ranging from patents and copyrights to nationalistic customs.

Although every nation has a battery of restrictions on imports, Japan is a special target, partly because of its success in penetrating foreign markets but also because of its widespread barriers to the purchase of foreign-made goods. The literature is filled with anecdotes about how tulip bulbs are excluded on health grounds or how imported automobiles are minutely examined for the slightest scratch. These barriers exist because of long held customs and behavior patterns of the Japanese people. So exasperated was Willy de Clerg, the European Economic Communities Commissioner for External Relations, that he said: "The plain message is that unless Japan opens up its market to the rest of the world and breaks down the autarchic structures that inhibit fair international competition, there can be no stable multilateral trading relationship."[14]

Subsidies to export industries are a competitive tool used by countries around the world, including the United States. The popular A320 airbus, produced by Airbus Industrie in France, is said to have received $3.4 billion in government development money.[15] No industry is more subsidized than agriculture. Agricultural subsidies encourage overproduction and create

[14]Clyde H. Farnsworth, "Europe Assails Trade Pattern," *New York Times,* July 4, 1986.
[15]Rahul Jacob, "Export Barriers the U.S. Hates Most," *Fortune,* February 27, 1989.

gluts in world markets which lead to further export subsidies, import restrictions, and more trade restrictions. GATT, as noted previously, is organized to arrange negotiations to reduce trade restrictions, but European agricultural countries and the United States have exempted their farm programs from GATT rules.

DEVIATIONS FROM FREE TRADE POLICY

Despite the asserted free trade policy of the United States and the strong free-trade rhetoric of government officials, deviations from free trade policy have been many and significant. The post-World War II boundless optimism of U.S. managers, and the extraordinary economic power of the United States around the world, favored free trade policies. As this nation's economic clout has eroded, and as U.S. industry has been battered by foreign competition, protectionist pressures have led to more and more import restrictions. Classic illustrations are the quotas imposed on steel and on Japanese automobiles.

Steel   For the past two decades, our steel imports have exceeded our exports, and the steel industry has persistently asked for and received protection. In 1984, for example, steel imports amounted to a new high of 26.4 percent of the domestic steel market. The government set steel import quotas and pressed other nations to stop subsidies on their steel exports to this country. At the same time, our industry modernized its equipment and increased productivity to such an extent that the cost of steel dropped 30 percent. The result has been a drop in the share of our domestic market held by foreign exporters. But it is still around 20 percent, and the steel industry continues to press for extension of the quota system.

Steel producers argue that they need protection from subsidized steel from abroad while they continue to modernize their plant and equipment. They have a point, because foreign subsidies to foreign steelmakers are huge, and they can land some basic steel shapes and forms on our shores at prices below our low-cost producers. One observer concluded that the European Community spent about $35 billion in steel subsidies during the past decade.[16]

There are many, however, who strongly oppose the extension of steel quotas. Without restraints, they say, steel prices in this country would have been much lower. Manufacturers opposed the quotas on the grounds that steel prices to them were higher, and this resulted in higher prices for their finished products, from refrigerators to canned tomatoes. The cost to consumers has been, as a result, billions of dollars. Higher steel prices also weaken our competitive position abroad. Some also argue that while jobs in the steel industry may have been saved with quotas, the quotas resulted in lost jobs in other industries as a result of the higher prices.

[16]Robert Kuttner, "Why Scrap a Steel Policy That Works?" *Business Week,* May 22, 1989.

Automobiles In 1977, imported car sales were 18 percent of total U.S. domestic sales. Foreign imports have grown steadily since and are now around 30 percent of the market. From 1978 to 1981, U.S.-made automobile and truck sales fell almost 50 percent, to a low of 6.2 million in 1981. There was a significant decline in jobs in the automobile industry. Since then, the industry has revived, and both sales and jobs have grown, but not to the previous peaks.

Severe pressures were put on the government in the late 1970s to restrict imports. In the face of this threat, the Japanese in 1981 imposed "voluntary" limits on their exports of cars and light trucks by about 7 percent. Voluntary quotas have been extended each year since, and an agreement was reached to limit exports to the United States. At first the quota was 1.68 million vehicles a year, but now the total is 2.3 million a year. When the threat of Japanese imports was first recognized, the complaint was that the Japanese were "dumping" in the United States. As facts became known, it was clear that the Japanese had a distinct advantage over U.S. manufacturers with respect to productivity per man hour, labor costs per car, quality, and a very favorable yen to dollar exchange rate.[17] Indeed, these advantages permitted the Japanese to drop an auto on our shores at a profitable price that was from $1,200 to $1,800 under the cost of a comparable U.S. car!

Much of the demand for protectionist legislation has eroded as a result of a 50 percent decline in the value of the yen relative to the dollar (from early 1985 to mid-1989) and the improved productivity and quality of the U.S. automotive industry. U.S. companies can now produce automobiles at prices comparable to those of the Japanese, and also of good quality. Yet the Japanese government decided to keep the so-called voluntary quotas again in 1990 at 2.3 million cars a year. They said a major reason was the political sensitivity in the United States to Japanese imports. Some observers think also that the quotas prevented unnecessary competition among Japanese companies to export to this country.

Other Protectionist Measures Hundreds of other products enjoy government protection, including bicycles, sheet glass, watches, sugar, stainless steel flatware, velvet carpets, motorcycles, and machine tools. In addition, there are "Buy American" laws that require government agencies to purchase products made in this country. The Federal Buy American Act of 1933 requires federal agencies to pay up to a 6 percent differential for domestically produced goods. Many states have Buy American laws.

Export Curbs and Aids Some government programs discourage U.S. exports. In addition to restrictions for national security and diplomatic goals (mentioned above), the following programs have been said by business to discourage exports: taxation of income earned abroad by U.S. citizens living

---

[17]William J. Abernathy, Kim B. Clark, and Alan M. Kantrow, *Industrial Renaissance: Producing a Competitive Future for America*, New York: Basic Books, 1983.

abroad and working for American companies; the Foreign Corrupt Practices Act, which we will discuss shortly; uncertainty over availability of foreign tax credits; uncertainty about the application of antitrust laws to joint international ventures; antipollution controls that raise costs; and laws that prohibit foreign sales of products prohibited for sale in the United States, such as drugs not certified by the FDA.

But there are generous benefits available to some manufacturers in exporting their products. One of the best known is the Export Import Bank of the United States. This independent government agency helps finance U.S. exports of goods and services, either through direct loans to foreign buyers or through guarantees that assure repayment of loans made by U.S. exporters and private banks. The total in loans that the bank can have outstanding at any one time is $25 billion. There are other financial aids, such as the Overseas Private Investment Corporation, which insures MNCs against political risks in foreign countries, provides tax incentives to export, trade promotion programs, and information from both the federal government and U.S. embassies about trade opportunities and threats. Agricultural subsidies should be mentioned here. They amounted to about $25 billion in 1988, much (but not all) of which directly or indirectly subsidized exports.

FREE TRADE THEORY VERSUS REALITY

It is clear from what has been said that there is a gap between free trade theory and government practice. The reality is that the global economy is a mixture of free trade and protectionism. It always has been. In such a world, how far can the United States go in lowering its trade barriers? Clearly, it cannot be the only major free trade zone in the world. So far as economic theory is concerned, the words of Paul W. McCracken, a highly respected economist, are provocative: "Professors," he observed, "would quickly lose their zeal for open trade if universities found that their strained budgets would be relieved by dismissing high-priced domestic professors and importing cheaper (and better?) pedagogy."[18]

Free trade theory depends on a number of basic assumptions in order to work as postulated, not the least of which is pure competition. Unfortunately, this and other assumptions upon which free trade theory rests do not always square with the real world. As a result, no one practices or desires free trade in the classic textbook sense. This inevitably leads to the pragmatic approach described above. To quote an article title, "The Gospel of Free Trade is Losing Apostles."[19] However, few would argue with the idea that it is in the interests of U.S. and world consumers to strive to achieve free world trade.

[18]Paul W. McCracken, "Light at the End of the Budget Tunnel," *The Wall Street Journal*, March 19, 1985.
[19]Karen Pennar, "The Gospel of Free Trade is Losing Apostles," *Business Week*, February 27, 1969:89.

SHOULD WE HAVE A DOUBLE STANDARD FOR EXPORT PRODUCTS?

Constance Cooper, a Canadian, sued Shiley Inc. because she feared a heart valve sold by the firm would be defective and she would die. She said that every time her heart beat she heard the tiny clicks of two mechanical valves implanted in her heart. "You wake up every night," she said, "and you just want to hear those clicks perfectly. You just hope you're going to wake up in the morning."[20] In December 1989, Shiley paid Cooper an undisclosed sum in settlement.

Shiley, a subsidiary of giant Pfizer Inc., won approval of the FDA to sell its heart valves not only in the United States but abroad, in April 1979. These mechanical valves were the predecessors of the valves implanted in Constance Cooper. They became the world's most widely used mechanical valves to replace diseased or damaged human heart valves. The valves developed fractures, and a new valve was made. In 1980, the FDA rejected a request that this valve be sold in the United States, but the agency gave Shiley permission to export it. Some 5,600 valves were exported, and Constance Cooper got one.

These valves also developed fracture problems and failed. How many people died as a result is not known. But the FDA has received reports of 181 deaths involving this valve and its predecessors.

Should the United States impose its strict standards on foreign customers of our pharmaceutical companies? Today there are many drugs and medical devices prohibited for sale in the United States that are sold abroad by our companies. Some consumer advocates say this should stop. The industry says we cannot and should not try to impose our standards on other countries.

FOREIGN PAYOFFS

Following the Watergate exposures, the Securities and Exchange Commission (SEC) began an investigation in 1974 to determine to what extent corporations had been illegally involved in making corporate contributions to former President Nixon's 1972 reelection campaign. The SEC investigations revealed illegal contributions but turned up, more importantly, deceptive accounting practices intended to cover up illegal foreign payments. Many of these payments were not illegal under United States law, but withholding material information from shareholders was. The SEC "invited" corporations to make voluntary disclosure of this activity. More than 400 corporations responded and disclosed that they had made almost $1 billion in questionable payments, mostly foreign. This disclosure immediately opened a Pandora's box of complex and troublesome questions concerning international investment of MNCs, United States foreign policy, applicable laws, and morality.

THE SPECTRUM OF FOREIGN PAYOFFS

At one end of the spectrum of payoffs are lubrication bribes involving relatively small amounts of money. They range from tips for services rendered to

---

[20]Douglas Frantz, "For Export: A Double Standard?" *Los Angeles Times*, December 12, 1989.

"requests" for money to stimulate someone to perform. In this category are payments to speed clearances of goods at ports of entry, certifications required, and so on. They are called "honest" graft, "tokens of appreciation," "contributions," and so on. They carry different names: *mordida* ("the bite"), *kumshaw* ("thank you"), *jeitinho* ("the fix"), and so on. They are accepted around the world as legitimate for services rendered. These payments are often sanctioned to offset low salaries in foreign countries.

At the other end of the spectrum is extortion. The chairman of Gulf Oil Corporation reported that South Korea's S.K. Kim, financial chairman of the Republican party, threatened the company's $300 million investment (mostly in refining and petrochemicals) if the company did not make a $10 million contribution to the party. Bob Dorsey, chairman of Gulf, eventually haggled the amount down to $3 million. This, of course, was blackmail.

In between the two extremes are payments made for all sorts of situations, such as to reduce inflated taxes, to get or retain business, to avoid threats and harassment, to obtain favors from officials that are denied to competitors, and to influence foreign governments' political actions.

LEGISLATION CONCERNING PAYOFFS

As a result of payoff disclosures, Congress passed the Foreign Corrupt Practices Act (FCPA) in 1977.[21] Here is a brief summary of the provisions of the act.

• Companies must make and keep accounting records that accurately and fairly reflect transactions. These records must be kept in "reasonable detail." "Reasonable detail" is defined as a level of detail that "would satisfy prudent officials" weighing the costs and benefits of control systems.

• It is a crime for a U.S. firm or its officers to bribe officials of foreign governments, foreign political party officials, or candidates of foreign political parties by offering gifts or payments for the purpose of getting those officials to exert influence on behalf of the U.S. firm.

• Third-party bribery is prohibited. It is unlawful to make payments to intermediaries or consultants "while knowing" that this person will transfer all or a portion of the money to foreign officials or political party candidates to influence acts or decisions on behalf of the U.S. firm. "Knowing" means that the firm is "substantially certain" or "aware of the high probability" that a payment to an intermediary will be repaid to a foreign official as a bribe.

• Excluded from criminal penalty are "grease" payments made to any foreign official when such payments are intended to expedite "routine government action" such as processing paperwork, obtaining licenses and permits, providing police protection, scheduling inspections, unloading cargo, or per-

---

[21]Pub. L. 95-213, December 19, 1977, 91 Stat. 1494, codified as amended at 15 U.S.C. Secs. 78dd-1 to -2. Amended in 1988 in the Omnibus Trade and Competitiveness Act of 1988, Pub. L. No. 100-418, 102 Stat. 1415. For analysis of the FCPA see Adam Fremantle and Sherman Katz, "The Foreign Corrupt Practices Act Amendments of 1988," *The International Lawyer*, Fall 1989, and O. Ronald Gray, "The Foreign Corrupt Practices Act: Revisited and Amended," *Business and Society*, Spring 1990.

forming "actions of a similar nature." The dividing line between "grease" payments and impermissible "corrupt" payments is reached when the foreign official exercises significant discretion in a situation where business is being obtained or retained.

• U.S. firms may make any payments that are "lawful under the written laws and regulations of the foreign...country" and payments that can be defended as "reasonable and bona fide" expenses related to "promotion, demonstration or explanation of products or services" or to "the execution or performance of a contract with a foreign government."

• U.S. firms must see that all foreign subsidiaries in which they have 50 percent or greater ownership comply with all provisions of the act. With less than 50 percent ownership, a U.S. firm must proceed in good faith to use its influence and make the subsidiary comply.

• Corporations may be fined up to $2 million for criminal violation of the FCPA and up to $10,000 for civil violations. Individual managers may be fined up to $1000,000 for willful criminal violations and may be imprisoned up to 5 years, or both.

Prior to passage, the FCPA was strongly opposed by the business community, which feared that U.S. companies would be handicapped in overseas competition against foreign companies unrestrained by antibribery laws. Polls of business executives taken shortly after passage of the law showed, however, that most did not feel they had lost business because of the FCPA. A special White House task force appointed by President Carter, however, concluded that lost business as a result of the act amounted to $1 billion a year and criticized the federal government for needlessly handicapping U.S. firms.

Over the years federal regulators have not been exceptionally zealous in enforcing provisions of the FCPA. Companies may obtain advisory opinions, called "review letters" from the Department of Justice (DOJ). When a review letter states that a transaction will not lead to an enforcement action, the company is free to proceed. Many firms also have obtained opinion letters from law firms regarding their transactions. Although the DOJ has opened as many as twenty investigations of foreign bribery by corporations, no prosecutions have been recorded. The SEC has been somewhat more active. Since the FCPA's passage in 1977 it has brought one criminal prosecution for violation of the antibribery section as well as 109 injunctive actions and twenty-four administrative proceedings for violations of the accounting sections. The largest enforcement action was when Donald G. Crawfrd, a Texas oil millionaire, agreed to pay a fine of $3.75 million for bribing officials of Pamex, the Mexican national oil company. But neither agency has used the FCPA to advance an activist agenda. The Reagan and Bush administrations have placed little emphasis on FCPA enforcement.

American Corporations
in South Africa

South Africa is a land of great and often stunning contrasts; of fertile green valleys and harsh near-desert conditions; of rugged mountains and endless silver beaches along two oceans; of hot summers and cold winter conditions; of bustling twentieth-century cities and settlements of hovels; of great wealth and bitter poverty; of dynamic growth and artificial restrictions to growth; of freedom for some and denial of basic human rights for the majority.

—*Traveler's Guide to Central and Southern Africa*[22]

The writer of this travelogue might well have included one other "stunning contrast," that between the goals of American corporations doing business in South Africa and the goals of activist critics who believe their business there is unethical. Corporations believe their economic activity advances the welfare of all of South Africa's citizens. Critics, however, believe that the presence of U.S. firms in South Africa adds legitimacy and support to an official government policy of racial discrimination called apartheid (literally "living apart"). A series of discriminatory laws passed since 1913 by whites prescribes a policy of separate development for the four officially recognized racial categories in the country's population of 34.3 million. The population includes:

• *25.5 million black Africans:* The blacks are composed of ten major ethnic groups, including Zulu, Xhosa, North and South Sotho, Tswana, Shangaan, Swazï, North and South Ndebele, and Venda. Non-Africans often believe that South African blacks are homogeneous, but some animosities exist among these native groups, and each is composed of many separate tribes. The most cohesive, the Venda, have twenty-seven distinct tribes. Cultural differences exist among the various black ethnic groups, and four main African languages are spoken.

---

[22]Gill Garb, ed., *Traveler's Guide to Central and Southern Africa,* London: IC Magazines Ltd., 1981, p. 152.

- *4.9 million whites:* One-third of the South African white population is an English-speaking people of British descent, and two-thirds are Afrikaners, or descendants of the white pioneers who settled the South African interior in much the same way as European immigrants settled the American frontier. These pioneers were a mixture of Dutch, French Huguenots who left Europe to escape religious persecution, Germans, and English. A language, called Afrikaans, developed during the colonization period and is a unique evolution of Dutch mixed with the tongues of other settlers. Today, Afrikaans is the official language of South Africa.

- *3 million coloureds:* "Coloured" is an official term denoting those of mixed race. Most coloureds trace their ancestry from the intermarriage of early male Dutch settlers in the Cape Province with women of the indigenous, brown-skinned San and Khoikhoi natives. A great shortage of white European women in the early settlement years led to frequent interracial marriage.

- *884,000 Asians:* The Asian community consists mainly of Indians who are concentrated in the province of Natal. They were originally brought to the country in the 1870s as indentured servants to work on sugar plantations in the 1870s because African men could not be induced to labor in cane fields. This category includes Chinese also.

THE HISTORY OF SOUTH AFRICA

To understand South African society today, it is essential to know its colorful and humanly costly history. The original inhabitants of the area were tribes of hunters and gatherers. By 1652, when the Netherlands (Dutch) East India Company established the first permanent white settlement in Cape Town, some of these tribes had developed agricultural and cattle-raising cultures.

Early Dutch settlers established a fort at Cape Town in 1652 to provision ships passing around the Cape of Good Hope. Soon the Dutch began to trade with the native population, and a few hardy employees of the Netherlands East India Company were given free land by the company to farm and raise stock. These were the first Dutch farmer-settlers, known as Boers. It was at this time that the first policies of racial segregation were established. The white Dutch settlers gradually expanded from the small Cape Town settlement, displacing local Africans who were not allowed title to land or political rights in the new white community. Although native residents remained free, the Dutch colonists imported slaves from elsewhere in Africa and from Indonesia.

It is important to note that native African cultures in an "iron-age" stage of cultural development had been thrown in contact with European cultures in the early stages of industrial development. The Europeans possessed a military technology that was far superior to the primitive warfare styles of the Africans, and when resistance was encountered, the Dutch settlers massacred opponents with modern firearms. As the Boers expanded to settle new lands in the interior, they fought frequent battles with black natives. There

were few casualties for the settlers and many for the Africans. To this day, white South Africans celebrate Covenant Day on December 16, in recognition of the Battle of Blood River in 1838, when 3,000 Zulu tribesmen attacked 500 Boer settlers. The Zulu ranks were decimated while the whites suffered not a single casualty, and the Boers, who were fervent Calvinists, took this as a sign that God favored the cause of white supremacy in South Africa. Today, Covenant Day is an annual reaffirmation of this belief.

With the defeat of the Dutch by the British in the Napoleonic Wars, South Africa suddenly came under British rule. Boer settlers were angered when the British imposed new taxes and freed their slaves. The Boers responded by trekking farther into the interior to establish two independent republics. Conflict between the rebellious Boers and the British culminated with the victory of the British in the bitter Anglo-Boer War of 1899 to 1902. But Boer opposition was so strong that following their battlefield victory, the British nonetheless conceded self-government to the territory known as South Africa and its stubborn white settlers. At first, the government was dominated by the English, but in elections in 1948, the Afrikaners' National Party achieved an electoral victory. Since 1948, the political interests of the Afrikaners (as the descendants of the Boers now call themselves) have been dominant.

Over the years of their struggles with native Africans and the British, the Afrikaners developed a cohesive ideology. They believed that their group, the descendants of the Boer farmers who fought to settle the land, was predestined by God to rule.[23] They believed that whites were culturally superior to blacks, coloureds, and Asians. They believed that the races could not be expected to live in harmony because of vast social and cultural differences. And over the years they developed a fierce in-group loyalty, leading the white Afrikaner elite to adopt a tone of secretiveness and cultural arrogance.[24]

In the 1950s, this Afrikaner ideology was translated into a series of apartheid laws that established the framework of a racially segregated society. Some laws set up a system of "petty apartheid" that resembled the old Jim Crow laws in the American South, wherein restaurants, hotels, train stations, post offices, rest rooms, and other public facilities were segregated. Interracial sexual acts and marriages were prohibited. Today much of the petty apartheid framework is gone, making overt discrimination less noticeable in the large cities frequented by foreign visitors.

Other laws, however, set up a continuing and repressive system of "grand apartheid." All South Africans are legally classified by race as black, white, coloured, or Asian. Until recently, a complex web of forty-three pass laws controlled the movements of blacks within the country. They had to carry passbooks identifying them as black, were forbidden to live or remain overnight in white areas, and were required to register with employers if they took jobs away from tribal homelands. These homelands occupy about 14 percent of South African territory, have black governments, and are declared to be officially independent nation-states, although their constitutions prohibit armed forces. Blacks were assigned citizenship in one of these homelands based on their tribal designation and were not citizens of South Africa. Blacks cannot vote in South African elections, but have self-rule within their homelands. Finally, a series of enactments extends widespread power to the South African police to prohibit assembly, outlaw black opposition groups, and detain suspected opponents of apartheid—all without standards of evidence as rigorous as in the United States.

In defense of apartheid, whites argued that they conquered and colonized the territory comprising South Africa and had a legal right to rule. The apartheid system, they said, was the best solution for governing a nation of such diverse inhabitants. Democracy could not work in a multiracial, fragmented society like South Africa; it works best in a homogeneous political culture

---

[23]The development of a theology in support of apartheid by the Dutch Reformed Church in South Africa is deftly described in a passage from James A. Michener's historical novel of South Africa, *The Covenant*, New York: Fawcett Crest Books, 1980, pp. 969–972. This sweeping work also brings the rest of South Africa's historical development to life. In 1986 the Dutch Reformed Church officially recanted its support of apartheid.

[24]Chester A. Crocker, "South Africa: Strategy for Change," *Foreign Affairs*, Winter 1980/81.

and is a mistake where unusually vast differences in language, religion, cultural heritage, education, and race exist. They also argued that the system was less repressive than other African governments. Blacks in South Africa had a higher economic standard of living than blacks in other African countries. Blacks throughout the African continent have suffered under impoverished black leadership in countries emerging from colonial rule. Some black African nations have not only been poorly run but are brutally repressive as well. Such situations arise where no democratic tradition exists and ageless tribal rivalries reassert themselves within modern parliamentary frameworks. Soon opposition parties and tribes are viciously repressed by the dominant tribe.

SOUTH AFRICA TODAY

Under pressure from the outside world and black resistance groups, the South African government has made cosmetic reforms which leave the basic pillars of apartheid intact. In 1984, for example, a new constitution gave the vote to coloured and Asian citizens, who could elect separate, advisory parliaments to represent their racial categories. Blacks, however, were given no vote and no parliament. Only whites, of course, could vote for members of the dominant white parliament. The implementation of this new parliamentary scheme resulted in violent rioting in black urban townships throughout South Africa, and the government was forced to institute a long-term "state of emergency" giving it broad powers to suppress black critics and the news media. In 1986, the government abolished the hated pass laws and blacks were allowed to move freely about the country, if not live in white areas. Opponents of the regime were not placated. They saw that the bulk of the framework of laws segregating the races was intact. They argued that superficial reforms could no more cure racism in South Africa than cancer can be cured by a bandage.

For much of the 1980s, a stalemate existed between the white government and its opponents. The government was unable to successfully implement constitutional reforms designed to preserve the essence of apartheid. The African National Congress, a black anti-apartheid group dedicated to violent resistance against the white government, conducted guerilla raids, sabotage, car bombings, and world-wide political opposition. Yet the group was never able to start a real revolution. Military and police forces were too strong, and many blacks were economically well off and not inclined to fight.

As this stalemate dragged on and international economic sanctions braked the economy, white South Africans increasingly realized that the apartheid system had failed as a political solution for governing diverse population groups. In 1990, South African President F. W. de Klerk took dramatic actions. He lifted a thirty-year ban on black political demonstrations; lifted bans on sixty anti-apartheid groups, including the violence-prone African National Congress and the South African Communist Party; integrated beaches and called for rescinding the law that segregated many public facilities; freed prominent political prisoners, including Nelson Mandela, a long-imprisoned revolutionary of mythic stature to blacks; and initiated negotiations with the African National Congress and other groups to shape a new, as yet undefined, South African system.

U.S. CORPORATIONS IN SOUTH AFRICA

South Africa welcomes American multinationals, and as of early 1990, 123 U.S. firms have direct investment there. Some of the largest are Minnesota Mining & Manufacturing Co., United Technologies Corp., Johnson & Johnson, and International Paper. About 5,000 others have trading arrangements, such as distributorships. Coca-Cola, Ford, and IBM, for example, sell their products through licensing arrangements with businesses owned entirely by South Africans and have no permanent employees or assets in the country.

Total direct foreign investment by U.S. companies is about 6 percent of the total capital invested in South Africa and about 18 percent of all foreign investment there.[25] This is a far smaller commitment than that of British companies, other European companies, and Japanese companies. (In order to court Japanese business, incidentally, South Africans classify Japanese businessmen as "honorary whites" rather than Asians and allow them to use white facilities and move freely in white areas without harassment.) U.S. firms employ roughly 120,000 black African workers—about 2 percent of the black labor force.

In 1950, direct foreign investment by U.S. firms was $140 million. Today it stands at $1.6 billion, down from a high of $2.63 billion in 1982, according to U.S. Commerce Department estimates. This is less than one-half of one percent of all U.S. foreign direct investment. The figure does not include bank loans (which totaled $3 billion in 1987), stock held by U.S. citizens (in the range of $4 to $6 billion), or indirect ownership of South African companies through wholly owned subsidiaries of U.S. firms on foreign soil. Total U.S. economic involvement, then, is far greater than the $1.3 billion figure.

ECONOMIC SANCTIONS ARE APPLIED

As conditions in South Africa deteriorated in 1985, the debate about policy with respect to U.S. corporations and trade became polarized. All sides wanted apartheid ended, but two paths to this goal each had strong support.

Anti-apartheid groups called for *principled disengagement* to require U.S. corporations to end investment in and trade with South Africa. Disinvestment would end direct tax subsidy and symbolic corporate support for apartheid. Trade sanctions would destabilize the South African economy, weakening white support for apartheid and leading to negotiations for democracy with nonwhites.

Corporations and the Reagan administration, on the other hand, called for *constructive engagement,* a policy which encouraged U.S. firms to stay in South

[25]David Brock, "Pondering the Cost of Sanctions," *Insight,* July 14, 1986.

Africa as a means of building leverage to pressure a recalcitrant Afrikaner class for reform.[26] The companies argued that they were a progressive force improving the life of all races. The Department of State favored the presence of U.S. corporations to increase diplomatic influence. South Africa has always been seen as an important strategic ally in world politics because (1) it is the major source of a number of strategic minerals, (2) its location on the southern tip of the African continent gives it control of the oil sea lane from the Persian Gulf, through which the bulk of the Western world's oil supply passes, and (3) it is a bulwark against the expansion of communist influence in southern Africa.

But in 1986, Congress passed the Comprehensive Anti-Apartheid Act to restrict economic involvement with South Africa. President Reagan vetoed it, but large majorities in both the House and Senate overrode his veto, and it became law.[27] This law prohibited new direct investment by U.S. corporations; banned export sales of petroleum, munitions, and nuclear materials or technology to South Africa; banned import of a wide range of South African natural resources and finished products; and prohibited landings by South African airliners at U.S. airports. In 1989, Congress also prohibited U.S. corporations from continuing the long-standing practice of deducting South African taxes from their U.S. income taxes.[28]

Together, these laws comprise the strongest economic sanctions of any country. But other countries have similar laws. Five other countries—Japan, West Germany, Italy, France, and Canada—prohibit new corporate investment, and the European Economic Community asks for voluntary restraint.[29] Since 1973, the Organization of Petroleum Exporting Countries (OPEC) has boycotted South Africa. These countries, and others, also restrict a range of trade activity similar to that in the U.S. law, but generally not as extensive.

Have sanctions hurt the South African economy? There is disagreement. The South African government denies adverse impact. A 1988 study by the Chamber of Commerce concluded that the sanctions "have had little effect

---

[26]The two best explanations of the policy of constructive engagement as national policy are Chester A. Crocker, "South Africa: Strategy for Change," *Foreign Affairs*, Winter 1980/81 and Ronald Reagan's single public statement, "U.S. Economic Relations With South Africa: Apartheid, Some Solutions," speech delivered to the American people, Washington, D.C., July 22, 1986, in *Vital Speeches of the Day*, August 15, 1986. The term "constructive engagement" subsequently fell into official disuse, but it still characterizes a distinctive policy approach standing in contrast to approaches that advocate severing economic relations.

[27]P.L. 99-440; 22 U.S.C. Secs. 5001–5116 (Supp. IV 1986). The vote in the House was 313 to 83; the vote in the Senate was 78 to 21. The large majorities were formed by a coalition of groups in Congress, each with different motives. They included the Congressional Black Caucus, which supports black causes; young Republican conservatives trying to attract black support for the GOP; a bloc of Democrats who were afraid to vote against the bill in an election year; and moderate Republicans, who wanted to shape a new alternative to presidential policy. See Michael Clough, "Southern Africa: Challenges and Choices," *Foreign Affairs,* Summer 1988, pp. 1071–72.

[28]Section 10231, Part IV, Title X of the Omnibus Budget Reconciliation Act of 1987. P.L. 100-203.

[29]For a discussion of sanctions by European countries see Martin Holland, "Disinvestment, Sanctions, and the European Community's Code of Conduct in South Africa," *African Affairs,* October 1989. In 1990, Britain elected to unilaterally lift its embargo on new investment after failing to persuade other European Community nations to do the same.

on the South African economy as a whole."[30] In 1987, the year following the imposition of U.S. sanctions, the South African economy grew by 2.6%, up 0.5% from 1986. And, in spite of a decrease in trade with the U.S., South African imports and exports increased, due to growth in trade with countries such as Taiwan and Japan.

Yet after 1987 economic growth slowed; inflation, unemployment, and interest rates rose. A 1988 study by the General Accounting Office stated that world sanctions were causing massive trade problems for South Africa, reducing both imports and exports. The fall in imports was slight, but exports were cut by 7%.[31] A 1990 study estimated that world sanctions had cost South Africa $32 to $40 billion, including $11 billion in net capital outflows and $4 billion in lost export revenues.[32] And to evade the ban on oil shipments by OPEC countries and other nations, South Africa, by its own admission, has to pay a premium of $2 billion each year for oil.[33]

It is probable that sanctions have contributed to sluggishness in the South African economy, but they have not crippled it. Statistics can be used to support both pro-investment and disinvestment policy preferences. As a policy tool, the Anti-Apartheid Act may not be powerful enough to pressure South Africa into meaningful reform of apartheid. Its limited trade sanctions are easily circumvented, and Presidents Reagan and Bush have only weakly enforced the law.[34] Its impact has been largely symbolic, and today South Africa continues to be by far the most industrialized economy on the African continent, shoring up the faltering economies of many neighboring black nations.

THE ARGUMENT FOR U.S. CORPORATE INVESTMENT

American corporations have resisted disinvestment pressure over the years, making the following arguments.

First, American firms are committed to ending apartheid and act as a liberal force in the country. Indeed, there is a long record of corporate resistance to racial laws. In the 1960s, IBM and General Motors defied the law to integrate employee cafeterias and use black supervisors. After 1977, up to 130 companies followed a set of social responsibility guidelines for South African operations drawn up by the Rev. Leon Sullivan, a black director of GM. Every year, American firms spent millions on training, education, housing,

[30]"Statement on Proposed Additional U.S. Economic Sanctions Against South Africa," submitted to the Senate Foreign Relations Committee, Washington, D.C.: Chamber of Commerce of the United States, June 24, 1988, p. 9.

[31]Allan I. Mendelowitz, *U.S. Sanctions Against South Africa*, Washington, D.C.: General Accounting Office, June 24, 1988, p. 15.

[32]William Claiborne, "South Africa's Quiet Revolution," *Washington Post National Weekly Edition*, January 22–28, 1990, p. 24.

[33]The Africa Fund, *Questions and Answers on South Africa Sanctions*, New York: The Africa Fund, 1989, p. 3.

[34]For a study of enforcement problems see, for example, U.S. General Accounting Office, *South Africa: Enhancing Enforcement of the Comprehensive Anti-Apartheid Act*, Washington, D.C.: Government Printing Office, July 1989.

health care, and other benefits for blacks to fulfill their duties as signatories of the so-called Sullivan Principles. Although Rev. Sullivan abandoned the principles which bear his name in 1985 and called for a complete withdrawal of U.S. corporations, companies still in South Africa adhere to a similar set of principles today.[35] American firms have also needled the South Africans about racial policies. Mobil published newspaper ads calling for a new non-racial democracy headlined, "There Is a Better Way." GM once offered to pay the legal fees of black employees arrested on white-only beaches near its Port Elizabeth assembly plant.

When U.S. firms leave, their liberalizing presence is lost. For example, General Motors left South Africa in 1986, selling its subsidiary to the white South African managers who ran it. The subsidiary was renamed Delta Motors, but it continues to manufacture the same GM cars and trucks under license. Sales increased from 24,000 vehicles in 1986 to 40,000 in 1988. Conservative whites, who had refused to buy GM cars due to its stand on Port Elizabeth's beaches, returned as customers, and Delta Motors also began to sell cars to the South African military and police, a market legally forbidden to GM.[36]

Second, American firms argue that apartheid will end sooner in a climate of economic growth than in a climate of constriction. Blacks have borne the greatest immediate burden under U.S. sanctions. Thousands of black workers have been laid off in industries hurt by the Anti-Apartheid Act, such as coal mining, agriculture, and iron and steel. The vast majority of public opinion polls in South Africa show large majorities of blacks opposed to trade boycotts and the pullout of foreign companies. In a 1989 Gallup poll taken in South Africa, 82 percent of blacks rejected foreign sanctions as a stimulus to change, and 85 percent thought that disinvestment by U.S. firms was a bad idea.[37] Black self-interest was forcefully stated by James Nycoya, president of the South African Black Taxi Association, in testimony before a U.S. congressional committee: "I ask you to hear our voices...before you decide what is good for us. Before you decide that black children must go hungry so you can be on the right side of history."[38]

And third, American firms argue that disinvestment pressures subordinate corporate policy to the goals of activists, church groups, and minority shareholders who sponsor get-out-of-South Africa shareholder proposals. These activists use corporation assets as a lever to force a foreign government

[35]The evolution of the Sullivan Principles is described in Karen Paul, "Corporate Social Monitoring in South Africa: A Decade of Achievement, an Uncertain Future," *Journal of Business Ethics,* June 1989.

[36]ICCR Brief, "White Wheels of Fortune: Ford and GM in South Africa," *Corporate Examiner,* vol. 18, no. 6 (1989).

[37] See "Opinion Outlook: Views on National Security," *National Journal,* August 5, 1989, p. 2004. See also Donald W. Caldwell, "Attitudes in South Africa," *Public Opinion,* January/February 1988, p. 55. For a summary and assessment of similar polls see Meg Voorhes, *Black South Africans' Attitudes on Sanctions and Disinvestment,* Washington, D.C.: Investor Responsibility Research Center, June 1988.

[38] In "Statement of Mobil Oil Corporation," in Hearings, *op. cit.,* p. 521.

to change its policies. Most American managers believe this is misguided, even after they have left South Africa to avoid the "hassle factor" of continued operations there.

THE ARGUMENT AGAINST U.S. INVESTMENT

In the United States, as in other countries, a long-standing anti-apartheid movement exists. One early success of this movement came as long ago as 1971, when Polaroid stopped distributing film in South Africa due to pressure from black employees who objected to its sale for use in photographs for government-required black identification. Since then the movement has gained strength, and its political activities have forced hundreds of companies to end or curtail activity.

Critics object to the role that American corporations play in supporting the South African government and economy. Although U.S. corporations are a reformist influence and generally follow antidiscriminatory employment practices, their presence buttresses a racist regime. In a commencement address at Hunter College, Archbishop Desmond M. Tutu, a black South African, addressed the U.S. corporation's defense of its presence in these uncompromising terms:

> I would be more impressed with those who made no bones about the reason they remain in South Africa and said honestly, "We are concerned for our profits," instead of the baloney that the businesses are there for our benefit. We don't want you there. Please do us a favor; Get out and come back when we have a democratic and just South Africa....
>
> It is true that many foreign corporations in South Africa have introduced improvements for their black staff... American companies, especially, have begun to speak out more forthrightly against apartheid than has been their wont, and they would be the first to admit that they got a considerable jog to their consciences from the disinvestment campaign. There has been progress, but we do not want apartheid ameliorated or improved. We do not want apartheid made comfortable. We want it dismantled.[39]

There are many ways that U.S. corporations have supported the South African economy. For example, Caltex processed oil for South Africa, and Fluor Corporation built three coal-to-oil conversion plants that give the nation considerable energy independence. Babcock and Wilcox, Combustion Engineering, and General Electric built nuclear reactors. IBM, Unisys, and Control Data at one time supplied most of the computers used in South Africa, and IBM 370 computers, for example, were once used by the Interior Department in Pretoria to maintain the population registry in which whites, coloureds, and Asians are classified.[40]

---

[39] Desmond M. Tutu, "Sanctions Against Apartheid: Which Side Are You On?" *The Corporate Examiner*, 1986, vol. 15, no. 5.

[40] Richard Leonard, "Hardware, Software and Ingenuity for Apartheid: U.S. Computer Companies in South Africa," *The Corporate Examiner*, vol. 18, no. 1, 1989.

Activists in the U.S. have emphasized three techniques for applying pressure to U.S. corporations. First, they have lobbied all levels of government for laws that restrict investment and trade. By 1990, over sixty-five city, county, and state governments had passed laws prohibiting investment of government funds in corporations still operating in South Africa. Second, they have introduced shareholder resolutions calling for disinvestment and/or disengagement at corporate annual meetings. None has passed, but few publicly held corporations doing business in South Africa can escape a debate over such a resolution. And third, activists have started consumer boycotts. Coca-Cola elected to leave South Africa late in 1986, when the Southern Christian Leadership Conference threatened a black consumer boycott if the company did not leave by Martin Luther King's birthday, January 15, 1987. The most extensive boycott has been an ongoing effort against Royal/Dutch Shell and Shell USA which is sponsored by church groups and unions in the U.S.

Because of this active opposition, in addition to racial turmoil, legal prohibitions against further investment, loss of tax write-óffs, and a slowdown of the South African economy, 177 U.S. firms left South Africa between 1985 and 1990.

APARTHEID AT THE CROSSROADS

What change will take place in South Africa? President de Klerk has established a climate in which significant change could occur. He and others in the majority white party, the National Party, set forth the outlines of a new "dispensation" that might be acceptable to whites in a platform statement made public prior to national elections in 1989. Their vision is one of a system in which blacks share power, but do not dominate whites. How can this be accomplished? Only if black demands for a democratic system with one-person, one-vote majority rule are rejected. Then, the National Party favors a system in which all racial groups have guaranteed rights. One such group right would be the freedom to choose a communal lifestyle. For example, if whites chose to live in geographic or occupational segregation from blacks they would have the right to do so. Blacks would not participate in the new government as a single mass, but would be divided into ten tribal groups, each with group participation rights. In additional to the other traditional groups—whites, coloureds, and Asians—an "open group" of people unwilling to be classified would also exist. All population groups would decide their own affairs through self-government, and issues of common interest would be decided through a consensus process in which all groups would participate. Where consensus could not be reached, a judicial body would act as a referee. No group, of course, would be allowed to dominate the white group.

White-driven reform efforts in South Africa are calculated to reduce international and domestic pressures by presenting the appearance of movement toward a negotiated end to apartheid. Yet the end is not yet arrived. In the country's 1989 parliamentary elections, a large majority of moderate and conservative whites voted for parties with platforms that would preserve some aspects of apartheid.[41] As a pessimistic analyst notes, "the outlook for South Africa is change but no solution."[42] Others are more optimistic. De Klerk has been praised for moving boldly and creating a real, constructive opportunity for change. One diplomat has called him the "Gorbachev of southern Africa."[43]

In the meantime, American corporations continue to feel pressure to leave. But should the domestic American political climate change, many companies which have left South Africa would likely return. A large number of companies have finessed their departure by leaving behind franchises and licensing agreements. Their products are still sold in South Africa through cooperative South African businesses. The engineering firm Fluor Corp. has placed its assets in trust in anticipation of eventual return. But the return of these companies is not likely until major changes in the political, legal, and social climate take place in both South Africa and the United States.

QUESTIONS

1 What is your assessment of the positive and negative aspects of corporate involvement in South Africa?
2 Is it unethical to make profits in foreign countries where public policy is contrary to American ethics and not democratically determined?
3 Should all American corporations withdraw from South Africa, and should they be required to break all commercial ties when they do?
4 Is disinvestment or trade boycott an effective pressure for change of racial laws in South Africa?
5 Should managers of American firms advocate political change in foreign countries where they do business?

---

[41]In the September 6, 1989, elections, 48 percent of whites voted for the National Party and 31 percent for the Conservative Party, a reactionary party that takes a hard line on preserving apartheid. Only 21 percent voted for the Democratic Party, a leftist party committed to ending apartheid. For a discussion of the election see Raymond Bonner, "Choices," *The New Yorker*, December 25, 1989.

[42] Bruce W. Nelan, "Changes in South Africa," *Foreign Affairs*, vol. 69, no. 1 (1989/90), p. 151.

[43] Former British Foreign Secretary David Owen, quoted in David B. Ottaway, "De Klerk: South Africa's Gorbachev?" *Washington Post National Weekly Edition*, February 19–25, 1990.

13

Corporate Global Competitiveness

The Ford Motor Company has grown from a tiny wagon factory in Detroit in 1903, staffed with ten people, to the second largest industrial corporation in the world, as measured by sales. In 1989, its sales totaled $96.9 billion and its profits were $3.8 billion.

Ford has manufacturing plants, assembly plants, and sales affiliates in twenty-four countries of the world. It has other business relationships with automotive producers in nine countries and has a total network of more than 10,500 dealers in 200 countries and a worldwide employment of 360,000 people.

In addition to producing cars and trucks, farm and industrial tractors, industrial engines, agricultural and construction machinery, steel, glass, and plastics, the company is involved in banking, finance, insurance, automotive replacement parts, aerospace, land development, equipment, and car leasing. The historic spark and economic fuel of the company's worldwide growth, however, always has been the motor vehicle.

The company and its subsidiaries are divided into three groupings: Ford Automotive Group, Ford Financial Services Group, and Diversified Products Operations. Ford's worldwide automotive and tractor manufacturing and marketing business is grouped into four principal regions: North America, Europe, Latin America, and Asia-Pacific. Ford Direct Market Operations represents a fifth regional grouping that is largely engaged in overseas markets where Ford has no operating affiliates.

One of the major elements of Ford's current strategy is to continue to strengthen its coordination of multinational resources into an integrated international complex that will provide the company with a unique opportunity to meet global competition. To strengthen its position in the major automotive markets, the company today is increasing the utilization of Ford design, engineering, and manufacturing worldwide and is teaming with other manufacturers and suppliers to share the development and production costs for new products.

Closely related to this strategy is expanding relationships with Mazda, the large Japanese automotive manufacturer. Ford and Mazda are cooperating in a close and mutually beneficial relationship directed toward the improved utilization of product development, manufacturing, distribution, and human resources. Mazda will continue to work with Ford affiliates in the Asia-Pacific region and is working with the company to develop a minicar to be built by Kia of South Korea. Mazda also is assisting in the design of the process and the vehicle at the new Ford plant in Hermosillo, Mexico, and at Ford's plant in Taiwan. The company also will purchase a significant portion of the production from Mazda's new assembly plant being built in Flat Rock, Michigan.

Ford has widespread operations throughout Western Europe, which puts it in a superb position to compete in the unified Europe scheduled to emerge in 1992. Ford opened its first overseas branch in France in 1908, and its first national company and assembly plant outside North America in Great Britain in 1911. Today there are fifteen Ford national companies in Western Europe employing more than 115,000 people in automotive and tractor operations. Ford was the fourth largest seller of cars in Europe in 1988, with 11.5 percent of the market. Ford's assets in Europe are $15 billion, and the company expects to invest $10 billion more over the 1989–1993 period.

In addition, Ford has embarked on a series of moves designed to improve its overall strength by developing new sources of earnings and strengthening its existing nonautomotive businesses. This part of Ford's strategy has been employed thus far in the acquisitions of First Nationwide Financial Corporation and Sperry New Holland, the world's largest manufacturer of specialized farm equipment. In addition to its equity position in Mazda (25 percent) and its outright purchase of First Nationwide and Sperry New Holland, in the last five years Ford has taken equity positions in fifteen other companies, principally in high-technology companies, and consummated joint ventures with component suppliers.

As a global company, Ford has a reputation for conducting its worldwide operations in a socially responsible manner. It commands respect for its integrity and its contributions to host governments around the world. In each country where it operates, the company's policy is to abide by the country's laws with respect to local content regulations, import-export credits, fuel and safety regulations, repatriation of profits, labor laws, and all other applicable laws, rules, and regulations. In turn, Ford provides the host country with a tax base, employment, payroll, training, new technology, and development of the country's infrastructure. Such operations are extremely complex, but Ford's years of experience with various customs regulations, tariffs, and shippers provide for a relatively trouble-free flow of components, parts, and whole vehicles among various countries.

Ford is one of a number of U.S.-based companies that have shown enviable muscle in the global competitive arena. Unfortunately, there are many other managers in our companies that have neither done very well in the global marketplace nor expressed interest in entering the arena. As will be discussed in this chapter, there is growing urgency for much of our industry to become more aware of the mounting global threats to our companies as well as the vast new opportunities opening in the global marketplace.[1]

In this chapter we examine the rise of the new global competitive environment and the posture of our companies today in that competition. We look at how our best companies maintain a superior competitive posture. The evolving international economic market will increasingly be determined by the interaction of business and governments around the world, including the United States. Business in the United States has no higher social and economic responsibility than to do what is necessary to meet this challenge successfully. At the end of the chapter we will discuss what business, government, and our educational institutions must do to meet the global competitive challenge.

INTRODUCTION

In the last chapter we examined the trade position of the United States in world markets and noted the huge persistent trade deficits and rising demands for protectionism. These are manifestations of much deeper and more serious problems facing the United States. The blunt fact is that the United States has seen its worldwide competitive position seriously erode.

Roger Smith, chairman and chief executive officer of General Motors Corporation, has phrased the challenge this way:

> America is now in the midst of one of its greatest challenges in history—a competitive struggle that will determine whether our standard of living remains the envy of the world and whether we retain our current role as the world's preeminent economic power. This challenge is less visible than the wars that in our past threatened our very existence as a nation and our fundamental freedoms. But its outcome is no less vital to our future.
>
> The central question facing us is whether America can compete successfully in the world marketplace. With all we have going for us, can we restore our industrial competitiveness? Or will we let it slip away—and along with it our national wealth and power?[2]

This issue is not new. In the early 1980s, there were a spate of books, congressional hearings, and official commissions dealing with the subject. At that time the focus was on what became known as "industrial policy," meaning essentially that government policy had to take a lead role in reversing the decline. The fourth edition of this book, published in 1985, contained a chapter entitled "Industrial Policy." That concept lost its vogue, and relevant parts of the subject were discussed throughout the next edition. Now, atten-

---

[1]This was prepared partly from personal communications with George E. Trainer, former director of the International Public Affairs Office of Ford, and "Ford Around the World," a press release dated August 1989 by the International Public Affairs office of Ford, Dearborn, Michigan.

[2]Roger Smith, "Global Competition—A strategy for Success," in Jerome M. Rosow, ed., *The Global Marketplace*, New York: Facts on File, 1988, p.33.

tion to our global competitiveness picks up some of the basic thrust of the old industrial policy debate and adds other dimensions. This chapter presents a thumbnail sketch of the essence of current thinking on global competitiveness.

RISE OF GLOBAL COMPETITION AND COMPANIES

International trade has taken place for centuries, but globalization of competition in world markets is a relatively new phenomenon. Professor Michael Porter places the rise of global competitors from 1950 to 1970.[3] Many forces have brought about this phenomenon.

One important force is a worldwide convergence of consumer needs and preferences, expecially in what Kinichi Ohmae calls the "Triad." The "Triad" is composed of the European, Japanese, and North American economies.[4] This is a market of some 640 million affluent people, in which many consumer needs and preferences are much the same. Consumers get the same kind of information and want products of the same quality and quantity, such as cameras, soft drinks, watches, computers, chemicals, drugs, and so on. The world has become homogenized.

During the last quarter century, world gross national product has grown explosively, especially in the developed countries and in the Triad. Merchandise trade (exports and imports) has grown even more rapidly. Today, about 50 percent of free world trade takes place in the Triad. These data reflect, of course, rapidly rising demand from affluent consumers.

To exploit this growing demand, companies sought competitive advantage by cutting cost and improving product quality. They knew from experience that the larger the production of a single unit, up to a point, the lower would be the cost per unit, since fixed costs would be spread over more units. Costs were also reduced as companies integrated worldwide acquisition of raw materials and components so as to find the lowest cost for each element of the finished product. The growth of larger corporations with worldwide operations resulted, in part, from this drive for lower product costs.

The strategic objective of lower cost and higher quality was more achievable by a virtual revolution in manufacturing, distribution, and quality. For example, the wider use of robotics, automation, and new technology in product design facilitated cost reduction and quality improvement. Transportation costs were reduced with new technology of ship containerization and more efficient aircraft. Tariff barriers, as noted in the last chapter, were reduced, and economic pacts like the European Community facilitated trade and investment. Marketing systems around the world became more rather than less similar. Countries improved their infrastructures and, again as

---

[3]Michael E. Porter, "Competition in Global Industries: A Conceptual Framework," in Michael E. Porter, ed., *Competition in Global Industries*, Boston: Harvard Business School Press, 1986.

[4]Kinichi Ohmae, *Triad Power: The Coming Shape of Global Competition*, New York: The Free Press, 1985.

noted in the last chapter, became more cooperative with large foreign-based corporations.

Coinciding with these developments was a revolution in communications technology that permitted virtually instantaneous communications, including face-to-face meetings of people. Isaac Asimov reminds us that Queen Isabella learned of Columbus's discovery only after five months. Europe learned of Lincoln's assassination in two weeks, but the world learned of Neil Armstrong's first step on the moon in 1.3 seconds.

Other forces have also been operating. For example, capital flows throughout the world are much smoother and faster than in the past. Improvements have been made in the techniques of corporate management, such as strategic planning and quantitative decision making from capital expenditures to inventory control and quality control.

Porter points out that the forces underlying globalization have been self-reinforcing. Thus, globalization of firms' strategies has contributed to the homogenization of consumer needs and preferences. Suppliers are stimulated to globalize their strategies. James E. Olson, late chairman of AT&T, said, "[t]he growth in telecommunications and data processing markets worldwide is a direct result of the globalization of industries across the board..."[5]

The world is not completely homogenized, of course. There still are demands in different countries for specialized products from machinery to automobiles. This is due to many factors, such as varying tastes, customs, laws, or beliefs among groups in the different countries. There still is market segmentation around the world, and many firms seek to exploit this fact. Illustrative products to meet such niches are Mercedes automobiles and Rolex watches.

The intensity of global competition has been increased by the ease with which technology is transferred around the world and quickly introduced into new products. For this reason even the lesser developed countries of the world have been able to enter the competitive global arena with great success. Illustrative are the competitive capabilities of firms in South Korea, Hong Kong, Taiwan, and Singapore.

The winner in this global competition has been Japan. Many U.S.-based companies have adapted skillfully to this new environment, but many more have not. We turn now to the global competitive posture of the United States today.

THE UNITED STATES GLOBAL COMPETITIVE POSTURE TODAY

There is broad agreement everywhere that since World War II, the dominance of the United States as the number one competitive power in the world has steadily declined. At the end of World War II, all the advantages were on our side. Most of the manufacturing capacity of the world was devastated,

---

[5]James E. Olson, "Toward a Global Information Age," in Jerome M. Rosow, *The Global Marketplace*, New York: Facts on File, 1988, p. 99.

but ours was honed into an efficient mass producer of goods. The United States market was eight times larger than the next largest. Our technology was superior, our workers were skilled, and our managers were among the world's best. We were the richest nation in the world and could afford high investment and consumption. These conditions were exceptional, of course.

As other nations recovered economically after the war, it was inevitable that the relative economic position of the United States would decline. This, of course, did take place. But the slippage was accentuated by growing competitive weaknesses. While many of our MNCs adapted with great skill to the changing post-war environment, many did not. On balance, the global competitive posture of the United States is now weak.

The *Harvard Business Review* conducted a survey among its readers in 1987, asking them this question: Do you think there is a competitiveness problem? Among the 4,000 responses, 92 percent believed U.S. competitiveness was deteriorating. Ninety-five percent believed that diminished competitiveness would hurt America's economic performance in the foreseeable future. Eighty-nine percent thought the problem represented a threat to the nation's standard of living and economic power. Almost 90 percent placed the blame on U.S. managers, and virtually all said the solution would come through more effective management and attention by business to international trade. Government was blamed for part of the problem, but only 59 percent faulted the government.[6]

There are many dimensions to our competitive position, a few of which we illustrate as follows.

The Council on Competitiveness has constructed four indices to measure our competitiveness: standard of living, trade, productivity, and investment.[7] The Council uses the index to compare the competitive position of the United States with the competitive positions of 1) seven other major countries, 2) other countries of the world, and 3) Japan and West Germany. The indices show that, in every case, our performance since 1972 has been poorer than that of other major countries.

For two years MIT examined the competitive position of the United States; it published its findings in mid-1989. It concluded that "American productivity is not growing as fast as it used to, and productivity in the United States is not growing as fast as it is elsewhere, most notably in Japan."[8]

The twin deficits—budget and trade—are also often used to illustrate our position in the world. Our annual federal budget deficits range about $150 billion, and our total federal debt is over $3 trillion. (We discussed the trade deficit in Chapter 12.) The significance of these debt figures is debatable.

[6]"Competitiveness Survey: HBR Readers Respond," *Harvard Business Review*, September–October 1987.

[7]For an explanation of these indices see *Competitive Index*, Council on Competitiveness, May 1988.

[8]Michael L. Dertouros, Richard K. Lester, Robert M. Solow, and the MIT Commission on Industrial Productivity, *Made in America: Regaining the Productive Edge*, Cambridge, Massachusetts: The MIT Press, 1989, p. 26.

Some authorities believe that neither has great significance.[9] Others think they have many adverse implications for our economic and political power.[10] For example, from an economic point of view the budget debt has, in light of our low savings rate, forced the Treasury to raise interest rates to attract foreign lenders. Higher rates, of course, raise the cost of doing business. This adversely affects our competitive position, since our rates have been about double those in Japan. Many other consequences flow from the federal debt, not the least of which is the possibility that it sucks away investment funds that otherwise might be put in plant, equipment, and research and development to improve our competitive position.

In Chapter 12 we noted how some industries have suffered from foreign competition. We add to this record the results of the MIT Commission's studies of competitive postures of eight major U.S. industries. They were automobiles; chemicals; commercial aircraft; consumer electronics; machine tools; steel; textiles; and semiconductors, computers, and copiers. In every one of these industries, the study concluded, "... foreign competitors have captured significant segments of the U.S. market and challenge American companies in all world markets."[11]

Most American products, whether the producers market solely in the United States or compete abroad, suffer the sting of foreign competitors. To this must be added the production by foreign companies of products in the United States to compete with U.S.-made products. Japanese automobile companies have built nine automobile plants in the United States and Canada (which now has a free trade agreement with the United States). These plants are expected to make about 13 percent of all domestic cars produced in this country in 1989.[12] Siemens AG, a large West German company, currently has fifty-two manufacturing facilities in the United States, which represent a major part of the company's $1.7 billion investment here.

We have many strengths in our global competitive posture. To begin with, American universities, especially in graduate technical training, are generally considered to be the world's best. The world sends thousands of its students to this country for technical training. The proportion of foreign students in technical schools to domestic students has grown rapidly in recent years.

The United States is a leader in many critical technologies. Booz-Allen & Hamilton in 1988 asked 282 senior executives around the world to identify the leading countries in technology. They compared Japan and the United States in major emerging technologies, with this conclusion. The United States was the leader in supercomputers, software engineering, artificial intelligence, computer-aided design and engineering, telecommunications,

---

[9]Marshall Robinson, "America's Not-So-Troubling Debts and Deficits," *Harvard Business Review*, July–August 1989.

[10]Benjamin M. Friedman, *Day of Reckoning: The Consequences of American Economic Policy Under Reagan and After*, New York: Random House, 1988.

[11]Dertouros, Lester, and Solow, *op. cit.*, p. 49.

[12]James B. Treece and John Hoerr, "Shaking Up Detroit," *Business Week*, August 14, 1989.

and genetic engineering. The Japanese were determined to be leaders in robotics, and had a narrow lead in microelectronics and computer-integrated manufacturing. It is noteworthy that a similar survey five years before by Booz-Allen showed the U.S. and Japan to be neck and neck in these emerging technologies! The United States still leads in superconductivity, laser and fiber optics, and high-performance materials (metal alloys, plastics, and other substances necessary for breakthroughs in product design and performance). However, the Japanese were perceived to be a close second to the United States in some of these technologies. Some respondents rated the Japanese ahead in several of the technologies.[13]

The United States has a worldwide reputation for many high-quality products. *Fortune* magazine conducted a survey among many experts in different fields to identify U.S.-made products considered to be the finest of their kind. Among a long list of products were these: agricultural equipment, aerospace products, computers, pharmaceuticals, medical instruments, laser angioplasty catheter heads, satellites, locomotives, and brain electrical activity mapping systems.[14]

There are many companies in the United States with superior products, managements, distribution systems, vision, planning systems, human resources, and other qualities to be strong global players. This list would include, not in any order of importance, IBM, Hewlett-Packard, Coca-Cola, Johnson & Johnson, Caterpillar, Ford, 3M, Boeing, General Electric, and many more, including smaller firms. Such companies as these have much to teach other firms that have not yet awakened to the global competitive struggle that lies ahead for the United States. Not only have the best firms penetrated foreign markets, but they maintain strong positions in them. The Japanese market is perceived to be hard to penetrate, and it is. However, IBM, as an example, has 25 percent of the Japanese computer market, Shick razors enjoy 70 percent of the market, Polaroid cameras and film have about 75 percent of that market, Johnson & Johnson has 25 percent of the bandage market, Coca-Cola has 30 percent of the carbonated soft drink market, and McDonald's has 30 percent of the fast-food hamburger sales.[15]

The United States should be unbeatable in global competition. It has some 15 million companies, a figure that no other nation comes close to matching. In 1987 it had over 800,000 scientists and engineers, more than twice the number in Japan. Its market is over twice the size of Japan's, and is roughly equal to that of all Western Europe. We spend twice as much on research and development (R&D) as does any other country. Our work force is highly skilled. We are politically stable. But, as we have said, our present global competitive posture is worrisome. We now address briefly the question: why is this so?

---

[13]Booz-Allen and Hamilton, "Asia Pacific Competition," Booz-Allen & Hamilton, Inc., 1988.
[14]Christopher Knowlton, "What America Makes Best," *Fortune,* March 28, 1988.
[15]Damon Darlin, "Myth and Marketing in Japan," *The Wall Street Journal,* April 6, 1989.

WHY THE UNITED STATES IS BEHIND IN GLOBAL COMPETITION

In its study, the MIT Commission concluded that there were important weaknesses in the U.S. competitive position in six categories.[16] A sampling of reasons for our weakness in each of these areas follows.

OUTDATED STRATEGIES

In the post-World War II era, it was all that our companies could do to satisfy an enormous domestic pent-up demand for goods. Our market was large, unified, and familiar. The foreign market, on the other hand, was small, segmented, and protected with tariff walls. Our total foreign trade at the time was in the range of 5 percent of our total internal trade. The legacy of this era led to the strategy of concentrating on the home market because it was so profitable and seemed to be less risky than venturing abroad.

This led to a strategy of indifference to foreign markets and competitors. Many of our companies saw no need to be concerned with foreign consumer needs and tastes. Since firms were strongly entrenched in the home market, there was an underemphasis on product quality. Foreign technology and sales strategies were discounted.

SHORT TIME HORIZONS

Our managers typically have felt strong pressures to emphasize short-range profits. Managers in Japan, Western Europe, and other highly industrialized countries of the world tend to think in longer terms. The Booz-Allen study asked managers in the United States and Japan the interval of time over which a CEO's performance is currently measured. In the United States, 59 percent said performance was measured for one year or less. The comparable figure for Japanese managers was 2 percent! In the United States, only 10 percent of the managers said performance was measured in terms of five or more years. The comparable number in Japan was 43 percent! Furthermore, when asked the interval of time over which a CEO's performance should be measured, 45 percent of the United States' managers one year or less, and only 13 percent said five years or more. In Japan, 66 percent said two to four years, and 34 percent said five or more years.[17]

Excessive emphasis on the short run can have all sorts of adverse consequences for a company. It can, for example, lead to less emphasis on R&D and fixed plant investment, because it takes time for the results to be translated into profits. The Booz-Allen study asked managers the average time required for a firm's investment in technology to return a profit. In the United States, 41 percent of the managers said three years or less, compared with 19 percent of the Japanese managers.[18] For two decades, capital investment in

[16]Dertouros, Lester, and Solow, *op. cit.*
[17]Booz-Allen & Hamilton, Inc., *op. cit*, p. 5.
[18]*Ibid.*, p. 6.

the United States, as a percentage of net output, has been considerably less than in either Japan or West Germany. Similarly, R&D has been sluggish, and productivity of industry has been in the doldrums for the past six years. These conditions are not all due to a short-range point of view in decision making, but that has had an important impact. R&D and productivity are two core conditions determining our competitive position, and deserve special attention.

RESEARCH AND DEVELOPMENT

The volume of total R&D in the United States is greater than that of any other nation in the world, but its growth has slowed down considerably in recent years. In 1970, total U.S. R&D was $26 billion; it will be $132 billion in 1989, according to an estimate of the National Science Foundation. After adjustment for inflation, however, the growth from 1970 to 1989 is less impressive. In 1982 dollars, the total was $62 billion in 1970 and almost doubled to $105 estimated for 1989. In real terms, the total R&D grew only from $90 billion in 1984 to $105 billion in 1989.

The great bulk of total R&D spent in the United States is by the federal government and industry. The federal expenditure in 1982 dollars was $9 billion in 1970 and $11 billion in 1989 (estimate). The level has been virtually the same in the past six years. The industry contribution was $51 billion in 1970 and $76 billion in 1989 (estimated). The percent change from year to year of industry R&D has declined precipitously in 1982 dollars following 1984.

The ratio of aggregate R&D expenditures to GNP was not much different among the U.S., Japan, and West Germany. In the U.S. it was 2.6 percent in 1987. In Japan it was 2.9 percent, and in West Germany it was 2.8 percent. To repeat what was said above, the actual total spent was far higher in the United States than in the other two countries.[19] The question arises: why is not the United States superior in product innovation and new product development?

TECHNOLOGY TRANSFER

"The United States is still unarguably," in the words of the MIT Commission, "the leader in basic research. The scale of its scientific enterprise is unequaled, and it is second to none in making new discoveries."[20] The United States lags behind its foreign rivals because it has not exploited inventions and new discoveries to produce new products as quickly as its rivals have. The base of the great economic strength built by the United States in the past was new discovery and comparatively speedy introduction to new products. Now, foreign nations are much ahead of this country's companies in quickly translating new technology into better products with higher quality.

[19]National Science Foundation, *National Patterns of R&D Resources: 1989*, Washington, D.C.: National Science Foundation, 1989.
[20]Dertouros, Lester, and Solow, *op. cit.*, p. 67.

We allowed our superb manufacturing talents, proven during the war, to slip. In contrast, the Japanese created a powerful machine to take new technology and use it quickly to produce new products. In a two-year study financed by the National Science Foundation, Mansfield found that Japanese and U.S. companies spent about the same amount of money and time to carry out an innovation based on internal technology development. However, Japanese firms spent 25 percent less time and 50 percent less money in carrying out an innovation based on external technology.[21]

In many instances, Japanese firms took technology developed in this country and got to market much quicker and at much less cost than U.S. companies. Well-known examples are robotics, television, radios, and automobiles. At the same time, the Japanese paid much more attention to product quality, shop floor control, and manufacturing flexibility than the typical American company. This has also been true of other countries, such as West Germany.

The MIT Commission drew the following conclusion about the weakness of American firms in this area:

> American companies evidently find it difficult to design simple, reliable, mass-producible products; they often fail to pay enough attention at the design stage to the likely quality of the manufactured product; their product-development times are excessively long; they pay insufficient attention to manufacturing processes; they take a reactive rather than a preventive approach to problem solving; and they tend to under-exploit the potential of continuous improvement in products and processes.[22]

PRODUCTIVITY

As noted earlier, a significant index of a nation's economic strength is the productivity of its work force. The most frequently used index of productivity is dollars of output (adjusted for inflation) of goods and services per worker. The level of productivity is the result of a great many factors, such as capital available, efficiency of machinery and tools, education of workers, skills of workers, commitment of workers, capabilities of their managers, and others. Productivity per worker in the U.S. began to slow down in the late 1960s and early 1970s. For two decades prior to that time, our annual productivity increased about 3 percent. In the two decades since then the rate has been a little over 1 percent. Another productivity index which measures how efficiently the economy makes use of both labor and capital inputs (called the labor productivity index) has followed a course similar to the above index. These are overall measures for the entire economy. Of course, different industries and companies show different trends.

These are discouraging trends, and are made more worrisome when contrasted with foreign countries. Since 1979, productivity in the United States has been lower than in Japan, West Germany, and the United Kingdom.

---

[21]Edwin Mansfield, "Technological Creativity: Japan and the United States," *Business Horizons,* March–April 1989.

[22]Dertouros, Lester, and Solow, *op. cit.,* p. 68.

One positive development in the United States has been a sharp increase in manufacturing productivity. Following a slump extending to 1973, the annual rate of growth was 4.2 percent from 1981 through 1987. Thereafter it dipped a little. One negative note in these statistics is that a good bit of growth in this index was achieved by closing inefficient plants and laying off workers in others.

HUMAN RESOURCES

There appears to be a pervasive failure, says the MIT Commission, to cultivate and nurture our human resources prior to the time people enter the work force and during their years of work. This is one of the important causes of low labor productivity in the United States. Low productivity is not due to a decline in the work ethic, they add, as has been amply proven in many companies. In some plants our workers are equal to if not better than those in the rest of the world. In some of our automobile and steel-making plants, for example, productivity is as high as it is anywhere in the world. So the work ethic has not been lost in this country. Inefficient workers are more a product of poor training and retraining to meet new challenges in the workplace.

The MIT study observed: "There seems to be a systematic undervaluation in this country of how much difference it can make when people are well educated and when their skills are continuously developed and challenged."[23] One result is that our educational system through high school produces students who score poorly on standard tests compared with students in Japan, West Germany, and other countries. Indeed, employers complain that too many workers when they enter the work force are virtually illiterate, have difficulty with elementary mathematics, and read very poorly, even though they have a high school diploma.

Many companies have training programs to teach new employees job requirements, but many do not. Those companies with carefully planned continuous training programs are few. In contrast, in Japan and West Germany, in-depth training programs are used to develop general transferable skills as well as specialized capabilities. On leaving school in West Germany, a student enters a three-year apprenticeship program in a firm under the direction of an instructor. The worker is also obliged to spend time outside the firm taking vocational school classes. There is more of a pattern of continuous retraining of workers in Japan and West Germany than in the United States.

Top level executives often display little understanding of and interest in foreign countries. Too many are ignorant of the customs, language, values, and behavioral patterns of peoples in other countries. This is a competitive disadvantage in meeting global competition when competitors are well informed about the United States and speak the language fluently.[24]

---

[23]*Ibid.*, p. 22.
[24]This point is addressed by Philip West, "Cross-Cultural Literacy and the Pacific Rim, *Business Horizons*, March–April 1989.

FAILURES IN COOPERATING AND COMMUNICATING

The MIT Commission emphasized several different levels on which this shortcoming appeared. Coordination among functions is disjointed in many companies. Important decisions are not integrated, and this results in all sorts of problems in designing, producing, and distributing products. For example, the Commission sees a growing trend of division between technical and managerial professionals. This can result, of course, in inadequate interjection of technical considerations in decision making. To save a few pennies, a new material may be rejected in a machine in favor of a poorer quality one. Well-planned and executed integration among engineering, manufacturing, sales, and finance should enable a company to develop a better product more quickly, at a lower cost, and with better quality.

It is important to note that the traditional adversarial relationships between management and labor have often had an adverse impact on worker productivity, product quality, product cost, and speed of output.[25] Here again there are noteworthy instances of excellent management-union relationships. But in contrast with the Japanese and West Germans, our labor-management relations have been frequently turbulent, as have British and French labor-management relations.

BLURRED GLOBAL PERSPECTIVE OF MANY TOP MANAGERS

A study made by Korn/Ferry International with Columbia University Graduate School of Business asked 1,500 top executives in twenty countries their views of the level of competition, and their concerns as well as challenges, they anticipated in the year 2000. There were significant differences among the major countries which shed light on our competitive posture.

U.S. executives say they expect the level of foreign competition in the twenty-first century to be much lower than domestic competition. They are more concerned about high levels of government regulation. Indeed, they view this as the most serious threat of all. They believe more opportunities will exist in production technology than do executives from other regions, and anticipate a shortage of qualified personnel to exploit this opportunity. They think education and training of personnel will be deficient. Surprisingly, American executives look for the unification of Europe in 1992 to have negligible impact on their corporations.

Japanese executives say that their number one growth strategy for the twenty-first century will be the development of new businesses. They expect to use their growing technological and market research to create new businesses. They foresee no shortage of available capital or personnel. They see no threat in government regulation. The executives, significantly more than those from other areas of the world, envision an increase in intensity of competition in virtually all of its aspects. "... There can be little question that in

---

[25]On this point see Thomas A. Kochan, Robert B. McKerie, and Henry C. Katz, *The Transformation of American Industrial Relations*, New York: Basic Books, 1986.

the year 2000 Japanese firms will be even more implacable competitors than they are now," observes the study.[26]

Western European managers anticipate a greater premium on product quality than those in other regions. They think getting qualified personnel will be a key corporate challenge. They see a decline in union power. They identify changes in information and communications as the most critical challenge in the twenty-first century. Managers in West Germany and the United Kingdom rate changes in product and production technology to be less important than do the respondents from other regions. They are not worried about government regulations, but predict a higher level of foreign competition in the year 2000 than any other group except the Japanese. They say hostile takeovers will be a threat. They expect half their revenues to come from nondomestic sources. This contrasts with 20 percent reported by American mangers. They are naturally concerned about the unification of European trade, and anticipate that deregulation of trade barriers among European nations will permit significant growth for some firms but bring about mergers and insolvency for others.

This is a thumbnail sketch of the results of the Korn/Ferry-Columbia study, but it reveals the insularity of American managerial attitudes toward international business. It is a mental state that discounts the importance of the changing international environment to their businesses. "What is most disturbing," concludes the study, "is that they do not acknowledge this liability, and so risk selecting a successor with the same narrow vision."[27]

This is a formidable list of weaknesses in the U.S. global competitive posture. There are many others, but enough has been said, however, to underscore the failure of many American managers. Our managers have had the capability to reverse most, but not all, of these weaknesses. To reverse the trend presents an imposing challenge for our managers, government, and educational institutions. Fortunately, we have many well-managed companies that have been very successful in international competition. They have lessons from which other managers may learn. We turn now to them.

WHAT HAVE OUR BEST COMPANIES DONE TO BECOME AND STAY COMPETITIVE IN THE WORLD MARKET?

The MIT Commission identified companies that were successfully competing in the international marketplace. Summarized here are the types of strategies which they employed to sharpen their competitive advantages.[28] Before noting them, it must be said that there is no one strategy which accounts for competitive strength. Nor do all the companies adopt the same strategies: strategies are tailored to particular circumstances. If there is any one overarching strategy that explains global competitive prowess, it is to think globally in formulating and

[26]Joint Study by Korn/Ferry International and Columbia University Graduate School of Management, *Reinventing the CEO*, Korn/Ferry International and Columbia University Graduate School of Business, 1989, p. 24.

[27]*Ibid.*, p. 54.

[28]Dertouros, Lester, and Solow, *op. cit.*

implementing strategies in such areas as overall company goals, R&D allocations, resource coordination, product design, product manufacture, marketing, and market share.

SIMULTANEOUS IMPROVEMENT IN QUALITY, COST, AND DELIVERY

The successful firms did not deal piecemeal with quality, cost, and service, but coordinated policies and practices with each. The results of this were products of high quality and low cost, speedy design of products, faster translation of new technology into production, and better customer service.

STAYING CLOSE TO THE CUSTOMER

This is a lesson that Peters and Waterman stressed in their best seller, *In Search of Excellence*.[29] Companies that perform this activity will naturally have up-to-date information about customer needs and preferences. They can pick up differentiated signals in the marketplace, respond quickly to different segments of the market, and enhance customer loyalty.

CLOSER RELATIONS WITH SUPPLIERS

Taking a lesson from the Japanese, the better companies are forging stronger ties with suppliers. Heretofore, as in the automobile companies, suppliers generally were those with whom the companies forced the lowest cost deals. If another supplier produced a lower cost product, the first one was no longer used. Companies are giving suppliers a larger role in product design. They place more emphasis on component quality, and work with the suppliers in perfecting components. They seek long-range relationships mutually satisfactory to both parties. Finally, they are installing just-in-time delivery systems. The JIT, as it is called, integrates the flow of components from suppliers into production schedules so that the delivery of the components is made at the precise moment they are needed in the production cycle. In this way, the need for stocking inventories is eliminated. All these strategies should produce higher quality finished products at lower cost.

USING TECHNOLOGY FOR STRATEGIC ADVANTAGE

The successful companies have integrated technology with their financing, manufacturing, marketing, and human resources planning. This seems an obvious requirement for excellence, but it is surprising how many companies perform these functions isolated from each other. We are reminded of an old cartoon which showed the wood cabinet of a floor television set, but the space for the tube and other parts was blank. The caption read: "We have designed the TV set, now let manufacturing produce it." Such practices do not lead to the best results. General Motors was much disappointed with the

---

[29]Thomas J. Peters and Robert H. Waterman, *In Search of Excellence: Lessons from America's Best-Run Companies*, New York: Harper & Row, 1982.

initial results of its new high-technology plants because the new technologies were not integrated into the manufacturing processes and work force, the organizational design, and human resource practices. Today all our major automobile companies link all these functions.

FLATTER AND LESS COMPARTMENTALIZED ORGANIZATIONS

Virtually all firms studied tried to integrate functions in the organization and reduced layers of management. By this strategy, better linkage was created and the internal processes in the company were speeded. The payoff, of course, was a better product at lower cost and quick response to changing market conditions. Some of the firms set up special project teams to design and manufacture a product. Some years ago we studied successful project teams in the aerospace industry and discovered that when teams were freed from beauraucratic surveillance and routines, they were able to create a prototype for a new product having advanced technology in less time and at less cost than with traditional organizational arrangements.[30]

INNOVATIVE HUMAN RESOURCE POLICIES

The successful firms introduced human resource policies that promoted participation, teamwork, trust, flexibility, employment security, and a sharing of economic risk. They sought employee inputs to decision making, introduced profit-sharing plans, and considered job security a high priority. These companies knew also that such results would not be achieved without strong performance in technology, product design, quality control, and so on. Innovative human resource practices, they knew, facilitated excellence in these areas, but also depended upon them for proper implementation. For example, technically inferior products that lose markets and profits reduce the ability of a company to maintain job security.

Many companies reward managers who are knowledgeable about global markets. IBM, for example, will not promote managers beyond a certain level unless they have acquired substantial international experience. In some units of Citicorp, executives will not be advanced unless they are fluent in more than one language.

CONCLUDING COMMENT

These are but a few of the strategies the most successful companies employ to win in the global market. There are many other winning strategies associated with finance, inventory control, distribution systems, and government relationships.

The successful companies recognize that all of the chosen strategies are linked. All reinforce others. If a major link is weakened, the whole chain will

---

[30]George A. Steiner and William G. Ryan, *Industrial Project Management*, New York: Macmillan Company, 1968.

weaken. Managements realize also that it is a formidable task to introduce and implement such policies in a large organization that has traditionally followed outmoded policies and practices. Roger Smith voiced this point in the following comment:

> We are trying to change our whole corporate culture—to move a giant worldwide organization toward a more flexible, decentralized management in order to gain better decisions and greater participation by employees at every level. But developing the plan is really the easy part for any corporation. The hard part is implementing it in a management environment that has been so successful for so long that the traditionalists in the organization find it difficult to see why we should change at all. Managers must believe in the plan, buy into it, and make it work. And you have to give it time to work.[31]

These companies realize that, once introduced, the new strategies require strong commitment on the part of everyone to maintain enthusiasm for and high performance of the policies. Finally, these companies understand that environment is constantly changing and that their strategies also must be constantly evaluated to make sure they are appropriately responsive to the new conditions.

GLOBALIZATION AND STRATEGIC ALLIANCES

Our larger MNCs, particularly, have long forged alliances with foreign businesses. In the past few years, however, there has been a rapid expansion of alliances. Two basic reasons caused this surge: intensification of global competition, and the decision to create a unified European community.

Alliances are long-term formal arrangements between companies that link their businesses to pursue specific purposes. They fall short of merger and include cross-licensing arrangements, supply agreements, joint ventures, marketing agreements and other similar arrangements.

In the recent growth in numbers of alliances, a shift in emphasis is noticeable. In the past, many alliances were for tactical purposes, such as to provide facilities and local knowledge (e.g., H. J. Heinz Company's forming joint ventures with local companies to distribute Heinz products in Thailand, China, Zimbabwe and other lesser developed countries). More strategic alliances have been formed in recent years. Illustrative is the arrangement between Inland Steel and Nippon Steel to build jointly what they describe as "the world's most advanced continuous cold steel mill" at New Carlisle, Indiana. Inland is to get Nippon Steel's technology and some long-range capital to provide a better final product. Nippon will get a part of the plant's output and will be enabled to leap over import quotas to supply Japanese auto plants in the United States.[32]

Corning Glass Works is a veteran and skilled alliance builder. Six joint ventures help Corning to market optical fiber throughout Europe. Corning's

---

[31]Smith, *op. cit.*, p. 36.
[32]Louis Kraar, "Your Rivals Can Be Your Allies," *Fortune*, March 27, 1989.

medical diagnostic equipment and supplies division was in need of fresh technical know-how. It teamed up with Ciba-Geigy of Switzerland to form Ciba Corning Diagnostics in order to get Ciba's technical knowledge. Corning saw its $250 million-a-year business in making glass bulbs for TV sets wither along with production of TV sets in the United States by American companies. The Japanese began to build TV plants in the United States. To get better access to these companies, Corning formed a joint venture with Asahi Glass of Japan, to give Asahi access to Corning's plants in the U.S. and Mexico and to allow Corning to take advantage of Asahi's good relationships with Japanese tubemakers who have moved here. Corning has also allied with Samsung of South Korea in a joint venture to produce glass products. Corning's global tie-ups extend to other parts of the world—Great Britain, France, West Germany, Belgium, China, and Australia.[33]

A major reason for the formation of alliances stems from the fact that, as in the case of Ciba Corning Diagnostics, more and more products rest on many critical technologies, and few companies can afford to maintain a cutting edge in all of them. Alliances also are much less expensive than building new factories. They make it possible for a company to meet new market demands more quickly than if it had to create new marketing and distribution systems. Such systems are both time-consuming and costly. Through alliances, companies can share risks as well as costs in developing new technologies. They facilitate technology or skill transfer. They can avoid wasteful duplication of facilities, utilize by-products, share distribution channels, improve personal interactions, retain entrepreneurial employees, and overcome trade barriers, as noted with Inland and Nippon Steel. This, of course, does not exhaust the list of motivations for forming alliances.

Ohmae sets the case for alliances simply in these terms. "Globalization mandates alliances, makes them absolutely essential to strategy...the simultaneous developments that go under the name of globalization make alliances—entente—necessary."[34] This has been behind the recent formation of worldwide alliances by American firms. But a special urgency to alliance formation has been added with the decision to unify Europe.

THE WESTERN EUROPEAN COMMON MARKET

In 1992, if matters proceed as planned, customs and tariff and nontariff barriers will be lowered or removed among the twelve European nations comprising the union. Also removed will be individual country laws and policies affecting trade, and others will be enacted in their place. All is designed to create a single unit around which trade will be free of government restraints. This market will have 340 million consumers (including East Germany), a GNP a bit smaller than that of the United States, and vigorous global competitors.

[33]Kraar, *op. cit.*

[34]Kenichi Ohmae, "The Global Logic of Strategic Alliances," *Harvard Business Review,* March–April 1989.

European Common Market Countries—1992 (as of March 1990).

The 1992 unification will open great opportunities and produce serious threats for individual firms. It is natural, therefore, for companies to begin to plan now to exploit the opportunities and avoid the threats. The merger, acquisition, and alliance-forming frenzy now washing over Europe reflects the expectation that the unification will in fact take place in 1992 as scheduled. Not all the pieces will be in place, but the framework is now being erected.

Opportunities will present themselves for making larger production runs to permit a firm to spread costs over more units and thus cut cost per unit and prices. There will be opportunities to profit by exchanging technologies, consolidating to reduce managerial overhead, and so on. Threats will exist also. The serious threat of widespread, vigorous competition will be an obvious one. Price competition will be widespread among many products that are today priced differently in different European countries. A Volkswagen Golf, for example, costs 55 percent more, before taxes, in Great Britain than in Denmark, and 29 percent more in Ireland than in Greece. So intense will be the competition in Europe after 1992 that the former chairman of Great Britain's Imperial Chemical Industries has predicted that within ten years, half of Europe's factories will close and half of its companies will be swallowed up in mergers.[35]

Consolidation of European food companies is moving rapidly. MAC Group, a management consulting firm, says that sixty-seven of the largest European food companies made fewer than twenty acquisitions a year in the early 1980s. After 1985, the number jumped to forty a year, and it is expected to go higher.[36] Nestlé, for example, has been very active and has acquired many companies in Europe, as well as in the United States. In automobiles, telecommunications, paper, electronics, and many other industries, the frenzy proceeds.

An important result of this activity for American firms is, of course, that they will face in Europe many large and powerful competitors. There is another concern for American companies, and that is the prospect that new barriers will be erected around the market to inhibit their exports. In Brussels, the headquarters of the unification planning, there are some 12,000 bureaucrats who are interacting with thousands of others from the twelve nations involved to forge policies, procedures, and regulations for the new unified market. Consultants say potential land mines are everywhere for American companies.

Many executives fear the development of "Fortress Europe." They believe that politicians and businesspeople see European unification as the road to General de Gaulle's old dream of Europe without Americans. These fears are not without justification. Early in 1990, the European Commission announced that computer chips will have to be fabricated within the European

[35]Eric G. Friberg, "1992: Moves Europeans Are Making," *Harvard Business Review*, May–June 1989.

[36]Reported by Stewart Toy, Richard A. Melcher, and Lois Therrien, "The Race to Stock Europe's Common Supermarket," *Business Week*, June 26, 1989.

community. This ruling sends the message that the Commission wants high-tech investments, technology, and jobs to stay in Europe. The so-called principle of reciprocity is also being articulated. It says that the community will give access to foreign companies on the same terms that foreign governments give access to European companies in the same industry. The message here is that the European countries do not want to be exploited from abroad in the same fashion that some of our industries have been. There seems to be movement toward a goal of "Europe for Europeans."[37]

Managers of many American corporations, as noted above, are alert to events in Europe and have been busy aquiring companies and building alliances. General Electric, for example, has been engaged in a battle with Great Britain's GEC and West Germany's Seamons to take over Plessey, a British defense and electronics supplier. Many other American companies, however, are still to make their moves.

CONSORTIA

The National Cooperative Research Act of 1984 relaxed our antitrust laws to permit competing manufacturers to form consortia to engage in research and development. Joint associations of various kinds have been formed for many years but not with competitors. That would have been declared illegal under our antitrust laws. Since the new legislation was passed there have been about 500 applications to the Department of Justice to form consortia under the act, and about 100 have been authorized. The most well-known are in the semiconductor industry.

One of the earliest and best known is Microelectronics and Computer Technology Corp. (MCC). It was formed by nineteen companies, including Boeing, 3M, and DEC, and seeks to develop advanced computer and microelectronic technologies, including artificial intelligence. A larger and more ambitious consortium was established in 1987 with SEMATECH (Semiconductor Manufacturing Technology). Its mission is to provide the semiconductor industry in the United States with the capability of achieving world leadership in chip manufacturing by 1993 using American-made equipment and materials. Its 1990 budget is $223 million, which includes $100 million from the federal government and $123 million from fourteen chip-making companies that formed the consortium. It has 550 employees, mostly scientists and other professionals on loan from member companies.[38]

While the National Cooperative Research Act applies only to research and development, there is every expectation that the Department of Justice will

[37]Philip Revzin, "European Bureaucrats Are Writing the Rules Americans Will Live By, *The Wall Street Journal,* May 17, 1989.
[38]For information about SEMATECH, see John M. Ols, Jr., et. al., "Federal Research: The SEMATECH Consortiuim's Start-up Activities," United States General Accounting Office, Washington, D.C., November 1989. For an analysis of 137 consortia filed with the Department of Justice since 1984, see William M. Evan and Paul Olk, "R&D: A New U.S. Organizational Form," *Sloan Management Review,* Spring 1990.

broaden the act to permit manufacturing. If not, several bills pending in Congress would do so, and there is a strong likelihood of their passage.

What is behind these consortia? MCC was formed in response to a Japanese consortium formed in 1981 to develop the "fifth" generation of computers that would respond to ordinary language and analyze problems like humans. It was making progress, and MCC was set up to overtake the Japanese in semiconductor manufacturing. SEMATECH also was established to offset the technical advances made through massively funded Japanese consortia. There are many different reasons why other consortia have been established. For example, the Center for Advanced Television Studies was created to promote independent domestic research in television science and technology. Some have been created to share risks involved in developing new technology innovations. Some have been created to share complementary technical knowledge. Other consortia have been formed among companies engaged in agriculture, automobiles, biotechnology, chemicals, glass, and petroleum.

Professor Bruce Scott puts the case for American companies to form consortia to combat foreign consortia as follows: "Competing American-style with Japan and Korea—that is, each rival U.S. company operating alone against all competition—is like joining a poker game where the other players cooperate to drive you out."[39] If several of the players, as is the case in Japan, have deep pockets or access to them, you cannot win the game. Among other things, this view leads Scott and, increasingly, many other observers to scrap free trade market ideology in certain cases. As Scott puts it:

> Nations that continue to subscribe to the old theory of totally independent companies operating in uncoordinated "free" markets will cede R&D- and capital-intensive new industries to countries that opt for coordinated R&D and industrial muscle building. At best, the complacent will be left to operate in low- or middle-technology, stagnant or declining sectors.[40]

Not everyone agrees that such consortia (as well as joint ventures and alliances mentioned earlier) are a benefit to the United States. Professor Robert Reich sees a potential that the Japanese will get research findings through the individual semiconductor companies. He argues that since most of them have some sort of alliance with a Japanese company (e.g., Texas Instruments has joined with Hitachi, and Motorola has allied with Toshiba) our technology will get into the hands of strong competitors.[41] That is possible, but these alliances are for specific purposes and need not result in free exchange of all technology. Others argue that if the need is so urgent, why do not individual companies step up to the plate and undertake research? Why team up? The counter argument is that no single company, not even IBM, has the resources to make the financial commitments needed. Others decry the con-

---

[39]Bruce R. Scott, "Competitiveness: Self-Help for a Worsening Problem," *Harvard Business Review*, July–August 1989, p. 118.

[40]*Ibid.*, p. 118.

[41]Robert B. Reich, "Put a Brake on High-Tech Alliances," *Los Angeles Times*, March 20, 1989.

sortia on the grounds that they will lead to monopoly. That is unlikely, since many companies are involved. Furthermore, what is the alternative?

Some of these alliances have yielded positive results, but many have failed to meet expectations. Corning, an example of successful alliance-building, received handsome dividends from its alliance with Ciba. Many of the alliances of our automobile manufacturers with Japanese companies have been successful. On the other hand, the results of the semiconductor consortia are mixed. There have been some successes and some shortcomings.[42] Professor Kathryn Harrigan, an expert on joint ventures, studied corporate alliances at home and abroad over a ten-year period ending in 1985. She found that 57 percent of them did not work out well. Nevertheless, she says, "[w]ithin a decade, most companies will be members of teams that compete against one another."[43]

Why is it that so many alliances fail? Many causes of failure are unique to a particular alliance; others tend to be general in certain types of situations. Professor Rosabeth Kantor sees a clash between the traditional adversarial role of American managers in competitive situations, and the cooperative mode alliances usually require for success. In the one role, managers seek control and fear to be dominated. In the other, they lose some control over the affairs of the alliance.[44] American managers do not like to lose control. They are impatient and easily frustrated when partners do not meet their expectations. Ohmae says they "fear the alliance will turn out to be a Trojan horse that affords potential competitors easy access to home markets."[45] For some joint ventures, the underlying causes of failure were different management styles, disputes over quality and labor practices, unfulfilled expectations, and in some cases plain bad luck.[46] While it is not typical to find that international alliances run smoothly to the satisfaction of the partners, where there is good will and a strong interest in achieving the objectives set for the alliance there are usually ways to make it work."[47]

STRATEGIES TO MEET THE GLOBAL COMPETITIVE CHALLENGE

Since 1983, there have been literally dozens of official commissions, research studies, and reports prepared by authorities in their respective fields concerning the global competitive posture of the United States.[48] These docu-

---

[42]Lee Smith, "Can Consortiums Defeat Japan?" *Fortune,* June 5, 1989.

[43]Quoted in Kraar, *op. cit.*

[44]Rosabeth Moss Kanter, "Becoming PALs: Pooling, Allying, and Linking Across Companies," *Executive,* August 1989.

[45]Ohmae, "The Global Logic of Strategic Alliances," *op. cit.*

[46]Stephen Phillips, "When U.S. Joint Ventures With Japan Go Sour," *Business Week,* July 24, 1989.

[47]Kathryn Rudie Harrigan, "Making Joint Ventures," Part I, *Management Review,* February 1987; David Lei, "Strategies for Global Competition," *Long Range Planning,* February 1989. For a comprehensive analysis of joint ventures see Kathryn Rudie Harrigan, *Managing for Joint Venture Success,* Lexington, Massachusetts: Lexington Books, 1986.

[48]For a summary reference list of over thirty of these books and commission reports see Dertouros, Lester, and Solow, *Made in America, op. cit.* A selected few are cited.

ments contain hundreds of specifications for industry, government, and other institutions, such as educational and financial. No brief summary of the recommendations of these studies can do justice to their richness. Here we will present a few of the major highlights.

THINK GLOBALLY

The President's Commission on Industrial Competitiveness correctly observes that the ability of the United States to compete globally lies within the private sector. To meet the new challenges, business has a responsibility to think globally. The Commission believes more business leaders must broaden their vision to think in global terms with respect to company goals, resource deployment, and investment in human resources, and to develop better coordination of company goals throughout their organization. There must be a clear recognition that the global company integrates resources throughout the world and competes in world markets. There must be clear recognition of the fact that the company is operating in different environments, with different cultures, laws, customs, business behavior, values, and consumer tastes. In short, managers should replace parochial thinking with global thinking.

BALANCE SHORT-TERM AND LONG-TERM THINKING

The MIT Commission, as others have, emphasized the fact that U.S. managers were much less willing than the Japanese to undertake large investments that did not pay off in the near term. There are many causes of this, but whatever they are, the end result is a tendency to incur less R&D, to build less new plant, or to develop fewer new products. The MIT Commission reported that the Japanese have been able to penetrate our markets because they enjoyed a number of advantages, such as superior manufacturing techniques and low capital costs; but in every case the Commission studied, "their longer time horizon was a key factor in their success."[49] It is essential that our managers take a longer range view in decision making. This will not be easy, since pressures on them are for short-range results.

IMPLEMENT GLOBAL STRATEGY

Global thinking must be followed by effective implementation of policies and strategies growing out of global thinking. This means the establishment of an effective organization to perceive opportunities and threats in the evolving environment, a reward system tailored to global performance, development among managers of the skills to succeed in dealing with different cultures, and learning to function successfully with alliance partners.

[49]Dertouros, Lester, and Solow, *op. cit.*

GIVE HIGH PRIORITY TO THE IMPROVEMENT OF PRODUCTION PROCESSES

The MIT Commission, and others such as the National Academy of Engineering, strongly urge the integration of and, if feasible, concurrent work on R&D, product design, manufacturing, communication systems, and human resource deployment. In this coordination, top priority must be given to quality control and flexible manufacturing where that is appropriate. The end result sought should be quick transfer of technology to finished products which cost less than those of competitors, are of higher quality, and beat competitors to the market.

IMPROVE HUMAN RESOURCE MANAGEMENT

This area needs much attention from top management, from workers, and from outside institutions such as educational institutions and unions. The coming shortage of managers with the abilities and background to run global businesses presents a unique challenge. Required is new thinking about job rotation and challenging assignments for managers. Another necessity is to plan and execute continuous education for managers both in-house, such as GE's Crotonville, and through outside organized seminars and educational institutions. The Korn/Ferry-Columbia survey strongly urged management to make human resource planning an intricate part of strategic planning; to add the human resource officer as a part of the top management team; and to strengthen the capability of the human resources function to assess, recruit, and deploy executives from around the world.

Many of the reports stress the need for improved training of workers. This recommendation ranges from strengthening secondary education generally to providing better and more continuous training of workers by the companies that employ them. It is clear that challenges ahead will demand workers who have the skills required in complex production processes. It is equally clear that rapidly changing technologies will necessitate continuous sharpening of those skills. Finally, it is clear that our educational system is not producing people with the needed skills, nor is that system—or industry—constantly retraining workers to meet new technical work requirements.

RECOMMENDED STRATEGIES FOR GOVERNMENTS

As might be expected, the many reports and studies suggested a long laundry list of changes in government (federal, state, and local) strategies, policies, and regulations. Here are a few, in no particular order of priority. The President's Commission on Industrial Competitiveness recommended modification of the antitrust laws to permit certain types of mergers and other business relationships that would promote national objectives. The Business-Higher Education Forum recommended a National Commission on industrial competitiveness, which was formed.

A high priority should be placed on science and technology as a key force in improving the competitiveness of American industry in global markets. This recommendation leads to many others, such as the following:

- Emphasize public policies that strengthen our science and technology
- Increase not only basic research expenditures of government but also funding for product innovation and development
- Encourage more joint consortia to permit companies to engage in collective research and, under certain circumstances, other activities like production
- Increase the tax credit for R&D

Renewing our educational system should have a high priority. This would include revitalization of the nation's elementary and secondary educational system. This requires a joint effort of the federal and state governments, and one in which industry makes important contributions. Universities should place more emphasis on manufacturing, engineering, product innovation, and international management. The Business-Higher Education Forum recommended a policy of federal stipends to encourage the best students to pursue graduate study in engineering.

CONCLUDING COMMENT

There is widespread agreement that we have a serious global competitive problem. If the many weaknesses in our competitive posture are not corrected, the adverse impacts will impoverish the United States relative to other nations which improve their technology and productivity more quickly to meet global market conditions. This places a heavy responsibility on business, government, and our educational institutions.

Caterpillar Inc.

For fifty years, the Caterpillar company was a highly profitable and powerful player in the world market for earth-moving and other construction equipment. Its dominant strategy was to produce in the United States and sell abroad, where it held as much as 40 percent of the global market in the early 1980s. Then disaster struck, and Caterpillar, as one major strategy for recovery, decided to assemble equipment in other countries and ship to those manufacturing facilities low-cost components from around the world. The company also reversed an old policy and bought equipment from low-cost overseas producers for sale with the "Cat" label on it. This is the story of the transformation of Caterpillar from an exporter only of finished products to a global company with integrated assembly plants and distribution systems throughout the world.

HISTORY OF CATERPILLAR

Farmers in the large grainfields of California were having trouble plowing at the turn of the century. They were using large, heavy steam tractors, the wheels of which sank into the fine, moist earth of the delta lands in the Sacramento Valley. Benjamin Holt, whose company had been building combines for years, decided to try the idea of a "treadmill" machine, one which laid its own roadbed, to solve the problem. He made the first track out of wood and tested it successfully in 1904. He later acquired the trademarks "Caterpillar" and "Cat" for his equipment.

By 1915, Holt had its machines in twenty countries. They became the standard artillery and supply tractor during World War I for the United States, Great Britain, and France. During World War II and subsequent wars, they became standard heavy earth-moving and construction machines for the U.S. military services. The famous Sea Bees of World War II relied heavily on them.

In 1925, the Holt Manufacturing Company merged with the C. L. Best Tractor Company to form the Caterpillar Tractor Company (later it became Caterpillar Inc.) with headquarters in Peoria, Illinois, where it still remains.

Production of agriculture equipment was abandoned in favor of construction equipment when that market appeared to have greater growth potential for the company. Understanding the financial losses of "down-time" for expensive construction equipment, the company adopted a priority strategy of making only high-quality machines and providing excellent service of them. This strategy has been dominant ever since. Throughout the years, Caterpillar has been the undisputed champion worldwide of quality earth-moving equipment.

Caterpillar began foreign production in 1950 when it launched its first joint venture in Great Britain to produce parts. This venture implemented a strategy to leap over barriers raised by tariffs, import controls, and foreign exchange shortages in lesser developed countries. The same and other reasons led later to more overseas manufacturing plants.

Today, Caterpillar is the world's largest manufacturer of earth-moving, construction, and materials handling equipment. It is also a major producer of diesel and gas turbines. In 1989, its total sales were $11.1 billion and its profits were $497 million. It had about 60,000 employees.

The company's products are made in seventeen plants in the United States and fifteen plants in other countries. It has plants in Europe, Canada, Mexico, Indonesia, Japan, and India. Some are wholly owned and some are joint ventures. Products are also produced under license in many other countries of the world. A worldwide network of 195 independently owned dealers and company-owned dealerships is a source of great strength to the company. These dealers operate 1,100 branch stores in more than 140 countries and employ 74,000 people. Approximately 50 percent of the company's revenues come from abroad.

In addition to its manufacturing plants and dealer network, the company has several subsidiaries to buttress its operations. The Caterpillar Financial Services Corporation was formed in 1981 as a leasing and financing agency. Caterpillar Insurance Co., Ltd., provides various types of insurance for dealers. Formed in 1983, the firm does not write insurance but is only a broker and servicing company. The Caterpillar World Trading Corporation, formed in 1984, expedites sales in countries having foreign exchange shortages. The company also has established other subsidiaries for other purposes, such as to engineer custom machines and to invest in new products with profit potential for the company.

CATERPILLAR'S ORDEAL IN THE EARLY 1980s

In 1982, for the first time in fifty years, the firm registered a deficit. Revenues fell from $9.1 billion in 1981 to $6.5 billion in 1982, and profits dropped from $579 million in 1981 to a deficit of $180 million in 1982. Sales dropped further in 1983, and the deficit rose to $345 million. There was some recovery in sales in 1983, but profits were even more negative, at $428 million. In three years the company's equity was reduced by 28 percent, and 30,000 people lost their jobs. Ten plants were closed, and the value of the company's stock fell by $3.7 billion (57 percent) by late 1984.[50] What happened?

To begin with, there was a worldwide crumbling of Caterpillar's markets. There was a global recession in 1982 that led to a sharp decline in demand in major markets served by the company, such as road construction, mining, airport construction, and energy-related construction.

A major problem was caused by an overvalued dollar. Beginning in 1980, the U.S. dollar began a sharp increase in value relative to major foreign currencies. This made Caterpillar's exports progressively more costly for foreign customers. This in turn gave strong competitors like Fiat Allis in Europe and Komatsu in Japan a distinct pricing advantage. In 1981, Komatsu had about a 15 percent price advantage over Caterpillar through its efficient manufacturing and policy of sacrificing profits to gain market share. With the rise in the value of the dollar, the advantage rose to about 40 percent in 1982 and held that through 1984. Caterpillar found its market share dropping and that of Komatsu rising. Caterpillar had to lower its prices, and this, with the decline in demand, painfully affected sales and profits.

In October 1982, the UAW called a strike at Caterpillar which was long and bitter. The strike virtually shut down U.S. operations, although foreign operations were unaffected. Management wanted to freeze wage rates, which at that time were the highest in the industry; when benefits were added, the company claimed the total was 90 percent higher than wage costs of Komatsu. The union resisted the freeze. It was not until April 1983 that a settlement was reached.

Some of Caterpillar's problems were self-inflicted. Management was characterized as being overconfident, conservative, highly inbred, and stodgy. "Quite frankly, our long years of success made us complacent, even arrogant," said Pierre C. Guerindon, an executive vice president of the company.[51]

Other problems hit the company. In 1982, it was forced to cancel a $90 million order from Russia for pipe-laying equipment. This order was for a gas pipeline from Siberia to Western Europe. The U.S. government put an embargo on all U.S. company shipments to build the line. The ban was decreed by President Reagan to exert pressure on Russia to relax martial law in Poland. Komatsu picked up the order.

The acquisition in May 1981 of Solar Turbines International was more burden than advantage in 1982. The acquisition gave Caterpillar a major position in the gas turbine market much more rapidly than if the firm had built its own plants. However, the $220 million price tag, plus the added capital expenditures required for operations, placed a burden on Caterpillar at a financially difficult time.

[50]Robert S. Eckley, "Caterpillar's Ordeal: Foreign Competition in Capital Goods," *Business Horizons*, March–April 1989.
[51]Quoted in Kathleen Deveny, "For Caterpillar, The Metamorphosis Isn't Over," *Business Week*, August 31, 1987.

KOMATSU LTD.

As mentioned, Komatsu became an indomitable competitor to Caterpillar. It burst into world prominence in the 1970s with the opening offered by Caterpillar's pricing policy. In addition, Komatsu extended liberal free tryouts to attract prospective customers, and it kept its engineers on constant alert to deal with any equipment problems. It expanded its product line, although that never became as extensive as Caterpillar's. Like Caterpillar, it placed emphasis on product quality. Its weakest link was a dealer network inferior to that of Caterpillar's, and it had heavy transportation costs in shipping machines from Japan. The result of this early rivalry was a change in market share. In 1979, Caterpillar had world sales three times greater than those of Komatsu, but during the next half dozen years Komatsu's market share rose steadily at the expense of Caterpillar's.

Caterpillar did not compete effectively against Komatsu. Even in Japan, where it had a joint venture with Mitsubishi Heavy Industries, Ltd. to make heavy excavating equipment for the Japanese market, its products suffered from high costs and high prices.

Komatsu management made it very clear early in the rivalry that its main objective was ending Caterpillar's dominance. It adopted a plan to do this called "Maru C," meaning "Encircle Caterpillar."

In 1985, Komatsu began operations in a plant in Great Britain which had been closed by Caterpillar a few years earlier after severe, acrimonious controversy with British labor unions. Komatsu reportedly bought the plant to circumvent anti-dumping legislation aimed at stopping foreign manufacturers from competing with low-priced products in the European market. Also, of course, it gave Komatsu a base in Europe from which to compete with Caterpillar.

In 1985, Komatsu opened a manufacturing plant in Tennessee, and in 1987 it pooled these facilities in a 50–50 joint venture with Dresser Industries Inc. to form Komatsu Dresser Co. This firm began as a $1 billion enterprise. The Japanese managed manufacturing and were responsible for most of the technology, while Dresser provided some plants and marketing. Some analysts viewed the marriage as one of desperation, because Dresser's construction equipment plants were operating at half capacity, and Komatsu's share of the U.S. market was falling. In 1986, Komatsu held about 20 percent of the U.S. market, but by 1987 it had lost three-quarters of that share. It was also thought that at the time Komatsu feared protectionist legislation and found this joint venture a way to avoid it if it came.

Komatsu Dresser, now the second largest company in the United States construction equipment market, is headquartered in Libertyville, Illinois, some forty miles outside Chicago. The company has four U.S. plants, two in Canada and two in Brazil. It employs over 5,000 people. The firm builds machines that move dirt, such as crawler tractors, wheel loaders, and hydraulic excavators. The dealer and product lines of Komatsu and Dresser will remain separate, but manufacturing will be joint. A question arises as to why Dresser turned over manufacturing to the Japanese. The answer seems to be, according to some analysts, that Dresser recognized it had much to learn from the Japanese.[52]

CATERPILLAR'S STRATEGIES

The crisis of the early 1980s and the competition with Komatsu energized the management of Caterpillar to formulate and implement a number of strategies to dig itself out of the hole. Here are the main ones, in no order of priority.

Cost Reduction   The firm's immediate reaction to adverse conditions in 1982 was to cut production schedules and substantially reduce employment. A 22 percent cost-reduction program was started and was almost achieved in three years. Price reductions, discounting, and other actions were also taken to reduce costs. From 1983 to 1987, plant space was cut one-third by closing ten plants and rearranging others.

Plant Modernization   In early 1986, the company announced a second round of cost reduction. One key strategy of this program was a $1 billion five-year plan to modernize plant and facilities. A major objective of this plan, called "Plant With a Future" (PWAF), was to increase efficiency and reduce costs by an additional 15 to 20 percent.

Caterpillar has prided itself on being a leader in the design, installation, and operation of large, multimillion dollar metal-cutting systems, flexible manufacturing systems, and automated production lines. The PWAF is adding a new dimension to these systems. The company is spending large sums on robots, laser technology, CAD/CAM numerical control machine tools, automated factory systems, and other automated equipment. The ideal sought is a worldwide computer linkage of Caterpillar's thirty plants with suppliers and dealers through a single integrated electronic information network. This system will enhance the ability of Caterpillar to anticipate demand more quickly, to buy components and supplies at the lowest cost around the world, and to satisfy special customer orders more rapidly and at lower cost.

There have been many positive results of the PWAF plan. For example, in Grenoble, France, automation has cut the time needed to fill orders for machinery parts from twenty to eight days. Inventory levels have been slashed and plant floor space significantly reduced. However, costs have escalated to such a degree that the outlays now are projected at $1.8 billion and rising. Also, delays in integrating the new equipment have been encountered, and the system is not expected to be functioning at the ideal level until 1992 or 1993.[53]

Product Quality   Caterpillar has rededicated itself to producing high-quality products. The company has for decades enjoyed a reputation for

[52]Jerry Flint, "The Enemy of My Enemy," *Business Week*, November 14, 1988.
[53]Brian Bremmer, "Can Caterpillar Inch Its Way Back to Heftier Profits?" *Business Week*, September 25, 1989.

quality. Peters and Waterman, in their best seller *In Search of Excellence*, underscored this reputation for quality. They said: "When we say anything about Cat in the presence of two senior agriculture executives we know, they both become misty eyed with reverence."[54] William Naumann, past chairman of Caterpillar, said that from the very beginning the company made a basic decision which to this day permeates all aspects of Caterpillar's operations. "We adopted a policy," he said, "that a Caterpillar product or component—no matter where it was built—would be equal in quality or performance to the same product or component built at any other location, whether in this country or abroad."[55] He believed that this policy of assuring product reliability, quality, and uniformity was basic to the success of the company. There is no doubt that he was right.

Substantial research and engineering (R&E) expenditures have supported product quality as well as new product development. Even in 1982, when the company was in financial trouble, the R&E budget was $376 million, up from $363 in 1981. However, about 10 percent was later deferred. Since then the level has been around $300, plus or minus a little, although there has been a decline relative to sales. In 1982 R&E was 5.8 percent of sales, and in 1988 it was 3.2 percent, still a very respectable level.

Foreign Assembly and Product Purchases As noted earlier, Caterpillar in 1983 reversed a long-held policy of not purchasing finished machines abroad for resale in the United States or elsewhere. To implement the new policy in 1983, the company contracted to buy lift trucks in South Korea, hydraulic excavators from West Germany, paving machines from a small Oklahoma company, and logging equipment from Canada, and put the "Cat" logo on them.

A second fundamental strategic change was made when the company decided to assemble products in foreign countries and buy parts and components from low-cost producers around the world. This replaced the older strategy, as we noted, of manufacturing its own parts and components and shipping finished products from the United States to foreign customers. By 1990, the company expects it will be making fewer than 50 percent as many parts in-house as in 1980.[56]

Product Line The company doubled its product line. At the same time, old products were improved. Another important product line strategy was to shift sharply from heavier construction (and very expensive) equipment to smaller machines. This change was due to the conviction that growth in the demand for the larger machines was limited. The change in strategy puts further pressure on Caterpillar, because competition is strong and profit margins are thin in this market. The broadening of the product line, however, will strengthen the company's competitive position.

[54]Peters and Waterman, *op. cit.*, pp. 171–172.
[55]*Ibid.*, p. 172.
[56]Eckley, *op. cit.*

Caterpillar's Strong Dealer Network   Caterpillar's dealers are solidly established in their markets and loyal to Caterpillar, even in times of economic difficulty. This is due not only to the superior product that they sell but also to Caterpillar's devotion to them.

In 1982, for example, when some dealers got into financial difficulty, Caterpillar worked closely with them and extended special assistance. Such attention was reflected in a very low turnover rate of dealers in the troubling year 1982.

Caterpillar looks upon its dealers as partners, even through most of them are privately owned. As noted above, Caterpillar has established several subsidiaries to aid dealers in moving and financing their sales. This has helped dealers to continue their close relationships with customers. Such interweaving of interests has been one other reason for the enviable dealership network that supports Caterpillar.[57]

Employee Involvement   Multi-functional problem-solving teams are used widely in the company as a part of employee involvement programs. An outstanding example is the team approach which successfully developed the 1.1 liter engine: the four-cylinder 3114 and the six-cylinder 3116. So highly regarded is this engine that General Motors took it apart, compared it with that of competitors, and signed a five-year contract to put only 3116 engines in a new line of medium-duty trucks, beginning with the 1990 models. This engine was developed by teams of employees representing different functional groups from around the world. There was constant communication among the teams, and lots of traveling. Said program manager Bud Edward: "It's a different culture from how we operated in the past when departments worked independently from each other. There were some rough spots crossing functional lines, but in the end, we got excellent results."[58]

In the fall of 1989, there were over 2,000 people in more than 200 teams that had started or completed some 1,600 programs, ranging from redesign of work areas to new systems that reduce paper flow. Top management says these teams are designed to facilitate employee cooperation and communication at all levels, with one common goal: "to involve employees in getting the job done easier and better than ever before."

Relations With Unions   Relations between management and the United Automobile Workers (UAW) have improved, as evidenced by the fact that since 1983 there have been two agreements reached without a work stoppage. Union leaders reportedly and understandably have been concerned with plant automation that reduces jobs. But a growing and profitable company does provide more job security for those that are left.

---

[57]Jim Croce, Joe Girty, Moses Okpamen, and Roger Unger, "Caterpillar Tractor Company," Case 13, in George A. Steiner, John B. Miner, and Edmund R. Gray, *Management Policy and Strategy*, 3rd ed., New York: Macmillan Publishing Company, 1986.
[58]"1.1 Liter: Cat's New Little Engine Takes on the World," *Caterpillar World*, no. 2, 1989, p. 20.

Anticipating European Unification in 1992   Special note should be made of Caterpillar's awareness of and preparation for the unification of Europe in 1992. Management claims that as long ago as 1985 it gave serious attention to the prospects of unification when, in that year, the European Commission issued its "White Paper" proposing the unification.

Caterpillar established a European dealer organization shortly after World War II, and in 1951 started its first European manufacturing facility. Since then, Caterpillar's presence has expanded, until today the company employs 11,000 people at nine European facilities in six countries. Dealers employ another 11,000. Europe is Caterpillar's largest market outside the United States.

Varying rules and regulations among European countries with respect to products prevents product standardization. For instance, in the United States there are few requirements governing the driving of earth-moving machines on roads between job sites. In England and France, however, flashing lights are required on roofs of the equipment when traveling on highways. But in Germany such lights are outlawed, because only emergency vehicles can have them. Backhoes to be shipped to Germany, where there are the most stringent road requirements, require modifications costing $2,000 per vehicle.

Caterpillar personnel are working with Community officials to eliminate as many of this type of barrier as possible. Caterpillar dealers throughout the twelve member countries have formed a "1992 Task Force" to keep abreast of events concerning such issues as changing laws, equipment service, training, cost reduction, and how customers will react when the trade barriers are removed. For example, on the latter issue, the question is how soon customers will be willing to cross country borders to purchase equipment.

RESIDUAL PROBLEMS

At this writing (early 1990), the company is faced with many problems. For instance, there is the problem of global competition. Komatsu, of course, is a major competitor, but there are many others. In Europe there is Fiat Allis of Italy, a strong competitor that uses Hitachi technology in making excavators. A. B. Volvo in Sweden and Mercedes-Benz of West Germany compete in diesel trucks. J. C. Bamford Ltd. of Great Britain is a strong competitor in the backhoe market. In the United States, while Caterpillar is "king of the hill," there are strong competitors such as Komatsu Dresser.

While labor relations are comparatively friendly, a question remains about the union's attitude as factory automation proceeds. Major questions arise about what more should be done to prepare to exploit the opportunities and avoid the threats inherent in the economic unification of Europe in 1992. There is need for joint ventures and more acquisitions, but Caterpillar's experience in making such arrangements has not been broad or always outstanding. While exchange rates are more satisfactory to the company today than a few years ago, a question arises as to what should be done if the dollar increases again in value. (It is now strengthening.) The company has the problem of completing and perfecting the manufacturing modernization program. It is concerned about the potential threat of trade restrictions here and abroad, an important worry for a company whose sales depend heavily on foreign operations. Raw material costs are rising. The price of steel is rising, for example, and this metal is a large cost item for the company.

Such questions led George A. Schaefer, chairman and chief executive officer of the company, to establish a Strategic Planning Committee (SPC) to assist in the formulation of new strategies. The work of the SPC follows.

CATERPILLAR'S STRATEGIC PLANNING COMMITTEE

In June 1987, Caterpillar for the first time set up a Strategic Planning Committee. It was composed of nine senior managers who represented a number of important functional areas. Since then, the number of managers has been raised to eleven. The CEO is the chairman of the committee, which makes recommendations to him and to a five-member Executive Office, where the final strategic decisions are made.

The SPC's goal is to evaluate, for top management consideration, Caterpillar's existing strategies, and then to develop significant options, alternatives, and opportunities for the company's growth and profitability. The SPC is also charged with designing a strategic planning system that can be institutionalized when the SPC completes its work.

The CEO has said that what he wants to come out of the whole process is "a clearly stated, integrated, and customer-oriented corporate strategy—one that is precise, well-communicated, and well-understood throughout the organization."[59]

As a foundation for its deliberations, the SPC hired management consultants, examined the changing environment, studied the lessons taught by companies that had undergone significant change, and talked at length with executives of those companies. These were well-known firms such as Ford, Boeing, American Express, and Eastman Kodak.

Two products of the SPC were a mission statement and a vision statement. The mission statement has been widely distributed throughout the company. It is set forth in four sentences, as follows:

• Provide differentiated products and services of recognized superior value to discriminating customers worldwide.
• Pursue businesses in which we can be a leader based on one or more of our strengths.
• Build and maintain a productive work environment in which high levels of personal satisfaction can be achieved while conforming to our "Code of Worldwide Business Conduct and Operating Principles."
• Achieve growth and above-average returns for stockholders resulting from both management of ongoing businesses and a studied awareness and development of new opportunities.

[59]George A. Schaefer, "Remarks to Machinery Analysts of New York," June 1, 1989.

Schaefer observed that there are four key phrases in this mission statement: provide differentiated products and services, be a leader, maintain a productive work environment, and achieve growth and above-average returns. "These four phrases," he said, "describe what Caterpillar is trying to accomplish as an ongoing business institution. This mission statement will serve as guidelines in evaluating the appropriateness of any strategic alternatives we develop."[60]

The vision statement is much more detailed, and was distributed to most of the salaried employees. It is a picture of what the company should look like in the year 2000 if all the strategies formulated are implemented effectively. Schaefer set forth essentials of this vision, as follows:

• The company will grow through developing its current profitable businesses and expanding into new related businesses from this base. It will continue to be a leader in its core businesses and move into only those areas the company knows best in terms of technology, distribution, and markets.

• The company will become more decentralized and probably organized in strategic business units, with a general manager having full profit and loss responsibilities for each unit.

• The customer will still be the central focus of attention. All actions will be evaluated in terms of their impact on customers.

• Serving specific market segments, rather than the generic marketplace, will be the company's posture.

• The independent dealer will remain the cornerstone of the company's marketing effort.

• Caterpillar will continue to be a technology leader in all of its businesses. The product line, as well as processes, materials, testing, transportation, distribution, and service diagnostics, will be technologically superior to the competition.

• Manufacturing facilities will be located in key industrialized locations. These facilities will incorporate flexible technology to improve productivity and minimize costs, while maintaining uniform, high levels of product quality.

• Product quality will improve with a program of continuous attention to quality for all products.

• Information technology will link customers, dealers, suppliers, and manufacturing operations.

Schaefer concluded: "Perhaps the magnitude of this change in such a short period of time is unprecedented not only for Caterpillar but for any capital-intensive business such as ours."[61]

FINANCIAL ANNOTATIONS

The historical financial strength and recent profits of Caterpillar have made possible financing of the strategies described above without excessive bor-

[60]*Ibid.*
[61]*Ibid.*

rowing. Long-term debt rose to $2.3 billion in 1982 to relieve the cash drain of that period. It gradually dropped to $1.4 billion in 1988. In the meantime, however, debts of subsidiaries rose from zero in 1982 to $425 million in 1988. Total long-term debt as a percentage of stockholder ownership declined from 42.8 percent in 1982 to a low of 29.4 percent in 1987, but rose slightly to 34.0 percent in 1988. This is a conservative ratio in light of the heavy leverage of many companies today.

Employment has fallen from 73,249 in 1982 to about 60,000 in 1989, reflecting the increased efficiency of operations since sales in the same period rose from $6.5 billion to $11.1 billion. Wages, salaries, and employee benefits, however, remained about the same during this period.

Financial analysts project a modest profit increase for Caterpillar for 1990 compared with 1980. This, they say, is due to the heavy development and modernization expenditures currently being made, plus rising raw material costs. As the modernization programs mature, however, in a few years there should be a signifigant profit payoff. In the meantime, the stock of Caterpillar has lagged much behind the average of a diversified group of machinery companies.[62]

QUESTIONS

1 Briefly trace the early history of Caterpillar.
2 What caused Caterpillar's crisis in the early 1980s? Should the company have foreseen it?
3 What strategies did Caterpillar formulate and implement to overcome the crisis?
4 Contrast these strategies with earlier strategies of the company. Were they correct in light of the changing environment of the company?
5 Appraise Caterpillar's strategies as it anticipates the unification of Europe in 1992.
6 What grade would you give the company's mission statement? Explain.
7 What dominant strengths and weaknesses do you see for Caterpillar as it moves toward the year 2000?
8 Komatsu has been a tough aggressive competitor and made no secret of its intent to vanquish Caterpillar. A question arises as to the point at which aggressive competition become unethical behavior. How do you draw the line?

[62]Bremmer, *op. cit.*

Pollution and the Environment

CHAPTER
14

Industrial Pollution and Environmental Policy

Ill fares the land, to hastening ills a prey,
Where wealth accumulates and men decay.

So wrote Oliver Goldsmith in 1770, recognizing that environmental pollution has been a concern through the ages. In the United States, knowledge of environmental degradation has focused widespread attention on the responsibility of business as a consumer of environmental quality, a scarce resource. How do companies today protect the environment? Here is one story.

In 1959 Ohio Edison Co. started construction of the W. H. Sammis electric power generating plant on the banks of the Ohio River. This was eleven years before passage of the Clean Air Act in 1970. Over the next fifteen years the company built seven coal-fired boilers at the plant; these heated steam.

During coal combustion, unburned particles called fly ash are created. If not removed by pollution control equipment, they lower visibility, promote atmospheric changes, and cause human respiratory illness. In the years before strict federal emission standards, Ohio Edison voluntarily installed electrostatic precipitators designed to remove 97 to 99 percent of the fly ash from the exhaust stream. Coal combustion also releases sulfur dioxide (SO_2) gas, and the company controlled SO_2 emissions by burning coal with a low sulfur content.

This pollution control strategy worked until the Arab oil embargo in 1973 led to a shortage of high-quality coal. By the mid-1970s, the plant was burning lower-quality coal because it was cheaper and more plentiful. But this lower-quality coal had a high ash content and a low sulfur content. Although the low sulfur content lessened SO_2 emissions, it aggravated the fly ash problem because high sulfur coal contains more iron particles that can be charged in the field of an electrostatic precipitator. Without these tiny pieces of iron in the ash, the antipollution equipment was far less efficient.

Thus, the plant developed a reputation as a source of pollution. The electrostatic precipitators were overwhelmed by fly ash from the low-quality coal and sometimes removed as little as 25 percent. This often left the plant far short of the federal standard of 99.4 percent particulate removal. In 1981, Ohio Edison paid $1.7 million in fines for violations of Clean Air Act standards and faced federally imposed deadlines for higher particulate abatement. Ultimately, the company undertook a $440 million retrofit. It erected four enormous "baghouses" on a reinforced concrete deck three football fields long over the highway in front of the plant. These baghouses are dust-collection systems that operate on the same principle as vacuum cleaners. They entrap particles in the airstream of the boiler exhaust that flows through fiberglass bags and remove about 99 percent of the fly ash. Sulfur dioxide emissions are controlled by burning higher-quality, low-sulfur coal. Two of the boilers, however, also have electrostatic precipitators to increase particulate removal capacity and allow burning of lower-quality coal.

A Herculean effort has been required to meet increasingly stiff pollution abatement standards set by the federal government and the state of Ohio. The $440 million spent retrofitting the Sammis plant is the most any company in North America has spent for this purpose and equaled the cost of the plant's original construction. At its 2,100-acre Bruce Mansfield Plant in Shippingport, Pennsylvania, Ohio Edison had to devote 1,800 acres to pollution control equipment—86 percent of total area. The air quality control equipment there eats up 50 percent of the plant's operating cost and uses 5 percent of the electricity it generates. As a result of such mandatory efforts throughout the company's generating system, 20 percent of a customer's electric bill pays for environmental protection.

The story of Ohio Edison illustrates the huge expenditures required of firms in many industries to meet rapidly escalating environmental protection standards. Ohio Edison's outlays are larger than most but not atypical for large companies with industrial operations that foul the environment. In this chapter, we discuss the growth of environmental concern in the United States, the passage and content of environmental regulations, and the response of business. Understanding the phenomenal surge of regulation in the area of environmental quality will help explain why Ohio Edison felt compelled to make such huge capital expenditures for pollution abatement.

ENVIRONMENTAL DEGRADATION: SOURCES AND CAUSATION

It is incorrect to say that pollution is caused entirely by industrial and other human activity. There are natural sources for many contaminants. Particulates causing atmospheric turbidity come from dust, forest wildfires, and volcanoes. Anaerobic decay and photochemical aerosol formation by plants are natural sources of hydrocarbons contributing to air pollution. Only about a

The W. H. Sammis plant on the bank of the Ohio River. The dust-collection system sits atop a reinforced concrete deck about the size of three football fields. Note the four-lane highway running under the deck. (Courtesy of Ohio Edison.)

third of sulfur oxide comes from human activities; most comes from sulfide compounds formed in decay of organic matter and from the sulfates in sea spray. About nine-tenths of all airborne carbon monoxide comes from "natural" sources. Water picks up trace elements of metals, asbestos, and other pollutants in its flow over rocks, gravel, and sand. Background ionizing radiation capable of mutating DNA comes from uranium ore and cosmic rays.

Fissures on the ocean floor that geologists call seeps continuously spill oil and natural gas, causing hydrocarbon pollution. Geologists estimate that thousands of seeps off the California coastline near Santa Barbara spill up to eight tons of hydrocarbons into the air each day and are responsible for much of the area's air pollution. A few volcanoes, such as Krakatoa in the East Indies and Katmai in Alaska, have put more sulfuric contaminants into the air than all the products of combustion since the beginning of civilization.

Human activity—particularly economic activity in agriculture, energy production, and manufacturing—burdens the environment with additional pollutants. Some *anthropogenic,* or human-generated, pollutants are not found in nature. These include, for instance, chlorinated hydrocarbon pesticides such as DDT and the fluorocarbon aerosols in air conditioners. Most pollution from industrial activity, however, simply adds to the normal background levels of naturally occurring substances. Thus, ambient concentrations of lead, hydrocarbons, ionizing radiation, and other naturally occurring substances may reach artificially high levels dangerous to human health.

Anthropogenic emissions of carbon dioxide are high enough to endanger the global climate. Carbon dioxide occurs naturally in the atmosphere. But since 1958, when systematic measurement began, the concentration of carbon dioxide in the atmosphere has risen from 315 parts per million (ppm) to 352 ppm. This rise is the result of combustion of wood and fossil fuel to energize economic activity. It is of great concern because atmospheric carbon dioxide absorbs heat radiated from the earth back toward space. This is the so-called greenhouse effect, which perpetuates the delicate heat balance necessary to preserve the narrow climatic conditions in which life flourishes. Since the 1890s, the mean average global temperature has gone up about one degree due to rising carbon dioxide levels. Some climatologists predict that temperatures will increase two to nine degrees more by the year 2050.

Although the existence of industrial activity is a direct cause of environmental damage, there are other fundamental causes. One is population growth. Between 1900 and 1990, world population grew from 1.2 billion to 5.5 billion. It continues to rise at an exponential rate, and each birth creates new demands for energy, food, and industrial products. A second ecological insult is urbanization, a worldwide phenomenon which concentrates pollutants in small areas where they are less easily dispersed. A third polluting force is affluence. In the industrialized countries it has encouraged great waste, and in poorer, less industrialized countries it is an ideal which often makes industrialization a priority over environmental protection.

The operation of these forces is illustrated by the decade 1970 to 1980 in the U.S. During these years, the population grew 12 percent, urban areas grew by 11 percent (since almost all the 23 million new people lived in them), and real disposable personal income grew by 33 percent. A few statistics illustrate the impact of these changes on natural resources. Solid waste production rose by 18 percent (with a 72 percent increase in discarded plastics), water consumption increased by 22 percent, farm output rose 23 percent, the number of motor vehicles in use increased 31 percent, production of chemicals rose 68 percent (including a 42 percent rise in pesticides), electric power production ran up 72 percent, and industrial production increased 123 percent.[1]

Finally, cultural and political factors are also an underlying cause of pollution. Deeply rooted shortcomings in our values and institutions were succinctly identified twenty years ago by the Council on Environmental Quality. The reader may agree that these shortcomings, noted in 1970, are only partially overcome today. They include:

> Our past tendency to emphasize quantitative growth at the expense of qualitative growth; the failure of our economy to provide full accounting for the social costs of environmental pollution; the failure to take environmental factors into account as a normal and necessary part of our planning and decision making; the inadequacy of our institutions for dealing with problems that cut across traditional political boundaries; our dependence on conveniences, without regard for their impact on the environment; and more fundamentally, our failure to perceive the environment as a totality and to understand and to recognize the fundamental interdependence of all its parts, including man himself.[2]

THE DAMAGING ENVIRONMENTAL EFFECTS OF POLLUTION

In the 1930s, a brick-manufacturing plant was built in the vicinity of a tribal pueblo near Santa Fe, New Mexico. A small private railroad was started to move materials between the plant and the main rail line nearby and the company operated a steam locomotive on it. When the boiler and pipe insulation on the locomotive needed replacement, workers discarded the old, asbestos-bearing insulating materials near the tracks, where it was found by members of the tribe and brought back to the pueblo. It was put to many uses. Asbestos pads were used for worktable insulation by silversmiths making Indian jewelry. Dancers at religious festivals scraped and pounded their deer-hide leggings with crumbling, asbestos pipe insulation to whiten them, an action that released clouds of floating asbestos fibers.

Gradually, the Indians found more uses for asbestos, and when the trackside windfalls proved inadequate, tribe members who did construction work started scavenging at their job sites for more. The result of this exposure was revealed years later by U.S. Public Health Service researchers, who discovered a cluster of five cases of malignant mesothelioma (a tumor in the

---

[1] These percentages are based on figures in *The Statistical Abstract of the United States, 1988,* 108th ed., Washington D.C.: Government Printing Office, December 1987, various tables.

[2] Council on Environmental Quality, *Environmental Quality: Annual Report,* Washington, D.C.: Government Printing Office, 1970, p. vii.

lining of the chest cavity) between 1970 and 1982 among the 2,000 Indians in the pueblo.[3] This is roughly 1,000 times the normal incidence rate for this asbestos-related tumor in a population of such small size. Investigation revealed that four of the five victims were silversmiths, and all five had actively participated in ceremonial dances. All have died.

Like the residents of this tiny pueblo, we are now subject to a wider range of contaminants and to larger quantities of pollutants than were our ancestors in the pristine, preindustrial world. Concern centers on five adverse health effects associated with industrial pollution: the induction of cancer (carcinogenicity), the induction of permanent genetic changes in cells (mutagenicity), the induction of nonhereditary birth defects (teratogenicity), noncancerous disease processes in bodily organs,[4] and behavioral impairment.

Sometimes the harmful effects of pollution are hard to pin down. Despite abundant studies, the health effects of ozone, a constituent of urban smog to, which millions are daily exposed, are unclear. Ozone is a highly reactive gas; it reacts rapidly with bioorganic compounds when it is inhaled and comes in contact with cells and fluids in the respiratory tract. A number of short-term effects, such as inflammation and reduced lung capacity, have been discovered, but they appear to be reversible once exposure stops. Some medical experts suspect that ozone causes permanent lung damage, but this remains unproven.[5] There is no evidence that breathing ozone causes lung cancer.

Adverse human health effects are only part of the cost of degradation. Global effects on property, weather, plants, and animals have also been documented. As noted, atmospheric carbon dioxide threatens to cause significant global warming. Destruction of tropical rain forests and degradation of other lands has not only made numerous species extinct, but since trees remove carbon dioxide from the atmosphere and fix carbon in their cells, this defoliation has made the ecosystem less able to reverse carbon dioxide build-up. Sulfur dioxide and nitrogen oxides from industrial air emissions cause growing acidity of rain. Depletion of the ozone layer by upper atmospheric chemical reactions with manufactured fluorocarbon molecules exposes the earth to unaccustomed doses of cosmic rays which are destructive of plant and animal tissues. These problems are serious because they portend the loss of important environmental life-supporting capabilities.

[3] Richard J. Driscoll, Wallace J. Mulligan, Daniel Schultz, and Anthony Candelaria, "Malignant Mesothelioma: A Cluster in a Native American Pueblo," *New England Journal of Medicine*, June 2, 1988, p. 1437.

[4] These include damage to the nervous system (neurotoxicity), suppression of host defense mechanisms (immunotoxicity), liver injury (hepatotoxicity), kidney damage (renal toxicity), and harm to other tissues. Medical studies have also demonstrated that some toxic chemicals are synergistic; that is, in combination with another chemical both become more toxic than they would be individually because one chemical significantly alters the metabolism and resulting bioactivity of the other. Examples are asbestos and cigarette smoke, toluene and trichloroethylene, or PCBs and benzene hexachloride.

[5] For two overviews of ozone studies see Morton Lippmann, "Health Benefits from Controlling Exposures to Criteria Air Pollutants," in John Blodgett, ed., *Health Benefits of Air Pollution Control: A Discussion*, Washington, D.C.: Congressional Research Service, February 27, 1989, and Beverly E. Tilton, "Health Effects of Tropospheric Ozone," *Environmental Science and Technology*, March 1989.

THE ROLE OF BUSINESS IN POLLUTING THE ENVIRONMENT

Industrial activity, broadly defined, is the source of enduring pollution problems, yet for most of the period since the 1850s, when industry began to transform societies, there has been little concern for protecting nature. Carelessness abounded. Copper ores in Butte, Montana, in the 1870s were roasted in open pits that produced fumes of sulfur and arsenic and smoke so thick that streetlamps burned on city streets at midday. Cows grazing in nearby areas had their teeth coated with fugitive copper fallen from the air. Isaac Edinger, a nearby rancher of that time, said:

> I used to carry a few of those gold-colored teeth in my pocket all the time because no one would believe me, and I'd have to show 'em. When they were shown they always wanted to keep the evidence, and I'd have to get a new supply every time I went back to the slaughterhouse.[6]

Ignorance of toxic effects, combined perhaps with ruthless exploitation of workers, led to the Gauley mine disaster in the 1930s, when a subsidiary of Union Carbide drilled a four-mile-long tunnel through a mountain of virtually pure silica. Long hours of drilling and blasting in unventilated shafts exposed 2,000 unprotected workers, mostly blacks, to enormous concentrations of silica dust. In 1936, four years after the tunneling ended, a congressional investigation revealed that 476 workers already had died of silicosis and estimated that many of the rest were destined similarly to perish.[7]

Industrial practices used for decades, with the expansion of scientific knowledge, have been pronounced unsafe or environmentally degrading. In retrospect, it is evident that workers in the asbestos industry who were exposed to high levels of airborne asbestos fiber faced grave danger of lethal illness. During a major, secret federal government push in the 1950s to develop a stockpile of nuclear weapons, uranium was mined in ways now considered environmentally unacceptable. The radioactive waste products of this mining, abandoned ore piles known as tailings, are found in proximity to twenty-two abandoned uranium mills in eight western states and constitute major health hazards. Indian miners were paid $50,000 to $80,000 a year to work underground uranium mines, and many perished of lung cancer attributable to exposure to radon daughters in unventilated shafts.[8]

Major environmental abuses by industry have, of course, continued through the 1980s. Sensational accidents, such as the leak of methyl isocyanate at a Union Carbide pesticide plant in Bhopal, India, killing 2,400 in 1984; the release of radionuclides by a mismanaged Russian reactor with a mature fuel supply at Chernobyl in the USSR, killing 31 in 1986; and the release of 11 million gallons of crude oil from the grounding of the *Exxon Valdez* illustrate catastrophic failures

---

[6] C. B. Glasscock, *The War of the Copper Kings: Builders of Butte and Wolves of Wall Street*, New York: Grosset & Dunlap, 1935, p. 86.

[7] U.S. Congress, House Committee on Labor, *An Investigation Relating to Health Conditions of Workers Employed in the Construction and Maintenance of Public Utilities*, 74th Congress, 2d Session, January 16–29, 1936.

[8] Sandra E. Bregman, "Blessing or Curse? Uranium Mining on Indian Lands," *Environment*, September 1982.

of industrial processes to contain pollutants. Yet pollution from these and other dramatic incidents is insignificant compared to the cumulative emissions of on-going, routine business activity.

Most industrial pollution in the 1990s is undramatic, garden variety degrada-tion. Many industrial processes are inevitably polluting and leave their specific signature on the environment. Agriculture leaves pesticide residues in ground-water, electroplating produces air emissions of chromium, paint factories dis-charge cadmium-contaminated waste water, petrochemical plants evaporate hy-drocarbons and benzene, and semiconductor manufacturing adds toxic solvents such as trichloroethylene to waste water. State of the art control devices are never 100 percent efficient, and so these industries and others leave their char-acteristic pollution signature on air, land, and water.

In addition, it is virtually impossible for an industrial plant not to pollute in many small ways. Dust escapes through wall vents. Oil may drip from the engine of a warehouse forklift and later be washed into a drain. Gophers can dig through dikes built around chemical storage tanks so that rainwater per-colates through the earth, carrying small amounts of dissolved toxic residues from minor spills during fluid transfer into and out of the tank. Dust from ductwork cleanouts may escape into the air. In short, a typical large plant has as many potential sources of pollution as the absent-minded professor has for error. Industrial activity is inevitably messy.

THE ENVIRONMENTAL MOVEMENT

The roots of the American environmental movement go back to the conser-vation movement of the 1800s, which was started to protect western lands from unregulated mining, timber cutting, and grazing. *Conservationists* be-lieved that resources should be harvested responsibly and with restraint to satisfy human needs. This thinking permitted a trade-off between nature and industrial growth and came to dominate public policy. A competing *preserva-tionist* view held that humanity should live in awe of nature, preserving it rather than consuming it. This ideal was, of course, out of tune with nine-teenth century values.

A modern environmental movement flowered in the 1960s. The seeds of this movement were sown by a century of human improvidence in relating to nature. A number of forces converged early in the decade to give birth to a mass movement, including early scientific studies of pollution; publication of popularizing books such as Rachel Carson's study of pesticides, *Silent Spring;* a new emphasis on quality-of-life; and a growing wave of cynicism toward business.[9] The first photographs from space allowed humanity to see planet earth and were galvanizing.

Environmentalists of the 1960s rediscovered preservationist notions and promoted a number of basic ideas. First, they condemned the logic of eco-nomic growth and materialism; one writer referred to U.S. business as "cow-

[9] Boston: Houghton Mifflin, 1962.

boy capitalism" which exploited resources as if they were limitless.[10] Second, because spaceship earth has limited resources, a new spirit of international cooperation was necessary. Third, many argued that technologies such as aerosols, nuclear power, and petrochemical refining created hazards well out of proportion to benefits. And fourth, some took the apocalyptic view that irreversible harm had already occurred.[11]

Ideas such as these were the framework of an ecological populism that decisively changed government policies, business incentives, and popular values. In the late 1970s, similar ideas motivated a strong, radical political movement in West Germany known as the Green Party. A Green movement spread to other countries, and by 1990 Greens had elected members of parliament in nine European countries and the European parliament. Today, the Greens are more moderate and their message of environmental protection is increasingly popular with the electorate.

Environmentalism had a more difficult birth in Eastern Europe and Russia, where until the 1990s socialist governments prioritized industrialization and virtually ignored pollution control. In Poland, for example, by the end of 1985 almost all river water was unfit for drinking. The Polish Chemical Society reported in 1988 that because of exposure to high levels of lead and other pollutants, 30 to 45 percent of schoolchildren suffered substandard health.[12] Yet until the late 1980s, scientists and journalist were pressured by the government to suppress alarming reports, and the hardy few who participated in demonstrations were given two-year jail terms. Since 1989, however, Poland has had a Green party modeled after the West German Green Party.

Likewise, in the Soviet Union the emphasis on industrialization since the Stalin years led to monumental pollution problems.[13] But repression of ecological protest was ruthless. When, for instance, party leaders in Leningrad proposed a huge dam on the Gulf of Finland in 1970, which would have devastated the ecology of a delta area, many scientists and environmentalists objected. Some dissenters were killed; others lost their jobs or were stripped of party membership. After the advent of *glasnost,* or openness, in the mid-1980s, greater concern for the environment has been evident in the Soviet Union, and hundreds of thousands of Soviet citizens have massed in environmental protests since the first big rally in 1987. In 1988, for example, from 50,000 to 100,000 Latvians, Lithuanians, and Estonians linked hands to show outrage at high effluent levels in the Baltic Sea. Nevertheless, it was not until 1989 that the Soviet Union passed a law mandating heavy fines and facility shut-downs for polluters, and environmental impact statements for major development projects are still not required.

[10] Kenneth Boulding, *Economics as a Science,* New York: McGraw-Hill, 1970.

[11] See, for example, Paul R. Ehrlich, *The Population Bomb,* New York: Ballantine, 1968.

[12] Noted in Jackson Diehl, "Choking on Their Own Development," *Washington Post National Weekly Edition,* May 29–June 4, 1989, p. 9.

[13] See Hilary F. French, "The Greening of the Soviet Union," *World Watch,* June 1989, and "Industrial Wasteland," *World Watch,* November/December 1988. See also William Mueller, "Green Reds," *The Amicus Journal,* Summer 1989, and Anthony Cortese, "Glasnost, Perestroika, and the Environment," *Environmental Science and Technology,* October 1989.

Many underdeveloped nations, anxious to create affluence, have ambitious development plans that prioritize industrialization and neglect environmental protection. In Brazil, the government has pursued a conscious policy of subsidizing rain forest destruction to relocate workers on cattle ranches away from crowded urban slums. In China and India, governments are promoting domestic auto production to boost economic growth. These two countries have 38 percent of the world population, but account for only 0.5 percent of auto registrations.[14] What will be the environmental cost of successful manufacturing-based development should these countries succeed in emulating the U.S. and Western Europe?

EVOLUTION OF A NEW ENVIRONMENTAL ETHIC

What is the proper relationship between business and nature? Throughout the history of Western civilization, nature has been regarded as an adversary to be conquered, wilderness has been the raw material from which profits stem, natural resources have been used for financial gain, and nature has been a depository for the toxic detritus of industrial activity. Ironically, the rapacious and arrogant attitudes of industry toward nature may be partly responsible for the current high standard of living and political dominance of Western culture. But the environmental ethic of the past, which ascribes few rights to nature and few obligations to business to protect it, is fading.

Today, the outlines of a new, expansive environmental ethic for business are emerging. The development of new ethical conceptions is the by-product of pollution damage, resource depletion, new scientific understandings of nature, public opinion unified in support of environmental quality, and the scholarly work of a critical mass of intellectuals interested in preserving nature.

Aldo Leopold, a naturalist, was a pioneer in thinking about an expanded environmental ethic. A seminal statement of a new "land ethic" in his 1949 book, *A Sand County Almanac*, inspired later generations of environmental ethicists. He wrote:

> All ethics so far evolved rest upon a single premise: that the individual is a member of a community of interdependent parts. His instincts prompt him to compete for his place in the community, but his ethics prompt him also to cooperate (perhaps in order that there may be a place to compete for).
>
> The land ethic simply enlarges the boundaries of the community to include soils, waters, plants, and animals, or collectively: the land...
>
> In short, a land ethic changes the role of *Homo sapiens* from conqueror of the land-community to plain member and citizen of it. It implies respect for his fellow members and also respect for the community as such.[15]

---

[14] Michael Renner, "Rethinking Transportation," in Brown et al., *op. cit.*, p. 100.

[15] New York: Ballantine, 1970, pp. 239–40. A more radical form of the land ethic, called "deep ecology," was set later forth by a Norwegian philosopher, Arne Naess. Naess' work has been as important to ecophilosophy as that of Leopold. See his two articles, "The Shallow and the Deep,

The evolving environmental ethic has two components. First, it gives moral standing to nonhuman, nonconscious beings. The traditional Western notion of rights is competitive; when *Homo sapiens* compete for rights with plant and animal species, we always win. To illustrate our lack of charity, philosopher Peter Singer has popularized the concept of "speciesism," or "a prejudice or attitude of bias towards the members of one's own species and against those of members of other species," that is analogous to racism or sexism.[16] The racist and sexist believe that skin color and sex determine the worth of people; the speciesist extends this concept in the belief that the number of one's legs or whether one lives in trees, the sea, or a condominium determines one's rights to life and environmental quality. The new school of environmental philosophy, however, argues that the human species, though vested with enormous power to alter the biosphere, is simply one among many. Other species have intrinsic value independent of any economic usefulness for industry. Buttressing this view is a remarkable theory developed by James Lovelock, a British chemist. Lovelock's theory, called the *Gaia hypothesis* (named after the Greek earth goddess Ge), holds that the earth itself is alive because "the Earth's living matter, air, oceans, and land surface form a complex system which can be seen as a single organism and which has the capacity to keep our planet a fit place for life."[17] Under the new environmental ethic, then, damage to nature is evil; harmonious coexistence is good. Hence, corporations have a duty to protect ecological systems, including animals and nonsentient objects, for their own sake.

A second part of the emerging environmental ethic is expansion of the human right to environmental quality. People, it is alleged, have the right to a pollution-free environment. Article One of the Constitution of Pennsylvania, for instance, states: "The people have a right to clean air, pure water, and to the preservation of the natural scenic, historic, and aesthetic values of the environment." Because pollution causes harm, a corporation has a moral obligation not to pollute and a duty to protect this human right to health. Corporations should not knowingly introduce damaging or dangerous elements into the environment.

Environmental ethicists are antagonistic to traditional business ethics that use utilitarian notions of overall benefit to justify economic development where such development causes some environmental damage. Industry customarily has argued that although pollution is harmful, the economic benefits of jobs, products, taxes, and economic growth often outweigh environmental damage. Therefore, there is a net benefit to society in industrial development. This ethical outlook clashes with newly developing notions that all members of "spaceship earth" are fellow travelers with rights. Extinc-

Long-Range Ecology Movement. A Summary," *Inquiry* (Spring 1973) and "A Defense of the Deep Ecology Movement," *Environmental Ethics* (Fall 1984).

[16]In *Animal Liberation,* New York: Avon, 1975, p. 7.

[17]J. E. Lovelock, *Gaia: A New Look at Life on Earth,* New York: Oxford University Press, 1987, p. x. This book was first published in 1979.

RADICAL ENVIRONMENTALISTS

The activities of ecological guerillas, who carry on the vigilante tradition of the Old West in the fight against pollution, illustrate just how sharply divergent the values of industry and environmentalists can be.

The archetype was "The Fox," who operated in Illinois in the late 1960s. The Fox struck corporate polluters about thirty times, plugging drainpipes and smokestacks. Once he appeared unannounced (and presumably unwelcomed) in the eighteenth-floor executive offices of USX Corporation to pour a bottle of foul-smelling effluent from one of the company's drains onto the white carpet. His exploits inspired others to sabotage bulldozers, yank surveyors' stakes, saw billboards, dynamite power line towers, and burn forests before they could be logged.

The environmental organization Greenpeace is renowned for intrepid forays against whale-hunting fleets, but its members also have committed criminal acts in the United States, such as plugging waste water drainpipes from chemical plants and refineries. Of late, a secretive, radical group named Earth First! has been pounding long, metal spikes into trees in areas of virgin timber. When hit by power saws, these spikes can cause gruesome in-juries. In 1988, a twenty-three-year-old hook tender in a Louisiana-Pacific sawmill in Northern California was brutally injured when a 52-foot band saw hit an 11-inch spike in a log. The worker was wearing a hard hat and Lexan face shield, but a piece of shrapnel from the blade penetrated the protective gear, slicing his jawbone, knocking out teeth, and cutting one jugular vein. Coworkers held him to-gether for an hour until an ambulance arrived. He lived but required extensive reconstructive surgery.

Radical environmentalists defend their actions. They speak for nature, they say, for creatures who are mute and defenseless in the face of corporate exploitation. They give plants and animals a voice. Polluters have broken the law for years—both nature's law and statutory law—so when they take the law into their own hands, they are simply fighting under the same rules as their corporate foes. Naturally, the business community condemns irresponsible vandalism and criminal endangerment of human life. Louisiana-Pacific called the spiking incident a "terrorist" act and offered a reward of $20,000 for arrest and conviction of the tree spikers. A member of Earth First! responded that the real terrorists were the companies "cutting down thousand-year-old redwood trees to make picnic tables."

tion violates the rights of species. Deforestation violates the rights of trees. Business decisions that do not accommodate these rights ignore costs and benefits to nonhuman, nonsentient members of the environmental community. Traditional developmental ethics of business also clash with the notion of human rights to a pure environment. The more absolute such rights are thought to be, the more constraint there may be on business activities that trade environmental quality for economic development. A carcinogenic particle that invades lung tissue may violate a person's right to health, but normal industrial processes cause some toxic pollution. Today a tension exists between the emerging, idealistic environmental ethic and the pragmatic, moderately exploitative industrial ethic.

PUBLIC OPINION ABOUT THE ENVIRONMENT

Since the 1960s, hundreds of opinion polls have monitored public attitudes on environmental issues. Although questions asked, methodology, and current events differ for these polls, important trend findings emerge.

First, the public regards the environment as an important issue, but it is a second-order issue behind bread-and-butter economic issues. To illustrate, in a 1989 Gallup poll, large majorities revealed that they worried a "great deal" about water pollution (72 percent), toxic waste (69 percent), and air pollution (60 percent). Yet only 4 percent said environmental issues were the most important national problem; by comparison, 34 percent named economic problems such as unemployment and deficit spending, and 27 percent picked drug abuse.[18] So, although the public shows enduring concern for the environment, this concern is, in the words of one opinion analyst, "not terribly intense."[19]

Second, however, the public is remarkably unified in its support for environmental protection. Pollution is experienced by everyone; it is visible and threatening. Unlike issues that divide rich and poor or liberals and conservatives, environmental protection is strongly supported in all age, regional, party, educational, religious, racial, and income groups. Pollster Louis Harris once remarked that "not a single major segment of the public wants environmental laws made less strict," and he remains correct.[20] There are a few population categories where opinion differences are clearly different, although over the years environmental values have been stronger in the Northeast than in the South and weaker among the less educated and blacks.

Third, the public rejects compromises between environmental quality and other goals. Thus, over the years, large majorities have favored preserving species regardless of cost, reducing air pollution even if some factories must close, and spending more to improve the environment even if taxes must be increased.[21]

Finally, we note that Americans are critical of business for laxity in environmental protection. A 1988 Roper poll found only 37 percent of respondents feeling that business satisfactorily met its responsibility to reduce pollution, and placed neglect of the environment at the top of its list of criticisms of business.[22]

ENVIRONMENTAL LAWS AND REGULATIONS

In the 1970s, newly powerful environmental lobbies were instrumental in translating the civic groundswell for environmental protection into an unprecedented string of victories in Congress. New laws established major regulatory programs, tightly controlling business for the first time. The streak

---

[18]Andrew Kohut and James Shriver, "Environment Regaining a Foothold on the National Agenda," *Gallup Report*, no. 285 (June 1989), p. 2.

[19]Riley E. Dunlap, "Polls, Pollution, and Politics Revisited: Public Opinion on the Environment in the Reagan Era," *Environment* (July/August 1987), p. 36.

[20]In "Public United in Concern About Environment," *Common Cause*, June 1982, p. 15.

[21]Illustrative are Kathy Bloomgarden, "Managing the Environment: The Public's View," *Public Opinion*, February/March 1983; "Environmentalists: More of a Political Force," *Business Week*, January 24, 1983; and "Issues Poll Results—1985, " *Common Cause Magazine*, May/June 1985; and Dunlap, *op. cit.*

[22]Noted in Frederick W. Allen and Roy Popkin, "Environmental Polls: What They Tell Us," *EPA Journal*, July/August 1988, p. 10.

began with passage of the National Environmental Policy Act in December 1969, an environmental Magna Carta that required environmental impact statements for all federal projects. It ended with the Comprehensive Environmental Response, Compensation, and Liability Act in December 1980, which established the "Superfund" program to remediate toxic waste disposal sites. Table 14-1 lists the notable statutes of this era.

These laws, passed with bipartisan support in Congress in what came to be called the "environmental decade," created a broad statutory base for industry regulation and changed forever the managerial task of coping with pollution. Since 1980, new laws have, of course, been passed. For example, the Emergency Planning and Community Right-to-Know Act of 1986, passed after toxic substance accidents at Bhopal and Chernobyl, requires businesses using toxic chemicals to report accidental discharges and to provide information to local emergency planning committees about routine on-site use of hazardous chemicals. And the original legislation has been amended, often adding new goals. But virtually all government oversight of business derives from the basic mandates and regulatory philosophies of the 1970s laws.

THE ENVIRONMENTAL PROTECTION AGENCY

A huge federal regulatory apparatus administers the corpus of legislation passed in the 1970s. Twenty-one agencies and departments have environmental regulatory programs. Most of the principal programs are presided over by the crown jewel of this extensive network, the Environmental Protection Agency (EPA). But some critical programs are located elsewhere. To illustrate, the protection of endangered species is entrusted to the Department of Interior, and an independent regulatory commission, the Nuclear Regulatory Commission, is empowered to set rules governing nuclear power plants.

The EPA was created in 1970 by President Richard Nixon. The duties of the EPA are to administer federal environmental laws, set standards for emissions of polluting substances, monitor compliance, and do research on pollution. The EPA may enforce standards directly on corporations, but in practice it delegates some or all of its enforcement authority to the states. The states are permitted by most statutes to set standards that are stricter, and states such as California and New Jersey are more stringent than federal regulators in many areas.

In its short twenty-year life, the EPA has deteriorated from a prime example of effective regulation into a classic case of a poorly managed bureaucracy imposing arcane, contradictory, and needlessly expensive laws on business. Early in its history, the EPA adopted a vigorous program of prosecuting polluters. During its first two years, it undertook more than 1,000 enforcement actions and meted out more than $9 million in fines to surprised companies (including a $7 million fine to Ford Motor Company for cars that exceeded exhaust emission standards). In November 1971, a dramatic emergency ac-

TABLE 14-1   MAJOR ENVIRONMENTAL REGULATORY STATUTES: 1969–1980

National Environmental Policy Act	1969	Declared environmental quality a federal policy goal, required environmental impact studies, and established the Council on Environmental Quality.
Clean Air Act (and Amendments in 1977)	1970	Authorized air quality standards, auto emission limits, state implementation plans, air quality regions, monitoring of stationary source pollution, and research.
Occupational Safety and Health Act	1970	Set up the Occupational Safety and Health Administration to enforce health and safety standards and oversee state health and safety programs.
Noise Pollution and Control Act	1972	Directed the EPA and FAA to limit noise from industrial activity and products and from transportation equipment.
Federal Water Pollution Control Act Amendments	1972	Set a national goal of eliminating all pollutant discharges into U.S. waters by 1985. Industry was required to conform to emission technology standards; a massive sewage treatment construction grant program was authorized; and the EPA was required to set effluent standards and issue discharge permits.
Federal Environmental Pesticide Control Act	1972	Required registration of pesticides by the EPA; required applicants for registration to submit extensive data; authorized the EPA to restrict or ban pesticide uses, and set up labeling requirements.
Marine Protection Research, and Sanctuaries Act	1972	Required the EPA to set up a permit system for ocean dumping, prohibit dumping of hazardous materials (including radioactive waste, but amended in 1982 to permit dumping of radioactive waste as regulated by the EPA), and preserve marine sanctuaries free from industrial activity and dumping.
Endangered Species Act	1973	Created a comprehensive program to identify animal and plant species on the verge of extinction and protect them. Enforced by agencies in the Department of Interior, Commerce, and Agriculture.
Safe Drinking Water Act	1974	Authorized the EPA to set and enforce national standards for drinking water.
Hazardous Materials Transport Act	1974	Authorized the Department of Transportation to regulate shipment of hazardous materials. Prohibited shipment of radioactive materials in passenger planes.
Resource Conservation and Recovery Act	1976	Established EPA regulation of solid and hazardous waste disposal; authorized the EPA to define hazardous waste materials and to encourage and supervise state programs.
Toxic Substances Control Act	1976	Established a national control policy for chemicals posing a risk to the environment. Authorized the EPA to set chemical testing and licensing procedures, to ban excessively risky chemicals, and to set up record-keeping requirements for chemical manufacture.
Federal Mine Safety and Health Act	1977	Established the Mine Safety and Health Administration in the Department of Labor to regulate mine safety and health, enforce and set standards, and undertake a rigorous inspection schedule for mines.
Surface Mining Control and Reclamation Act	1977	Regulated strip-mining operations and set standards for reclamation of abandoned mines by a newly established Office of Surface Mining Reclamation and Enforcement in the Interior Department.
Department of Energy Organization Act	1977	Created a new cabinet-level Department of Energy to administer national energy policies including nuclear waste management, energy conservation, and energy impacts on the environment.
Comprehensive Environmental Response, Compensation, and Liability Act	1980	Established a $1.6 billion Hazardous Substance Response Trust Fund and taxes on the chemical and oil industries. Required the EPA to identify and remediate dangerous dumpsites of high priority and to establish disposal standards for hazardous substances.

tion vividly underscored the agency's powers. It shut down all factories in heavily industrialized Birmingham, Alabama, for twenty-four hours during a temperature inversion in which air pollutants were building up to dangerous concentrations.

Throughout the Nixon, Ford, and Carter presidencies, the agency developed an excellent reputation for standard-setting, enforcement, and technical expertise. But it had difficulty digesting the amount of work imposed on it as new laws were enacted by Congress. A brief review of the march of laws in Table 14-1 may lead the reader to conclude that some indigestion at the EPA was understandable. In fact, Congress was responding to public pressure by enacting laws with unrealistic goals and imposing unreasonable schedules for attaining them. For instance, the goal of the Federal Water Pollution Control Act Amendments of 1972 to eliminate all pollutant discharges into American waters by 1985 was sheer fantasy, because the technology required to purify all industrial effluents did not exist at the time (and does not yet exist). In 1970, Congress gave the EPA sixteen months to set standards for hazardous air pollutants, but it was not until 1988 that standards were first set for six of eighty-six toxic air pollutants.[23] By the late 1970s, the agency was being criticized for paperwork backlogs, delays in issuing standards, tardy research to classify hazards, and inflexible enforcement.

With the advent of the Reagan administration, the EPA got into more trouble. During his 1980 presidential campaign, Reagan called the EPA staff "environmental extremists" and advocated easing its grip on industry. When elected, he appointed a new administrator, Anne Gorsuch, who had a long record of opposition to EPA programs at the state level. He also imposed a $400 million budget cut and a 14 percent staff reduction between 1980 and 1982—a time when statutory requirements for performance were still growing. During these years, the agency made many more exemptions from standards than usual, and pressure on industry eased. Dollar sales of air pollution monitoring equipment, one indicator of EPA enforcement activity, dropped 58 percent between 1980 and 1982.[24] Later, the agency was tarnished by scandal when Gorsuch was accused of delaying or hastening Superfund toxic waste cleanups to help Republicans in the 1982 midterm elections. She had to resign in 1983.

Throughout the 1980s, the EPA faced a continuing avalanche of new statutory duties as Congress reauthorized and amended basic laws, each time expanding their scope. The Reagan administration continued to give the

---

[23]This timetable was mandated by Sec. 112 (b) of the Clean Air Act of 1955 as amended in 1970. See Bureau of National Affairs, *U.S. Environmental Laws*, Washington, D.C.: BNA, Inc., 1988, p. 457. Standards set are for ammonia, ethyl chloride, acetaldehyde, propylene, naphthalene, and propylene oxide. See *Regulatory Program of the United States Government, op. cit.,* p. 380. Some critics of environmental law argue that when Congress delegated rulemaking and standard setting to the EPA it was simply passing the buck and avoiding politically difficult decisions. This may have benefitted business, because the decreased visibility of EPA decisions enabled industry to retard and water down actions. See, for instance, David Schoenbrod, "Environmental Law and Growing Up," *Yale Journal on Regulation,* Summer 1989, pp. 362–67.

[24]Barbara Bry, "Sales of Air-Pollution Monitoring Gear Drop," *Los Angeles Times,* March 8, 1983.

agency starvation budgets. The first Bush administration budget in 1989 hiked the EPA budget $1.4 billion from its $5 billion 1988 level. But adjusted for inflation, this is less than the agency got in 1979.

Entering the 1990s, the EPA is overwhelmed, accused of being disorganized, inflexible, slow, and ineffectual.[25] A former administrator says it suffers from "battered agency syndrome."[26] The basic problem is not budgetary constraints, but the regulatory laws themselves. Let us take a closer look at them.

ENVIRONMENTAL LAWS

How well have the laws worked? A fair overall assessment, shared by many, is that they have been only a modest success.[27] And, as we shall see, there is growing realization that the corpus of existing regulation is grossly inadequate to the task of obtaining further progress.

In some areas, the laws have brought great progress. Public exposure to airborne lead, polychlorinated biphynols (PCBs) in electrical transformers, and the pesticide DDT has been largely eliminated. The unpermitted discharge of toxic effluents from factories into water bodies has virtually ceased. In other areas, such as air pollutants that cause urban smog, progress has been modest. Since the 1970s, particulate emissions (essentially dust) have been cut over 60 percent, but other emissions have been cut only in the 20 to 40 percent range, with almost all the progress coming between 1970 and 1980 and little gain since.[28] Nitrogen oxides, a product of high temperature combustion, have actually increased. Of course, stabilization or modest gain represents an achievement against a backdrop of twenty years of population growth and a 57 percent increase in the GNP (in constant 1982 dollars). In some areas, the laws have been ineffectual. Despite billions of dollars in appropriations, the Superfund law has been ineffective in cleaning toxic waste sites. The volume of garbage is increasing. Nitrate pollution of ground water has increased. And no standards have been set for regulating air emissions of most toxic chemicals.

Why haven't the laws worked better? There are a number of reasons. Some problems, such as regulation of cancer-causing chemicals, are too big. It takes three to five years and costs roughly a million dollars to conduct standard carcinogenesis tests on a new chemical with rats or mice. International

---

[25] Anthony Ramirez, "EPA Should Clean Up Its Own Act," *Fortune*, November 6, 1989, p. 139.

[26] William Ruckelshaus, quoted in Bruce Ingersoll, "Tough Environment," *Wall Street Journal*, January 20, 1989, p. R22.

[27] See, for example, Barry Commoner, "Let's Get Serious About Pollution Prevention," *EPA Journal*, July/August 1989; Lester B. Lave and Eric H. Males, "At Risk: The Framework for Regulating Toxic Substances," *Environmental Science and Technology*, April 1989; Gregg Easterbrook, "Cleaning Up," *Newsweek*, July 24, 1989; and various statements by members of the Environmental Protection Agency, for example, "An Interview with William K. Reilly," *EPA Journal*, March/April 1989.

[28] *Statistical Abstract of the United States: 1988, op. cit.*, figures derived from Table No. 332. See also EPA, *National Air Quality and Emissions Trends Report*, Washington, D.C.: Government Printing Office, 1989.

laboratory facilities can accommodate tests of only about 300 chemicals each year.[29] Yet every year, industry creates and markets almost 2,000 new chemicals. It is no wonder that the EPA cannot, for example, effectively enforce risk standards for pesticides.

Environmental protection statutes are sometimes confusing and contradictory. For example, different laws rely on different standards for regulating industry pollution. The Clean Air Act requires that the EPA regulate toxic emissions with standards that provide an "ample margin of safety" for public health. The Clean Water Act and the Safe Drinking Water Act, on the other hand, require water quality standards to be set so that there is "no risk" to public health. Still other laws, such as the Toxic Substances Control Act and the Federal Insecticide, Fungicide, and Rodenticide Act, permit balancing health benefits against pollution control costs, something prohibited in setting water effluent standards. More confusion exists in laws where Congress has enacted guidelines for selecting pollution control devices. In the Clean Air Act alone, Congress prescribes three different standards for choosing control technology: "best system of continuous emission reduction" (section 111), "lowest achievable emission rate," (section 173), and "greatest degree of emission reduction [with technology that the EPA] determines will be available" (section 202). The Clean Water Act also has three different standards. In practice, this enormously complicates regulations. For example, in 1989 the EPA promulgated water pollution standards for companies that form metals by processes such as pouring molten metal into a mold. During these processes, water comes in contact with various metals and picks up contaminants. The EPA set contaminant levels for various pollutants, such as oil and grease and metal traces, for fourteen different metal forming processes.[30] These levels had to be different for each of three different control technology standards in the Clean Water Act, i.e., "best practicable control technology currently available," "best available technology economically achievable," and "new source performance standards." This resulted in forty-two complex charts listing parts-per-million standards for a dozen metals, or 504 charts in all!

Another shortcoming is that the legal framework is inadequate to deal with trans-media pollution, or pollution that moves between water, air, and/ or ground. For example, since the 1970s, control devices that remove small particles from coal boiler exhaust have produced huge quantities of sludge. This sludge is a mixture of water and chemical impurities found in coal, including toxic metals and radioactive particles. It must be disposed of by the ton in landfills, some of which may be classified as hazardous waste sites.[31] Waste dumps may re-release toxic aromatic compounds back into the atmo-

---

[29]Lester B. Lave and Arthur C. Upton, "Regulating Toxic Chemicals in the Environment," in Lave and Upton, eds., *Toxic Chemicals, Health, and the Environment*, Baltimore: Johns Hopkins University Press, 1987, p. 282.

[30]See 54 FR 13606, April 4, 1989.

[31]One analysis of trace metal contaminants (arsenic, barium, cadmium, chromium, lead, mercury, selenium, and silver) in leachate from six utilities found, however, that levels were below those set under the Resource Conservation and Recovery Act to define hazardous waste. See

sphere. Typically, statutes direct that a pollutant be controlled in one medium without full consideration of its migration to another, reflecting the more limited understanding of the 1970s. Departments in the EPA are organized along media lines, which contributes to a fragmenting of regulatory effort and makes the agency even less able to respond flexibly to cross-media transfers. In the example used above, inspectors from one department would enforce stack gas emission standards on the company running the coal-fired boiler under authority of the Clean Air Act, other inspectors would issue permits for transportation of sludge to approved disposal sites under authority of the Resource Conservation and Recovery Act, and still others would regulate the dumps themselves, under one of three other laws. Some experts believe that a single statute covering all types of pollution would be preferable to the splintered authorities extant now.

Space permits only brief mention of some other problems. There is too much emphasis on command and control regulation, which deprives EPA enforcement of needed flexibility. The arcane science used to set standards is increasingly intelligible only to experts in narrow fields. The laws are so complicated that they invite litigation, and regulators may be tied up in court for years by companies or environmentalists who disagree with agency actions. The philosophy of most environmental laws, adopted to reflect thinking in the 1970s, is to use end-of-the-pipe control devices to stop pollution, but today this approach is seen as severely flawed, for two reasons. First, control devices are never 100 percent perfect (and in most cases far less than that) and so some pollution remains. Second, pollutants caught in control devices are in many cases not destroyed, but simply trapped and eventually transferred to another place in the environment (one exception is high-temperature incineration, which breaks complex, toxic molecules down into harmless water vapor, oxygen, and simple carbon compounds). Experts today believe that redesign of manufacturing processes to prevent hazardous emissions and discharges is a superior philosophy. Examples of reengineering will be discussed in the following chapter.

Finally, the laws reflect Congress' political priorities, and these may diverge from the reality of environmental degradation. For example, although discharges from factories create little water pollution today, Congress continues to mandate the use of expensive new effluent-cleaning technology. In the meantime, pesticide and fertilizer runoff from farmland, the source of 60 percent of new water pollution, is virtually uncontrolled. The reason? Congress lacks the fortitude to impose an economic burden on the farm lobby.

Where the laws do provide strong authority, they are sometimes compromised in the enforcement process. For example, the EPA sets standards to control pollutants such as sulfur dioxide. These are called ambient air quality standards and they specify a concentration of the pollutant which can be measured, above which a violation occurs. For sulfur dioxide, this is 0.03

C. A. Wentz, *et al.*, "Use of Fly Ash as a Waste Minimization Strategy," *Environmental Progress*, August 1988, p. 200.

parts per million in one cubic meter of air. But the EPA has ruled that ambient air only begins outside company property. In some cases, companies have simply purchased more property so that they can emit more pollutants and have them diluted in a larger airspace before reaching the plant boundary where concentrations must be within EPA limits. One copper smelter in Utah bought adjoining property from the Bureau of Land Management so that it could raise its sulfur dioxide emissions by 72 tons a year. After the purchase it owned 120 square miles surrounding the smelter stack which the EPA excluded from ambient air measurement.[32]

PRINCIPAL AREAS OF ENVIRONMENTAL POLICY

Here is a brief overview of five dominant areas of legislation. In each area we describe the basic nature of problems, current public policy, and crucial concerns for business.

AIR QUALITY

To control air pollution, Congress passed the Clean Air Act. First passed as a weak research measure in 1963, it was forcefully amended in 1970, empowering the EPA to set air quality standards for the principal pollutant classes, to approve state plans for achieving the standards, and to minimize pollutants from new stationary and mobile sources.

Under the act's authority, the EPA has acted to reduce six air pollutants, called "criteria pollutants," which are responsible for urban smog. They are lead, carbon monoxide, volatile organic compounds (substances such as gasoline vapors which react with sunlight in the air to form ozone), sulfur dioxide, particulates, and nitrogen dioxide. To regulate emissions of these pollutants, the EPA divided the nation into 247 air-quality control regions; each was required to meet national standards by 1975. A second major amendment to the Clean Air Act was passed in 1977 to extend this deadline to 1987, but by 1990 more than 150 of the 247 regions still violated EPA standards with respect to one or more of the six criteria pollutants. The EPA also set stringent standards for reduced auto emissions, which led to emissions reductions of 90 percent for carbon monoxide and 75 percent for sulfur dioxide from uncontrolled 1970 levels. But in the meantime, the number of autos and miles traveled increased so rapidly that total emissions only leveled off.

For industry, the EPA has established emission levels, control technologies, and reduction timetables for the six criteria pollutants and for eight toxic pollutants in addition. The Clean Air Act requires the EPA to control emissions of toxic air pollutants such as dioxin, chloroform, and cadmium, because many are carcinogens and thought to be especially hazardous to public

[32]A critical report by the General Accounting Office has recommended that the EPA redefine ambient air; see *Air Pollution: EPA's Ambient Air Policy Results in Additional Pollution*, Washington, D.C.: Government Printing Office, July 1989.

health. In 1987, industry released 2.4 billion pounds of these hazardous pollutants, and they caused an estimated 2,000 cancer deaths in the general public.[33] But the EPA has yet to set standards for 321 of 329 identified toxics. Even without strong standards for toxics, air emission reduction is the most expensive area of pollution control for business.

A typical large factory has many sources of air emissions. For utilities and smelters, combustion in furnaces is a major source of criteria pollutants, which must be controlled. At other plants, diesels, turbines, and gasoline engines power machinery and need emission controls.

Industry uses a wide array of devices such as reactors, mixers, cookers, distillers, and spray booths, and must control emissions from each. For example, EPA air-emission standards for kraft pulp mills apply to the "digester system, brown stock washer system, multiple-effect evaporator system, black liquor oxidation system, recovery furnace, smelt dissolving tank, lime kiln, and condensate stripper system."[34] The "Standard for Particulate Matter" in kraft pulp mills is instructive of the detail with which these devices are regulated. Particulates are only one of a number of pollutants that must be controlled.

§ 60.282 Standard for Particulate Matter

(a) On and after the date on which the performance test required to be conducted by § 60.8 is completed, no owner or operator subject to the provisions of this subpart shall cause to be discharged into the atmosphere:
   (1) From any recovery furnace any gases which:
      (i) Contain particulate matter in excess of 0.10 g/dscm (0.044 gr/dscf) corrected to 8 percent oxygen.
      (ii) Exhibit 35 percent opacity or greater.
   (2) From any smelt dissolving tank any gases which contain particulate matter in excess of 0.1 g/kg black liquor solids (dry weight) [0.2 lb/ton black liquor solids (dry weight)].
   (3) From any lime kiln any gases which contain particulate matter in excess of:
      (i) 0.15 g/dscm (0.067 gr/dscf) corrected to 10 percent oxygen, when gaseous fossil fuel is burned.
      (ii) 0.30 g/dscm (0.13 gr/dscf) corrected to 10 percent oxygen, when liquid fossil fuel is burned.[35]

About a dozen mechanical and chemical control devices exist to remove gases, particles, and odors from plant emissions. They range from baghouses, which force exhaust streams through filters, to electrostatic precipitators, which give particles in the air a negative charge so that they collect on a positively charged plate for later removal. Often equipment must be spe-

---

[33]See James E. McCarthy, *Hazardous Air Pollutants*, Washington, D.C.: Congressional Research Service, 1988, and U.S. Environmental Protection Agency, *Unfinished Business: A Comparative Assessment of Environmental Problems*, Washington, D.C.: Government Printing Office, February 1987.
[34]40 CFR 311.
[35]*Ibid.*, p. 313.

cially designed to be effective with the specific air pressure, volume, temperature, or chemical composition of emissions from an industrial process. The customizing adds to its cost.

Overall, despite two decades of regulation, the nation still suffers from serious air quality problems. Urban smog and toxic pollutants are not yet controlled to the level of public expectation. In addition, the existing Clean Air Act is seriously deficient in addressing some other pressing problems.

• Acid rain is a worldwide problem. In the U.S. it is principally a problem in the Northeast. Its primary cause is massive emissions of sulfur dioxide and nitrogen oxide by coal-fired power plants in the Midwest. It results in acidification of water bodies and soils, and although scientific controversy exists about its seriousness, much damage is attributed to it. Current EPA controls on sulfur dioxide and nitrogen oxide emissions as criteria pollutants are inadequate to prevent acid rain.

• Global warming is another worldwide problem felt in the U.S. Though scientific uncertainty exists about its inevitability, it is thought to be likely because of increased concentrations of certain gases in the atmosphere. There are roughly a dozen gases released by industrial activity which act in the atmosphere to retain terrestrial radiation and promote heating.[36] Of these, carbon dioxide, which is released by burning fossil fuels and by forest burning, has increased the most. The EPA has no regulatory program to reduce carbon dioxide emissions.

• A third international pollution problem is the presence of chlorofluorocarbons (CFCs) in the upper atmosphere, where they cause chemical reactions that destroy stratospheric ozone. While the ozone in urban smog is unwanted, ozone in the upper atmosphere screens out powerful ultraviolet rays harmful to living tissue. In 1990, the U.S. signed the Montreal Protocol, an international agreement which mandates a 100 percent reduction in CFC production among signatory nations by the year 2000. This has not been opposed by large CFC manufacturers such as Du Pont, because public pressure is strong and they have developed substitutes for many CFC applications. Until signing of the Montreal agreement, the EPA had no program to reduce CFC emissions.

• Indoor air pollution from radon causes an estimated 5,000–20,000 cases of lung cancer each year, and other indoor pollutants such as natural gas, formaldehyde, cigarette smoke, and household chemicals cause another 3,500–6,500 cancers annually.[37] Indoor pollutants are, therefore, a greater health risk than all toxics emissions released by industry combined. Most city dwellers spend 90 percent of their time indoors. The Clean Air Act does not cover indoor pollution, and the EPA has no regulatory program to address indoor pollution comparable to its program of regulating industrial point sources.

---

[36]These include, in addition to carbon dioxide, methane, chlorofluorocarbon compounds, and halon compounds.

[37]John D. Graham, David R. Holtgrave, and Mary Jean Sawey, "The Potential Health Benefits of Controlling Hazardous Air Pollutants," in Blodgett, *op. cit.*, p. 171.

- Electromagnetic radiation from high voltage transmission lines, radio waves, computers, microwave transmitters, mobile telephones, medical scanners, radars, and hundreds of other sources pose an unknown threat to public health. Studies to date hint at a weak association between heavy exposure and childhood leukemia, brain tumors, miscarriages and biological abnormalities in test animals. The EPA is studying the possibility of setting standards for exposure to radiofrequency radiation under a statute aside from the Clean Air Act.[38]

The existing Clean Air Act is inadequate and must be amended again. In April 1990, the Senate passed a comprehensive clean air bill. Its provisions were aimed at combatting major air pollution problems. In simplified form, the bill attacked the acid rain problem by requiring large sulfur dioxide emission cuts from the dirtiest power plants by 1995, and put a nationwide cap on emissions by the year 2000; it attacked the urban smog problem by requiring strict new auto emission standards and reformulation of gasoline to add methanol or ethanol (to lower hydrocarbon emissions); it attacked toxic industrial emissions by requiring 75 to 90 percent reductions by the year 2000, and threatened plant shutdowns if they were not achieved; and it attacked the ozone depletion problem by mandating a complete ban on chlorofluorocarbons. At this writing, a similar clean air bill is being debated in the House. If this legislation becomes law, as political commentators predict, it will break a decade-old deadlock on revision of the clean air laws and stiffen regulatory requirements considerably.

WATER QUALITY

The Clean Water Act of 1972 (as amended in 1977 and 1987) is the basic law for fighting water pollution. Its purpose is "to restore and maintain the chemical, physical, and biological integrity of the nation's waters." Since 1972, regulatory efforts have substantially reduced deterioration of streams, rivers, and lakes, to the point where only 10 percent of surface waters fail to meet the statutory criteria of being "fishable and swimmable."

The EPA regulates three classes of water pollutants: conventional pollutants such as suspended solids, oil and grease, and fecal coliform bacteria; nonconventional pollutants such as ammonia, sulfides, phosphorus, and nitrogen; and toxic pollutants such as heavy metals, polychlorinated biphenyls, halogenated aliphatics, phthalate esters, and polycyclic aromatic hydrocarbons. It has established effluent guidelines for approximately twenty heavily polluting industries which, when fully implemented, will reduce release of toxic chemicals by about 95 percent.

Every industrial plant uses water, and sources of pollution are numerous. Large plants must purify sanitary waste water from restrooms, cafeterias, and laboratories and often set up sewage treatment plants for this purpose.

[38]See "Federal Radiation Protection Guidance for Public Exposure to Radiofrequency Radiation," in *Regulatory Program of the United States Government, op. cit.*, pp. 393–94.

Storm water runoff is a significant pollution threat, and in plants where surfaces are contaminated with oil, grease, or other pollutants, this water must be collected and treated. Cooling systems introduce heat into water and must be partially drained from time to time of low quality water that needs treatment. The greatest source of industrial water pollution, however, comes from waste water from production processes. Used as a washing, scrubbing, or mixing medium, this water is contaminated with a wide variety of dissolved solids and particles. As with air pollution, there are effluent control techniques ranging from the use of screens to remove large particles to complicated chemical and biological treatments.

In some industries, such as petroleum refining, ink formulating, and electroplating, pollutants cannot be completely removed from process waste water. For these industries the EPA issues permits allowing discharges limited to levels set by the agency. These permits contain complex effluent limitations that take into account the amount, temperature, turbidity, and chemical constituents of waste water discharge. They usually contain sampling and reporting requirements and have an expiration date. Polluting firms have been required to meet a series of deadlines for improved water quality as control device technology advances.

A major source of water pollution not systematically regulated is "nonpoint" pollution. This occurs when rainfall collects pollutants from agricultural chemicals, construction sites, mines, and oil-coated roads, and transports it into water bodies. In 1990, almost 65 percent of water pollution stemmed from nonpoint sources, and only 9 percent came from industrial sites (sometimes called point sources).[39] Nonpoint sources are virtually uncontrolled, and it will be many years before regulatory actions meet this challenge, because the Clean Water Act lacks a coherent philosophy for tackling the problem and delegates remedial action to the states.

TOXIC CHEMICALS

Industrialized society depends on a staggering array of chemicals. Underlying concern about the presence of toxic chemicals in the environment is the phenomenal growth of the chemical industry since World War II. The industry grew from sales of $13.7 billion in 1947 to sales of $113 billion in 1977. Since then, sales have more than tripled. This growth was accompanied by the development of new synthetic compounds and a petrochemical revolution that has made fuels, solvents, pesticides, plastics, and other oil byproducts ubiquitous in the environment.

Approximately 60,000 chemicals are used in industrial production, and 1,000 to 2,000 new ones are developed yearly. Many cause health problems and property damage. Of the 60,000 commonly used industrial chemicals, twenty-eight are known human carcinogens, and about 10 percent of roughly 6,000 suspect chemicals tested to date cause cancer in animals. In addition, arteriosclerosis,

[39]Easterbrook, *op. cit.,* p. 36.

heart disease, hypertension, emphysema, behavioral disorders, and kidney disease may result from exposure to poisonous chemicals.

The Toxic Substances Control Act (TSCA) of 1976 gives the EPA authority to control the manufacture, processing, distribution, use, and disposal of existing chemicals. The EPA may require manufacturers to test designated chemicals for toxic effects and to maintain records and reports. In addition, industry must submit a "premanufacture notification" to the EPA at least ninety days prior to manufacturing or importing a new chemical. The chemical industry has complained about disruption of new chemical development caused by premanufacturing notice delays. The EPA has set stringent guidelines for phasing out most uses of asbestos, and it has stopped the manufacture and sale of polychlorinated biphenyls (PCBs). It has developed a basic inventory of 55,000 chemicals now manufactured, but has made little headway in assessing the risks of most.

The Federal Insecticide, Fungicide, and Rodenticide Act (FIFRA), as amended, gives the EPA authority to balance the benefits of pesticide use against health risks and set tolerance levels for crop residues and farm worker exposure. But there is broad agreement that regulation has been ineffective. There are roughly 50,000 pesticides on the market. They are formulated with 600 active ingredients, which are the specific chemicals intended to kill pest organisms. In 1971, Congress asked the EPA to evaluate the safety of these active ingredients, but by 1989 tolerances for residues in food and for human exposure had been set for only 125.[40] In addition, the EPA does not evaluate inert ingredients, of which there are thousands. Inert ingredients are used to dissolve and stabilize active ingredients. When FIFRA was amended to require setting of tolerance levels, pesticide manufacturers succeeded in having inerts excluded, claiming they were trade secrets. However, many inerts are more toxic than some active ingredients, and, in a remarkable Catch-22 situation, one such inert, carbon tetrachloride, is so hazardous that it is banned as an active ingredient but nevertheless present in some formulations as an inert.

The EPA has been slow to evaluate pesticides because each review requires almost one year, and because 1980 budget cuts have reduced the EPA's pesticide staff by almost one-third. Even when the EPA determines that a pesticide is exceptionally hazardous, legal authority under FIFRA is so weak that it cannot get it off the market. A cancellation order sets in motion a regulatory appeals process lasting almost two years. In the meantime, the manufacturer may continue to sell inventory, and crop use may continue unless an emergency suspension is issued. In 1986, the EPA tried just such a suspension for the pesticide dinoseb, but could not make it stick. The agency determined that dinoseb caused excessive risk of birth defects, lowered male reproductive capacity, and might cause sudden death to exposed farm work-

---

[40]Sonia L. Nazario, "EPA Under Fire for Pesticide Standards," *Wall Street Journal,* February 17, 1989.

ers. Before suspending dinoseb, the EPA conducted a risk benefit study as required by FIFRA. But in a landmark case brought by fruit and vegetable growers, an Oregon district court second-guessed the EPA research methodology and held that the agency had not fully calculated benefits to the growers and the regional economy in the Northwest.[41] The court held that the EPA had made an "error of judgment." This blow to the agency has discouraged future suspensions.

The inadequacy of pesticide regulation is another example of how the complexity of environmental regulation has overwhelmed the statutes of the 1970s. And nobody seems to know how to rewrite the law. Pesticide regulations are so abstruse that only one or two members of Congress understand them. Environmentalists who do are now at loggerheads with pesticide manufacturers and farmers over more stringent controls. And the history of regulation in this area is that when major amendments pass, the EPA faces years of court challenges by industry before it can impose stricter standards. In the meantime, the EPA has estimated that between 6,000 and 70,000 cancers are caused annually by exposure to only the one-third of pesticides on the market which the EPA has evaluated so far.[42]

SOLID AND HAZARDOUS WASTE

Solid waste is the detritus of production and consumption. It includes sludge from waste water treatment, household garbage, old automobiles and appliances, and wastes from agricultural, animal, mining, and industrial processes. Today we have billions of tons of solid waste, a residuum of affluence, convenience packaging, disposable products, and a rising population. In addition, stringent air and water pollution control standards have caused industry to accumulate solid wastes in antipollution equipment. Radioactive solid waste from nuclear reactors and tailings of uranium and phosphate mining are also a disposal problem. There are more than 100,000 industrial hazardous waste land disposal sites.

When water comes in contact with solid waste, it removes soluble materials, forming a polluted liquid called leachate. Leachate may contain toxic and carcinogenic chemicals, viruses, metals, bacteria, and decaying organic matter. A leachate plume may form if water is present and, moving underground as fast as two feet a day, enter a groundwater aquifer and pollute it. To avert serious hazard to drinking water supplies from this process, Congress in 1976 passed the Resource Conservation and Recovery Act, mandating government control of solid waste from generation to ultimate disposal.

In 1984, the Hazardous and Solid Waste Amendments to this act set stringent deadlines for EPA action to control hazardous waste dumping and applied the program to much smaller companies than before, that is, those

---

[41]*James M. Love v. EPA,* 26 ERC 2064 (1987).
[42]Sonia L. Nazario, "Pesticide Regulation, Mainly the States' Job, Is Spotty and Weak," *Wall Street Journal,* January 18, 1989. See also Margaret E. Kriz, "Pesticidal Pressures," *National Journal,* December 10, 1988.

dumping the equivalent of half of a fifty-five-gallon drum per month. Firms must identify their hazardous waste, obtain EPA identification numbers for it, use an approved manifest system when they truck wastes away from plants, label all wastes kept on site, and meet strict record-keeping requirements. This program cost business $6 billion a year in the 1980s but is predicted by EPA officials to cost at least $20 billion a year in the 1990s.

As in other areas, the EPA has made slow progress in regulating hazardous waste. It has issued criteria identifying most, but not all, hazardous wastes from industrial processes and has set up guidelines for safe disposal. However EPA action to date has lagged far behind statutory deadlines, and in 1990 less than half of all hazardous waste producers were in compliance with federal handling standards.[43]

In the 1970s, a number of conspicuous hazardous waste accidents were blamed on business. In 1973, for instance, Michigan Chemical Company accidentally shipped an extremely toxic chemical, polybrominated biphenyl (PBB), to the Michigan Farm Bureau, where a worker who thought it was a growth stimulant put it into feed for dairy farm animals. More than 9 million Michigan residents ate contaminated meat, milk, and eggs, and eventually about 150,000 contaminated farm animals had to be destroyed. In the Love Canal area of Niagara Falls, New York, Hooker Chemical Corp. was blamed for improper waste disposal practices that exposed nearby residents to toxic chemicals. President Carter declared Love Canal a disaster area.

Incidents such as these led Congress to pass the Comprehensive Environmental Response, Compensation, and Liability Act (CERCLA) of 1980. This legislation set up a $1.6 billion "Superfund" to pay for cleaning abandoned hazardous waste sites. (In 1986, Congress reauthorized the act with a $9 billion fund.) The EPA has identified 29,500 hazardous waste sites needing cleanup and established a priority list for cleaning the worst sites.

Although Superfund accounts for half of the EPA's financial resources and busies one-third of its people, the agency has been so slow and incomplete in its remediation of dumpsites that a 1988 report to Congress said the program was "largely ineffective and inefficient."[44] The report found that, on average, it took thirty-six months to get a dump on the priority list, and another nine to twelve years before cleanup was finished. Many cleanings were found to be "cheap, impermanent remedies," due in large measure to poor management by the EPA.[45] One problem was that Superfund had created a booming business for private contractors who worked on dumpsites. The EPA paid

[43] For more information see U.S. General Accounting Office, *Hazardous Waste: New Approach Needed to Manage the Resource Conservation and Recovery Act*, Washington, D.C.: Government Printing Office, July 1988.

[44]U.S. Congress, Office of Technology Assessment, *Are We Cleaning Up? 10 Superfund Case Studies—Special Report*, OTA-ITE-362, Washington, D.C.: Government Printing Office, June 1988, p. 1. Other commentators outside government use stronger, less flattering language to describe Superfund, as the titles of recent articles suggest; i.e., Stanton S. Miller, "Superfund: An Environmental Boondoggle," *Environmental Science & Technology*, April 1989, and Betsy Carpenter, "Superfund, Superflop," *U.S. News & World Report*, February 6, 1989.

[45]*Ibid.*, Office of Technology Assessment, p. 12.

such low salaries that managers in charge of multiple cleanup projects earned as little as $25,000 a year. Experienced senior staff often left for higher salaries in companies, and recent college graduates with only two or three years experience were running operations.

In all, only 34 of 1,175 dumpsites on the Superfund priority list had been cleaned up by late 1989.[46] Despite huge appropriations, then, Superfund is not the panacea that Congress intended it to be. It is one more example of weak environmental regulation. Nevertheless, for individual companies, cleaning disposal sites can mean enormous expenditures. In 1988, a Michigan pigment manufacturing subsidiary of Swedish Nobel Industries was forced into liquidation when the cost of cleaning up such a site was more than twice its annual sales.

OCCUPATIONAL HEALTH

In 1970, Congress passed the Occupational Safety and Health Act "to assure so far as possible every working man and woman in the nation safe and healthful working conditions and to preserve our human resources." The act set up an agency in the Labor Department called the Occupational Safety and Health Administration (OSHA), giving it authority to reduce health and safety hazards in the workplace by establishing and enforcing standards, requiring employers to keep records and report on hazards, and encouraging states to set up occupational health and safety programs. OSHA has authority over about 4.6 million workplaces. A team of about 1,000 inspectors conducts workplace inspections. OSHA may propose fines of up to $10,000 and prison terms of up to six months for offenses by employers.

Millions of workers are exposed to occupational hazards from pollutants. The famous have perished with the obscure. The great philosopher Spinoza, who ground lenses for a living and wrote in his spare time, died from lung infection caused by prolonged exposure to glass dust. The death in 1936 of Marie Curie, discover of radium, is blamed on radiation burns. In 1898, asbestos entrepreneur H. W. Johns, founder of the roofing company that grew into the giant Manville Corp., died of chronic lung disease. More than 800,000 workers are regularly exposed to carcinogens, and certain occupations have a high cancer risk. Two hundred years ago, a British physician named Percival Potts found a high incidence of scrotum cancer among chimney sweeps, attributable to their exposure to coal tar in chimneys. Women who painted radium on watch dials to make them glow in the dark often licked their brushes to sharpen points and died in excessive numbers from cancers of the mouth and bone. Asbestos workers and workers exposed to benzine seeping out of older coke ovens show elevated lung cancer rates when compared with the general population.

Cancer is not the sole illness, of course, that workers risk. Hundreds of illnesses may be caused or aggravated by occupational exposures. OSHA sets

[46]*Rand Research Review,* "Rating Superfund's Progress: In a Word, 'Super-Slow,'" Fall 1989, p. 7.

standards for worker exposure to lead, vinyl chloride gas, formaldehyde, carbon monoxide, cotton dust, and mercury. Unlike EPA standards, which limit emissions from sources such as smokestacks and valves, OSHA standards typically limit worker exposure to a substance to levels averaged over an eight-hour shift. Sometimes production equipment may be reengineered to lower emissions. When this is excessively expensive or technologically impossible, as is often the case, workers are permitted exposure to greater risks than is the general public. A glassblower, for example, may be exposed to concentrations of nitrogen oxides twenty-five times greater than permitted in ambient air quality outside the shop. Exposure to hazards such as mercury vapor, diesel fumes, petrochemical vapors, and airborne lead is typically regulated by installing exhaust systems under ducts or hoods that collect fumes, by mixing fresh air with polluted air to dilute toxic concentrations, or by rotating workers in and out of the workplace—sometimes on the basis of blood tests showing concentrations of a contaminant.

The protective organizational machinery established by the OSH Act embodied the ethical principle that workers have a right to a healthy work environment and employers have an obligation to provide it. During its first years, OSHA was criticized for excessive zeal, for enforcing trivial standards, for the officiousness of its inspectors, and for imposing unreasonable costs on business. In the early 1970s, it emphasized job safety, but in the last decade prevention of health hazards for exposure to toxic substances has received higher priority. It is estimated that between 50,000 and 100,000 workers die at work each year from diseases attributable to contact with toxic chemicals, wastes, fumes, and dusts.[47] If correct, this would be more than the roughly 10,500 workers who die each year in accidents.

It is hard to tell whether OSHA activity has increased workplace safety, since reporting requirements have changed over the years and recent job safety statistics are not comparable with those from the 1970s.[48] OSHA, however, works under handicaps similar to those of the EPA. It has a low budget and too few inspectors to conduct adequate workplace inspections. It is also hamstrung by flaws in its underlying statutory authority. For example, agriculture is the most dangerous occupation for workers. Each year there are more deaths, injuries, poisonings, and respiratory illnesses among agricultural workers than those in any other industry. Over 300 of the 1,500 fatalities in 1988 were children. Yet OSHA is prohibited from regulating farms because farming interests did not want federal interference and wrote an exemption into the Occupational Safety and Health Act when it was passed. Industry also succeeded in getting a provision allowing OSHA to base en-

---

[47]By Sen. Howard Metzenbaum, quoted in David Shernoff, "Workers at Risk," *Multinational Monitor*, October 1988, p. 21.

[48]For an analysis of OSHA in an international context see Richard E. Wokutch and Josetta S. McLaughlin, "The Sociopolitical Context of Occupational Injuries," in William Frederick, ed., *Research in Corporate Social Performance and Policy*, vol. 10, Greenwich, Connecticut: JAI Press, 1988, and Richard E. Wokutch, Douglas S. Spadaro, and Bong-Gyu Park, "The Regulation of Occupational Safety and Health in Japan and the U.S.," paper presented at the Academy of Management, Washington, D.C., August 1989.

forcement only on industry-wide statistics. The Bureau of Labor Statistics, which provides OSHA with job safety data, is prohibited from giving OSHA figures on individual companies. Because of such counterproductive prohibitions, OSHA is unable to effectively guarantee workplace safety on a broad front.

CONCLUDING COMMENT

Pollution problems stemming from industrial activity are serious. In its current state, industrial processes are inherently damaging to the environment. Existing environmental laws have brought large reductions in some pollutants and have prevented much deterioration. But today there is wide realization that they are inadequate for further progress and revisions are needed.

In the following chapter we take an in-depth look at how regulatory decisions are made under existing regulatory programs.

Owls, Loggers,
and Old Growth Forests

There may come a time when we will have to opt for a choice between an owl and a human being.

Senator Mark Hatfield

The secretive Northern spotted owl lives in remote sections of coastal forest in Washington, Oregon, and upper California. Since the 1800s, timber harvesting has reduced the owl's habitat by as much as 80 percent, threatening its extinction. Now, environmentalists trying to save old growth forests from the ax have focused on the owl's plight. But they face powerful opposition. The health of the Pacific Northwest wood products industry depends on harvesting old growth timber to keep sawmills running.

Early victories have gone to environmental forces, but the timber industry has mounted a formidable campaign to keep the supply of timber coming and is by no means down for the count. We begin to explore this complex situation with a trip into the forest.

OLD GROWTH

An old growth forest is one that has developed undisturbed through stages. In nature, a forest usually begins when fire destroys the vegetation on an expanse of land. At first, opportunistic plant species such as wildflowers invade the area, their seeds blown in by wind. In a few years these pioneers are displaced by dense shrubs which create more shade than the wildflowers can tolerate. In turn, shrubs are shaded out by red alders, aspens, or other fast-growing deciduous trees. The dominant tree species is the one that can propagate in the shade of these early trees and persist to ultimately supplant all competitors for nutrients. This species is called the climax species. In the

499

conifer forests of Washington and Oregon it tends to be the Douglas fir; in California it is the coast redwood.

It may be centuries before the climax species takes over. Some large forest stands in the Pacific Northwest are over 1,000 years old, and a commonly accepted definition of old growth is a stand that has developed without catastrophic disturbance for 175–250 years or more. These old growth forests are unique ecosystems dominated by large, live trees rising 200 to 300 feet through an uneven, multilayered canopy. Dead trees, called snags, stand in place, and the floor is littered with decaying logs. Some snags have fallen in streams, damning and diverting the water flow.

Ancient forests are more structurally and biologically complex than younger forests. Snags and logs, for example, provide habitat niches for a variety of plant and animal life. During the 200 to 500 years it takes a large log to disintegrate, it may nurse an expansive population of bacteria, insects, lichens, plants, and small animals which utilize the stored moisture and nutrients in the dead wood. First come boring insects that open pathways into the log. Then microorganisms such as fungi invade the wood, followed by mites, spiders, and the beetles that feast on them. Birds come to catch insects. As the wood fragments, ferns and small hemlocks force their roots in and tap stored moisture. Soon mice and wood rats find homes, attracting predators such as the Northern spotted owl. Eventually scavengers that feed on dead vegetation and animal feces arrive.[49] Put poetically, in the downed tree, "Decay is merely a counterpoint, life and death a single process, like a mirror fugue conceived by a composer even better than Bach."[50]

Old growth forests achieve great natural beauty and inspire comparisons with cathedrals. They have much richer biotic communities than younger forests and are repositories for species which have adapted to ecological niches created only under old growth conditions. The spotted owl is one such species.

THE NORTHERN SPOTTED OWL

The northern spotted owl *(Strix occidentalis caurina)* is a perch-and-dive predator with a wingspan of two feet and a weight of about one and a half pounds. Its body is mottled brown with patches of white, making it nearly invisible as it roosts in the cavities of tall conifers. Its habitat ranges from British Columbia in the north to the redwood stands above San Francisco in the south.

The modern owl family emerged as a separate evolutionary line 70 to 80 million years ago. Since then, owls have developed anatomy and behavior suited for efficient predation of small mammals and reptiles. At one time

---

[49]Chris M. Maser and James M. Trappe, eds., *The Seen and Unseen World of the Fallen Tree,* Portland, Oregon: U.S. Forest Service, General Technical Report PNW-164, 1984.

[50]David Kelly and Gary Braasch, *Secrets of the Old Growth Forest,* Salt Lake City: Peregrine Smith Books, 1988, p. 39.

The Northern Spotted Owl. (Photo by Stephen Tuttle. U.S. Fish & Wildlife Service.)

owls came into competition with the line of raptors which became hawks, falcons, and eagles. Both phyletic lines hunted small prey by diving upon it and grasping it with sharp talons. But habitat confrontation was avoided in a way that allowed both to exploit the same prey resources. Hawk-like species became diurnal hunters, and owls became nocturnal hunters. Hence, by day the spotted owl roosts in the cavities of standing snags; it emerges to hunt only after sunset. One study of 62 pairs found that on average they left their roosts 14 minutes after sunset to forage and returned at 21 minutes before sunrise.[51]

The northern spotted owl, like other owls, is well adapted to nighttime activity. It has a large head with a relatively large brain compared to other birds, and big, round eyes. "Indeed," notes one biologist, "the heads of owls are basically little more than brains with raptorial beaks and the largest possible eyes and ears attached.[52] The spotted owls' eyes have rod-rich retinas which provide exceptionally acute black-and-white vision in low-light conditions. They can locate and dive on scampering mice in illuminations as much as thirty times below the lowest reported human visual threshold. Their hearing is similarly acute. Without benefit of vision, they can locate tree squirrels or mice which make small rustling noises in frequency ranges inaudible to humans. Their brains calculate time lags of microseconds in the arrival of sounds at each ear, enabling them to fly unerringly to a sound source through dark of night. The northern spotted owl, despite its sedentary daytime roosting, has a high metabolism and hunts actively through the night. Prey species are mainly small mammals such as flying squirrels, wood rats, rabbits, mice, and tree voles. It also eats over twenty species of birds and some reptiles.

Northern spotted owls exhibit a wide range of social behavior. They have courtship rituals, and pairs bond for extended periods. They communicate with postural signals, displays of aggression, and a variety of hoots and calls. They are territorial, and announce their presence with a series of four hoots. These low hoots have long wavelengths especially suited for penetrating dense foliage. Reproduction occurs in the spring, when the female lays an average of two eggs in a nest. After hatching, the young owls are cared for by the parents for one month before flying off to mate and establish their own territories.

Spotted owls prefer old growth forest habitat. They find the dense vegetation useful for protection from predators such as the great horned owl and the barred owl. Thick, multi-layered forest canopy also provides thermal cover, creating a climate which protects them from extremes of heat and cold. Owls nest in the cavities of standing snags, and a large mass of fallen trees creates conditions which support abundant prey to satisfy their voracious appetites.[53] The spotted owl plays an important role in the ecology of the old growth forest by culling small mammal populations to keep them vigorous and genetically fit.

Research bears out the owl's overwhelming preference for old growth. In one study of 1,502 spotted owl sightings in Oregon, 1,282 were in old growth, 191 in a combination of old growth and mature forest, and only 67 in

[51]E. D. Foresman, E. C. Meslow, and H. M. Wight, "Distribution and Biology of the Spotted Owl in Oregon," *Wildlife Monographs,* No. 87 (1984).

[52]Paul A. Johnsgard, *North American Owls: Biology and Natural History,* Washington, D.C.: Smithsonian Institution Press, 1988, p. 42.

[53]Elliott A. Norse, *Ancient Forests of the Pacific Northwest,* Washington, D.C.: Island Press, 1990, p. 78.

stands younger than 100 years old.[54] In Washington, a similar study found that 97 percent of spotted owls lived in old growth/mature forest, with no known reproductive pairs in second-growth areas.[55] Spotted owls are thought to be at a disadvantage competing with more aggressive barred owls in more open areas of young growth. Using radiotelemetry, ornithologists have determined that the forest territories of spotted owl pairs average about 5,500 acres.

LOSS OF OLD GROWTH MAY IMPERIL THE SPOTTED OWL

The expansion of American civilization has come at the expense of forests. When the pilgrims landed at Plymouth Rock, the land mass destined to become the continental United States had 850 million acres of forest. By the 1920s, only 138 million acres of virgin forest remained, roughly 16 percent of what had existed.[56] The rest had been burned, grazed, cut, radically disturbed, or converted to other uses. Reduction of forest area stopped in the late 1970s and, on balance, regeneration now exceeds consumption.

The first logging of the Northwest coastal forest began in the 1860s and, since then, somewhere between two-thirds and four-fifths of old growth acreage in Washington, Oregon, and California has been lost to timber harvest, land conversion, and fire.[57] Today, about 30 million acres of forest exist, down from about 94 million acres early in the 1800s. And only 7.7 million acres of old growth remain. Much of this is not contiguous; rather, it is a checkerboard of stands of old growth mixed with clearcut timber harvest areas, young growth, and tree farms growing mainly one species such as the Douglas fir.

Of these 7.7 million acres, 2.8 million acres are in national parks or wilderness areas closed forever to timber harvest. Little remaining old growth is on private land; virtually all is on federal land managed by the U.S. Forest Service and the Bureau of Land Management. These agencies are required to open forests for "multiple use" activities such as logging, mining, recreation, and geothermal development. Hence, each year they hold hundreds of timber auctions in which private logging companies bid for the right to fell specially picked stands of timber. Once the high bidder has been selected, timber harvesting proceeds based on precise regulations describing boundaries, logging techniques, and the restoration and replanting that is necessary. Current policy permits clearcutting, or the felling of all trees in an area, followed by replanting with seedlings, which are reharvested when they reach marketable size. Even-age planting and short logging rotations preclude regeneration of old growth conditions.

[54]"Proposed Threatened Status for the Northern Spotted Owl," *Federal Register*, Vol. 54, June 23, 1989, p. 26668.

[55]*Ibid.*, p. 26668.

[56]Figures for forest size are from Michael Williams, *Americans and Their Forests: A Historical Geography*, Cambridge: Cambridge University Press, 1989, pp. 3–4.

[57]Daniel Simberloff, "The Spotted Owl Fracas: Mixing Academic, Applied, and Political Ecology," *Ecology*, August 1987, p. 766.

WOOD IN THE AMERICAN ECONOMY

The overall importance of wood in the economy should not be underestimated. The foundation of the wood products industry consists of companies that fell trees and turn logs into lumber, plywood, poles, and highly processed forms such as molding, flooring, wooden doors and windows, and furniture. Nationwide, this industry employed 500,000 and made shipments worth $59 billion in 1989. The average American house contains 17,600 board feet of lumber and finished products, the equivalent of ten old growth Douglas firs. In the 1980s, there were 1.5 million new housing starts each year.

In the mid-1800s, a process for making paper from wood fiber was perfected, and since then the fortunes of the paper products industry have been connected with timber operators. In 1989, this huge industry was the tenth largest in the United States, employing 625,000 and making shipments of $130 billion.[58] Each year, 300,000 acres of forest must be harvested to supply the paper just for the Sunday *New York Times*, and the average American uses nearly 600 pounds of paper.

The federal government expedites timber harvest by building logging roads to open sites, receiving money from the sales in return. Since federal timberland is not on state and local tax rolls, Congress has provided that 25 percent of gross receipts from timber sales be paid to local counties to support schools and road construction. Recently, it has been revealed that many timber sales lose money, meaning that, in effect, the taxpayers are subsidizing the forest products industry, which gets sawtimber at below market value.[59]

Although millions of acres of old growth remain closed to logging, there are reasons for concern about survival of the spotted owl. First, its historical habitat has been decimated and what remains is shrinking. If the federal government continues timber sales at the present rate, virtually all legally marketable old growth will be gone by the year 2050, and the spotted owl's habitat will decline from its current 7 million acres to roughly 2 million acres.

Second, because much remaining old growth exists in islands surrounded by logged areas and immature forest, as little as 50 percent of remaining old growth is suitable habitat for the owl.[60] Even if the owls can subsist in patchwork old growth stands, wildlife biologists note a risk that gene pools of isolated subpopulations will be inadequate. In 1989, there were an estimated 1,550 breeding pairs of spotted owls in the Pacific Northwest and an unknown number of unmated birds.[61] According to the "50/500 law," if the

[58]Employment and shipment figures are from *U.S. Industrial Outlook, op. cit.,* pp. 6-1 and 10-1.

[59]See Brian P. Crowley, *Forest Service Cost Accounting for Timber Sales,* Washington, D.C.: U.S. Government Accounting Office, 1990, and Margaret E. Kriz, "Last Stand on Timber," *National Journal,* March 3, 1990, p. 510.

[60]"Proposed Threatened Status..." *Federal Register, op. cit.,* p. 26671.

[61]"Protection Proposed for the Northern Spotted Owl," *Endangered Species Technical Bulletin,* July 1989, p. 1. In early 1990 the U.S. Forest Service said there were only 949 known owl pairs. *Los Angeles Times,* "28,000 Jobs May Hang on Ruling on Owls," May 18, 1990.

TIMES CHANGE

The early colonists had remarkably different attitudes toward the forest from our attitudes today. To them, the forest was a dark, mysterious, unproductive area filled with dangerous wild animals and savage natives. They set out to clear it, using lumber for firewood, housing, and industrial products such as wagons or ships. Land redeemed from forest clearing was converted to farms, roads, and towns. Forest destruction represented progress, civilization, and the taming of the wilderness. It was even a moral imperative since, as one historian notes, "social order and the Christian concept of morality seemed to stop at the edge of the clearing."[62] In the second half of the last century, the forest products industry was the second or third largest in the nation in any given year. Backwoodsmen and lumberjacks became noble symbols of American character, only to be supplanted by the romanticized caricature of the western cowboy.

---

breeding population drops below 50 owls, the gene pool will be too limited to continue species fitness; if it drops below 500 owls, genetic variation will be insufficient to permit continued evolution in the face of environmental change.[63] In fact, two subspecies, the Northern spotted owl and the California spotted owl *(Strix occidentalis occidentalis)* are separated by only a 12–15 mile gap in forest habitat between the Shasta and Lassen National Forests in northern California.[64]

And third, the spotted owl has a very low reproductive efficiency. A mated pair produce an average of 0.50 young per year. And there is a first year mortality rate of 88 percent among juvenile owls.[65] In one radio-telemetry study of forty-eight juvenile owls, only three were known to be alive after three years—a mortality rate of 94 percent.[66] Proximity of old growth to clearcutting has subjected both adult and juvenile spotted owls to increased predation by great horned owls, natural enemies which thrive in more open forest areas.

PROTECTING THE SPOTTED OWL

Environmental groups seeking to preserve old growth for its beauty and biological diversity are campaigning to save the spotted owl. The importance of the owl for environmentalists is: (1) its intrinsic value as a species with the right to survive, (2) its role as a predator maintaining an intricate forest ecosystem not yet fully understood by scientists, and (3) its use of old growth as a habitat, which makes saving it a convenient pretext for saving the ancient timber.

[62]Williams, *op. cit.*, p. 11.
[63]Simberloff, *op. cit.*, p. 771.
[64]There is a third subspecies, the Mexican spotted owl *(Strix occidentalis lucida)*, which lives in the forests of northern Arizona, Utah, Colorado, Texas, and parts of Mexico.
[65]Simberloff, *op. cit.*, p. 768.
[66]"Proposed Threatened Status…" *Federal Register, op. cit.*, p. 26667.

Little was known about the reclusive spotted owl before early studies in the 1970s. When it became clear that forest destruction clouded its future, Washington and Oregon listed it as a threatened species and California listed it as a sensitive species. State laws, however, provide only weak protection. Because of a requirement in the National Forest Management Act of 1976 to maintain populations of vertebrate species, the U.S. Forest Service in 1986 developed a long-term plan for protecting owl habitats from fragmentation by timber sale. The plan called for protecting 550 habitat areas, each between 1,000 and 2,000 acres, for an unspecified number of owl pairs.[67] The number of habitats was increased to 750 in 1988, but this was still far below a recommendation of the National Audubon Society to maintain 1,500 habitats in sizes ranging from 1,400 acres to 4,500 acres. The Forest Service admitted that the probability of spotted owl survival under its long-term plan after 100 years was "low" to "very low."

In 1987, environmentalists petitioned the Department of the Interior to list the northern spotted owl as an endangered species under the Endangered Species Act of 1973. The Act defines an *endangered species* as one that is "in danger of extinction throughout all or a significant portion of its range."[68] It also permits the listing of a *threatened species* which is "likely to become an endangered species within the foreseeable future throughout all or a significant portion of its range. . . ."[69] Listing decisions must be made solely on scientific evidence of species survival; economic and political factors do not have relevance. Once a species is listed—and there were 427 endangered and 135 threatened in 1990—it is entitled to a great deal of protection. Under threat of civil and criminal penalties, a listed species may not be collected, hunted, harassed, or harmed in any way. Federal agencies are required to coordinate their actions to protect the species. If the listed species has a geographically defined "critical habitat," the Secretary of the Interior is empowered to protect that as well. Restoration plans for recovery of the species must be implemented by the U.S. Fish and Wildlife Service.

In practice, once a species is listed there is little flexibility to compromise its survival for human economic benefit. In 1978, the Supreme Court interpreted the Endangered Species Act rigidly. Chief Justice Warren Burger wrote:

> One would be hard pressed to find a statutory provision whose terms were any plainer than those in Section 7 of the Endangered Species Act. Its very words affirmatively command all federal agencies "to insure that actions authorized, funded, or carried out by them do not jeopardize the continued existence" of an endangered species or "result in the destruction or modification of habitat of such species. . . ." This language admits of no exception.[70]

[67]U.S. Department of Agriculture, *Draft Supplement to the Environmental Impact Statement for an Amendment to the Pacific Northwest Regional Guide*, 2 vols., Portland, Oregon: U.S. Forest Service, 1986.
[68]16 U.S.C., Section 1532(6).
[69]16 U.S.C., Section 1532(20).
[70]This quote is from the majority opinion in *TVA v. Hill*, 437 U.S. 174.

This firm stand inspired Congress in 1978 to set up a special seven-member cabinet-level Endangered Species Committee empowered to exempt federal projects from the act even if a species would be made extinct. Exemption may be granted if (1) there is no reasonable and prudent alternative to the proposed action, (2) the benefits of the proposed action clearly outweigh the costs, and (3) the project is in the public interest. However, no exemption has yet been made. Thus, listing of the spotted owl as a threatened or endangered species would drastically curtail timber harvesting in old growth forests.

But in December 1987, the Department of the Interior refused to list the spotted owl as endangered or threatened.[71] It ruled that while close observation was warranted, the owl's numbers had not yet dwindled to a critical point. This was a blow to environmentalists and a victory for the Pacific Northwest forest products industry. While the owl's survival was clearly precarious, the Department of the Interior may have backed away in order to save the Endangered Species Act from a gutting. Listing the spotted owl would have virtually halted Pacific Northwest timber sales, generating a political firestorm.

Environmentalists did not give up. The Sierra Club, on behalf of twenty-three environmental groups, filed a lawsuit challenging the decision not to list the spotted owl. In 1988, a district court held that the Department of the Interior had acted arbitrarily and capriciously and ordered it to review its decision.[72] After further study, the agency reversed itself, and in 1989 issued a preliminary ruling that listing the spotted owl as a threatened species throughout its range was warranted.[73] It initiated a twelve-month hearing process required before the listing could become final. In the meantime, environmental groups systematically challenged timber sales on federal lands, managing to get court injunctions stopping 166 of 425 sales proposed by the Forest Service in 1989. These injunctions, based on the need to save irreplaceable owl habitat pending the listing, reduced the timber harvest from 5.4 billion board feet to 2.4 billion, drastically cutting the supply of timber to Pacific Northwest sawmills.

THE PACIFIC NORTHWEST WOOD PRODUCTS INDUSTRY

These timber injunctions have been disastrous in Oregon, where 44 percent of the economy is dependent on forest resources, and in Washington, where 28 percent of the economy is so derived. Hundreds of little towns scattered throughout these states and northern California are solely dependent on local mills and logging operations.

Since 1988, thirty-five mills have been closed in Oregon, California, and Washington, causing a loss of over 2,500 jobs.[74] Some stories from Oregon,

[71]"Finding on Northern Spotted Owl Petition," *Federal Register*,vol. 52, December 23, 1987, p. 48552.

[72]*Northern Spotted Owl v. Hodel*, No. C88-573-Z, W.D. Wash., May 5, 1988.

[73]"Proposed Threatened Status..." *Federal Register*, op. cit., p. 26666.

[74]Richard Martin, "No Hoot for Northwest Mills: Preserving an Owl's Habitat," *Insight*, June 19, 1989, p. 19, and Mark A. Stein, "Timber Shortage Putting Jobs, and Trees, at Risk," *Los Angeles Times*, January 29, 1989.

where seventy towns are dependent on just one or two sawmills, illustrate the anger and hardship that exists.

- In Sweet Home, population 6,890, three of the town's eight mills closed due to timber sale injunctions, costing 150 residents their jobs. Yellow ribbons fly from houses in support of loggers. Workers paste small yellow dots on dollar bills to make visible their spending in the local economy. Bumper stickers on cars read "SAVE A LOGGER/ EAT AN OWL" and "I LIKE SPOTTED OWLS...FRIED."[75]

- In Glendale, an independent sawmill is the largest employer. In 1989, its supply of logs from federal forests dropped by 75 percent, and the swing shift had to be eliminated. Forty families left town, and bumper stickers read: "IF IT'S HOOTIN', I'M SHOOTIN'."[76]

- In Clackamas County, residents have seen the land available for timber sales at Mt. Hood National Forest cut from 1 million acres to 467,000 acres due to wilderness preservation plans. In 1989, court injunctions put even this land off limits to loggers. The county received $6 million in timber harvest revenues from 1988 sales, but unless the injunctions are lifted, it expects to receive only $350,000 in 1990.[77] Its schools will be hard hit.

- Senator Mark Hatfield (R-Oregon) describes his experience giving the last high school commencement address in tiny Valsetz, where the only mill had just closed: "Instead of the usual smiles and laughter at such an event, there were tears and sadness in the faces of the members of that small community....In two weeks the bulldozers came in, and today there is not a sign left of community life because we are now finding underbrush taking over."[78]

Old growth timber is of central importance to mill town economies because there is no available substitute. In the 1950s, most of the old growth and much younger growth on private lands was harvested to meet spectacular lumber demand created by the post-World War II housing boom. Areas logged and replanted then will not mature for reharvest until after 2010. Thus, most consumable timber in the Pacific Northwest is old growth on federal lands. The wood from large old trees has a tight grain, and makes lumber of exceptionally high quality. Since an industry slump in the early 1980s, sawmills have increased productivity by making capital investments for equipment that processes large logs efficiently. These investments were based on the assumption that there would be a steady timber harvest on federal lands for the next fifty years. If sawtimber is unavailable, or if smaller

---

[75]Mark A. Stein, "Loggers See Spotted Owl as a Harbinger of Doom," *Los Angeles Times,* July 7, 1989.

[76]Jonathan B. Levine, "The Spotted Owl Could Wipe Us Out," *Business Week,* September 18, 1989, p. 99.

[77]Hearing, *U.S. Wood Products Competitiveness: Timber, Taxes, and Trade,* Joint Hearing before the House Committee on Small Business and the Senate Committee on Agriculture, Nutrition, and Forestry, testimony of Jim Geisinger, president, Northwest Forestry Association, July 8, 1989, p. 259.

[78]Remarks in the *Congressional Record,* October 7, 1989, p. S 12960.

logs must be substituted for large old growth logs, modernized mills will lose their cost advantage.

Although small Pacific Northwest towns are hardest hit, the spotted owl battle has nationwide impact. During 1989 there was a rise of 5 percent in the price of lumber, matching a 5 percent decline in softwood log production. Employment in sawmills decreased about 4.1 percent.[79] This may be only the beginning. One industry estimate is that if the spotted owl is added to the endangered species list, the cost will be 130,000 jobs, loss of $1 billion in timber revenue for the federal government, and loss of $400 million in income for local county school districts.[80]

THE OWL CONFLICT DEFIES RESOLUTION

By mid-1989, lumber mills were on the brink of complete shutdown. To avert a crisis, Senator Hatfield of Oregon and Senator Brock Adams (D-Washington) sponsored a bill that released for harvesting 1.1 billion board feet of the 1.8 billion then under injunction. The bill also directed the Forest Service to minimize fragmentation of old growth stands and supported continued research on the owl.[81] It reopened timberlands for one year.

Then, in 1990, the Department of the Interior issued a final rule listing the northern spotted owl as a threatened species throughout its range from British Columbia in the north to San Francisco Bay in the south.[82] This was done after the most exhaustive review of biological data ever undertaken for a species listing. Environmentalists felt they had won a great victory. They believed the owl's official threatened status would save vast expenses of ancient forest.

But only four days after the listing was published their hopes were dashed. The Bush administration announced that logging on federal lands would proceed as usual while an interagency task force chaired by Secretary of Agriculture Clayton Yeuter met to recommend to President Bush (1) changes in the Endangered Species Act and (2) a long-term timber management plan that balanced the preservation of the owl with the needs of industry. Thus, the threatened status of the owl did not resolve the conflict between preserving and consuming old growth.

The battle for the forest, then, continues. Environmentalists continue to believe that forest preservation is an imperative. As one conservationist notes, remaining old growth stands are "the only blueprint of the ancient forest that we have, the entire genetic code with all its parts functioning."[83] Its rescue from slow destruction is worth considerable economic discomfort. A spokesperson

---

[79]*U.S. Industrial Outlook, op. cit.*, p. 6–5.

[80]Mark Stein, "Expected Protection of Owl May Sharply Curb Logging," *Los Angeles Times*, April 26, 1989.

[81]See the *Congressional Record*, July 26, 1989, p. S 8796, and October 7, 1989, p. S 12959.

[82]"Determination of Threatened Status for the Northern Spotted Owl," *Federal Register*, vol. 55, July 26, 1990, pp. 26114–26194.

[83]Quoted in Jim Stiak, "Old Growth!" *The Amicus Journal*, Winter 1990, p. 35.

for the Wilderness Society asks: "Do we really want to sacrifice our nation's heritage for a few more years of cutting?"[84]

Industry advocates, on the other hand, point out that timber, even old-growth timber, is a renewable resource. They have advanced plans to protect more owl habitat, but are not willing to concede its survival at the expense of jobs and state economies. Rising in the Senate, Senator Hatfield has scolded "those who like to isolate themselves in a little cocoon and talk about theoretical and esoteric subjects," and cautioned, "let us not forget we are talking about human problems."[85] Residents of logging communities have rebelled against the intrusion of environmental groups into local affairs. A resident of Sheridan, Oregon, wrote: "Oregonians cannot be the guinea pigs for the rest of the country's moral conscience, and we cannot be expected to provide a sanctuary for every rare animal and plant species in the country."[86] A logger's wife in Underwood, Washington, wrote:

> My family consists of my husband, myself and our 1 ½ year old son. My husband is the fourth generation of a logger....If the spotted owl were to win the debate our family would be torn apart. We'd have to file bankruptcy and lose everything; we wouldn't have enough money saved to even relocate....The atmosphere in our community is that of panic....right now I don't feel we're getting the respect we deserve as American citizens.[87]

QUESTIONS

1 Was the Department of the Interior justified in listing the northern spotted owl as a threatened species?
2 What alternatives, if any, exist for resolving the conflict between environmentalists and the timber economy?
3 If there continues to be a direct conflict between the Pacific Northwest economy and preservation of the spotted owl, which should take precedence?

[84]Quoted in Stein, "Timber Shortage...," *op. cit.*
[85]*Congressional Record*, October 7, 1989, p. S 12959.
[86]Karen-Alicia Robertson, "Oregon: Put Through the Mill," *New York Times*, November 27, 1989.
[87]*Congressional Record*, October 7, 1989, p. S 12964.

15

Environmental Policy Issues

In the early 1980s, an aging copper smelter in Tacoma, Washington, operated by Asarco, Inc., was releasing 310 tons of airborne arsenic annually. Arsenic compounds are liberated from copper ore at high temperatures and are a common emission from smelters. Airborne arsenic is a carcinogen associated with lung cancer. Most of the emissions traveled downwind and fell in a circular area roughly twelve miles in diameter, encompassing an affluent suburb. Studies using recently developed techniques to measure risk conservatively estimated that the emissions caused four additional lung cancers each year in Tacoma, where the incidence rate of 70 to 90 annually was already 20 percent higher than the national average.

The plant, which had operated since 1905, employed 600 workers and contributed about $35 million to the area economy. In 1983, the EPA ordered Asarco to install $4.4 million of abatement equipment to lower arsenic emissions to 189 tons a year. But it estimated that the remaining arsenic fallout would still cause one additional lung cancer per year in Tacoma. The study on which this estimate was based assumed that no level of arsenic exposure—no matter how minute—is safe. Asarco, in contrast, argued that a threshold exists below which exposure is safe, and said that because of competitive conditions the cost of further abatement would force plant closure.

At public hearings in Tacoma, the EPA gave residents a choice. Did they want the EPA to strictly enforce new arsenic emission standards on the smelter, forcing it to close, or were they prepared to accept the risk of one more annual lung cancer death in exchange for economic benefits from the smelter? At one hearing, a smelter worker in his seventies rose to say that he had been exposed to so much arsenic during his forty years at the plant that his sweat was sometimes green, but he felt fine and didn't believe it was harmful. A young mother rose to blame airborne arsenic for the leukemia death of her child. Others were confused, angry, and upset at the stark choice. The EPA administrator said: "Listen, I know people don't like these kinds of decisions. Welcome to the world of regulation."[1]

Soon residents of Tacoma began sporting buttons saying "Both!" at community meetings. A compromise with smelter management was ironed out in which arsenic emissions would be lowered to the extent economically feasible to allow continued operation. In 1985, however, a glut of cheap foreign copper dropped copper prices below the level at which the smelter could operate profitably, and it closed.

As illustrated in the preceding chapter, effective implementation of environmental statutes has been difficult. In this chapter we discuss general problems embodied in Tacoma's regulatory dilemma. We focus on how risks are assessed and managed and how costs of abatement are balanced against benefits. Later, we discuss suggestions for improving environmental regulation, including how market incentives are used by the EPA. And we also look at some abatement measures taken by specific companies.

THE PROCESS OF MANAGING RISKS POSED BY INDUSTRIAL POLLUTION

The story of the Asarco smelter, a story that typifies the hard choices faced by EPA administrators, teaches that regulating noxious emissions is a complex task. The first step in many regulatory decisions is to estimate accurately the risks to human health or to the biosphere posed by a pollutant. As we shall see, this is not easy. In what follows, the focus is on assessing risks to health from carcinogens, which is the leading edge of environmental risk assessment. Other health risks and risks to natural ecology are seldom calculated with as much effort and precision as are risks of contracting cancer.

ANALYSIS OF ENVIRONMENTAL RISKS

There have been many attempts to assess and state risks. For example, paper products manufactured from bleached pulp—including writing paper, newspapers and magazines, baby diapers, and toilet tissue—contain trace amounts of the carcinogenic chemical dioxin. When we touch these products, dioxins may pass from them to our skin and thence into our tissues. What is the risk of getting cancer? A recent estimate is 1 in 1,000,000 over a three-year period.[2] A calculation of the annual risk of contracting cancer from

---

[1] Quoted in Eleanor Randolph, "What Cost a Life? EPA Asks Tacoma," *Los Angeles Times*, August 13, 1983. Looking back, the EPA now considers the Tacoma hearings a failure; see Caron Chess and Billie Jo Hance, "Opening Doors: Making Risk Communication Agency Reality," *Environment*, June 1989, p. 15.

[2] Russell E. Keenan and Michael J. Sullivan," Assessing Potential Health Risks of Dioxin in Paper Products," *Environmental Science and Technology*, June 1989, p. 643. This estimate is based on assumed use each day of six diapers, seven tissues, sixty sheets of toilet paper, three sanitary pads, ten paper towels, and ninety sheets of paper.

drinking water contaminated with 1,530 parts per billion of the industrial solvent trichloroethylene is 1 in 2,173.[3] The EPA has estimated that living by the boundary of a plastics plant emitting the maximum levels of vinyl chloride gas permitted by law and breathing the outdoor air twenty-four hours a day for seventy years creates a cancer risk of 1 in 170.[4] These risks may be compared with a 2 in 100 lifetime risk of dying in an auto accident and a 2 in 10 of succumbing to cancer.[5]

How accurate are environmental risk estimates? One of the most famous risk assessments grew out of a 1975 study sponsored by the U.S. Atomic Energy Commission to estimate the risks of nuclear reactor operation. The Rasmussen Report, named for Normal C. Rasmussen, the chair of the reporting committee, estimated that an accident causing loss of core coolant, meltdown, and breach of containment was likely to occur only once in 10 million years of reactor operation. This probability is about the same as an individual walking down the street being struck by a meteorite. However, only eleven years later, such an accident occurred in the Soviet Union!

The Chernobyl reactor fire released fallout equivalent to thirty-six atomic bombs of the type dropped on Hiroshima. Thirty-one people died of radiation exposure and 116,000 people living within thirty kilometers of the plant received an estimated three percent of the lethal dose. Wind and rain deposited the long-lived radionuclides cesium 187 and iodine 131 across the globe, raising background levels of radiation in every country. Some experts believe that as many as 28,000 cancer deaths will result, about half in the Soviet Union and Eastern Europe. One set of risk estimates gives a range of 4 to 8 out of 100,000 in Poland and 4 to 8 out of 100 million in the U.S.[6] Other experts, however, predict zero fatalities.

The difference in these risk predictions lies in assumptions about how data from radiation deaths of high-dosage Hiroshima survivors can be applied to a situation in which radiation exposure is lower. Those who predict many deaths believe that lower doses of radiation cause progressively fewer deaths, but continue to kill. Those who predict few or no deaths believe there is a threshold below which small doses of radiation do not cause cancer. State-of-the-art medical research provides no proof for either theory. This uncertainty is characteristic of risk predictions for other carcinogens.

METHODS OF ASSESSING RISK

The source of uncertainty about cancer risks lies in the limited range of experimental methods available to risk scientists. It would be unethical to ex-

---

[3]David E. Burmaster and Robert Harris, "Groundwater Contamination: An Emerging Threat," *Technology Review*, July 1982, p. 60.

[4]50 FR 1182 (1985).

[5]Curtis C. Travis and Holly A. Hattemer-Frey, "Determining an Acceptable Level of Risk," *Environmental Science and Technology*, August 1988, p. 874.

[6]Christoph Hohenemser and Ortwin Renn, "Chernobyl's Other Legacy," *Environment*, April 1988, p. 6.

pose human populations to toxic chemicals, and other techniques for assessing cancer causation are flawed.

These include *animal tests,* in which animals such as mice, rats, dogs, guinea pigs, monkeys, goats, minks, or trout are repeatedly exposed to a compound through diet, inhalation, or other means for several months to a year or more, a period covering an appreciable span of the animal's life. As many as a thousand animals may be divided into groups with various exposure levels. They are then dissected, and tumors on various organs are counted.[7] If excessive tumors are present, the chemical is carcinogenic to the animals. The assumption is then made that the chemical can also cause cancer in humans at lower exposure levels over longer time periods. Such tests were used to determine, for example, that nitrosodiethanolamine, a synthetic chemical found in metalworking fluids used to minimize corrosion during machining, is a strong carcinogen. Based on animal tests, the Environmental Protection Agency estimated that a metalworker with frequent exposure to such fluids has a 1 in 100 risk of cancer over forty years of work.[8]

But such conclusions are made using unproven assumptions of parallel disease processes. In some cases, test animal physiology is so different from that of humans that disease processes may be unique. For example, gasoline vapor causes kidney tumors in male rats, but the biological mechanism causing the rat tumors has recently been shown to be unique to rats, casting doubt on EPA risk assessments which assume gasoline vapor is an exceptionally potent human carcinogen posing a 1 in 175 lifetime risk of cancer to exposed individuals.[9] Because carcinogenesis is not fully understood, it is an additional, unproven assumption that human cancer may result from lower exposures to a compound than were administered to small mammals.

Another way of determining health risks from environmental substances is through *epidemiological studies,* or studies of human mortality (death) and morbidity (sickness) in a sample population. Epidemiological studies, which are analogous to opinion polls, are used to establish a relationship between some business activity and a wide range of degenerative conditions. A typical study showed the following associations:

• High bladder cancer rates near factories producing dyes and pigments, drugs, perfumes, cosmetics, and toiletries.

---

[7]EPA studies require that benign and malignant tumors be added together for conservative calculations of cancer risk, unless benign tumors are of a type which cannot progress to malignancy. Other abnormalities, such as fibrotic effects, are noted too. Animals are also used for acute toxicity tests in which a single dose of a compound is administered in differing amounts to separate groups of animals. They are watched for a few hours to a week, their symptoms and deaths recorded. In this way the toxicity of a chemical may be estimated.

[8]Office of Management and Budget, *Regulatory Program of the United States Government: April 1, 1988 to March 31, 1989,* Washington, D.C.: Government Printing Office, 1989, p. 405.

[9]John D. Graham, David R. Holtgrave, and Mary Jean Sawey, "The Potential Health Benefits of Controlling Hazardous Air Pollutants," in John Blodgett, ed., *Health Benefits of Air Pollution Control: A Discussion,* Washington, D.C.: Library of Congress, Congressional Research Service, February 27, 1989, pp. 178–79.

• High lung cancer rates near factories manufacturing industrial gases, pharmaceuticals, soaps and detergents, paints, pigments, and synthetic rubber.
• High liver cancer rates near factories making synthetic rubber, soaps and detergents, cosmetics, printing inks, and some organic chemicals.[10]

Epidemiological studies, though valuable, also have shortcomings. In particular, people are exposed to literally thousands of substances in the environment, and individual exposures vary. Exposures to contaminants such as air pollutants present only in small amounts are difficult to relate to cancer. People in a city may have moved in and out of the area. Because lung tumors and other cancers have latency periods of up to forty years, current exposures may not be the damaging ones, and no records exist for concentrations of air toxics prior to the 1970s. Death certificates may be inaccurate, particularly when a number of diseases contributed to death. Overall, the results of epidemiological studies are valuable, but their accuracy is subject to doubt. One expert believes that "a negative epidemiologic study, even when many people are studied, can miss a 20 percent increase in cancer."[11]

Mutagenic tests judge carcinogenicity by exposing bacterial strains such as *Salmonella typhirurium* or animal cells such as Chinese hamster ovary cells to suspected cancer-causing agents and measuring damage to genetic material. In one such test, the Ames test, 90 percent of chemicals which cause genetic mutations are also found to be carcinogenic by other methods. Like animals, however, bacteria strains and cells are only surrogates for human tissues, and extrapolation from them is of uncertain accuracy.

In some cases, accidental exposure of human populations to a chemical produces direct evidence of disease. In 1968, for example, 1,291 Japanese were exposed to rice oil contaminated with polychlorinated biphenyls, a chemical used in the manufacture of electrical equipment. They suffered from symptoms of chronic toxicity such as eye discharge and swelling, acne, jaundice, numb limbs, muscle spasms, impaired vision, and bowel disturbances. After three years, 50 percent failed to improve. Animal tests have shown PCBs to be carcinogenic, and after five years nine of the exposed Japanese had died from cancer, a number which researchers concluded was possibly excessive.[12] As the case of PCBs illustrates, many carcinogens also cause a wide range of acute and chronic health problems.

THE EPA RISK ANALYSIS PROCEDURE

Even though disagreement about risks exists, a legal framework of regulations requires that the EPA act to reduce them. Because risk decisions are

---

[10]Laurent Hodges, *Environmental Pollution*, 2nd ed., New York: Holt, Rinehart and Winston, 1977, p. 12.
[11]Michael Gough, "Estimating Cancer Mortality," *Environmental Science and Technology*, August 1989, p. 929.
[12]EPA, *Ambient Water Quality Criteria for Polychlorinated Biphenyls*, Washington, D.C.: Government Printing Office, October 1980, p. C-72.

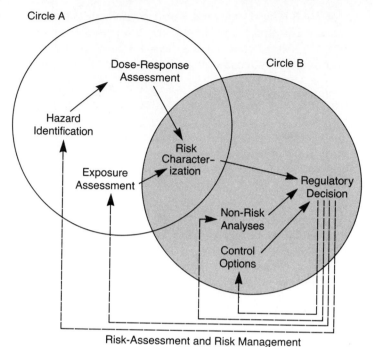

FIGURE 15-1 EPA risk-analysis procedure. (*Source:* Environmental Protection Agency.)

complex, the EPA has developed a systematic procedure for risk management. This procedure, diagramed in Figure 15-1, has two parts.

The first part of the analysis is *risk assessment,* in which an estimate of the danger of an environmental pollutant is measured. As represented by Circle A on the diagram, it includes the following elements.

• *Hazard Identification* is the process of gathering and evaluating evidence that a substance causes an adverse health effect. Animal tests may show, for example, that a chemical such as dioxin or benzene is carcinogenic.

• *Dose-Response Assessment* is the process of determining how toxic or hazardous a substance is at different levels of exposure. Saccharine causes cancer in laboratory animals only at very high doses, whereas exposure to small amounts of asbestos leads to malignant tumors in animals. Often the judgment of potency must be stated within a broad range and cannot be measured exactly. It has been particularly difficult, for instance, to relate airborne particulate levels to the onset of pulmonary disease.

• *Exposure Assessment* is undertaken to estimate how much of a substance humans will come in contact with. This step usually involves monitoring emissions, but may involve mathematical modeling to estimate air or water dispersal of a contaminant. The pertinent time period for assessing degree of exposure may vary from a lifetime, as with airborne hydrocarbons, to short-term peak exposures, as with asbestos.

• *Risk Characterization* is the final step, during which the overall risk assessment is made. In practice, two risk estimates are made. One is based on the *most exposed individual* concept, which calculates risks for a hypothetical person living at the factory fence and breathing high emissions around the clock for seventy years. This figure represents an upper range of disease. A second figure is based on the *public health standard*, which estimates risks for the general population, in which most individuals will have lower exposure levels. In some cases, such as pyrobenzines from coke oven emissions, there is great danger to most exposed individuals, i.e., the workers who toil in proximity to leaky furnaces, but little danger to the general population. The EPA has estimated that coke oven workers face a 3.4 in 100 lifetime risk of cancer, whereas the yearly risk to the public is less than 1 in 500 million.[13]

The second part of the EPA risk analysis procedure is *risk management*. It entails making regulatory decisions about risks on the basis of the earlier risk assessment. Whereas risk assessment is largely a scientific process, risk management is the administrative art of identifying and choosing regulatory alternatives. It is best to keep risk management separated from risk analysis. This is so because the objective determination of risk levels may be separated from the political or emotional factors that go into an enforcement (or risk management) decision. Separation avoids the temptation of distorting risk assumptions to fit predetermined regulatory preferences.

There are three basic elements in risk management, as shown in Circle B in Figure 15-1.

• *Control Options*, which are the alternatives available to mitigate the risk, must be defined. Technical data, such as control device engineering, may open or limit options. Public opinion or pressure from industry groups may define politically acceptable options. In recent years, for example, public consensus has strongly backed reduction of carcinogenic pollutants released by industrial activity, at enormous cost, despite a consensus of scientific opinion that this has little impact on overall cancer rates. The most comprehensive review of cancer mortality to date attributed only about 2 percent of cancer deaths to industrial pollutants, and another 4 percent to occupational exposures.[14] Estimates in medical literature are that 25 to 40 percent of cancer mortality is caused by cigarette smoking, yet, due in part to tobacco industry lobbying, far less is spent to eradicate smoking than to control factory emissions. Statutes also define control options. The Toxic Substances Control Act, for instance, gives regulators a range of choices in regulating chemicals. Depending on the toxicity and exposure risk of a particular chemical, the manufacturer may be subject to a spectrum of regulatory controls. At one end of this spectrum, the EPA may prohibit further production and use of a chem-

---

[13]See Graham, *et al., op. cit.,* pp. 178–79.
[14]See R. Doll and R. Peto, *Journal of the National Cancer Institute,* vol. 66, 1981. In 1987, EPA employees estimated that only 2–7 percent of cancers were caused by industrial pollution and occupational exposures combined. See EPA, *Unfinished Business: A Comparative Assessment of Environmental Problems,* Washington, D.C.: Government Printing Office, 1987, p. 6.

ical. At the other end, it may require only record keeping for a chemical of low toxicity. In the middle, the agency may do such things as require a warning label or specify quality-control steps in the production process.

• *Non-Risk Analyses* refers to the use of cost-benefit and risk-benefit analyses as methods of supporting control options. Under some statutes, but not all, the agency must consider the benefits of a regulatory action compared to its costs, and may consider the costs and benefits of alternative actions. Cost-benefit analysis is considered at length in the next section. The EPA must also consider new risks that may arise from an abatement action. For instance, when the pesticide ethylene dibromide (EDB) was banned for use on crops to control nematodes, the EPA assessed the toxicity of potential substitutes and found that they posed less risk to human health than did EDB (largely because they broke down more easily on the surface of fields and did not cause ground water contamination, as EDB did). But because all substitute nematocides were also hazardous to human health, the risk-benefit ration was close.

• *The Regulatory Decision*, of course, is the action taken. It naturally affects future calculations in the risk analysis procedure, as is shown by the interconnecting lines in Figure 15-1.

COST-BENEFIT ANALYSIS

Cost-benefit analysis is a decision-making technique that consists of systematically comparing the costs and benefits of a proposed action—in this case, an environmental regulation. If benefits are greater than costs, the action is desirable, other things being equal. The most rigorous forms of cost-benefit analysis assign common values, such as dollar amounts, to all costs and benefits so that they may be compared using a common denominator.

Cost-benefit analysis has been used in rudimentary form in government since the nineteenth century, but achieved its modern, elaborate form in the evaluation of alternative weapons systems by the Pentagon during the 1960s. The EPA began doing cost-benefit studies as early as 1971, and during that decade cost-benefit considerations were built into environmental statutes such as the Clean Water Act. Because of opposition by environmentalists to weakening standards due to cost consideration, other laws, such as the Clean Air Act, specifically forbid cost-benefit analysis, for instance in determining safe public exposure levels for toxic air pollutants.

In 1981, as noted in Chapter 9, President Reagan issued Executive Order 12291, stating that new regulations should be implemented only if benefits to society outweigh costs.[15] Thereafter, "major" regulations with an economic impact of $100 million or more required a "regulatory impact analysis" (RIA), essentially a cost-benefit analysis, from the sponsoring agency before going into effect. The analysis had to show estimates of benefits exceeding costs. Since 1981, the EPA has conducted many RIAs. Obviously, the requirement of a cost-benefit study in some cases directly contradicts statutes and court

[15]*Federal Register*, February 19, 1981, pp. 13193–98.

decisions forbidding the EPA to incorporate cost-benefit studies into its decisions.[16] The EPA resolves these contradictory demands by calculating costs and benefits, but excluding this information from decision making. In such RIAs a disclaimer is included, stating that the results were not considered by the EPA in setting or revising standards.

In recent years, typical RIAs have run several hundred pages and cost an average of $670,000.[17] In an RIA, the calculation of costs usually includes costs to industries for abatement measures, inflation, plant closures, lost jobs, property damage, medical costs, and the value of statistical lives lost. The accounting is very detailed. For example, the expected number and types of cancers are calculated from risk data. They are then described in terms of age groups affected; disabilities likely to result; their length, medical costs, lost productivity, foregone wages; and estimates of pain and suffering. The value of a statistical life is usually based on discounted value of future earnings lost, which sums a person's wages over the remainder of his or her expected lifetime. Because of inflation, current dollars received are worth more than future ones. Therefore, the Office of Management and Budget requires the value of future wages to be discounted by 10 percent. All costs and benefits accruing in future years must also be discounted by a rate of 10 percent.[18]

Benefits include public health gains, lives saved, property damage avoided, productivity gains, and economic benefits such as higher land values or increases in tourism to a cleaner area. In recent years, the EPA has valued lives at between $400,000 and $7 million, based on wage rate studies. After all benefit-cost calculations are made for alternative regulatory stan-

---

[16]See, for example, *EPA v. National Crushed Stone Association*, 66 L. Ed. 268 (1980), in which the Supreme Court rejected an industry attempt to inject cost-benefit measures into regulation when it ruled that the EPA was not required to consider costs in enforcing the Clean Water Act's requirement that industry use the "best practicable control technology currently available." See also *National Resources Defense Council v. EPA*, 824 F.2d 1146 (1987), in which Judge Robert Bork prohibited the EPA from considering control costs in determining exposure levels for toxic air pollutants that protected public safety. Other agencies are similarly restricted by environmental statutes. In the famous "snail darter" case, *Tennessee Valley Authority v. Hill*, 437 U.S. 153 (1978), the Supreme Court ruled that the Endangered Species Act required the Department of the Interior to protect endangered species regardless of cost consequences. In two other cases, *Industrial Union Department, AFL-CIO v. American Petroleum Institute*, 65 L. Ed. 2d. 1010 (1980), and *American Textile Manufacturers Institute v. Donovan*, 425 U.S. 490 (1981), the Supreme Court limited the Occupational Health and Safety Administration in the Department of Labor in using cost considerations. Congress, said the court, had not intended to compromise worker health protection with consideration of costs imposed on industry. OSHA was, however, required to demonstrate significant health risks before imposing expensive protective measures.

[17]Figures derived from data in Ralph A. Luken, "Weighing the Benefits of Clean-up Rules Against Their Costs," *EPA Journal*, March 1988, p. 9.

[18]This discount rate is higher than the range of 2 to 6 percent that many economists believe is more accurate. The result of using a high 10 percent discount rate is that overall benefits are reduced and costs loom larger. This is so because in most pollution reduction programs, costs, such as for the installation of expensive abatement equipment by industries, usually come sooner than benefits. Hence, costs are discounted less. Some have said this is, in effect, a bias against regulation. See, for example, EPA, *Costs and Benefits of Reducing Lead in Gasoline: Final Regulatory Impact Analysis*, Office of Policy Analysis, EPA-230-05-85-006, February 1985, pp. I-23–24. Some have suggested that it is inappropriate to discount benefits at all, because in the future people may value environmental quality more than we do now.

> In the realm of ends everything has either a *price* or a *dignity*. Whatever has a price can be replaced by something else as its equivalent; on the other hand, whatever is above all price, and therefore admits of no equivalent, has a dignity.
>
> *Source*: Immanuel Kant; *Foundations of the Metaphysics of Morals* (1785).

dards, Executive Order 12291, when applicable, requires the EPA to choose the alternative having "the least net cost to society."

CONTROVERSIAL ASPECTS OF COST-BENEFIT ANALYSIS

Cost-benefit analysis is attractive as a method of evaluating regulatory impacts and expenditures; however, it has important shortcomings.

First, it is hard to identify all costs and benefits in a project. When a firm spends money for pollution control, it also may redesign a production process to make it more energy-efficient. Is the expenditure a cost or a benefit? Where benefits are measured in dollar amounts, how is one to value a clear sky, a fishable stream, fragrant air, or extra years of life? These values are subjective and necessarily involve disagreement. It is hard to assign a dollar amount to untraded goods such as aesthetic beauty or a human life.

Policy choices in environmental regulation often have consequences for mortality rates and, therefore, implicitly place a value on life. Although pricing life evokes a callous image, it is a hard reality that decisions about pollution abatement programs must be made. Zero-discharge standards could prevent some risks to human health, but only at an astounding price. Society cannot afford the infinite expenditures necessary to reduce pollution to the no-risk level. Expenditures below this level indicate policies that compromise between preserving lives and maintaining a higher standard of living for everyone.

Methods of calculating the value of human life are discordant with widely held public values of fairness and equity. If life value is based on wages earned through the remainder of a lifetime, an objection is that workers in some jobs have low wages due to discrimination. Whites may earn more than blacks, men more than women, working husbands more than housewives. As one critic notes, such calculations run "directly contrary to the egalitarian principle, with origins deep in the Judeo-Christian heritage, that all persons are equal before the law and God."[19] EPA valuations of life are also based in part on earnings surveys of dangerous occupations which try to measure the wage premium paid to attract people to risky work. One problem with this approach is that wage determinations may not be based on accurate risk estimates. Some critics of life valuation have criticized all ap-

[19]Thomas O. McGarity, "Health Benefits Analysis for Air Pollution Control: An Overview," in Blodgett, *op. cit.*, p. 55.

proaches, arguing that the very process of monetizing human life belittles its intrinsic value.[20] An example, perhaps, is one study of premature babies which found that, for infants under 900 grams, the costs per survivor exceeded the child's probable lifetime earnings. The inference of this study is that babies under 900 grams should be allowed to die.[21]

A related set of criticisms comes from environmentalists, who dislike cost-benefit approaches because they trade off environmental quality. One critic, Steven Kelman, writes that "there may be many instances where a certain decision might be right even though its benefits do not outweigh its costs" and points out that the Bill of Rights and the Emancipation Proclamation were not subject to cost-benefit study because the moral rights they represented were absolute.[22] Another writes: "If the value of each endangered species or population must be compared one by one with the value of the particular development scheme that would exterminate it, we can kiss goodbye to most of Earth's plants, animals, and microorganisms."[23] The root of all such objections is the elevation of efficiency as a criterion that trumps all others. For many, of course, maximum efficiency is not a measure of the good society.

A second general difficulty with cost-benefit analysis is that the benefits and costs of a program may affect different parties and, therefore, may not be truly comparable. A reduction in particulate emissions from a factory may impose large costs on the business and on consumers of its product. But benefits from cleaner air accrue to local real estate agents as clean air raises property values, to pollution-control equipment manufacturers who profit from abatement, and to individuals whose medical bills are lower. Weighing diverse cost-benefit effects in this way is subjective and raises complicated issues of justice.

A third criticism of cost-benefit analysis is that it unnecessarily complicates the regulatory process. After the Reagan administration stressed cost-benefit approaches, some objected that RIAs increased the expense of regulating, delayed needed regulations while study was undertaken, and made the decision process more complex and dependent on arcane methods and technical experts. The process created a barrier to public participation in regulatory decisions. While it is correct that RIAs are highly technical reading, John Luken, chief of the EPA's Economic Analysis Branch, has recently written that they result in dramatic cost savings.[24] For example, in 1985 new scientific data indicated that reducing lead content in gasoline beyond its already substantially reduced level would create large environmental and health benefits. But no law required further reduction, and since the public was uninformed, there was no political pressure to do so. However, the EPA con-

---

[20]See McGarity, *op. cit.,* p. 57, note 91.
[21]In McGarity, *op. cit.,* p. 58.
[22]"Cost-Benefit Analysis: An Ethical Critique," *Regulation,* January/February 1981, p. 31.
[23]Paul Ehrlich and Anne Ehrlich, *Extinction: The Causes and Consequences of the Disappearance of Species,* New York: Random House, 1981, p. 10.
[24]*Op. cit.,* p. 12.

ducted a benefit-cost analysis, which confirmed that lowering lead in gasoline from 1.1 gram per gallon to 0.1 gram per gallon would produce monetized benefits of $7.9 billion between 1985 and 1992 as opposed to costs of just $607 million—a total net social benefit of $7.3 billion. This study enabled the EPA to justify and take regulatory action.

ARGUMENTS IN FAVOR OF COST-BENEFIT ANALYSIS

Although cost-benefit analysis has an image problem and limited precision, its use may be advantageous for several reasons. First, it is a framework for fully categorizing the impacts of a policy. It disciplines thinking, but should not be expected always to result in clear choices. Judgment is still required, even though cost-benefit analysis may show some alternatives more desirable than others. After cost-benefit studies are completed, decision makers still may use ethical criteria in decisions.

A second advantage of cost-benefit analysis is the reverse of the critics' charge that it is cold-blooded. In fact, cost-benefit analysis may inject rational calculation into highly emotional arguments and thereby lead to compassionate decisions that protect nature and minimize human suffering more than intuitive decisions based on emotional considerations.

And third, cost-benefit analysis may help regulators locate the proper level of regulation by recognizing the importance of marginal abatement costs. The bill for pollution abatement is rising rapidly because, as a general rule, control costs rise steeply as full cleanup is approached. In some cases, it may cost as much to reduce pollution for the last 3 to 5 percent as it did to clean up the first 95 to 97 percent. Figure 15-2 shows this. The pulp and paper industry, for example, spent about $3 billion to comply with EPA water emission control standards and achieved a 95 percent effluent reduction in 1983. However, to reach a 98 percent reduction would cost an additional $4.8 billion, or a 160 percent increase in costs to achieve only a 3 percent increase in benefits.[25] In cases such as this, cost-benefit analysis can identify efficient regulatory goals to prevent skyrocketing costs that produce trivial benefits. It provides an artificial but valuable test of efficient resource allocation for regulators not subject to a market mechanism.

MARKET INCENTIVES IN ENVIRONMENTAL REGULATION

Environmental protection is expensive. Total expenditures in the United States now run over $75 billion a year. About one-third is paid by governments, with most expenditures at the state and local level. A municipal waste incinerator can cost up to $500 million, and a public drinking water system can cost $100 million for even a medium-sized city.[26] Most federal expenditures have been grants-in-

---

[25]Murray L. Weidenbaum, *Regulation and the Public Interest*, Contemporary Issues Series, no. 4, St. Louis: Center for the Study of American Business, Washington University, 1983.

[26]Arthur Koines, "Under the Environmental Regulation Layer Cake," *EPA Journal*, July/August 1989, p. 19.

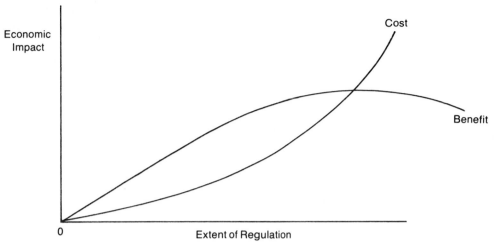

FIGURE 15-2   Benefit-cost analysis of regulation. *(Source:* Murray L. Weidenbaum, *Benefit-Cost Analysis of Government Regulation,* St. Louis: Center for the Study of American Business, 1981, p. 3. Reprinted with permission of the Center for the Study of American Business, Washington University.)

aid to the states. The other two-thirds is paid for by business in new capital expenditures and operating costs. The largest single area of business expenditure is air pollution abatement, which is nearly matched by water pollution abatement. Together, expenditures on air and water account for about 85 percent of business's pollution bill; solid waste disposal costs lag far behind at only 15 percent. Since 1975, just five industries (paper, chemicals, petroleum, primary metals, and public utilities) have made almost 75 percent of total capital expenditures by business for pollution abatement.[27]

Although these expenditures are accompanied by many benefits, these benefits may be noneconomic goods and may be realized only in the future. In an era of unprecedented federal budget deficits, it is unlikely that federal spending for environmental quality can be significantly increased. The politically powerful industries which foot most of the business sector abatement bill have balked at increased expenditures under current statutes, because it is now clear that the kind of command and control regulation required by most of the 1970s era laws often imposes unreasonable expense. Therefore, regulators, environmentalists, and others have proposed greater reliance on market incentives to achieve cost-efficient progress. In this section, we discuss market-based alternatives to traditional command and control regulation.

AIR EMISSIONS POLICIES AS AN EXAMPLE OF MARKET INCENTIVE REGULATION

Typically, the EPA has enforced the provisions of the Clean Air Act on industry by prescribing control equipment and emissions limits for each point

[27]Bureau of the Census, *Statistical Abstract of the United States: 1988,* 108th ed., Washington, D.C.: Government Printing Office, December 1987, Table 342.

source in a plant. Experience has shown, however, that the cost of controlling the same amount of a pollutant from two different sources can vary considerably. It may, for example, cost $1,000 a ton to remove hydrocarbons from the exhaust gases of one industrial process and 100 times that much, or $1 million, to remove one ton from another industrial process, depending on the nature of that process and the level of control already achieved. Therefore, the EPA has adopted four innovative policies to give business flexibility in controlling overall emissions of the six criteria pollutants (lead, carbon monoxide, volatile organic compounds, sulfur dioxide, particulates, and nitrogen dioxide) and to reduce compliance costs.

First, in 1976, the EPA adopted a policy allowing *emission offsets*. Under the Clean Air Act, new sources of pollution are prohibited in areas such as southern California, where large air basins fail to meet federal ambient air quality standards. If the law had been strictly enforced, no new factories could have been built, and economic growth would have been choked off, not only in southern California, but in most other large cities. Under the EPA's emission offset program, however, new factories may be built provided they utilize the "best available" control technologies and produce pollution "offsets" from existing sources. Under this offset policy, for example, a General Motors assembly plant employing 5,000 was built in Oklahoma City (a "nonattainment area") when four local oil companies agreed to install floating roofs in oil storage tanks to reduce hydrocarbon emissions from evaporation. This reduction more than offset hydrocarbon emissions from paint-spraying booths in the new auto plant. GM paid for the floating roofs. Total hydrocarbon emissions in the area were reduced at a fraction of the cost of achieving zero emissions at the new GM plant. Over 2,000 offsets have been made.

A second, and similar, regulatory innovation is the *bubble concept*, first introduced by the EPA in 1979. It works this way. Traditionally, the EPA monitors and limits individual sources of air pollution in a factory. But rather than measure emissions from each stack, valve, paint sprayer, or dust source, under the bubble concept a single limit is placed on an entire industrial complex—an imaginary bubble overarching all point sources. The company is then allowed to choose which sources to control, with which technologies, and at what level, so long as overall plant emissions limits are not exceeded.

An example is the compliance bubble the EPA approved for a utility, Central Illinois Public Service. The utility operates two identical boilers for power generation, both of which are subject to sulfur dioxide (SO_2) emission limitations of 1.2 pounds per million BTU heat input. The first boiler burns high-sulfur coal, and sulfur emissions are controlled with expensive flue gas desulfurization equipment capable of lowering stack emissions below the 1.2 pound limit. The second boiler does not have flue gas emission controls, but met the 1.2 pound SO_2 emission standard by burning low-sulfur coal. The utility proposed to switch the second boiler to locally available, less expensive coal with a higher sulfur content that would result in emissions of 1.8 pounds of SO_2. It further proposed to overcontrol the first boiler so that the *combined* flue gas emissions of both boilers totaled only 1.1 pounds of SO_2. The EPA approved the bubble, which lowered total annual sulfur emissions by about 3,100 tons and saved the utility $22 million in coal purchase costs.[28]

A third innovation is *emissions banking.* Under the EPA's air emissions banking policy, established in 1982, firms may overcontrol emissions or shut down polluting sources and receive credits for the amount of pollution not emitted. Credits may be stored in an emissions "bank," which acts as a clearinghouse, and later used by the firm that owns them or sold to another firm that may use the credits to emit more pollutants. A firm may buy emission credits because they are often cheaper than installing expensive abatement equipment. For example, Borden Chemical Company once bought the rights from B. F. Goodrich Co. to emit twenty-five tons of hydrocarbons annually at a price of $2,500 per ton. Borden claimed that emission control at its facilities would have averaged $5,800 per ton.[29]

The most active emissions bank is in Louisville, where eighteen factories have deposited emission credits equal to 26,000 tons per year of air pollutants. Nine firms have purchased emission credits at the bank, and nineteen have used banked credits to make internal offsets. Only five states have approved banking programs, and some other states prohibit the practice.

A fourth form of emissions trading is *netting.* A hypothetical example is useful to explain netting. A firm that increases sulfur dioxide emissions from a coal-fired boiler by more than 250 tons per year would, in most states, be required to obtain a type of permit that is difficult and expensive to qualify for. A typical major new source permit application requires research using computerized air modeling to show how the pollutant will disperse, and most applicants must also do studies of existing air quality. All this can cost up to $25,000, and averages $15,000.[30] Permits for major new sources have taken as much as ten years, and it is not unusual for a major permit to take two or three years of work with regulators. If, however, the firm is able to reduce sulfur dioxide emissions from another boiler on the factory grounds by, say, 50 tons per year, the *net* increase in emissions is only 200 tons, and the firm need apply for only a new minor source permit. These permits are much quicker, simpler, and less expensive. But the main savings in netting occurs because major new sources of pollution are faced with stringent emission limits requiring costly control devices. Avoiding classification as a major new source is estimated to have led to average cost savings of $100,000 to $1 million, in addition to permitting cost savings for the more than 5,000 netting transactions to date.[31] The difference between using a bubble and netting is that emissions may not increase under a bubble, but may be raised under a netting agreement.

[28]Council on Environmental Quality, *Environmental Quality: Annual Report,* Washington, D.C.: Government Printing Office, 1985.

[29]Richard Greene, "Selling Dirt," *Forbes,* May 24, 1982.

[30]Robert W. Hahn and Gordon L. Hester, "Where Did All the Markets Go? An Analysis of EPA's Emissions Trading Program," *Yale Journal on Regulation,* Winter 1989, p. 135.

[31]*Ibid.,* pp. 135–36.

These four forms of market incentive regulation have seen limited use. Environmentalists oppose them, believing that since clear air is a basic right, polluted air should not be for sale at any price. Another aspect of these transactions that galls them is the implication that polluters become responsible for decisions trading off environmental quality against economic development. But legal challenges have been turned aside.[32] It is likely that as pollution control costs soar in the 1990s, market incentives to reduce emissions will be increasingly attractive as an alternative to traditional command and control regulation.[33]

ENVIRONMENTAL LAWSUITS

Most enforcement of environmental statutes is done by regulatory agencies which may threaten large civil fines and criminal fines and jail sentences for noncompliance. Under the Clean Water Act, for example, when the EPA determines that a company has exceeded effluent discharges, it may go to court seeking fines of up to $25,000 per day.[34] In setting the penalty, the court is required to appraise the following:

> ...the seriousness of the violation or violations, the economic benefit (if any) resulting from the violation, any history of such violations, any good-faith efforts to comply with the applicable requirements, the economic impact of the penalty on the violator, and such other matters as justice may require.[35]

Although civil fines are the traditional method of bringing polluters to heel, federal and state prosecutors may seek criminal indictments. In U.S. law, criminal liability exists when deliberate intent, or prior knowledge of injury to society or nature from an illegal act, is present. In court, the burden of proof in criminal cases is heavier, i.e., "beyond a reasonable doubt" as opposed to the civil standard of a "preponderance oft he evidence." Under the terms of the Clean Water Act, a person who knowingly violates the law and discharges pollutants capable of causing personal injury or property damage into a sewer or water body is subject to a criminal fine of between $5,000 and $50,000 or imprisonment of up to three years or both. A manager who releases a hazardous water pollutant that places anyone in imminent danger of death or serious bodily injury is subject to a fine of up to $250,000 or impris-

---

[32]A court challenge by the Natural Resources Defense Council against netting transactions in nonattainment areas, *NRDC v. Gorsuch*, 685 F.2d 718 (D.C. Cir. 1982), was successful but soon overturned in *Chevron v. NRDC*, 467 U.S. 837 (1984). The legal status of market incentive air emissions policies is today unquestioned.

[33]See Timothy E. Wirth and John Heinz, *Project 88, Harnessing Market Forces to Protect Our Environment: Initiatives for the New President*, Washington, D.C., December 1988.

[34]33 U.S.C. 1319, Sec. 309 (c).

[35]33 U.S.C. 1319, Sec. 309 (d). This wording is typical of that found in other federal statutes. The Clean Air Act alone is more specific; defining the economic value of a delay as "the quarterly equivalent of the capital costs of compliance and debt service over a normal amortization period, not to exceed ten years, operation and maintenance costs foregone as a result of noncompliance, and any additional economic value which such a delay may have...[minus legitimate compliance expenditures]" [42 U.S.C. 7420, Sec. 120(d)(2)].

An analysis of environmental offenders published by the New Jersey Division of Criminal Justice indicates that a typical environmental criminal is a lower-level employee who does not fully understand the consequences of illegal dumping and comes to believe that circumventing the law is an unspoken norm in the industry or company. An actual case from the report illustrates this:

After several promotions, [a yard worker in a waste handling facility] found himself laboring near the wa-

ter's edge, secluded from the rest of the facility, connecting waste-filled tanker trucks to a grounded hose. Coworkers and supervisors alike maintained the hose was linked to underground holding tanks.

The worker's confidence in this explanation was shaken after witnessing wastes surfacing in the abutting waterway. The worker, at first, questioned the legitimacy but became satisfied with procedures as being part of the normative structure. When reality eventually set in, he was now a fairly long-standing participant in the criminal activities and decided it prudent to remain silent.[36]

onment for as much as fifteen years. The company involved may be fined up to $1 million.[37] All these penalties may be doubled if they are for second convictions, so a manager could wind up being fined $500,000 and imprisoned for thirty years!

The EPA now has a squad of forty-eight environmental police (called E-Men within the agency) who investigate and apprehend outlaw polluters. Since 1982, the environmental crimes section of the Department of Justice has gotten 385 pleas and convictions, 279 against individuals, resulting in $13 million in fines and 200 years of jail terms.[38]

The primary factor in the rise of intentional pollution cases has been the rising cost of toxic waste disposal. Since passage of the Resource Conservation and Recovery Act, which mandates strict disposal standards, the cost of disposing of some wastes has risen to as much as $500 for a 55-gallon drum of chemicals. Simply analyzing a drum of unidentified organic chemicals to determine how best to dispose of it costs from $200 to $600. Not all companies can afford such charges and begin to covertly hide, bury, and spill hazardous wastes.

Other legal methods of sanctioning corporate polluters exist. Most major environmental statutes permit private citizens to sue corporations for violating pollution laws. There are over 100 such citizen lawsuits each year. Most

[36]In David Wann, "Environment Crime: Putting Offenders Behind Bars," *Environment*, October 1987, p. 45.

[37]33 U.S.C. 1319, Section 309(c). Naturally, managers committing a pollution crime are subject to prosecution under federal statutes aside from those in environmental laws. These include aiding or abetting a crime, accessory after the fact, misprision (concealment) of a felony, conspiracy to defraud or commit an offense against the United States, submitting false statements to government agencies, mail fraud, obstruction of government agency proceedings, and others. L. Lee Harrison, ed., *The McGraw-Hill Environmental Auditing Handbook*, New York: McGraw-Hill, 1984, "Introduction," p. 2-5.

[38]These figures are taken from Stephen J. Hedges, "Enviro-Cops on the Prowl for Polluters," *U.S. News & World Report*, October 9, 1989, p. 23; Raymond B. Ludwiszewski, "Reagan Team Fought Pollution in the Courts," *Wall Street Journal*, October 5, 1988; and Jill Abramson, "Government Cracks Down on Environmental Crimes," *Wall Street Journal*, February 16, 1989.

are part of a bizarre ritual encouraged by a peculiarity of the Clean Water Act. Factory discharges of pollutants into water bodies are based on permits which set daily limits on the amount of any substance which may be released. Exceeding this amount is a violation of the statute, and in Section 309 Congress sets civil fines as high as $25,000 per day! The Clean Water Act also mandates detailed reporting of effluents to the EPA—so detailed that the company must itself document those occasions when, due to equipment failure, accident, or other cause, it has released more pollutants than its permit allows. These records must be available to the public.

Environmental groups have trained students to pour over company reports to find violations. Then, acting as a "citizen," these groups sue the company. The firm's reports of effluent limit violations have standing as legal evidence in courts and are used to convict the companies. Fines assessed can be huge. Bethlehem Steel Corp., for example, once paid $1.5 million in a citizen lawsuit for polluting Chesapeake Bay. But assessment of the fine does not conclude the comedic ritual. If the corporation pays the fine to the environmental group that initiated the citizen suit (instead of to the federal treasury), the payment is tax deductible. Therefore, an estimated 65 percent of the fines have gone to fund the Sierra Club and a handful of other groups.[39] James Thornton, a lawyer with the Natural Resources Defense Council, chortles that: "It's like shooting fish in a barrel, and we've shot a lot of fish."[40] But some in industry call it extortion.[41]

Tort law, a body of civil law used for redressing wrongful acts, is also a powerful check on corporations.[42] Court-ordered awards for damages, injury, illness, and risk of latent illness caused by environmental pollution are increasing in number. Theories of tort law such as nuisance, negligence, trespass, and strict liability for ultrahazardous activity have been used to seek judgment against companies. Highly publicized "toxic tort" lawsuits have been filed against Union Carbide by the victims of the gas leak at Bhopal, against the chemical companies that made Agent Orange by Vietnam war veterans, and against Manville Corp. and other asbestos manufacturers by workers exposed to asbestos materials. Less publicized cases include an Oregon suit in which Martin Marietta Co. was ordered to pay damages because emissions from an aluminum smelting plant damaged fruit trees, and a Kentucky suit in which B. F. Goodrich was held liable for the death of a nearby resident exposed to vinyl-chloride gas emitted from a plastics plant.[43] The

---

[39]This figure refers to an assessment made of such fines between 1983 and 1985. See Barry Meier, "'Citizen Suits' Become a Popular Weapon in the Fight Against Industrial Polluters," *Wall Street Journal,* April 4, 1987. For an example of one such arrangement in which the National Resources Defense Council settled suits against four companies see *NRDC Newsline,* "Water Pollution Cases Settled on East Coast," December 1989, p. 6.

[40]*Ibid.*

[41]See Michael S. Greve, "Congress's Environmental Buccaneers," *Wall Street Journal,* September 18, 1989.

[42]For an explanation of the concept of a tort and of the law of torts see William L. Prosser, *Law of Torts,* St. Paul, Minnesota: West Publishing Co., 1971, Chapter 1.

[43]J. Raymond Miyares, "Controlling Health Hazards Without Uncle Sam," *Technology Review,* July 1983.

resident had a rare liver cancer associated in medical literature with exposure to the gas.

The liability system brings strong pressure to bear on industry, providing an incentive to limit pollution in order to minimize lawsuits. In the aftermath of the Love Canal controversy, $16 billion in personal-injury lawsuits were filed against Occidental Chemical Corp. by 1,345 residents![44] But the tort system has shortcomings as a mechanism for regulating business. Widespread environmental lawsuits could overwhelm the courts. Current evidentiary rules make it difficult for victims to prove damages, since the link between illness and past exposure to a pollutant is often a matter of scientific speculation. This is especially the case when the illness has a long latency period and other disease-causing factors have intervened. Courts historically have required that injured people show with a "reasonable degree of medical certainty" that a company was responsible for their illness.[45] Litigation is costly, slow, and unpleasant; there are many opportunities for corporations to win delays. And some states still have statutes of limitation as short as two to seven years, meaning that victims of latent illnesses and genetic defects may have no standing to sue when their illnesses become manifest.

ENVIRONMENTAL IMPAIRMENT INSURANCE

Insurance is another alternative for deterring socially irresponsible corporate behavior. In 1982, the EPA enlisted the help of insurance companies in regulating toxic waste when it established a policy requiring hazardous-waste dump operators to prove their ability to finance the costs of permanently closing dump sites. Any company operating such a dump would have to buy insurance coverage for both "sudden" and "non-sudden" pollution accidents (the latter term referring to slow leaks and manifestation of long-term health effects). If a company cannot buy insurance, it may post a surety bond in an amount stipulated by the EPA and insure itself.

In theory, this policy would shift part of the regulatory burden from the EPA to the insurance industry, which would need to accurately assess the risks of toxic pollution incidents, charge adequate premiums, and insist on safe handling of toxins. The EPA knew that, historically, insurance carriers have provided financial incentives to corporations to act safely. At the turn of the century, when unsafe steam boilers frequently blew up in manufacturing plants, insurance companies, which had to pay the accident claims, helped to develop the safety boiler. Insurance has also worked to compliment regulation in areas such as auto, marine, and fire safety. But it has not worked well in the pollution field. Its cost has skyrocketed, and policies are often unavail-

---

[44]These cases were settled in 1983, and the settlement figure is not public knowledge.

[45]See, for example, *Jones v. Ortho Pharmaceutical Co.,* 209 Cal. Rptr. 456 (1985); *Wells v. Ortho Pharmaceutical Co.,* 788 F.2d 741 (1986); *Ferebee v. Chevron Chemical Co.,* 736 F. 2d 1529 (1984); and *In re Agent Orange Product Liability Litigation,* 611 F.Supp. 1223 (1985). For an overview of evidentiary requirements see Stephen W. Jones, "Problems of Causation in Toxic Torts," *Defense Counsel Journal,* July 1988.

able. Today an annual premium of $250,000 is typical for $2 million of coverage—if a company can find an insurer.[46]

The main reason that environmental liability insurance is always expensive and often difficult to get is the fear insurance companies have of tort liability. Court decisions based on the theory of joint and several liability in the pollution field scared insurers, who found themselves footing large medical and cleanup bills for policyholders who were minor parties in hazardous waste spills. In addition, the courts sometimes expansively defined the insurers' liability to the policyholder. For instance, some insurers were forced to pay for cancers caused by exposures twenty to thirty years before, even though coverage had long since lapsed. Finally, pollution risks are hard to define. New and unknown dangers are constantly discovered, and future damage claims are potentially astronomical. Conspicuous accidents, such as the Bhopal methyl isocyanate gas leak that killed and injured thousands of Indians, have also made insurers wary.

CORPORATIONS IN AN ENVIRONMENTAL ERA

In years past, corporations were far less conscious of environmental protection. Steel mills ran without air emission controls; solvents such as carbon tetrachloride were used in normal maintenance and drained away without treatment. Today such trespass against nature is illegal and unconscionable, and increasingly minor sloth is forbidden. Until a few years ago, for example, normal track construction for a railroad included the use of wooden railroad ties impregnated with toxic chemical preservatives to deter insect activity and weathering. Small diesel spills at fuel stops were of little concern. No more. In railroading and other industries, the present business environment is one of strong public pressure to abate pollution and of increasing minute regulatory oversight of operations. Costs of environmental protection will almost certainly rise through the 1990s, because existing laws mandate increased abatement for all forms of industrial pollution. The possibility even exists, though it is remote, that new scientific findings about changes in atmospheric chemistry caused by industrial emissions could reveal extreme danger to the biosphere. In such an event, draconian requirements to, for example, cut carbon dioxide emissions by 50 percent before the year 2010 could become law. In this section, we discuss three ways that businesses adapt to an era which prioritizes environmental protection. These are (1) complying with laws, (2) preventing pollution, and (3) managing public pressures.

MANAGING COMPLIANCE AND ENVIRONMENTAL PROTECTION POLICIES

Corporations need a systematic effort to institutionalize environmental protection requirements. The effort begins with top management leadership, in-

---

[46]Terry R. Galloway, "Destroying Hazardous Waste On Site—Avoiding Incineration," *Environmental Progress*, August 1989, p. 179. For an overview see Kenneth S. Abraham, "Environmental Liability and the Limits of Insurance," *Columbia Law Review*, June 1988.

cluding statements from top executives about the importance of compliance with environmental laws. Union Carbide and several other companies also have committees on the board of directors to manage environmental affairs.

A corporation also needs policies and procedures to insure compliance with environmental laws. They direct action and provide a standard by which to measure performance later. One company that has developed a comprehensive policy is ARCO, a company which has, generally, earned the respect of environmental groups for its actions to protect nature. ARCO's policy suggests basic guidelines that managers elsewhere should consider.

Atlantic Richfield Company Environmental Protection Policy

Realizing that the world's natural resources of air, water and land are vital to mankind's global existence, progress, and continued development, we consider environmental protection to be a paramount concern in our total activities, domestic and international. Therefore, it is our policy to:

• Manage our operations with diligence and with an awareness that our goal is to protect the environment by employing the best control mechanisms, procedures, and processes which are proven technically sound and economically feasible.

• Entrust each line manager with responsibility for the environmental performance of his or her activity.

• Comply with all environmental legislation, regulations and standards, and provide self-monitoring to insure compliance.

• Assist all levels of government in the promulgation of sound, cost-effective environmental laws, codes, rules and regulations, based on scientific facts and needs.

• Consider the expense of environmental protection as a legitimate cost of doing business in modern society, assuming environmental regulations are uniformly applicable throughout an industry.

• Encourage and support—with technical ability, time, and money—environmental programs and research efforts sponsored by trade associations and other organizations seeking solutions to technological and ecological problems.

• Train our employees in environmental matters, actions, and responsibilities relating to their particular assignments.

• Secure ecological guidance in our long-range planning, using recognized consultants and employing the services of experts of various disciplines.

• Enhance communication and understanding with our stockholders, civic groups, environmental and conservation organizations, universities, and the general public through publications, speakers, exhibits, demonstrations, and the media.

• Maintain a Corporate Environmental Protection Group to review, advise, coordinate, and implement environmental protection activities and programs.

Organizational changes insure responsibility for compliance with policies and law. To illustrate, at Allied Chemical a Corporate Environmental Affairs Department has been set up, headed by a vice president who reports to Allied's senior vice president for operations, to assist Allied's operating units in complying with statutes. This department meets regularly with managers to explore environmental problems, and sends out environmental surveillance teams to inspect Allied facilities and monitor legal compliance. A risk assessment committee in the department reviews hazards posed by company products and operations. A final stimulus to environmental protection at Allied is the requirement that up to one-third of a middle manager's bonus depends on meeting environmental objectives. Other companies have similar management systems.

POLLUTION PREVENTION

Compliance with pollution control laws is one method of minimizing adverse environmental impacts. But both companies and regulators are increasingly emphasizing strategies of pollution prevention. Ordinary control technologies isolate or neutralize harmful pollutants after they have been created by an industrial process. Pollution prevention, on the other hand, occurs when industrial processes themselves are modified to eliminate contaminants. Pollution is prevented because it is not generated.

Manufacturers have often found that a close look at operations reveals numerous opportunities to prevent pollution. In many such cases, interventions are profitable. For example, manufacturers of copper parts dip them in a "pickling" bath of chromic acid and oxidizers to brighten them. In the process, the bath is saturated with copper ions and is gradually degraded until it loses its cleaning efficiency. A decade ago, this bath was simply thrown out and processed through expensive water clarification equipment, which failed to remove all trace metals before releasing wastewater into streams and rivers. Today, an electrolytic process is used to recover copper from the bath, which is then used over again. The recovered copper metal is then sold as No. 1 copper scrap. In Charlotte, North Carolina, the Duke Power Company had been trucking barrels of PCB-contaminated oil to a solid waste disposal site, paying almost $200,000 per year to dispose of it. The EPA, however, permits destruction of PCBs in incinerators which reach temperatures of 1,832 degrees Fahrenheit. Investigation determined that the fuel-oil flame in boiler systems at Duke Power's electrical power plants was 2,400°. The company began to mix PCB-contaminated oil with ordinary fuel oil, saving $400,000 a year in new fuel oil costs and foregoing land disposal bills.

In 1975, Minnesota Mining and Manufacturing (3M) Corporation began a program called Pollution Prevention Pays. It required aggressive auditing of manufacturing processes to seek waste reduction opportunities. By 1989, the program had saved 3M an estimated $300 million and reduced waste by over 100 million tons.[47] A simple example of the 3M program in operation is that

---

[47]Cynthia Pollock Shea, "Doing Well by Doing Good," *World Watch*, November/December 1989, p. 27. For other examples of pollution prevention see Michael G. Royston, *Pollution Prevention Pays*, Oxford: Pergamon Press, 1979, and American Management Association, *Toward Pollution-Free Manufacturing*, New York: AMA, 1986; and, for a technical treatment, Marvin Drabkin and Edwin Rissmann, "Waste Minimization Opportunities at an Electric Arc Furnace Steel Plant Producing Specialty Steels," *Environmental Progress*, May 1989.

of a circuitry plant in Columbia, Missouri, that cleaned oil residue from copper sheeting by spraying the sheeting with several toxic chemicals that created a hazardous effluent. Research showed that a machine which scrubbed the copper plating with pumice using a brush system did the same job without creating 40,000 pounds of hazardous liquid waste and sludge each year. The brushing machine cost $59,000 and paid for itself in three years. Many other companies have such a program today and use environmental audits to discover changes which will lower costs and prevent pollution.

MANAGING PUBLIC PRESSURES

In the winter of 1987, Eastman Kodak learned that methylene chloride contamination from one of its factories in Rochester, New York, had entered well water in a bordering neighborhood. The company believed itself only partly responsible, and did not think that the low concentrations discovered presented a health problem. In April 1988, local newspapers learned of the contamination and stirred up local residents, the city charged Kodak with violating hazardous waste disposal laws, and in 1990 the company paid $2.15 million in fines.

The only effect of the methylene chloride established with certainty was lowering of property values for homeowners. So Kodak has initiated a Value Protection Plan. It guarantees property values in the neighborhood for ten years by offering home buyers mortgages 3 percent below market rate and $5,000 home improvement grants. If any house fails to sell, Kodak agrees to buy the home for its appraised value prior to discovery of methylene chloride pollution plus an amount equal to average appreciation of homes in the rest of Rochester. It even pays moving expenses, closing costs, and a $500 miscellaneous fee. So far, forty homeowners have moved, but only six vacant houses have been purchased. This plan has cost Kodak "tens of millions of dollars" with many years yet to go, and was necessitated in large measure by the error of delay in disclosing the problem to the community.[48]

The Kodak story illustrates the high public relations and financial costs of even small pollution incidents. Major accidents can cost hundreds of millions and lead to extensive litigation. This potential has led many companies to conduct a wide spectrum of community relations activities. Others have produced biodegradable, recyclable, or otherwise environmentally attractive consumer products. Wal-Mart Stores in 1989 elected to emphasize "environmentally sound" products because of rising customer concern about the environment.[49] In the process of coming to grips with the strength of public feeling for environmental protection, a few firms have produced remarkable examples of corporate social responsibility.

An illustrative case is that of Monsanto's efforts to rescue the Illinois mud turtle, a small, reclusive reptile six to nine inches long that exudes an offen-

---

[48]Marc S. Reisch, "Firms Boost Community Programs to Fight Chemicals' Poor Image," *Chemical & Engineering News,* December 5, 1988, p. 15.

[49]National Wildlife Federation, *Conservation Exchange,* "Growing 'Greener'," Winter 1989–90, p. 5.

sive odor from its musk glands and remains burrowed in underground hideaways nine months of the year. The turtle lives on a swampy, 2,000-acre tract near Monsanto's agricultural chemical plant at Muscatine, Iowa, and at one time was a candidate for the endangered species list, with only 200 known specimens extant. During a census, Monsanto discovered that a nearby lake vital to the turtle's habitat was drying up. Although the operations and proximity of its agricultural chemicals plant had no effect on the turtles or their habitat, Monsanto launched a $500,000 project to save them. Raccoons and skunks were trapped and removed from the acreage so that they would not eat turtle eggs, and a fleet of tanker trucks brought 80 million gallons of water to the sinking lake from the nearby Mississippi River. Belatedly, it was discovered that the site probably was populated by more than 2,000 specimens of the Illinois mud turtle![50]

In a similar effort, Florida Power & Light Co. has taken extraordinary measures to protect twenty-five to thirty crocodiles which live and breed in a grid of cooling canals at its Turkey Point nuclear power plant. Crocodiles are an endangered species, and the plant is one of only three known breeding grounds in the U.S.[51] The company, which employs an ecologist to manage impacts on wildlife, once kept a power plant running for eleven winter days solely to provide warmth for about 100 manatees. The manatees, or sea cows, are another endangered species. They had clustered in a cooling canal seeking heat from coolant water.

CONCLUDING COMMENT

Only in a fairy tale world could Congress pass an environmental law, set up an agency to enforce it, and be assured that the agency would soon restore environmental quality. In the real world, regulatory decisions are based on a series of guesses, assumptions, and political considerations piled atop each other. In this chapter we have tried to illustrate the complexity of such decisions as well as the business response to them. We believe that abatement of industrial pollution is an exceptionally difficult art. Legislators, scientists, regulators, managers, and citizens are moving up a learning curve, but it will be many years before anyone can say confidently that abatement efforts are focused on the highest risk problems and that expenditures are reasonably cost-effective. In the meantime, many pollution problems are worsening.

[50]Harvey Berman, "Industry Saves a Turtle," *Environment*, March 1981.
[51]Eric Morgenthaler, "A Florida Utility Wins Naturalists' Praise for Guarding Wildlife," *Wall Street Journal*, May 7, 1987, p. 1.

Cost-Benefit Decision at Bluebird Smelter

Bluebird Smelter is owned by a large, national mining company and located in Bluebird, a town of 12,000 in western Montana. The smelter, which has been operating profitably for thirty-five years with 100 employees, processes copper ore arriving by railroad. Its most distinguishing feature is a tall, brick stack, visible for miles and used as a landmark by nearby residents, which emits a visible plume and often leaves a faint, smudgy pall over Bison Valley, the geological basin in which Bluebird is located.

Bucolic Bison Valley has about 25,000 residents and attracts retirees from big city life and wealthy weekenders who build retreats or buy small farms in the area. The economy of Bison Valley has been primarily agricultural, but tourism is an important—if small—component, as is Bluebird Smelter.

Bluebird Smelter is the only major industrial pollution source in the valley. Fugitive and stack emissions from the smelter include gases such as sulfur dioxide, nitrogen oxides, carbon monoxide, and volatile organic compounds such as tuolene; particulates of lead, copper, iron, beryllium, inorganic arsenic, and asbestos fiber; and droplets of sulfuric acid. Trace radionuclides released from ore-bearing material at high temperatures subject the environment to small amounts of radioactivity. On sunny days, when the air is still, and during periods of temperature inversion over the valley, the action of the sun on smelter emissions contributes to photochemical smog similar to that in urban areas. Auto emissions and agricultural activities also are sources of photochemical oxidants, but smelter emissions are a much greater contributor to the smog.

Due to smelter emissions, the air shed in Bison Valley was classified by the Environmental Protection Agency as a "nonattainment area" in 1974. An area is so classified under Section 171 of the Clean Air Act when national ambient air quality standards for criteria pollutants are exceeded. Because of smelter emissions, the twenty-four-hour maximum levels of particulate matter and ozone were exceeded an average of ninety-four days a year.

While new stationary sources of pollution in nonattainment areas are required by Section 111 of the Clean Air Act to use "the best system of continuous

535

emission reduction" available and to offset their emissions by reducing other emission sources in the area, old stationary sources such as Bluebird Smelter are allowed by Section 110 to operate under a permit system when "necessary technology or other alternatives are not available" to lower their emissions to levels that would improve air quality and permit the air basin to meet EPA standards.

However, because of the plant's conspicuous presence, dramatized by the tall stack, visible plume, and a lingering odor from sulfur dioxide emissions, a small, local environmental group called the Earth Riders made the plant a target of protest in the 1970s. Lawsuits and political pressures by the Earth Riders led to installation in 1977 of costly pollution control equipment at the smelter that reduced sulfuric and particulate emissions by roughly 75 percent from an uncontrolled state. This improved air quality, but visible pollution, adverse health effects, and crop damage continued.

After 1977, Bluebird Smelter was granted a series of variances from federal and state emission standards because the company let it be known that further abatement expenses would force smelter closure. From the 75 percent control level, control costs escalate rapidly, and further controls—say to the 90 percent level—would cost more in total than the original 75 percent reduction. These massive expenditures would push the plant into long-term financial loss. Today, Bison Valley is in violation of criteria air pollutant standards an average of forty days a year. This is an improvement, but the area still has more twenty-four-hour periods of violation than major industrial cities, with the exception of Houston, Pittsburgh, and Los Angeles.

Some smelter emissions are classified by the EPA as hazardous air pollutants. By 1989, the EPA had set standards for public exposure to arsenic, asbestos, beryllium, and radionuclides. But although annual public exposures to these substances in Bison Valley exceeded EPA standards, the agency placed a low priority on regulating air toxics. For many hazardous pollutants, the EPA had yet to set standards or, as in the case of nickel, copper, and toluene, had elected not to regulate them even after standards were set. Within the agency, it was believed that only about 2,000 cancers per year in the United States were attributable to all hazardous air pollutants combined. Definitive health tests for other illnesses had not been done. Therefore, the agency elected not to impose heavy costs on installations such as Bluebird Smelter.

Many townspeople told reporters from big-city papers that they wanted jobs and were willing to tolerate a little dirty air. Local observers thought that closure of the smelter would throw Bison Valley into an economic recession. Despite opposition and organized protest by the Earth Riders, the Bluebird City Council passed five resolutions asking for variances from air-quality standards for the smelter and sent them to state and federal agencies. When several Earth Riders chained and locked themselves to railroad tracks leading to the smelter, demanding that ore shipments cease and the plant close down, the mayor of Bluebird, a veterinarian, placed a placard in his office window offering "Free rabies shots to Earth Riders. No appointment necessary."

In 1990, a state public health official conducted an epidemiological study of the region, because it offered a unique opportunity for observing the health effects of a single, major source of industrial pollution. Using standard mortality tables, the official determined that there had been twenty-five "excess" deaths in Bison Valley over the five-year period between 1984 and 1989. These were deaths from emphysema, lung cancer, tuberculosis, pneumonia, and ischemic heart disease over and above those naturally occurring in a population not exposed to similar industrial pollution. Such results were not surprising given the existing sulfur dioxide and particulate levels. The unique element in the situation was that the cause was a single source rather than a collection of sources mixing together, as in most industrial and urban areas. What could not be determined, of course, was which deaths were the "excess" ones. The extra five fatalities averaged each year were part of a group of several hundred deaths, most of which were statistically "expected."

A group of economists from a prestigious research institute in another city picked the Bluebird Smelter as a test case for a research project on the health effects of pollution. The figures that they produced led to debate among the various local groups involved in the controversy. The researchers looked at the operation of Bluebird Smelter in terms of costs and benefits to the community and to society. Exhibit 15-1 shows their basic calculations.

The Earth Riders seized upon the study, arguing that if total costs of smelter operation exceeded benefits, then a clear-cut case had been made for closing the plant. It was already operating at a loss—in this case, a net social loss of $605,000. Thus, in the eyes of the environmentalists, Bluebird Smelter was in social bankruptcy.

The smelter's managers and members of the Bluebird City Council, in contrast, ridiculed the study for making unrealistic and simplistic assumptions.

EXHIBIT 15-1 ANNUAL BENEFITS AND COSTS OF BLUEBIRD SMELTER

Benefits	Value
Payroll for 100 employees at an average of $23,000 each	$2,300,000
Benefits paid to workers and families at an average of $1,000 each	100,000
Income, other than wages and salaries, generated in the valley by the company	4,600,000
Local taxes and fees paid by the company	125,000
Social services to community and charitable contributions	20,000
	Total $7,145,000

Costs	Value
Excess deaths of five persons at $1 million each*	$5,000,000
Other health and illness costs to exposed population	450,000
Crop and property damage from pollutants	1,200,000
Reduction of aesthetic value and quality of life	500,000
Lost revenues and taxes from tourism	600,000
	Total $7,750,000

*Calculated on the basis of recent court decisions compensating victims of wrongful death in product liability cases in western states. The figure reflects average compensation.

They questioned whether the costs were meaningful, citing estimates of the value of a human life made by other economists that were much lower than $1 million. They argued that health risks posed by the smelter were less than those of smoking cigarettes, drinking, or riding motorcycles and that benefits to the community were great. They even suggested that important costs had been left out of the calculations, such as sociological and psychological costs to workers who would be laid off if the plant closed.

The debate raged, and the smelter continued to operate.

QUESTIONS

1 Do you believe that the costs to society of smelter operation outweigh the benefits?
2 Do you believe that the cost figures in the researchers' calculations, particularly those representing human life, are accurate? What are some alternative ways to calculate the value of human life? Could the social benefits exceed social costs if different values were used?
3 Are any important benefits or costs not included in the analysis of the smelter's operation? What are they?
4 Is the cost-benefit method of decision making an appropriate tool for deciding whether to close the smelter?
5 List and explain several alternative solutions to this controversy. Which is best and why?

The Exxon Valdez Oil Spill

On March 24, 1989, the *Exxon Valdez (EV)* oil tanker struck Bligh Reef in Prince William Sound about twenty-eight miles from Valdez in southeastern Alaska (see Exhibit 15-2). It caused the largest oil spill in U.S. territorial waters in our history (but not the largest in the world).[52] Eleven million gallons of crude oil gushed from the tanker bottom into the clear waters of the Sound, with serious consequences for the ecology and economy of the area. The disaster inflamed many old and created important new policy issues for governments; for the oil industry, especially Exxon; for environmentalists; and for the people of Alaska.

THE PRINCE WILLIAM SOUND

The Sound is a remote, pristine fjord, an estuary-type ecosystem of breathtaking beauty. It is circled by spectacular rugged glaciated mountains, rising to 15,000 feet, and glaciers. It is one of the richest concentrations of wildlife in North America, including five species of threatened or endangered marine mammals that frequent the area. It is 100 miles in diameter and about the size of Massachussetts. Within the Sound are fifteen islands, each over fifteen square miles, hundreds of streams and inlets, many bays and marshes, and a few reefs. Its ragged and rocky shoreline measures several thousand miles. Six large hatcheries that spawn millions of fish are harbored in its bays. Hundreds of thousands of birds live or pass through the Sound on their migratory journeys. To many people, the Sound is one of the natural wonders of the world.

In the northeastern part of the Sound sits the fishing village of Valdez, which is also the terminus of an 800-mile pipeline extending to Prudhoe Bay on the north slope of Alaska. Prudhoe Bay is a major source of oil for the United States, and it was this oil that filled the *EV*.

[52]Other larger oil spills were as follows: *Atlantic Empress* and *Aegean Captain* collided July 19, 1979, off Trinidad and Tobago and spilled 92 million gallons of oil; on August 6, 1983, the *Castillo de Beliver* spilled 77 million gallons off Cape Town, South Africa; on March 16, 1978, the *Amoco Cadiz* ran aground off the coast of northwest France and dumped 68 million gallons of oil on the beaches; and on March 18, 1967, the *Torrey Canyon* grounded off Land's End, England, and spilled 37 million gallons of oil. There were at least four other spills in the 30 million gallon range.

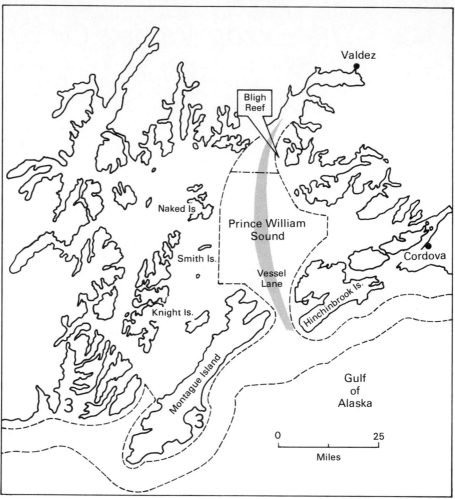

EXHIBIT 15-2   Prince William Sound and the point of spill. (*Source: Hearing Before the Subcommittee on Coast Guard and Navigation of the Committee on Merchant Marine and Fisheries, House of Representatives,* 101st Congress, 1st Session, on *Topics Concerning the Exxon Valdez Oil Spill into the Prince William Sound of Alaska,* April 6, 1989, p. 272.)

GROUNDING THE *EXXON VALDEZ*

Some facts are clear about the grounding of the *EV*, but many are not and will remain the subject of sharp controversy and legal battles for years to come.[53] The *EV* left Valdez at 9:15 pm on March 23 with a local harbor pilot aboard. The pilot left the ship at 11:24 pm as it approached prescribed ship-

[53]Details about the grounding can be found in the following: *Hearing Before the Committee on Commerce, Science, and Transportation, United States Senate,* 101st Congress, 1st Session, on *Exxon Valdez Oil Spill and its Environmental and Maritime Implications,* April 6, 1989; and *Hearing Before the Subcommittee on Coast Guard and Navigation of the Committee on Merchant Marine and Fisheries, House of Representatives,* 101st Congress, 1st Session on *Topics Concerning the Exxon Valdez Oil Spill into the Prince William Sound of Alaska,* April 6, 1989.

ping lanes and before it reached Bligh Reef, a standard procedure. At 12:04 am on March 24, the *EV* went aground on Bligh Reef (see Exhibit 15-2).

Captain Joseph Hazelwood left the bridge before the grounding to take care of paperwork in his cabin. Before leaving the bridge, he took the tanker outside normal traffic lanes to avoid icebergs in the area and notified the Coast Guard of his action. The ship was turned over to third mate Gregory T. Cousins, who was told by Hazelwood to turn back into the traffic lanes beyond Busby Island, where a buoy light warned of dangerous shoals. Seven minutes before the accident and immediately after the ship passed Busby Island, Cousins said he ordered rudder correction, but the vessel took too long to respond and the ship hit the reef. Why the ship did not respond sooner is not clear. Questions have been raised about the capability of Cousins to handle a ship the size of *EV*, but Exxon claims he was licensed and qualified.

The *EV* is longer than three football fields and carried over 53 million gallons of crude oil. Going at 11 to 12 knots when it hit the reef, it suffered a 600-foot gash in its hull, and rocks punched large holes in the ship's bottom. The gush of oil into the Sound was so rapid that it caused three-foot waves on the water's surface. Cousins immediately called Hazelwood, who tried to free the ship but could not do so.

Ten hours after the grounding, Hazelwood failed a blood test administered by the Coast Guard. Testimony is clear that he had been drinking before the *EV* left port (two beers, he claims), but witnesses testified that he was not drunk aboard ship. Some hypothesized that he failed the test because of his drinking after the spill, but this is a question which will not be settled until court hearings, if then.

Since his college days, Hazelwood had been a heavy drinker of alcohol, although those who knew him said he always knew when to stop. His drinking did not stop his advancing rapidly with Exxon. He became a ship captain only ten years after graduating from the New York Maritime College. Arrested twice in 1984 for drunk driving, Hazelwood entered a twenty-eight-day alcohol rehabilitation program. He joined Alcoholics Anonymous and attended meetings regularly through 1988. Exxon claims that after the rehabilitation program the company closely monitored Hazelwood's behavior, including his command of the *EV*, which began in 1987. After the ship went aground, Exxon fired Hazelwood.[54]

THE DISASTER AND CLEANUP

When the *EV* was speared by Bligh Reef, it was seen as a major disaster by all observers. The oil quickly contaminated vast areas of the Sound; sea birds died by the thousands in the muck; sea otters and sea lions perished; the salmon, herring, and halibut appeared to be in imminent danger of contamination and death; and the beautiful shores of the Sound were awash with crude oil.

[54]Richard Behar, "Joe's Bad Trip," *Time*, July 24, 1989.

Despite years of planning and solemn pledges of assurance that even major oil spills could be contained rapidly and effectively, no one apparently was prepared to deal with a spill in the Sound as large as that of the *EV*. Problems ranged from shortages of equipment and skilled personnel to inadequate communications and management.

The primary responsibility for responding immediately to oil spills in the Sound rested with Alyeska Pipeline Service Co., an eight-company consortium that operates the Valdez oil terminal. It had a detailed contingency plan, approved by the federal government, Alaska, and the associated oil companies, but it proved incapable of handling a spill of the magnitude of the *EV*'s.

The contingency plans assumed a "most likely" spill of from 42,000 to 84,000 gallons. This probable spill assumption was based on experience from the opening of the oil line in 1977 to the time the plan was formulated. During this period, 8,700 tankers had hauled over 245 billion gallons of oil, spilling only 210,000 gallons. The plan said it would be inadequate for a large spill and, unfortunately, that was accurate.

Alyeska's response capability was severely weakened by its failure to continue field exercises to test its ability to respond to a major spill in the Sound. A round-the-clock team had been assigned to oil-spill cleanup, but was abandoned in 1981. The responsibility for cleanup was then assigned to other personnel of the company as an additional duty. Also, at the time of the *EV* spill, Alyeska's response barge was undergoing repairs. When it was made ready for action it was loaded with the wrong equipment. Instead of barrier booms to fight spills, it had emergency pumps to suck oil off tankers into smaller vessels. Reloading the boat and preparing it again for action lost precious hours.

It was not until 2:30 pm on March 24 that Alyeska's first containment equipment reached the grounded vessel. At 3:23 am the Coast Guard arrived at the stricken *EV* and estimated that the ship had already lost about 6 million gallons of oil.

Later that day, Alyeska tested a toxic chemical dispersant designed to dissolve oil. The test failed because the props of the helicopter used for the test blew the dispersant too widely for effectiveness. At this time, the Coast Guard and the state of Alaska rejected Exxon's request for widespread use of the chemical, a fact which Exxon insists seriously delayed cleanup efforts. Eventually, tests were successful, and authority was given for the agent's use. However, at the time less than 10,000 barrels of dispersant were available, far too little to deal with the spillage.

The cleanup proceeded on day two, but not enough skimmers were available. These machines suck up oil trapped in containment booms and pump it into accompanying barges. By the time skimmers and booms were in place, the oil had so widely dispersed that skimming was difficult, and only about 50,500 gallons were recovered. Furthermore, the cold water had begun turning the oil into a mass resembling chocolate mousse, which clogged the type of skimming equipment on hand.

Problems in assembling cleanup crews, coordinating their work, and communicating with many agencies interested and involved in the disaster further delayed the work.

On the third day, strong winds up to 70 miles an hour significantly disrupted cleanup efforts. Skimmer boats had to retreat into sheltered inlets. Coordination of crews was very difficult, a problem accentuated by a breakdown of electronic communications equipment. The winds also drove the oil slick 30 to 40 miles down the Sound. Winds so scattered the oil that dispersants became ineffective.[55]

As the slick spread, it became clear that the spill was out of control. By day seven the slick extended 90 miles down the Sound and covered over 100 square miles of water. By day 14 it was 180 miles down the Sound, by day 30 it was 280 miles, and by day 56 it was 470 miles.[56] At this time, the oil spread over 1,000 square miles of the Sound. Fearful of fish contamination, the State of Alaska in May closed the $12-million-a-year herring fishing industry, and in mid-June salmon fishing in the areas in the path of the spill was prohibited. Shrimp and black cod fisheries were also closed.

Within a few days, the area was flooded with people and equipment from federal and state government agencies, Exxon worldwide resources, and volunteers. At the peak of activity, in mid-summer, Exxon employed 14,000 people, 1,400 boats, and 85 aircraft. In addition, of course, were hundreds if not thousands of other people who volunteered or were employed by private and public agencies. Two observers described the scene this way:

> In some areas of Prince William Sound, cleanup activities are so frenetic that bays sheltering workers have come to resemble floating military encampments. Skiffs turn inshore waters into busy highways. Some coves drone like busy municipal airports as helicopters and small planes ferry in supplies or wing off on reconnaisance missions.[57]

All sorts of methods were used to clean up the mess. A squad of workers in yellow rain suits sprayed the rocks and shore with hot water to loosen the oil, and others then employed high-pressure hoses to push the oil residue to the water's edge. Workers then used cold-water hoses to flush oil to skimmers, where it was sucked into tanks. Some skimmers used an absorbent conveyor belt to pull thick "mousse" on board. Rollers then scrapped off the muck from the belt and moved it into barges. Hundreds of workers used hand methods to clean shorelines, from blotting oil with paper towels to digging gummy oil out of the ground with rakes and shovels.

---

[55]Ken Wells and Charles McCoy, "Out of Control: How Unpreparedness Turned Alaska Spill Into Ecological Debacle," *The Wall Street Journal,* April 3, 1989.

[56]Jerry Adler, "Alaska After Exxon," *Newsweek,* September 18, 1989. There seems to be a consensus that about 11,000,000 gallons of oil were spilled. The reader should know, however, that estimates vary greatly about such matters as miles of shoreline damaged with oil; birds, fish, and marine animals killed; the extent of ecological and economic damage; and costs. We believe that the estimates cited in the case are in the ballpark of reality.

[57]Ken Wells and Alanna Sullivan, "Stuck in Alaska: Exxon's Army Scrubs Beaches, but Many Don't Stay Cleaned," *The Wall Street Journal,* July 27, 1989.

Environmental Protection Agency scientists introduced a new cleanup method called bioremediation. This is a technique of spraying a nitrogen-phosphorus fertilizer mix on oil-laden shores. The substance promotes growth of microorganisms that are naturally present in the environment to degrade the oil.[58]

Exxon planned to complete its cleanup by mid-September, a schedule approved by various government authorities. This time of the year is a "natural deadline," because it marks the beginning of blustery cold winter weather which prevents effective cleanup operations.

IMPACT OF THE SPILL ON WILDLIFE

The birds, fishes, and marine animals in the Sound suffered egregiously from the oil spill. These creatures cannot live with oil. They were coated with oil and died in vast numbers. Experts believe that at least 100,000 birds died, including 150 eagles. At least 1,000 otters perished. There are no estimates for other mammals such as sea lions, seals, walruses, or whales, or how many fish perished or were so contaminated that they became a danger to other species that ate them.

Even a speck of oil on a bird's feathers can poison it, as it ingests the toxic substance during preening. Also, when oil coats feathers, they lose their insulating capability and deadly hypothermia sets in. Eagles ingest oil when they scavenge oil-soaked prey, causing possible kidney and liver damage. Also, the eagles, as well as other birds, carry the toxic substance to their nests and contaminate eggs and young birds.

Sea otters have very little body fat, and when oil mats their fur they lose buoyancy and insulation until they freeze to death or drown. Oil will also blind an animal. Many otters died because oil impaired their lung, kidney, and liver functions. No one knows how much damage was done to organisms at the bottom of the food chain.

Unfortunately, early spring is one of the worst times of the year for an oil spill. Birds are nesting, seals and sea lions are preparing to pup, and brown bears are stirring. Plankton begins to multiply. Millions of one-inch pink salmon, hatched in December, are about to be placed in pens floating in the bay, where they will feed on plankton until ready to be released into the Sound on their journey to the open sea.

Strenuous efforts were made by Exxon as well as voluntary groups and individuals to save as much wildlife as possible. For example otter rescue centers were established quickly by volunteers and Exxon. Early in the cleanup, as many as fifty boats were bringing otters to rescue centers for treatment. In April, however, the U.S. Fish and Wildlife Service ordered amateur otter rescuers to cease their activities because otters are mean and bite. Many people thought this was an incomprehensible order, but it stuck, and the number of rescue boats declined substantially. The fact remains that otters can be dangerous. One helicopter pilot almost lost his craft because an otter that had been thought dead suddenly revived, chewed through a sec-

[58]Bryan Hodgson, "Can the Wilderness Heal?" *National Geographic*, January 1990, p. 39.

tion of steel sheeting, and went on a rampage in the cockpit before being subdued.[59] Professional rescue centers continued their life-saving work.

Hundreds of paid workers and volunteers swarmed to the area to clean birds covered with oil. Scrubbing the birds with detergents and brushes, they saved thousands, but only a fraction of those contaminated.

LONGER-RANGE IMPACTS OF THE OIL SPILL ON THE SOUND

Although the short-range devastation of the oil spill was serious, the longer-range consequences appear to be minimal, from the perspective of the total environment of the Sound. Intensive investigations by scientists and others are now being undertaken by the state of Alaska, various federal agencies, and private organizations. Eventually, therefore, we shall have a thorough understanding of the long-range impacts. Most of the current investigators are now pledged to secrecy in light of pending legal battles. Most others who are free to talk support the view expressed above.

Representatives of the National Geographic Society visited the Sound immediately after the spill and were appalled at the devastation. Five months later they said they were surprised at the extent of the revival. One observed: "Incredibly, I found pink salmon spawning in a stream that had been choked with oil, and I smelled fresh seaweed on a pebble beach where native bacteria had eaten much of the oil away."[60]

Other observers agreed with this assessment. For example, Richard Barrett, head of Alaska's Division of Environmental Health laboratory, said: "We have tested 5,000 fish sent in by state inspectors and by native subsistence fisheries, and so far we have found no crude-oil contamination."[61]

The National Oceanic and Atmospheric Administration (NOAA) conducted numerous tests of fish contamination throughout the Sound and concluded: "So far we have found no hydrocarbons in their flesh, except for a few pink salmon from Kodiak that contained some traces in the parts-per-billion range."[62] The NOAA found no substantive effects on herring spawning, pink salmon, or salmon spawning.

Few seals and sea lions died after being touched with oil. Unlike otters, they rely on subcutaneous fat for warmth and do not freeze when their fur is oiled. Also, they do not groom like otters and do not, therefore, ingest oil. Lloyd Lowry of the Alaska Department of Fish and Games observed: "Harbor seals that look like they have been rolled in creosote are alive and acting normally."[63] Whales appear to have been unharmed.

While the initial impact on some species of birds was disastrous, the long-range effects appear to be unnoticeable. Impacts on nesting and body func-

---

[59]Charles McCoy, "Heartbreaking Fight Unfolds in Hospital for Valdez Otter," *The Wall Street Journal*, April 20, 1989.
[60]Bryan Hodgson, *op. cit.*, p. 8.
[61]*Ibid.*, p. 16.
[62]*Ibid.*, p. 12.
[63]Michael Satchell and Betsy Carpenter, "A Disaster That Wasn't," *U.S. News & World Report*, September 18, 1989, p. 63.

tions from ingestion will take time to develop and assess, but today they appear to be negligible, in light of the millions of birds and scores of species found in the area. Small marine organisms on shore were badly damaged by the crude oil, but after six months they appeared to be thriving.

The breakdown of oil after a spill favors a rapid fading of adverse impacts on life. As much as 25 percent of the oil evaporates within twenty hours of a spill and removes much of the toxicity in the oil. As time passes, solar radiation intensifies the evaporation process. Water combines with the oil to form an emulsion like mousse, as we noted previously. Eventually, wind and waves shape this mousse into pancakes which break up into tar balls. Some of the balls wash up on the shore. These are degraded biologically by microorganisms and leave asphalt-like hydrocarbons which are unsightly but not toxic. The cold water of the Sound and the composition of Prudhoe Bay crude produce tar balls that do not sink to the bottom of the Sound unless the oil picks up sand, rocks, or shells. Hence, bottom fish such as halibut and bottom organisms are little affected by the spill.[64]

Two observers described the beaches and water in the Sound in September 1989 this way: "Despite the oleaginous assault, the sublime beachscapes of Prince William Sound remain startlingly beautiful. Steep, spruce-covered mountains plunge down to craggy headlands and smooth-rock beaches. The blue-green water is clear. Gone are the devastating scenes of oil-slicked otters drowning by inches, and sea birds struggling to fly. The only visible traces of the Exxon Valdez oil are an occasional rainbow sheen on the water and dark bands of weathered oil, much like bathtub rings, along about 10 percent of the Sound's coastline."[65]

Oil scars remain on the most heavily damaged shores today, but experience with other spills leads to the conclusion that eventually nature will completely clean the environment. Scientists from the National Science Foundation and the NOAA studied the long-range impacts of the *Amoco Cadiz* disaster, which dumped 68 million gallons of oil on the beaches of France in 1978. They found that within three years most of the major impacts had disappeared, but the most heavily affected areas did not fully recover for ten to twelve years.[66] Some scientists believe recovery in the Sound will take half these two times with bioremediation.

The immediate economic consequences of the spill were felt unevenly. Many boat owners lost heavily when they were prevented from fishing. Others reaped handsome windfalls when Exxon hired them and their boats for the cleanup. All eventually were compensated by Exxon for their losses. Anyone in the Sound wanting to work on the cleanup could do so at good pay. Workers were paid $16.69 an hour for so-called "rock polishing" and cashed weekly pay checks of $1,800. Many individuals and businesses suffered because of the spill but the millions of dollars spent on the cleanup created a boom-town atmosphere.

[64]Bryan Hodgson, *op. cit.*, pp. 34–35.
[65]Satchell and Carpenter, *op. cit.*, p. 63.
[66]Hodgson, *op. cit.*, p. 12.

The long-range economic results remain to be felt. The tourist trade, for example, has declined, but no one knows for how long. The money spent by Exxon creates its own economic developments, with consequences not predictable.

COSTS OF THE SPILL

Preliminary figures for the dollar costs of the immediate cleanup have been announced by Exxon, but it is impossible to determine all costs, using that word in its broadest sense. These costs include the loss of wildlife; the consequences of shattering the tranquil, isolated way of life of the 6,000 people in the Sound; the results of the scorched image of oil companies, especially Exxon; the consequences of public policies which certainly will follow events in the Sound; and the polluted environment.

In July 1989, Exxon estimated that the cleanup cost would be $1.3 billion, one-third of which would be paid by insurers. Even to a company the size of Exxon (see the short study at the beginning of Chapter 1), this is a heavy cost. (Later estimates boosted the cost to $2 billion.) The company did not break down the total cost, but the bulk of it went to the army of workers, ships, and aircraft directly employed in the cleanup. The state of Alaska was paid $14.5 million, and the Coast Guard a comparable amount, in partial payment on their larger claims. Fisherman received compensation of $40 million, and municipalities $480,000. It will cost an estimated $25 million to repair the damaged tanker.

These costs, while large, will be substantially increased by lawsuits, adverse consumer reaction resulting in lost sales and profits, and new government regulations necessitating new expenditures for Exxon. The Department of Justice is expected to indict Exxon on criminal charges under provisions of the Clean Water Act, which provides stiff penalties for owners of vessels discharging oil into navigable waters of the United States. If found guilty, Exxon could suffer extremely large dollar penalties, and if managers are found to have been willfully negligent they may wind up in jail.

This is not the limit of Exxon's legal exposure. By early 1989, 150 suits, including 58 class actions, were filed against the company by local businesses damaged by the spill, environmentalists who seek a multi-billion-dollar cleanup fund, consumers who charge that gasoline prices were raised because of the spill, shareholders who say Exxon's mismanagement cost them dearly in the stock market, and opportunists who claim various losses. For instance, chiropractors allege they lost business because unemployed fisherman had fewer backaches than when working.[67]

Finally, there is damage to Exxon's image. As noted at the beginning of Chapter 1, this company has enjoyed an excellent reputation as a soundly managed firm that was socially responsible. That image was shattered.

---

[67]Michele Galen and Vicky Cahan, "Getting Ready for Exxon Vs. Practically Everybody," *Business Week,* September 25, 1989.

INDUSTRIAL GROWTH VERSUS ENVIRONMENTAL PRESERVATION

The *EV* oil spill raises new and exacerbates old oil policy issues. Indeed, the spill may be remembered more for its impact on public and oil company policy than for its damage to the Sound's environment.

The spill has intensified an old conflict between industry and environmentalists. An immediate consequence of the spill was to halt passage of a bill in the Congress to authorize oil exploration in the Artic National Wildlife Refuge (ANWR). This bill had the support of the Bush administration and many in the Congress. The ANWR lies about sixty miles east of Prudhoe Bay on Alaska's north slope and has promise of becoming a significant source of oil.

Environmentalists have been opposed to oil exploration in the ANWR because drilling rigs, buildings, storage pools, roads, and trucks would severely damage the fragile tundra. Now added to this objection is fear of the ecological consequences of big oil spills, like that of the EV.

Proponents of exploration in the ANWR point out that while there are still huge reserves of oil at Prudhoe Bay, the flow of oil will decline during this decade. ANWR, therefore, could take its place. Prudhoe Bay provides 25 percent of the nation's total production of oil and 40 percent of the crude oil on the West Coast. Our total oil production is declining, and we are becoming more dependent on foreign oil imports. This subjects the nation to many problems, such as higher oil prices and further imbalance in our foreign trade. So, argue the proponents of oil exploration, there are powerful economic reasons for drilling in the ANWR.

Similarly, for years there has been a conflict between environmentalists and those who favor drilling off our coasts. This argument also has tilted in favor of environmentalists because of the *EV* spill.

HOW SHOULD OIL INDUSTRY MANAGEMENTS RESPOND TO DISASTROUS OIL SPILLS?

There is a growing body of literature relating to crisis management, but Lawrence G. Rawl, CEO of Exxon, did not know about it or ignored it. He admitted, after being battered severely by shareholders who demanded his resignation, that "[o]ur public image was a disaster once that ship went on the rocks."[68]

Rawl's first public comment about the tragedy came one week after the accident, and then he said, "I don't want to point fingers, but the facts are, we're getting a bad rap on that delay," when speaking of the cleanup.[69] He later apologized to the public for the spill on a national television news program. Instead of going to Valdez, he sent a shipping executive and public relations personnel to field questions. It was not until President Bush sent three representatives to survey the spill that William Stevens, president of Exxon Co., U.S.A., went to Alaska. Rawl has persisted in blaming the Coast Guard and Alaskan officials for delaying Exxon's use of a dispersant agent,

[68]Stratford P. Sherman, "Smart Ways to Handle the Press," *Fortune,* June 19, 1989.
[69]*Ibid.*

although before congressional committees he said Exxon assumed full responsibility for the accident.

Rawl's low profile early in the disaster stands in sharp contrast to other successful managerial responses to crises. When deaths from cyanide-laced Tylenol were discovered in 1982, Chairman James Burke of Johnson & Johnson met with reporters within forty-eight hours to discuss the tragedy. A day after the Bhopal chemical leak in India (see the case at the end of Chapter 6), Chairman Warren Andersen held a news conference and then flew to India.

There are many lessons these and many other executives could have taught Exxon's management. Roger Ailes, former media adviser to President Bush, says it is imperative that executives have attitudes that will lead to correct behavior in crises. He says: "Many executives don't see public relations as part of their job description. They should." The first step, he says, is to acknowledge that the public has a legitimate interest in the company's affairs, "not just the public but employees, investors, bankers, legislators, regulators, neighbors, friends, and family."[70]

Ailes advises heads of corporations to develop a deep understanding of the media to know how to speak to journalists as well as television interviewers, how and with whom to share information, when to invite and/or respond to reporters, when to seek or accept invitations to appear on television, and how to use public relations staff effectively. Such rules have day-to-day applicability to corporate managers but are doubly important in times of crisis. There are many more guidelines, such as: respond quickly in facing the facts of a crisis, tell the truth, admit mistakes, don't blame others for your mistakes, and honestly seek means to rectify the crisis.

CONCLUDING COMMENTS

The *EV* spill raises a long list of significant and controversial issues: political, social, technical, legal, environmental, and economic. At present, there are many unanswered questions about precisely what happened to cause the *EV* to ground and about the subsequent flawed cleanup process. Questions arise about the long-range extent of damage to the environment, some of which will not be completely clear for years to come. The full impact of the spill on the lives, culture, and values of the people of the Sound will perhaps never be known. We await with uncertainty the long chain of consequences, good and bad, of new regulations which the spill makes inevitable.

QUESTIONS

1 From the facts in the case, who would you say was to blame for the oil spill and its devastation?
2 Discuss the costs of the *EV* spill, using cost in a broad sense. Do you think the costs likely to be incurred by Exxon will match the damages of the spill?

[70]*Ibid.*

3 Do you agree with the argument that since nature eventually cleans up even major oil spills, we should not restrict oil exploration because we badly need the oil?

4 Even Lawrence Rawl said that the company's handling of public relations after the oil spill was deplorable. Do you agree? If so, what do you think the company should have done?

5 Do you think that good public relations management in the event of crises is mere cosmetics to hide business failings, or a needed measure to put crises in proper perspective?

6 What new regulations, if any, do you believe the federal government, the states, and the oil companies should impose to prevent oil tanker accidents and spillage and to respond more effectively to spills once they occur?

SEVEN

Business and the Consumer

CHAPTER
16

Consumerism

The International Business Machines Corporation (IBM) has been built on three cornerstones—respect for the individual employee, customer service, and excellence in the performance of every job. These three principles were repeatedly emphasized by Thomas J. Watson, Sr., who led the company and its predecessors from 1914 to 1956, and by his son Thomas J. Watson, Jr., who led the company from 1956 to 1971. They are still the foundation of IBM's great success.

These three principles are interrelated. Management of IBM has been strongly committed to them, and they are institutionalized in the beliefs and behavior of people throughout the organization.

Our interest here centers on IBM's concern for consumers. In a little book called *A Business and Its Beliefs,* Thomas J. Watson, Jr., wrote:

> Years ago we ran an ad that said simply and in bold type, ''IBM Means Service.'' I have often thought it our very best ad. It stated clearly just exactly what we stand for....We want to give the best customer service of any company in the world.[1]

He went on to explain that this concept became reflex behavior in IBM. ''IBM's contracts,'' he continued, ''have always offered, not *machines* for rent, but machine services, that is the equipment itself and the continuing advice and counsel of IBM's staff.''[2] This policy means that IBM is committed to giving the best service possible, not some of the time, but all of the time. It means answering every customer complaint within twenty-four hours, not when convenient. It means marshaling all the resources of the company if necessary to solve a customer's problem.

[1]Thomas Watson, Jr., *A Business and Its Beliefs,* New York: McGraw-Hill, 1963, p. 29.
[2]*Ibid.,* p. 32.

This policy is regarded as a major reason for the phenomenal growth, present size, and superior strength of the company. Today it is the world's largest producer of computers and office equipment. In 1989, it was the fourth largest industrial firm in the United States. Its sales were $63.4 billion and its net profit was $3.8 billion.

When John F. Akers became IBM's CEO in 1985, the company showed signs of competitive softness. Sales were down, due largely to a shift from main frame computers (the great strength of IBM and a large money marker) to micro and mini machines. IBM faced tough competition in this market for the smaller computers. Customers were impatient, and critics were growing in numbers. Internally, according to several analysts, "arrogance, inertia, self-delusion, and plain old corporate flab had left the No. 1 computer maker in no shape to cope with its worst earnings slump ever."[3]

One of Akers' top priorities in combating this situation was to reinvigorate the philosophy enunciated by Thomas Watson, Jr., and subsequent CEOs. "The result was a renaissance in attention to customers," said one IBM executive to the authors. Akers emphasized that "the final arbiter of all that we do around here is our customer." The policy is to view IBM's business from the customer's point of view and to identify with the customer. George Conrades, head of U.S. marketing for IBM, instructs salespeople: When the customer asks for something, "Just say Yes." His policy for his troops is to tackle whatever the customer asks: to service other brands, to tie other computers to IBM computers, or to recover lost data after a disaster.[4]

For many years, IBM has had a set of policies and programs to stimulate, train, and reward sales and service personnel. They are now considered to be more important than ever. Included, for example, are basic sales training programs that last for about one year, programs to teach sales personnel how presidents and financial officers of companies think, employee attitude surveys to determine perceptions of how customer services are being maintained, and full-scale evaluations of why each loss of a customer has occurred. In addition, employee rewards, including incentive compensation, are geared to customer satisfactions, which are routinely measured.

IBM's dedication to consumer interests is part of a growing trend. Until recent years, government efforts to protect consumer interests were intermittent. They usually were stimulated by a shocking exposé or a visible disaster. Today, consumers and their representatives are continuously aggressive in demanding and getting better treatment from business, both through legislation and voluntarily. The movement, called *consumerism,* is widespread, organized, and powerful. It has resulted in an extraordinary expansion of federal consumer protective legislation during the past two decades. Although the movement currently has lost some of its momentum, there is still powerful support for it in this country. Consumerism embraces a wide range of public issues and problems for business managers.

[3]Geoff Lewis, Anne R. Field, John J. Keller, and John W. Verity, "Big Changes at Big Blue," *Business Week,* February 15, 1988.
[4]Joel Dreyfuss, "Reinventing IBM," *Fortune,* August 14, 1989.

This chapter begins with a definition of consumerism and the underlying forces driving it, followed by a brief résumé of the most significant recent consumer legislation and the major characteristics of the current consumer movement. We then discuss selected public and private policy issues centering on products and services, and false and deceptive advertising. Special emphasis is given to product risk and liability. The chapter concludes with a description of business response to consumerism.

THE CONSUMER MOVEMENT

Consumerism is a movement designed to improve the rights and powers of consumers in relation to the sellers of products and services. It is a protest movement of consumers against what they or their advocates see as unfair, discriminatory, and arbitrary treatment. Consumerism is as old as business but has taken on new dimensions in recent years.

The current consumer movement began in the mid-1960s and has continued ever since, but with diminished momentum in the past half-dozen years. Its beginning can be marked by a special message of President Kennedy to Congress on March 15, 1962. Momentum picked up a little with a few new pieces of legislation in 1964 and 1965, and an important boost was given to the movement by the publicity associated with the publication in 1965 of Ralph Nader's polemic (*Unsafe at Any Speed*) about General Motors' Corvair auto. The American public, which for so long had been patient about product and service abuses, began to express itself in strident ways. There was no rallying motto, but had there been, it well could have been one recommended by Denenberg: *"Populus iamdudum defatatus est"* ("The consumer has been screwed long enough").[5] Politicians heard: A flood of bills inundated Congress, and many were passed.

Broadly, the current consumer movement, is a mix of people, ideas, and organizations that represent previously unrepresented groups or concerns with the objective of bringing about change or reform. It is based on the proposition, as expressed by President Kennedy in his message and later by President Nixon in a special message to Congress about consumers, that the consumer has certain rights and that these rights have been violated. The rights in question include the rights to make intelligent choices among products and services; to have access to accurate and useful information; to register complaints and be heard; to be offered fair prices and acceptable quality; to have safe and healthful products; and to receive adequate service.

So powerful was this movement in the 1960s and 1970s that it led to an unprecedented expansion of federal legislation to protect consumers. Twenty-one major pieces of legislation were passed in the ten years from 1965 through 1975.[6]

---

[5]Quoted in *Newsweek*, March 5, 1973, p. 60.

[6]For an excellent account of the politics behind the rise of consumerism and new legislation see David Vogel, *Fluctuating Fortunes*, New York: Basic Books, Inc., 1989.

FORCES BEHIND CONSUMERISM

It seems paradoxical that the American consumer is the envy of the world for the quality and abundance of the products and services he or she consumes, and yet is dissatisfied with those products and services. Why the paradox? There are many explanations.

This is an age of discontent, of skepticism, and of challenge to established authority. Today's consumers are much better educated than those of the past, and they challenge practices that previous generations bore in silence. They question the authority of the uncontrolled marketplace. This is an age, too, of vocal expression of discontent; and consumers, fed up with actual or perceived bad treatment at the hands of manufacturers, advertisers, merchants, and repair services, are voicing their complaints.

Are the complaints justified? Every consumer would say yes, because every consumer has been frustrated with a variety of consumption problems. Businesspeople, however, claim that dissatisfied consumers represent only a small fraction of the total.

Like most products, the consumer movement has gone through a life cycle and is now in its maturity stage. This is evidenced by the fact that there has been no new major consumer legislation passed by the U.S. Congress since the mid-1970s. During the Reagan administration, consumer regulations were deemphasized. In this period, various polls showed that consumer interest in new regulations had declined. Today, however, consumer complaints are growing about a wide range of perceived problems. For example, consumers protest what they believe are excessive insurance rates, especially for automobiles. They are troubled about health hazards of pesticides used to produce foods. They worry about air and water pollution, toxic waste disposal, oil spills, and faulty airplanes. They cannot make sense out of labels on food packages, and are confused about contradictory health claims on food labels.

This is a sample of consumer concerns that give momentum to growing consumer demands for better implementation of old laws and new laws for problems not covered by old regulations. We seem to be on an up cycle in the consumer movement. No one today can say how much momentum the movement will generate.

HIGHLIGHTS OF RECENT CONSUMER LEGISLATION

In previous chapters, especially Chapters 9 and 10, we discussed consumer protective legislation. Virtually all of the older laws are still in force and have been strengthened and expanded with new legislation that responded to the consumer movement of 1965 to 1975.

Outstanding among the older laws were those concerning railroad rates and services, monopolistic practices in industry, maintenance of fair competition, protection against adulterated drugs and foods, and honest dealings in finance. Outstanding among the newer laws were those concerning labeling and information about product content and services offered, motor vehicle safety standards, hazardous toys and articles, protection from contaminated foods, safety standards for inflammable fabrics, controls over atomic products, warnings about health hazards of smoking, limits on consumer liability in the use of credit cards, child-resistant packaging of hazardous substances, unreasonable risks of injury associated with any consumer products, standards for drinking water and air, standards for pension programs, and standards for warranties offered by manufacturers and retailers. As we shall note later in this chapter, these laws have been expanded significantly by liberal judiciary rulings that favor consumers.

With such protective armor on the statute books, in regulatory agencies, and in the courts of law, the consumer can hardly be said to be the prey today of malevolent people in business. Yet new issues and abuses, which demand new protections, appear daily.

MAJOR CONSUMER-PROTECTION AGENCIES OF THE FEDERAL GOVERNMENT

It is estimated that today there are more than fifty federal agencies and bureaus performing between 200 and 300 functions that directly affect consumers. These numbers are easily exceeded in state and local governments although, as noted above, the overwhelming power to protect consumers lies in the federal government and in courts. The six major federal consumer protective agencies, together with their basic missions, are as follows.

1 The FTC promotes fair competition in interstate commerce which, of course, benefits consumers. The agency protects consumers from false and deceptive advertising and unfair trade practices, regulates packaging and labeling of consumer products, and ensures appropriate consumer credit disclosure and reporting.

2 The CPSC sets safety standards for consumer products. These standards cover design, construction, contents, performance, and labeling of hundreds of products. The agency, of course, has power to enforce its standards.

3 The NHTSA establishes motor vehicle safety standards, determines automobile fuel economy standards, enforces laws concerning automobile speed limits, and prohibits tampering with odometers.

4 The FDA regulates the safety, effectiveness, and labeling of food, drugs, cosmetics, and medical devices to protect the public against potential health hazards from these products. It is also responsible for setting standards for radiation exposure.

5 The Food Safety and Quality Service (FSQS) regulates the meat, poultry, and egg industries for safety and purity by inspecting all meat, poultry, and eggs shipped in interstate commerce. It also administers truth-in-labeling laws for these products.

6 The EPA establishes standards for air quality and pollution (including motor vehicles); water quality and pollution; hazardous waste disposal;

cleanup of hazardous dumps; pesticides; hazardous chemicals; noise levels for construction equipment, transportation equipment (except airplanes), and motors and engines.

As pointed out in Chapter 9, these agencies have a powerful influence over free-market activities. Within their areas of authority, which are vast, they make decisions that affect the production, pricing, content, purity, and design of products and services. They can stop production of a hazardous item, such as a dangerous toy. They can force the recall of defective products, such as automobile tires. They can delay the introduction of a drug until it is approved.

CONSUMER ADVOCATES

One of the phenomena of today's consumerism, in contrast with that of the past, is the rise of consumer advocates. These self-appointed promoters of the consumer are numerous. Probably the most publicized advocates are Ralph Nader and his "Raiders," as his legal staff is called. His role has been partly like that of the muckrakers of the past. But it goes further, to active representation of the consumer in the courts, government agencies, legislatures, and corporations. He has been a thorn in the side of business, and some people in business consider him to be a dangerous radical. But many other people, including businesspeople, believe that he has sought to achieve his objectives through, not against, our legal and political systems. Many observers believe that he has distorted or exaggerated the facts in numerous cases, but others believe that his motives are beneficial. Edward Rust, when president of the U.S. Chamber of Commerce, said that he was in full agreement with Nader when he concerned himself with the production of better products and services. "I think we are forced to the conclusion," he said, "that his commitment is to make the system work."[7]

Nader's greatest triumphs came in the 1960 and 1970s with the passage of many new consumer-protectionist laws. His influence continued when many of his staff assumed important positions in the Carter administration. But he also thereby lost his experienced people. At the same time, business responded strongly and was no longer the easy target it had been in the 1960s. Academicians began to calculate the costs of much of the new legislation, in contrast to their previous calculations of costs of government indifference. As a result, the movement lost its thrust in the mid-1980s.

Sparked by his activities in the consumer insurance revolt in California in 1988, he and his organizations once again became vigorous. Dominant in his current agenda are insurance reform, automobile safety, setting up group-buying organizations to reduce prices to consumers, and reforming government. Not only does he want government to extract more royalties for graz-

---

[7]Edward B. Rust, "Ralph Nader—Friend of U.S. Capitalism," speech before National Insurance Men's Meeting, Chicago, excerpted in *Los Angeles Times*, September 26, 1973.

ing rights, cut costs of drugs, and charge broadcasters rent for airways, but he wants the government to run more like our corporations.[8]

There are many other important consumer advocacy groups aside from Nader's organization. The Consumer Federation of America, for example, was formed in 1967 to bring together about 200 organizations (mostly state and local) with consumer interests. This organization may well represent some 30 million people. Consumers Union, founded in 1936, is basically an organization that disseminates information, especially in its magazine, *Consumer Reports,* to consumers.

Fundamentally, consumer advocates are reformists. On balance, they probably have served the best interests of consumers, business, and the community. However, many of them are polemicists, and their "factual" assertions, arguments, and policy recommendations must be examined critically in that light.

BUSINESS-ORIENTED INTEREST GROUPS AND ORGANIZATIONS

To round out the picture of the interest groups that address consumer issues, we should mention many groups inside and outside of business organizations that have responded to consumer advocates, sometimes positively and sometimes negatively, and also have initiated programs in the interests of consumers. Business organizations such as the U.S. Chamber of Commerce and the Business Roundtable vigorously advance the business point of view, especially in legislative debates. Not-for-profit organizations such as the American Enterprise Institute are presumably objective but lean to conservative positions.

Also of importance are groups formed to deal with special problems. To illustrate, the Consumer Research Institute was created by the Grocery Manufacturers Association to study consumer complaints and inform grocery manufacturers about those it believes to be valid and widespread. The tobacco industry established the Council for Tobacco Research to study the effects of tobacco on health. To complete this abbreviated list of organizations, we note the Better Business Bureau, a long-established institution in cities and towns, which is supported by business interests to deal with consumer complaints. The above discussion underscores the point that there is no scarcity of consumer issues nor organizations to address them. We turn now to a few of the more pressing consumer issues.

CONSUMER PRODUCT ISSUES

A cluster of issues relate to products. Before discussing a few of them, it is important to comment on the cost/price/quality questions that intrude in both business and governmental decision making about products.

[8]Thomas A. Stewart, "The Resurrection of Ralph Nader," *Fortune,* May 22, 1989.

Generally speaking, the decision-making processes in business involve many complex trade-offs among various forces. For example, product quality is one variable in decisions concerning a product. The higher the quality sought, the higher the price that must be charged. The higher the price, the lower will be the demand for the product. The lower the demand, the fewer products will be produced. If more products are produced, the cost per unit can be reduced. At what point do price, potential sales, quality, product design, and other factors balance? Balancing such factors is an extremely intricate process for which there usually are no formulae to produce the decision. Human judgment is an essential, and generally final, determinant of a decision. This concept of trade-offs is very important in appraising the managerial response to consumerism.

Highly relevant in this discussion is a point made previously that government regulatory standards set without any reference to costs can be extremely and unnecessarily expensive to the general public. It seems that a sensible approach to regulation is to weigh the costs and benefits of a proposed regulation to determine whether the equation is balanced properly. Although a final standard may not be determined by the cost-benefit equation, the method raises appropriate questions about a standard. In government, as in business, decision makers must consider and balance a multiplicity of factors.

PRODUCT SAFETY

Product safety is one of the major issues facing business today. Despite the powerful agencies noted above that are concerned with product safety, the issue is still a burning one among consumers. The CPSC, for example, estimates that consumer products contribute annually to the deaths of 29,000 people and injure 33 million more. This is, of course, a worrisome matter.

The authority of the CPSC illustrates the scope of federal product safety regulations. This agency is directed by six major pieces of legislation to "protect the public against unreasonable risks of injuries and deaths associated with consumer products."[9] The more serious risks include amputation, electocution, burns, asphyxiation, and cancer. It regulates every consumer product except guns, boats, planes, cars, trucks, foods, drugs, cosmetics, and pesticides, which are in the province of other federal agencies. Even with these exclusions, its mandate is formidable, since it must oversee 15,000 classes of products, work with thousands of manufacturers, and address the complaints of millions of consumers.

To make its task manageable, the agency identifies each year a limited number of priorities. In FY 1987 and FY 1988 the list was riding mowers and garden tractors; all-terrain vehicles; child drownings in residential swimming

[9]The six laws are the Consumer Product Safety Act (1972), the Flammable Fabrics Act (1953), the Federal Hazardous Substances Act (1960), the Poison Prevention Packaging Act (1970), the Refrigerator Safety Act (1956), and the Toy Safety Act (1969).

pools; fire combustion toxicity; safety for older consumers; and poison prevention.

The agency works to prevent injury and death through these programs:

• Working with industry to develop voluntary safety standards.
• Issuing and enforcing mandatory standards, where appropriate.
• Banning products for which no feasible standards would adequately protect the public.
• Obtaining the recall or repair of products that fail to comply with mandatory standards or that present substantial hazards or imminent hazards to consumers.
• Conducting research on potential hazards.
• Conducting information and education programs.

There is no doubt that these programs have reduced injuries and deaths. Unsafe products have been recalled and redesigned. The educational programs initiated by the agency have alerted consumers to hazards and taught them to use products more safely. For example, the Commission claims that since its inception it has initiated over 1,500 product recalls or other corrective actions involving over 200 million products.

The CPSC, however, has been criticized for not doing enough. Critics claim that the agency relies too much on voluntary agreements with product manufacturers and has been too lenient in allowing industry to police itself. They look at the declining budgets of the agency and wonder, in light of the monumental and important task that it has, whether they are sufficient. The CPSC budget declined from $43 million in 1980 to $32 million in 1988, and is projected at that level through FY 1990. In the meantime, staff dropped from 978 to 519. Critics claim that during this period the Commissioners appointed to run the agency were more committed to deregulation than product safety.[10] Two commissioners said in their defense that they were conservatives who believed in a voluntary approach to enforcement.[11]

Another federal agency concerned with consumer product safety is the National Highway Traffic Safety Administration (NHTSA). This agency has authority over safety and emission features of automobiles. A short list of the items for which the agency has set safety standards includes: seat and shoulder belts, windshield defrosting and defogging systems, door latches and hinge systems, lamps, theft protection, head restraints, improved side-door strength, reduced flammability of interior materials, hydraulic brakes, improved bumpers, leak-resistant fuel systems, and many controls over engine exhaust emissions.

There is no doubt that such safety features reduce automobile injuries and deaths. On the other hand, these safety features have cost consumers. In ad-

[10]Michael deCourcy Hinds, "Troubles of a Safety Agency: A Battle to Keep Functioning," *The New York Times,* March 18, 1989; and Steven Waldman, "Kids in Harm's Way," *Newsweek,* April 18, 1988.
[11]Jeanne Saddler, "Consumer Safety Agency's Role Is Questioned Amid Charges Over Its Chairman's Leadership," *The Wall Street Journal,* September 23, 1987.

dition to the direct cost, which is well over $1,000 per car (or over $10 billion in a normal car production year), are alternative costs. It is argued, for example, that for the same amount of money, traffic accidents could be more effectively reduced by better marked roads and intersections, installing breakaway traffic lights and signs, padding abutments and concrete pillars, placing a cap on driving speeds, and taking more vigorous action against drunk driving.[12] All these programs should be pushed in the interests of consumer safety.

Two other agencies, the FDA and the EPA, have very important responsibilities for product safety and will be discussed later in the chapter.

RISK AND PRODUCT SAFETY

Consumer protection agencies face several questions. How safe is safe? How much risk should consumers be expected to assume? What is the role of government in balancing risk, safety, and other considerations in consumer protection? These are enormously difficult questions to answer. One might oversimplify by saying that the moment one jumps out of bed in the morning, one assumes risk and faces product safety questions. Chlorine can react with organic matter in drinking water to produce carcinogens. Stored peanuts can develop a mold that produces a potent carcinogen named aflatoxin. Aspirin is safe and therapeutic when properly used but when used improperly it can kill.

"Too safe" may involve costs so high that consumers cannot buy the product; "too unsafe" causes needless injuries and loss of lives. Acceptable risks must be tolerated. But what are such risks? What is a minimum risk? Can a $20 power tool be expected to be as safe as a $500 one? Are products supposed to be safe even when used by boobs and idiots?

In the last chapter we found that assessing environmental risks is an extraordinarily difficult problem. There are no general measures of minimally safe levels of many environmental substances. Much the same thing can be said for risks in product use.

Yet regulatory agencies of necessity have had to address the question: What is a "reasonable" risk? Edwards defined a reasonable risk:

> as one where a consumer (a) understands by way of adequate warning or by way of public knowledge that a risk is associated with the product; (b) understands the probability of occurrence of an injury; (c) understands the potential severity of such an injury; (d) has been told how to cope with the risk; (e) cannot obtain the same benefits in less risky ways at the same or less cost; (f) would not, if given a choice, pay additional cost to eliminate or reduce the danger; and (g) voluntarily accepts the risk to get the benefits of the product.[13]

[12]For a discussion of these points see Murray L. Weidenbaum, *Business, Government, and the Public*, Englewood Cliffs, New Jersey: Prentice Hall, 1986.

[13]Alfred L. Edwards, "Consumer Product Safety: Challenge for Business," *University of Michigan Business Review*, 1975, p. 19.

These are lofty but useful generalizations. Still, how is a reasonable risk established for a particular product? How does one calculate risks of safety for a large commercial aircraft with its thousands of parts or of the space shuttle? How far should an agency go in protecting consumers from specific product hazards? How far should the CPSC go, for example, in protecting consumers from hazards associated with electric lawn mowers? How far should NHTSA go in trying to protect drivers of automobiles?

THE DELANEY CLAUSE AND FOOD ADDITIVES

The Delaney Clause is a good illustration of the capacity of Congress to enact specific laws. It bars the approval by the FDA of any carcinogenic food additive. The clause allows no tolerance in prohibiting the addition to food of any substance known to produce cancer in any species, in any dosage, and under any circumstances. This clause, an amendment in 1958 to the Food, Drug, and Cosmetic Act of 1938, has raised enormous administrative problems.

The first major ruling under this clause was the decision by the Secretary of Health, Education, and Welfare to remove from the market after January 1, 1970 all cyclamate-sweetened soft drinks and soft-drink mixes. This ruling was made on the basis of research showing that six of twelve rats that were given the equivalent of fifty times maximum recommended lifetime daily consumption developed an ''unusual'' form of bladder cancer. (For a person to ingest as much cyclamate as the rats, it would be necessary to drink several cases of cyclamate-sweetened soft drinks every day for most of a normal human life span!) Since this decision was made, a number of other products have been removed from the market because of similar tests on laboratory animals.

One FDA decision that was not accepted, however, concerned saccharin, an artificial sweetener. In 1977, the FDA proposed to ban saccharin in processed foods and drinks, while permitting its continued sale to consumers who wanted to add it to food themselves for medical reasons. Soft-drink manufacturers, consumers, and others strongly objected to the ruling, and Congress delayed the ruling for two years. The Congress has extended the moratorium since then.

One can expect continuing controversy over the Delaney Clause. The FDA has primary responsibility for food safety with respect to 2,700 ''direct'' food additives, thirty-three color additives, and thousands more ''indirect'' additives that may get into foods through ingredients in packaging materials. The issue therefore is not a negligible one.

This point is confirmed by the fact that the Delaney Clause is an open invitation for ingenious toxicologists to find cause to outlaw even the most innocuous substances. Experimentalists, for example, have created tumors with hundreds of common food substances from eggs to salt. New instruments are capable of detecting traces of substances at the level of one part in a trillion. ''The result,'' says one observer, is that almost everything anyone eats can be shown to contain carcinogens. If, for instance, a tin can is soldered, and if the solder contains lead, and if lead is a carcinogen in test animals, and if detectable traces of it migrate into the contents of the can—all of which is indisputably the case—why, then, the FDA can be accused of being less than diligent if it doesn't outlaw tin cans.[14]

The FDA has found itself increasingly facing zealots who press for bans on substances that may save more lives than could be saved by a ban. For instance, one physicist calculated when the FDA was pressed to ban saccharin that the substitution of diet for nondiet soft drinks would increase life expectancy by 100 times more than the cancer risk of saccharin would reduce it. Secretary of Health and Human Services Margaret Heckler lamented that strict interpretation of the Delaney Clause had put her agency into a scientific straitjacket. She was referring specifically to a proposed ban on the dye used in lipstick. She said that a woman would have to ingest 600 lipsticks a day to consume the quantity of dye that causes cancer.

The FDA has sought to avoid banning substances that were in minuscule quantities in foods and that cause no harm.[15] A door was opened for the agency by the U.S. Court of Appeals for the District of Columbia Circuit in *Monsanto Company v. Kennedy*.[16] The court said: "There is latitude inherent in the statutory scheme to avoid literal application of the statutory definition of 'food additive' in those *de minimus* situations that, in the informed judgment of the Commissioner, clearly present no public health or safety concerns." Thus, under the de minimus legal doctrine, the FDA might know that a substance was present in a food but disregard it. (The de minimus doctrine means that the law does not concern itself with trifles.)

On her last day in office early in 1986, Secretary Heckler ruled that a chemical used to decaffeinate coffee could be allowed under the clause. This chemical, methylene chloride, was found to cause cancer in laboratory tests. In one case, rats were fed doses equal to 12 million cups of decaffeinated coffee a day. (This chemical is also an excellent solvent and flame suppressant and is used widely in paint removers, aerosols, and hair sprays.) In making her decision, the secretary was applying the de minimus doctrine to a new mathematical technique that the agency had been developing for many years called quantitative risk assessment. This technique enables scientists to infer the risks of additives to human beings from the data collected in laboratory tests. The calculation for methylene chloride, for example, showed that if a person drank no more than five five-ounce cups of decaffeinated coffee a day, there would be a one in 1 million chance that the person's risk of developing cancer would increase. This approach is in agreement with many opponents of the Delaney Clause who insist that the cancer impact on a human being is in the dosage of an additive, not the substance itself. Still, how-

---

[14]Tom Alexander, "Time for a Cease-Fire in the Food-Safety Wars," *Fortune*, February 26, 1979, p. 94.

[15]Richard M. Cooper, "Stretching Delaney Till It Breaks," *Regulation*, November–December 1985.

[16]613 F.2d 947, 954 (D.C. Cir. 1979).

ever, many public interest groups and consumer activists take the position that no level of risk is acceptable.

Some color additives—Orange No. 17, and Red No. 19—have been shown to produce tumors in animals, but the FDA has refused to ban them. The FDA claimed that it could except them under the de minimus doctrine. The agency said that the maximum risk to humans exposed to drugs and cosmetics containing the colors were, respectively, one in nineteen billion and one in nine million. The estimated risk, said the FDA, was well below the level of any other additive deemed to be safe. The FDA decision was challenged, and in 1987 a U.S. District Court in Washington, D.C., ruled against the FDA, saying that the Delaney Clause ruled out the type of discretion the FDA applied in refusing to ban the additives. Unless Congress changes the law, and it does not seem inclined to do so, the FDA is likely to go on trying to find means to avoid banning additives with no or little risk to humans, and the courts will decide how far, if at all, the Delaney Clause can be stretched.[17]

PESTICIDES AND UNAVOIDABLE CARCINOGENS IN FOODS

The District Court in the above decision closed the discretionary door on food additives. However, two other measures approved by the Court open wide the door to food hazards. The Food, Drug, and Cosmetic Act (1938) says that when the addition of any poisonous or deleterious substance to food is required in the production of it or cannot be avoided by good manufacturing practice, the Secretary of Health and Human Services "shall promulgate regulations limiting the quantity therein or thereon to such extent as he finds necessary for the protection of public health." The Secretary has designated the FDA to enforce this provision of the Act, and the FDA has interpreted this provision to permit it to establish "tolerance levels" for such substances.

This interpretation has been tested and approved by the Supreme Court. Two public interest groups and a consumer sued the FDA when it authorized the shipment of a harvest of corn to be used for livestock and poultry feed so long as aflatoxin in the grain did not exceed 100 ppb. Aflatoxin is a potent carcinogen, but the FDA said that in the small quantities allowed it was not injurious to public health. The plaintiffs obviously disagreed. In an 8-1 decision, the Supreme Court upheld FDA authority to establish minimum standards for poisonous and deleterious substances in food when the public health was protected.[18]

The second legal authority over hazardous substances in foods is the Federal Insecticide, Fungicide, and Rodenticide Act of 1947. This act authorizes the EPA to set maximum safe levels for pesticide residues in human and an-

---

[17]For a comprehensive analysis of the Delaney Clause see Richard A. Merrill, "FDA's Implementation of the Delaney Clause: Repudiation of Congressional Choice or Reasoned Adaptation to Scientific Progress?" *Yale Journal on Regulation,* Winter 1988.

[18]*Frank Young, Commissioner of Food and Drug Administration, Petitioner v. Community Nutrition Institute et al.,* no. 85–664, argued April 30, 1986, decided June 17, 1986.

imal food. The EPA also may ban or restrict the use of pesticides permanently or at selected times and places.

Both these measures and the Delaney Clause must be remembered in the controversy swirling about carcinogens in the food supply. They tend to overlap, and they each are embroiled in ever more arcane legal battles over the meaning of words and phrases. On the one side are those who insist that no known carcinogen must be tolerated in foods, irrespective of what that would cost. On the other side are those who insist that such action would impose intolerable costs on society that are unnecessary because tolerable limits do not impair the public health.

How safe is food? Most scientists believe that the cancer threat from pesticides is miniscule compared with everyday risks such as smoking, chloroform in ordinary tap water, or natural substances in foods. However, there are enough uncertainties about what is known about pesticides and other food hazards, as well as what happens in the processing and distribution of foods, to raise questions about the adequacy of current regulations and practices. This subject is far too big and complex to be treated here, but a few comments are appropriate.

The case of Alar, a chemical used to regulate the growth of some red apples, illustrates a worrisome type of consumer problem. In late February 1989, a public interest group published a report that said school children faced serious risks from eating chemically treated apples and apple products. The story was aired on talk shows and in the newspapers. Immediately, school boards removed apples from school lunches, grocery stores stopped selling apples, sales of apples and apple juice plummeted, and the FDA and EPA were accused of failure to stop the use of Alar.

The scientific community almost unaminously said the risks of cancer from eating apples treated with Alar were virtually nil. An ad hoc group of fourteen prominent scientists called the risks from approved agricultural chemicals negligible or nonexistent and said flatly that the "public's perception of pesticide residues and their effects on the safety of the food supply differs considerably from the facts."[19] The fact is that Alar does produce a possible carcinogen (daminozide), but in minute quantities. Anyway, only 5 to 10 percent of apple orchards were treated with Alar at the time.

A troubling aspect of the Alar incident is that a complicated scientific issue was decided by individuals throughout the country rather than by officials charged with the responsibility for determining what should and should not be tolerated in foods. The case was decided not upon any hard evidence but by a frightened public acting on incorrect media reports. Professor Bruce Ames, chairman of the biochemistry department at the University of California, Berkeley, tells us that many foods contain natural toxins at much higher levels than residues of dangerous pesticides. Fruits and vegetables produce such sustances, he says, to repel insects, fungi, and other predators. Ames points out that up to 10 percent of a plant's weight is made up of natural

---

[19]Malcolm Gladwell, "A Consuming Matter of Apples," *The Washington Post National Weekly Edition*, May 17, 1989.

pesticides.[20] The ordinary potato contains 150 chemicals before it is sprayed with pesticides. Most scientists affirm that by the time a food gets to the market, very little pesticide residue remains. In 1987, the FDA tested 14,492 food samples for pesticides. About one-third of the sample were fruits and vegetables and fewer than 1 percent had residues that exceeded the legally allowable EPA levels. In 57 percent of the items, no pesticides were found.[21]

Nevertheless, there are troubling aspects to hazards in the food chain. Restrictions in foreign countries on the use of pesticides and additives are not as strong as in this country, and we import as much as 25 percent of our fruit and vegetables. Little of this is tested when it arrives on our shores. Critics claim that EPA has no way to measure the combined effects of ingesting many different pesticides. A major concern of Frank Young, commissioner of the FDA, "is microbiological contaminantion of food."[22] The spread of bacteria is growing, and millions of people get some form of food poisoning each year. Few die from it, however, and all have the ability to avoid it. Most food poisoning comes from a few bacteria such as *salmonella* and *staphylococcus aureus*. An individual has the power to eliminate such germs by handling, storing, and preparing foods properly.

MANUFACTURING LIABILITY FOR DEFECTIVE PRODUCTS

Consumers sometimes are injured in using products. The question of liability long has been a matter of concern for the courts, business managers in the chain of manufacture and distribution, and, of course, consumers. Until recent years consumers had difficulties in collecting damages from anyone, especially the original manufacturer. More recently, however, laws and judicial rulings have expanded importantly the liabilities of manufacturers and have permitted consumers to collect greater damages from them. A discussion of some of the milestones in this evolution follows.

Until a few years ago manufacturers were well protected from consumer liability suits. An injured plaintiff proceeded to collect damages through either contract or tort law. Under contract law the disgruntled consumer had to plea that the manufacturer was bound by a warranty (implied or expressed) that the product was reasonably fit to do what it was supposed to do without injury to the user. In the absence of a direct contract between the manufacturer and the consumer, called "privity," the courts would argue that the plaintiff had no case against the producer but had to go to the retailer. If the retailer lost a suit, he or she would sue the wholesaler, and the wholesaler in turn, the manufacturer. This seldom resulted in redress to consumers.

If the injured consumer used tort law, he or she had to argue that a manufacturer was negligent in producing a product. This was very difficult to prove because courts of law found manufacturers not guilty if they exercised reasonable care in producing a product, whether or not it caused injury.

[20]Gisela Bolte and Dick Thompson, "Do You Dare to Eat a Peach?" *Time*, March 27, 1989.
[21]*Ibid*.
[22]Tufts University Diet and Nutrition Letter, Special Report, vol. 6, no. 6, August 1988, p. 3.

EXPANDING MANUFACTURER LIABILITY

The first major change occurred in 1916, when General Motors was held liable, irrespective of privity, for injuries resulting from the use of its products in the case of *MacPherson v. Buick Motor Company.*[23] In this case, a wheel was found defective when it fell off while the car was going fifteen miles per hour. In 1962, the court held that "it is highly unrealistic to limit a purchaser's protection to warranties made directly to him by his immediate seller. The protection he really needs," said the court, "is against the manufacturer whose published representations caused him to make the purchase."[24] As a result of such decisions, it is now possible for injured consumers to sue and have a good chance of collecting damages from manufacturers when they are injured by a product that is defective. Unfortunately, the courts have not been consistent in determining precisely what is a defective product.

There also have been important changes in tort law. Now it is held that a manufacturer is liable for unfit products that unreasonably threaten a consumer's personal safety. This is called strict liability under tort and means that liability exists when a wrong is done. In a crucial case in 1962, the doctrine held, and the court said: "A manufacturer is strictly liable in tort when an article he places on the market, knowing that it will be used without inspection, proves to have a defect that causes injury to a human being."[25] Thus, it is not necessary to prove fault on the part of the manufacturer. It is only necessary to show that the product was defective when sold, and caused injury.

Subsequent court decisions substantially widened the liability of manufacturers. A few illustrations in this evolution follow. General Motors Corporation, in a case in 1968, was held responsible for designing products that minimized risks of injury in a collision. If the company did not do so, said the court, it was liable for damages.[26] In 1975, the California Supreme Court said that when a manufacturer changed or improved a product line after the manufacture and sale of a product that caused an injury, the changed design was proof of a design defect in the original product.[27] A year later, a New York court said that even when an injured plaintiff knew of a danger inherent in using a product, that would not defeat the claim if the manufacturer could reasonably have guarded against the danger in designing the product.[28] In 1983, the New Jersey Supreme Court said in effect that the manufacturer had the responsibility for warning of dangers that were not only undiscovered but were scientifically undiscoverable at the time the products were first introduced for use in the workplace.[29]

---

[23]217 N.Y. 382, 111 N.E. 1050 (1916).
[24]*Randy Knitwear v. American Cyanamid,* 181 N.E.2d 402, N.Y.—(1962).
[25]*Greenman v. Yuba Power Products, Inc.,* 377 P. Cal.2d 897 (1963).
[26]*Larson v. General Motors Corporation,* 391 F.2d 495 8th Cir. (1968).
[27]*Ault v. International Harvester Company,* 117 California Reporter 812. Supreme Court of California, in Banc. December 12, 1974.
[28]*Micallef v. Miehle Co.* 384 N.Y.S. 2d 115. Court of Appeals of New York, April 8, 1976.
[29]*Bashada et al. v. Johns-Manville Products Corporation et al.,* 51 U.S. 2038 (N.J. Supreme Court, July 7, 1982).

In 1984, the court held a vaccine manufacturer liable because he did not identify specifically the risk of "serum sickness" that beset the plaintiff.[30] Astonishingly, there is no epidemiological evidence that the flu vaccine in question can produce that illness. A dissenting judge commented that "the practical consequence...is to impose so stringent a warning requirement as likely to render any future mass inocculation program infeasible, no matter how desirable."[31] That is precisely what happened. In the 1960s, there were about a dozen companies doing research in this area. Today there are two—Connaught Biosciences Inc., and Lederle Laboratories—and they were pressured to stay in the business by the government.

The scope of liability was further broadened by a concept of "joint and several liability." It works this way. The driver of a bumper car at Disney World was injured when her car was struck by the bumper car driven by her fiancé. The jury found the fiancé 85 percent responsible for the injury, the plaintiff 14 percent responsible, and Disney World 1 percent responsible. Later, but before the trial, the plaintiff married her fiancé. Under Florida law, the husband was immune from suit by the wife. As a result, Disney World had to pay for all of the damages not attributable to the plaintiff.[32]

Robert H. Malott, who headed a Business Roundtable task force on product liability, concluded that lawsuits against corporate defendants with deep pockets "have turned the courts, in effect, into an erratic, back door system of nationalized health and accident insurance, financed by corporate insurance premiums."[33]

GROWTH OF PRODUCT LIABILITY LAW SUITS AND AWARDS

Paralleling the widening of manufacturer liabilities has been a substantial increase in both legal suits and jury awards. Product liability filings in federal courts grew from under 2,000 in 1974 to about 14,000 in 1986, and leveled off in 1987 and 1988. Three products were the subject of most of this rise—asbestos, the Dalkon Shield, and bendecin. Without these product-related cases, the growth was from a little under 2,000 in 1974 to under 6,000 in 1981, and only slight growth since then. Comparable data are not available for state courts. Although cases initiated vary greatly among the states and in each state from time to time, the trends have been broadly the same.[34] No one knows the total cost of our liability system, but estimates are $40 billion a year and up, over half of which go for legal fees and other administrative costs.

These numbers add up to a "liability crisis," the severity of which has eased in the last few years, but the root causes remain.

[30]*Petty v. United States*, Eighth Circuit Court of Appeals (1984).
[31]Edmund W. Kitch, "Vaccines and Product Liability," *Regulation*, May/June 1985.
[32]*Walt Disney World Co. v. Wood*, 515 So.2d 198 (Fla. 1987).
[33]Robert H. Malott, "Let's Restore Balance to Product Liability Law," *Harvard Business Review*, May–June 1963, p. 24.
[34]General Accounting Office, "Product Liability: Extent of 'Litigation Explosion' in Federal Courts Questioned," Washington, D.C.: General Accounting Office, January 1989.

THE IMPACT OF PRODUCT LIABILITY

In an effort to determine the impacts of the product liability system on American firms, The Conference Board surveyed CEOs of both large and small companies.[35] Four out of ten of the respondents to the survey said the system had a major impact on their companies. By major impact is meant a significant rise in insurance and administrative costs, plant closing, employee layoffs, product withdrawal, discontinuance of research, a decision not to introduce a product, loss of market share, or movement of production to an overseas location. Thirty-eight percent of the CEOs said the impact on their firms was moderate, and only 20 percent said the impact was minimal. Fifty-eight percent of the CEOs whose firms had annual sales less than $50 million said the impact on them was major. Only 14 percent said it was minimal.

Table 16-1 shows that the most frequently cited adverse impact—47 percent—was discontinued product lines. We noted the case of vaccines. There are many others, for example football helmets, machinery, off-the-road vehicles, and small airplanes.

The second most important impact noted in Table 16-1 is deciding not to introduce a product. For instance, Richard Mahoney, CEO of Monsanto, says that his company developed a substitute material for asbestos but that he shelved this new phosphate-fiber product, fearing that plaintiffs' lawyers who had brought more than 75,000 suits over asbestos would next attack this substitute which Monsanto says is perfectly safe.

These and the other reports of adverse impacts are disturbing. Not noted in the table is management and staff time devoted to litigation. This was a complaint of many CEOs. A number of CEOs complained that the costs of product liability insurance put their companies at a disadvantage in world markets because the European code of product liability, for example, limits damage suits. The CEO of Dow Chemical said that his firm in 1986 had $100 million of insurance expenses in the United States, but only $20 million for

[35]E. Patrick McGuire, *The Impact of Product Liability*, New York: The Conference Board, 1988.

TABLE 16-1 PERCENTAGE OF COMPANIES REPORTING ADVERSE IMPACTS OF PRODUCT-LIABILITY COURT DECISIONS

Type of impact	Percent of firms reporting impact
Closed production plants	9
Laid off workers	16
Discontinued product lines	47
Decided against introducing new products	39
Decided against acquiring/merging	22
Discontinued product research	25
Moved production offshore	4
Lost market share	22

Source: E. Patrick McGuire, *The Impact of Product Liability*, New York: The Conference Board, 1988, p. 20. Based on responses from 264 companies.

comparable coverage overseas, where the company made half its total sales. In 1987, Dow defended 456 suits in the United States, compared with 4 outside this country.

BENEFICIAL EFFECTS OF PRODUCT LIABILITY EXPERIENCE

Nearly half the companies represented in The Conference Board survey said that actual experience with product liability had improved their products and warning materials. A third said they had redesigned their products, and a third said they had improved their product safety. The survey revealed that even among the companies that had not actually experienced liability problems, there was considerable improvement in product design, safety, and warning of use.

Many CEOs noted, however, that these results could not be entirely attributed to the liability system. There were many other reasons, including new technology, company image, competition, and the resurgence of the significance of quality in products.

BUSINESS EFFORTS TO REFORM PRODUCT LIABILITY LAWS

The business community has exerted pressure on both the Congress and state legislatures for reforming the product liability laws. None have been passed by the Congress, but a few states have acted. For example, fourteen states narrowed joint and several liability; thirteen states have modified laws concerning punitive damages; and a few states penalize attorneys for bringing frivolous suits to the court. Efforts to reduce awards for pain and suffering, however, have not fared well.[36] The future of limiting punitive damages is clouded by a 7-2 decision by the U.S. Supreme Court in June 1989. The case involved the Eighth Amendment to the Constitution, which prohibits levying excessive fines or the infliction of unusual punishment. The Court said that this clause limits government prosecutors, but it does not limit private citizens who sue other citizens or companies in court.[37]

The topic of product liability reform is high on the agenda of business. A significant recent set of recommendations was made in a comprehensive 174-page study by the Committee for Economic Development, an old and respected organization composed of top business leaders.[38] Some of the more important proposals of this study, and those contained in current bills before the Congress, are as follows.

- A cap should be placed on punitive damages.
- Plaintiffs should be required to prove a specific act of corporate negligence, as opposed to identifying only a product defect, which is all that is required in virtually every state of the union.

[36]*Ibid.*
[37]*H. J. Inc. v. Northwestern Bell*, 87–1252, U.S. 1989.
[38]Committee for Economic Development, *Who Should Be Liable? A Guide to Policy for Dealing with Risk*, New York: CED, 1989.

- Joint and several liability should be eliminated.
- Business should be allowed a so-called state-of-the-art defense. This means that liability for product safety should be based on the laws and technology at the time of production, and not on the retroactive application of current laws and technology to past production. Liability should not attach to unknowable risks at the time of production.
- The discretion of courts in granting awards should be narrowed to make awards more equitable, reduce incentives for litigation, and reduce uncertainty for all parties concerned.
- A federal product liability statute should be enacted to supersede the wide diversity in state laws.
- Manufacturers should not be liable when a product is unreasonably misused or used contrary to explicit warnings.

COMPANY PRODUCT SAFETY PROGRAMS

Many manufacturers have been concerned about product safety aside from the threat of legal action. For example, the chairman of a major agricultural equipment firm recently stated that: "We make frequent safety-oriented redesigns and improvements in product usage and warning information. While avoiding liability claims is one motivating factor, preventing death or serious injury and protecting the reputation of the product are more important."[39]

On the other hand, business has tried to prevent new legislation that would set government standards for product safety. A classic case was the vigorous battle waged by the automobile companies in the 1960s to stop passage of car safety legislation. The tactics used, however, backfired and strengthened rather than weakened the resolve of the Congress to pass tough new legislation for automobile safety.

Three powerful forces have been responsible for companies paying stricter attention to product safety. One is the sharp increase of product liability awards. Another is the need to implement existing federal and state safety laws. A third is the damage to a company's reputation, image, and profits from adverse publicity of product failure.

There is no one standard organizational arrangement for product safety programs. Some companies form an ad hoc task force to redesign a product or monitor a recall. A company may appoint a committee to bring together from time to time people in an organization involved in assuring product safety. A third approach is to delegate to some person on a part-time basis the job of monitoring product safety programs. A final method is to place the product safety responsibilities on an individual or a committee on a full-time basis.

Whichever approach is used, there are checkpoints that must be monitored in the process of production and distribution of a product. A few illustrations of the major checkpoints follow.

[39]McGuire, *op. cit.*, p. 18.

The designers of the product must be safety conscious and must test their ideas and designs against customer experience and court cases. The reliability of raw materials and components must be assured. Care must be paid to warranties, instructions to use a product, and labels on the product. The manufacturing process must follow established production and quality control procedures. For complex products, reliable dealers should be selected for distribution. Standards need to be established for satisfactorily servicing a product and handling complaints. A methodology to survey continuously consumer usage, complaints, product safety incidents, and product liability exposure must be in place.[40]

FALSE AND DECEPTIVE ADVERTISING

A wide range of policy issues surrounds the question of what information should be made available to consumers. This area covers not only information about the contents, use, maintenance requirements, and warranties associated with products, but also advertising. Fundamentally, the purpose of advertising is to make the consumer aware of the existence of a product or service, to inform the customer of the characteristics of the product or service, and then to persuade the customer to buy the product or service. Each of these segments of the information-policy area contains important policy questions, but because of space limitations we discuss only false and deceptive advertising. Mark Twain once said: "When in doubt, tell the truth. It will amaze most people, delight your friends, and confuse your enemies." American advertisers apparently have not heard or been convinced by Twain's recommendation.

FEDERAL TRADE COMMISSION GUIDELINES

The FTC was named by the Congress over fifty years ago as the primary watchdog over false and deceptive advertising, but in recent years the states have become much more active than the FTC in this area. The FTC has a mandate to prevent false, unfair, and deceptive advertising. What this means has been defined over many years in numerous FTC and juridical decisions.

Space permits only a few examples to reveal the scope of FTC guidelines. The agency says that an advertisement for a medicine that offers relief for a symptom is unlawful if it implies an ultimate cure for an illness. Warner-Lambert asserted that its Listerine mouthwash helped to prevent colds and sore throats. The advertising also used such phrases as "for colds," "kills germs by the millions," and "those (colds) we do catch don't seem to last as long," when Listerine mouthwash was used. The FTC said that this falsely implied that the mouthwash "will cure colds," which simply is not so.[41]

---

[40]E. Patrick McGuire, *The Product-Safety Function: Organization and Operations*, New York: The Conference Board, 1979.

[41]*Warner Lambert*, 86 F.T.C. 1398, 1489–90 (1975), *aff'd* 562 F.2d 749 (D.C. Cir. 1977) *cert. denied*, 435 U.S. 950 (1978).

On the other hand the FTC accepts certain types of puffery. The agency will not stop puffery when it appears obvious that consumers know it is exaggeration. Thus, "Coke is the real thing," or "Mac's hamburgers are the best in town," are accepted. But if the advertisement says "the lowest prices in town," the FTC wants solid evidence that this statement is true. Otherwise, it is unlawful.

Significant implications in advertising are unlawful when they cannot be substantiated. General Foods Corporation had to stop advertising Gainesburgers as having all the milk protein a dog needs. Dogs, said the FTC, have no special need for milk.[42] In 1987, the FTC issued a complaint charging that Kraft, Inc., was guilty in its advertising of implying things that were not true. The company said that a slice of Kraft Singles contains the same amount of calcium as five ounces of milk, and that Kraft Singles contains more calcium than do most imitation cheese slices. These claims are not true, said the FTC.[43] At this writing, the company is contesting the complaint. Although the FTC knife is sharp, it often takes years to cut.

If a product is contrasted with another one and the implication made is untrue, the FTC says this is contrary to its guidelines. Thus, when Aspercreme was compared to oral aspirin in advertisements, the implication was that Aspercreme is aspirin in cream form, according to the FTC. The advertisement was stopped. The FTC held that the advertisement had no express representation that Aspercreme contained aspirin, but the comparison of the words left the false impression that the creme did in fact contain aspirin.[44]

This is a small sample of a long list of guidelines that the agency has established over the years. Other guidelines have been set for the use of endorsements and testimonials, deceptive pricing, the use of the word "free" and similar representations, allowances and other merchandising payments and services, private vocational and home study school product guarantees, and bait advertising (that which is offered to get the consumer to buy something else).[45]

These established guidelines for the most part were not enforced during the Reagan administration. James C. Miller III was named chairman of the FTC in 1981 and stated that prior to his appointment the FTC had gone too far "to find implied claims that did not fit the common-sense meaning of the words." The FTC imputed claims of advertisers "that were never intended or were understood by only a small minority of consumers," he said.[46] These views led the FTC to focus on advertisements that were blantantly false, de-

---

[42]*General Foods Corp.* 84. F.T.C. 1572–1573 (1974).

[43]*United States of America Before Federal Trade Commission in the Matter of Kraft, Inc., A Corporation,* Docket No. 9208, April 3, 1989.

[44]*Thompson Medical Co.* 104 F.T.C. 648, 690, 792–793 (1984).

[45]For comprehensive but readable accounts of FTC guidelines see Ivan L. Preston, "The Federal Trade Commission Identification of Implications as Constituting Deceptive Advertising," *University of Cincinnati Law Review,* vol. 57, no. 4, 1989; and Dean Keith Fueroghne, *"But the People in Legal Said..."* A Guide to Current Legal Issues in Advertising, Homewood, Illinois: Dow Jones-Irwin, 1989.

[46]Bob Hickox, "Miller Restrains the FTC Bully," *The Wharton Magazine,* Spring 1982.

ceptive, or injurious to consumers. The agency found its target in small health food companies making false and deceptive claims for such offbeat products as wheat-germ oil, a protein supplement, and a vegetable pill. These companies, with only 1 percent of the food industry sales, were small players in the industry. There were very few FTC complaints against large national companies.

STATES MOVE AGGRESSIVELY

The attorneys general in the states were unhappy with what they called Washington's *laissez-faire* approach to advertising regulation. They became aggressive in bringing multistate lawsuits against large national advertisers and began to prepare guidelines of their own to fill what they said was a federal void in prosecuting false and deceptive advertising.

For example, in 1987 Procter and Gamble agreed to pay the state of California $350,000 because the state said that during the test marketing of Citrus Hill Plus Calcium orange- and grape-fruit juice beverages, these products were promoted as "juices" when they each contained only 60 percent real juice. The state of New York and Kellogg Company recently reached an agreement over the company's Rice Krispies cereal advertisements that claimed the food had "more energy-releasing B vitamins than ever" and as part of a good breakfast could "help give you some get up and go." The company admitted no liability or violation of law but agreed to pay the state $10,000 for the costs of its investigation. Other major, well-known national companies which changed ads because of state complaints include Campbell Soup Co., Coca-Cola, McDonalds Corp., Nestlé Carnation, Pepsi, Sara Lee, Seven-Up, and Pan Am Corp.

The National Association of Attorneys General has established guidelines for the air travel industry because they were concerned about practices of airlines such as offering air fares with many restrictions which were explained in small print at the end of advertisements; and what is called "unbundling." This refers to the practice of advertising a fare but listing separately in fine print other costs to be borne by a traveler such as security, immigration, and airport departure. Another set of guidelines has been prepared for car rentals, and others are expected. All states, of course, have their own laws governing advertising and have taken action to make companies conform to them.

THE FTC REACTS

The FTC in the Bush administration shows promise of more activity than has been seen in the past in this area. Aside from continuing the Kraft case mentioned above, it has filed a major complaint against Campbell Soup Co. for an allegedly deceptive advertisement touting health claims for its soups, a charge denied by the company. It is also looking into other health claims in advertising. It has filed a complaint against two national car-rental companies for violating consumer protection rules. One of the pressures for renewed FTC action comes from the advertising industry, which would rather deal with one federal agency than aggressive states which may have different sets of standards.

HEALTH CLAIMS IN ADVERTISING

Walk down the aisles of a supermarket and you may think you are in a drug store. The message on one food package tells you that it has high fiber and will reduce your chance of cancer; another claims it will lower cholesterol; another says it will help you ward off heart disease; another asserts it can free your arteries from clogging deposits; and another declares it will give you enough calcium to prevent brittle bones from forming. We all have been exposed to this blitz of medical advice on food packages—all to sell a product.

This wave of hyperbole started with an advertisement by Kellogg in 1984, when it got approval from the National Cancer Institute (NCI) to say in advertisements and on its packages of All-Bran cereal that the NCI believes "a high-fiber, low-fat diet may reduce the risk of some kinds of cancer." This was precedent-setting, since such health claims on foods were previously not within accepted guidelines. The FDA, which has authority over food labeling, was not happy with the move, but apparently was unwilling to challenge the NCI. It subsequently did try to establish guidelines for such advertising but could not get them approved by the Office of Management and Budget (OMB), an agency with power to review new proposed government regulations.[47]

Today, many claims go beyond nutritional advice and link eating a particular food with risks of contracting certain diseases, as noted above. Health advertisements make other types of claims which are deceptive half-truths. For instance, a soup advertisement may claim that the soup is low in fats and imply that it is healthy, but not specify that it also contains a day's allowance of sodium, which is not healthy. There is also great confusion among consumers about the meaning of such words as "light," "natural," "low calorie," saturated fats, unsaturated fats, fiber, and other words used in food advertising and labeling.[48]

In late 1989, the American Heart Association, concerned about the confusion and deception in disease-prevention claims on packaged foods, and distressed at the inaction of the FDA, launched its program to verify food health claims. The program met with criticism in the food industry and stern disapproval from both the FDA and the Department of Agriculture (which controls poultry and meats). As a result, the program was canceled in April 1990.[49]

---

[47]Carole Sugarman, "The New Chow Hounds," *The Washington Post*, September 21, 1988.

[48]For a good overview of these issues see Zachary Schiller, Russell Mitchell, Wendy Zellner, Lois Therrien, Andrea Rothman, and Walecia Konrad, "The Great American Health Pitch," *Business Week*, October 9, 1989.

[49]Natalie Angier, "Heart Association Cancels Its Program to Rate Foods, *New York Times*, April 3, 1990.

In the meantime, food labeling bills were introduced in both the U.S. House of Representatives and the U.S. Senate. Also, early in 1990 Health and Human Services Secretary Louis W. Sullivan announced that the FDA, which falls within his agency, is preparing and will propose major changes in food labeling to provide consumers with improved nutritional information.[50]

FOOD LABELING

Three types of problems exist with current food labeling. First is lack of useful nutrition information. Many food labels do not contain nutrition information. Those that do may not list the most important nutrients, or the information given may not be informative. Second, nutrition information and health claims may be misleading. Third, information may be incomplete or unclear about the ingredients in the food. It is not now required by law that every ingredient used in food processing be included on the label, nor is there a requirement that the quantities of major ingredients be specified.

To illustrate what might be done to improve labeling, Figure 16-1 is presented on the following page. It shows at the top how nutritional information might be shown in a more informative and useful way to shoppers. The label should give ingredient information which officials such as the Surgeon General and the FDA commissioner consider to be most important. At the bottom of the figure is a proposal for listing all the ingredients and showing the percentages of content for the most important ones.

THE CONSUMERS AFFAIRS DEPARTMENT (CAD)

In many companies, a Consumer Affairs Department (CAD) has been established to pull together intelligence about and attention to consumers. In other companies without a CAD, the same functions may be performed by implementation of policies through different staffs and divisions.

A survey of the American Management Association (AMA) revealed that 74 percent of the largest companies had established CADs since 1977.[51] Even 21 percent of the small companies reported creating such departments since 1982–83. Most of the CADs were headed by middle managers reporting to a senior officer, and 60 percent said their customer affairs objectives were part of the company's strategic plans.

The 267 companies in the AMA survey were asked which strategies were most effective in building a customer service program and assuring repeat business. The conclusion was "Make a quality product, or perform a quality service, and deliver it on time." To do this requires coordination among a

---

[50]Mariene Cimons, "FDA Plans to Increase Data on Food Labels," *Los Angeles Times*, March 8, 1990. For bills before the Congress see Bruce Ingersoll, "Food-Label Bill Clears House Panel," *The Wall Street Journal*, May 17, 1990.

[51]American Management Association. *Close to the Customer: A Research Report on Consumer Affairs.* New York: American Management Association, 1987.

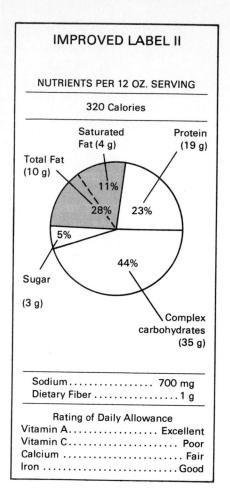

IMPROVED LABEL I
Nutrition Information per Serving
Serving Size .... 12 OZ.
Servings per Container 1
Calories 320
Total Fat................. High (10 g)
Cholesterol-
Raising Fat .... Medium (4 g)
Cholesterol .... Low (10 mg)
Sodium.............. High (700 mg)
Starch.................. High (35 g)
Dietary Fiber .... Low (1 g)
Sugar .... Low (3 g)
Other Nutrients and % of USRDA
Protein .... High (40%)
Vitamin A............... High (160%)
Vitamin C.......................(0%)
Calcium .... Low (5%)
Iron .... Medium (15%)

IMPROVED LABEL II

NUTRIENTS PER 12 OZ. SERVING

320 Calories

Saturated Fat (4 g)
Protein (19 g)
Total Fat (10 g)
11%
28%
23%
5%
44%
Sugar (3 g)
Complex carbohydrates (35 g)

Sodium................. 700 mg
Dietary Fiber .... 1 g

Rating of Daily Allowance
Vitamin A.................. Excellent
Vitamin C..................... Poor
Calcium .... Fair
Iron .... Good

MAJOR INGREDIENTS: Sugars 50% (sugar, corn syrup, dextrose), White flour (30%), Hydrogenated soybean oil (10%). Coconut fat (5%; a saturated fat).

OTHER INGREDIENTS: Gum arabic, Salt, Hydrolyzed vegetable protein (contains MSG), Egg, Artificial colors including Blue 2 and Yellow 5, Artificial flavors, Vitamins B-1 and B-6, BHT (preservative).

FIGURE 16-1 Proposals for improving nutritional and ingredient labeling on food packages. (*Source:* Charles P. Mitchell, Bruce Silverglade, and Lawrence F. Liebman, *Food Labeling Chaos: The Case for Reform,* Washington, D.C.: Center for Science in the Public Interest, July 1989.)

number of staff groups and departments. The CAD must work with those responsible for product safety, quality control, strategic planning, legal affairs, personnel, and distribution. What major functions should be and are being performed by a CAD?

1 The CAD should work with other staffs and departments to coordinate company actions to meet consumer objectives and strategies of the company. This means, of course, that the CAD should have access to relevant information in the company about consumers, and must be given authority to create the appropriate mechanisms to get it and use it. At Pepsi-Cola, the CAD is responsible for enforcement of all regulations concerning consumer affairs.

2 The CAD must listen to consumers and collect information about their needs, complaints, and expectations. Most of the companies reporting in the AMA survey use 800 telephone numbers. Procter and Gamble, for example, has had such a line since 1974, and says it employs 150 people on the program and makes 1 million contacts a year. Companies give this approach a very high rating in terms of effectiveness. Other preferred sources of information are: gathering data from selected "jury" groups of customers; mail/ phone questionnaires; comments and written responses from point-of-sales, trade shows, dealers, consumer panels, and the like. Most companies, especially the larger ones, according to the AMA survey, keep records of consumer complaints. Reports from them generally go to the top management.

3 The CAD should develop programs to assure effective communication between the company and consumers to build public confidence and understanding of company policy and practices. Three-fourths of the large companies in the survey say they disseminate consumer education materials and find it effective.

4 The CAD must be given authority to audit company-wide programs concerning consumer affairs to make sure that activities are in conformance with company policy.

5 The CAD may install or work with others in developing programs in the company to instill in employees a "consumer point of view." Special training programs for customer service and sales personnel are an important method for doing this. About 90 percent of the large companies and 75 percent of the small companies have such programs. The intensity and time devoted varies greatly, from a few weeks to continuously.

6 The CAD should develop or work with others in establishing links between rewards and performance goals. Four out of ten companies link performance in consumer affairs with rewards. Federal Express, for example, has its prestigious Golden Falcon Award, which is a gold pin and ten shares of the company stock. It is given for special meritorious service.

7 The CAD should have contingency plans for four types of unpleasant surprises. One should be for refuting promptly and effectively incorrect assertions or irresponsible actions by consumer activists and others. A second is for openly opposing legislative proposals that are demonstrably counterproductive. A third is for recalls of company products, whether initiated by government directive or company voluntary action. A final and very important one sets forth preferred policies, strategies, and implementation tactics to deal with disastrous tampering with company products in the distribution chain.

Putting these functions together results in a wide range of organizational and operational configurations among companies. Whatever the patterns, the above functions are needed for a first-rate consumer affairs posture.

Restrictions on Alcohol and Tobacco Advertising

It has been said that a drink is the best thing to take for a headache—provided that it is taken the night before. Of course, the person accepting this advice might want to have a cigarette—defined in an adage as "a fire at one end, a fool at the other, and a bit of tobacco between." In fact, alcoholic beverages and tobacco products have much more in common than being sources of humor.

- Both contain powerful, addicting drugs—alcohol and nicotine, respectively—which are a source of pleasure but may have pernicious effects on bodily organs.
- Both imperil users. There are an estimated 100,000 alcohol-related deaths and 390,000 tobacco-related deaths each year.
- Both sustain massive economic networks that combine producing corporations in oligopolistic industries, advertising agencies, broadcasters, publishers, farmers, labor unions, trade associations, and supportive government officials. Just as alcohol and nicotine spread throughout the body, so the industrial structure that makes and sells them weaves its financial sinews throughout the economy.
- Both are "rite-of-passage" products; that is, their use is associated with adulthood. Of course, use is not confined to adults.
- Both are heavily promoted by slick advertisements that associate their use with images of the good life.
- And both have been the target of campaigns to impose restrictions on their marketing, specifically by curbing all or some kinds of advertisement.

In the two associated cases presented here, we examine the ethical, political, legal, and medical issues associated with current campaigns to ban various forms of alcohol and tobacco advertising. We turn first to alcohol advertising.

PART I: ADVERTISING ALCOHOLIC BEVERAGES

To what lengths will marketers go to sell alcohol? The industry has come a long way from the 1960s, when promoters from E. & J. Gallo Winery prowled downtown alleys giving out free samples of Thunderbird wine to "opinion leaders" on skid row in order to entice them into switching brands.[52] But what has it come to? Critics today see all liquor advertising as reprehensible.[53] Alcohol sellers are under increasing attack, and anti-alcohol forces have advertising restrictions on the policy agenda. Would such regulation be constitutional?[54] Would it solve any of society's problems?

THE ALCOHOLIC BEVERAGE INDUSTRY FACES ADVERSITY

The alcoholic beverages industry is divided into three main segments. The largest, by far, is the manufacture and sale of beer, with domestic revenues of $40 billion in 1988; second is distilled spirits, with revenues in that year of $14.7 billion; and third is wine, with revenues of $7.2 billion.[55] The industry matured in a tremendous period of growth between 1960 and 1984, when sales of beer, wine, and distilled spirits more than doubled.

Its growth was fueled by baby boomers entering their prime drinking years and encouraged by advertising. Most beer advertising, for instance the Hamm's beer animations picturing bears at play, was low key and simple in the 1950s and 1960s. Most ads for distilled spirits and wine were similarly unsophisticated. All this changed with the injection of advertising techniques learned in cigarette marketing.

In 1970, Philip Morris, the largest U.S. tobacco company, sought to diversify into other businesses and acquired the Miller Brewing Company. At the time, Miller was a small brewer, with only 4.2 percent of the domestic beer market. But Philip Morris quickly revolutionized beer marketing with the introduction of market segmentation, target marketing, and image-oriented lifestyle advertising. By 1980, Miller had grown to be the second largest domestic brewer. More important, other beer, wine, and distilled spirits marketers adopted its more sophisticated advertising techniques and alcoholic beverage ads were transformed.[56] Sales boomed.

But recent trends in the industry environment have led to stagnating sales. Fewer people drink and those who do often drink less. A 1989 Gallup

---

[52]To this day, the "wino" market segment remains highly competitive. A number of manufacturers make cheap-ingredient wines with 18–21 percent alcohol content (roughly twice that of table wines) for down-and-out alcoholics. These brands are not heavily advertised, and their makers do not crave recognition for their efforts. In 1989, Gallo was under pressure by church and community groups to end sales of Thunderbird and another brand called Night Train Express.

[53]See, for example, Michael Jacobson, Robert Atkins, and George Hacker, *The Booze Merchants: The Inebriating of America,* Washington, D.C.: Center for the Study of Science in the Public Interest, 1983.

[54]For an overview of legal issues see Steve Younger, "Alcoholic Beverage Advertising on the Airwaves: Alternatives to a Ban or Counteradvertising," *UCLA Law Review,* April 1987.

[55]*Standard & Poor's Industry Surveys,* "Alcoholic Beverages," New York: Standard & Poor's Corporation, April 1989, pp. F29, F32, and F34.

[56]William Oscar Johnson, "Sports and Suds," *Sports Illustrated,* August 8, 1988, pp. 73–74; Eric Clark, *The Want Makers,* New York: Viking Press, 1988, p. 268.

poll revealed that only 56 percent of Americans drink, down from 63 percent in 1988 and the high of 71 percent in 1978.[57] This decline in drinking is partly the result of changing demographics. Most beer sales, for example, are to people under age thirty-five, but as baby boomers age there are fewer consumers in the prime beer-drinking years. Entering the 1990s, industry observers predict annual 4 to 6 percent declines in domestic beer production.[58] In addition, changes in social values and lifestyles have depressed demand. The rise of health and fitness values has encouraged moderation. Changing tastes have increased demand for diet sodas, decaffeinated coffee, skim milk, and bottled waters at the expense of alcoholic beverages. Since 1980 demand for distilled spirits has dropped an average of 2 percent annually, with most of the decline in whiskeys, which are perceived by the public as "heavy." "White" goods (gin, rum, vodka, and tequila) are perceived as "lighter" because of their appearance and their market share relative to whisky has steadily increased since 1970. Wine consumption has dropped most of all, hurried along by the falling dollar in the late 1980s, which raised prices of imported wines. In 1988, wine consumption fell by 5.9 percent.[59]

As a consequence of falling sales, competition in the three industry segments has grown fierce. A primary competitive weapon is extensive advertising and promotion. At the same time, a widespread competitive tactic is the introduction of niche products. Newly popular dry beers such as Michelob Dry, Bud Dry, and Lone Star Dry are designed to appeal to health-conscious consumers because of their lower sugar content, fewer calories, and less prominent aftertaste.[60] The introduction of new national brands requires, of course, heavy advertising outlays.

Lower consumption is also encouraged by a nationwide anti-alcohol movement. Industry was overpowered by a similar movement in 1919, when temperance groups secured ratification of the Eighteenth Amendment, which committed the federal government to enforce prohibition of liquor sales. Prohibition, of course, failed, and in 1933 the Twenty-first Amendment ended the sales ban and returned control of liquor sales to state governments, which today regulate sales and advertising in the absence of comprehensive federal legislation. Over time, the states have adopted a variety of controls, but most are permissive.

The new temperance movement was built on outrage about drunk driving deaths and growing knowledge of medical problems such as liver cirrhosis and fetal alcohol syndrome associated with alcohol abuse.[61] It is energized by activists in dozens of church, health, and citizens' groups. The anti-alcohol movement has many dimensions and targets. For example, a campaign by

---

[57]Diane Colasanto and John Zeglarski, "Alcoholic Beverages: Alcohol Consumption at Lowest Level in 30 Years," *Gallup Report*, no. 288, September 1989, p. 12.

[58]Michael J. Branca, "Brewing/Distilled Spirits Industry," *Value Line Investment Survey*, February 23, 1990, p. 1528.

[59]Bruce Keppel, "Wine Drinking in U.S. Continues to Decline," *Los Angeles Times*, July 6, 1989.

[60]Marj Charlier, "New Kinds of Beer to Tap a Flat Market," *Wall Street Journal*, April 20, 1989.

[61]See M. S. Berry and V. W. Pentreath, "The Neurophysiology of Alcohol," in Merton Sandler, ed., *Psychopharmacology of Alcohol*, New York: Raven Press, 1980, and Jean Kinney and Gwen Leaton, *Loosening the Grip: A Handbook of Alcohol Information*, St. Louis: Times Mirror/Mosby, 1987.

Mothers Against Drunk Driving in 1988 forced Hallmark Cards to withdraw graduation cards which jested about heavy drinking.[62] However, the movement has focused activities on restricting advertising and promotion tactics, and there is nationwide support for this. In 1985, for example, a petition campaign named Project SMART (Stop Marketing Alcohol on Radio and Television) collected over 700,000 signatures for a proposal to ban beer and wine ads on television and radio. (Distilled spirits, of course, never have been advertised on the broadcast media due to voluntary restraint by producers.)

THE CASE AGAINST BEER AND WINE ADVERTISING ON TELEVISION AND RADIO

According to anti-alcohol forces, there are a number of reasons why beer and wine advertisements should be banned from the airwaves.

First, ads increase consumption. Beer and wine companies would not spend over $1 billion a year without the expectation of some return. The companies argue that advertising is intended to increase market share by enticing existing drinkers away from competing brands. Yet beer and wine companies perceive themselves to be in competition with soft drinks and other beverages, and seek to promote drinking alcoholic beverages as an alternative to other refreshments. "Lite" beer commercials such as Miller's classic "Tastes Great—Less Filling" segments attempt to reposition beer as a competitor to soft drinks and educate consumers to believe that lite beers are low-calorie, light drinks that can be consumed more frequently and on more occasions than regular beer.

Second, the ads influence children and teenagers to start drinking because they are ubiquitous, frequently feature sports stars or celebrities admired by those under age twenty-one, and are made with models or actors who are young-looking. The ads also depict drinking as a route to social acceptance by peers and a necessary adjunct to having fun at parties. In 1988, for example, Miller Brewing Co. began a series of ads targeting young drinkers aged twenty-one to twenty-five with a series of thirty-second television spots. "Three out of four party animals preferred the taste of Miller Lite," announced one. Another said that Miller Lite was "served at 87 percent of the parties your parents would never attend."[63] Critics note that the science of promotion is not yet precise enough to reach *only* the targeted group of twenty-one to twenty-five-year-olds, and believe that they influence underage and potential drinkers also.

Third, many ads target heavy drinkers and encourage increased consumption. An example is the Michelob beer campaign based on the slogan, "Put a little weekend in your week." This ad and others like it suggest drinking all through the week, not just on weekends.

---

[62]One card pictured a refrigerator containing many beer cans and a single egg and was captioned: "Don't go to graduation without a good breakfast first." Another contained "Advice to the Graduate," which was: "Make sure your gown is comfortable and loose fitting. That way you can hide at least two bottles of champagne underneath." Jim Carlton, "Hallmark Bows to Protests About Graduation Cards," *Los Angeles Times*, June 2, 1988.

[63]Quotes are from *Los Angeles Times*, "Miller Aims for 'Party Animals' Aged 21–25," December 9, 1988.

EXHIBIT 16-1 (*Left*) Alcoholic beverage advertising sometimes associates drinking with romantic attraction and fitting in with others—important concerns for teenagers and young adults. (*Right*) This ad associates sexuality with the consumption of alcohol. (Copyright © 1983, Center for Science in the Public Interest.)

Fourth, sophisticated lifestyle advertising attempts to play on the viewer's emotional needs for popularity, success, romance, or having fun and puts beer, wine, and distilled liquor products in the position of fulfilling these needs. Young drinkers particularly are inclined to emulate. Therefore, ad agencies have associated alcoholic beverages with glamorous activities such as hang gliding, mountain climbing, and riding a roller coaster. Sexual images are a staple in alcohol ads, which frequently depict attractive models in suggestive situations or imply sexuality with body language, facial expressions, or camera angles (see Exhibit 16-1).

Finally, although individual commercials often have little impact, the cumulative mass of alcoholic beverage ads is an enveloping lesson that teaches children as they grow that drinking is all right and is associated with life's high notes. One study estimated that between the ages of two and eighteen, American children see 100,000 beer ads on television.[64]

All forms of targeting in alcohol promotion are anathema to the anti-alcohol forces. They decry college marketing programs in which companies advertise in college newspapers or magazines. Young readers are also targeted by ads in magazines such as *Rolling Stone* and the *National Lampoon*, and in rock group sponsorships such as Anheuser-Busch's sponsorship of

[64]Noted in Johnson, *op. cit.*, p. 78.

the rock opera "Tommy" performed by the Who at key concert facilities. They dislike ads in publications such as *Ms.* and *Working Woman*, which recruit more female drinkers. And they look contemptuously at advertisements aimed at minorities. But TV and radio ads are the most offensive because they can be more compelling and forceful than print ads, they come over air waves regulated for use in the public interest, and they reach teenagers and children as they enter homes along with family and sports programs.

ALCOHOLIC BEVERAGE ADVERTISERS DEFEND THEIR COMMERCIALS

Industry spokespeople defend advertising. First, they argue that advertising is not the cause of alcohol abuse in society. Alcoholism is a complex disease that is caused by personality, family, genetic, and physiological factors rather than by listening to commercials. Most people who drink are not harmed. And the preponderance of research shows that underage drinking is largely the result of peer pressure and lax parental supervision. Scholarly studies confirm this. In a recent review of research, it was found that virtually every credible study showed advertising had little or no influence over increased consumption.[65] Hence, the main result of an ad ban would be to deprive drinkers of truthful, relevant information without reducing alcohol abuse by a minority of alcoholics, who would be blithely unaffected.

Ad restrictions would also deprive the industry of an important competitive weapon. Both the beer and wine industries are dominated by a small number of giant producers who use nationwide broadcast advertising as a critical weapon in the war for market share. Beer, for example, is a mature product, and per capita consumption has been in decline despite modest total increases in barrels sold in the 1980s. The result is that brewers compete in internecine warfare for existing market share. Using national advertising campaigns as primary weapons, the seven largest brewers increased their combined share of the domestic market from 48 percent in 1970 to 98 percent in 1988.[66] Small local and regional brewers have been unable to hold onto their markets in opposition to giants such as Anheuser-Busch, which has a 43 percent domestic market share. Under these conditions, the dominant brewers use political contributions, lobbying efforts, and influence over the broadcasting, publishing, and advertising industries to keep an advertising ban off the congressional agenda and protect their advantage over weaker companies.

Second, anti-alcohol groups assume that the public is too stupid to make correct decisions. The proposal to restrict advertising is condescending. Peo-

[65]Reginald G. Smart, "Does Alcohol Advertising Affect Overall Consumption? A Review of Empirical Studies," *Journal of Studies on Alcohol,* July 1988. An example of a study that disagrees with this conclusion by showing that advertising promotes drinking is P. P. Aitken, "Television Alcohol Commercials and Under-age Drinking," *International Journal of Advertising,* vol. 8, no. 2 (1989).

[66]*Standard & Poor's Industry Surveys,* "Alcoholic Beverages: Stagnant Demand Sparks Competition," New York: Standard & Poor's Corporation, June 22, 1989, p. F5.

ple are not fooled by the association of alcohol consumption with attractive imagery. Would the critics expect brewers and vintners to associate their products with toxic waste, taxation, or traffic congestion? An advertising ban would wrongly imply to millions of drinkers that they were doing something wrong by having a beer or a glass of wine.

Third, the beer and wine industries have adopted voluntary codes of advertising to police their own behavior. Although compliance is not total, the codes have moved ad agencies away from the most crass commercials. For instance, the first of twenty guidelines set forth by the United States Brewers Association reads: "Beer advertisements should neither suggest nor encourage overindulgence." Others prohibit depicting driving after drinking or encouraging underage drinking. The guidelines of the Wine Institute prohibit, among other things, any suggestion that excessive drinking or loss of control is amusing, the use of "models and personalities in advertisements who appear to be under twenty-five years of age," or the use of "professional sports celebrities, past or present." In addition, the industry has begun to deflect critics by broadcasting messages of sensibility and moderation. A Coors Lite beer commercial, for example, while suggesting that Coors Lite is "The Right Beer Now" also depicts a beer drinker about to drive and cautions: "Absolutely, positively not now." Industry sponsors public service announcements and alcohol-abuse prevention programs such as the National Alcohol Awareness Week sponsored by Adolph Coors Brewing Co. in 1989 to educate college students about alcohol abuse. Industry advertisers recognize that advertising is a right and that it entails the corresponding duty of properly informing the public of alcohol's dangers. The industry, say its spokespeople, has stepped up to accept this responsibility. But it has never conceded that advertising causes abuse, as is colorfully put by an advertising company executive who argued that "trying to control drunk drivers by outlawing the advertising of alcohol makes as little sense as trying to control the Ku Klux Klan by outlawing bed linens."[67]

Fourth, broadcasters have argued that the loss of revenues from beer and wine ads would bring about a reduction in services for viewers. These ads are 4 percent of television ad revenue, 12 percent of radio, and 18 percent of minority-owned radio stations. One area of programming likely to suffer is sports programming, where beer and wine ads cluster.

Finally, the industry does not deny the practice of targeting younger drinkers, women, and minorities with specific advertising themes. It is natural that most ads are designed to appeal to younger drinkers, since they drink more than other age groups. In 1989, for example, 66 percent of those aged eighteen to twenty-nine drank, as opposed to only 41 percent of those over fifty.[68] Contemporary women do not see themselves as more gullible and dewey-eyed than men and, hence, are not in need of special protection from ads that might appear on sports programs with primarily male viewers.

[67]Clark, *op. cit.*, p. 285.
[68]Colasanto and Zeglarski, *op. cit.*, p. 14.

And heavy advertising in minority media outlets helps minority communities financially.

THE PROSPECTS OF AN ADVERTISING BAN

In 1985, both the House and Senate held hearings on the subject of banning beer and wine commercials from radio and television.[69] No legislation resulted, but political pressures by anti-alcohol forces led Congress in 1988 to require a health warning label on every container of alcoholic beverages sold.[70] In 1989, Surgeon General C. Everett Koop, in his final press conference, released a report which condemned alcohol ads for sending "the message that drinking is a normal and glamorous activity without negative consequences."[71] Koop recommended eliminating industry sponsorship of sporting events and rock concerts and a prohibition on advertising at college campuses. And late in 1989, the Senate passed an amendment restricting campus promotions, such as free beer from kegs, which encourage "illegal and irresponsible consumption."[72] These actions are signs that Congress may face further pressure to enact advertising and promotional restrictions.

PART II: ADVERTISING TOBACCO PRODUCTS

About 68 million Americans smoke cigarettes, and another 15 million use other tobacco products. But the number of smokers is steadily declining, as roughly 1,000,000 a year quit and 390,000 die of smoking-related diseases. Despite heavy advertising, the tobacco companies cannot recruit enough new smokers to replace those departing the ranks. Between 1988 and 1989, for example, the number of adult smokers dropped from 32 percent of the population to 27 percent.[73] Domestic consumption of cigarettes dropped by 2.4 percent.[74]

---

[69]See *Alcohol Advertising*, hearing before the Subcommittee on Children, Family, Drugs and Alcoholism of the Committee on Labor and Human Resources, United States Senate, February 7, 1985, and *Beer and Wine Advertising: Impact of the Electronic Media* from hearings before the Subcommittee on Telecommunications, Consumer Protection, and Finance of the Committee on Energy and Commerce, United States House of Representatives, May 21, 1985.

[70]This label reads: "GOVERNMENT WARNING: (1) According to the Surgeon General, women should not drink alcoholic beverages during pregnancy because of the risk of birth defects. (2) Consumption of alcoholic beverages impairs your ability to drive a car or operate machinery, and may cause health problems." By early 1990, implementation of the label requirement was still held up by wrangling between the industry and the Department of Treasury over details of print size and placement. See David Wessel, "Warning Labels on Alcohol: Just What Is 'Prominent'?" *Wall Street Journal*, May 5, 1989.

[71]Quoted in Alix M. Freedman, "Koop Urges Alcoholic-Beverage Curbs, Including Ad Restrictions and Tax Rise," *Wall Street Journal*, June 1, 1989.

[72]Joanne Lipman, "Alcohol Firms Retain Campus Presence," *Wall Street Journal*, October 6, 1989.

[73]*Gallup Report*, "Cigarette Smoking at 45-Year Low," number 286, July 1989, p. 23.

[74]U.S. Department of Commerce, *1990 U.S. Industrial Outlook*, Washington, D.C.: Government Printing Office, January 1990, p. 34–31.

THE TOBACCO INDUSTRY'S GRIM MARKETING ENVIRONMENT

In early America, smoking was largely a southern custom. During the Civil War, however, Union troops were exposed to the habit in occupied southern territory and smoked tobacco to fight boredom and stress. Upon returning home after the war, these new smokers created a national demand for southern smoking tobacco. Smoking never enjoyed unanimous approval in society; Mark Twain, for example, called it a "filthy habit." But for the century following the Civil War, it was widely accepted, and by the 1950s the majority of men smoked, along with about one-third of women.[75] In 1964, however, the Surgeon General of the United States released a report that warned of a strong association between smoking and lung cancer.[76] The report was a turning point for the industry, putting it on the defensive politically and soon ending the century-old growth of demand for its product.

Since then, the environment for marketing tobacco products has further deteriorated. In 1965, Congress required health warnings on cigarette packages, and in 1971 it prohibited cigarette ads on radio and television. Over the next decade, the health warnings on cigarette packages became more strongly worded, and medical research on the ill effects of smoking accumulated. In 1985, the Surgeon General called for a "smoke-free society" by the year 2000, and the first high-profile bills to prohibit all tobacco advertising were introduced in Congress. In 1986, smokeless tobacco ads were banned from the airwaves and in the same year a special review of medical literature by a select committee of the National Academy of Sciences concluded that "passive smoking," or the exposure of nonsmokers to tobacco smoke, increased the risk of lung cancer in nonsmokers by as much as 30 percent. This report provoked a growing militancy among nonsmokers. In 1990, smoking was banned on virtually all domestic airline flights. By this time, forty-one states and the District of Columbia had restrictions on public smoking and nine states, seventy cities, and thousands of companies restricted workplace smoking. State and federal excise taxes had increased to an average 34 cents per pack.

An additional burden to the industry are lawsuits by consumers who claim that using tobacco has injured their health. Tobacco firms deflected a series of such suits in the 1950s and 1960s, only to see a new crop of nearly 300 arise in the 1980s. The new suits sought to take advantage of changes in product liability law which made it easier for consumers to sue manufacturers of dangerous products such as asbestos.

The tobacco manufacturers successfully fought off the 1980s suits, however, by using two main lines of defense. First, they emphasized ambiguities in the medical research that links smoking with cancer, convincing juries that this research does not absolutely prove smoking to cause cancer. Second, they argued that smokers have adequate notice of the health dangers of

[75]*Ibid.*, p. 24.
[76]U.S. Department of Health, Education, and Welfare, *Smoking and Health: Report of the Advisory Committee to the Surgeon General of the Public Health Service*, Washington, D.C.: Government Printing Office, 1964.

smoking from warning labels on cigarette packs and have been well educated by the flood of information about smoking in the media. Therefore, they contend that smokers voluntarily accept the risks of smoking. The use of these two defensive arguments is awkward. It puts the companies in the position of saying that smoking is not dangerous while simultaneously asserting that smokers are adequately warned that it is dangerous.[77] By the early 1990s, most smokers' lawsuits had faded away, but despite the appearance of industry victory the litigation retained an active dimension as some lawyers continued to seek a theory of liability that would hold manufacturers accountable for tobacco-related illness.

COMPETITION IN THE TOBACCO INDUSTRY

In this climate, the market for tobacco products is shrinking. Domestic per capita consumption of cigarettes has declined each year since 1973, and aggregate consumption has fallen an average of 1.9 percent annually since 1981.

There are seven large tobacco manufacturers and two of them dominate the domestic market; Philip Morris Cos., with about 40 percent of domestic sales, and R. J. Reynolds Tobacco Co., with about 30 percent. Despite shrinkage in the U.S. market, industry profits have been high in recent years because the companies have raised cigarette prices, doubling the average retail price of a pack since 1982, and expanded foreign sales, most notably in Asia.

In an environment of shrinking consumption and growing consumer disfavor, the companies rely heavily on advertising to war with each other over market share. Advertising is also essential for launching new national brands and repositioning older brands. In recent years, brand advertising has been especially important for R. J. Reynolds, the second largest tobacco company. Its top-selling brands—Winston and Camel—have been losing market share to its rival Philip Morris' brands. Through new advertising themes, R. J. Reynolds has attempted to appeal to younger smokers and tried to start new brands that would appeal to population segments with many smokers. Tobacco marketers are thought to be exceptionally resourceful because of the difficulty of their task, and their work is state-of-the-art. The companies sponsor sporting events and art exhibits. They fill magazines, newspapers, and billboards with well-researched, visually striking appeals to the multiple motivations of smokers.

PROPOSALS TO RESTRICT TOBACCO ADVERTISING

Recently, the attack on tobacco has centered on advertising restrictions. Federal law already bans broadcast advertising, but anti-smoking forces want to go further. In Congress, bills to restrict tobacco ads have adopted three basic approaches.

[77]A comprehensive review of industry litigation strategy is a note in the *Harvard Law Review*, "Plaintiff's Conduct as a Defense to Claims Against Cigarette Manufacturers," November 1985.

1 Enact a restrictive format for advertisements. Illustrative is a 1989 bill by Representative Tom Luken (D., Ohio) requiring cigarette ads to be all text with no pictures. These so-called "tombstone ads" would have no pictures, models, slogans, or colors. Cigarette makers would be unable to make emotional appeals with words and images.

2 Allow states and cities to adopt restrictions. Current law, based on 1969 legislation, permits only federal regulation of tobacco ads. But a 1989 bill introduced by Senator Edward Kennedy (D., Mass.) would end federal preemption and expose industry to a welter of restrictions and challenges. This approach avoids a ban and does not affect advertisements in national newspapers and magazines.

3 Enact a partial or total ban. Although it would be possible to prohibit ads in some media, such as magazines, while prohibiting them in others, most legislative proposals have advocated a blanket ban on all forms of advertising and promotion. Three bills before Congress in 1989 would end all media ads as well as free sample giveaways, sponsorship of sporting events, and other marketing techniques. The Kennedy bill mentioned above would prohibit sponsorship of sporting events such as Philip Morris' Virginia Slims tennis tournaments.

Bills such as these have foundered so far, but each year they resurface. The debate over them pits cigarette firms and their allies, publishers and advertising agencies, against a coalition of health, religious, civic, and consumer organizations. Despite the unpopularity of tobacco products, the industry lobby opposing this coalition is formidable. The tobacco companies have 350,000 employees and provide an indirect livelihood for another 1.5 million, including tobacco farmers, distributors and retailers, matchbook makers, and grave diggers. In 1988, the companies spent $2.4 billion in advertising tobacco (roughly three times alcoholic beverage advertising), and paid $10 billion in taxes. In addition, the growing export of tobacco products improves the nation's trade balance.

This economic muscle is a major reason why recent presidents have opposed advertising restrictions. Yet one tobacco critic within the Bush administration, Dr. Louis W. Sullivan, Secretary of Health & Human Services, estimates that smoking-related diseases cost the nation $52 billion a year in lost productivity, health care expenses, and higher insurance premiums.[78]

It seems likely that further restrictions will come, but what will they be? Other countries have gone farther than the U.S. For example, Canada prohibits all advertising and promotion of tobacco, China bans newspaper and broadcast ads, and Ireland bans broadcast ads and prohibits only plain printed ads in one color. How long and in what way can the tobacco companies forestall similar limitations?

[78]"Smoking: All Clear (Cough, Cough)," *Los Angeles Times*, February 25, 1990.

THE CASE AGAINST TOBACCO ADVERTISING

The attack on cigarette advertising is like that on alcoholic beverage advertising. For one thing, say critics, smoking is harmful, and advertising increases consumption of tobacco. Since the early 1960s, epidemiological studies have shown a relationship between smoking and illnesses including cancer, heart disease, stroke, emphysema, immune deficiencies, and pregnancy disorders. In 1989, the Surgeon General issued a report concluding that one of every six deaths is caused by smoking, including 87 percent of lung cancer deaths, 82 percent of emphysema deaths, 21 percent of heart disease deaths, and 18 percent of stroke deaths.[79] Tobacco smoke contains forty-three carcinogens, which is why it is associated not only with lung cancer but with cancers in many sites such as the bladder, kidney, and pancreas. Advertising depicts smoking as an attractive, worthwhile pastime and encourages people to assume major health risks by starting, smoking more, switching to low tar brands instead of quitting, and restarting after quitting.

Second, tobacco ads are designed to recruit smokers in certain segments of society. Although smoking is in overall decline, certain population groups—blacks, Hispanics, blue-collar workers, women, youth, and the less educated—have a higher percentage of smokers. These groups are targeted by cigarette makers seeking growth segments, but critics object to targeting because of the implication that industry is creating victims. Here is how targeting works with these groups.

Blacks and Hispanics   The number of black and Hispanic smokers continues to rise. Cigarettes are heavily advertised in minority magazines and on billboards in minority communities. Rio, Dorado, and L&M Superior are special brands introduced for Hispanic smokers. About 75 percent of blacks smoke mentholated brands such as Kool, Newport, and Salem. Early in 1990, R. J. Reynolds tried to launch a new mentholated brand named Uptown to compensate for market share losses in its Salem brand, which was deemed too heavily mentholated for many black smokers. It was openly stated by the company that Uptown targeted blacks. Ads featured black couples in urban scenes. But the brand was withdrawn under fire from Health and Human Services Secretary Sullivan, who said: "Uptown's message is more disease, more suffering and more death for a group already bearing more than its share of smoking-related illness and mortality."[80]

Women   Smoking rates are declining among women, but more slowly than for men. Moreover, young women start smoking in greater numbers than young men. Virginia Slims was the first female cigarette, introduced in the 1960s by Philip Morris. It now leads among all "female" brands with a market share of

[79]U.S. Department of Health and Human Services, *Reducing the Health Consequences of Smoking: 25 Years of Progress. A Report of the Surgeon General,* Rockville, Maryland: U.S. Department of Health and Human Services, Publication no. (CDC) 89-8411, 1989, p. i and p. 161.

[80]James R. Schiffman, "After Uptown, Are Some Niches Out?" *Wall Street Journal,* January 22, 1990.

3 percent. To attract women, marketers have used new cigarette production technologies to make slim and ultra-slim brands (Capri and Superslims), flavored smokes (Chelsea and Spring Lemon Lights), and decorated cigarettes in packs with pastel colors, flowers, and other feminine touches (Newport Stripes 100s and Eve). Marketing themes targeting women, according to the head of a cigarette account at an ad agency, "try to tap the emerging independence and self-fulfillment of women, to make smoking a badge to express that."[81]

Youth   Advertisers also target young people, and the age at which smoking begins has fallen. About 90 percent of smokers adopt the habit before the age of twenty-one, and brand loyalty for cigarettes is higher than for any other major consumer product; 70 percent remain faithful to one brand.[82] Therefore, attracting a beginning smoker pays long-term dividends. The industry has a voluntary code of advertising principles requiring that ads not "appear in publications directed primarily to those under twenty-one years of age," and that models in cigarette ads shall not "appear to be under twenty-five years of age," yet many ads show young-looking models. And there are frequent ads in magazines such as *Hot Rod, Rolling Stone,* and *National Lampoon,* which attract teen-age readers. Of course, young models may not be necessary to attract teenagers to smoking. As one critic notes, "That fourteen-year-old models aren't used in these ads is irrelevant; eighth graders don't smoke cigarettes in order to look like eighth graders."[83]

A third and related concern of critics is that ads associated with targeted marketing are redolent with deception. Tobacco ads, like beer and wine ads, employ cleverly constructed "lifestyle" themes. These associate a contemptible product with success, adventure, romance, status, fun, and masculinity or femininity. The depiction of the macho, ruggedly independent Marlboro cowboy or the slightly rebellious, sassy, and liberated Virginia Slims woman is geared to satisfying strong emotional needs in targeted personality types. Cigarettes as physical objects are essentially the same from brand to brand, but advertising endows them with potent psychological magic. Thus an awkward male adolescent—or a middle-aged man—may smoke cigarettes to share the aura of strength, male sensuality, and acceptance by the opposite sex like the Camel man. The ads, in addition, imply that healthy, happy people in top condition smoke, thereby undermining health warnings on packages and advertisements (see Exhibit 16-2).

TOBACCO MARKETERS DEFEND ADS

The battle is joined by cigarette manufacturers. First, they argue that although they are extremely concerned about possible adverse health effects

---

[81]Anonymous quotation in Peter Waldman, "Tobacco Firms Try Soft, Feminine Sell," *Wall Street Journal,* December 19, 1989.

[82]Ronald Alsop, "Brand Loyalty is Rarely Blind Loyalty," *Wall Street Journal,* October 19, 1989, p. B1.

[83]David Owen, "The Cigarette Companies: How They Get Away With Murder, Part II," *Washington Monthly,* March 1985, p. 53.

EXHIBIT 16-2   This ad associates cigarette smoking with masculinity, adulthood, athletic activity, and peer-group acceptance. (Random House photo by Stacey Pleasant.)

from smoking, the evidence to date does not prove that smoking causes cancer and other diseases. Their point is a precise, technical one about the nature of proof in scientific inquiry. Although epidemiological studies show a *relation* between smoking and lung cancer, they do not prove that smoking is the *cause* of that lung cancer. Rather, they simply show an association between the two. The exact mechanism of cancer causation is not yet definitively explained by science. Until it is, the tobacco companies argue that other factors known to be associated with cancer, including everything from genes to smog, may have initiated a disease process.

The literature on smoking and health is vast. Inevitably, there is bickering about methodology and validity, as in every scientific field. Perhaps inevitably, some studies show no relation between smoking and cancer. For example, in a series of Scandinavian studies of identical twins, one of whom smoked and the other not, the smokers did not differ from the nonsmokers in the incidence of any illnesses, including lung cancer.[84]

In response to charges that targeting is reprehensible, the tobacco companies say that new brands provide useful alternatives for smokers. In response to the furor over Uptown, R. J. Reynolds argued that withdrawal of the

[84]Hans J. Eysenck, "Statement Regarding S. 772," in *Smoking Prevention Health and Education Act of 1983*. Hearing before the Committee on Labor and Human Resources, United States Senate, May 5, 1983.

brand deprived black consumers of additional choice. Companies also deny designing ads to snare new, young smokers. Although seven states have no minimum age for tobacco sales and fourteen states set the age lower than eighteen, the companies say that they do not target minors in marketing efforts. Whatever indirect impact tobacco ads have on children, there is face validity in this claim because no ads relating to unique life experiences such as first dates or Little League games appear. Research indicates that advertising ranks low among the factors leading teenagers to initiate smoking. For example, in studies of college students who smoked or used smokeless tobacco, the influence of advertising ranked ninth and eighth respectively out of ten factors leading to the decision to initiate tobacco use.[85] The most important factors were peer pressure, tobacco use by parents and siblings, and personality variables such as rebelliousness and extroversion. Advertising is designed to encourage brand switching and provide information to consumers about new products.

Tobacco firms also reject the argument that their advertising plays unfairly on emotional needs. Surveys going back to the 1970s indicate that over 90 percent of both teenagers and adults believe cigarette smoking harms health, and up to 95 percent believe it causes lung cancer.[86] Thus, they freely choose risk exposure. Cigarettes are not marketed differently from other products, and the ads are manipulative only in the sense that all advertising incorporates positive associations from life into product presentation. Millions see tobacco ads daily but do not become smokers. No statistics or research indicate that consumers are tricked by tobacco advertising, so the burden of proof still rests with those who would ban it. Many factors aside from advertising influence tobacco purchase decisions, including previous experience with the product, opinions of relatives and friends, and information from other sources such as churches, the government, schools, and the media. There also exists widespread skepticism toward ad content in American society. In short, adverting is not a disquieting, manipulative determiner of behavior.

Tobacco companies point out that there is little hard evidence that advertising increases consumption or that its elimination would result in declining consumption. The removal of cigarette ads from the broadcast media in 1971 was followed by years of increased consumption. Findings of research into the relationship between advertising expenditures and tobacco sales are similar to those regarding alcohol advertising. Most studies show no statistically significant correlation between expenditures for advertising and subsequent sales. The few that do show that advertising raises consumption find its impact is small.[87] Therefore, ad restrictions or bans would simply harm consumers by depriving industry of a competitive weapon.

---

[85]John P. Foreyt, statement submitted for record in *Tobacco Issues*. Hearing before the Subcommittee on Health and the Environment of the Committee on Energy and Commerce, House of Representatives, July 26, 1985.

[86]*Report of the Surgeon General, op. cit.*, p. 179.

[87]For an overview of the literature see *Ibid.*, pp. 503–504.

Finally, the industry and its advertising agencies have tried to portray smoking and tobacco advertising as a civil rights issue in which smokers are cast as a downtrodden minority, forced to resist the infringement of their right to smoke by imperious, strident foes of tobacco, "self-appointed arbiters of right and wrong."[88] In 1989, Philip Morris ran a televised series of public service advertisements on the Bill of Rights. But because the company used its name in the ads, critics claimed it was trying to endow the questionable right to smoke with the legitimacy of the hallowed amendments.

ALCOHOL AND TOBACCO ADVERTISING BANS: ARE THEY CONSTITUTIONAL?

Proposals for banning beer, wine, and tobacco product advertisements raise important constitutional issues. The First Amendment protects speech from government-imposed restrictions, but courts have distinguished *pure speech* from *commercial speech*. The former is defined as speech in the broad marketplace of ideas, encompassing political, scientific, and artistic expression, and is closely protected. The latter refers to advertisements and other speech designed to stimulate business transactions, and has received less protection. In both areas of speech, however, the general principle adopted by the courts to test restrictions is that the right of speech must be balanced against society's need to maintain the general welfare. The right of free speech is assumed to be a fundamental barrier against the growth of tyranny and is not tampered with or restricted lightly. So the courts ordinarily do not permit censorship of speech unless it poses a grave threat to public welfare, as it would, for example, if a speaker posed the threat of imminent violence or a writer published classified military secrets in time of war.

With respect to commercial speech, however, various restrictions have been permitted. For example, advertisements for securities offerings may appear only in the austere format of a legal notice, and, as noted, cigarette and snuff advertising has been barred from television and radio. These are not total bans, of course, only restrictions. Total suppression of commercial speech about legal alcohol and tobacco products, as called for in several bills now before Congress, raises major constitutional questions. Would the courts approve it?

In the case of *Central Hudson Gas & Electric Corp. v. Public Service Commission* in 1980, the Supreme Court struck down a New York regulation banning advertising by public utilities, a law that was intended to help conserve energy.[89] In the *Central Hudson* case, the Court developed its current theory of commercial speech. Justice Powell, writing for the majority, set forth a four-pronged test for determining when commercial speech could be restricted.

First, the advertisement in question should promote a lawful product or activity and must be accurate. If an ad is misleading or suggests illegal activ-

---

[88]Kenneth Roman, "The Neo-Prohibitionists," *Vital Speeches*, May 1, 1989, p. 441.
[89]447 U.S. 557.

ity, it does not merit protection. Second, the government interest in restricting the particular commercial speech must be substantial, not trivial or unimportant. Third, the regulation or advertising restriction clearly must further the interest of the government. In other words, it should definitely help the government reach a public policy goal. Fourth, the suppression of commercial speech must not be more extensive than is necessary to achieve the government's purpose. Any advertising ban passed by Congress would, no doubt, be challenged by industry and would have to pass this test.[90]

CONCLUSION

While advertising restrictions are debated, sales of both alcoholic beverages and tobacco products continue to drop. Both industries are spending somewhat less on promotion. The public favors greater restrictions. A *Wall Street Journal* survey in 1989 found that 48 percent favored and 31 percent opposed banning all beer and wine advertising from television; 42 percent favored and 34 percent opposed eliminating printed ads; and 54 percent favored and 24 percent opposed eliminating cigarette ads in magazines and newspapers (the remaining fractions in each case were undecided).[91]

The debate in Congress and society is complex, involving medical, religious, and ethical aspects. But in the end, two factors will be most central in resolving the issue of advertising restriction. The first is the relative political strength of the economic interests versus the political strength of reform groups. The second is the constitutionality of any restrictions on commercial speech that may be enacted, as determined by federal courts.

QUESTIONS

1 Are certain beer, wine, or tobacco ads misleading? What examples can you give? What specifically is misleading?
2 Do alcoholic beverage and tobacco companies that fight for their right to advertise also generally fulfill their corresponding ethical duty to be informative and honest?
3 Would a ban on broadcast advertising for beer and wine be constitutional? Apply the four-pronged test set forth by the Supreme Court in the *Central Hudson* case to reach a conclusion.
4 Would a total ban on tobacco advertising pass a similar test of constitutionality?
5 What other products are typically advertised in exaggerated, misleading, or manipulative ways? Would advertising restrictions be appropriate for them? What kind of restrictions?

[90]In 1986, proponents of an advertising ban were given heart by the Supreme Court's decision in *Posadas de Puerto Rico Associates v. Tourism Company of Puerto Rico* (54 LW 4960) allowing the Puerto Rican government to ban casino advertising.
[91]Alix M. Freedman, "Rebelling Against Alcohol, Tobacco Ads," *Wall Street Journal*, November 14, 1989.

EIGHT

Human Resources

CHAPTER
17

The Changing Internal Face of Organizational Life

In the late 1970s, AT&T experienced growing competition from some 200 cut-rate long distance telephone companies and a like number of telephone equipment manufacturers. Simultaneously, intellectual and political forces in favor of deregulation led to the breakup of the venerable "Ma Bell" into nine separate corporations on January 1, 1984.

The divestiture was upsetting for employees. A survey of AT&T workers revealed these feelings:

> [I was] angry, sad, a little scared about my future. Divestiture was a triumph of lawyers, bureaucrats, and financial manipulators over producers and servers.
>
> I felt like I had gone through a divorce that neither my wife nor my children wanted. It was forced upon us by some very powerful outside forces, and I could not control the outcome. It was like waking up in familiar surroundings (your home) but your family and all that you held dear was missing.
>
> My feelings were ambivalent....I was numb but I neither rejoiced nor shed a tear.

One of the most wrenching aspects of the change for employees was the necessary alteration of AT&T's corporate culture. The old culture, to which employees were accustomed, was highly paternalistic. It incorporated a deep sense of employees as family. People anticipated lifetime careers, and promotion was from within company ranks. A primary focus of the Bell culture was to provide high-quality, affordable customer service. Authority was centralized, and Bell employees had a high "level consciousness," that is, awareness of the status hierarchy of six management ranks. Bell managers focused their planning on regulatory matters, which dominated the competitive environment.

After the breakup, the company was far less regulated; most of its markets were fully competitive. It had to develop new products, sell them, and take unaccustomed risks to survive. Charles L. Brown, chairman at the time of the breakup, tried to change the corporate culture. To reduce reverence for the management hierarchy, he set up independent profit centers within management groups. He placed a new emphasis on marketing and product innovation to encourage competitive thinking in place of the old focus on regulatory compliance. He even told employees that it was no longer appropriate to refer to an aggressive firm with high-tech products as "Ma Bell." Brown used training programs, publications, policy statements, and employee awards to convert the culture.

But in 1988, Robert Allen, the third chairman since 1984, took the helm and concluded that the staid old AT&T culture was still too much in evidence. He made a renewed effort to change it. He gave middle managers more authority to make decisions. He reorganized the company again into nineteen business units which have authority to make major decisions on product lines. He extirpated petty, bureaucratic rules and procedures that slowed managerial action. He also signalled change by buying a leading manufacturer of modems to enhance the AT&T product line. In the past, it would have been unthinkable to go outside the company for a product.

It has been a difficult time for AT&T employees. They have been through deregulation, at least six reorganizations, three top management changes, and a shift in corporate culture. Clearly, the company is no longer the paternalistic guarantor of a lifetime job. Since 1984, AT&T has shed 18 percent of its employees to streamline operations, most in two large work force reductions of 24,000 and 32,000.

The AT&T transition represents in microcosm, the tremendous impact of environmental forces on the American work force today and the ways in which managements try to attune corporate cultures to competitive conditions. In this chapter we discuss these and other changes in the modern workplace.

THE NATURE AND MEANING OF WORK

Those who work are performing a timeless, basic task. We define work as sustained effort designed to produce something of value for other people. At an elemental level, work is essential. Humans must manipulate their environment to live. The underlying moral basis of work is that each person is a burden on society and should contribute a fair share of the expenditure of human energy necessary for survival.

Work has an important psychological dimension. The clinician Karl Menninger saw work as one of two constructive outlets for aggressive impulses, the other being play.[1] Psychoanalyst Harry Levinson speaks of work as a central means for accomplishing the "twin unconscious drives of love and hate." "The carpenter who hammers nails," says Levinson, "is not only discharging his aggressions but also building a shelter."[2]

---

[1]Karl Menninger, *The Vital Balance*, New York: Viking, 1963, p. 141.
[2]Harry Levinson, *Executive*, Cambridge, Massachusetts: Harvard University Press, 1981, p. 29.

Work may give one a sense of mastery, provide legitimate expression for inner drives, placate a stern conscience, or divert attention from emotionally harmful anxieties. Medical research shows that fired and laid-off workers are at greater risk of accident, illness, suicide, and divorce than those who remain employed. When, for example, General Motors closed its auto plant in Freemont, California, in 1982 and put 7,000 people out of work, numerous divorces and three suicides were attributed to the closure. A landmark, long-term study carried out between 1922 and 1971 showed an inverse relationship between economic conditions and admission to mental hospitals.[3] A more recent study found that 25 percent of unemployed men experience feelings of shame and humiliation.[4] Despite the generally salutary benefits of work, however, the workplace often is highly stressful and competitive. It may be difficult even for emotionally healthy people to adapt to its pressures, frustrations, and conflicts.

Work also has a social dimension. The concept of work has been different in other societies, past and present, from what it is in the United States today. In pre-Christian Greece and Rome, work—in the sense of hard physical labor—was associated with degradation and slavery. In medieval times and among deeply religious people thereafter, work and hard labor were viewed as service to God and the road to salvation.

In communist countries, work has political content. In the People's Republic of China, North Korea, Cuba, and Russia, constitutions require work as a duty to the state. In Article 60 of the 1977 Soviet Constitution, for example, it is stipulated that "labor in one's chosen field of socially useful activity and observance of labor discipline is the duty and a matter of honor for every Soviet citizen who is able to work."

In the United States, the meaning of work has been variable. In the pre-industrial, colonial period, farmers and artisans worked hard to survive, but their toil was softened by overtones of religious obligation that endowed work with dignity and by pride in their skills and crafts. Mundane tools such as saws, shovels, and knives had ornate engraving and were proudly passed from father to son. After 1850, the Industrial Revolution attracted farmers and immigrants to cities where they hoped to work their way to riches. Instead, they often found alienating work with low wages, long hours, tedium, danger, and pitiless supervision. In the early twentieth century, businesses applied "scientific management" to factories. Scientific management was a school of thought inspired by the influence of Frederick Taylor, an engineer who tried to increase worker productivity using time and motion studies to make tasks specialized, routine, and quick. Gone were the days of ornamental shovels. Taylor ushered in an era of utility.

Then, in reaction to this treatment of workers as machines, a school of thought developed that applied psychology to workers and encouraged em-

[3]Harvey M. Brenner, *Mental Illness and the Economy*, Cambridge, Massachusetts: Harvard University Press, 1976.
[4]M. J. Eales, "Shame Among Unemployed Men," *Social Science in Medicine*, vol. 28, no. 8 (1989), p. 788.

In the morning when thou risest unwillingly, let this thought be present—I am rising to the work of a human being. Why then am I dissatisfied if I am going to do the things for which I exist and for which I was brought into the world? Or have I been made for this, to lie in the bedclothes and keep myself warm? But this is more pleasant. Dost thou exist then to take thy pleasure and not at all for action or exertion? Dost thou not see the little plants, the little birds, the ants, the spiders, the bees working together to put in order their several parts of the universe? And art thou unwilling to do the work of a human being, and dost thou not make haste to do that which is according to they nature?

Marcus Aurelius, (circa A.D. 174–180) Meditations.

ployers to increase their productivity by nurturing their social needs. During World War II, the driving motive behind work became patriotism. From the end of the war through the 1950s, work was seen by Americans mainly as a source of status and income.

But by the 1970s, work came increasingly to be seen as a means of direct self-fulfillment. In a 1983 survey of 1,300 middle managers, for example, salary and regular promotions ranked seventh and eighth on a list of ten indicators of career success, behind self-fulfillment measures such as "achievement of personal life goals" and having the "opportunity and means for achieving a fulfilling, happy home and social life."[5] Today most workers continue to see work as a way to fulfill a variety of inner needs beyond simple survival, and they demand more than the grim drudgery that dispirited so many workers during the raw, early years of the Industrial Revolution.

THE CULTURAL CONTEXT OF WORK: THE CONTRAST BETWEEN AMERICAN AND JAPANESE WORKPLACES

Work and the workplace exist in a broad cultural context. Previously, we examined how attitudes toward work differ across time and place. Here we illustrate how cultural background determines in large measure how work is done.

Since World War II, the economy of Japan has developed impressively. Today Japan, which is America's largest overseas trading partner and increasingly its greatest competitor in international markets, has the third largest GNP in the world. Since World War II, the Japanese have had a productivity increase four times greater than that of the United States. Although growth of the Japanese economy has slowed since the first international energy shortage in 1973, between 1960 and 1973 growth in total factory productivity was 6.6 percent a year in Japan, the highest in the world and much in excess of the 1.9 percent in the United States.[6]

[5]George F. Breen, *Middle Management Morale in the '80s,* New York: American Management Association, 1983, p. 16.

[6]John W. Kendrick, "International Comparisons of Recent Productivity Trends," in *Quality and Productivity Improvements: U.S. and Foreign Company Experiences,* ed. Y. Krishna Shetty and Vernon Buehler, Chicago: Manufacturing and Productivity Center, 1983.

A critical element of this success is thought to be the unique nature of Japanese business organizations, which embody patterns of worker involvement different from those found in America. There has been enormous interest on the part of American business in transplanting elements of Japanese management to American corporations. Japanese managerial skills are thought to be closely associated with Japan's economic miracle.

In a best-selling 1981 book, *Theory Z*, William Ouchi explained major differences between Japanese and American company cultures.[7] In Japan, in the large industrial combines that employ about a third of the work force, work is the centerpiece of life, particularly for male employees. Workers have an ethic of extreme loyalty to employers and to the groups and teams in which most of them work. Responsibility for decisions, projects, and aspects of work such as quality control are assigned to groups, and these groups, rather than individuals with supervisory titles as in the United States, are held responsible by management for performance of duties. This intimacy of effort extends to inter-organization relations, and in Japan close relations exist between major firms, banks, government agencies, and hundreds of suppliers (which may go so far as to deliver parts right to worker stations in a factory).

The Japanese style of consensual decision making, known as the *ringisho* (RIN-gi-show) system after the name of a document passed around so that each manager can affix a seal of symbolic agreement to important decisions, differs considerably from the American custom of rapid executive decision followed by implementation and obedience. In a Japanese company, important policy changes are widely discussed and refined throughout the company until a consensus is reached. Japanese managers shun confrontation or argument. They do not like to be pushed into giving clear "yes" or "no" answers, and do not converse like American managers. The Japanese stress *haragei* (HA-ra-gay), or the "art of the stomach," a visceral, nonverbal communication process in which participants intuitively understand each other's feelings.

Most workers in the big industrial combines are given lifetime job security, which means in practice that barring malfeasance, workers are guaranteed a job from time of hire after schooling to at least age fifty-five. At age fifty-five to sixty, workers are severed from the company with a payment of three to six years' salary unless they go into one of the handful of top executive slots. The Japanese have met the problem of economic downturn, not by laying off workers as American companies do, but by paying less. In Japan, 40 to 60 percent of the typical paycheck is bonus compensation based on overall company performance. In recessionary times, therefore, worker pay can be lowered without violating union wage agreements. This system enables companies to guarantee jobs for thirty to forty years to some workers.

The work force in Japan is more homogeneous than that of the typical American company today, and important line positions are held exclusively by Japanese men. Women are paid lower salaries and expected to put home

[7]Reading, Massachusetts: Addison-Wesley, 1981.

and family before careers. Men are paid more, promoted sooner, and expected to place work before home. During their lifetime with the firm, Japanese workers are evaluated and promoted very slowly. The first promotion to assistant section head, for instance, usually comes between eight and twelve years after hiring. Employees follow nonspecific, nonspecialized career paths and learn various aspects of company operations.

The Japanese have a cultural tradition of obedience to authority. The extent to which workers devote their lives to their employers is shown by the loyalty and regimentation that a company may command. Workers are instructed to take calisthenics during the day; they may sing a company song or recite a company philosophy each morning; they live in company housing, wear company uniforms, and are likely to marry an employee of their company in a ceremony attended by top executives. Even in death, employees may remain part of the family by being buried in a corporate cemetery.

The Japanese have a strong work ethic in which they labor for the corporation with an intensity of effort which might be called fanaticism in America. A typical work schedule for managers is twelve hours a day six days a week plus several evenings spent socializing with peers after leaving the office. They also show loyalty and obedience to the employer of the kind seldom found in the West. At Taiyo Kogyo, a tent manufacturing company in Osaka, for instance, the workers assemble for a pep rally at 8:30 on Monday mornings, at which they recite company creeds. Creed number 7 is: "Once you've grabbed hold of a potential piece of business, never let it go, no matter what—even at the risk of your own life."[8] The devotion of the Japanese worker is vividly shown in an early morning scene described by an American visitor to Tokyo: "Along the curb, sanitation men carefully polish their tiny Isuzu garbage trucks. Imagine the response of American garbage men to such a directive—it would burn this page."[9]

The Japanese work ethic encompasses more than devotion and hard work. It also involves a perfectionism sometimes referred to as "pursuing the last grain of rice in the corner of the lunchbox." An American professor who toured Japanese factories quotes a Japanese scholar describing this fixation with quality.

"If you do an economic analysis you will usually find that it is advantageous to reduce your defect rate from 10 percent to 5 percent. If you repeat that analysis, it may or may not make sense to reduce it further to 1 percent. The Japanese, however, will reduce it. Having accomplished this, they will attempt to reduce it to 0.1 percent. And then 0.01 percent. You might claim that this obsession is costly, that it makes no economic sense. They are heedless. They will not be satisfied with less than perfection."

Indeed, in most of the Japanese factories I visited, the quality charts on the walls measured the defect rate not in percentages but in parts per million.[10]

The culture that harbors these organizational values evolved from a Japanese society of small villages with strong norms of individual subordination

[8]John Greenwald, "A Hard Day's Night," *Time*, August 1, 1983, p. 42.

[9]B. Bruce-Briggs, "The Dangerous Folly Called Theory Z," *Fortune*, May 17, 1982, p. 41.

[10]Robert H. Hayes, "Why Japanese Factories Work," *Harvard Business Review*, July–August 1981, pp. 62–63.

Who's Better?

U.S. News & World Report asked 10 leading scholars who have studied both Japanese and American workers to rate them on a variety of qualities. Although the experts disagreed on some issues, the comments are representative of their remarks.

U.S.	Concern for Quality	Japan
☐	Japanese workers possess an almost religious desire to do jobs well. They pay great attention to detail. Many Americans just want to finish the job.	●
	Initiative	
★	On an individual level, Americans are willing to take the lead. They are concerned with who gets credit for exceptional work.	☐
	Hard Work	
☐	The work ethic is strong in both countries, but the experts give the Japanese a slight edge because they routinely put in extra hours. Their company is the central focus of their lives.	●
	Honesty	
☐	Because of strong identification with their company, Japanese are less likely to steal office supplies or cheat on time cards and expense accounts.	●
	Ambition	
★	America's individualistic culture encourages workers to strive to get ahead. Japanese, though ambitious, try not to stand out, especially early in their careers.	☐
	Loyalty	
☐	The average Japanese worker expects to spend an entire career at one firm. Companies, in turn, take a paternalistic interest in employees.	●
	Basic Skills	
☐	Japan's schools produce graduates with good basic skills. Japanese learn discipline and good work habits that they transfer to the job.	●
	Advanced Skills	
★	A close call. Workers in both nations are highly educated, but the U.S. has more college graduates and white-collar professionals.	☐
	Reliability	
☐	Japanese are reluctant to show up late or call in sick, largely because they don't want to let down their bosses and co-workers. Many skip parts of their vacations.	●
	Cooperativeness	
☐	Japanese subordinate individual concerns to group needs. This fosters a spirit of togetherness that is especially effective on the assembly line.	●

Source: Adapted from Richard Aim and Maureen Walsh. "America vs. Japan: Can U.S. Workers Compete?" *U.S. News & World Report,* September 2, 1985. Copyright © 1985 U.S. News and World Report.

to group interest, low social-class mobility, and strong feudal loyalties of vassals to lords. In the United States, in contrast, our frontier tradition emphasized rugged individualism and high social mobility, not collective social control. Therefore, the American worker is animated by values of independence. Social control of individuals is not as strong here. Highly mobile workers have been accommodated by job specialization that makes individuals interchangeable production units rather than team members. Hierarchical and authoritarian decision making exists instead of a tradition of group consensus. American corporations lay off workers because they face union opposition to lowering wages during recessions. And quality control comes through specialized inspection and cost control functions rather than team planning. Hence, the evidence strongly suggests that the two divergent societies have sprouted two strikingly different corporate cultures, each of which is successful in its environment.

Some observers believe that many of the most successful American firms, companies such as IBM, Levi Strauss, Procter & Gamble, and Hewlett-Packard, have some of the characteristics of Japanese companies. These companies are said to use management skills and quality of worklife techniques that overcome the productivity problems inherent in antagonistic industrial relations. Ouchi calls these hybrids "Theory Z organizations" and says that they are characterized by long-term employment, consensual decision making, slower evaluation and promotion, the merger of informal group control with formal hierarchical control, broader employee career paths, and concern for the total needs of the worker, including family life.

We note in passing that due to cultural and historical differences, the large Japanese firm has an approach to social responsibility different from that of its U.S. counterpart. In Japan, pressure groups in the business environment are less strident and demanding, because there is a strong reluctance to challenge prevailing rules and authority. Questioning corporate leaders is thought inappropriate in a crowded country where cultural values teach the necessity of accomodating differences to get along. Hence, no strong consumer movement has ever emerged in Japan. Due to strong traditional values that stereotype women in submissive roles, the women's movement is weak. Labor unions mostly support management. Employees are very loyal, and because of Confucian ideals of obedience and fealty to authority do not challenge management or demand expansive rights. Civil rights groups are weak because minorities comprise less than one percent of the population. Thus, in Japan, corporate social responsibility is based on the charitable duty defined in Confucian ethics to minister to those in dependent relationships. In the U.S., on the other hand, the social environment of the corporation is more complex and challenging. The paternalistic approach characteristic of Japanese firms is inadequate. Large American firms are far less able to dictate the terms of their socially responsible actions.[11]

THE DOWNSIDE OF JAPANESE MANAGEMENT

Japanese management is not a wellspring of unadulterated contentment. If its inner flaws and stresses are exported in productivity improvement pro-

---

[11]We are indebted to Richard E. Wokutch for his discussion in "Corporate Social Responsibility: The Missing Link in Japanese Management Theory," *Academy of Management Executive*, May 1990.

grams, American workers may regret it. In Japan, dedication to organizational life starts in prekindergarten training sessions, where competition to get into the best schools begins. Children attend school six days a week, and this obsessive preparation foreshadows the long workdays and utter devotion of the Japanese male to his work. Japanese men place work before family life and commonly slight their families to meet group pressures to perform. The sacrifice inherent in this mania for work exceeds what is regarded as normal in the United States.

The strength that homogeneity provides for the Japanese work force is the result of sexist and racist tendencies in companies. Important line positions in Japanese companies are reserved for Japanese men. Women, men of other races (such as Caucasians), and men of other cultures (such as Koreans or Chinese) are screened out by formal and informal processes. Development and promotion rituals socialize men with common backgrounds into management teams and subtly exclude outsiders. These discriminatory personnel practices have been exported to Japanese-run companies in the United States. On the surface they violate American antidiscrimination statutes but have been held by the courts to be permissible under U.S. Treaties of Friendship, Commerce and Navigation that allow Japanese parent companies wide latitude in employing nationals in managerial and technical positions in U.S. operations. For example, in the case of *Sumitomo Shoji America, Inc. v. Avigliano,* the Supreme Court refused to permit a Japanese company to hire only male Japanese citizens for executive positions—only because Sumitomo Shoji America, Inc., a subsidiary, was incorporated in New York and technically a U.S. company.[12]

The discipline, conformity, and loyalty of Japanese workers is motivated by collectivist ideas, a strong work ethic, and stiff group pressure to conform. The latter takes its toll. Freelance journalist Satoshi Kamata studied Toyota Motor Company in Japan and one night met with workers from various plants who recalled twenty worker suicides over the past year. For example, a worker at a Toyota plant in Tsutsumi died in his company-owned quarters after taking an overdose of sleeping pills. He had been depressed from being berated for tardiness by his team leader and forced to "apologize to his fellow workers for the inconvenience he caused."[13] Other workers had hanged themselves, driven their cars into reservoirs, and thrown themselves into the sea. Not only does pressure exist to be productive, but Japanese are also expected to move through life with their age groups—never too far ahead, never too far behind. Like radical individuality, premature success in salary or position is the seed of rejection.

In Japan today there is less idealization of the management system than there was in the past. That faithful drone, the Japanese worker, is showing signs of rebellion against long hours, unquestioning loyalty, and group pressure. Increasingly, affluent younger workers are likely to refuse transfers that

---

[12]102 S.Ct. 2374 (1982).

[13]Satoshi Kamata, "Employee Welfare Takes a Back Seat at Toyota," *Business and Society Review*, Summer 1983, p. 31.

break up families, to demand more leisure time, or to switch to another company in mid-career.

In addition, some Japanese corporations now believe that pressures for conformity to group norms have stifled creative development of new, basic technology. Japanese work groups tend to ostracize individuals with unusual ideas, yet these ideas may be valuable. In 1989, Toyota Motor Corp. did a massive internal restructuring designed to break down group-oriented decisions and encourage individualistic thinkers. It began to base promotions on merit instead of seniority, reduced the number of approvals necessary for implementation of new ideas, reduced the number of middle managers, and deemphasized customs of deference to higher-ranking managers. These actions all move Toyota away from the classic but flawed form of Japanese management.

MANAGING JAPANESE-OWNED COMPANIES IN THE UNITED STATES

The primary exposure of Americans to the astringent of foreign management techniques has been in Japanese-owned businesses. Between 1977 and 1989, the number of workers employed by Japanese firms in the U.S. jumped from 60,000 to over 400,000. This is a small but growing percentage of the work force.

Most Japanese employers have tried to import customary workplace practices to U.S. operations. They demand the quasi-spiritual commitment to work found in Japanese workers. Employees at Three Bond Company in Torrance, California, for instance, are told that the first company rule is: "We shall be guided by the belief that faithful execution of our duties contributes to the greatest happiness of the greatest number, and that working for the prosperity of the company is at once working for the well-being of society, country, and mankind." Hourly workers are carefully screened for personalities compatible with teamwork. At Toyota's auto manufacturing plant in Georgetown, Kentucky, for example, assemblers must complete eighteen hours of interviews and testing, including group manufacturing sessions which evaluate interpersonal skills and an exam about their attitudes toward work. Less than 10 percent of applicants are hired. Many, but not all, Japanese companies also insist on the symbolic rituals of loyalty, including morning calisthenics, company songs, and company uniforms.

Blue-collar workers at Japanese plants typically work in teams where they make many decisions about their work that would be made by supervisors in American plants. In Japanese auto plants, all workers have authority to stop the motion of the assembly line, an act that would lead to discipline or firing if undertaken by an auto worker at Ford or GM. The egalitarian atmosphere in Japanese plants extends beyond the assembly line. Managers and executives may wear the same uniforms as workers, compete with them for open spaces in the parking lots, and eat lunch at the same cafeteria. The pace of work is typically grueling. A Honda plant is described:

> On the production line...workers are often closer to a run than a walk as they rush between parts benches and car bodies moving down the line. One worker jumps into a car, attaches a back-seat catch, wheels around to attach a piece of

waterproofing, and then, juggling an electric screwdriver, drives several screws into the frame. She then jumps out, dodges other workers, resupplies, and jumps into the next car. Her face is tight with concentration.[14]

Japanese companies have tried to avoid American unions. One reason is that unions in this country differ from Japanese unions in ways that Japanese managers find counterproductive. There are 74,000 unions in Japan, each organized around an individual company. Each year they conduct a "spring wage offensive," but their efforts are meek by U.S. standards. Union leaders are considered part of company management and would be shunned as disloyal if their actions hurt operations. When strikes do occur, they usually last only an hour or two at a time least likely to disturb production. Strong wage demands are seen as unpatriotic because they might weaken the Japanese firm in its competition against low-wage competitors in Taiwan and South Korea. Given this background, Japanese managers see American unions with their forceful wage and benefit demands and dead-serious strike threats as anathema. A second reason is that American unions insist on contract rules inimical to Japanese production practices. In a typical U.S. auto plant, for example, the United Auto Workers contract stipulates 175–200 job categories and prohibits workers in one category from performing work defined as being in another. In a typical Japanese auto plant, on the other hand, there are as few as four job categories, and the teamwork ethic demands frequent cross-over among them.

American managers also find work in Japanese companies to be unconventional. They work in proximity with Japanese career employees from the home corporation, yet many feel like outsiders. They are expected to work long hours. David M. Proctor III, the highest ranking American in the U.S. subsidiary of Dai-Ichi Kangyo Bank (the world's largest bank) arrives at his office at 6:30 a.m. and does not leave until 7:30 p.m. He says: "I'm somewhat guilty leaving at that hour because I'm the first to go."[15] Despite efforts, few Americans in Japanese subsidiaries are permitted access to the career ladder of the parent company in Japan. The Japanese are often seen as xenophobic, secretive, and prejudiced against women, minorities, and American workers. Thus, American managers are denied access to real power, which resides with the Japanese. An executive at Toshiba America's calculator division noted to a newspaper reporter that he soon discovered his inability to overrule a young Japanese assistant. Among the Americans at Toshiba, he said, "[t]here was a subtle understanding that if the order came from a Japanese— no matter what his title was—you had your work cut out for you."[16]

The success of transplanted management systems has been mixed, but generally positive. Where Japanese methods have been installed in start-up operations with a clean slate, they have been successful. One example is the

[14]Martin Tolchin and Susan Tolchin, "A Clash of Cultures," *Management Review*, March 1988, p. 50.
[15]Quoted in Jim Schachter and Nancy Yoshihara, "Bosses From Japan Bring Alien Habits," *Los Angeles Times*, July 10, 1988.
[16]Quoted in Jonathan Peterson, "Americans as 'Watched' Executives," *Los Angeles Times*, July 11, 1988.

joint venture called New United Motor Manufacturing, Inc. (NUMMI) set up in 1983 by Toyota Motor Co. and General Motors at the Freemont Plant in northern California. In order to study Japanese auto production techniques, GM entered this partnership and gave Toyota free reign in setting up the production system. Toyota, for its part, was attracted to the joint venture by the need to acquire a manufacturing plant in the United States.

Under GM management, the plant had been a nightmare of inefficiency. Drugs, sex, and alcohol were freely available in its parking lots. The grounds were littered with beer bottles. Absenteeism approached 20 percent on Mondays and Fridays. The plant closed in 1982 and reopened only after the UAW agreed to a nonadversarial, nonconfrontational relationship in which it accepted the Toyota teamwork production system with flexible work rules and few job classifications. In return, NUMMI granted workers top hourly wages and pledged not to lay off workers unless dire losses were sustained. When the NUMMI operation started, 85 percent of the workers came from the motley GM work force which had thrown together low-quality autos before 1982. But now, the Toyota system transformed them. They worked in teams of five to seven and decided how jobs could best be done by themselves, rather than following the dictates of time and motion study experts and floor supervisors. Several ideas inculcated by Toyota proved critical in the transformation. One was *jikoda* (gee-KO-dah), a principle by which each worker regards subsequent workstations as customers of his product and strives to attain perfect quality. Another was *kaizen* (KYE-zen), or continuous improvement, which exhorts workers to constantly seek small efficiencies in their work. And a third was *muda* (MOO-dah), or the philosophy of avoiding waste, which made inefficient use of space, energy, and materials sinful. The NUMMI plant has been a success. The Toyota Corollas and Chevrolet Novas it makes meet quality standards of plants in Japan, and absenteeism now runs only two percent. But it has been hard for GM to spread the NUMMI system to its other plants.[17]

Where Japanese techniques have been overlayed on existing situations, they sometimes have not been as successful as new operations. When Sanyo Electric Co. took over a Zenith Corp. television factory which made sets for Sears Roebuck & Co., it introduced the trappings of Japanese-style factory work. Initially, productivity and quality improvement was marked, but was largely a result of using better components from Japanese suppliers. The electrical worker's union balked at introduction of calisthenics and the company uniform. The union fought with management over many issues and struck twice by 1985. From 1985 to 1989, the plant ran up deficits of $60 million, and at this writing its continued operation is unlikely.

---

[17]Maryann Keller describes how GM has thus far been unable to spread the NUMMI system in *Rude Awakening*, New York: William Morrow, 1989, Chapter 6. On NUMMI see also Peter Ennis, "NUMMI Struggles to Close Culture Gap," *Tokyo Business Today*, September 1987; and Bill Childs, "New United Motor: An American Success Story," *Labor Law Journal*, August 1989. For more on the Toyota production system see Toyota Motor Corporation, *Toyota: A History of the First 50 Years*, Toyota City: Toyota Motor Corp., 1988, Chapter 4.

Such stories send signals about important elements of the work environment.

• *Norms, Values, and Assumptions:* All strong corporate cultures emphasize mutually reinforcing norms, values, and assumptions. At 3M, innovation is prized. Employees who have ideas can get funding and organizational sanctuary for their projects. If they successfully develop a new product, as did Art Fry, who developed Post-it Notes within the company, they even can share in its profits. At ITT under former CEO Harold Geneen, in contrast, entrepreneurship was sometimes the equivalent of insubordination. In the 1960s, when scattered groups of engineers began furtively working within the ITT organization to develop computer technology, Geneen unleashed organizational detectives who ferreted these people out and shut down their projects.

• *Physical Objects and Arrangements:* The physical layout of a workplace may be indicative of its culture. Open or closed offices suggest communication norms. So do the number of conference rooms. Some companies have abolished separate eating and parking areas for executives to introduce a more democratic feel. Authoritative and strongly hierarchical companies, in contrast, separate managers from workers, physically alter office spaces to make them more luxurious for higher-level occupants, and in a variety of ways reinforce organizational status with physical statements.

Corporate cultures are long-standing; some go back to the company founders. Henry Ford, for example, inspired a narcissistic management style at Ford Motor Company in which managers demanded complete, unquestioning obedience from subordinates.[19] For example, Ford assigned two men the same job and title to see which one survived the competition and abolished whole departments by firing all the executives in them. Today, the style lives on at Ford, although the company is trying to abolish it because managers believe that competing personalities and autocratic management hamper productivity. Thousands of Ford managers have been sent to workshops on participative management. But change is difficult. Ford has, over the years, selected naturally authoritarian managers. A study of 2,000 Ford managers once classified 76 percent as "noncreative types who are comfortable with strong authority."[20] (Only about 38 percent of the population at large would fall into this category.) The Henry Ford style may be contrasted with that of IBM founder Thomas Watson, who insisted that all employees call each other Mr., Miss, or Mrs. to show mutual respect. To this day, IBM retains a reputation for deferential treatment of employees and for employee loyalty.

In conclusion, it is not only the national culture that determines basic aspects of work, but the corporate culture as well. Corporate cultures vary widely with industry, competitive environment, and founders' attitudes.

[19]Anne Jardim, *The First Henry Ford: A Study in Personality and Business Leadership*, Cambridge, Massachusetts: MIT Press, 1970.
[20]Melinda G. Guiles and Paul Ingrassia, "Ford's Leaders Push Radical Shift in Culture as Competition Grows," *Wall Street Journal*, December 3, 1985.

EXTERNAL FORCES CHANGING THE WORKPLACE

As is by now evident, those who work today, especially those who work in large corporations, are caught up in changes wrought by powerful environmental forces. A listing of the most important changes follows.

TECHNOLOGICAL CHANGE

Technological change has many impacts on work. It affects the number and type of jobs available. Invention of the airplane, for example, created new job titles such as pilot and flight attendant. New machines are used by management to raise productivity and reduce costs. Automated teller machines at banks, for instance, increase the number of daily transactions possible and simultaneously reduce the number of employees necessary to handle them. Robots in auto manufacturing have made American companies more competitive in cost and quality with Japanese car makers.

Automation offers both benefits and drawbacks. It has a turbulent impact on employment because it creates jobs for the architects of the machine age while displacing traditional manufacturing and service jobs. In the coal mining industry, the use of longwall and continuous mining machines has eliminated 300,000 pick-and-shovel jobs since the 1950s. The 30,000 robots on U.S. assembly lines in 1989 have eliminated two-thirds of all assembly line jobs since 1980.[21] Where machines and robots are used for painting, handling toxic waste, or cutting meat in slaughterhouses, they eliminate drudge work and danger. Increasingly, however, machinery eliminates highly skilled work. Numerically controlled lathes and milling machines, for example, have reduced the need for skilled machine shop operators.

The growing application of computer technology affects most jobs. Computers make information more assessable, speed the performance of duties, and can move managers closer to production activity. But they may also impose more stress on workers whose job performance can be precisely measured. The exact performance record of a bank loan officer or stockbroker—hard to calculate at present—eventually may be clearer to superiors than ever before. Any employee who works at a computer terminal may have his or her performance recorded. One airline required reservationists working on a computerized system to average 109 seconds per call and 11 seconds between calls. Another measured bathroom breaks, allowing 12 minutes during each seven and one-half hour day.[22] These practices illustrate the unfriendly side of new technology in the workplace. It can be used to speed work, but it may also create stress and invade privacy. These tendencies have been present since the nineteenth century, but new technologies continuously open new avenues of psychological abuse and must be carefully adapted.

[21]Marvin Cetron and Owen Davies, *American Renaissance*, New York: St. Martin's Press, 1989.
[22]In Peter A. Susser, ''Electronic Monitoring in the Private Sector: How Closely Should Employers Supervise Their Workers?'' *Employee Relations Law Journal*, Spring 1988, p. 581. See also Barbara Garson, *The Electronic Sweatshop: How Computers Are Transforming the Office of the Future into the Factory of the Past*, New York: Penguin Books, 1988.

DEMOGRAPHIC CHANGE

Out of a 1989 population of 249 million Americans, about half, or 124 million, composed the labor force as either working or unemployed. The rest were retired, disabled, students, housewives, students, children, or not counted by the government because they got unreported wages. Demographic movements are altering the characteristics of this labor force; it is growing more slowly and aging.

The number of workers is continuously increasing. In 1950, the number of available workers was 62.3 million. By 1989, there were 123.8 million, but expansion is now slower than at any time since the 1930s because population growth has slowed. By the year 2000, it is predicted that the labor force will expand only to about 138.8 million.[23]

The labor force is also aging. High fertility rates following World War II created a "baby boom generation" born between 1946–1961. The presence of this generation now creates a bulge of workers in their thirties and forties. Because baby boomers are aging, between now and the year 2000 the number of workers aged thirty-five to forty-seven will increase 30 percent, and the number of workers aged forty-eight to fifty-three will increase a phenomenal 67 percent.[24] Simultaneously, there will be a dearth of younger workers. Since the 1950s, the nation's fertility rate has been declining, and the number of workers under age thirty will fall by about 10 to 12 percent in the 1990s. At the end of this decade, there will be a shortage of entry-level workers, and the demographic bulge of the postwar baby boom, now located at the middle-management level, will rise to upper management. There a new bottleneck will form as large numbers of ambitious people compete for fewer and fewer vacancies where the organizational pyramid constricts. Not all would-be CEOs can be accommodated.

STRUCTURAL CHANGE

Our economy is being reshaped by long-term trends common to industrialized nations around the world. They are illustrated by employment shifts between 1950 and 1986.

1 Farm workers declined from 12 percent of the labor force to 1.5 percent, as fewer and larger farms delivered the nation's food supply using intensive forms of crop and animal agriculture. For example, in 1920 the largest chicken farm in the country had a flock of 500 birds; today 100,000 birds are raised in a single poultry building, and large operations have several million birds at one time. New farming methods require huge capital investment, but produce efficiencies beyond smaller family farms.

2 Employment in the goods producing occupations declined from 78 percent to 22 percent. Many manufacturing operations have been displaced to

[23]Bureau of the Census, *Statistical Abstract of the United States 1989*, 109th ed., December 1988, Table no. 621. Other figures in this section are from Section 13 and from *Employment and Earnings*, September 1989.

[24]Hudson Institute, *Workforce 2000*, Indianapolis, Indiana: Hudson Institute, Inc., June 1987, p. 79.

lower wage countries. Also, workplaces have increased productivity with automation that replaces workers and lowers labor costs. Since 1980, for instance, General Motors has installed 4,000 new robots.

3 Service workers increased from 10 percent to 67 percent of the labor force. As manufacturing has become more efficient, the service sector of the economy has grown. Service jobs such as retailing and transportation add value to manufactured goods.

4 Blue-collar workers declined from 41 percent to 28 percent. This decline reflects a serious disruption in the labor market. In steel production, for example, foreign competition and automation have reduced blue-collar workers from a peak of 620,400 in 1953 to 275,000 in 1986, and the number continues to fall. Heavy manufacturing will continue to decline as an employer as the economy shifts to newer high-technology industries.

5 White-collar workers increased from 36 percent to 56 percent of the labor force, primarily because of growth in government and of technical positions in service industries. Unfortunately, the skills of surplus workers in "smokestack" industries often are not salable in these employment growth areas. This qualifications gap has been disproportionately burdensome to minority workers who, in the aggregate, have lesser job skills.

INTENSE COMPETITIVE PRESSURES

Competitive forces always have been strong in the U.S. economy, but they are arguably stronger in the 1990s, for several reasons. First, foreign competitors in Japan, the Far East, and Europe have taken advantage of low labor costs, high productivity, and a strong dollar to undersell American firms. Second, formerly protected companies in newly deregulated industries are now more exposed to market forces. And, third, a wave of hostile mergers and acquisitions has disciplined management to protect the value of the company's assets in the stock market.

These competitive pressures have many ramifications for employees. To lower costs, hundreds of corporations, including the largest, are pruning the ranks of middle management. One estimate is that over 500,000 of the roughly 28 million middle managers in the United States lost their jobs between 1984 and 1987.[25] Since 1980, for example, General Motors has eliminated 150,000 jobs—enough people to fill a stadium. In February 1989, an executive of McDonnell Douglas assembled all 5,200 supervisors, managers, and executives of the corporation's Douglas Aircraft subsidiary in a paint warehouse in Long Beach, California. He announced that none of them had a job any longer. If they wished to remain with the company, they could reapply for just over 4,000 positions in a new organization charted in advance. In order to qualify, they had to pass personality tests designed to measure teamwork skills.

[25]Rod Willis, "What's Happening to America's Middle Managers?" *Management Review,* January 1987, p. 24.

Layoffs and restructuring may exact a price. Loyalty to a company has been an enduring aspect of work in America, but some surveys show that loyalty is fading among middle managers. In a 1986 survey of 600 corporations, 65 percent of respondents said that their fellows were less loyal than they had been ten years earlier.[26] A second survey of managers at 1,900 companies found sharply diminished commitment to employers in the decade 1977–87.[27] The ebbing of loyalty extends to all employees. A 1989 *Time*/CNN/ Yankelovich national poll of employed adults reported that 63 percent saw employees as less loyal to their companies than they were ten years ago.[28]

CHANGING VALUES OF EMPLOYEES

Shifting social values are changing attitudes toward work, particularly among younger, highly educated workers. Our society has emphasized education, and the work force of the 1980s is more educated than ever. Since World War II, the number of workers with college degrees has more than doubled. The number of professional and technical workers nearly doubled, from 8.4 percent in 1950 to 15.8 percent in 1987.[29] Traditionally, workers valued jobs as sources of economic security and were motivated by the pursuit of money and status. They toiled for distant rewards and postponed immediate pleasures. So strong was loyalty to corporate employers that managers commonly sacrificed personal interests to work demands.

Workers today, however, have different values. To many, work is a quest for self-fulfillment, not income and status. Employees are more narcissistic, insistent on their rights, less accepting of authority, inclined to immediate gratification of desires, and not automatically loyal to the company. Survey findings reflect such changes. When 1,460 workers were asked which of sixteen different stakeholders was most important to the firm, "myself" was ranked first by supervisors, middle managers, those under forty years old, and the college educated.[30]

Because of these value changes, there is growing desire for increased quality of work life. Generally, quality of work life is a shorthand phrase for the concept of making work and workplaces more rewarding for human beings. Today there is agreement that a corporation that simply offers paid employment is not doing enough. There is, for example, a declining willingness to do meaningless work in authoritarian settings. Some people have wrongly

---

[26]Bruce Nussbaum, "The End of Corporate Loyalty?" *Business Week,* August 4, 1986.

[27]Gail Cook Johnson and Ronald J. Grey, "Signs of Diminishing Employee Commitment," *Canadian Business Review,* Spring 1988. The 1,900 companies were in both the U.S. and Canada.

[28]*Time,* "Ebbing Loyalty," September 11, 1989, p. 54. A recent survey of executives of the very largest companies, however, found that 80 percent said their companies had been good to them and, hence, they were "deeply committed" to their companies. It was a 1988 Roper Organization survey reported in Jerry Buckley, "The New Organization Man," *U.S. News & World Report,* January 16, 1989, p. 42.

[29]See *Statistical Abstract, op. cit.,* Table no. 642 and older editions for comparative data.

[30]Warren H. Schmidt and Barry Z. Posner, *Managerial Values and Expectations: The Silent Power in Personal and Organizational Life,* New York: American Management Association, 1982.

concluded that the work ethic has eroded. The drive to work is as strong as ever, but the moral and doctrinal elements of the old Protestant ethic have been replaced by strong economic and psychological needs. The demand today is for fulfillment of old demands for improved working conditions, including better pay and fringe benefits, safety and health, shorter hours, and elimination of incompetent supervision. In addition, workers demand greater control over their immediate work environment. For most employees it means meaningful work; the use of available skills; the chance to grow and achieve; the opportunity to find interesting and challenging work; facilities to do the assigned job correctly and well; the protection of a growing array of rights and entitlements; and an end to monotonous, meaningless tasks performed in isolation.

GROWING HETEROGENEITY OF THE WORK FORCE

The work force is becoming more heterogeneous. Minorities, immigrants, and women, propelled by powerful political movements and protected by antidiscrimination law, are becoming a larger percentage of all workers. Nonwhites have grown from 11 percent of the labor force in 1970 to 14 percent in 1987, and are predicted to be 16 percent by the year 2000. Women will comprise three-fifths of new entrants into the work force until the year 2000, rising from 45 to 47 percent of the total work force. Immigrants will be approximately 13 percent of new workers during this period.[31]

These new workers bring new aspirations and pose new challenges. Minorities and immigrants are overrepresented in less skilled and declining occupations. As the job mix shifts in favor of knowledge work, their assimilation becomes more difficult. In management ranks, assimilation will create conflict. In years past, white males dominated 95 percent of corporate management positions, even though constituting only 37 percent of the population.[32] Now white males must compete with a new mix of ambitious people.

In addition, an increasingly varied mixture of individual values in the work force may also cause stress. David Ewing, a scholar of the changing workplace, thinks our "variegated American culture" produces a hodgepodge of workers. "Some employees," he writes, "are materialistic, others are aesthetic; some are conservatives, others are heretics; some worship authority, others only tolerate it; some revel in teamwork and group membership, others prefer to go it alone in field selling or research; some 'think like farmers' whereas others 'think like Madison Avenue'."[33] These differences create dissidence. They make empathic relationships more difficult.

GOVERNMENT INTERVENTION

Government has injected new rules into the workplace. Historically, governments at all levels reflected the strong *laissez faire* content of American eco-

[31]Figures in this paragraph are from *Workforce 2000, op. cit.,* pp. 85, 89, and 95, and the *Statistical Abstract, op. cit.,* Table no. 621.

[32]John P. Fernandez, *Racism and Sexism in Corporate Life,* Lexington, Massachusetts: Lexington Books, 1981, p. 7.

[33]In *Do It My Way or You're Fired,* New York: Dutton, 1983, p. 4.

THE TRAP

Turn-of-the-century cartoonist Art Young drew this cynical view of the lopsided employment contract in the days before labor unions and laws protecting worker rights. (*Source:* Art Young, *The Best of Art Young.* New York: Vanguard Press, 1936, p. 53.)

nomic philosophy and were reluctant to interfere with the employment contract, or the agreement by which an employee exchanges his labor in return for specific pay and working conditions. But today, government intervention is extensive and growing. This has been a twentieth century trend.

Prior to the 1930s, the only government intervention was in state laws that limited female and child labor. Unquestionably, the advantage in the contract between employer and employee lay with the employer. Employees had little bargaining power; they could be fired at will and had to accept virtually any working conditions. The unchallenged dominion of employers led to negligent treatment of workers and created the labor union movement, a social movement to empower workers. The first federal law designed to redress the huge power imbalance favoring employers was the Norris-La Guardia Act of 1932, which struck down a type of employer-employee agreement that angry unionists colorfully labeled "yellow dog contracts." These were agreements that workers would not join unions. Employers virtually extorted signatures on them when workers were hired. Workers had little choice but to sign if they wanted to keep their jobs—and jobs were scarce in the 1930s. If union organizing began, employers went to court, where judges enforced the yellow dog contracts by prohibiting workers from holding union membership. But the Norris-La Guardia Act outlawed this tactic and encouraged unionism. It was soon followed by the Wagner Act of 1935, which guaranteed union organizing and bargaining rights.

After the 1930s, employers still dominated the work contract, but company power over wages and working conditions was increasingly checked by unions. Then, beginning in the 1960s, the trend toward more government regulation of companies reached into the workplace once more. And since then, new federal and state laws have been enacted to further protect employees. At the federal level, this is illustrated by six major laws.

- The *Civil Rights Act of 1964* prohibited discrimination against women and minorities and established an agency to enforce its provisions. It is discussed at length in the following chapter.
- The *Occupational Safety and Health Act of 1970* was passed to protect workers from chemical and radiation hazards as well as high injury rates in many industries. Stories of employer irresponsibility preceded passage of the act, which set up an agency to inspect workplaces and enforce standards.
- The *Employee Retirement Income Security Act of 1974* outlawed practices that cheated employees out of pensions; such practices included "weasel clauses," which stated that with any break in employment, such as a brief layoff, workers forfeited their previous contributions and had to start anew. It set many standards and requirements for corporate pensions.
- The *Worker Adjustment and Retraining Act of 1988* required companies employing more than 100 people to give sixty days' notification prior to plant closings or large layoffs.
- The *Drug Free Workplace Act of 1988* required firms with federal contracts to set up policies prohibiting drug use at work. This law, which does not make drug testing mandatory, followed Executive Order 12564 issued by President Reagan in 1986 to require drug testing for most federal employees. Both require employers to establish rehabilitation programs.
- The *Employee Polygraph Protection Act of 1988* prohibited the use of lie detectors to screen job applicants and narrowed legitimate grounds for using the tests to detect theft or sabotage among employees.

All these laws continue to redress the weakness of employees in the employment contract and expand their rights. This expansion requires further explanation.

THE EMPLOYEE RIGHTS MOVEMENT

In years past, employers could demand total dedication and obedience from employees. In 1878, a New York carriage shop adopted a list of rules for employees that stipulated among other things, "On the Sabbath, everyone is expected to be in the Lord's House," and, "All employees are expected to be in bed by 10:00 P.M."[34] Under the direction of Henry Ford, the Ford Motor Company set up a sociology department headed by a Detroit minister. It sent teams of investigators into workers' homes to certify the purity of their private lives. A second department, the service department, was formed to spy on workers at the plant. Workers were carefully watched for drinking, smoking, or criticizing the company, and many were summarily fired for offenses.[35] Throughout American history, in fact, employees have been subject to the whims of employers.

Although employees have political rights, such as the right to vote and speak freely, the Constitution protects citizens only from government infringement of these rights, not from infringement by private employers. If an employer restricts freedom of speech by banning an underground newsletter printed by employees and mailed to customers, the employees are not protected by the First Amendment because the guarantee of a free press in the First Amendment limits only action by government, not repression by a corporate employer. Professor David Ewing of Harvard argues eloquently that because of this rights gap, employees are deprived of important protections.

> For nearly two centuries Americans have enjoyed freedom of press, speech, and assembly, due process of law, privacy, freedom of conscience, and other important rights—in their homes, churches, political forums, and social and cultural life. But Americans have not enjoyed these civil liberties in most companies, government agencies, and other organizations where they work. Once a U.S. citizen steps through the plant or office door at 9 A.M., he or she is nearly rightless until 5 P.M., Monday through Friday. The employee continues to have political freedoms, of course, but these are not the significant ones now. While at work, the important relationships are with bosses, associates, and subordinates. Inequalities in dealing with these people are what really count for an employee.[36]

RIGHTS THAT EMPLOYEES DEMAND

There are many rights that workers feel entitled to today. Following are the major ones:

- the right to a job
- the right to protection from arbitrary or sudden termination
- the right to privacy of possessions and person in the workplace, including freedom from arbitrary searches, use of polygraphs, surreptitious surveillance, and intrusive psychological or medical testing

[34]Robert Ellis Smith, *Workrights,* New York: Dutton, 1983, p. 15.
[35]John D. Dahlinger, *The Secret Life of Henry Ford,* New York: Bobbs-Merrill, 1978.
[36]David W. Ewing, *Freedom Inside the Organization,* New York: Dutton, 1977, p. 3.

- the right to equal opportunity and nondiscriminatory treatment in personnel decisions
- the right to a clean, healthy, and safe environment on the job, including freedom from undue stress, sexual harassment, cigarette smoke, and exposure to toxic substances
- the right to be informed of records and information kept and to access to personnel files
- the right to freedom of action, association, and lifestyle when off duty
- the right to freedom of conscience and to inform government or media about illegal or socially harmful corporate actions
- the right to self-actualization through career advancement
- the right to collective bargaining and to strike
- the right to due process for grievances against the employer
- the right to free expression of sexual preference and choice of a romantic partner
- the right to participate in major decisions affecting one's job
- the right to freedom of political belief and expression, including the right to publish opinions related to occupation
- the right to adequate leisure time for personal and family activities
- the right to reject interdepartment and intercity transfers
- the right to choose clothing and hair style
- the right to fair play and fringe benefits such as medical and insurance
- the right to an adequate pension

THE TREND TOWARD MORE EMPLOYEE RIGHTS

Originally, all of these rights developed as moral rights due workers who toiled under autocratic managers. Many of these moral rights have become legal rights. Federal law prohibits discrimination, sets standards for pensions, prohibits disclosure of government data on workers to employers, sets rules for labor relations, and protects worker safety. State law encodes additional legal rights. Michigan, for example, bans discrimination based on height or weight. Twenty-one states have laws protecting corporate and government whistleblowers from reprisal. Courts also protect some rights not covered by legislation by applying doctrines of common law. The theory of intentional infliction of emotional distress, for example, has been used by workers who claim that emotional disorders have resulted from on-the-job stress. The current trend in common law, as in state and federal law, is expansion of employee rights.

The expansion of employee rights has steadily whittled down a broad range of management prerogatives. Although the march of rights shows no signs of slowing, the priority of various rights changes over time. For example, objections to conservative dress codes were more prominent in the rebellious 1960s, and discrimination was a more volatile issue in the 1970s than today. Events may spur sudden concern for a right. For a year after the chemical leak at Union Carbide's pesticide plant in Bhopal, a furor arose over the right of workers to have information about the toxic substances they worked with. Within six months, twenty-five states had passed "right-to-know" laws that required companies to disclose that information.

Fundamentally, employee rights must be balanced against corporate rights. Corporations have the right to protect their reputations and assets. Sometimes two legitimate rights conflict. For example, corporations have an important right to ensure the suitability and integrity of employees. Yet lie detectors, drug tests, personality tests, and AIDS antibody tests may entail a substantial encroachment on privacy and dignity. In addition, all these tests are subject to error and employees risk unfair job loss. Thus, two legitimate rights conflict, and a careful balance must be struck. The duty of an airline to provide safe transport may outweigh the privacy rights of pilots in a drug testing program. There may be less of an overriding need for the airline to invade the privacy of typists, whose rights to privacy may predominate.

Perhaps the most fundamental right of an employer is the right to hire and fire. We turn to this subject in the next section.

THE RULES OF AGENCY

In the United States there is a body of common law known as "agency" which governs employer-employee relationships. The general provisions of agency hold that employers and employees may enter into voluntary agreements of employment and that either party may freely terminate these agreements at any time.

While employed, an employee must act "solely and entirely" for the employer's benefit in all work-related matters or be liable for termination and damages. Furthermore, the law stipulates that when a conflict arises between an employee and employer, the employee must conform to the employer's rules. The common law of agency is derived from paternalistic English common law which, in turn, was influenced by Roman law that framed employment in terms of a master-servant relationship. Under agency, employers have had extensive rights to restrict employee freedom and to arbitrarily fire workers. An extreme interpretation of agency characterizes the history of American labor. It resounds in this oft-quoted statement by a Tennessee judge over 100 years ago: "All may dismiss their employees at will, be they many or few, for good cause, for no cause, or even for cause morally wrong without being thereby guilty of legal wrong."[37]

Recently, however, absolute discharge rights have eroded. Federal and state laws have restricted the right to fire employees for reasons related to age, sex, race, union activity, physical handicap, religion, or national origin. State whistleblowing laws restrict discharge in retaliation for criticizing an employer. In addition, state courts have introduced three common law exceptions to termination at will. First, an employee may not be fired for carrying out the intentions of public policy. In *Petermann v. International Brotherhood of Teamsters,* a California worker was asked by his supervisor to lie in

[37]*Payne v. Western A.R.R. Co,* 81 Tenn 507 (1884).

answering certain questions before a legislative committee investigating unions.[38] When the worker answered honestly, he was fired. Even though the employee was subject to firing at will in his position, the court did not uphold the termination, stating that it was an overriding public policy interest to have truthful testimony at legislative hearings. In *Sheets v. Teddy's Frosted Foods,* a quality control inspector in Connecticut was fired for protesting the company's intentional mislabeling of the weight of its food products, a practice which was illegal under the state's Food, Drug & Cosmetics Act. The court held that an employee should not be expected to have to choose between fraudulent behavior or continued employment, and found the discharge improper.[39]

Second, courts are limiting the employer's ability to fire if an implied covenant of good faith is breached. In *Cleary v. American Airlines,* an employee of eighteen years in a position subject to arbitrary dismissal was fired.[40] Company personnel policy contained a specific statement that the firm reserved the right to terminate an employee for any reason, but the court became convinced that the firing had occurred so that the airline could avoid payment of a sales commission to the employee. It awarded the fired worker punitive damages.

A third check on freedom to fire is recognized where an implied contract exists. In *Pugh v. See's Candies,* a vice president was fired after thirty-two years with the company.[41] But the court refused to uphold the firing because there was evidence that at the time of the man's hiring he had been promised permanent employment so long as his performance was satisfactory. As a result of such decisions, companies are carefully examining personnel manuals to remove implied promises of job tenure. One company has stopped calling its nonprobationary employees "permanent" employees. Instead, legal counsel has advised the term *regular* to avoid an implied promise of a long-term job.

CONCLUSION: TRENDS IN MANAGING WORKERS

Corporations face a dual challenge in managing the changing workplace. They must make employees more productive if they are to survive. At the same time, they must meet the expectations that increasingly varied and independent workers have about their jobs. This is being done in four general ways.

INCREASED WORKER PARTICIPATION

Historically, authoritarian management styles dominated American workplaces. But since the 1960s, managers have tried to temporize with changing worker values by encouraging employees to participate in decisions. Over

[38]344 Cal. App.2d 25 (1959).
[39]427 A.2d 385, Connecticut, 1980.
[40]168 Cal. Rptr. 722 (1980).
[41]*Pugh v. See's Candies,* 161 Cal. App.3d 311 (1981).

the years, there have been a number of faddish efforts to increase participation. Legions of managers have, for instance, attended training programs on how to develop consultative leadership styles. (Skeptics say that a manager will be sent to such a program if he is the type who says, "Joe, get your butt moving." After the program, he will say, "Joe, how's your new baby?... Great, now get your butt moving.") Job enrichment programs were popular in the 1970s. Job enrichment is based on the theory that workers in dull, repetitive jobs with little prestige receive ego gratification and become more productive if given more self-determination. Jobs were redesigned to give workers more control over their environments and more decisions to make.

Since the late 1970s, quality circles—called quality-control circles in Japan—have been started in 6,000–10,000 American corporations. They are small groups of workers who meet voluntarily off the production line to study and solve production problems. Typically, these groups are composed of two to twelve workers and meet for one hour a week. They may request information and cost data from management and have the authority to implement solutions to workplace problems.

By the mid-1980s, the quality circles had evolved into self-managing teams of workers. Self-managing teams in manufacturing are usually composed of five to fifteen employees who make products by dividing tasks among members and rotating them. Self-managing teams differ from quality circles because they reorganize the work process from an assembly line watched by supervisors to a group project controlled mainly by peers. Teams take over tasks such as scheduling, ordering parts, and job assignments. When they succeed, they increase productivity and quality while eliminating the need for supervisors who are paid nominally more than workers.

The team concept, like quality circles, is inspired by similar teams in Japanese companies. It has spread rapidly from manufacturing to banks, insurance companies, hospitals, and other industries, and appears to be the wave of the future. Teams have rendered spectacular successes. In the early 1980s, A. O. Smith Corp., an auto chassis manufacturer, suffered enormous quality problems with a traditional assembly line setup. In 1981, for example, 20 percent of Ford Ranger frames needed repair as they came off the assembly line. Dictatorial foremen argued with bored workers and union stewards; absenteeism was high. Quality circles introduced after 1981 brought modest improvement, but fundamental conflicts remained. In 1987, however, A. O. Smith introduced self-managing teams, of five to seven workers each, which build individual frames. Each team has an elected leader who performs managerial duties; the ratio of line foremen to workers dropped from 1 to 10 in 1987 to 1 to 34 in 1989. Defects have dropped from 20 percent to around 3 percent.[42]

CHANGES IN ORGANIZATION STRUCTURE

Until the 1950s, the vast majority of large corporations were organized along bureaucratic lines. Today, corporations are experimenting with a variety of

---

[42]John Hoerr, "The Cultural Revolution at A. O. Smith," *Business Week*, May 29, 1989, p. 68.

less hierarchical structures. The primary motive is increased flexibility in an unpredictable competitive environment. The basic prescription is the loosening of traditional bureaucratic structures which tend to be rigid and slow in responding to change.

At the extreme, W. L. Gore & Associates uses a team management approach with its 4,000 employees in which no person holds a position of formal authority. In this system, followers gravitate naturally toward leaders, and individuals volunteer for projects.[43] Most large companies, however, are making less drastic changes, including rethinking the balance between centralization and decentralization, restructuring, delegating more authority to lower levels, increasing the autonomy of divisions and business units, and more directly measuring and rewarding profit performance.

Many companies, in addition, are streamlining their work forces by shedding large numbers of managers. When companies delete layers of supervisors and middle managers, as many are doing, authority for decisions rests closer to the production process. To maintain productivity with fewer people, companies adopt new, flatter organization structures which have fewer supervisory levels and wider spans of control for remaining managers. This expands individual responsibilities and sometimes creates additional stress. A manager at General Electric describes what "delayering," or removal of an entire level of management in his Medical Systems Group, feels like:

> Quite honestly, I feel overworked. I work hard, and sometimes I don't enjoy it, anymore. Before the delayering. . . . I had a total of ten people who would report to me, and four of them were other managers who had people reporting to them. After that, I wound up with twenty people. . . . I'm usually here at 7 A.M., and I leave at 6 at night.[44]

Corporations also are learning to develop more flexible structures to permit innovation. New projects may be located in sanctuaries outside the formal organization structure so that the formal organization is not challenged by them. These sanctuaries sometimes are called "skunk works" (after the top-secret project center at Lockheed where the U-2 and stealth fighter were developed).

CHANGING CORPORATE POLICIES

Like organization structures, corporate policies are being changed to accommodate the needs and values of the contemporary worker. Selection, retention, and promotion decisions are examined systematically to help employees meet career needs. Few corporations offer job security, but many have flexible employment policies. Flex-time plans let workers decide what hours they will keep, job sharing programs allow two or more people to fulfill the

[43]John Naisbitt, *Megatrends: Ten New Directions Transforming Our Lives*, New York: Warner, 1985.

[44]John A. Byrne, "Caught in the Middle," *Business Week*, September 12, 1988, p. 83. For a discussion of restructuring see Frank Caropreso, *Organization Designs for the 1990s*, New York: The Conference Board, 1989.

requirements of a single job, and a few companies allow new parents to work at home for a while. Many companies offer day care for children; fewer give maternity leaves for mothers (or fathers).

Mainly because of rising health-care costs, but partly to meet demands from a new generation of fit workers, corporations increasingly adopt health-conscious policies, including no smoking areas and smoking bans, company-sponsored recreational programs, and bans on junk food in office vending machines. When workers have health problems, they get traditional medical and dental benefits. In addition, over 8,000 corporations offer employee assistance programs (EAPs) for stress, alcoholism, drug addiction, and family problems.

Career counseling, flexible work programs, and EAPs are a few examples of the policy changes that accommodate the new self-concern and independence of workers.

STRATEGIC CONSIDERATIONS

In years past, the problems and needs of employees were largely relegated to personnel and industrial relations offices. These offices experimented with behavior modification, job enrichment, participatory decision making, and other techniques designed to enhance productivity. Today, however, a new philosophy of human resource management is emerging: that human resources are as important as finances or marketing and should be considered in any major strategic decisions. When a company makes plans to greatly expand or contract, enter new markets, or reorganize, it should take into consideration the human resource implications of its actions. Will there be enough skilled workers? Will jobs remain for long-time employees? Can the company recruit successfully in new locations?

This kind of strategic thinking is revealed in the start-up manufacturing facilities of the Japanese. They often locate plants in fiercely non-union areas and away from urban areas containing minorities.

Drug Testing of Employees: Employers' Rights versus Employees' Rights

A drug is a chemical introduced into bodily tissues to produce physical, mental, or emotional change. Each year Americans spend nearly $40 billion on prescription drugs used for medicinal purposes.[45] Each year Americans also spend more than twice this amount, an estimated $100 billion, on illicit drugs taken for nonmedicinal purposes.[46] The possession, manufacture, importation, and distribution of these drugs is illegal under the Controlled Substances Act of 1970, yet Americans spend more on them than they do on gasoline.

The two most widely used illegal drugs are marijuana and cocaine. Once a month or more, about 20 million Americans use marijuana, and 6 million use cocaine. Many cocaine users use "crack," or cocaine boiled down into small crystals to be smoked and so named because of the crackling sound it makes when heated. Crack is an ingenious product innovation of the illicit international commodity cartels that supply cocaine. After 1985, "crack" transformed cocaine use from an expensive $100-a-day habit of declining incidence among the wealthy into a $5–$15-a-dose habit accessible to a huge mass of consumers with modest or low incomes. Drug abuse hits hardest in younger age groups. Recent studies show that 65 percent of those between the ages of 18 and 25 have used illicit drugs and another 20 percent ingest them regularly.[47] Drug use declines sharply after age 35.[48]

---

[45] *Statistical Abstract of the United States*, 108th ed., 1988, estimates and figures based on Tables 137 and 1265.

[46] Figure cited in Louis Kraar, "The Drug Trade," *Fortune*, June 20, 1988, p. 27. A lower figure, $50 billion, is cited by Gustavo A. Gorriti in "How To Fight the Drug War," *The Atlantic Monthly*, July 1989, p. 71.

[47] These studies are summarized in William F. Banta and Forest Tennant, *Complete Handbook for Combating Substance Abuse in the Workplace*, Lexington, Massachusetts: Lexington Books, 1989, p. xix.

[48] In 1985, for example, 21.9% of those aged eighteen to twenty-five used marijuana once a month or more, but only 2.2% of those over thirty-five did so. Similarly, 7.7% of those eighteen to twenty-five used cocaine, but only 0.5% of those over thirty-five did so. Alcohol abuse declines only slightly. Figures are from Bureau of the Census, *Statistical Abstract of the United States*, 108th ed., December 1987, Table 180.

Control of illegal drugs and their societal impacts is a central public policy issue, with debate focusing on four alternative solutions: (1) limiting the supply of drugs by law enforcement action against drug kingpins, smugglers, and dealers; (2) limiting the demand for drugs by prosecuting users; (3) limiting demand by education and rehabilitation of users; and (4) legalizing abused drugs, thereby permitting multinational corporations to take the profits away from criminals. The prominence of the issue is reflected in the actions of two presidents. In 1986, President and Mrs. Ronald Reagan made a national television address to say that drugs were undermining the nation's vitality. The President noted a White House study showing that between 12 and 23 percent of American workers had a drug problem. He suggested—and later implemented—a drug testing program for federal employees, and Mrs. Reagan urged that people "just say no" to drugs. President Reagan focused the nation's efforts on the interdiction of smuggled drugs, particularly cocaine. But this policy is widely agreed to have failed. Between 1986 and 1989, the supply of cocaine increased, its street price fell from almost $35 per kilogram to $20 per kilogram, and its purity increased. In 1989, President George Bush in his first television address warned that drugs are "the gravest domestic threat facing our nation today" and announced a $7.9 billion federal control program.[49] This program, like the Reagan program, focused heavily on law enforcement aimed at criminals in the drug trade. In announcing it, he went against some advisors who considered the drug war a political loser because it was unwinnable. But opinion polls showed the public approved, and also showed that Americans perceived drug abuse as the nation's top problem.[50]

EMPLOYEE DRUG ABUSE IN CORPORATIONS

Drug abuse has been an enormous problem for employers. In 1986, *Time* magazine reported estimates that 10 to 23 percent of U.S. workers used drugs on the job.[51] Statistics gathered from callers to a cocaine help line, 1-800-COCAINE, showed that 76 percent of cocaine users were employed, 45 percent stole from employers, family, or friends to get drug money, and 3 to 7 percent used an illegal drug daily.[52] In 1989, the Bureau of Labor Statistics reported that 11.9 percent of nearly 4 million job applicants in a broad spectrum of industries tested positive for drug use.[53] And in a 1990 Gallup Poll,

[49]George Bush, "National Drug Control Strategy," *Vital Speeches,* October 1, 1989.

[50]A *Washington Post*-ABC News Poll in September 1989, for example, showed that 82 percent favored his proposals and 74 percent wanted an even bigger program. *Washington Post National Weekly Edition,* September 18–24, 1989, p. 37. Three polls on drug abuse as a problem are a *Wall Street Journal*/ABC News Poll cited in Michel McQueen and David Shribman, "Battle Against Drugs Is Chief Issue Facing Nation," *Wall Street Journal,* August 22, 1989; a Gallup poll cited in *Los Angeles Times,* "Americans Want Tougher Drug Laws," August 15, 1989; and a Yankelovich poll cited in, "Opinion Outlook," *National Journal,* February 24, 1990, p. 477.

[51]Janice Castro, "Battling the Enemy Within," *Time,* March 17, 1986, p. 53.

[52]Victor Schachter and Thomas E. Geidt, "Cracking Down on Drugs," *Across the Board,* November 1985, p. 30.

[53]David Wessel, "Evidence Is Skimpy That Drug Testing Works, but Employers Embrace Practice," *Wall Street Journal,* September 7, 1989.

one-fourth of workers had seen coworkers use drugs at work in the past year.[54]

Across the country, employers experience drug-related problems. A company doctor at Rockwell International Corp. estimated that 20 to 25 percent of the workers at the company's Palmdale, California, space shuttle assembly plant worked under the influence of drugs or alcohol between 1981 and 1983. At Eastern Airlines, baggage handlers are the focus of a federal investigation concerning drug shipments from Colombia. General Motors, the nation's largest employer, discovered in 1986 that one out of five employees on the second shift at its Adrian, Michigan, assembly plant used alcohol or drugs at work. At other plants, drugs were sold in parking lots, cafeterias, and supply rooms. Dealers often worked as forklift drivers who had access to large areas of the plants. A computer operator at American Airlines cost the company $19 million while on a marijuana high by neglecting to enter data in the computerized reservation system. In January 1987, a Conrail engineer who had been smoking marijuana rolled his string of locomotives past a warning light and onto the same track as a high-speed passenger train carrying 600 people. The collision killed 16 and injured 176. It cost Conrail and Amtrak $106 million.

Perhaps the biggest cost of drug abuse in companies is the low-level incompetence that characterizes addicted employees. Such employees almost always exhibit one or both of two pernicious medical effects. The first is distortion of time, which is seen in the inability of the employee to follow normal time patterns for job activities. The second is lack of motivation, which is seen as lack of interest in normal performance standards. Both effects stem from imbalances of brain chemistry caused by the chronic presence of marijuana, cocaine, or other drugs in the bloodstream.[55] Supervisors are trained to suspect drug abuse when employees show patterns of behavior such as:

- frequent tardiness and absences from work, especially on Mondays and Fridays and near holidays;
- poor concentration, forgetfulness, missed deadlines, and frequent mistakes;
- mood changes, including a wide range of states that interfere with personal relationships such as depression, withdrawal, hostility, and overexcitability; and
- risk taking and frequent accidents.

It is clear that every day an army of drug users descends on factories and offices across the nation. Drugs are concealed in clothing and lunch boxes. They often can be bought from coworkers, but if not, a messenger service may send them in. The mail rooms of multinational corporations have been centers of worldwide drug distribution. Cocaine is preferred over other drugs for use at work because it can be easily hidden, leaves no odor, manifests no visible signs of impairment when the user is high, and often gives a

---

[54]Cited in Cindy Skrzycki, "Drugs in the Workplace," *Washington Post National Weekly Edition,* January 1–7, 1990.

[55]Banta and Tennant, *op.cit.,* p. 45.

feeling of enhanced performance. Workers smoke crack in cigarettes and sniff cocaine powder in elevators and restrooms. They ingest LSD and hallucinate for the rest of the day. They steal, engage in acts of prostitution, and sell drugs to others to support their habits. Occassionally, employees drop dead from drug overdoses.

The cost of drug abuse in business is difficult to calculate. In 1989, the Chamber of Commerce estimated an overall cost of $60 billion.[56] Whatever the figure, the components include lost productivity, elevated accident rates, extra worker compensation claims, higher insurance premiums for employers, higher absentee and sick leave rates, the loss of trained workers who are fired or die, the administrative costs of antidrug programs, and the costs of beefed-up plant security. Human costs are not, of course, included in any of these categories and are extra, unmeasured, and tragic losses.

EFFORTS TO REDUCE DRUG ABUSE BY EMPLOYEES

A wide range of antidrug measures is available to employers trying to stop drug abuse. They include these.

Antidrug policies are the foundation for all efforts to rid the workplace of drugs. The Drug Free Workplace Act of 1988 requires private employers with federal contracts over $25,000 to have comprehensive policies designed to prevent drug abuse. Effective policies usually include: (1) the prohibition of specific conduct, such as using or possessing illegal drugs at work, (2) the procedure used to test for illegal drug use, and (3) the consequences of violation, such as termination, suspension, or referral to an assistance program. The policy needs to be well considered, because there are many alternatives. For example, employers should define whether company premises include parking lots and employees' vehicles in parking lots. They must decide what kind of screening tests will be used and whether they will be scheduled or random. In addition, large companies must tailor their policies to varied locations. State and local laws on drug testing vary widely. To illustrate, random testing is permitted in Idaho, but prohibited in Iowa; San Francisco prohibits companywide urine testing, but Los Angeles does not.

Employee education and rehabilitation are used by many corporations and federally mandated for defense contractors. A wide variety of films and training programs may be used for education. Companies have gotten few voluntary self-referrals to assistance programs. Most candidates for rehabilitation emerge from testing programs, and success rates are low. It is not unusual for a firm to spend $50,000 or more on an addict for hospitalization and sick leave, only to have that person fail in recovery and be terminated.

Employee searches may include searches of lockers, workstations, desks, and purses. They seldom include bodily searches, which anger workers and create litigation. Drug-sniffing dogs are extremely effective in locating contraband. Even when drugs are packed in containers of moth balls, dogs can

[56]U.S. Chamber of Commerce, "Drug Testing," *1989 Congressional Issues,* Washington, D.C.: USCC, 1989, p. 25. This figure was also reported by the White House Conference for a Drug Free America in its *Final Report,* Washington, D.C.: GPO, June 1988.

find them.[57] And dog sniffs, which do not require opening purses or toolboxes, are not as intrusive as physical searches of person and property. Searchers are often ineffective in deterring drug use because employees secrete drugs in common areas. Drug-sniffing dogs can find them, but ownership cannot be established. Where dogs are not used, employees may tape drugs to parts of their bodies where they elude discovery. Searches, of course, will not stop drug users who dose themselves before coming to work.

Surveillance can detect drug use, but has many pitfalls. It is difficult to keep undercover agents a secret in the long run. For example, if a lawsuit results from their work, they will testify in court. The mistrust that spying creates can shatter employee morale. In addition, company employees working as amateur sleuths are not trained to gather evidence and may make errors such as participating themselves in drug use to catch drug users.[58] Professional detectives and former police officers may not be attuned to corporate life and may make their own mistakes, such as striking or handcuffing employees. Such actions intrude on rights protected by common law and generate expensive lawsuits. Also, watching employees will not reveal who has used drugs or alcohol before arriving at work. Still, many companies do spy without publicizing it.

Written drug tests are available from a dozen or more vendors of employment tests. They ask job applicants and employees whether they have used drugs, what kind, and how often. Some drug users can be screened out because they answer honestly, but others lie. The validity of these tests is unproven, but at $10 or so they are the least expensive drug test.

Polygraphs, or lie detectors, were often used in the past to ferret out drug use. The accuracy of such tests has long been questioned, however, and the Employee Polygraph Protection Act of 1988, enacted in response to these questions, limits their use so severely that most employers no longer use them for drug screening.

Physical exams, sometimes called fitness-for-duty exams, are performed by a person trained to conduct them. Alcohol and drug use alters reflexes, blood pressure, and eye movement in ways which may be detected by a trained observer. A test called the "rapid eye test," for example, reliably reveals abnormalities associated with drug use, such as expanded pupil size, diminished reactivity to light, and diminished corneal reflex. This test takes only about two minutes and involves less invasion of privacy than some other tests. Only a few companies now use physical exams because their validity has not yet been established through court and arbitration challenges.

Blood tests are useful primarily for alcohol abuse testing. They are expensive and exceptionally intrusive and are rarely used by employers due to legal challenges. Their main advantage is that they can determine the approximate time a drug was used.

[57]Kimberly A. Kingston, "Hounding Drug Traffickers: The Use of Drug Detection Dogs," *FBI Law Enforcement Bulletin*, August 1989, p. 31.

[58]I. John Vasquez and Sharon A. Kelley, "Management's Commitment to the Undercover Operative," *FBI Law Enforcement Bulletin*, February 1989.

Saliva tests exist to test for marijuana use, but they are unreliable. They are useful only up to three hours after marijuana is smoked, and rinsing the mouth can remove detectable residues.

Hair analysis can detect drug use for as long as thirty days prior to removal of a hair for testing. However, it takes about seven days for substances indicative of drug use to appear in the hair. Hair analysis is used primarily in forensics. The seven-day lag in detection makes it less useful for screening job applicants and awkward for screening employees.

Urinalysis detects the presence of drugs or chemical by-products of drugs in the urine, usually within an hour of ingestion. Urine testing has become the favored method of employers for catching drug users and is discussed at length in the following section.

URINE TESTING

There are several basic types of urine tests. The first is the immunoassay test, best illustrated by the EMIT test, which stands for enzyme-multiplied immunoassay technique. This is an inexpensive test costing about $15 which can be done quickly with modest laboratory equipment and technician training. In this test, several ingredients are added to a urine sample. Telltale chemical reactions indicate the presence of metabolites, or chemical by-products produced by the body from drugs such as marijuana. In a variation of this test called a radioimmunoassay (RIA), a radioactive isotope is added to urine to measure the presence of a drug.

Manufacturers of EMIT and RIA tests claim that they are 95 to 99 percent accurate when used correctly. But in actual testing, inaccuracy is greater. These tests are particularly susceptible to a false positive result if a person has recently used any of ten common over-the-counter drugs, including dextromethorphan, an ingredient in Vicks Formula 44, and perylamine, an ingredient in Midol. Poppy seeds, found in bagels and other baked products, may cause false positives for morphine and cocaine. An additional flaw of immunoassay tests is that they cannot detect hallucinogens such as LSD.

A second test, thin layer chromatography or TLC, is more precise than the EMIT or RIA tests but is more time consuming, more expensive (about $25 per test), and requires a highly trained technician to interpret results. Therefore, this technique is less often used for mass employee screening and is frequently held in reserve to double-check a positive result on an immunoassay test. In this test, urine is placed near the bottom of a vertical plate that stands in a trough of solvents. The solvents climb the plate by capillary action, and after reaching the urine specimen, they carry it upward. Various chemical components in the urine—including drug compounds—are soluble at different rates and therefore move upward at varying rates. A skilled technician can interpret the pattern of movement on the plate to determine if a drug is present. The technician may also spray the plate with a reagent that causes color changes in the presence of drugs. It takes much experience to read these plates accurately, and errors sometimes are made.

A third type of test is done with a mass spectrometer. It is the most accurate and, at a cost of nearly $100, the most expensive. In this test, components of urine are separated by gas chromatography. The various chemical constituents of the urine flow by a mass spectrometer in gaseous form. The spectrometer measures the relative proportions of molecules in the urine and produces a pattern on a photographic plate that can be interpreted by computer. Done properly, this test is virtually 100 percent accurate. Gas chromatography/mass spectrometry tests are so sensitive that they have detected cocaine and a by-product, cinnamolycocaine, in the urine of people who have drunk one or two cups of coca leaf teas imported from Peru. Five doctors writing in the *Journal of the American Medical Association* cautioned that individuals in urine testing programs should be warned not to drink these teas.[59]

One shortcoming of urine tests is that they can be thwarted by employees who tamper with samples. A small amount of table salt, bleach, laundry soap, ammonia, or vinegar causes screening tests to miss drug residues in the urine. For this reason, employees giving urine samples must be closely supervised. In addition, efforts have been made to substitute drug-free urine samples for a person's own, tainted urine. A person may carry a small sample in his or her clothing and pour it into the test vial if not closely watched. If there is hot water in a bathroom where an employee is being asked to give a sample, he or she can warm the sample to body temperature. In one situation where no hot water was available, a woman carried a condom of unsullied urine in her vagina to keep it at body temperature until the switch was made.

Because these games are played, many corporations require urination in the presence of an observer, a particularly demeaning mode of testing. An additional problem with urine testing is that it cannot indicate whether an employee is high or impaired. Cocaine and heroin can be detected for up to three days after last use and marijuana up to two months after last use. This means that a person who used cocaine at a party on Saturday night could be nailed by a drug test on Tuesday morning when feeling hale and working productively. But a colleague who had taken LSD that morning, and was hallucinating and dangerous, would not be detected with an EMIT or RIA test.

WHY CORPORATIONS FAVOR DRUG TESTING

Corporations that test for drugs find four compelling reasons.

First, in some cases it is required by law. The Department of Defense requires defense contractors to test employees who have access to classified material or hold otherwise "sensitive" positions. The Department of Transportation requires urine testing, including random testing, by airlines, railroads, trucking companies, and maritime firms, and sets forth precise rules for testing procedure. These rules cover well over four million workers. Two

---

[59]Ronald Siegel, Mahmoud A. Elsohly, Timothy Plowman, Philip Rury, and Reese T. Jones, "Cocaine in Herbal Tea," *Journal of the American Medical Association*, January 3, 1986, p. 40.

other laws which lack a specific mandate for testing nevertheless imply legal obligation. The general duty clause of the Occupational Safety and Health Act requires employers to provide safe working environments. And the Drug Free Workplace Act requires defense contractors to "make a good faith effort" to rid their facilities of drugs. In the public sector, drug testing of federal employees is required under Executive Order 12564, issued by President Reagan in 1986.

Second, experience shows that drug testing deters drug use and lowers costs. When a large oil service company in Louisiana began testing job applicants in 1983, 29 percent were rejected. But as word spread, the figure dropped to 15 percent in 1984; it had fallen to 3 percent by 1987.[60] Chevron Corp. had the same experience. In the early 1980s, a third of job applicants tested positive, but only 2 percent did so by 1989. When Southern Pacific Railroad instituted drug testing, its accident rate went down by 60 percent. Other companies have had similar experiences.

Third, corporate drug testers argue that urinalysis is a practical method of testing for drug use. Although urine tests are intrusive, they are less so than alternatives such as drug-sniffing dogs, polygraphs, searches through handbags and desks, undercover investigations, entry and exit searches, and closed-circuit TV monitors in restrooms. When done correctly, urine tests are reliable. Good programs follow the Rule of Two, in which two positive tests are required before action is taken. The first test, an inexpensive screening test, is followed by a second and more sophisticated confirming test on the same vial of urine. Cutoff levels for positive results can be set reasonably high to avoid unnecessarily stigmatizing innocent employees. For example, a person sitting with others smoking marijuana on Saturday night may show a level of metabolites in the urine of up to 10 ng/ml (nanograms per milliliter) as late as 5 P.M. on Monday. By establishing the cutoff point for a positive test result at 20 ng/ml or higher, that person will not be branded a drug user.[61] Also, by carefully selecting a properly certified testing laboratory, human errors may be minimized. Overall, if the testing program is done with respect for employee concerns, it will be accepted as reasonable.

Fourth, there is a social responsibility argument for drug testing. As employers screen applicants and employees, it will become harder for drug abusers to make a living. Employees have no right to use drugs such as heroin, cocaine, LSD, marijuana, hashish, morphine, PCP, and designer drugs. Their use is illegal and an inconvenience to corporations. Thus, business is helping society by reducing criminal activity and combating drug abuse. From an individual standpoint, if companies can catch a drug-using employee early, it might save his or her career.

---

[60]Banta and Tennant, *op. cit.*, p. 25.

[61]Cocaine and PCP may also be passively ingested in the presence of smokers and show up in urine tests later. Some federal agencies and states set the cutoff points employers may use for positive test results. See Banta and Tennant, *op. cit.*, p. 90, for a table of recommended screening levels.

WHY SOME EMPLOYEES OPPOSE DRUG TESTING

As compelling as these arguments are, drug testing in general and urine testing in particular raise difficult questions. Critics point out that the right of an employer to protect assets and property must be balanced against the rights of individual employees to a reasonable amount of privacy. Opponents of drug testing have included individual employees, labor unions, and the American Civil Liberties Union. The opponents make telling points.

First, urine tests are intrusive—unreasonably intrusive. Susan Register, an employee at a Georgia Power Company nuclear plant, describes what happened to her when asked to give a urine sample.

> I walked into the bathroom with a company nurse and sat down on the commode. The nurse said, "Stand up, we're going to do it differently today."
>
> The nurse made me bend over at the waist and hold my right hand in the air. My blue jeans were around my ankles. I had a bottle in my left hand between my thighs. If you were a woman you could understand how hard it would be to get urine this way. I was barely hitting the bottle. I wet all over my pants and my left hand.[62]

Susan Register's experience is probably not typical and may even be rare, but supervised urination, whether visual as in this case, or auditory, as is sometimes the case when an observer listens behind a partition while urination is done, is inherently demeaning. As a federal appeals court noted:

> There are few activities in our society more personal or private than the passing of urine. Most people describe it by euphemisms if they talk about it at all. It is a function traditionally performed without public observation; indeed, its performance in public is generally prohibited by law as well as social custom.[63]

And the author of a law journal article has written that:

> [I]n our culture the excretory functions are shielded by more or less absolute privacy, so much so that situations in which this privacy is violated are experienced as extremely distressing, as detracting from one's dignity and self esteem.[64]

In addition to the act of sample collection, there are two other potential privacy invasions in urine testing. In order to avoid false positives based on the presence of other drugs in the urine, employees are asked to list all prescription and over-the-counter drugs taken in the last thirty days. This reveals their private, off-duty lives and medical histories. Also, chemical analysis of urine (or blood) can reveal more than drug use. Employers could test it and discover medical conditions such as pregnancy, clinical depression, diabetes, and epilepsy. For all these reasons, civil libertarians believe urine testing smacks of Big Brother.

Second, the tests are unjust in the sense that they violate ethical standards of fair treatment. Testing is a dragnet; many innocent employees are tested for each drug abuser detected. A presumption of guilt is placed on everyone,

---

[62]Harry Weinstein, "Drug Tests: Privacy vs. Job Rights," *Los Angeles Times*, October 26, 1986.
[63]*National Treasury Employees Union v. Von Raab*, 816 F.2d 175.
[64]Charles Fried, "Privacy," *Yale Law Journal*, volume 77, p. 487.

and workers must prove their innocence. If there is an overriding necessity to prohibit drug abuse—among airline pilots or train engineers, for example—then it may be permitted. But indiscriminate testing of clerical staff and plant workers is an evil greater than the drug abuse that it seeks to remedy. Moreover, drug testing may be used to harass workers. In some cases, workers who have tested positive have been singled out over and over for repeated testing while their coworkers have not, even when later tests have been negative for drug abuse.

Third, urine tests are faulty. Inaccuracies arise from lab errors, mixed-up specimens, and false positives due to legal drugs in the body. These errors are common, and false accusations cost individuals their jobs. Errors by screening labs are a particularly difficult problem. With the boom in urine testing by employers, the labs have sprung up like mushrooms following a rainstorm. Contracts are frequently let based on low cost of screening. The result is an incentive to cut costs and training for lab technicians. A series of studies over a nine-year period conducted by the Centers for Disease Control showed a "substantial" number of errors by screening labs for six commonly misused drugs, including falsely negative and positive screenings.[65]

LEGAL ISSUES IN DRUG TESTING

Legal precedent on drug testing is relatively young and still developing, but the clear trend is to uphold it where it is part of a previously announced and carefully formulated policy. Here is a short briefing on legal issues.

Since the Bill of Rights of the U.S. Constitution restrains only government actions, public employees are protected by these provisions, whereas employees in private businesses are not. This is a major legal difference; public employers must meet stricter guidelines for testing. The Fourth Amendment guarantees protection to public employees against "unreasonable search and seizures," and courts have generally held that urine tests and other forms of testing, such as blood tests for HIV antibodies, are a form of search and seizure. The Fifth Amendment guarantees "due process of law" and protects against self-incrimination. Public employers must guard against firings that violate these rights.[66] Since 1988, federal agencies have adhered to testing guidelines issued by the Department of Health and Human Services. These guidelines attempt to elevate due process for government employees to an impeccable level and stipulate testing procedures in detail.

There have been many court challenges to federal urine testing programs. Two of the most significant cases concerned whether testing programs were "reasonable" under the Fourth Amendment. In *Skinner v. Railway Labor Executives' Association*, the Supreme Court was asked to decide whether railroad workers could be forced to submit to mandatory urine and blood tests for

---

[65]Hugh J. Hansen, Samuel P. Caudill, and Joe Boone, "Crisis in Drug Testing: Results of CDC Blind Study," *Journal of the American Medical Association*, April 26, 1985.

[66]These rights are, of course, extended to state, county, and local employees through the Fourteenth Amendment.

drugs and alcohol following accidents, even if there were no signs they had been using drugs.[67] In a 7-2 decision, the Court ruled that the clear public interest in railroad safety outweighed the privacy rights of employees. In dissent, Justice Marshall argued that the testing program violated general guidelines for search and seizure developed by the Court over many years. For example, no warrant was required prior to testing. He compared the decision with the Court's 1940s decisions upholding the assignment of Japanese to relocation camps during World War II and noted that, "when we allow fundamental freedoms to be sacrificed in the name of real or perceived exigency, we invariably come to regret it.[68]

A second case decided by the Supreme Court, *National Treasury Employees Union v. Von Raab,* involved a urine testing program of the U.S. Customs Service. It required applicants for positions in which they would interdict drugs, carry guns, or work with "classified" material of interest to criminals to submit to a urine test. In a 5-4 decision, the majority argued that the national drug crisis, together with the special gravity of drug enforcement work, justified weighing the public interest in drug-free customs agents more heavily than the interference with the agents' civil liberties. Thus, testing was "reasonable" under the Fourth Amendment. Justice Antonin Scalia, writing in dissent, warned that the Court was too cavalier in sacrificing basic constitutional privacy rights. He quoted these famous lines written by Justice Louis Brandeis in 1928: "The greatest dangers to liberty lurk in insidious encroachment by men of zeal, well-meaning but without understanding."[69]

These two decisions do not apply to private employers, who may search employees or spy on them and, within broad limits, fire them at will. Thus, reasonable search and seizure requirements established for government employees do not restrain corporate drug testing (although they may serve as an inspiration). Nevertheless, the law does limit corporate testing in two other ways. First, many states have adopted laws and constitutional provisions that set legal limits to testing. And second, private employers are open to common law actions by employees based on doctrines such as negligence, defamation, assault and battery, emotional distress, invasion of privacy, or wrongful discharge. Employees have sued using all these legal theories. Some have won in court, but there is no clear common law trend to invalidate drug testing programs. Only where employees have been treated with obvious contempt, or where judges are strict civil libertarians, have corporate testing programs been held to violate common law. Union contracts also may limit drug testing programs.

QUESTIONS

1 Should urine testing (or other types of testing) be permitted among public and private employees to prevent drug abuse? What reasons can you give in support of your answer?

---

[67]57 LW 4324.

[68]At 57 LW 4333; the relocation-camp cases are *Hirabayashi v. United States,* 320 U.S. 81 (1943), and *Korematsu v. United States,* 323 U.S. 214 (1944).

[69]In *Olmstead v. United States,* 227 U.S. 479.

2 If you believe that urine testing in some form might be acceptable, write down the outlines of a sound testing program. Who should be tested? Employees? Job applicants? Should there be random testing? Should people in all job categories be tested? How frequently should tests be administered?

3 As a manager with responsibility for conducting a testing program, what would be your response to the following situations?

   a An employee who tests positively for marijuana on a Monday morning but has a spotless ten-year work record

   b An airline pilot who refuses a random test

   c A job applicant who tests positively for cocaine use

   d An employee who tests positively for cocaine use

   e An employee who comes do your office the night before an announced urinalysis and admits that he regularly uses a hallucinogenic drug off the job

   f A productive worker who gives no outward sign of drug use but who is named as a drug abuser at work in an anonymous tip

   g An employee involved in a serious work accident who refuses to take an immunoassay test based on her belief in a right to privacy

CHAPTER

18

Minorities, Women, and Antidiscrimination Law in the Workplace

How does a large corporation cope with seething tensions in its work force that stem from compliance with antidiscrimination laws? White males worry that less qualified minorities and women may leapfrog ahead of them through unfair, preferential promotion programs. Minorities fear that they will be regarded as unqualified as they advance. Women are angered at subtle male efforts to place them in submissive roles.

In 1968, Merck & Co. set up an office of equal employment affairs to handle equal employment and affirmative action issues. Merck is a large, multinational corporation headquartered in Rahway, New Jersey. In 1989 it had sales of $6.6 billion and ranked 70th on the *Fortune* 500 list. Its 34,000 employees are engaged in the development, production, and marketing of pharmaceuticals and other chemical products.

By 1970, Merck, like many other companies, had established affirmative action programs to comply with government requirements. Unlike other companies, however, Merck started a sweeping program to inform its employees about affirmative action issues, to allow them free expression of their feelings about discrimination or favoritism toward minorities, and to build support for affirmative action policies. The training sessions in this program had three phases. In Phase I, executives and managers at all Merck facilities met in small groups to discuss the creation of equal opportunities for all employees. In Phase II, supervisors, shop stewards, and union officials undertook the same training. Approximately 1,000 line managers and supervisors were trained to act as group discussion leaders so that they could conduct one-day workshops for other Merck employees. In Phase III, which began in 1982, all remaining 16,000 U.S. employees at sixty-one locations met in groups of ten to fifteen people for one day. During these sessions, Merck employees saw video tapes that depicted employees—men and women, black and white, young and old—discussing experiences and feelings related to discrimination, sexual harassment, and preferential treatment. The discussions that followed were often heated. Many workers felt that for the first time they could verbalize feelings about sensitive relations with coworkers.

- "Just knowing other people's attitudes were a lot like mine was surprising." [a black man]
- "The vignettes are excellent because I think we all see a little bit of ourselves in these films. I think some of the messages were a surprise to some employees; for example, discrimination can be exhibited in the question of who gets the coffee or calling someone 'honey.'" [a white male manager]
- "The important factor in career advancement is still qualifying for the job. You could actually feel the ice melting during the discussion. And long after, it's obvious that attitudes are more positive." [a black female manager]
- "Because so much attention is being focused on blacks and women, it's easy to feel you are being treated as a type and not as an individual. Phase III helped by talking about individual concerns." [a black woman]
- "I had never even heard of affirmative action until Phase III." [anonymous]

The program has been helpful in developing supportive attitudes among employees. Surveys showed that 70 percent of employees taking it felt more positive toward affirmative action and equal employment programs than previously. Three percent felt more negative. And 27 percent reported no change in their feelings. Other companies have adopted the Phase III program under arrangements by which they pay royalties to Merck. Merck donates these royalties to minority and women's groups.

The Merck experience underscores the management problem arising because minorities and women are entering the workplace in larger numbers. In this chapter, we discuss this phenomenon.

MINORITIES IN THE WORKPLACE

Since the Constitution was ratified in 1789, no nation has accepted more immigrants than the United States. Only about half our population today is descended from settlers in the United States before 1789. The rest are immigrants and descendants of immigrants from many nations and several races. A huge wave of 35.3 million immigrants arriving between 1851 and 1930 provided labor for industrialization of the country. A new, smaller wave of immigration began in 1960 and continues today. Between 1960 and 1988, 12.6 million legal immigrants have entered; about 600,000 a year in the 1980s.[1] It is estimated that as many as 6 million illegal aliens have also entered.

All large immigrant groups, past and present, are represented in the labor force. Some, such as the Irish, Germans, Italians, English, and Polish, have been assimilated into the middle-class mainstream of American society. Oth-

---

[1]These figures are derived from the Bureau of the Census, *Statistical Abstract of the United States 1990*, 110th ed., Washington, D.C.: Government Printing Office, January 1990, Table no. 7.

ers, particularly nonwhites, or those with ethnic loyalties, and recent arrivals, are not yet fully assimilated. Members of these groups may be victims of racial and ethnic discrimination in the workplace. Although many groups may literally be minorities, discrimination in the workplace historically has been most persistent against five sizable groups: blacks; native Americans; Asians, including Chinese, Japanese, and recent Vietnamese immigrants; Hispanics, including Puerto Ricans, Mexican-Americans, Cubans, South and Central Americans, and other Spanish-surnamed people from countries such as Spain; and Jews.

Racial and ethnic minorities are a growing part of the labor force. One estimate is that between 1985 and 2000, about 29 percent of new workers entering the labor force will be nonwhites, and that the percentage of nonwhites will increase from 13.6 percent to 15.7 percent. Immigrants will constitute 22 percent of new workers.[2] One problematic aspect of this increase is that nonwhite and immigrant workers tend to fill less skilled jobs, but the fastest growing occupations tend to require more education and skill. Hence, these two groups may experience growing hardship in the labor market. In 1986, for example, Hispanics were 6.6 percent of the workforce. They were only 3.7 percent of managers, but 22 percent of domestic servants and 22 percent of sewing machine operators. In 1990, blacks were 10.2 percent of the labor force. They were only 7.4 percent of managers and administrators, but 23 percent of service workers.[3]

RACISM AND SOCIAL DISCRIMINATION

Racism, defined broadly, is the belief that each race has distinctive cultural characteristics and that one's own race is superior to other races. It persists when myths and stereotypes about inferiorities are expressed in institutions of education, government, religion, and business. Racism leads to social discrimination, or the apportioning of resources based on group membership rather than individual merit.

There is a long history of racism and discrimination in the United States. Early in American history, blacks from non-Western, little understood African cultures were enslaved in large numbers and thought to be inferior to whites.[4] After the freeing of the slaves, the idea that whites were superior to blacks was institutionalized in segregated schools and restrooms and at water fountains; in literacy tests that disenfranchised blacks; in restrictive cov-

---

[2]These estimates are in a study done for the Department of Labor, William B. Johnston and Arnold E. Packer, *Workforce 2000*, Indianapolis, Indiana; Hudson Institute, June 1987, p. 89 and p. 95. See also Amanda Benett, "As Pool of Skilled Help Tightens, Firms Move to Broaden Their Role," *Wall Street Journal*, May 8, 1989, and Jonathan S. Leonard, "The Changing Face of Employees and Employment Regulation," *California Management Review*, Winter 1989.

[3]*Statistical Abstract of the United States: 1990, op. cit.*, Table no. 645, and *Employment and Earnings*, February 1990, pp. 15 and 30.

[4]The first slaves were brought to Jamestown colony in 1619. By independence in 1776, there were 500,000, and by 1800 about 1 million. Thereafter, the slave trade grew rapidly, and there were 4 million black slaves at the onset of the Civil War in 1860. See *Report of the National Advisory Commission on Civil Disorders*, New York: Bantam Books, 1968, pp. 207–210.

enants, or deeds that prevented whites from selling property to blacks in certain neighborhoods; and in discriminatory job policies that kept blacks in menial positions. Racism insulates the power of a privileged group—in this case the white American—from challenge. All these devices added up to an institutionalized structure of racism.

Similarly, from the earliest meetings of the settlers and Indians in colonial Virginia to nineteenth-century military conquests, American Indians were widely treated as an inferior race. Hispanic people have been the victims of *la leyenda negra*, an ancient prejudice against Hispanic peoples, obscure in origin and perhaps related to their darker skins (although there are many light-skinned Hispanics, who often prefer to classify themselves as white).

Many immigrants arriving in periods of major influx have met prejudice. With the exception of forced immigration by blacks from African countries, most new arrivals between 1776 and 1900 came from northern and western Europe. These immigrants were said to be from Nordic, Teutonic, or Anglo-Saxon stock in the racially descriptive language of that era, and their ancestry was similar to that of earlier colonists. They were rapidly assimilated into the workforce because their appearance and cultural heritage were familiar. Small influxes of Chinese laborers between 1850 and 1890 led to nativist fears and discriminatory treatment. For instance, the California state constitution, adopted in 1874, prohibited Chinese from voting and made it illegal for corporations to hire them. When the first Japanese immigrants came to America in the 1890s, suspicion of their motives and loyalties led to overt discrimination.

Then, after 1900, the nation was hit by a huge wave of immigrants from southern Europe, Italy, Russia, and Poland. These new immigrants were ethnically dissimilar to the old stock which had populated the colonies. Their influx led to social tensions and discrimination founded on popular racial theories of the Progressive era. For example, it was widely believed that behavior was transmitted through the germ plasm and not altered by the environment later, implying that strange, culturally deviant behavior was inborn. Nativist fears led to laws that severely restricted immigrants from all but northern European countries. Eventually, however, these immigrants were assimilated into American culture.

Today, the face of immigration has changed again. Immigration law amendments in 1965 permitted entry in large numbers from Asian and Latin American countries. Since 1980, only 11 percent of immigrants have been of European ancestry; most, 46 percent, have been Asians, and 40 percent have been Hispanic. These immigrants, like those of past years, have sometimes settled in ethnic enclaves and have faced prejudices. But the process of assimilation is at work for them also. Between 1981 and 1987, for example, the number of other Americans not wanting Hispanics as neighbors dropped from 18 percent to 9 percent.[5] The Chinese and Japanese, perhaps because of

---

[5]*Gallup Report,* "Prejudice: Cults Lead List of Groups 'Not Wanted as Neighbors,' " January–February 1987, p. 21.

their lighter skins, say some observers, have not suffered as much discrimination as other minority groups. Poverty, racism, and lack of privilege have characterized their lives, and still do for some. But economically, Asian groups have fared well. The Chinese and Japanese now have incomes above the average for all Americans.

DISCRIMINATION IN THE WORKPLACE

Discrimination against members of minority groups has inevitably entered the workplace. Its extreme form was the slavery that existed from colonial times to 1865. Slavery was always a racial phenomenon as well as an economic one. No whites were ever enslaved, even when it would have been legal. In lesser form, discrimination against other immigrant groups and women has marked business life and still exists. Although blatant bigotry is rare today, it may occasionally be found. In 1989, for instance, the U.S. government filed charges against two U.S. subsidiaries of Recruit, a Japanese placement firm, for using secret codes to screen people by sex, age, and race for corporate clients. If clients such as IBM Japan wanted Caucasians, the recruiter wrote "talk to Mary" on the job order. "Talk to Adam," denoted a preference for men. And "Suite 20 through 35" meant ages 20 to 35.[6]

This kind of prejudice is increasingly rare. There still exists, however, subtle, ingrained racism in corporate life. For example, hiring and promotion policies that treat all applicants equally may discriminate against minorities who are qualified for positions but less qualified than competing whites who benefitted from racial discrimination in education and hiring. Corporations such as Corning Glass Works and Union Carbide, which moved their headquarters to small town settings, may force minority employees to live in cultural isolation, away from supportive ethnic enclaves in metropolitan areas. Similarly, Honda Motor Co. was criticized for locating auto assembly plants in rural communities away from black population centers in cities. When it set up an assembly plant in Marysville, Ohio, it hired only workers living within thirty miles of the plant, a rule which screened out the region's largest pool of black labor in Columbus, thirty-five miles away.[7] Buddy systems among whites often exclude minorities. In the oil field supply and service industry, social contacts and friendships within a white, male, "old boy" network have been a barrier to minority-owned firms. Much oil field business is transacted at private clubs with restricted membership policies. Minorities also may be perceived according to stereotypes rather than actual performance. A black or a woman manager who is aggressive may be thought pushy, whereas a white manager with the same style may be called decisive.

---

[6]Jim Schachter, "Two Firms Linked to Recruit Accused of Discrimination," *Los Angeles Times*, June 1, 1989.

[7]In 1988, Honda reached a settlement with the Equal Opportunity Employment Commission in which it agreed to pay $6 million to 377 blacks and women who were denied jobs at three Ohio plants between 1983 and 1986. The details of the EEOC investigation and the agreement reached with Honda regarding future hiring policy was kept secret as a condition of the settlement.

Discrimination in the workplace is persistent. Discrimination against blacks, for instance, continues to be perceived despite strong social trends away from racist attitudes. In a 1944 poll, only 42 percent of the population felt that "blacks should have as good a chance as white people to get any kind of job," but by 1972, 96 percent of those responding to the same question favored equal hiring.[8] But this attitude shift has not translated into uniformly equal treatment. In a 1987 survey, 37 percent of whites and 71 percent of blacks felt that blacks do not have "the same opportunities as whites in employment."[9]

Examples of direct discrimination toward individuals are anecdotal and subjective. But broad statistical disparities document the difficulty that some minorities have in breaking through barriers. The 1987 firing of Al Campanis, Dodger vice president of player personnel, for saying that blacks "do not have the desire to be in the front office" and are not good swimmers because they "don't have buoyancy" illustrates the intolerance of society for openly racist remarks. But society did tolerate twenty-six major league teams in that year without a single black manager. Only one black, Henry Aaron, personnel director of the Atlanta Braves, held an executive position with any team.[10]

In corporate management, like major league sports, blacks, who are 12 percent of the population, are statistically underrepresented. A 1985 survey showed that less than one percent of the top managers of some of America's largest companies were minorities.[11] In 1988, only one black headed a *Fortune* 1000 company. A survey of 400 *Fortune* 1000 companies in 1986 showed that only 9 percent of all managerial positions were held by minorities.[12] In 1989, blacks owned only 449 of 25,300 auto dealerships.[13] One roadblock to black ownership is that older dealerships, including the most desirable, rarely come on the market. Instead, they are sold in "sweetheart deals" to the friends and business associates of the owner. Blacks face more physical danger on the job and are more likely to die from job-related illness or accident. A study of 6,500 rubber workers, for instance, found that 27 percent of black workers, but only 3 percent of white workers, toiled in compounding and mixing operations—jobs marked by high exposure to toxic chemicals associated with elevated rates for six types of cancer. A study of steelworkers

[8]Tom W. Smith and Paul Sheatsly, "American Attitudes toward Race Relations," *Public Opinion*, October/November 1985, p. 15.

[9]This was a *Time*/Yankelovich poll, "Attitudes in Black and White," *Time*, February 2, 1987, p. 21. An NAACP poll in 1989 found that 66 percent of blacks felt they did not get equal pay for equal work in comparison with whites; in Lee May, "Blacks, Whites Disagree Over Basic Racial Issues," *Los Angeles Times*, January 12, 1989.

[10]Ross Newhan, "The Action Doesn't Look Affirmative," *Los Angeles Times*, April 9, 1987. Newhan also notes a survey by the *Detroit Free Press* in 1985 showing that 50 percent of black players were outfielders. Only 8 percent were pitchers and 5 percent were catchers, "two of the thinking men's positions."

[11]*Korn/Ferry International's Executive Profile: A Survey of Corporate Leaders in the Eighties*, Korn/Ferry International, October 1986, p. 23.

[12]These figures are quoted in Colin Leinster, "Black Executives: How They're Doing," *Fortune*, January 18, 1988, p. 109.

[13]Faye Rice, "The Rise of Black Auto Dealers," *Fortune*, August 14, 1989, p. 68.

found cancer rates for blacks far elevated over those for whites because blacks, who have less seniority, work in less desirable jobs near coke ovens, where carcinogens are most numerous.[14] Compared to whites, blacks today also have lower average incomes, less access to desirable jobs, higher unemployment, and fewer promotional opportunities. They have shorter life expectancies, less education, higher infant mortality, and a greater likelihood of living in poverty than other racial and ethnic groups in the United States.

FEDERAL REGULATION TO PREVENT EMPLOYMENT DISCRIMINATION

Today there exists a massive legal and regulatory apparatus to protect employees' civil rights in companies and government agencies. It has not always existed.

When the Constitution was ratified in 1789, it sanctioned the practice of slavery in Article I, Section 2, which counted slaves as three-fifths of a person for purposes of apportioning seats in the House of Representatives. This language was rendered obsolete by the three Reconstruction Amendments; the Thirteenth Amendment abolished slavery, the Fourteenth guaranteed citizens "due process of law" and "equal protection of the laws," and the Fifteenth outlawed race as a barrier to voting. The original constitution also protected slavery in Article I, Section 9, which forbade Congress to stop the importation of African slaves before 1808. This passage was rendered obsolete by the passage of time.

In 1866, 1870, and 1871, Congress passed civil rights acts intended to prohibit employment discrimination, but until very recently, courts narrowly defined these acts to apply only to state government employees, not workers in corporations. Not until almost 100 years later, with the passage of the Civil Rights Act of 1964, were corporate employees given significant protection from employment discrimination. We turn now to a discussion of its most important section, Title VII.

TITLE VII OF THE CIVIL RIGHTS ACT OF 1964

The cornerstone of the structure of laws and regulations enforcing equal opportunity is the Civil Rights Act of 1964. Title VII prohibits discrimination in compensation, terms, or conditions of employment because of an individual's race, color, religion, sex, or national origin. Conditions of employment include hiring, promotion, training, disciplinary action, firing, layoffs, bonuses, working conditions, and selection procedures. Title VII also provided for the establishment of the Equal Employment Opportunity Commission (EEOC), an independent regulatory commission, to enforce its provisions. All companies with fifteen or more employees have to report annually to the EEOC the number of minorities and women on each step of the employment

---

[14]Morris Davis, "The Impact of Workplace Health and Safety on Black Workers," in *Occupational Safety and Health*, Frank Goldsmith and Lorin E. Kerr, eds., New York: Human Sciences Press, 1982, pp. 204–205.

ladder. The act holds employers responsible for any discriminatory acts that occur in the workplace. The Equal Employment Opportunity Act of 1972 extended coverage of Title VII to state and local government employees, to employees of educational institutions, and to the federal bureaucracy.

The overall purpose of Title VII is to remove barriers to equal employment opportunity. It does not require that minority workers be hired simply because they belong to a protected class, but it does require removal of discriminatory barriers to their hiring and advancement. Employers are not required to redress racially imbalanced work forces or to change established seniority systems. When the Civil Rights Act was being debated in 1964, its congressional opponents claimed that it would require employers to fire white workers and hire minorities to achieve proper racial balances. In order to get the bill passed, its supporters included an amendment stating that such actions were not mandated. If an employer had been discriminating prior to the act, the act required only the removal of that discrimination. The employer did not have to go further and change the composition of a work force to what it would have been had there been no discrimination.

Where employer discrimination still exists and can be proved, however, federal courts are empowered under Title VII to remedy the situation. Courts may use their power of injunction to prohibit an illegal activity, as in the case of one firm where new workers were hired only upon recommendation of a member of the existing, all-white work force. Courts may order individuals rehired or give them back pay after they have been unjustly fired. In addition, Section 706(g) of Title VII empowers judges to "order such affirmative action as may be appropriate," and courts sometimes have established numerical hiring goals for minorities and timetables for their achievement in cases where discriminatory practices have been long-standing and egregious. In 1975, for example, a New York district court ordered a sheet metal workers' local union to achieve a 29 percent nonwhite membership (based on the percentage of nonwhites in the New York City labor pool) by 1981. The court did so because the union had a nonwhite membership of only 3.19 percent and a long history of discriminatory barriers to minority employment, including entrance tests unrelated to job requirements, special training sessions to prepare relatives of white members for entrance examinations, and membership-size restrictions designed to bar minorities. A long court battle by the union ended in 1986 when the Supreme Court, in *Local 28 v. Equal Employment Opportunity Commission* (478 U.S. 421), upheld the validity of numerical goals as a remedy for this pattern of prejudicial hiring behavior.

Basically, two legal theories are accepted by the courts to demonstrate discriminatory employment barriers under Title VII. The first is the *theory of disparate treatment*. Disparate treatment exists where an employer bestows less favorable treatment upon employees because of their race, color, religion, sex, or national origin. For example, a retail store that refused to promote minority warehouse workers to sales positions because it preferred white salespeople to serve its predominantly white customers would be guilty of this type of discrimination. Proof in disparate treatment cases usually requires establishing a motive to discriminate. The second legal theory is the *theory of disparate impact*. Disparate impact exists where an employment policy is apparently neutral in its impact on all employees but, in fact, is not job-related and prevents individuals in protected categories from being hired or advancing. An example would be the requirement that applicants for a manual-labor job pass an English comprehension test in a geographic area where many minorities have poor English language skills.

The Equal Employment Opportunity Commission (EEOC) resolves complaints of workers who claim to have suffered discrimination. It may investigate these claims, but it does not have the power to fine employers. So if informal settlements cannot be reached, it must bring lawsuits and rely on court-ordered remedies for enforcement.

During the 1970s, the EEOC had an aggressive enforcement policy and sued large corporations on behalf of classes of their employees who had suffered from bias. In 1973, for example, AT&T was forced to pay $36 million in back pay to women and minorities who were unfairly denied promotion.[15] In the 1980s, however, the EEOC dropped class actions directed against large corporations and concentrated instead on the complaints of individual victims of discrimination. It did so to move closer to the Reagan administration's civil rights policy of racially neutral application of the laws. The Reagan administration promoted the view that Title VII should be used to redress cases of individual discrimination, not to give advantage to protected groups in which many individuals had not suffered discrimination. In 1985, the EEOC also dropped the use of timetables and numerical goals in hiring agreements with employers. The EEOC processes about 60,000 bias claims each year. This is a large number, but critics contend that its enforcement is inadequate to control discrimination in the workplace.[16] Since the EEOC has a huge backlog, resolution of a claim may take up to four years. In the meantime, the employee faces blackballing and forms of subtle retaliation by the employer which are difficult to remedy.

EXECUTIVE ORDER NUMBER 11246

A second major law protecting employees from discriminatory employment practices is Executive Order 11246, issued by President Lyndon Johnson in 1965. It requires federal contractors and subcontractors to take affirmative action "to ensure that applicants are employed, and that employees are treated during employment without regard to their race, color, religion, sex, or national origin." President Johnson derived the authority to require affirmative action of federal contractors from the Federal Property and Administrative Services Act of 1949, which directs the executive branch of government to buy goods and services in the most efficient way. The President construed

---

[15]*Equal Employment Opportunity Commission v. AT&T*, 365 F.Supp. 1105 (1973).

[16]See, for example, Rubye S. Fields, "Lack of Enforcement: A Barrier to Equal Opportunity," *Management Review*, December, 1987. For a defense of the EEOC and explanation of its enforcement philosophy in the 1980s see Juan Williams, "A Question of Fairness," *The Atlantic Monthly*, February 1987.

the act to prohibit discrimination, an inefficient use of human resources. As originally promulgated, Executive Order 11246 simply underlined the concept of employee equality found in Title VII of the Civil Rights Act of 1964. However, in 1971, the Labor Department—which had authority for administering the executive order through its Office of Federal Contract Compliance Programs (OFCCP)—issued Order Number 4.

The now historic Order Number 4 applies to companies that have federal contracts over $50,000 and fifty or more employees. It requires these companies to analyze major job categories—especially officials and managers, professionals, technicians, sales workers, office and clerical workers, and skilled craftworkers—to determine if they are utilizing women, blacks, Hispanics, Asians, Native Americans, and other minorities in the same proportion as they are present in the area labor force. If minorities are underutilized, companies must establish Labor Department-approved goals for hiring, retention, and promotion, and timetables for goal achievement. About 200,000 corporations, and virtually all the *Fortune* 500 companies, have contracts to supply goods and services to various government agencies. In effect, Executive Order 11246 (with Order No. 4) imposes widespread affirmative action requirements.

The Labor Department does not establish rigid hiring quotas for companies. Instead, it requires a contractor to set up hiring goals and make a "good-faith" effort to achieve them. This effort is checked in required reports and may involve anything from job fairs to summer employment for minority high school students. Generally speaking, adequate progress is defined by the Labor Department as a final hiring total that meets the "80 percent" rule. This rule is met if a company has hired minority groups at the rate of at least 80 percent of the rate at which it hires from the demographic group (usually white males) that provides most of its employees. If, for example, it hires 20 percent of all white males who apply for a particular job category, it must then hire at least 16 percent (80 percent of 20 percent) of all blacks who apply, 16 percent of all women, and so on. If its records prove that hiring has met this standard, it is likely that the federal government will have no complaint, but that is not assured. If a company fails to comply, the Labor Department may cut off federal contract payments. The threat is real, but remote. Between 1980 and 1988, only five firms were disbarred.[17]

In 1985, the Reagan administration tried unsuccessfully to emasculate Executive Order 11246. Attorney General Edwin Meese III drafted a proposal to require only voluntary affirmative action goals for federal contractors in place of federally enforced quotas and timetables. But the proposal met strong opposition from civil rights groups, and large corporations were lukewarm. In one survey of 104 big corporations, 99 said they would continue using numerical goals and timetables even if the government did not require them.[18] The proposal failed, and even though the Reagan administration cut the

[17]Jube Shiver, Jr., "Affirmative Action?" *Los Angeles Times*, July 7, 1989.
[18]Joe Davidson and Linda M. Watkins, "Quotas in Hiring Are Anathema to President Despite Minority Gains," *Wall Street Journal*, October 24, 1985.

OFCCP budget, fairly rigorous enforcement continued. The number of firms cited for serious violations of affirmative action rules rose from 1,121 in 1981 to 1,779 in 1988.[19]

OTHER IMPORTANT ANTIDISCRIMINATION LAWS

In addition to Title VII and Executive Order 11246, other federal laws protect women, ethnic or racial minorities, and other disadvantaged groups in the workplace. Briefly, they include the following.

The Equal Pay Act of 1963 prohibits pay differentials between male and female employees with equal or substantially equal duties in similar working conditions. It does not override pay differences due to legitimate seniority or merit systems. It covers fringe benefits also. Since 1979, the EEOC has had responsibility for enforcing this act.

The Age Discrimination in Employment Act of 1967 prohibits discrimination against people over age forty. After that age, it is illegal to base personnel actions on age. As the work force ages, age bias lawsuits have become the fastest-growing category of discrimination complaint. The average lawsuit is brought by a white male in his fifties who was dismissed in corporate downsizing and has reason to believe his age was a factor in the dismissal.[20] Since passage of this act, casual remarks about a person's age or jokes about "the old man" have led to expensive lawsuits by over-forty workers who are subsequently terminated.

The Vocational Rehabilitation Act of 1973 requires federal contractors and subcontractors to develop affirmative action programs for hiring handicapped people. A handicapped person has "a physical or mental impairment which substantially limits one or more of such person's major life activities."[21] In practice, this legal definition of handicapped applies to about 600 medical conditions, including symptomatic and asymptomatic HIV infection.[22] Persons with these conditions who are able to perform basic job duties without endangering others are termed "qualified handicapped" and protected under the law. Companies are required to make "reasonable accommodations" to them. In the case of AIDS victims, for example, courts have relied on med-

---

[19]Shiver, *op. cit.*, p. 5. However, a Democratic staff report of the House Committee on Education and Labor in 1988 concluded that the Reagan administration permitted lax enforcement of E.O. 11246. See David T. Croall, "Affirmative Action in the Late 1980s," *Labor Law Journal*, August 1988, p. 523.

[20]A study done at Syracuse University for the American Association of Retired Persons showed that 84 percent of plaintiffs were white males, 68 percent of cases dealt with dismissal or involuntary retirement, and 54 percent of plaintiffs were between the ages of fifty and fifty-nine. Sydney P. Freedberg, "Forced Exits? Companies Confront Wave of Age-Discrimination Suits," *Wall Street Journal*, October 13, 1987.

[21]P.L. 93–112, Sec 7(8)(B)(i).

[22]In a 1988 memorandum, the Department of Justice held that both symptomatic and asymptomatic HIV-infected individuals suffered from a protected handicap (401 FEP 2021, October 6, 1988). State and federal court decisions have also converged on this view. See Cynthia F. Cohen and Murray E. Cohen, "AIDS in the Workplace: Legal Requirements and Organizational Responses," *Labor Law Journal*, July 1989, p. 412.

ical opinion that risk of contagion to coworkers is negligible. To reasonably accommodate AIDS victims, companies may be required to give AIDS education programs to those who work with them and to provide flexible work schedules. In one case, a female quality control inspector who complained of fatigue while standing all day was allowed to sit on a stool to do her work. Workers with AIDS are not protected, of course, if they are too ill to work.

The Vietnam-Era Veterans' Readjustment Assistance Act of 1974 is similar to the Rehabilitation Act in requiring federal contractors to develop affirmative action programs for hiring, training, and promoting the nation's 6.9 million Vietnam veterans.[23] Some companies actively seek Vietnam veterans by making contacts at military bases and university veterans' counseling services. The law is administered by the OFCCP.

The Pregnancy Discrimination Act is a 1978 amendment to Title VII passed by Congress to reverse *General Electric Co. v. Gilbert,* a Supreme Court decision holding that a company which paid for the vasectomies of male employees was not legally biased against women even though it failed to cover medical costs and provide disability insurance for pregnancies.[24] It prohibits employment discrimination based on pregnancy, childbirth, or related medical conditions. As long as a woman can still perform work, she may not be required to resign or take a leave of absence for any pregnancy-related condition, including having an abortion. It is enforced by the EEOC.

The Immigration Reform and Control Act of 1986 was passed to control the influx of illegal immigrants by making employers responsible for checking the residency status of workers. Companies with four or more employees must document the immigration status of newly hired employees and job applicants. Hiring an undocumented alien carries a fine of $250 to $10,000 per offense, and repeat offenders may be imprisoned for up to six months. Hispanic groups feared that companies would discriminate against "foreign-looking" applicants, so Congress required employers to document the status of all job applicants and imposed fines of up to $2,000 for hiring discrimination on the basis of national origin or citizenship. However, in 1990 a study found that 19 percent of 4.6 million employers surveyed admitted to bias against job applicants who looked or sounded like foreigners.[25]

There is an important loophole in the law—employers are not required to verify the authenticity of documents which establish legal status. So a huge black market sprang up for phony driver's licenses, green cards, and birth certificates. In one case, Immigration and Naturalization Service (INS) inspectors raided the 1928 Jewelry Company factory in Burbank, California, and found that the entire work force of 190 had used counterfeited documen-

---

[23]In 1990, there were 7.3 million Vietnam-era veterans, but only 6.9 million were in the labor force. *Employment and Earnings,* February 1990, p. 17.

[24]429 U.S. 125 (1976).

[25]U.S. General Accounting Office, *Immigration Reform: Employer Sanctions and the Question of Discrimination,* GGD-90-62, March 29, 1990.

tation. The company's owners claimed they thought the papers were legitimate. They replaced all the workers and were never fined.[26]

The Americans With Disabilities Act of 1990 protects workers with mental and physical impairments, including those with AIDS, from job discrimination and extends to them the protections granted to women and ethnic, racial, and religious minorities in Title VII of the Civil Rights Act of 1964. It prohibits employers from asking if job applicants have disabilities or from using screening tests which have adverse impact on the disabled. Employers may ask only about ability to perform specific work. Companies are required to make "reasonable accommodations" for disabled workers including, for instance, provision of devices which allow deaf workers to communicate visually. But they are not required to make accommodations imposing an "undue burden." Thus, an existing two-story building does not have to be rehabilitated to include elevators. Restaurants, hotels, stores, and other service establishments, must accommodate the impaired among the public. When fully implemented in 1994, the law will apply to all businesses with more than 15 workers.

SOME OBSERVATIONS ON THE LAWS

Altogether, this thorough body of legislation protects a *majority* of the work force from discrimination. It covers white women, blacks, Hispanics, American Indians, handicapped males, white male Vietnam-era veterans, and all workers over the age of forty. At some point in their lives, if they live long enough, all people fall under the protection of federal employment legislation.

Also, there are two fundamental and sometimes opposing mandates in federal antidiscrimination law that exist in uneasy partnership.

- First, employers must not discriminate against an individual on the basis of race, sex, religion, age, national origin, pregnancy, physical handicap, or veteran status.
- But second, employers who have maintained discriminatory employment practices (even unintentionally) and federal contractors who have fewer females or minority group members than are available in the area work force may be asked to take affirmative action to preferentially recruit, hire, train, and promote such persons.

The net result of the simultaneous existence of these mandates is that managers may be asked not to discriminate against anyone, while at the same time they are required to give preference to individuals from a variety of groups constituting the majority of the work force.

---

[26]Pauline Yoshihashi, "Employer Sanctions and Illegal Workers," *Wall Street Journal*, May 26, 1989. For more on the law see Charles E. Mitchell, "Illegal Aliens, Employment Discrimination, and the 1986 Immigration Reform and Control Act," *Labor Law Journal*, March 1989; Peter Skerry, "Borders and Quotas: Immigration and the Affirmative-Action State," *Public Interest*, Summer 1989; and Carol Matlack, "Working Around a Law," *National Journal*, July 11, 1987.

THE JAPANESE APPROACH TO EQUAL OPPORTUNITY

Japan is a remarkably homogeneous society, undisturbed by the racial and ethnic tensions of America. But Japanese women have faced high barriers in companies.

In the post-World War II years of economic growth, Japanese companies have put women into low-paying office jobs. Job ads require them to be young, single, and living at home. When hired, they often become "office ladies," trained to answer telephones, bow at the proper angle to visitors, and do menial jobs for men in managerial positions. Women have been discouraged from managerial work because the long hours might impair marriageability. In Japan, the primary role of a woman is that of homemaker and childrearer. With women in charge of the home, Japanese men work their notoriously long hours and this system is thought by some experts to have helped the Japanese dominate world markets.[27]

Two forces now challenge this situation. First, affluence has led more women to enter the marketplace. And second, international pressure has made the Japanese self-conscious about sexism. Hence, in 1985 the Japanese Diet passed the Equal Employment Opportunity Law. Its approach to ending discrimination is radically different from the U.S. approach, and of interest for that reason.

The law makes it an obligation for companies to eliminate sexism in hiring, promotion, pay, and other areas of employment. Unlike our Title VII, however, it is not coercive and does not open employers to lawsuits. In Japan, concerted action is difficult without strong group consensus. Since the new law threatens the centuries-old sexual division of labor, it is felt that companies cannot be forced to end discrimination. So the new law is constructed as an educational, persuasive, and gradual method of introducing a new social idea around which enlightened consensus can form. When workers have complaints, the act requires only mediation and arbitration in which both the company and the woman compromise and neither loses face. The American-style lawsuit is proscribed. In Japan, a person bringing a lawsuit is ostracized and the defendant suffers embarrassment, so this enforcement technique is ruled out.

The Ministry of Labor issued modest guidelines for compliance with the act. It then announced that sometime in the future, when attitudes are more receptive to female equality, it will issue stricter guidelines. In the meantime, there is only slow progress. Between 1977 and 1987, the number of women in supervisory positions rose only half a percent, from 0.7 to 1.2 percent, and average monthly wages for women are only 52 percent of men's.[28] Discrimination is less open now, but it remains. The Japanese path is as different from the American path as are the two cultures, but of course it may be equally long.

THE CONTROVERSY OVER AFFIRMATIVE ACTION

Recall that under Title VII of the Civil Rights Act of 1964, courts may order affirmative action programs and, likewise, the Labor Department may require affirmative action from federal contractors under the authority of Executive Order 11246.

Corporate America has an enormous investment in affirmative action. Atlantic Richfield Co., for example, employs twenty-four people to manage forty-five separate affirmative action plans. Yet many in our society believe that affirma-

[27]See Loraine Parkinson, "Japan's Equal Employment Opportunity Law: An Alternative Approach to Social Change," *Columbia Law Review*, April 1989, p. 629.

[28]"Japanese Women Making Strides in the Workplace," *Journal of Japanese Trade and Industry*, no. 1, 1989, p. 5.

tive action programs, especially those that contain numerical goals for utilizing minorities, are objectionable, because in favoring blacks or other minorities they create so-called reverse discrimination against whites. They transform laws written to prohibit discrimination based on race into race-conscious laws that mock the ideal of color-blindness. They are also attacked by minority groups, which argue that affirmative action clouds the real achievements of minorities. There is always the suspicion that advancement has come because of affirmative action requirements and not individual ability.

These criticisms have been present since passage of the Civil Rights Act in 1964, but in the ensuing twenty-five years society supported affirmative action, and it has become institutionalized. By the end of the 1980s, however, support for affirmative action was wearing away, for four reasons.

First, for eight years the Reagan administration pursued litigation strategies based on the principle that only individual victims should benefit from antidiscrimination laws, not classes and groups. Under Reagan, enforcement of affirmative action by federal contractors was deemphasized, and the EEOC dropped its class action suits against large companies. The Bush administration has not shown the dogmatic opposition of its predecessor to affirmative action, but momentum has slowed and will be difficult to renew in the face of other trends noted here.

Second, there is growing acceptance of the idea that statistical disparities of income, opportunity, and occupation between groups result from innocent forces rather than malicious discrimination. "Nowhere," writes conservative intellectual Thomas Sowell, "do people have the same preferences, behavior, or performance."[29] Women may be underrepresented in blue-collar jobs because they decide in large numbers against pick and shovel work. Since the median age of American Jews is forty-six and that of Puerto Ricans is eighteen, there is bound to be a greater percentage of medical doctors among the Jews. American Indians are underrepresented as managers because Indian cultures do not inculcate values fostering wage work or business careers.[30] In short, random distribution of ethnic and racial groups is a fiction, and statistics showing the lack of many group members in a job category need not imply discrimination.

Third, the climate of liberal public opinion which long supported affirmative action has dissipated. Recent polls show that large majorities of both whites and blacks oppose preferential treatment for minorities at work. A 1988 *Newsweek*/Gallup poll, for example, found only 14 percent of whites and 40 percent of blacks in favor of affirmative action.[31]

---

[29]In *Compassion Versus Guilt*, New York: William Morrow and Co., 1987, p. 151.

[30]This is one observation of a recent report by the National Commission for Employment Policy. See Roger G. Ainsworth, *An Overview of the Labor Market Problems of Indians and Native Americans*, NCEP Research Report No. 89-02, Washington, D.C.: Government Printing Office, January 1989, p. 11.

[31]"Black and White: A Newsweek Poll," *Newsweek*, March 7, 1988, p. 23. A 1987 Gallup poll showed only 29 percent of a national sample in favor of plans that preferred minorities and women to "better qualified men and whites" in employment situations. "Majority Opposes Supreme Court Ruling in Affirmative Action Case," *Gallup Report*, no. 260, May 1987, pp. 18–19.

And fourth, the Supreme Court, the final arbiter of affirmative action, has begun to make proof of job discrimination more difficult. Over his eight years in office, President Reagan appointed four conservative justices. The last, Anthony M. Kennedy, appointed in 1988, created a five-member conservative majority on the nine-member court. Over the years, affirmative action cases have badly split the court, but until 1988 a 5-4 liberal majority often prevailed in civil rights cases. Because of this, the court upheld affirmative action plans over the years which were well-tailored to legal guidelines. In 1989, however, closely split decisions were controlled by the conservatives, who set higher standards for proving the existence of employment discrimination. In the following section, we review the court's course in affirmative action cases.

AFFIRMATIVE ACTION ON TRIAL

In the first affirmative action case of note, *Regents of University of California v. Bakke* in 1978, the Supreme Court ruled in a muddled, divided, and lengthy opinion in favor of a white male, Allan Bakke, who claimed to be the victim of reverse discrimination.[32] In this case, the University of California Medical School at Davis had reserved sixteen places out of 100 for entering minority students. Bakke complained that he had superior qualifications for admission than many of the minorities admitted, and the Supreme Court of the United States agreed with him when he said that he had been the victim of reverse discrimination. In a split decision, the Court ordered the university to admit Bakke, and it did so. The court forbade quota reservations of places for minorities and separate, insulated evaluations of minority applicants without comparison with other applicants. It held, however, that race could be a consideration in admissions, in these words: "The State has a substantial interest that may legitimately be served by a properly devised admissions program involving the competitive consideration of race and ethnic origin."

In another case in which the Court upheld a race-conscious remedy, Brian Weber, a thirty-one-year-old laboratory analyst with ten years' service at the Kaiser Aluminum & Chemical Corporation plant in Gramercy, Louisiana, charged the company with reverse discrimination. He claimed that he applied in April 1974 for a crafts-retraining program that would double his pay and provide him with a much better job. He was not selected, however, because the program called for at least 50 percent black trainees. As part of its voluntary affirmative action program, Kaiser set up dual seniority ladders—one for blacks and another for whites. Those admitted to the training program were picked alternately from the top of each ladder until the positions were filled, with the result that several blacks with less seniority than Weber were chosen. Weber claimed reverse discrimination based on a literal reading of Title VII, which clearly states that employment decisions based on race are

An exception to this pattern is a survey of 4,209 managers by John P. Fernandez (*Racism and Sexism in Corporate Life,* Lexington, Massachusetts: Lexington Books, 1981) which shows high levels of minority support for affirmative action. See p. 37.

[32]438 U.S. 265.

unlawful. In 1979, in *United Steelworkers of America v. Weber*, the Supreme Court ruled against Weber's claim and upheld the selection procedure—but only indirectly.[33] The Court did not rule in favor of discriminating against white males. It held that the Kaiser affirmative action program, being voluntary and not court-ordered, was a private matter and within the "spirit of the law," which was to advance minorities.

The Court also established important general guidelines for evaluating affirmative action programs that it would frequently return to in later years. It stated that any race-conscious relief for past discrimination would be subject to great scrutiny based on these criteria. First, a plan must be designed to break down old patterns of racial or sexual discrimination. Second, the plan must not unnecessarily trammel the interests of white (or male) employees or create an absolute bar to their advancement. In the *Weber* case, for example, whites were still admitted to the training program along with blacks. Third, the plan must not require the discharge of white (or male) workers and their replacement with black (or female) workers. Finally, the plan should be flexible and temporary, so that numerical hiring quotas and hiring goals, where they are used, can be dropped when the effects of past discrimination are overcome.

In a third case of major significance, the Supreme Court upheld another type of race-conscious remedy for past discrimination, namely "set-aside" programs for minority contractors. In 1977, Congress passed the Public Works Employment Act, which established a $4 billion fund for public-works construction programs in an effort to spur the economy. The act reserved 10 percent of this $4 billion appropriation for minority businesses. These so-called set-asides created problems. For one thing, there were all kinds of fraudulent schemes by companies posing as minority owned. For another, studies showed that construction costs had increased. This was because minority firms, although not always low bidders, had to be given contracts anyway. When the set-asides were challenged, the Supreme Court ruled that it was within the power of Congress to consider race-conscious criteria to remedy past patterns of discrimination against minority contractors in the construction industry. In *Fullilove v. Klutznick* in 1980, the Court rejected the contention of white contractors that this "reverse discrimination" was an inappropriate remedy.[34]

In other cases, however, the Supreme Court has refused to uphold affirmative action remedies. In 1981, the Memphis Fire Department was forced to lay off firefighters because of budgetary problems. The fire department had been following an affirmative action plan, and under a district court order, recently had hired blacks for one of every two vacancies. Because of the operation of a seniority system, however, many new blacks would be laid off, and the progress made under the affirmative action program would be lost. The district court that mandated the original affirmative action hiring program ordered the Memphis Fire Department to alter its se-

[33]443 U.S. 193.
[34]448 U.S. 448, 100 S. Ct. 2758.

niority plan in order to retain blacks and lay off more whites—even though the whites had more seniority. In *Firefighters Local Union No. 1784 v. Stotts* in 1984, a 6-3 Supreme Court majority held that the seniority system should be maintained in its original state, even if many recently hired blacks were laid off. The justices held that the intent of Congress in Title VII was to prohibit tampering with ongoing seniority systems.[35]

This case raised the hopes of some opponents of affirmative action that the Court might be ready to rule in favor of a color-blind interpretation of Title VII. If it would condemn race preference in layoffs, was it ready to prohibit race consciousness in hiring and end court-ordered affirmative action programs? The answer was no. In several 1986 cases the Supreme Court further defined the conditions under which affirmative action was acceptable and, although the majorities were weakened by concurring opinions and dissents were strong, it upheld the concept of affirmative action in hiring as a remedy for past discrimination.

The first case was *Wendy Wygant et al. v. Jackson Board of Education.* There a Michigan school district had adopted a layoff plan in which seniority would be followed, except that at no time could the number of minority teachers laid off exceed the minority employment percentage in the district. As a result, white teachers with more seniority than black teachers were laid off. The Court struck down the layoff plan, stating that it imposed too great a burden on those teachers laid off. Justice Powell, writing for the majority, argued:

> While hiring goals impose a diffuse burden, often foreclosing only one of several opportunities, layoffs impose the entire burden of achieving racial equality on particular individuals, often resulting in serious disruption of their lives. That burden is too intrusive.... Other less intrusive means of accomplishing similar purposes—such as the adoption of hiring goals—are available.[36]

Thus, even though the Court struck down a layoff provision giving preference to minorities, it implied that preferential hiring plans could be acceptable as a remedy for racial imbalance in a work force. The Court confirmed this stand in four other cases.

In *Local 28 v. EEOC* (1986)[37] and *Local No. 93 v. City of Cleveland* (1986)[38] the Court upheld affirmative action programs utilizing goals and timetables to overcome flagrant patterns of hiring discrimination by unions. In *United States v. Paradise* (1987), the Court upheld an affirmative action plan adopted by the Alabama Department of Public Safety, which required that 50 percent of the promotions to the rank of corporal be given to blacks.[39] And in *Johnson v. Transportation Agency, Santa Clara County, California* (1987), the Court upheld an affirmative action plan that permitted supervisors to consider the sex of an applicant as one factor in promotion decisions until the agency work

---

[35]467 U.S. 561.
[36]4 LW 4484, 476 U.S. 267.
[37]478 U.S. 421.
[38]478 U.S. 450.
[39]480 U.S. 149.

force had enough women in various job categories to approximately equal the 36.4 percent of women in the area labor market.[40]

In these cases the Court argued that a compelling societal interest in ending past patterns of egregious discrimination justified hiring and promotion programs that favored minorities and women. The Court relied heavily on the criteria developed in the *Weber* case and approved affirmative action plans that remedied past discrimination, did not absolutely bar the advancement of whites and men, did not require the discharge of whites or men, and were flexible and temporary.

Throughout this period a minority on the Court penned a series of dissents. The dissenters argued that the prohibition against employment discrimination in Title VII, taken literally, was absolute and prohibited affirmative action programs that utilized race and sex as the basis for preferential treatment. For example, Justice Scalia wrote these words of dissent in the *Johnson* case:

> The Court today completes the process of converting [Title VII] from a guarantee that race or sex will *not* be the basis for employment determinations, to a guarantee that if often *will.* Ever so subtly, without even alluding to the last obstacles preserved by earlier opinions that we now push out of our path, we effectively replace the goal of a discrimination-free society with the quite incompatible goal of proportionate representation by race and by sex in the workplace.
>
> In effect, *Weber* held that the legality of intentional discrimination by private employers against certain disfavored groups or individuals is to be judged not by Title VII but by a judicially crafted code of conduct, the contours of which are determined by no discernible standard....We have been recasting that self-promulgated code of conduct ever since—and what it has led us to today adds to the reasons for abandoning it.[41]

With the appointment of Justice Anthony Kennedy in 1988, a conservative block of five justices emerged on affirmative action cases.[42] They predominated for the first time in January 1989, striking down a program adopted by the City of Richmond, Virginia, which awarded 30 percent of city construction work to minority-owned contractors. Evidence showed that in Richmond, where the population was 50 percent black, less than one percent of contracts were being awarded to black companies and that six contractors' associations had virtually no minority members. Nevertheless, in *City of Richmond v. Croson,* the Court held that these statistics alone failed to prove past

---

[40]480 U.S. 616. A Gallup poll taken shortly after this decision showed that only 29 percent of the public approved it, including only 32 percent of women. "Majority Opposes Supreme Court Ruling in Affirmative Action Case," *Gallup Report,* no. 260, May 1987, p. 19.

[41]55 LW 4394.

[42]In addition to Kennedy, this bloc included Chief Justice William Rehnquist, Antonin Scalia, Sandra Day O'Connor, and Byron White. These five joined to dominate William Brennan, Thurgood Marshall, Harry Blackmun, and John Paul Stevens in civil rights cases. Blackmun and Stevens sometimes sided with conservative majorities, further weakening the liberal bloc. Then, in 1990, Justice William Brennan retired owing to failing health. His departure cost the liberals their long-time leader.

discrimination.[43] Also, since Richmond's set-aside program entitled black, Hispanic, Asian, Indian, Eskimo, or Aleut contractors anywhere in the country to participate, it was not narrowly tailored and violated the rights of white contractors. The effect of this ruling was to cast doubt on minority set-aside laws in thirty-six states and 190 cities and counties, and in his dissenting opinion Justice Marshall accused the majority of launching "a grapeshot attack on race-conscious remedies in general."[44]

He was prescient. In June 1989 came three more rulings that showed the Court was less willing to support race-conscious affirmative action. In *Wards Cove Packing Company v. Antonio*, the Court made it easier for companies to turn aside employee lawsuits based on statistical disparities in the work force.[45] Workers at an Alaskan salmon cannery brought suit because unskilled jobs on the canning line were filled almost entirely by nonwhites, whereas higher-paying skilled jobs and managerial positions were dominated by whites. Frank Antonio, an Alaskan native, brought suit against the cannery, alleging disparate impact. The Supreme Court held that, contrary to past statistical disparity cases, Antonio would have to prove that the company had no legitimate business reason for hiring minorities on the canning line. Previously, it would have been up to the company to prove that "business necessity" required the hiring practices in question. The *Wards Cove* case had the effect of taking the burden of proof away from the employer in disparate impact cases and putting it on the employees alleging discrimination. In dissent, Justice Blackmun wrote that the Court was taking "major strides backwards in the battle against race discrimination."[46]

In *Martin v. Wilks*, the Court allowed white firefighters in Birmingham, Alabama, to reopen a district court-approved fire department affirmative action because they alleged it discriminated unfairly against whites.[47] The plan established strict hiring and promotion goals for black firefighters, and had been adopted because only 42 of 453 firefighters and none of 140 lieutenants, captains, and chiefs were black in a city over 50 percent black. Until this case, no court-approved affirmative action plan had ever been reopened by whites claiming reverse discrimination. In permitting a rehearing, the Court paved the way for white victims of reverse discrimination to block and stall other plans around the country.

Finally, in *Patterson v. McLean Credit Union*, the Court made it harder for minorities to sue employers over racial discrimination.[48] Brenda Patterson, a

---

[43]822 F.2d 1355, 57 LW 4123. Justice Stevens went with the conservatives in a 6-3 decision. In March, the Court affirmed an appeals court ruling which struck down a Michigan law requiring that 7 percent of state contracts be given to minority firms and 5 percent be given to firms owned by women. The court had held that the state legislature had failed to prove past discrimination before passing the law. The case was *Milliken v. Michigan Road Builders Association*.

[44]57 LW 4149.

[45]827 F.2d 439, 57 LW 4583.

[46]57 LW 4593. This was a 5-4 decision.

[47]833 F.2d 1492, 57 LW 4616. This was a 5-4 decision.

[48]805 F.2d 1143, 57 LW 4705.

black teller at the McLean Credit Union, was ordered by her employer to do menial tasks such as sweep the floor and dust, whereas white tellers did not do this. Her white supervisor bullied her and said that "blacks are known to work slower than whites."[49] She sued the company, using a section of the Civil Rights Act of 1866 providing that "all persons...shall have the same right...to make and enforce contracts...as enjoyed by white citizens."[50] The significance of this 1866 law is that it covers 11 million workers in 3.7 million firms with fewer than 15 employees. Such small firms are exempt from EEOC oversight and their employees are not covered by Title VII of the Civil Rights Act of 1964. The Court decided that, contrary to past precedent, this part of the law did not cover racial harassment on the job after an employment contract had been made. Once hired, Patterson had no remedy against later racial bigotry by her supervisor. In dissent, Justice Brennan noted that the supervisor's harassment belied "any claim that the contract was entered into in a racially neutral manner" and criticized the majority for "a needlessly cramped interpretation" of the law.[51]

These cases, among others, showed that the Court majority was willing to narrow the permissible range of affirmative action.[52] They made it easier to challenge affirmative action plans by both public and private employers and made it harder for minority employees to prove discrimination.

The decisions in the 1989 cases, in which the new conservative court majority dominated, angered civil rights advocates. In early 1990, a bill called the Civil Rights Act of 1990 was introduced in Congress to overrule the objectionable decisions. If passed, it would reverse the *Wards Cove* decision by shifting the burden of proof in statistical disparity cases back to employers. It would reverse *Martin v. Wilks* by prohibiting whites to challenge court ordered consent decrees after they go into effect. And it would reverse the *Patterson* decision by redefining the right "to make and enforce contracts" as prohibiting post-hiring racial harassment and discrimination. In addition, the bill would, for the first time, allow victims of intentional discrimination to get punitive damages. All told, the Civil Rights Act of 1990 is a swift and broad repudiation of the Supreme Court's 1989 decisions involving civil rights in the workplace. The bill's backers believe its provisions are needed to restore civil rights which have been lost. In just one year following the *Wards Cove* decision, for example, over 300 employee discrimination cases were dropped because they could not meet the elevated burden of proof requirements for

[49]57 LW 4708.

[50]This is Section 1981.

[51]At 4716 and 4711.

[52]Two other cases of note did not repudiate prior Supreme Court decisions. In *Watson v. Fort Worth Bank & Trust,* a unanimous court (which nonetheless produced two separate majority opinions and two concurring opinions among eight participating justices) held that employers were entitled to use subjective judgment in promotion decisions. In doing so, it turned away a black woman who alleged discrimination in promotion policy because only whites were promoted (789 F.2d 791, No. 86-6139, 1988). And in *Price Waterhouse v. Hopkins,* the Court held in the case of a woman turned down in her bid for promotion to partnership in an accounting firm that she was discriminated against because a senior partner advised her to dress and act in a more feminine manner if she wanted to be promoted (825 F.2d 458, 57 LW 4470).

HOMER PLESSEY'S RIDE INTO HISTORY

For most of the twentieth century, the Supreme Court permitted blatant racial discrimination. Let us go back 100 years to tell the story of how it all started.

The East Louisiana Railway Company was required by an 1890 state law to have separate coach cars for blacks and whites on its trains. The managers and conductors of the company were subject to criminal penalties, including jail terms, if they did not enforce this law.

On June 7, 1892, Homer Adolph Plessy, who was seven-eighths Caucasian and one-eighth African blood, bought a first-class ticket to travel from New Orleans to Covington. Boarding the train, he took a vacant seat in the white coach. He was asked by the conductor to move to the "nonwhite" coach. Plessy refused and was forcibly taken off the train to a New Orleans jail.

Plessy brought suit, claiming he was entitled to "equal protection of the laws" as stated in the Fourteenth Amendment to the Constitution. In 1896, in *Plessy v. Ferguson,* the Supreme Court disagreed, holding that as long as accommodations for blacks were equal to those of whites, blacks were not deprived of any rights. This ruling created the fa-

mous "separate but equal" doctrine which was the legal foundation for segregation in the South.

There was a lone dissenter. Justice Harlan, in a principled argument, lectured the Court majority.

> Our Constitution is color-blind and neither knows nor tolerates classes among citizens. In respect of civil rights, all citizens are equal before the law. The humblest is the peer of the most powerful. The law regards man as man, and takes no account of his...color when his civil rights as guaranteed by the supreme law of the land are involved.[53]

For fifty-eight years, the Supreme Court majority ignored Harlan's argument. Finally, in 1954, the Court outlawed segregated schools and invalidated the "separate but equal" principle in the *Brown v. Board of Education* case.[54] At last Homer Plessy was vindicated. The *Brown* decision ushered in an era of judicial willingness to take race into account to end discrimination, not to perpetuate it. But in 1989, the Supreme Court began to move away from any consideration of race as a relevant factor in employment practice. It has not yet overturned the legality of race-conscious affirmative action, but one day it might.

showing discrimination. And in just eight months following the *Patterson* decision 96 cases alleging racial discrimination in small companies had to be dropped.

ETHICAL ISSUES IN AFFIRMATIVE ACTION

The legal debate about affirmative action is paralleled by an ethical debate. How can discrimination against white males, which inevitably must take place in affirmative action programs, be justified? There are three directions of ethical argument in which debate commonly proceeds.

First, there are utilitarian considerations. Utilitarian ethics require calculations about the overall benefit to society, as opposed to the costs, of reverse discrimination. Is affirmative action an effective policy for providing the greatest good for the greatest number of people? Advocates say yes. Prefer-

[53]163 U.S. 537.
[54]347 U.S. 483.

ential treatment of blacks, women, and other minorities enriches society by bringing fuller utilization of labor, demonstrating compassion, and shoring up political stability (because unhappy, unemployed, poor people riot). Opponents, however, argue that affirmative action promotes inefficiency. Employers must hire less trained, less qualified workers. Employees protected by legislation suffer diminished self-esteem when they are made to feel undeserving of their positions. In the end, it is impossible to establish precisely the relative weights of costs and benefits. No convincing conclusion about overall impact on society will soon be forthcoming.

Second, ethical theories of justice have been used to raise questions about the ultimate fairness and equity of affirmative action. It is fundamentally unethical, argue some, to distribute power and economic rewards unequally in a democratic society by using racial, ethnic, and sexist criteria. Although open discrimination is less than in the past, subtle forms of discrimination remain in our institutions. And past discrimination has created handicaps for women and minorities that put them at current disadvantage. Blacks, for example, have not had access to equal education with whites. Early in American history they were enslaved. Thus discrimination in favor of blacks is thought by some to compensate for past injustice and deprivation. In 1963, President Lyndon Johnson used a colorful analogy to make this point.

> Imagine a hundred-yard dash in which one of the two runners has his legs shackled together. He has progressed ten yards, while the unshackled runner has gone fifty yards. How do they rectify the situation? Do they merely remove the shackles and allow the race to proceed? Then they could say that "equal opportunity" now prevailed. But one of the runners would still be forty yards ahead of the other. Would it not be the better part of justice to allow the previously shackled runner to make up the forty-yard gap or to start the race all over again?[55]

However, with affirmative action, the penalty for past injustices falls on the current generation of white males—probably the least racist and discriminatory of all generations. Affirmative action may compensate for past economic deprivation, but of course it cannot compensate for pain and suffering among those long dead. Is it just and fair, then, to impose it, in view of these obvious inequities?

And third, affirmative action may be examined in light of ethical doctrines stipulating that humans possess important rights that the good society protects. Are there minimal levels of rights to equal treatment that cannot be abridged? Advocates of affirmative action argue that when the rights of minorities and white males conflict in the personnel process, the rights of minorities should be given precedence. Discrimination in favor of blacks, women, and others is benevolent of intention, unlike the evil discrimination of whites against blacks in the past. It is necessary to mint a new right, the right of preferential treatment for suffering minorities, and to exercise it until equality prevails. There is some validity to this argument, but discrimination

---

[55]Quoted in Robert A. Fullinwider, *The Reverse Discrimination Controversy: A Moral and Legal Analysis,* Totowa, New Jersey: Rowman and Littlefield, 1980, p. 95.

against whites perpetuates the distribution of rewards and power on the basis of race, which is a discredited doctrine.

There is no easy resolution to the contradictory appeals of these ethical arguments. Philosopher Robert K. Fullinwider notes that "earlier patterns of racial discrimination and oppression in our nation were so egregiously offensive that people could unite in condemning them without being forced to formulate with precision the principles upon which their condemnation rested,"[56] Reverse discrimination, however, is a more subtle evil and requires us to further refine our ethical thinking.

Some years ago, Father Theodore Purcell, a leading scholar in this area, devised guidelines to avoid ethical dilemmas in pursuing equal opportunity goals.

1 Minority persons must be qualified for the job under consideration by a single standard of minimum qualifications applicable to everyone.

2 If the minority person is *more* qualified, pick the minority person.

3 If the minority and majority persons are *equally* qualified and minorities are underrepresented on the job, pick the minority person.

4 If the minority person is *less* qualified in job-related abilities, then two considerations may be made.

First, if the job is not very sensitive or important regarding the safety and efficiency of the company or the welfare of fellow workers or customers, pick the less qualified person. As you move toward more job importance, however, greater merit should take precedence.

Second, if only a small gap exists between majority and minority persons, pick the minority. But as the qualifications gap widens, greater merit should take precedence.[57]

WOMEN IN THE WORKPLACE

Social trends and economic necessity have combined to bring about an unprecedented movement of women into the workplace. During World Wars I and II, women moved into the labor force in large numbers to help the war effort, becoming about one-fourth of the total work force both times. Following World War I, women returned to traditional roles in the home and on the farm, but after World War II they stayed on the job.

Because of economic necessity, feminist attitudes, and high divorce rates, the number of women in the work force has continued to rise. The number of women employed rose from 32 percent in 1970 to 46 percent in 1980 to 58 percent in 1990. The number of working women will increase through the 1990s and is projected to be 63 percent of all women by the year 2000.[58] Al-

---

[56]*Ibid.*, p. 8.
[57]Theodore V. Purcell, "Management and Affirmative Action in the Late Seventies." In *Equal Rights and Industrial Relations,* Industrial Relations Research Association Series, 1977, pp. 97–98. The passages here are paraphrased from lengthier text.
[58]These participation rates are from the *Statistical Abstract of the United States: 1990, op. cit.,* Table no. 625, and *Employment and Earnings,* February 1990, p. 8.

though much of the influx has been to low-paying, low-status service jobs, 27 percent of working women are managers or professionals.[59] In the late 1980s, women held only about 3 percent of senior management positions, leading some women to say they that a "glass ceiling" thwarted their career advancement.[60] This "glass ceiling" was an invisible barrier analogous to subtle male discrimination, which was as hard to pin down as it was effective in limiting women.

The entry of many women into the labor force has challenged employers and created the need for new policies. The challenges lie in the feminist assault on male dominance of corporate life. In addition, some special needs of women have had to be recognized. One example is the frequent need that women have to balance their dual role as mother and employee. Women lose time from work due to pregnancy and are frequently absent to care for sick children. Studies show that women managers are more costly to employ than men because of this absenteeism and their tendency to leave the company to raise a family. Women are not less productive than men, but their days and years away from work reflect traditional family solutions which distribute the burdens of childrearing preponderantly to women. The time women take away from the workplace slows their careers. In an effort to keep women on the job by accommodating their roles as mothers, companies have begun to experiment with child-care programs, extended leaves, flexible scheduling, job sharing, telecommuting, and alternative career paths—fast track for career women, a slower "mommy track" for career-and-family women.[61] These accommodations cause friction in high-achievement corporate cultures. One company which has experimented heavily with programs for women is North Carolina National Bank. CEO Hugh L. McColl Jr. notes the dilemma for women.

> The typical NCNB employee is a high-energy, competitive, self-motivated individual. In a corporate culture made up of a lot of these sort of people, it is difficult to accept a teammate who has cut back their work schedule, no matter what the reason.[62]

Corporations have also developed policies that reduce their liability for sexual harassment. Some companies, such as Levi-Strauss and Westinghouse, have sponsored employee training programs on premenstrual distress. And companies increasingly realize that they must contend with new possibilities for romantic relations among workers as the sexes step into more proximate and equal work conditions.

[59]*Employment and Earnings,* February 1990, p. 30.

[60]This figure is from a Korn/Ferry International study forthcoming in July 1990. It is an update of *Korn/Ferry International's Executive Profile: A Survey of Corporate Leaders in the Eighties,* Korn/Ferry International, 1986. See Cindy Skrzycki, "Throwing Stones at the Glass Ceiling," *Washington Post National Weekly Edition,* March 5–11, 1990.

[61]For more on alternative career paths see Felice N. Schwartz, "Management Women and the New Facts of Life," *Harvard Business Review,* January–February 1989; Elizabeth Ehrlich, "The Mommy Track," *Business Week,* March 20, 1989; and Catherine E. Olofson, ed., "Management Women: Debating the Facts of Life," *Harvard Business Review,* May–June 1989.

[62]In "What a Caring Company Can Do," *Across the Board,* July/August 1988, p. 40.

GENDER ATTITUDES AT WORK

Throughout recorded history, men and women have been socialized into distinctly different sex roles. The male was traditionally aggressive, logical, the breadwinner, and dominant. Women were objects of sexual desire, emotional, homemakers, and submissive. For centuries, a comfortable symmetry of sex roles existed. These traditional attitudes were carried from family and social life into the workplace, where they defined male-female relationships.

Consider, for example, these statements from older books giving career advice to women. Writing in 1929, Miriam Simons Lueck in *Fields of Work for Women* reinforced the traditional homemaker stereotype by suggesting that women were more interested in being wives than managers.

> Men maintain, not entirely without reason, that women want the honors and the salary, yet shirk the actual responsibility....Employers insist, and events support their statement, that just when they have a woman trained to·take over her share of executive responsibility, she marries.[63]

Catharine Oglesby, in her 1932 book, *Business Opportunities for Women*, accepted the image of women as sex objects and frivolous gossips concerned mainly about their appearance:

> The majority of business women have definite hours reserved by their hairdresser and manicurist. These stand week in and week out. They enjoy all the importance of a "heavy date," and business obligations are fitted around them....Whenever a group of women gather to chat the subject is usually *clothes*.[64]

In the 1960s, a powerful, worldwide feminist movement arose that challenged male domination in Eastern and Western cultures. Feminists argued that women were equally capable of holding traditionally masculine jobs and attacked a range of cultural impediments to equality. Men no longer were obliged to open doors for working women because even manners were thought to subtly assert male dominance. Women no longer accepted the submissive role of guest at business lunches, and took their male counterparts out. And, of course, women's political organizations pushed laws fighting sex discrimination and promoting equality in work and pay.

As a result of the feminist movement, two competing sets of values now exist in the workplace. The new feminist perspective of equality, widely held by women workers, clashes with traditional stereotypes of sex roles still prevalent among men. Some men still feel that women are too emotional to manage well; that they lack the ambition, aggressiveness, and toughness to excell in business; that male executives' wives dislike their husbands' working and traveling with women; and that women cannot display the sustained career drive of men due to pregnancy, child rearing, and family obligations. Inherent in all these stereotypes are basic attitudes of male dominance and superiority.

---

[63]Miriam Simons Lueck, *Fields of Work for Women*, New York: D. Appleton, 1929, p. 15.
[64]Catharine Oglesby, *Business Opportunities for Women*, New York: Harper & Brothers, 1932, p. 28.

Yet evidence suggests that such stereotypes, in the aggregate, are inaccurate. Sex-difference studies done over many years clearly show genetic, hormonal, behavioral, and aptitude differences between men and women. They document, for example, greater aggressiveness in men due to higher levels of the hormone testosterone, earlier math aptitude in males, and greater willingness of women to express a range of emotions.[65] Yet the overriding lesson of these studies is that sex-differences, while they exist at statistically significant levels, are small in terms of practical behavior. There is much overlap between men and women in aggressiveness, math aptitude, emotionality, and other personality characteristics. Individual capacities are unpredictable and may be shaped by the business environment. One recent study shows that women rate higher in some historically masculine, job-related values than their male colleagues. In this large survey, women were more likely than men to prioritize a job-related function over a family function and to relocate their families for a promotion. They were less likely than men to reject a promotion that changed their lifestyle. Women were more willing to work long hours than were men.[66] A variety of other studies and surveys indicate that women are not different from men in the way they work. A study analyzing the decision styles of 279 women managers, for example, found that the women were, like male managers, predominantly left-brain and tended to use the same decision-making methods as men. It concluded that "from a decision-style perspective, women are as capable of performing managerial jobs as men."[67] Of course, studies such as these cannot erase stereotyped perceptions that men have of working women.

THE PERSISTENCE OF TRADITIONAL STEREOTYPES

The clash of traditional male stereotypes with new feminist ideals of equality in work roles has been much studied. Its existence is documented by years of survey data and a continuing stream of anecdotes by candid men and angry women. Apparently, though, the gap between male and female attitudes is narrowing, and women are more widely accepted by men than in the past. For example, surveys of executive attitudes about women in business were conducted in 1965 and again twenty years later in 1985. The results, published in the *Harvard Business Review*, showed that sexist male attitudes toward women were receding. The number of men expressing an "unfavorable basic attitude" toward female executives fell from 41 percent in 1965 to 5 percent in 1985. The surveys also showed that:

• In 1965, 9 percent of the men surveyed agreed that "men feel comfortable working for women." By 1985, 21 percent agreed.

[65]For a summary of studies on these and other subjects see Paul Chance, "Biology, Destiny, and All That," *Across the Board*, July/August 1988.
[66]Gary N. Powell, Barry Z. Posner, and Warren Schmidt, "Women: The More Committed Managers?" *Management Review*, June 1985.
[67]James D. Boulgarides and Alan J. Rowe, "Success Patterns for Women Managers," *Business Forum*, Spring 1983, p. 23.

- In 1965, 54 percent agreed that "women rarely expect or want authority." By 1985, only 9 percent agreed.
- In 1965, 61 percent felt that "the business community will never wholly accept women executives." But by 1985, only 20 percent agreed.[68]

Other repeated surveys also show sexism receding. In one, the percentage of men agreeing that women are not as career-oriented as men dropped from 52 percent in 1981 to only 29 percent in 1988.[69] In another, the number of men preferring to work for another man instead of a woman dropped from 63 percent in 1975 to only 29 percent in 1987.[70] However, a third recent study of almost 30,000 corporate employees shows that most people retain some biases. When presented with a list of six stereotyped views of women for agreement or disagreement, 91 percent of men and 73 percent of women agreed with at least one of them.[71]

THE ORGANIZATIONAL DOUBLE STANDARD

Traditional stereotypes of women underlie differential, discriminatory treatment. Here we discuss several important ways that women in corporate life have not been treated equally with men.

OCCUPATIONAL SEGREGATION

Women are more likely to work in some kinds of jobs than in others. Within corporations and in the economy as a whole, women's jobs generally are lower in status and pay than typically male jobs. Women also have less occupational diversity that men do. Most women work in food and health services, clerical, and professional job classifications. And most women in the professional category are either registered nurses or teachers. A majority of both men and women are in work situations where they have daily contact mostly with coworkers of the same sex.[72]

Despite a great deal of occupational concentration in traditionally feminine work roles, the huge influx of women into the workplace has led them into traditionally male occupations. In the past decade, for example, three mostly male occupational categories—insurance adjuster, computer operator, and typesetter and compositor—have come to have a majority of women. Women are integrating other occupations; they are now, for instance, 50 percent of accountants and auditors.[73] Some feminists worry that if women predominate in new job categories, those jobs will be devalued in pay and pres-

[68]Charlotte Decker Sutton and Kris K. Moore, "Executive Women—20 Years Later," *Harvard Business Review*, September/October 1985.

[69]Alma S. Baron, "What Men Are Saying About Women in Business: A Decade Later," *Business Horizons*, July/August 1989, p. 52.

[70]"Women's Perception of Job Bias Grows," *Gallup Report*, January–February 1987, p. 18.

[71]John P. Fernandez, "New Life for Old Stereotypes," *Across the Board*, July/August 1988, pp. 24–25.

[72]Barbara A. Gutek, *Sex and the Workplace*, San Francisco: Jossey-Bass, 1985, Chapter Two.

[73]*Statistical Abstract of the United States: 1990, op. cit.*, Table no. 645.

tige relative to remaining male bastions. They believe that sexist attitudes downgrade the prestige of feminized work. A striking illustration given by one feminist scholar is a study in the *Dictionary of Occupational Titles* which ranked the job of marine mammal handler as more complex and calling for more skill than the job of kindergarten teacher.[74] Is caretaking for dolphins a more complex activity than educating children?

DIFFERENTIAL TREATMENT IN THE WORK PROCESS

Many workplaces, including those in large corporations, have masculine cultures. In them, managers display the values and behavior patterns characteristic of the traditional male role. When this role is established as the norm, women who behave differently are nonconformists and may be perceived as failing to meet behavioral standards. Women in such settings face a dilemma. If they adopt the male standard of behavior, they may be scorned as unfeminine by men who expect traditional role behavior. This is what happened in a prominent incident in which a woman who was the top contract winner in the accounting firm of Price Waterhouse was denied promotion to partnership by male partners who, in written reviews, described her as "macho" and suggested that she "overcompensated for being a woman." The man assigned to inform her of her rejection advised her to "walk more femininely, talk more femininely, dress more femininely, wear make-up, have her hair styled, and wear jewelry."[75] She brought a successful Title VII suit against the firm. If, on the other hand, women display stereotypic feminine behavior, they may be seen as lacking in male virtues.

Nowhere is the pervasive, controlling influence of masculine corporate culture better illustrated than in the image of the secretary. The job of the secretary is defined by traditional sex-role expectations. Women are 98 percent of all secretaries, and the image of the secretary is synonymous with traditional female sex roles.[76] As a worker she is perceived as the office wife of her boss; as a woman she is often made a sex object by jokes about sexy secretaries.[77]

Contrariwise, the role of boss is defined in a masculine way. Since women do not have wives, it becomes difficult for a woman to become a boss. And if she is a boss, can she remain "feminine" and have an office-wife? Visitors to the company who hold traditional sex-role images of the office environment

---

[74]Discussed by Christine A. Littleton in "Equality and Feminist Legal Theory," *University of Pittsburgh Law Review*, Spring 1987, p. 1048.

[75]*Price Waterhouse v. Ann B. Hopkins*, 618 F.Supp. at 1117, 57 LW at 4471 (1989).

[76]*Statistical Abstract of the United States: 1990, op. cit.*, Table No. 645. We are indebted to Rosemary Pringle's *Secretaries Talk: Sexuality, Power, and Work*, London: Verso, 1989, for this analysis of sexual stereotypes.

[77]Sample: The boss caught his secretary and one of his executives in a bit of sex in one of the storerooms during a coffee break.

"Okay," the boss growled, "what's the meaning of this?"

"Well," the girl explained, "neither of us likes coffee."

From a joke book containing many more, Joey Adams, *Speaker's Bible of Humor*, New York: Doubleday, 1972, p. 233.

may perceive women executives as secretaries. Men fear emasculation from assuming feminine secretarial roles and expect teasing.

Masculine work values are a challenge for women in many ways and result in differential treatment. Some women managers have not had problems. But many are faced with the subtle, sexist dimension of male job culture. Men are more likely to interrupt women at meetings than the reverse. They may apologize for swearing in their presence, forget their presence in decision-making groups, and proposition them. Women are less likely to participate in informal group activities, such as having a drink after work, when valuable information about organizational life may be shared. It is more difficult for them to find mentors. A male mentor may be hesitant, fearful that his relationship with a woman will be awkward and misunderstood as a romantic interest. Women in a position to mentor may be scarce.

Much male insult and awkwardness arises from the continued male perception of female coworkers as submissive objects. Men who are conditioned to see women as lovers or wives may subconsciously place women coworkers in the same category. These men may find it difficult to work for a female boss or include women in formerly male gatherings.

THE PAY GAP

Pay is an area in which the organizational double standard has a long historical record. For example, an 1883 survey in Philadelphia showed that women were paid less for a typical seventy-eight-hour work week than men were paid for one ten-hour day.[78] At Westinghouse in the 1930s, all plant jobs were classified as either "male" or "female" jobs, and an official company *Industrial Relations Manual* instructed that "female" jobs rated equal to "male" jobs in terms of skill, physical effort required, responsibility, and working conditions were to be given lower compensation. This was justified, the *Manual* said,

> because of the more transient character of the service of the women, the relative shortness of their activity in industry, the differences in environment required, the extra services that must be provided, overtime limitations and the general sociological factors not requiring discussion herein.[79]

In 1989 the average woman still earned only 72 cents for every dollar earned by a man. The average annual income for men was 28 percent higher than for women. Within major job classifications, women earned less than men. And jobs typically dominated by women paid less than male-dominated jobs. Male dominance of more powerful and career-enhancing jobs in business is only one reason for the male-female pay gap. Another is that the entry of many women into the labor force in recent years means that they often have lower seniority.

---

[78]Dara Demmings, "Comparable Worth: A Matter of Simple Justice," *The Corporate Examiner,* June 1983.
[79]*Ibid.,* p. 3B.

Women are protected against pay discrimination based on sex by the Equal Pay Act of 1963, which prohibits paying women less than men for jobs which are identical or not substantially different. Recently, however, women's rights advocates have developed the idea of *comparable worth* for equalizing pay with male occupations. Basically, comparable worth is the theory that lower-paying jobs held by women may be comparable in their content, effort, and responsibility with nonidentical higher-paying jobs typically held by men. In a comparable worth study done in the Washington state government, for example, points were assigned for the "knowledge and skills, mental demands, accountability, and working conditions" in relatively low-paying jobs held mainly by men or mainly by women. The resulting tally indicated that the job of "laundry worker," usually held by a woman making $1,114 per month, received the same point total as the normally male "truck driver I," which paid $1,574.[80] Advocates of comparable worth argue that nonidentical but comparable jobs should be paid equally. If there is a wage differential between "men's jobs" and "women's jobs," it is evidence of sex discrimination by the employer.

The Equal Pay Act prohibits sex-based pay discrimination only for jobs that are identical or nearly identical within the same facility. It is too narrow to uphold the idea of comparable worth. Therefore those who advocate comparable worth, including women's groups and state employee unions, have argued that Title VII of the Civil Rights Act of 1964 is broader and prohibits pay differentials among both identical and comparable jobs where these jobs are held mainly by opposite sexes. Most courts have rejected this argument. Opponents of comparable worth, including business groups such as the Chamber of Commerce, believe that the wage differential between roughly comparable men's and women's jobs is determined in the labor market and is not the result of discrimination. Comparable worth is seen as inherently subjective, disruptive to the labor market, and unnecessary because the wage gap between men and women is closing without it.[81] Nevertheless, comparable worth advocates have won major victories. Seven states now have comparable worth laws for government employees, and in 1988 the House of Representatives passed a bill requiring a comparable worth study of jobs in the federal bureaucracy (but the Senate failed to act).

SEXUAL HARASSMENT

Sexual harassment is a problem faced by some working women. Although various permutations of harassment exist, including homosexual and lesbian harassment, the major problem today is harassment of women by male superiors.

[80]David G. Tuerck, "Fair Pay for Women: Comparable Worth or Incomparable Work?" Speech before the Federalist Society, Boston University Law School, Boston, Massachusetts, March 25, 1986.

[81]See U.S. Chamber of Commerce, *1989 Congressional Issues*, Washington, D.C.: U.S. Chamber of Commerce, 1989, p. 14, or Dick Armey, "Comparable Worth: A Bad Idea That Won't Die," *Wall Street Journal*, September 26, 1988.

In her landmark book *Sexual Shakedown,* Lin Farley defined sexual harassment as "unsolicited nonreciprocal male behavior that asserts a woman's sex role over her function as a worker."[82] This definition encompasses a wide range of behavior. Minor forms of harassment include suggestive stares, gratuitous touching, referring to women as "honey" or "sweetie," and off-color jokes. The tendency of older men to treat younger women as daughters, a tendency that makes a female manager's job sticky when subordinates are older men, also fits Farley's definition. More serious forms of harassment are unwanted propositions for sex, lewd remarks, and physical assault.

In a survey of both men and women, researcher Barbara Gutek found that 53 percent of women and 7 percent of men had experienced sexual harassment. Gutek found, furthermore, that men and women reacted very differently to sexual overtures, with 67 percent of men saying they would feel flattered by a proposition to have sex, whereas only 17 percent of women felt that way. Women also were more likely than men to perceive various actions in a range of verbal and physical acts as sexual harassment.[83]

Forms of sexual harassment may reinforce the sexist double standard in organizations. By treating a woman as a sex object, a man places her in the stereotypical role of submissive female. Harassment affects women at all levels in the corporation and many are afraid to report it because it may be a case of their word against a supervising male's. Sexual harassment may contribute to a pattern of female job loss that interrupts careers and lowers incomes. Women who have had to quit a job because of it lose seniority, access to fringe benefits, and salary. Furthermore, women who are considered unattractive may lose economically if selection and promotion processes favor women who are sexually alluring. In addition, women who are harassed are less productive, take more sick leave, and frequently request transfers.[84] All this is costly to the organization.

In November 1980 the EEOC issued guidelines for employers for determining the nature of sexual harassment in the workplace that is prohibited under Title VII of the Civil Rights Act of 1964. Basically, these guidelines hold that sexual behavior is harassment if it is required for an employee to continue and advance in a job or if it creates an upsetting work atmosphere for the employee. The EEOC Guidelines on Sexual Harassment are as follows:

> Unwelcome sexual advances, requests for sexual favors, and other verbal or physical conduct of a sexual nature constitute sexual harassment when:
> 1 submission to such conduct is made either explicitly or implicitly a term or condition of an individual's employment,
> 2 submission to or rejection of such conduct by an individual is used as the basis for employment decisions affecting such individual, or
> 3 such conduct has the purpose or effect of unreasonably interfering with an individual's work performance or creating an intimidating, hostile, or offensive working environment.
>
> *Source:* Equal Employment Opportunity Commission, 1980.

[82]New York: McGraw-Hill, 1978, pp. 14–15.
[83]*Sex and the Workplace, op. cit.,* p. 46.
[84]Sharon W. Walsh, "Confronting Sexual Harassment at Work," *Washington Post,* July 21, 1986.

These guidelines have since been upheld and refined by the courts. In the case of *Meritor Savings Bank v. Vinson* in 1986, the Supreme Court decided that employers may be liable for the harassing acts of their employees that create a hostile working environment.[85] It did not make clear under what circumstances liability arises but hinted that a clear management policy against harassment and a workable grievance procedure are important in reducing liability. Without this kind of management oversight, a company could be held responsible for the harassment of an employee of which it had no knowledge. Therefore corporations around the country have developed training programs, policies, and oversight procedures by which to protect themselves from liability.

CONCLUDING COMMENT

Discrimination in the workplace has existed throughout American history. The first national effort to end it began with the Emancipation Proclamation freeing slaves and included constitutional amendments and civil rights laws passed following the Civil War. This first attack focused on racial discrimination, and, although slavery ended, the effort to reduce other forms of workplace bias floundered because laws were not strictly enforced.

In the 1960s a second effort to eradicate discrimination began with passage of the Civil Rights Act of 1964. Since 1964 further legislation and thousands of court decisions have greatly reduced job bias against minorities and women. Today, the accumulated corpus of antidiscrimination law is massive, complex, and not easily understood in its entirety. But it works.

More progress needs to be made. Although penalties in the law have scared most employers into abandoning openly biased job actions, prejudicial attitudes still show in subtle ways. Strengthened affirmative action remedies face more resistance from whites and conservatives than in the recent past. But despite this, it will be difficult to slow the momentum of antidiscrimination law, and progress will continue.

[85] 54 LW 4703.

A New Plant Manager

A senior executive at Federal Chemical Corp. is reviewing the records of three candidates who have applied for promotion to a newly vacant plant manager position. Federal Chemical has a work force of 9,000 employees. It is not operating under either a court-ordered affirmative action plan or a voluntary plan negotiated with any of its unions.

What follows is a brief sketch of the reviewing executive's impression of each candidate and basic information from their folders.

EDGAR MARTIN (32 YEARS OLD)

Martin is a graduate of Ivy League schools. He is energetic, polished, ambitious, and the son of a U.S. senator. During the 1986 elections, he organized a company-wide get-out-and-vote drive.

B.A.	Princeton University 1978, *cum laude* (chemistry major)
M.B.A.	Columbia University 1980
1981–83	Peace Corps. (Kenya)
1983–85	Sales representative, Eastern Division of Federal Chemical
1985–87	Special assistant to the President of Federal Chemical
1988–89	Production supervisor, Western Division
1990–91	Assistant Plant Manager, Midwestern Division
1990	One of three employees receiving an Outstanding Productivity Award

THOMAS WASHINGTON (58 YEARS OLD)

Washington is a graduate of a small agricultural and technical school in the South (the same school the Rev. Jesse Jackson graduated from). He has been a loyal, competent employee for 17 years. He is hard working and methodical.

B.A.	North Carolina A & T 1951 (mechanical engineering)
1952–54	U.S. Army (Korea)
1955–58	Laborer, Bekins Van Lines

1958–59	Unemployed
1960–61	Laborer, Bekins Van Lines
1962–68	Driver, Bekins Van Lines
1969–70	Unemployed
1971–73	Machinist, Western Division, Federal Chemical
1974–75	Plant foreman I
1976–79	Plant foreman II
1980–86	Plant foreman III
1987–91	Assistant plant manager

MARTHA OLIVERAS (56 YEARS OLD)

Oliveras has been with the company for 34 years. She is very popular with coworkers. She cohosts a local radio program on drug abuse one evening a week and works with community groups on anti-drug projects.

B.A.	University of Michigan, 1953 (English literature)
M.B.A.	Pepperdine University, Los Angeles, California, 1983
1957–76	Secretary, purchasing department, Rocky Mountain Division, Federal Chemical
1977–80	Administrative assistant, R&D Office
1981–83	Technical assistant, testing laboratory
1984–86	Sales representative, Western Division
1987–89	Sales manager, Western Division
1990–91	Assistant plant manager

QUESTIONS

1 Which of these three candidates would you choose for the position of plant manager? Why?

2 Are issues of discrimination, sexism, or affirmative action raised in this case?

3 Review the section in this chapter entitled "Ethical Issues in Affirmative Action," and use one or more of the arguments presented there to defend the candidate of your choice. What are the strongest arguments for other candidates and why are they less convincing?

4 Review Father Purcell's guidelines for preferential treatment set forth in this chapter. Is your decision compatible with them when they are applied to the three candidates for promotion here?

5 Under what circumstances could serious legal problems exist if either of the passed-over candidates filed a lawsuit?

Martin v. Wilks

This is the story of more than twenty years of lawsuits over discrimination by the Birmingham Fire Department. Over this time, social values about discrimination have changed markedly, so that although the litigation still continues it has a much different meaning today. When the suits first started, blacks were fighting a racist white establishment to get a foothold in a fire department which had no black firefighters. Today they are fighting to retain a program of preferential treatment which has made them 25 percent of firefighters and guaranteed them promotions over whites who score higher on qualifying exams. What is fair to both blacks and whites? You be the judge.

THE CITY OF BIRMINGHAM, ALABAMA

Birmingham is located in a valley in north central Alabama, bordered by southern ranges of the Appalachian Mountains. Prior to the Civil War, the valley where the city now stands was covered with many cotton fields worked by black slaves. But in the post-Civil War years Birmingham became a major mining and iron and steel-making center. The area has a unique combination of iron, limestone, and coal deposits, the three critical natural resources needed for steel production. After the 1870s, the city grew rapidly, and by the early 1960s had a population of 350,000. Its economy was expansive, but there were problems—air pollution, traffic congestion, urban decay, and a festering climate of race relations. Blacks were 40 percent of the population. Jim Crow laws segregated public facilities such as drinking fountains, rest rooms, and parks. Downtown merchants had "Colored Only" signs on their facilities. Blacks could shop in department stores but could not sit at lunch counters. They sat in the backs of buses; whites sat in front. There was an undercurrent of danger. In 1956, Nat King Cole was beaten on stage during a singing performance. Another time, a group of drunken white men kidnapped a black man, took him to a rural shack, and castrated him. One black who grew up in that era recalls: "Life then was frightening—you had to guard against so much...."[86]

---

[86]Tony Jackson, battalion chief, Birmingham Fire Department, quoted in Barry Siegel, "Battling to Climb the Ladder," *Los Angeles Times*, February 7, 1990, p. A15.

The economics of racial segregation went against blacks also. Steel firms were hotbeds of discrimination, hiring blacks mainly as unskilled laborers; only one of six blacks worked in a skilled position as compared to three out of four whites. At $3,000, the annual income of blacks averaged only about half that of whites. There were no black police officers or firefighters.[87] These careers were open only to whites.

In the early 1960s, the civil rights movement had yet to inflame public opinion. But racism in Birmingham was destined to stoke the fires. The city first made headlines in 1961 when a group of activists called "Freedom Riders" rode through the south on a bus. In defiance of local custom, white Freedom Riders sat in the back of the bus and blacks in front. At bus stations, the blacks used white restrooms and vice versa. At the Birmingham bus station a crowd of whites had collected to meet the bus. In a headline-making melee, the Freedom Riders were viciously assaulted; one was paralyzed for life.

In 1963, Rev. Martin Luther King led massive demonstrations in Birmingham to integrate lunch counters and force merchants to hire black salespeople. The white community resisted. Thousands of blacks were arrested, including King, and Police Commissioner Eugene "Bull" Connor's men used fire hoses, electric cattle prods, and police dogs on peaceful demonstrators. For days, Birmingham was a cynosure of media attention, and brutal assaults on blacks were broadcast around the world. The Ku Klux Klan rallied outside the city. Firebombs exploded at black homes. With world opinion hanging in the balance, President John F. Kennedy eventually sent federal troops to calm the situation.

PASSAGE OF THE CIVIL RIGHTS ACT OF 1964

Within a month of the Birmingham demonstrations, President Kennedy announced on national television that he was sending a new civil rights bill to Congress. It would outlaw segregation in public facilities, education, federal programs, and employment.[88] The bill passed, becoming the landmark Civil Rights Act of 1964. Title VII of the law forbade discrimination in any aspect of employment. It read, in part:

It shall be an unlawful employment practice for an employer:

1 To fail or refuse to hire or to discharge any individual, or otherwise to discriminate against any individual with respect to his compensation, terms, conditions, or privileges of employment, because of such individual's race, color, religion, sex, or national origin.

2 To limit or classify his employees or applicants for employment in any way which would deprive any individual of employment opportunities or otherwise

[87]Figures in this paragraph are from Juan Williams, *Eyes on the Prize*, New York: Penguin Books, 1988, p. 181.

[88]For an overview of the ten titles of the bill and floor debate over its passage see *Congressional Quarterly*, "Humphrey Opens Civil Rights Debate with Detailed Defense," April 3, 1964, pp. 655–657.

adversely affect his status as an employee, because of such individual's race, color, religion, sex, or national origin.

Section 703 (a)

Title VII, opposed by southerners in Congress, would haunt Birmingham's whites, including Robert "Kenney" Wilks, the son of a steelworker. In 1963, as a high school student, Wilks had watched Bull Connor's men subdue the civil rights demonstrations on television. By 1989, Wilks was a forty-year-old firefighter battling black coworkers in a reverse discrimination lawsuit. His claim? He was unfairly discriminated against for promotion to lieutenant in the Birmingham Fire Department. Less qualified blacks were promoted ahead of him, he argued, because of their race. They were getting preferential treatment under Title VII of the Civil Rights Act of 1964, but unfairly so.

BIRMINGHAM GRAPPLES WITH JOB DISCRIMINATION

The case of *Martin v. Wilks* has its origin in a controversy over tests given to applicants for firefighter jobs. Here is the story of that controversy.

In 1945, Jefferson County, Alabama, the county in which Birmingham is located, set up a Personnel Board and asked it to determine the fitness of applicants for jobs in local government agencies. The Personnel Board adopted a system wherein applicants for the Birmingham Fire Department were given tests. Those passing the tests were ranked on eligibility lists in the order of their exam scores. When openings for firefighters occurred, the Personnel Board sent the names of the top three on the eligible list to the department. The department then chose one of the three for a twelve-month probationary appointment.

Prior to passage of the Civil Rights Act of 1964, the process of determining eligibility of job candidates at the Personnel Board was, not surprisingly, strongly discriminatory against blacks. Proof of this lay in the fact that there were no black firefighters in a city where 40 percent of the population was black. After 1964, the Personnel Board came under pressure to make blacks eligible for fire department positions, because around the country discrimination lawsuits against government agencies had resulted in expensive damage and back pay awards.

In 1968, after an outside study recommended less discriminatory testing procedures, the Personnel Board adopted a new fitness test for firefighters, called Firefighter Test 20-B. This was a paper-and-pencil test with 120 multiple-choice questions. It had been developed by the International Personnel Management Association to be nondiscriminatory and was used in other cities. To encourage black applicants, the Personnel Board also began paying the $10 charge for physical exams and dropped a $1.50 charge for the screening tests.

COURT ACTION TO INTEGRATE THE FIRE DEPARTMENT

But to say progress in hiring blacks was slow would be a striking understatement. It was not until 1968 that Birmingham hired its first black firefighter; a second was not hired until 1974, when a total of nine were hired. This progress was too sluggish to go unchallenged, and lawsuits against the city and the Personnel Board arose.[89] These cases were consolidated as *Ensley Branch, National Association for the Advancement of Colored People (NAACP) v. George Seibels.* Seibels was the Mayor of Birmingham at the time.

At a 1976 trial before Federal District Court Judge Sam C. Pointer, lawyers for failing black applicants presented statistical evidence that the written test was discriminatory. Although the Personnel Board was not accused of intentionally discriminating, it was accused of using a test which had an adverse impact on blacks. Title VII of the Civil Rights Act of 1964 prohibits using tests if the operational effect is to screen out minorities unless the tests can be shown to measure "job-related" skills.[90]

Figures compiled by the Personnel Board, shown here, indicate that only 24 percent of black applicants passed the test as compared to 83 percent of whites.

FIREFIGHTER TEST 20-B: 1972–1974

	Black	White
Total applicants	285	1,530
Failing test	216	267
Passing test	69	1,263
Hired	9	215

Further, even blacks who passed had lower scores than whites, and 90 percent of them wound up on the bottom half of the eligibility list. Not surprisingly, only 3.2 percent of blacks were hired, as compared to 14.1 percent of whites.

The Equal Employment Opportunity Commission (EEOC) had developed guidelines for determining when selection rates for minorities were illegally low. They read:

> A selection rate for any racial . . . group which is less than four-fifths (4/5) (or eighty percent) of the rate for the group with the highest rate will generally be regarded as evidence of adverse impact. . . .[91]

Based on this standard, sometimes called the "80 percent rule," the testing and selection of firefighters was in violation of Title VII. Blacks passed the

---

[89]The Ensley Branch of the National Association of Colored People sued George Seibels, the Mayor of Birmingham. John W. Martin, a black applicant for firefighter, sued the City of Birmingham on behalf of other applicants. The U.S. government sued Jefferson County. These cases were consolidated as *Ensley Branch, NAACP v. Seibels* in the U.S. District Court, Northern District of Alabama, 14 FEP 670 (1977).

[90]Prior to the trial, the Supreme Court of the U.S. had ruled that Duke Power Company of North Carolina could no longer require passing scores on a general intelligence test and a mechanical aptitude test for workers who wanted transfer to higher-paying blue-collar jobs at a power station. The use of the two tests had the effect of keeping blacks in low-paying jobs, and there was no evidence that they measured abilities needed for higher-paying jobs. This case was *Griggs v. Duke Power Company*, 401 U.S. 424 (1971) and the part of Title VII in question is 42 U.S.C. Sec. 1981.

[91]14 FEP 673.

test at a rate only 29 percent of that of whites and were hired at a rate of only 23 percent of that of whites. These anemic figures were, of course, far short of the 80 percent guideline established by the EEOC.

The only way that Firefighter Test 20-B could be upheld was through validation—that is, a study which shows that scores are related to job performance. The Personnel Board had commissioned such a study in 1972, and it was completed four years later. Judge Pointer ruled, however, that it failed to validate the test as predictive of the ability of applicants to do the firefighter job, and held that use of 20-B was "no longer permissible."[92]

In his 1977 opinion, Judge Pointer also prescribed an affirmative action remedy for the illegal exclusion of blacks which had occurred due to use of the 20-B test. Immediately, ninety-one black applicants were to be added to the eligibility list.[93] Thereafter, when job vacancies opened, at least one of every three applicants added to the eligibility list had to be black until the number of blacks on the list reached 14 percent of the total. Following that, one of every seven applicants added to the list had to be black.[94]

Then, in 1979, a new trial was held in Judge Pointer's court in the case of *U.S. v. Jefferson County,* in which the Justice Department, joined by the NAACP and individual blacks, was suing the Personnel Board for the discriminatory effects of a broader array of selection policies, including eighteen written tests aside from the Firefighter Test 20-B; the imposition of height, weight, and educational requirements; restriction of firefighter job announcements; and promotional policies which required favorable evaluations from white superiors. In this case, as in the previous case, the selection practices were attacked for disparate impact, in violation of Title VII.

However, in 1981 Judge Pointer delayed his decision in *U.S. v. Jefferson County* while the parties in the case—the City of Birmingham, the NAACP and black litigants, and the U.S. government—negotiated a consent decree.[95] A consent decree is a voluntary agreement that settles a lawsuit and works like a contract when accepted by the court. In its final form, the consent decree permanently enjoined the City of Birmingham from any further racial discrimination and required the following.

---

[92]14 FEP 686.

[93]This number was derived in the following manner. White applicants passed the test at a rate of 82.6 percent. If black applicants had passed at the same rate, 235 would have been added to the eligibility list rather than the 69 who had been. White applicants passed at the rate of 82.6 percent, and 80 percent of that rate is 66.1 percent. A total of 285 blacks had taken the test. If they had passed at 80 percent of the white rate (i.e., 66.1 percent of 285), 150 would have passed. Subtracting the 69 who did pass from the 150 who would have passed had the test not been discriminatory yields a total of 91, the exact number Judge Pointer ordered to be added to the eligibility list.

[94]The Personnel Board appealed this decision, but the U.S. Court of Appeals upheld the finding that the tests were discriminatory and violated Title VII. It also asked the lower court to reconsider the case and take tougher remedial measures, on the grounds that the Personnel Board should have known it was discriminating unfairly long before the court had found it legally culpable. See *Ensley Branch of the N.A.A.C.P. v. Seibels,* 616 F.2d 812 (1980).

[95]This is oversimplified to keep the exposition simple. Actually, there were two consent decrees, one between the City of Birmingham, black plaintiffs, the NAACP, and the U.S. government, and another between the Personnel Board and the plaintiff parties.

1 The Personnel Board was to place black firefighter applicants on the eligibility list at a rate commensurate with the percentage of black applicants.

2 The Birmingham Fire Department would hire one black applicant for every white hired.

3 One black would be promoted to the rank of lieutenant for every white promoted. A black lieutenant would be promoted to one of the next two fire captain openings. Further promotions of blacks would be made at a percentage rate equal to the number of blacks at the level from which such promotions normally come.[96]

These rules were to be in effect until the fire department achieved a labor force that was 28 percent black, matching that of Jefferson County. In essence, until this goal was reached, the fire department would give 50 percent of its jobs and promotions to blacks. It was a deliberately race-conscious program designed to make up for sins of the past. And it was so typical of other consent decrees and court-ordered affirmative action plans in cities across the United States that one observer said it was simply "plain vanilla."

Upon learning of the consent decree, whites in the Birmingham Fire Department became apprehensive and outraged that less qualified blacks would be hired and promoted. Billy Gray, a white male lieutenant and president of the Birmingham Firefighters Association (BFA), the union that represented the white majority in the department, objected to Judge Pointer's decision. Although Gray and the BFA had no standing as parties in the case, Judge Pointer convened a fairness hearing to hear their objections.

At the hearing, the whites argued that preferential treatment for blacks would create an impermissible "reverse discrimination." Reverse discrimination was permitted in Title VII affirmative action plans, but only upon court order after a legal finding of past discrimination had been made. Since the case of *U.S. v. Jefferson County* was to be resolved by a consent agreement rather than a judicial opinion on the charges of discrimination by the Personnel Board, no such finding had been made. Therefore, reasoned the white firefighters, quotas for blacks were illegal. In addition, the plan would "benefit individuals who personally never were the victims of any discrimination by the city" and "disadvantage those who personally never were the beneficiaries of such discrimination."[97]

Judge Pointer rejected these arguments. He stated that the affirmative action plan was based on sufficient finding of discrimination during the trial. Specifically, he noted that Firefighter Test 20-B had been shown to be discriminatory. In 1981, the year the consent decree had been negotiated, only 42 of 453 firefighters (9.3 percent) and none of the 140 officers were black. These statistics, said Judge Pointer, provided "more than ample reason" to conclude that the city "would be in time held liable for discrimination."[98] The plan was also consistent with guidelines for affirmative action set forth by the

---

[96]The consent decrees also required affirmative action for women as well as blacks.
[97]*U.S. v. Jefferson County*, 28 FEP 1836.
[98]28 FEP 1838.

Supreme Court. Specifically, it did not completely "preclude the hiring or promotion of whites and males," and it was limited in time.[99] In addition, Judge Pointer stated that "intervention [by the firefighters] at this time as parties to the litigation is clearly untimely and must be denied."[100]

RESENTMENT IN THE FIRE DEPARTMENT

Robert Wilks had joined the fire department in 1968, one year after graduating from high school. In 1982, after fourteen years of service, he was bucking for promotion to lieutenant, just at the time the consent decree, with its 50 percent quota for blacks, was implemented. In that year there were eight lieutenant vacancies. Candidates take a qualifying test, and to their raw score is added one point for each year of service. The Personnel Board, acting to meet the quota in the consent decree, certified as eligible eight white firefighters ranking 1 through 8 in combined scores, then skipped over fifty-two other whites and certified five blacks, all of whom ranked 60th or lower.

Then, Wilks' worst fears were realized. Although he ranked eighth on the promotion list, he did not make lieutenant. After taking the top four whites, the city passed over fifty-six more to promote four blacks. The fire department got its first black officers.

In 1983, Wilks filed suit, asking the district court to halt use of the consent decree. In a five-day trial in 1985, his attorneys once again argued that promotion of less qualified black firefighters was impermissible reverse discrimination because Title VII permitted court-ordered affirmative action only when there was a specific finding of discrimination. But Judge Sam C. Pointer accepted a motion to dismiss Wilks' case without considering his claim. The judge noted that Wilks' claims had been aired at the earlier fairness hearing held before the consent decree became final. Wilks was now bound by the decree, said Judge Pointer; he and other white firefighters no longer had legal standing to challenge it.[101] "The City Decree is lawful," he stated, and "if the City of Birmingham made promotions of blacks to positions as fire lieutenant...because the city believed it was required to do so by the consent decree, and if in fact the City was required to do so by the consent decree, then they would not be guilty of racial discrimination...."[102] Wilks appealed Judge Pointer's refusal to hear his claim.

In the meantime, blacks continued their climb up the promotion ladder. In 1983, there were five vacancies, and Wilks ranked third. But because of the

[99]28 FEP 1837. These were main guidelines set forth for affirmative action plans by the Supreme Court majority in *United Steelworkers of America v. Brian Weber*, 433 U.S. 193.

[100]28 FEP 1839. Judge Pointer's decision was upheld by the U.S. Court of Appeals, Eleventh Circuit, after appeal by the City of Birmingham and the white firefighters in *U.S. v. Jefferson County*, 720 F.2d 1511 (1983). The appeals court refused to grant an injunction against the consent decree because there were no major errors and the whites had "made no showing of possible irreparable injury" (at 1520).

[101]United States District Court for the Northern District of Alabama, No. CV-84-P-0903-S. Motion to dismiss by Jefferson County Personnel Board granted.

[102]Quoted from Judge Pointer's December 1985 bench opinion by Justice Stevens in *Martin v. Wilks*, 57 LW 4623 and 4622.

consent decree, the city picked the top two whites, then bypassed seventy-six other whites to select blacks ranked 80th, 83rd, and 85th. And 1984 was no different. Wilks ranked 9th, but was passed over for blacks ranked as low as 86th.[103] Finally, in 1986, Wilks made lieutenant. By then, of course, blacks who had leapfrogged over him were being promoted to captain and battalion chief.

But the wheels of justice were still in motion.

WILKS WINS HIS APPEAL

The question of whether white males could challenge civil rights settlements after they went into effect had arisen frequently in lower courts. But since the 1960s, every federal appeals court had rejected these after-the-fact appeals. Then, in 1987, the U.S. Circuit Court of Appeals for the Eleventh Circuit, located in Atlanta, broke rank, ruling that Wilks had the right to be heard.[104]

Always before, courts had precluded white challenges under the doctrine of "impermissible collateral attack," which immunized employers following court-approved affirmative action plans from discrimination charges. But Wilks and other white firefighters had not been official parties to the consent decree, which had been negotiated between the City of Birmingham, the Personnel Board, black litigants, and U.S. attorneys supporting the blacks. In breaking with precedent and allowing whites to challenge an operating consent decree, the court said: "The policy of encouraging voluntary affirmative action plans must yield to the policy against requiring third parties to submit to bargains in which their interests were either ignored or sacrificed."[105] The appeals court ordered Judge Pointer's district court to hear Wilks' claims of reverse discrimination.

For blacks, women, and minorities, this was an ominous decision. If allowed to stand, not only could Wilks challenge Birmingham's consent decree, but all across the nation whites facing reverse discrimination might reopen, tinker with, and possibly destroy similar plans. If this occurred at a time when conservatives appointed by Ronald Reagan dominated the Supreme Court on civil rights cases, then gains for women and minorities since passage of the Civil Rights Act of 1964 would be threatened. Because of this danger, black firefighters, led by John W. Martin, appealed Wilks' victory to the Supreme Court. The case became that of *John W. Martin v. Robert K. Wilks*.[106]

THE SUPREME COURT DECIDES

Oral argument before the Supreme Court took place in Washington, D.C., on January 18, 1989. Attorneys for the black firefighters argued that Wilks had been given fair opportunity to contest the 50 percent quota for blacks in 1981,

[103]Siegel, *op. cit.*, p. A14.
[104]*In re Birmingham Reverse Discrimination Employment Litigation*, 833 F.2d 1492 (1987).
[105]833 F.2d 1498.
[106]No. 87-1614, together with *Personnel Board of Jefferson County v. Wilks* (No. 87-1639) and *Arrington v. Wilks* (No. 87-1668).

when the district court held a hearing on objections. At the time, the firefighters' union, which represented Wilks, had fought the decrees "tooth and nail" and had been overruled.[107] In addition, said Robert D. Joffe, a New York attorney representing the blacks, permitting a reopening of the consent decree would create "massive problems" nationwide as whites brought suit to destroy affirmative action plans.[108]

Birmingham attorney Raymond P. Fitzpatrick, representing Wilks, argued that the white firefighters deserved a chance to prove that the city's actions were outside "the bounds of permissible affirmative action."[109] The whites had been unfairly "denied their day in court," he said."[110]

After a wait of six months, the Supreme Court issued an opinion on June 12. It was divided 5-4, but Wilks and the white firefighters won.[111] They would have their day in court to prove illegal reverse discrimination. Chief Justice William Rehnquist wrote the majority opinion, representing the block of conservative Reagan-appointed justices which had begun to dominate civil rights cases only in 1989.

Rehnquist's short opinion focused on the narrow, technical area of "preclusion law," that is, legal theory about when court decisions are binding and challenge is precluded. He noted that even though the white firefighters had objected to the consent decree through their union, they had never been a formal party to it. He argued that, generally speaking, "one is not bound by a judgment...in which he is not designated as a party," and noted a "deep-rooted historic tradition that everyone should have his own day in court."[112] Finally, he ordered Judge Pointer's court to hold a trial to judge the discrimination claims of the white firefighters.

Justice John Paul Stevens wrote a lengthy dissenting opinion in which other members of the minority joined. He said it was "unconscionable" to subject the City of Birmingham to a new lawsuit simply for following a lawful settlement that sought to eradicate a long history of racial discrimination. He added that:

> The white respondents in this case are not responsible for that history of discrimination, but they are nevertheless beneficiaries of the discriminatory practices that the litigation was designed to correct. Any remedy that seeks to create employment conditions that would have obtained if there had been no violations of law will necessarily have an adverse impact on whites, who must now share their job and promotion opportunities with blacks. Just as white employees in the past were innocent beneficiaries of illegal discriminatory practices, so it is inevitable that some of the white employees will be innocent victims who must share some of the burdens resulting from the redress of the past wrongs.[113]

[107]57 LW 3517.
[108]57 LW 3516.
[109]57 LW 3517.
[110]*Ibid.*
[111]*Martin v. Wilks,* 57 LW 4616. Voting in the majority with Chief Justice Rehnquist were Associate Justices White, O'Connor, Scalia, and Kennedy. Voting in the minority were Stevens, Brennan, Marshall, and Blackmun.
[112]57 LW 4619.
[113]57 LW 4626.

REACTION TO THE DECISION

Lieutenant Robert Wilks was pleased. Interviewed on the NBC Evening News, he said, "I feel that I am paying the price for something I had nothing to do with."[114] William Bradford Reynolds, former assistant attorney general for civil rights in the Reagan administration, applauded the decision, calling it "a ringing affirmation of America's unyielding commitment to civil rights for all its citizens, whatever their race." "All who have a claim of discrimination," he wrote, "whether it moves in forward gear or reverse, shall have access to the courts."[115]

Blacks were dismayed. Benjamin L. Hooks, executive director of the NAACP, said: "Night has fallen on the Court as far as civil rights are concerned. We are seeing the unraveling of gains we thought were secure. This is a bad decision, another reminder of the Reagan legacy that will haunt this nation for years."[116] Rev. Joseph E. Lowery, president of the Southern Christian Leadership Conference in Atlanta, accused the Supreme Court of trying "to hide racism under a cloak of legalism."[117] Most newspaper editorials around the country were against the decision (see box).

Meanwhile, back in the Birmingham Fire Department, a sense of uncertainty prevailed. Over the years, the consent decree had wrought considerable change. Between 1982 and 1989, the number of black firefighters climbed from 42 to 160 out of 650. In 1982 there had been no black officers, but in 1989 there were 29 lieutenants, 9 captains and one battalion chief. Hence, blacks were 25 percent of the overall force and 6 percent of the officers. Would this trend continue?

White and black officers interviewed by newspaper reporters were philosophically divided. Charles Brush, the white president of the firefighters' union, told a *New York Times* reporter: "We would be the last people to say that there wasn't ever discrimination in Birmingham. But we aren't the people who did it. We have to have a system that stresses more than numbers and race."[118] Black lieutenant Carl Cook, in turn, responded to a *Los Angeles Times* reporter with this little allegory about the First Alabama Bank.

> Your daddy goes there, robs that bank. Then he buys a house on a hill with the stolen money. Buys mom a mink, you a Jaguar. The FBI arrives, wants to take Dad, his house, the mink, the Jaguar. You say, "No sir, not fair. I didn't rob the bank. I want to keep the car." Point is, all these things you have is a result of what happened before, something that wasn't right. When it's time to pay the piper, now it's unfair.[119]

---

[114]Quoted in Charles Mohn, "Minority Advocates Fear Gains Will Be Lost," *New York Times,* June 13, 1989, p. B5.

[115]"Stripping Away the Quota Barnacles," *Los Angeles Times,* June 28, 1989, Part II, p. 7.

[116]Quoted in Mohn, *op. cit.,* p. B5.

[117]*Ibid.,* p. B5.

[118]Quoted in Ronald Smothers, "Ruling on Firefighters Debated in Alabama," *New York Times,* June 14, 1989, p. A18.

[119]In Siegel, *op. cit.,* p. A15.

EDITORIAL OPINION ON *MARTIN V. WILKS*

Here is a sampling of newspaper editorials on the case from around the country. Most editorials were critical. All appeared on June 14 or 15, immediately after the ruling was released.

PRO

Martin v. Wilks...should go far toward settling one very important matter: Civil rights belong to all citizens, regardless of their race or sex, and they may not be violated with impunity, even with the approval of trial judges.

The Providence Journal

To assume that the court's decisions have gravely weakened U.S. civil rights would be a mistake. If Congress objects to the Supreme Court's interpretions, it can amend the law....Also, Congress may be forced to draft its legislation in less vague language, revealing its true intent in passing new laws and leaving less to the interpretive powers of the appointed justices.

Houston Chronicle

CON

[T]he Birmingham decision sends an unmistakable signal to minorities and women that the court is bent upon the total negation of affirmative action...[T]he Supreme Court majority has set back the clock on the evolution toward the kind of color-blind and gender-neutral society it mistakenly presumes already to exist.

Fort Worth Star-Telegram

In effect, cases involving consent decrees might never end....Underlying such logic is the disturbing notion that classes of people who have long suffered from discrimination deserve no special consideration to help catch up.

St. Louis Post-Dispatch

In its latest ruling against affirmative action, the Supreme Court virtually ignores evidence that bias hasn't been eliminated in the Birmingham, Ala. Fire Department, the better to indulge gripes of so-called "reverse discrimination"—that remedies for the effects of segregation discriminate unfairly against whites and men.

The Atlanta Journal

Justices Antonin Scalia, Byron White, Anthony Kennedy, Sandra Day O'Connor and William Rehnquist have determined that affirmative action programs are inherently bad and legal rulings that support them should be weakened or eliminated.

Syracuse Herald-Journal

The ruling may...prompt government employers to scale back affirmative action programs that might—someday—adversely affect some whites.

The Courier Journal

Employers will be less likely now to implement training programs or hire and promote minorities and women for fear of litigation by white workers.

The Kansas City Star

The decision has already resulted in challenges to consent decrees in cities and counties across the country. It is too early to tell whether these will be successful in ending court-enforced quotas in affirmative action programs.

QUESTIONS

1 Do you agree with the decision of the Supreme Court to permit Robert Wilks and the other firefighters to bring their reverse discrimination complaints to trial?

2 Does this decision weaken civil rights protection in employment for blacks, as critics have charged?

3 Do you think that the consent decree requiring that 50 percent of new firefighters and officer promotions be reserved for blacks is fair to both races? If unfairness exists, what would be a better solution?

4 In a new trial, should Robert Wilks and the other white firefighters prevail in their reverse discrimination complaint? What reasons can you give for your conclusion?

5 Based on your reading of this case and the discussion of affirmative action law in the preceding chapter, do you believe that the Supreme Court is ready to interpret Title VII in a new, literal way and end *all* racial discrimination, even that which favors blacks to redress a history of racist exclusion by employers?

The Sales Career of Cotton Springfield

Frank Converse, personnel director for the Chicago Metals Company, saw his job as an adventure. And today there was already enough excitement to justify that outlook.

In the morning mail Converse received a letter from Cotton Springfield, the company's only female sales representative. It read:

Dear Mr. Converse:

This is written as a last resort. During the six months I have been working the southeastern sales territory, I have been cruelly victimized by arrogant, chauvinistic men. These men have shown me depths of male crudity and rudeness that previously I could only have imagined to exist. This sexual harassment must stop!

I have been subjected to unwanted, crude behavior by customers. When we go to dinner they tell boorish, sexually explicit jokes. They call me "honey" and "girl." More than once I have been pinched or patted on the behind. A customer in Memphis sent me a lewd, sexually suggestive Valentine card. One night in Little Rock a buyer followed me to my motel room. He was married, too! In Birmingham a customer inquired about my sexual proclivities. These and similar actions have created a hostile, interfering, and offensive working environment.

When I am in Chicago, Vice President of Sales John Turner harasses me. In his office, he jokes about having "heart-to-breast" talks with me, he has inquired about my sexual proclivities; and sometimes he compares our work relationship to the state of wedlock. When we walk together, he touches my arm to guide me, thereby asserting his male superiority. It is the responsibility of the Company to end explicitly harassing behavior toward employees, especially harassment based on gender distinctions.

In the interest of keeping my job and keeping up sales, I have not yet revealed my anger to my male tormenters. But I cannot hold it in much longer. Many nights I have returned to my room to cry. I have a diary in which I have recorded these painful experiences and my feelings. Please help me, or it will be necessary to take more drastic action.

Sincerely yours,

Cotton Springfield

This was not a pleasant letter, but for Converse, worse was yet to come. Shortly before lunch he received a phone call from Helen Gibson, Anthony Gibson's wife. It wasn't the first call from Mrs. Gibson that Converse had received, and he hated to take them. It was always the same complaint.

"I'm certain my husband is having an affair with that Cotton Springfield," said Helen Gibson.

"We've been all through this," replied Converse. "I'm convinced you're wrong. Ms. Springfield is a fine young woman."

"You don't know what I know instinctively."

"No, and what's that?"

"You don't have to live with it. I do. Would you want your wife in a situation of constant temptation?"

"Helen, I don't have much choice. Springfield is an excellent saleswoman. All of us—even Anthony—support her. Certainly you know we can't remove her from her job based on groundless fears."

"Groundless fears! Anthony says Cotton keeps telling him she is lonely. She tells him about her boyfriends and what they do in bed. You and your [expletive deleted] affirmative action. It's going to wreck my marriage. Who has washed and ironed Anthony's clothes for the twenty-two years he's been with Chicago Metals? Me! Who ran the house and raised the kids while he was away at work helping to pay your salary? Me! Who went out at night with customers and their wives for years so Chicago could get a sale? Me! I've contributed, so now what rights do I have in this company, Frank?"

Later, as he wiped up the coffee he had spilled on his desk during Helen Gibson's call, Converse reflected on the situation.

Chicago Metals had a modest sized, elite corps of sales representatives who travel throughout the country demonstrating Chicago's capability to serve clients through the application of unique metals technologies. The job of the sales force is to show a prospective client that one or more of the company's processes can fulfill a need. Each sales representative, although based in Chicago, is teamed with a partner and assigned one of seven sections of the United States. It is necessary to have two representatives working together because the work is too difficult for only one person to perform. It is common for a sales team to be on the road for two to three weeks at a time.

Of the fourteen sales representatives, not one had been a woman until eight months ago, when Converse had agreed with the recommendation of the vice president of sales, John Turner, to promote Cotton Springfield, a Vassar-educated, promising, twenty-five-year-old company legal librarian. Cotton was single and attractive, and her buoyant personality made a successful career in sales a likely prospect. She was eager for the opportunity. In an abstract sense, Converse was pleased with this decision, because it not only contributed to Springfield's career development, but fulfilled government guidelines that specified that women and minorities should be hired in certain job categories, including sales. Thus, Springfield was placed in the sales job instead of one of several male candidates, all of whom had had a few years of sales experience.

After a six-week sales training program, Ms. Springfield was assigned to the only existing opening. She was teamed with Anthony Gibson, a forty-two-year-old veteran in the Chicago Metals sales force who worked the southeastern sector, which included Missouri, Arkansas, Mississippi, Kentucky, Tennessee, Alabama, Georgia, and the Carolinas.

On the day the assignment was announced, Gibson came to Converse's office with an ardent plea for reconsideration based on his feeling that Cotton Springfield was not qualified and would cause problems. First, he said, she had no technical background or experience in the metals business and "doesn't know carbon steel from the kitchen sink." If she didn't know the product, she couldn't do the job, and neither her education at an elite college nor her subsequent experience in the company law library gave her any background in metallurgy or engineering.

In addition, Gibson argued, his successful sales routine involved entertaining prospective buyers, who were all male, after business hours, and the normal evening ritual included lots of off-color jokes, obscene language, and other male pastimes, such as taking in a pornographic movie. Said Gibson: "How a proper and refined little filly like Cotton can handle that, I just don't know." He also pointed to a related potential difficulty. The southeastern sector encompassed a population with conservative lifestyles and values. What would many of his customers conclude when the representative of Chicago Metals arrived with a sexy young traveling companion in tow? His and the company's image might be tarnished in the eyes of prospective customers. The inevitable kidding about their sharing a motel room might have a serious edge that would prove costly to the company. Male horseplay was okay, but to some of the "old boys" in southern companies, this might be going too far.

Gibson then became even more serious and reported an angry confrontation with his wife, who had railed bitterly against the prospect of her husband traveling across the country with a young and attractive woman for an extended period. She had threatened to leave him rather than face the ridicule of acquaintances who would assume that the two salespersons had more than aluminum in common. Gibson felt it unfair that he should be subjected to this pressure in addition to the normal pressures of a demanding occupation.

"Naturally I have nothing personal against Cotton," said Gibson as he rose to leave, "but I think you ought to reexamine your decision. She is being promoted because of her sex and not her competence, and we both know it. Why don't you save me from problems with my wife and customers, and save yourself and Cotton the heartache of her getting in way over her head?" Although completely in earnest, he dispelled the gravity of the situation by winking and adding that of course he "wouldn't mind her company on lonely nights on the road," if things couldn't be changed.

At the time, Converse had sympathized with the salesman, but he was not sure what action, if any, he should take. Every year Chicago Metals had to fill out an EEO-1 form, and among other disclosures, Converse was required to present employment data by job category, including "sales." The *Affirmative Action and Equal Employment* guidebook on Converse's desk seemed to preclude sexual discrimination in the sales force. It stated in part that:

> For all practical purposes, almost all jobs must be open legally to men and women. The "bona-fide occupational qualification" (BFOQ) exception of Title VII is narrowly construed by EEOC and the courts. The burden of proof is on the employer to establish that the sexual characteristics of the employee are *crucial* to successful performance (such as model, actor, or actress). Only when the essence of the business enterprise would be undermined by not hiring a member of one sex exclusively is a BFOQ justified.

Converse had no doubt that women could be as effective sales representatives as men. Cotton Springfield had been given an extensive training program to inform her about Chicago's products, sales techniques, and the new territory. During the program, Springfield attended a four-hour presentation by a psychologist in the personnel department on "Emotional Problems of Women in Traditionally Male Work Roles."

About the time of Springfield's promotion, the company was attacked for sexual discrimination by the National Organization of Women. The company came to NOW's attention when an article in *Ms.* magazine criticized an incident in which the company decided against hiring a woman as a lathe operator because she was pregnant and would need to take a leave of absence for childbirth near the production deadline on a big order. Currently, Chicago faced two EEOC suits involving alleged discrimination against women. This was not unusual for a company of Chicago's size, but the suits ate up staff time and could result in nasty fines.

The legal implications of Springfield's letter worried Gibson. He remembered that she had been Chicago's legal librarian. The phrasing in part of the letter indicated that she was familiar with criteria that courts had used recently in sexual harassment cases. Had she consulted a lawyer?

Converse did not want to let Gibson or any of the other salesmen go. They were too good, and the jobs were so lucrative that voluntary resignations were rare. It would be unfair to force a man out, and the next retirement was eight years away. Therefore, he could not hire another woman to travel with Springfield. He hesitated to transfer a salesman to the southeastern sector and put Gibson in another area of the country because Gibson had spent years developing and polishing contacts, as had the salesmen in other sectors. In addition he was not sure that other salesmen would be more accommodating to the idea of working with a young woman.

Yes, he thought, my job is an adventure.

QUESTIONS

1 Was Springfield's promotion to sales representative a correct decision? Was it handled properly by the company?

2 Evaluate Springfield's letter in terms of the EEOC's sexual harassment guidelines discussed in this chapter and in terms of landmark sexual harassment litigation, such as *Bundy v. Jackson, EEOC v. Sage Realty Corp., Ferguson v. Du Pont,* or *Meritor Savings Bank v. Vinson.*[120] If she takes legal action, is it likely that the company will be held liable for exposing Springfield to a harassing work environment? Is her harassment by Vice President Turner actionable?

3 What action should Converse take now?

4 Do some research on women in business. Is Cotton Springfield's experience typical of the barriers and problems of women entering sales or other areas of business today? What should Springfield do?

---

[120]*Bundy v. Jackson,* 641 F.2d 973, 24 FEP 1155 (1981); *Equal Employment Opportunity Commission v. Sage Realty Corp.,* 25 Emp. Prac Dec. 529 (1981); *Ferguson v. Du Pont,* 3 FEP 795 (1983); and *Meritor Savings Bank v. Vinson,* 54 LW 4703 (1986).

Corporate Governance

19

Reforming Corporate Governance

TRANS UNION

Until recently, courts would not hold directors liable for their decisions if they had exercised prudent business judgment. If a director acted in good faith and was not guilty of self-serving behavior, fraud, or gross negligence, he or she was not held liable for honest errors or mistakes in judgment. In 1985, this immunization from stockholder suits was shattered by Delaware's Supreme Court in the milestone decision of *Smith v. Van Gorham*.[1]

In this case, W. Van Gorham, chairman of Trans Union Corp., a Chicago-based company leasing tank cars, told his board of directors for the first time about a deal he had quietly negotiated. The deal was to sell the company to the Marmon Group, Inc., which was controlled by the Pritzker family, for $690 million. This amounted to $55 a share, which at that time was approximately $20 over the market price and about twice book value. Two hours after he told the board, the board approved. Stockholders sued in Delaware, where Trans Union had gotten its charter. They said the board acted too quickly on too little information and should have received more for the stock.

The Delaware Supreme Court decided the case in January 1985 and agreed with the stockholders. The directors, said the court, had breached their duty to shareholders when they agreed to sell the company too hastily and without seeking enough information and advice to reach a responsible decision. The court held the directors personally liable for paying the stockholders the difference between the price paid for the company and what the company was really worth. The case was finally settled in 1986 for more than $23 million, most of which was paid from insurance and by the Pritzker family. But individual directors paid substantial sums.

[1]488 A.2d 858 (Del. 1985).

This case sent shock waves through corporate America. For the first time, the court held directors personally liable for actions which seemed to directors to be well within the range of good business judgement. All the directors of Trans Union were experienced businessmen who also had important stock holdings in the company. For the first time, the court said directors would be personally liable if they did not take enough time to evaluate properly, in the judgment of the court, the proposals placed before them.

This case illustrates some of the difficult problems facing managers in governing a company. But there are many others which will be addressed in this chapter. The chapter begins with a definition of governance and contrasts it with management. We then discuss the core issues in corporate governance, including a brief analysis of its current legal framework and how the process operates in fact. Then, major proposals for reform are examined in two areas: federal chartering, and reforming the structure and functioning of the board of directors. The chapter concludes with a brief discussion of the threats to governance of takeovers. The Unocal case at the end of the chapter is an integral part of this chapter, in that it deals with governance in a takeover situation and also includes a discussion of the impact of takeovers on managers, shareholders and employees.

GOVERNANCE DEFINED

Corporate governance ensures that long-term strategic objectives and plans are established and that the proper management structure (organization, systems, and people) is in place to achieve those objectives, while at the same time making sure that the structure functions to maintain the corporation's integrity, reputation, and responsibility to its various constituencies.[2]

Another useful definition is that of Robert K. Mueller, Chairman of the Board, Arthur D. Little:

> Governance is concerned with the intrinsic nature, purpose, integrity, and identity of the institution, with a primary focus on the entity's relevance, continuity, and fiduciary aspects. Governance involves monitoring and overseeing strategic direction, socioeconomic and cultural context, resources, externalities, and constituencies of the institution.[3]

In these definitions, governance is the concern of the board of directors of a company. However, top management is also clearly involved. But management has other dimensions that are quite distinct from the operations of the typical board of directors. Management is a hands-on operational activity. It is concerned with supervising day-to-day action and with the prudent use of scarce resources to achieve desirable aims. The typical board of directors of a corporation does not become involved in such activities. While governance is

---

[2]National Association of Corporate Directors, *Evolution in the Boardroom*, NACD Corporate Director's Special Report Series, August 1978.

[3]Robert K. Mueller, "Changes in the Wind in Corporate Governance," *Journal of Business Strategy*, Spring 1981, p. 9.

shared by boards of directors and top management, our focus in this chapter is essentially but not exclusively on boards.

CORE ISSUES IN REFORMING CORPORATE GOVERNANCE

The fundamental source of demands for reforming corporate governance is dissatisfaction with the power relationships among the boards of directors, managers, stockholders, state governments as chartering authorities, and constituents of corporations.

If the responsibility of corporate managers is not clarified to the satisfaction of the public, it is likely that there will be government regulation of corporate governance. As Courtney Brown, a former business school dean and member of a number of corporate boards, said, the prudent corporation will prepare itself now to convince the public that its internal structures and procedures are designed to assure consideration of a wide spectrum of "publics" in its decision making.[4] These other "publics" include the long list of stakeholders that were identified in Chapter 1 (Figure 1–6).

The critics of corporate governance assert that these interests are not being met adequately. Furthermore, they argue, the way in which corporations are governed today permits abuses that call for government control. For example, they assert that the large corporations have harmful market and nonmarket impacts, the government of large companies more resembles an autocracy than democracy, boards do not do the job they are supposed to do in running companies, there is much too much secrecy in decision making, the system permits payoffs and crimes, companies violate the rights of employees, officers are not accountable for their individual actions, and corporations have too much power. Most observers—even friendly ones—worry that corporate boards are dominated too much by management. Not everyone would accept all these criticisms, but they are the basis, among other legitimate criticisms, for reforming the governance structure and processes of our corporations.

Demands for reforming corporate governance are not new. Nor are demands solely those of radicals. Prominent businesspeople, for example, have condemned some practices. Consider the following.

Harold S. Geneen, longtime chairman of the board and CEO of ITT, said recently: "Among the boards of directors of *Fortune* 500 companies, I estimate that 95 percent are not fully doing what they are legally, morally, and ethically supposed to do. And they couldn't even if they wanted to." He said that the major responsibility of the board is "to sit in judgment on the management, especially on the performance of the chief executive, and to reward, punish, or replace the management as the board sees fit."[5] The tendency of CEOs to dominate directors was referred to colorfully as the

---

[4]Courtney C. Brown, *Putting the Corporate Board to Work*, New York: Macmillan, 1976, p. 9.
[5]Harold S. Geneen, "Why Directors Can't Protect the Shareholders," *Fortune*, September 17, 1984.

"mushroom concept" by John T. Connor, when he was chairman of Allied Chemical. "Put him in a dark place," said Connor of a director, "feed him plenty of horse manure, and when his head rises up through the pile to get attention or ask a question, cut it off quickly and decisively."[6]

Changes in the structure and operation of boards of directors during the last decade have been in response to such criticism and have muted them somewhat. But criticisms persist, and many of them are justified.

THE CORPORATE CHARTER

Today, all American corporations except a few quasi-public enterprises chartered by the federal government (for example, the Tennessee Valley Authority) are given charters of authority by the state in which they are incorporated. At the Constitutional Convention of 1787, the Founding Fathers debated a federal chartering power but decided that existing state controls were adequate to regulate corporate activity.

In the early history of the United States, state assemblies and legislative bodies issued special charters to corporations one at a time on an ad hoc basis. Corporations were supposed to do something of general value, such as build a turnpike or operate a grain mill. For this value to society, the people contributing capital were given power to purchase and hold property collectively, to sue and be sued collectively, and to enjoy limited liability, and corporations were often, but not always, given the right of perpetual life. The corporations were not generally liked in the American colonies, and every effort was made to restrain them.

Between 1790 and 1800, the states granted about 300 charters. One-half were for transportation companies, and most of the remainder were for finance enterprises. In 1790, exactly three charters were given to manufacturing companies, and the total for this category rose to nine in 1800.[7]

The demands for the corporate form, however, were strong, and the states were disposed to grant more and more charters. This led to general incorporation laws. If corporations met the law, they could get charters routinely rather than go through the legislative process. In 1799, Massachusetts passed a general incorporation law for companies engaged in building aqueducts. In 1811, New York passed the first general incorporation law for manufacturing companies, and in 1837, Connecticut passed the first general incorporation law for any lawful purpose.

Over the years, the states have become progressively more permissive in corporation law to attract the tax revenues of large companies. Delaware has been the long-time victor in this competition and has chartered almost half of the largest industrial corporations in this country. Corporate charters estab-

---

[6]John T. Connor, "An Alternative to the Goldberg Prescription," Remarks before the American Society of Corporate Secretaries, March 14, 1973.

[7]John P. Davis, *Corporations,* Reprint, New York: Capricorn, 1961. Originally published c. 1897. See also E. A. J. Johnson and Herman E. Kroos, *The Origins and Development of the American Economy,* New York: Prentice-Hall, 1953.

lish the powers of the corporation to engage in business. The Delaware law today is so broad that it virtually permits a corporation to engage in any business that is legal.

Corporate charters also specify the rights and responsibilities of stockholders, directors, and officers. Fundamentally, corporate charters lodge control over the property of the enterprise in stockholders who own shares in the assets of the company and vote those shares in naming a board of directors to run the firm. The directors have a fiduciary responsibility to protect the interests of the shareholders. They are responsible for appointing officers to run the day-to-day affairs of the company. The legal line of power runs from the state, to shareholders, to directors, to managers.

The charters also include detailed provisions about such matters as annual meetings, methods of choosing directors, and authority of directors to issue stock. For instance, charters are specific about calling meetings of shareholders, declaration of dividends, election and removal of officers, proposing amendments of the articles of incorporation, and so on. Such charter provisions are meant to protect the interests of shareholders. A vast body of law that seeks to do the same thing has also been created over time.

THE STRUCTURE AND DUTIES OF BOARDS OF DIRECTORS

STRUCTURE

The average corporate board had thirteen members in 1988.[8] But the actual number of members ranges from three to thirty or more. Boards of many not-for-profit organizations are generally much larger than those of profit enterprises. Giovanni Agnelli, founder of Italy's huge Turin-based Fiat conglomerate, once observed: "Only an odd number of directors can run a company, and three is too many."[9] That is an extreme position, but some large firms do have small boards. Banks and other financial institutions tend to have larger boards than industrials.

Board membership may include both inside (management) directors and outside (nonmanagement) directors. In recent years, the number of outside directors on boards has grown because of pressures to put members on the board who are independent of the CEO. Eighty percent of the 500 large companies surveyed in a Korn/Ferry research study stated a preference for a majority of outside directors. The average company had three inside and ten outside directors.

Korn/Ferry reports that the number of boards with women members rose from 11 percent in 1973 to 58 percent in 1988. During the same period, boards with ethnic-minority representation grew from 9 percent to 33 percent. The percentage of former government officials and academicians now on boards is higher than it was a decade ago. In 84 percent of the companies in the study, the chairman of the board is also the CEO.

[8]Korn/Ferry International, *Board of Directors: Sixteenth Annual Study, 1989*, Korn/Ferry International, 1989.

[9]Paul Betts, "Heads Begin to Roll at Fiat," *Paris Financial Times*, June 18, 1980.

Typically, board members are suggested by the CEO to the board for its approval. This was so in 81 percent of the companies in the Korn/Ferry study. The nominees are then presented to the shareholders in the annual call to the stockholder meeting, and management solicits the proxies of the stockholders. A proxy is a permission given by each stockholder to the management to vote the stock as the management sees fit. Most stockholders give their proxies to management, which in turn votes the stock at the annual meeting.

In this model, which differs from the classical legal line of appointment noted earlier, managers choose directors. It is easy to see how it is possible in such a situation for corporations to develop what Adolph Berle called "self-perpetuating oligarchies,"[10] Nevertheless, the legal authority for selecting managers rests with the board, and many boards have exercised that power by ousting management that has not performed as it should. In smaller corporations, the stockholders typically still choose directors, who in turn choose managers.

Boards are divided into committees, a practice that has grown over the past decade. Today, 98 percent of companies have audit committees, the functions of which will be noted later. More than 89 percent of the boards have compensation committees that make recommendations to the board concerning pay and bonuses of top executives of the company. More than 77 percent have executive committees that are authorized by the board to decide on behalf of the board about matters needing attention between board meetings. There has been a surprising increase in nominating committees, from 2.4 percent in 1973 to 60 percent today. These committees make recommendations to the board and the CEO about new members. Generally, the CEO's wishes dominate the selection offered to the stockholders. Other committees are: finance; public affairs; corporate ethics; benefits; corporate strategy; legal affairs; conflict-of-interest; science, technology and research; and personnel or human resources. Not all companies have all these committees.

DIRECTOR DUTIES

Corporate charters require that corporate affairs be "managed" by a board or "under the direction of a board." The board of directors clearly is the ultimate corporate authority except for matters that must have the approval of shareholders, such as the election of the board itself or an increase in capitalization.

The Business Roundtable, in a pamphlet entitled *The Role and Composition of the Board of Directors of the Large Publicly Owned Corporation*, says the four outstanding responsibilities of boards and directors are as follows.[11]

1 To select the CEO and his or her principal management associates. A corollary function, of course, is to replace managers who do not perform to the expectation of the board.

[10]Adolf A. Berle, Jr., "Second Edition/Corporate Power," *The Center Magazine*, January 1969.
[11]Business Roundtable, *The Role and Composition of the Board of Directors of the Large Publicly Owned Corporation*, New York: The Business Roundtable, January 1978.

2 The board is accountable for the financial performance of the enterprise. It is not in a position, of course, to conduct day-to-day operations of the company, but it is responsible for continuously checking on corporate financial results and prospects. The board should consider and act upon any major commitment of corporate resources. It should consider corporate strategic plans and major strategies.

3 "It is the board's duty to consider the overall impact of the activities of the corporation on 1. the society of which it is a part, and 2. the interests and views of groups other than those immediately identified with the corporation. This obligation arises out of the responsibility to act primarily in the interests of the share owners—particularly their long-range interest."[12]

4 The board should see that policies and procedures are designed in the corporation to promote compliance with laws on a sustained and systematic basis at all levels of operating management.

Cutting across these functions are requirements to make sure there is an appropriate flow of information to the board and that internal policies and procedures of the company are fully capable of responding to board decisions. Peter Drucker has added several dimensions to these functions if a board is to be effective. They are: asking crucial questions; acting as a conscience, a keeper of human and moral values; giving advice and counsel to top management; serving as a window on the outside world; helping the corporation to be understood by its constituencies and by the outside community; and assuring management competence.[13]

These responsibilities are generally accepted by directors and managers. How boards discharge them, however, varies greatly from board to board.

VARIATIONS IN BOARD FUNCTIONING

At one extreme are boards that meet only to fulfill their statutory requirements. At the other extreme are active boards that are involved in setting corporate objectives, strategies, and policies, and in overseeing the performance of the company and its managers. Critics charge that there are far too many boards that operate in a perfunctory manner and that not enough actively fulfill all their responsibilities as set forth above.

However, there is little question that more and more boards are more and more active in discharging the full range of their responsibilities. There is great pressure to do so. They are being driven in this direction because of mounting legal liabilities, threats of government regulation, social pressures, takeover threats, the need for corporate reconstructuring, stockholder pressures, growing competition in the global marketplace, and various other forces.

William May, the retired chairman of American Can Co., and a board member of about a dozen boards over the years, underscores the major

---

[12]*Ibid.*, pp. 11–12.
[13]Peter F. Drucker, "The Bored Board," *Wharton Magazine*, Fall 1976.

changes taking place in the functioning of boards. He recalls earlier boards as pleasant gatherings of congenial peers. "We'd combine meetings with lunch and a glass of sherry, or maybe something stronger," he said. "The chairman would describe what had happened, give some numbers and a projection, and we'd all go home." Those days are gone. At American Can, May had to contend with corporate raider Carl Icahn, who had acquired 4.9 percent of the company's stock in 1982. As a director of Manville Corporation, he helped take the company into bankruptcy proceedings, and he had to defend himself against stockholder suits. "It took a lot of hours out of my life that I could have spent much more profitably and enjoyably....I'd think four or five times before going on another board."[14]

Of special interest to readers of this book is a marked departure by outside directors from the traditional one-dimensional focus on shareholder representation. The Korn/Ferry study revealed that "90 percent of the outside directors...surveyed see themselves as having a responsibility to represent the interests of other corporate constituencies. Foremost among these are employees (cited by 85 percent), communities (cited by 78 percent), and customers (cited by 69 percent)."[15] This is in contrast, says Korn/Ferry, to CEOs who still see the board as representing shareholders exclusively.

LEGAL LIABILITIES OF BOARDS OF DIRECTORS

Following the Trans Union case discussed at the beginning of this chapter, pressures were placed on state legislatures to limit the liability of corporate directors. Delaware responded with a law that went into effect on July 1, 1986. This law allows corporations chartered in Delaware to insert in their charters a provision to relieve directors of all liability to company or shareholders for mere negligence. Liability does attach, however, to any breach of the director's loyalty to the corporation or its stockholders; acts of omissions of good faith; and any transactions in which directors derive improper personal benefit. Most states have adopted or have pending such legislation.

Legal opinion is that such laws will not appreciably reduce stockholder suits. Plaintiffs usually sue on the grounds not of negligence but of bad faith, self-dealing, or disloyalty. They use negligence, which has various legal meanings, only as a last resort.[16]

PROPOSALS FOR REFORMING THE BOARD OF DIRECTORS

The list of proposed reforms of boards of directors is long and includes suggestions from friends of the institution as well as its harsh critics. Here are a few of the more frequent and significant proposals.

[14]Amanda Bennett, "Board Members Draw Fire, and Some Think Twice About Serving," *The Wall Street Journal*, February 5, 1986.

[15]Korn/Ferry International, *op. cit.*, p. 2.

[16]Leo Herzel, Richard W. Shepro, and Leo Katz, "Next-to-Last Word on Endangered Directors," *Harvard Business Review*, January–February 1987.

FEDERAL CHARTERING

Some argue that the time is ripe for federal chartering of larger corporations. Some argue that state incorporation laws are too permissive and that state governments are unable or unwilling to exercise needed controls over corporations. As the law now stands, giant corporations such as Ford, Chrysler, Texaco, IT&T, Du Pont, and Boeing, which do business in all fifty states and worldwide, may be chartered in Delaware and be subject to that state's corporation law. It is preposterous, argue corporate critics, to go on letting little New Jersey charter Exxon, the world's largest industrial corporation.

Other critics advocate federal incorporation to make sure that corporations uniformly address themselves to meeting more fully the new demands that society is placing on the corporation.

Advantages of Federal Chartering   The foremost critic advancing the idea of federal chartering is Ralph Nader. He and others believe that federal chartering of corporations would provide society with an important constraint on managerial power, making corporations more accountable to society than they now are. Nader points out that there is plenty of evidence of corporate abuses, as reported in detail in the *Wall Street Journal* over the years. For example, "looting of shareholders, worker health and safety hazards, seriously mistreating consumers, contaminating community water and air, demanding preferential subsidies which unfairly burden smaller taxpayers, lobbying for direct preferential tax treatment, and pouring money into Congressional campaigns to gain influence not based on the merits."[17] Nader is not alone. Professor Bruce R. Scott suggested federal chartering to have companies "guarantee employment security for all employees with at least ten years' service, subject to safeguards in case of gross negligence or misbehavior."[18]

Disadvantages of Federal Chartering   But serious doubts and drawbacks exist. First, federal chartering may confuse the political goals of critics with the economic goals of enterprise and hamper the achievement of both by placing new regulatory costs on business and tinkering further with a market no longer "free" because of existing regulation.[19]

Second, federal chartering would require the creation of a new, powerful regulatory authority in government exceeding traditional boundaries of government authority. Would such regulation be heavy-handed, as is much government action today? Would business subvert the new agency to corrupt or counterproductive ends? What would be the performance criteria for the diverse business operations to be regulated? Would massive new regulations

[17]Ralph Nader, "Reforming Corporate Governance," *California Management Review*, Summer 1984, pp. 126–127. See also his *Taming the Giant Corporation*, written with Mark Green and Joel Seligman, New York: Norton, 1976.

[18]Bruce R. Scott, "Can Industry Survive the Welfare State?" *Harvard Business Review*, September–October 1982.

[19]Peter H. Aranson, "Federal Chartering of Corporations: An Idea Well Worth Forgetting," *Business and Society Review/Innovation*, Winter 1973.

and tough implementation result in so much uncertainty and restraint on corporations that they could not function efficiently? These questions need to be answered before a federal chartering law is passed.

Finally, defenders of business note that corporate power is accountable and restrained. Millstein and Katsh, in their book *The Limits of Corporate Power*,[20] explain how the large corporation is hemmed in by economic constraints, a formidable array of legal and regulatory requirements, an "adversary-minded press," and general public opinion. The Business Roundtable earlier concluded that "contrary to some misconceptions, sanctions for management misconduct are in fact imposed and constitute an impressive system of deterrence,"[21]

Concluding Comment There is no doubt that federal incorporation would improve control over corporations in such matters as pollution, discrimination, anticompetitive practices, unethical conduct, and so on. However, there are plenty of other remedies to deal with such matters in the absence of federal chartering. Why launch a new, federal program with all of its dangers when abundant current remedies exist for controlling corporations? Critics argue, of course, that such controls are not sufficient. Their opponents say that they are and that if more are needed, the federal government can be depended upon to impose them.

STRENGTHENING STOCKHOLDER DEMOCRACY

The role of the stockholder in theory is strong, but in practice power has shifted away from the stockholder. Critics of managerial autonomy assert that greater stockholder democracy, or stockholder control, is needed for legitimate governance. It is necessary, they say, to meet the long-range interests of shareholders, to conform with legal doctrine, and to assure public understanding and acceptance of the governance system. In pursuit of such objectives, reformers call for more information for stockholders on the grounds that they may participate more wisely in the affairs of the enterprise. Opponents argue that stockholders now get a great deal of information, provided at great cost, especially to smaller firms. The typical stockholder of a larger corporation is not interested in getting more information, they believe.

Reformers want shareholders to vote on specific issues, such as social responsibilities, that are not subject to shareholder ballot. Opponents concede that there is merit in having stockholders vote on major issues affecting their interests but that shareholders now vote on such vital questions as the choice of directors and important resolutions brought to the annual stockholder meetings. For a large company, the reality is that intrusion of stockholders in the decision-making process would be completely inconsistent with the types

---

[20]Ira M. Millstein and Salem M. Katsh, *The Limits of Corporate Power*, New York: Macmillan, 1981.

[21]Business Roundtable, *The Role of Corporate Directors, op. cit.*, p. 3.

of demands on managers to operate corporations and would probably work to the detriment of stockholder interests.

INSTITUTIONAL INVESTOR PARTICIPATION IN GOVERNANCE

The above issue takes on a new dimension when one considers the growing power of institutional investors in the market, particularly pension funds. Today, pension-fund assets total $2.6 trillion, up from $444 billion in 1975. These funds today own well over 60 percent of the stock of our largest corporations.

Pension fund managers got together in 1986 and formed the Council of Institutional Investors (CII). It endorsed a "Shareholders' Bill of Rights" that demanded a voice in all "fundamental decisions which could affect corporate performance and growth." The CII acted because many members had been hurt financially in corporate takeover wars and wanted to protect themselves. The bill of rights calls for stockholder approval of board decisions concerning takeovers.[22]

Many people feared when the CII was formed that the pension fund managers would get together and vote as a bloc. That has not happened, nor have these managers organized to exert any across-the-board pressures on directors. Rather, they have influenced directors by their mere existence, and they have from time to time gotten together to persuade directors to take actions to protect their interest. For example, a small group got together to persuade Texaco to put on the board one director from a list of nominees suggested by the managers. Texaco did so. Also, these managers helped persuade Texaco to settle a lawsuit with Pennzoil Corp.

In 1989, the CII launched Directors Project to become more active in expressing its concerns to directors. It wrote to five companies—Sears, Emerson Electric, SmithKline Beckman, American Greetings, and Scott Paper—asking for a meeting with management. Along with the self-invitation went a three-page letter with a list of questions that might lead to reforms in both the composition and practices of boards.

Sarah Teslik, CII's executive director, said that the initiative did not reflect a desire on the part of the fund managers to second-guess managers, but that as shareholders they felt a responsibility to ask whether the boards were operating properly. "Our goal is to ask if there's anything we can do to make (the system) work better," she said.[23] This, of course, is subtle, but has leverage behind it.

Institutional investors undoubtedly will become more active in influencing corporate managers. This trend, of course, reflects their interests in protecting their huge holdings of corporate securities. It also reflects pressures of outside groups for them to become more active. For example, New York

---

[22]Quoted in Judith H. Dobrzynski, Michael Schroeder, George L. Miles, and Joseph Weber, "Taking Charge: Corporate Directors Start to Flex Their Muscle," *Business Week,* July 3, 1989, p. 68.

[23]*Ibid.*

State Governor Mario M. Cuomo formed a task force to study issues raised by the emergence of pension funds as a major force in society. The task force strongly urged more participation of fund managers in corporate governance. These managers, said the report, had a duty to monitor governance of firms in which they had large holdings. They also had "the duty to play a constructive role in corporate governance, including the process of evaluating and voting proxies. They also had a responsibility to communicate to their stakeholders what they were doing in the governance area." The task force recommended to the governor and the New York state legislature that new language in the laws governing pension funds be drafted to make these responsibilities obligatory.[24]

STRENGTHENING THE AUDIT COMMITTEE

In 1968, a New York court held directors liable for misleading or inaccurate financial statements.[25] This case stimulated more boards to create and strengthen existing audit committees. In January 1977, the New York Stock Exchange amended its rules and mandated that each domestic company listed on the exchange establish and maintain an audit committee comprised solely of outside directors.

There is no general agreement about the duties and responsibilities of the audit committee. The committees first established dealt somewhat narrowly with reviews of financial statements prepared by outside auditors and made recommendations to the board about who the outside auditors should be. Many audit committees still have only this limited perspective.

Critics argue that the committee functions should be expanded, an idea shared by many outside directors. Critics say that the audit committee should take on other responsibilities such as the following: approve important professional services provided by outside auditors; review management responses to independent and internal auditors' recommendations; review all important financial statements before they are released to the public; help management educate the board about the company's accounting practices, internal audits, financial reporting practices, and business ethics policies; ensure proper lines of communications among directors and independent accountants, internal auditors, and financial management; and assume other responsibilities concerning the financial affairs of the company, such as adjudicating financial conflicts of interests of company executives.

SEPARATE THE BOARD CHAIRPERSON AND THE CEO

When Harold Williams was chairman of the SEC, he proposed that the CEO not chair the board of directors because of the chairperson's ability to control

---

[24]*Our Money's Worth. The Report of the Governor's Task Force on Pension Fund Investment*, June 1989, A Project of the New York State Industrial Cooperation Council.

[25]*E. Scott v. BarChris Construction Corporation* (S.D.N.Y. 1968).

the agenda and reduce the independence of other members. Very few executives approved this idea. One who did, while chairman of Armco, Inc., was C. William Verity, Jr. He said this would be a "clear way to avoid any appearance of conflict of interest between what's good for the current management of a company and what's good for the company as a whole, its shareholders, and other constituencies."[26]

There is, however, powerful opposition to separation of the two top executive roles. The Business Roundtable,[27] for instance, opposed such a move in its statement on governance. Critics of the idea point out that successful although it is when the two top people get along well, there are many unpublicized cases of failure. If the CEO and board chairperson positions are split, and if rivalry or dislike develops between the two, then the split works to the detriment of the business, and the board functions less well. Reginald Jones, who held both offices for General Electric, is a strong critic of decoupling. He concluded:

> In a word, separation of the offices of CEO and board chairman will work only if the occupants of the two offices are compatible and collaborate fully and in good faith. But if a CEO is prepared to cooperate with a colleague who is board chairman, he is also highly likely to serve the board faithfully in the capacity of chairman.[28]

It is probably wise not to establish a flat policy to separate the board chairperson and the CEO. In some circumstances it makes sense to separate the two positions; in others, and in probably a majority of cases, the interests of all concerned are best served when the two positions are combined.[29]

PROPOSALS FOR SPECIAL-INTEREST DIRECTORS

Proposals repeatedly are made for special-interest directors on boards. Recommendations have been made for board representation of the general public, environmentalists, consumers, employees, the government, women, and minorities. The thought behind such suggestions, of course, is that boards of directors either don't give these interests enough attention or ignore them altogether, that such interests must be fully represented on boards of directors, and that the only way to make sure that they are is to have special representatives on the boards to advance them.

There is strong opposition to special-interest directors both in the business and academic worlds. Opposition arises from the conviction that directors are responsible for the long-range viability of the corporation and the effec-

---

[26]C. William Verity, Jr., "Multiplication by Division: An Organic View of the Changing Role of the Board Chairman in Corporate Governance," *University of Michigan Business Review*, January 1979.

[27]Business Roundtable, *The Role of Directors, op. cit.*

[28]Reginald H. Jones, "Challenges to Business Leadership," *The Wharton Magazine*, Fall 1978.

[29]For further pros and cons see Paula L. Rechner and Dan R. Dalton, "The Impact of CEO as Board Chairperson on Corporate Performance: Evidence vs. Rhetoric," *The Academy of Management Executive*, May 1989.

tiveness of the corporation in meeting its fundamental objectives. Special-interest directors might politicize or polarize the board and embroil decision making in constant bickering and indecision, it is argued. The most likely result, it is said, would be that the real decision making would take place before official board meetings, and special-interest directors would be frozen out of any real power. The focus of special-interest representatives on the board would be in the interests of a particular group and not in the interests of the corporation. Serious conflicts in the board would be an inevitable result. They argue that special-interest directors would be chosen for their ability to represent groups and not for their capabilities in making prudent business decisions. Introducing a variety of noneconomic objectives into the board's decision-making process would place other groups on the same plane as stockholders and introduce the idea of accountability to new constituencies. The fiduciary duty of the special-interest directors would be to the constituency they represent and not the shareholders. Not only the legality, but also the morality, of this position would be in question. Directors would, in effect, be accountable to no one if the doctrine of stockholder primacy were compromised. The result would be deterioration in corporate governance.

UNION REPRESENTATION ON BOARDS

An important exception to the opposition of managements to special-interest representation on boards has been the recent election of union leaders to corporate boards of directors. Management's acceptance of union representation on boards has been a phenomenon of the last decade. The most publicized union appointment was at Chrysler Corporation. Chrysler appointed UAW president Douglas Fraser to its board in 1980. When Chrysler got into deep financial difficulties, it asked the UAW to make significant wage concessions. They did and one of the trade-offs was an offer by Lee Iacocca, chairman of the board of directors of Chrysler, to nominate Fraser to the board. Fraser's acceptance was not a new thought to him, since in 1976 he said it would be refreshing to have the point of view of workers in the atmosphere where all the decision are made which affect every Chrysler worker. "Maybe we could save them (the board members) from some of their own mistakes," he added.[30]

This was the first appointment to a major corporation in the United States of a union leader. Fraser's appointment and a few others at the time led to sharp controversy about the desirability of having union representation on boards of directors. Most labor union leaders were distinctly opposed. Rank-and-file workers expressed no enthusiasm for the idea. Business leaders generally were adamantly opposed to it.

When union representatives have been elected to corporate boards, the primary reason has been union concessions at the bargaining table or pro-

---

[30]Douglas Fraser, *San Francisco Chronicle,* May 7, 1976.

grams to give employees equity positions as a motivating force for greater loyalty and productivity. By means of stock ownership plans, employees have frequently become major shareholders. In the Chrysler case, for instance, the Loan Guarantee Act of 1979, under which the government underwrote a $1.5 billion bailout loan to the firm, established an Employee Stock Ownership Plan (ESOP) which was calculated at the time to result in a 15 percent stock ownership for employees in four years.

Opposition to union representation in business circles is based on a concern about conflict of interest and the traditional adversarial relationship between management and labor. Opponents point out that legally the directors have a fiduciary responsibility to represent all shareholders equally. How, they ask, can a labor leader sit on a board of a company and then negotiate with other members of the industry without conflict of interest? They argue also that union access to confidential information may weaken management in its bargaining with unions. The National Labor Relations Act imposes a specific duty on union officials to represent their members fairly. How can they do this and also represent stockholders fairly? Managers are also concerned about their ability to maintain open and candid discussion at board meetings when union officials are present. They ask: whose interests do they represent? Workers distrust management as well as labor representatives who associate closely with management.

But advantages are claimed for union representation. Workers have easier access to key decision makers, and they, in turn, have access to the views and concerns of workers. This can, of course, lead to more realistic decision making, to the advantage of both groups. In reviewing his Chrysler experience, Fraser pointed to a number of instances in which this advantage was achieved. If management wants more cooperation from unions, they might want to understand the thinking that prevails in the workplace. If a company wishes to alter the traditional adversarial relationship between management and labor, union representation on the board is one way to do so. It has long been accepted that workers respond much better to implementing strategies and tactics if they have had some voice in their formulation, and representation gives them a voice. Board membership is not the only way to achieve all these advantages, but it is an important way.

The presence of union representation on boards in Europe has been common practice for many years. In the 1970s, six nations—West Germany, Sweden, Norway, Denmark, Austria, and Luxembourg—passed laws requiring representation on the boards of major companies. Since then, the policy has spread to other European countries. Some people believe that this movement will cross to the United States, but most observers do not agree. But more corporations may invite union leaders to be board members. The number of companies with employee stock ownership plans has grown significantly. This movement, together with the growth and financial power of pension funds set up for employees, inevitably will exert pressures for employee representation on boards of directors.

REPACK THE GOLDEN PARACHUTES[31]

Golden parachutes are special compensation agreements that provide generous severance and benefit payments to top executives of a company in the event the company changes hands. These arrangements are made by boards of directors. Stockholder approval is not required. They first appeared in the early 1970s along with the wave of corporate takeovers that began then. Golden parachutes have since multiplied; it is now estimated that from one-third to one-half the 1,000 largest corporations have them.

The first widely criticized parachutes were given to William M. Agee as chairman of the Bendix Corporation and fifteen of his top executives during his attempt to take over Martin Marietta in 1982. Agee reportedly asked his board to complete the agreement during the takeover battle. The parachute guaranteed Agee an annual salary of $805,000 for five years. This was not as inflated as some parachutes have been since then. Michael Bergerac, chairman of Revlon, pulled a parachute worth $36 million when his company was acquired by Pantry Pride in late 1985.

Golden parachutes vary considerably. All include severance pay but vary with respect to stock options, continuation of general benefits (for example, medical insurance), moving costs, schedule of payments, consulting agreements, and so on.

Stockholder suits to rescind parachute agreements have multiplied in recent years, and some have succeeded. For instance, in one settlement, forty-four executives of Signal Companies (which merged with Allied Corporation) agreed to relinquish an estimated one-half of their $50 million worth of parachutes. Shareholders forced City Investing to cut back its agreements by $10 million.

Ceilings were placed on golden parachutes by Congress as part of the 1984 Deficit Reduction Act. The law now provides that a 20 percent tax be levied on any parachute that is more than three times an executive's average annual compensation in the previous five years. Parachutes awarded since then generally have been for no more than 2.99 times the average annual compensation. This law did not slow down the practice. It legitimized golden parachutes.

There are a number of major arguments in favor of golden parachutes. For example, they alleviate takeover anxiety in executives who might lose their jobs; they encourage managers to stick with the company during takeover attempts; stockholders of the company can afford to be generous because stockholders of the acquiring company will pay for them; and they are necessary to assure objectivity of managers during merger negotiations.

But Peter Scotese, chairman of the executive committee of Springs Industries, says that such arguments are flawed because they "legitimize giving

---

[31]For an excellent summary of research on this subject see H. Singh and F. Harianto, "Top Management Tenure, Corporate Ownership Structure and the Magnitude of Golden Parachutes," *Strategic Management Journal*, Summer 1989. For a more detailed analysis of what is included in golden parachutes and their pros and cons see also Philip L. Cochran and Steven L. Wartick, "Golden Parachutes': A Closer Look," *California Management Review*, Summer 1984.

million-dollar bribes to executives for doing what they were paid to do anyway,"[32] It is also argued that hostile takeovers usually occur when top management is not doing its job, and why compensate them for that? It is said that they lower rather than raise the resistance of managers to takeover attempts. It is argued that they are really excessive compensation. Finally, they create a poor image for business.

Many managers agree with Scotese when he says that the only way to avoid further shareholder antipathy and government regulation is rigorous self-monitoring of golden parachutes. If directors do nothing, says Scotese, there will be restrictive and punitive legislation—and it "will be richly deserved." Arch Patton, a pioneer of executive compensation at McKinsey & Company management consultants, agrees that parachutes frequently have been abused. "It's the greed factor surfacing," he says.[33]

GOVERNANCE ISSUES IN MANAGEMENT LEVERAGED BUYOUTS (LBOs)

On October 19, 1988, at a dinner meeting the evening prior to a formal session of the board of directors, F. Ross Johnson, President and CEO of RJR-Nabisco, Inc. (RJR), offered to buy the company for $75 a share. From all accounts, the board members were stunned by the proposal and the offering price but did not object. Four days later, Kohlberg Kravis and Roberts & Co. (KKR) put in a bid for the company of $90 a share, which totalled $20.7 billion. Henry Kravis, chairman of KKR, who had been following the affairs of RJR for some time, said he could not tell from the bid of Johnson's whether he wanted to put the company up for sale or own it. "If the latter," said Kravis, "the one thing we were very certain of was that the management group was stealing the company."[34] As it turned out, the final bid was $109 a share for a total of $25.1 billion, the largest takeover in American corporate history. Johnson and his small group of executives also bid $109, but the board awarded the company to KKR.

One of the reasons the board awarded the company to KKR was that the label "greed" attached to Johnson. This began with the very low initial bid, but became entrenched when on November 5 *The New York Times* published an article that gave some of the details of the compensation package contained in Johnson's revised bid. For a modest equity in RJR, Johnson and his small management group would wind up owning a large part of the company if the financial projections specified were achieved. At the time it was generally believed the projections would be met, and if so, the value of Johnson's group equity would be $2.5 billion dollars. Johnson said this num-

---

[32]Peter G. Scotese, "Fold up Those Golden Parachutes," *Harvard Business Review*, March–April, 1985, p. 170.

[33]Clemens P. Work, "Are Golden Parachutes Turning Platinum?" *U. S. News & World Report*, January 3, 1986.

[34]Michael O'Neill, "Greed Really Turns Me Off," *Fortune*, January 2, 1989. See also Judith H. Dobryzynski, "Was RJR's Ross Johnson Too Greedy for His Own Good?" *Business Week*, November 21, 1989.

ber was much too high, and anyway, the figures were negotiable and any gains would be distributed among many managers, not just a few.

This story focuses squarely on the question: Should top managements of companies be involved in leveraged buyouts (LBOs)? Before discussing this question, it should be noted that the United States has been involved in recent years in a frenzy of acquisitions and mergers, many of which have been financed by huge issues of bonds. The word "leverage" refers to the use of bonds or debt to pay for the common stock of the company to be taken over. The acronym LBO encompasses a variety of transactions concerned with acquisitions and mergers.[35] LBOs by managements of their own companies are made to "take the company private." This means buying the stock and retiring it. In this event, the top management has bought and owns its company. Often the debt is partly repaid by selling assets of the acquired firm.

Why would managers want to do this? The answer, of course, is both money and the satisfaction of running their own company. While the numbers of LBOs are not large in proportion to our corporate population, the issues associated with them are significant. Some large and well-known companies have gone private—R. H. Macy, Borg-Warner, Owens-Illinois, and Beatrice.

The interests of stockholders and managers inevitably conflict in management takeovers. The stockholders are interested, of course, in higher prices for their holdings. Managements, in an LBO, are interested in buying the firm for the lowest price. If managements have a fiduciary responsibility to shareholders, and they do, there is a clear conflict with managerial self-interest.

LBOs by managers are often justified by a claim that the company can be run more efficiently as a private company. It is quite true that many companies have operated much more profitably after going private than before. There are many reasons why this may happen. The managements sell off unprofitable subunits, discharge managers and other unneeded employees, negotiate wage concessions with workers, cut executive perquisites such as company airplanes, reorganize more efficiently, reduce research and development expenditures (R&D), and cut advertising. Important also is tax reduction when using debt rather than equity. (Interest on debt is tax-deductible, whereas dividends are not.) When huge debt is incurred to buy the company, this deduction can be very important.

Some of the actions of managers after a takeover may be aimed at boosting profits to sell the company later. In this event, some inappropriate actions may be taken, such as cutting too deeply into R&D. But a further question arises, as cogently put by Alfred Rappaport, chairman of the Alcar Group: "Why is it that managements get so damn economically insightful after a company goes private?"[36]

---

[35]For a fuller definition of LBO see Carolyn Kay Brancato and Kevin F. Winch, *Leveraged Buyouts and the Pot of Gold: Trends, Public Policy, and Case Studies*, Report Prepared by the Economics Division of the Congressional Research Service for the Subcommittee on Oversight and Investigations of the Committee on Energy and Commerce, U.S. House of Representatives, Washington, D.C.: U.S. Government Printing Office, December 1987.

[36]Quoted in Dan R. Dalton, "The Ubiquitous Leveraged Buyout (LBO): Management Buyout or Management Sellout?" *Business Horizons*, July–August 1989, p. 40.

Some LBOs are made with the clear objective of restructuring the company to sell later for a profit. For example, the Leslie Fay Companies, makers of women's apparel, went private in 1982 for $58 million and then went public in 1986 for $521 million. In cases such as this, the troubling question arises: Did shareholders get full value for their holdings when management bought them out?

Different types of LBOs raise many other important questions. We now turn to some of the major ones, and follow with the case of T. Boone Pickens' attempted takeover of UNOCAL.

TAKEOVERS AND TAKEOVER THREATS CHANGE GOVERNANCE

Everyone accepts the need for companies to merge when both parties believe that the marriage will be beneficial to the various interests involved and so long as there is no conflict with antitrust or other laws. Most mergers and acquisitions are friendly. It is the hostile takeover that raises profound public policy issues about corporate governance, the free market, capitalism, and ethical business behavior. A few of the critical issues raised by such takeovers follow.

DO TAKEOVERS CORRECT POOR MANAGEMENT PERFORMANCE?

Raiders claim that they correct poor corporate management by stimulating weak managers to do better when a takeover threat is initiated or by actually taking over a company and running it more efficiently. This assertion raises many questions. When is a company poorly managed? Do hostile takeovers really improve corporate management? Do hostile takeovers benefit stockholders?

Unfortunately, there is no generally accepted measure of managerial performance. The typical standard used by those defending raiders is the price of stock on the market. They believe or say they believe that if the stock price is high, management is efficient. If the price is low, it reflects poor management performance. This can be a defective measure. We all are aware of how fluctuations in market stock prices can change radically, for many reasons, while managerial performance remains unchanged. But aside from that, management that focuses on the future of a company may in the process reduce short-term profits for long-term advantage. Other things being equal, this lower profit will be reflected in lower stock prices. Managers who emphasize the long run will expand research and development expenditures, increase capital outlays, hire talented scientists and engineers, concentrate on strengthening their marketing and distribution systems, fund new operating centers (at home and abroad) through their unprofitable initial stages, maintain a strong work force, and fully fund their pension programs. If managers focus solely on short-term stock prices they can raise them, other things being equal, by increasing their short-term profits. This can be done easily, aside from perfectly legal accounting manipulations, by doing exactly the opposite of what was just described for managers with a long-range managerial perspective. Which is the better managed company? In which company will the stockholders most likely have the greatest stock appreciation over time?

Of course, not all takeover targets have had satisfactory managerial performance. There are many instances of inept management that showed indifference to shareholder interests, declining profits, weak balance sheets, low employee morale, bloated staffs, excessive salaries and wage rates, outrageous perquisites among executives, seriously flawed decision-making processes and strategies, and low stock prices. Takeover efforts have on occasion stimulated improvement in such poor managerial performance.

The question of whether or not takeovers result in improved management, using that term broadly to include all operations of a company, has not been settled. There are many studies, some of which will be noted shortly, concerning profits and financial results to shareholders. Although these are a popular measure of management performance, they are far from conclusive. There is no scientific evidence that merged firms, whether hostile or friendly, have over time been more efficient than they would have been had they remained independent. Raiders and their defenders can proclaim that a takeover will redeploy assets more efficiently, sharpen distribution and marketing systems, improve productivity of employees and increase profits. But for every case where profits have increased after a hostile takeover, just the opposite can be cited. Before presenting results of research concerning profitability and stock prices it is informative to note several general impacts, both beneficial and damaging, on managements and their companies.

A number of hostile takeovers, especially when organized by those who are more intent on making money than running a business, have indeed quickened the flow of adrenalin of managers and brought better performance. For example, Walt Disney Productions changed its management following successful resistance to a takeover bid by Saul P. Steinberg. The bid was halted in 1984 when Disney paid Steinberg $325 million for his stock, $60 million of which was profit. Disney stock plummeted but subsequently more than doubled. Erwin D. Okun, a Disney spokesman, said that about sixty new executives were hired that "set this place afire." He added: "At the lowest hour of the attack someone told me that good might come of all this. I thought he was crazy. Now I think he was visionary."[37] Had Steinberg kept his stock, he would have had a paper profit in 1989 of $1.7 billion on his 16.2 million Disney shares.

More frequently, however, targeted companies that have finally freed themselves from takeover specialists have found themselves weakened and handicapped by the wounds of the battle. Some companies have adopted a "scorched earth" tactic to thwart a hostile takeover and have subsequently suffered as a result. For example, in 1982, Brunswick Corporation, of Skokie, Illinois, was an unwilling target of Los Angeles-based Whittaker Corpora-

---

[37]Leslie Wayne, "Costs of Escaping a Takeover," *New York Times*, January 20, 1986.

tion. To defend itself, Brunswick sold its valuable Sherwood Medical Division to American Home Products Corporation. Whittaker broke off the battle. But Sherwood had been the best potential growth division of the company, and its loss adversely affected the fortunes of Brunswick. Management was hobbled, and stockholders suffered.

Pickens (1986) claims, "[w]hen Mesa has tried to take over a company, we have really wanted to acquire it and run it."[38] But too many raiders seem more interested in making quick profits than in the management of the takeover targets. British raider Sir James Goldsmith, who has profited substantially in a number of his forays, says takeovers are "for the public good, but that's not why I do it. I do it to make money."[39] Some raiders clearly are interested in acquiring a company to sell off its assets because they believe that by doing so, they can acquire cash in an amount far greater than their investment in the takeover. If they fail in their takeover attempt, the price of their disengagement may be "greenmail." ("Greenmail" is a term used to describe the practice of a corporate raider acquiring a block of a company's stock, threatening takeover, and then agreeing to sell back the stock to the company at a premium price.) This is precisely what occurred when Goldsmith attacked Goodyear Tire and Rubber Company and pocketed a profit of $93 million in a settlement with the company in 1986.

Harold M. Williams, former chairman of the SEC, doubts that mergers and acquisitions of the last decade resulted in greater efficiencies of operation. He suspects that a case can be made "that many acquired companies were run less efficiently and had consistently negative effects on the acquirers' balance sheets for years afterward." He believes the rash of mergers and acquisitions at inflated prices had less to do with managerial operating efficiency than with such factors as: depressed stock prices on the market resulting from inflation and the fears of inflation; accounting procedures and tax laws that benefited raiders; the lure of growing faster and easier by acquisition than by internal growth; and the sudden availability of billions of dollars as a result of new aggressive bank lending and new financing methods, such as "junk bonds." ("Junk bonds" are sold to the public by investment bankers to help raiders acquire stock in targeted companies. These bonds carry interest rates from 3.5 to 5.5 percent over top grade corporate bonds. This does not mean the bonds are literally junk. They have high rates to reward high risk because they are not as secure as high-grade corporate bonds. If the raider acquires a company, sale of the company's assets may be used to pay off some of the bonds.) Williams concludes:

> To be fair, there certainly are positive aspects to some takeovers, and a free market for corporate control is valuable. But the phenomenon is negative on a variety of scores. There are serious problems of equity, of the best use of management time, of the erosion of shareholder rights, of corporate accountability, and of the delegitimization of the free-enterprise system.[40]

[38]Pickens, "Takeovers and Mergers," *op. cit.*
[39]Stewart Toy, *op. cit.*
[40]Harold M. William, "It's Time for a Takeover Moratorium," *Fortune*, July 22, 1985.

DO STOCKHOLDERS BENEFIT FROM TAKEOVERS?[41]

There is no doubt that takeover activity raises stock prices. In defending his attempted takeover of Unocal (see following case). T. Boone Pickens, for example, contended that he served the Unocal stockholders well. "We did a hell of a job for Unocal's stockholders in this deal," he said.[42] The stock price rose from $35 to $48. Professor Michael Jensen summarized the results of more than a dozen studies and concluded from them that shareholders who surrendered their stock in successful takeovers profited with a premium of 30 percent.[43] David Ruder, chairman of the Security and Exchange Commission, said his staff calculated that more than $20 billion in premiums were paid to stockholders in LBO transactions during 1980–87.[44]

It should be noted, however, that stockholders can lose even when they sell for a profit. They lose if the company accepts a price less than the true value of the firm. They can also lose when executives buy them out and then after a few years resell the company to the public at a higher stock price than they paid.

How about stockholders of acquiring companies? Two researchers found that on the average, "accounting and investor returns decrease significantly in the four years after acquisition activity compared with their levels in the four years before such activity."[45] These data are for all mergers. Data for LBOs alone could be different.

How about stockholders of firms where the takeover bid failed? A study of thirty-three such firms found that shareholders received abnormal returns of 31 percent with the initial announcement of the bidding. At the time of the termination announcement, however, the losses were about 10 percent. This loss did not completely offset the gains from the initial announcement. During the next three years, there was little change in stock price.[46]

The longer-range record is also mixed. A study of 6,000 mergers occurring between 1960 and 1975 concluded: "Although individual exceptions existed, our statistical materials provided no support for the assertion that acquired unit operating efficiency rises on average after acquisition."[47] Data do not ex-

---

[41]This and the next section were extracted from George A. Steiner, "The KKR-RJR Nabisco Blockbuster Leveraged Buyout," in John F. Steiner, *Industry, Society and Change: A Case Book,* New York: McGraw-Hill Book Co., 1991.

[42]James B. Stewart and Laurie P. Cohen, "Golden Era for Raiders May be Waning," *The Wall Street Journal,* May 22, 1985.

[43]Michael Jensen, "Takeovers: Folklore and Science," *Harvard Business Review,* November–December 1984.

[44]David S. Ruder, "Statement Before the House Committee on Ways and Means Concerning Leveraged Buyouts," January 31, 1989.

[45]Karen L. Fowler and Dennis R. Schmidt, "Tender Offers, Acquisitions, and Subsequent Performance in Manufacturing Firms," *Academy of Management Journal,* December 1988, p. 972.

[46]Richard S. Ruback, "Do Target Shareholders Lose in Unsuccessful Control Contests?" in Alan J. Auerbach, *Corporate Takeovers: Causes and Consequences,* Chicago: The University of Chicago Press, 1988.

[47]Quoted in F. M. Scherer, "Testimony Before the Committee on Ways and Means, U.S. House of Representatives, U.S. Congress," March 14, 1989. Details of the study are in F. M. Scherer and David J. Ravenscraft, *Mergers, Sell-offs, and Economic Efficiency,* Washington, D.C.: The Brookings Institution, 1987.

ist to extend this study to the present. During the same time period, 46.6 percent of acquisitions consummated ended in divestiture.[48] Another study concluded that for every 100 mergers between 1980 and 1987, 37.5 percent were divested.[49] Through the period 1960 to 1988, many acquired companies were profitable but were divested for a variety of reasons, such as that the firm did not fit into the business of the acquired company, or a new strategy did not include the acquired company. Many, however, were unprofitable.

The record of companies going private is spotty, but one study of seventy-six companies concluded that operating income as a percentage of assets improved relative to pre-restructuring by 1.8 percent in the year after restructuring, and by 5.6 percent in the second year after restructuring.[50] These numbers are positive but not recordbreaking.

Critics say that after a takeover the pressure is on managers, especially in light of the heavy debt usually incurred in the takeover, to cut all postponable expenditures. The National Science Foundation studied twenty-four firms that had been taken over. These were large spenders on R&D. After the takeovers their R&D expenditures dropped.[51]

HOW DO OTHER STAKEHOLDERS FARE?

Research on how other stakeholders fare in takeovers is even more spotty and ambiguous than the above. Bondholders may find the bond rating of the company lowered as a result of the newly incurred debt. This happened to RJR-Nabisco bondholders after being taken over by KKR. The Metropolitan Life Company sued RJR, claiming that its $360 million in bonds fell 20 percent.[52]

Employees typically have suffered in corporate takeovers. In too many instances, employees have been discharged without notice; or find if they keep their jobs, strong pressure is put on them to make concessions on wages and salaries as well as benefits. This is especially true when the motive of a raider is to cut costs and sell assets to reduce the heavy debt load incurred to make the takeover. In many cases managerial careers have been shattered. One illustration of what may happen in an LBO is that of Safeway Stores. In 1986, this publicly held company was sold to a group of buyout specialists headed by KKR and members of Safeway management. The stockholders sold their shares to the buyout group at a price 82 percent higher than three months before the takeover. Investment bankers and lawyers were paid $90 million for their work. Four years later the buyout group sold shares for 10 percent of the company for an amount four times their cash investment. In the meantime, tens of thousand of employees lost their jobs. One survey in Dallas

[48]Scherer, *op. cit.*

[49]*Ibid.*

[50]*Ibid.*

[51]Erich Bloch, "Testimony Before the House Ways and Means Committee, U. S. Congress," March 14, 1989.

[52]Morey W. McDaniel, "Bondholders and Stockholders," *Journal of Corporate Law*, December 1987.

showed that a year after the takeover, 60 percent of the employees who lost their jobs had not found full-time employment.[53]

Communities are certainly hurt if a company is sold off piecemeal to make a profit, or if cost-cutting measures result in substantial employee layoffs in a small community. In the case of Winston-Salem, headquarters of RJR, people were unhappy even though the takeover resulted in many of them becoming instant millionaires. Their concern: an old way of life had been disrupted.[54]

DEFENSES AGAINST HOSTILE TAKEOVERS

In December 1985, the Belzberg family of Canada sent Arvin Industries Inc., of Columbus, Indiana, a letter saying that it had accumulated 4.9 percent of the company's stock and that it was considering buying much more. Arvin is one of the two largest companies in Columbus, Indiana. It makes mufflers, exhaust pipes, catalytic converters, and a number of other industrial and electronic products. Its sales in 1986 were nearly $1 billion, it registered a $41 million profit, and it employed 2,000 people. It is an unusually strong supporter of community projects. Indiana granted the company its charter.

Arvin appealed to the Indiana state legislature for help in opposing this hostile takeover attempt. The legislature, in response, passed an anti-takeover bill called the Control Share Acquisition Chapter. The bill mandated that a company that acquires 20 percent of an Indiana company loses the shares' voting rights unless the other shareholders vote to reinstate them. A strong motivation for this bill was the desire of legislators to protect companies in smaller Indiana cities from hostile takeovers that might weaken the companies to the detriment of the local communities.

Six days after the Indiana law went into effect, CTS Corporation, which had announced a tender offer for Dynamics Corporation of America, an Indiana company, took the case to the U.S. Supreme Court. Lower courts in the past had repeatedly struck down such laws. The Department of Justice and the Securities and Exchange Commission filed briefs urging the Supreme Court to do the same. The court did no such thing.

In April 1987, the Court rejected the suit of Dynamics and upheld the Indiana law by a 6-2 vote (*CTS Corporation v. Dynamics Corporation of America*). The Court said that "[a] state has an interest in promoting stable relationships among parties involved in the corporations it charters, as well as in ensuring that investors in such corporations have an effective voice in corporate affairs." There was no doubt, said the Court, that Indiana was trying to protect shareholders of Indiana corporations, and it had a right to do so. "It does this," said the Court, "by affording shareholders, when a takeover offer is made, an opportunity to decide collectively whether the resulting change in

[53]For an account of the Safeway Stores story see Susan C. Faludi, "The Reckoning: Safeway LBO Yields Vast Profits but Exacts A Heavy Human Toll," *The Wall Street Journal*, May 16, 1990. See also Victor Kirk, "What About the Workers?" *National Journal*, February 18, 1989.

[54]Robert E. Dallow, "Tobacco City's Old Retainers Oppose Buyout," *Los Angeles Times*, December 1, 1988.

voting control of the corporation, as they perceive it, would be desirable." Furthermore, said the Court, "[n]othing in the Constitution says that the protection of entrenched management is any less important a 'putative local benefit' than the protection of entrenched shareholders...."[55]

This case is a strong affirmation of the right of individual states to protect the corporations they charter when, of course, there is no contradictory federal law. The case leads to the conclusion that the Court has entered the hostile takeover game and approves granting managers broad protection against raiders, given the same conditions as existed in Indiana.

Since the Indiana law was declared constitutional by the Supreme Court, more than thirty states have passed laws similar to Indiana's. These laws feature two important provisions to repel hostile takeovers. One is the Indiana requirement that when raiders accumulate a certain percentage of stock, usually 20 percent, they must get approval from the remaining stockholders before they can vote their stock. The other is to impose a lengthy moratorium on the sale of acquired assets of the company. The time period varies from state to state.

The state of Delaware set a standard in this connection when it passed a law in February 1988 that requires that anyone acquiring from 15 percent to 85 percent of a Delaware-registered company must wait three years before selling off assets or merging the acquired firm with another one. Such a law does not prevent friendly takeovers, but strikes at raiders whose motive is quick profits.

Target companies have also prescribed poison pills to repel raiders. These take on all kinds of characteristics. Generally, however, they weaken the enterprise when it is taken over. For example, a takeover may trigger a 100 percent stock dividend to all stockholders except the raiders; the company may set up employee stock ownership plans and by various arrangements provide employees with stock ownership; or the managers might forge a "suicide pact," as was done when Borden, Inc., thwarted a takeover. The pact provided that in the event of a takeover, twenty-five top executives of the company would quit if any one of them were fired. Courts of law have accepted such repellents, but not always.

WHAT SHOULD BE DONE ABOUT TAKEOVERS?

Strong pressures have been put on the government to take action against LBOs, especially when they are hostile, greenmail is involved, or raiders seek a quick profit by selling off assets. There is naturally strong opposition to any government action by defenders of the idea that takeovers are only a part of a dynamic capitalism and market forces will deal with any abuses.

Numerous bills have been introduced in Congress, and the House Ways and Means Committee held extensive hearings in 1988. Nothing has been passed by the Congress, and little action is likely. An important reason is that

---

[55]*CTS Corporation v. Dynamics Corporation of America*, 55 LW 4478 (April 21, 1987).

those measures most likely to deal with abuses, aside from current federal and state laws, would create more harm than good. A prime illustration is the demand that double taxation of dividends be removed. Another is that the tax deductability of bond interest be eliminated.

Dividends are not tax deductible by the corporation and are taxed when received by shareholders. One suggestion is to give individuals a tax credit for dividends received or if a dividend tax is paid by corporations. If implemented, this would eliminate a major advantage of junk bonds (whose interest costs are tax deductible) over equities and dampen enthusiasm for the use of such bonds to finance LBOs.

This proposal has disadvantages. One is that the U.S. Treasury says it would lose from $20 to $25 billion a year. The budgetary problems of the United States alone rule out this suggestion.

Another popular suggestion is to eliminate the tax deductibility of corporate debt. This would, of course, chill the heavy usage of junk bonds to finance LBOs. If this deductibility were disallowed and applied to current junk bond debt, it would throw into bankruptcy many companies now barely able to meet interest costs on their debt. If the regulation applied only to new junk bonds, it would put newly formed companies with junk bond financing at a great disadvantage with competitors who use junk bonds. Also, U.S. companies would be at a disadvantage with foreign companies whose laws permit tax deductibility.

Many other proposals have been made, such as to outlaw greenmail, to require a cooling-off period between the time an intention to acquire is made and the offer to buy is made, to force buyers to notify the Securities and Exchange Commission of any intention to make a change that will have a deleterious impact on a community, and to require boards of directors to submit any bona fide tender offer to stockholders for a vote. All these and other suggestions face formidable obstacles in defining terms, and potentially create serious problems.

What should be done? We should move cautiously. The great majority of mergers and acquisitions are friendly and for legitimate economic reasons. To stifle this process would sap the vitality of our economic system. On the other hand, there are areas of abuse which need attention. Recent legislation has moved in the direction of correcting some of them. The question, of course, is: Are these laws enough?

T. Boone Pickens, Jr., Stubs His Toe on Unocal

T. Boone Pickens, Jr., chairman of Mesa Petroleum Co., Amarillo, Texas, has become a folk hero in some quarters and in others, such as corporate boardrooms, a hobgoblin, to use a milder epithet. He asserts: "I am the champion of the small stockholder....Many American companies are heavily undervalued, and I blame their management entirely."[56] He claims that his takeover attempts on giant corporations have benefited stockholders and have spurred managers to improve their performance. He is fond of pointing out that 750,000 stockholders have improved their financial performance by sharing $6.5 billion produced by his raids on four big oil companies in the years 1983 and 1984.[57] Unocal was one of the companies over which Pickens waged a hostile takeover attempt. This is the story of what happened and the important controversies about corporate governance that this and similar battles raise.

Unocal Corporation is the parent of Union Oil Company of California. It is a fully integrated, high-technology energy company, dealing worldwide in all major aspects of energy production. Its primary activity is the development and production of crude oil and natural gas resources throughout the world. In 1985, its total revenues were $11.6 billion, and it employed over 20,000 people. Net crude oil production averaged 251,300 barrels per day, and its natural gas production averaged 1,084 million cubic feet per day.

PICKENS ATTACKS UNOCAL

In October 1984, Pickens and Mesa formed a partnership with Texas investors referred to as Mesa Partners II or the Pickens Group. They targeted Phillips Petroleum and Unocal for takeover and began accumulating stock in the companies. In December, Pickens narrowed his target to Phillips and

[56]Stewart Toy, "The Raiders," *Business Week*, March 4, 1985.
[57]T. Boone Pickens, Jr., "Takeovers and Mergers: A Function of the Free Market," *The Diary of Alpha Kappa Psi*, September 1986. See also T. Boone Pickens, Jr., *Boone*, Boston: Houghton Mifflin Company, 1987.

stopped acquiring Unocal shares. Shortly before Christmas, Phillips, to avoid takeover, agreed to purchase Pickens' shares at a price that netted him $89 million profit.

Following the Phillips victory, the Pickens Group began accumulating Unocal stock. By mid-February 1985, they had accumulated 5 percent of Unocal's total outstanding shares and notified the SEC of their holdings, in conformance with that agency's rules that stock acquisition over the 5 percent mark be reported. Pickens continued to accumulate stock on the open market and on April 8 announced a $3.46 billion bid for a controlling interest in Unocal. The tender offer for outstanding shares was $54 per share up to 64 million shares. That would give Pickens 50 percent of the company stock and control of it.

In the meantime, Unocal officers decided to fight the hostile takeover attempt aggressively. Fred L. Hartley, the feisty and outspoken chairman of Unocal, in speeches and public announcements denounced the "corporate raiders" and said that they were destroying corporations. The management of Unocal planned its battle strategy with highly skilled lawyers and investment bankers. The first specific move, a "shark repellent," was to adopt a policy that anyone wishing to nominate a director or bring up business at Unocal's forthcoming stockholder meeting (scheduled for April 29) had to give at least thirty days' notice. Pickens could not meet this schedule and, if it held, would have been prevented from getting his representation on the Unocal board of directors. Pickens, of course, challenged this ruling in court. On April 14, the Unocal board of directors unanimously rejected the Pickens tender offer, saying that it was "grossly inadequate."

The Pickens Group considered what might be necessary beyond the $54 tender offer to acquire the company. Discussions with investment bankers and banks led to the conclusion that it was possible to float $3 billion of junk bonds and raise an additional $1 billion in bank loans to buy more stock of Unocal.

On April 16, Unocal announced that it would acquire up to 87.2 million shares of its common stock for senior secured notes and cash with an aggregate par value of $72 per share. This offer was conditioned on the Pickens group getting 64 million shares. The Pickens shares were excluded from this offer. This was, of course, another "shark repellent."

On April 19, Unocal announced another "shark repellent." The board authorized the formation of a Master Limited Partnership to hold most of the assets of the company's Gulf region. It would involve nearly half the company's domestic oil and gas reserves. Units of this partnership could be distributed all at once to Unocal shareholders in the event of a change in corporate ownership. That would leave Pickens with an enormous debt in acquiring Unocal shares and a company half the size he thought he was acquiring. The Master Limited Partnership sold units to the public when it was formed.

On April 29, a Delaware chancery court judge granted a temporary restraining order prohibiting Unocal from excluding Pickens from its $72 exchange offer. On May 2, the Delaware Supreme Court delayed hearing an appeal of the chancery court ruling and sent the case back to that court for rehearing.

In the meantime, on April 28, a U.S. district court in Los Angeles ordered Unocal to delay its annual meeting to May 13. This gave both sides an opportunity to solicit proxies from shareholders. Chairman Hartley and Unocal employees launched a massive campaign. At the meeting on May 13, Pickens and Hartley, instead of tossing barbs at one another as most people expected, were outwardly cordial. Both had some reason to believe that he had won. As it turned out, Pickens decisively lost the shareholder vote to block the election of three Unocal directors favored by management. But on the same day, the Delaware lower court upheld its earlier ruling that Pickens must be included in the $72 Unocal offer. On May 17, however, the Delaware Supreme Court reversed the lower court ruling and said that Unocal had a legal right to exclude Pickens from the $72 offer. The court in this case made the point that the defensive measure was "reasonable in relation to the threat posed." It held that there was a "destructive threat" to the shareholders posed by the "junk bond" tender offer.[58]

The time for compromise had arrived. Pickens, of course, could go on offering a price per share higher than Unocal. Unocal could match the offer. This jockeying would make no sense to either party and eventually would bankrupt both. A third possibility, of course, would be for Unocal to find a "white knight." (A "white knight" is a third company, friendly to the target company, that agrees to acquire all or part of the target company and whose tender offer is accepted by the target company.)

On May 20, Unocal and Mesa Partners II arrived at a settlement. Among the agreements were the following: (1) Unocal would buy only 7.8 million of Mesa's shares under terms of the $72 exchange offer; (2) Pickens would stop all attempts to acquire control of Unocal or to influence its policies and would not buy any new shares of Unocal for twenty-five years; and (3) Unocal would seek to maintain its present level of cash dividends to stockholders.[59] The latter provision, of course, was to protect Pickens, who still held substantial amounts of Unocal's stock.

SOME FINANCIAL IMPLICATIONS FOR UNOCAL

The financial price Unocal paid for defending its freedom was $4.16 billion in new debt. Fees to investment bankers totaled about $25 million, and legal costs were somewhat less than $10 million. At the time of settlement the Pickens Group stood to lose from $40 to $80 million, depending upon how much it could sell its shares for and what its costs for waging battle were. Its accumulated shares averaged $44.72 each, and the stock price closed at $35.875 on May 21, the day after the Unocal directors approved the settlement. This was a severe blow to Mesa. It contrasted with a pretax profit of

[58]*Unocal Corp. v. Mesa Petroleum Co.* (1985).
[59]*Seventy Six,* May–June 1985.

about $598 million, which Mesa calculated that it had made since 1982 in unsuccessful attempts to take over Cities Service, General American Oil, Superior Oil, Gulf Oil, and Phillips Petroleum.[60]

The debt accumulated in the battle pushed Unocal's debt from 18 to 75 percent to total capital, roughly double the industry average at the time. Hartley lamented, "[e]very day when we open up the building here we first write a check to our friendly banks and private investors for $2 million."[61] To get needed cash, Unocal drastically cut its exploration expenditures (1985 was 47 percent under 1984). It laid off employees, retired others, and sold assets. With oil prices depressed and large interest payments, Unocal's net income for 1986 was projected to be around $140 million, or some 60 percent under that of 1985. (Actually, it turned out to be $176 million in 1986.) Hartley understandably was bitter about the whole experience. "It would seem," he said, "that we have a real failure in our capitalistic system and a real failure of our morals, and manners, and ethics, and integrity in our society if one has to maintain a hell of a high debt in order to protect oneself from the financial barbarians."[62]

Unocal's revenues and profits grew after 1985, and its debt has been reduced. But the debt reduction has been a drag on the company. From a peak debt of $6.1 billion in October 1985, the company has reduced it consistently, until it was $4.6 billion at the end of 1988. This brought the debt/equity ratio down from 79 percent to 68 percent, still high compared with 1984. Profits have risen, but without debt interest payments (amounting to $451 million in 1988) they would have been much higher. In 1987, profits were $181 million, and in 1988 they were $480 million. Earnings per share of stock rose from $1.51 in 1986 to $4.12 in 1988. They were $4.03 in 1986. Unocal's stock price rose to $50 per share in 1989.

QUESTIONS

1 Define hostile takeover, greenmail, junk bond, poison pill, and white knight.
2 Defend the position that Pickens took in the Unocal case. Defend Hartley's position. With which do you agree? Why?
3 Can managers who stubbornly resist a takeover tender offer be defended even though the offer amounts to a large premium over the current market price of the company's shares?
4 Corporate raiders justify their actions by claiming that taking over a company will throw out inefficient management and make the company more efficient. Is this correct?
5 Do stockholders generally benefit from hostile takeovers? How about other stakeholders?

---

[60]Nancy Rivera and Debra Whitefield, "Unocal Win May Dampen Takeovers," *Los Angeles Times,* May 22, 1985.
[61]John Heins, "It's Not as Much Fun," *Forbes,* November 17, 1986.
[62]Nancy Rivera, "Unocal Will Trim Capital Spending, Hartley Says," *Los Angeles Times,* June 3, 1985.

Index